THE CATHOLIC CHALLENGE TO THE AMERICAN ECONOMY

THE CATHOLIC CHALLENGE TO THE AMERICAN ECONOMY

Reflections on the U.S. Bishops' Pastoral Letter on Catholic Social Teaching and the U.S. Economy

Edited by
Thomas M. Gannon, S.J.

• *with the final text of the pastoral letter* •

MACMILLAN PUBLISHING COMPANY
A Division of Macmillan, Inc.
New York

Collier Macmillan Publishers
London

Macmillan Publishing Company
A Division of Macmillan, Inc.
866 Third Avenue, New York, N. Y. 10022

Collier Macmillan Canada, Inc.

Library of Congress Catalog Card Number: 86-28448

Printed in the United States of America

printing number
1 2 3 4 5 6 7 8 9 10

Library of Congress Cataloging in Publication Data

The Catholic challenge to the American economy.
   1. Catholic Church. National Conference of Catholic
Bishops. Pastoral Letter on Catholic social teaching and
the U.S. economy. 2. Economics—Religious aspects—
Catholic Church. 3. Sociology, Christian (Catholic)
4. United States—Economic conditions—1981–
5. Catholic Church—Doctrines. I. Gannon, Thomas M.
BX1795.E27C37 1987   261.8′5   86-28448
ISBN 0-02-911260-5
ISBN 0-02-911270-2 (pbk.)

Contents

THE CATHOLIC CHALLENGE TO THE AMERICAN ECONOMY

Introduction
Thomas M. Gannon, S.J.

Among many economists and social observers it has become almost commonplace to observe that the American and world economies are in the midst
of a profound structural transition that calls into question not only traditional
techniques for managing economic affairs, but also for conceptualizing the
workings of both the economy and government. There are few signs that this
transition is over or that it has become any more predictable. In fact, some
theorists have argued that renewed economic growth is uncertain even in
the long run. Precisely because this situation has such profound effects on
the everyday lives of so many people, and because of the basic choices with
which it confronts us, it has also raised serious moral questions that involve
our basic understanding of human nature—the individual, the family, community and society—and of human purpose, what we are called to become
individually and collectively. More and more people inevitably are coming
to see that the wisdom of their different religious traditions has something
to offer in the debates and conflicts over the best responses to alternative
policy choices, precisely because these policies seriously affect the lives of
us all—our material well-being as well as our motivations and fears, hopes
and desires.

We are not accustomed, however, to thinking about the moral and religious
dimensions of economic policies. We are more familiar with the claim that
economics is a complicated science, that policy decisions are technical issues
best left to experts, and that morality concerns personal matters and individual
choice. Consequently, in learning to recognize the moral and religious dimensions of economic life, we confront the difficult task of rethinking the
scope of ethics and of economics, as well as the nature of the mission of
religious communities in the larger society.

To appreciate what is at stake in the current economic situation and in
our efforts to rethink its moral and religious dimensions, it is useful to consider
the question of economic growth. Ever since publication of *The Wealth of
Nations* in 1776, growth has been recognized as the distinctive characteristic

1

of a capitalist society, at once its chief glory and its principal concern. As Adam Smith pointed out, the process of accumulating wealth brought about a social result previously unknown in history—the extension of "improvements" to the lower ranks of people. As Ricardo was soon to add, though, and Marx to hammer home, growth also brought about social changes along with material betterment. In Ricardo's view, the process of growth seemed likely to terminate in a stagnant state in which wealth would be transferred mainly to the hands of landowners. In Marx's view, the accumulation process was not only inherently unstable, bringing with it recurrent periods of business ruin, but eventually destined to create the conditions for the eruption of a new, anticapitalist social order.

In our own time, growth continues to receive mixed reviews. On the one hand, it has increasingly come to be recognized as the most important precondition for social harmony, indispensable for maintaining high employment and providing the rising consumption standards everyone has come to expect of capitalism. On the other hand, our renewed efforts to stimulate growth have also incurred the bitter criticism of social theorists who are concerned about the continuing uneven distribution of the social product and repeatedly draw attention to substantial pockets of poverty and misery amid the general plenty. The continuation of poverty in an affluent society alienates sections of the population from society at large and underlines the moral hollowness of an economic system that has otherwise been so generally admired.

Regardless of which side of the argument lies one's sympathy, there is no denying the fact that industrial capitalism in the West has produced a better material life for larger numbers of people than any other system in history. Furthermore, if by human betterment one means both higher standards of living and social institutions that protect liberty and human rights, then some form of capitalist arrangement is surely a better risk than any known alternative.

Yet something about growth seems fraudulent; something about the riches it purports to bring is illusory. Over 12 years ago, Richard Easterlin in a much-quoted study examined a wide variety of interviews on well-being conducted in the United States and elsewhere over the last 30 years and noted that an improvement in American incomes had been accompanied by no change at all in the percentage of persons reporting themselves as "happy."[1] Similar polls disclose no shift toward "happiness" when we compare rich countries with poor ones. If capitalist growth has made us twice as rich as our parents, four times as rich as our grandparents and incalculably richer than our colonial forebears, why are we not twice as content, engaged, or hopeful as our parents and ancestors?

Economic theorists and practitioners have generally been oblivious to such concerns as hope and happiness. They have perceived the free market largely as an atomistic interaction governed by abstract rules, whereby enlightened self-interest dictates that each agent make "the highest worthwhile contribution to the common pool from which each will win an uncertain share."[2] This perception has not only brought about a highly sophisticated articulation of the mechanics of economic interactions, but has also contributed to a policy framework more concerned with manipulating internal processes than with ultimate outcomes. In assuming that the morality of the economic system lies in "abstract rules (that) operate as ultimate values because they serve ... individuals in the pursuit of their temporary aims,"[3] economists may have convincingly demonstrated the superior efficiency of American-style capitalism, but they have also undermined its essential moral foundations by denying the existence of any transcendent purpose. It was Adam Smith, after all, who pointed out that even though with sufficient competition self-interest would lead to the common good, this was true only if most people in the society accepted a general moral law as a guide for their behavior, that is, if there were a moral base for the society at large.

Certainly, it is legitimate for economists to be inattentive to transcendent moral concerns in pursuing a clear and empirically grounded explanation. It should also be understood that the mechanics of an economic system do not constitute the whole reality of the social system, but comprise, rather, a skeletal abstraction useful for certain important though limited purposes. The transformation of methodological abstraction into structural explanation, in which a partial reality masquerades as the fullness of truth, only serves to confirm Marx's assertion that capitalism breeds "no other nexus between man and man than naked self-interest," where all transcendent values are drowned "in the icy waters of egotistical calculation."[4] Such misplaced argumentation distorts the fact that a capitalist economic system is an essential, but subordinate, part of a wider moral-political order, a part whose fate is inextricably linked to the ethical and cultural health of Western civilization as a whole.

Wilhelm Ropke has argued convincingly that, since "people do not live by cheaper vacuum cleaners alone," any economic order that forgets humanity's transcendent nature contains within itself the roots of its own decay.[5] Hence, the protagonists of capitalism need to pay equal attention both to the efficiency of that system and to the equity it must generate if it is to achieve the proximate goal of enhancing the participation of all citizens and the ultimate goal of contributing to the common good, including increasing human fulfillment and freedom.

These misgivings suggest the possibility that the current economic problems of the West, particularly in the United States, are as much moral as economic. They result both from an inability to control the new forms of conflict as groups struggle for larger shares of the gross national product (GNP) in a situation of more limited productivity, and from the erosion of a societal moral base, which economists have simply assumed was there. New social conflict is a byproduct of this erosion and of our concomitant inability to bring about widespread agreement over distributing the fruits of the economy. This problem is exacerbated by the pressures of international competition, the relative decline of America's global economic contribution, the persistent adversarial patterns in America's economic culture, as well as the challenges of the Reagan administration to the welfare state. Not only is this conflict a key factor in the present economic situation, but critics have argued that it may also require increased regulation that could undermine the free market system. Obviously, this struggle erodes fellowship and forces reconsideration of the meaning of free choice in consumption.

This volume brings together a series of original, critical reflections on the moral and religious dimensions of the American economy. Its objective is to analyze and discuss the principal themes of the 1986 pastoral letter of the American Catholic bishops, "Catholic Social Teaching and the U.S. Economy." This letter, like the bishop's 1983 pastoral, "The Challenge of Peace," represents a significant event both in American public life and in the presentation, extension and application of a tradition of Catholic social teaching that has been developed in a series of papal social encyclicals, begun by Leo XIII in 1891 with *Rerum Novarum* and continued through the Second Vatican Council's Constitution on the Church and the Modern World (*Gaudium et Spes*) to John Paul II's *Laborem Exercens*. These sources provide a rich body of material, largely conceived in response to the problems of industrialization, social strife and decolonization as these affected Western Europe over the last 100 years. However, this material lacks the clarity and precision associated with other themes of Catholic moral teaching, such as the just-war theory. Many of the specific recommendations found in earlier papal encyclicals are outmoded; many were designed to address problems of European, not American, society. Some, like those in John Paul II's encyclical on human work, are so generic that they are compatible with a wide variety of institutional arrangements.

Another building block of the bishops' pastoral on the economy is American Catholicism's long history of involvement with many of the issues considered in the letter. As leaders of an immigrant church, Catholic bishops and priests were in the forefront of the struggle for economic justice, exercising what has more recently been termed the "preferential option for the poor." The American labor movement owes a large part of its origin to Catholic auspices. In contrast with Europe, American Catholicism never lost the working class and still retains a strong identification with it. At the same time, Catholics were just as affected as everyone else by the economic crises of the late 1970s: galloping inflation and unemployment, increasing global interdependence and the shifting national and international division of labor, the collapse of liberal assumptions and policies based on the promise of continued unlimited growth, and the attendant dilemmas of the welfare state under advanced capitalism.

The bishops experienced the consequences of this crisis not at the theoretical or empirical level, but at the pastoral level of everyday life: increased family breakdown; higher rates of crime, suicide and mental illness; feelings of helplessness among their people and loss of human dignity for those without work. By the early 1980s, awareness was growing among both Catholic and non-Catholic religious leaders that the elaboration of any economic strategy involves making moral decisions about the kind of people we are, the kind of people we want to become, and the kind of world we want to leave to our children. For the bishops who believe that promoting integral human development lies at the very core of the church's mission, these questions are not only moral but religious as well, for they touch on the matter of where God is present in our lives and what fidelity to God demands of us in the present debate over economic rights and economic justice.

While these were some of the considerations that led the Catholic bishops to write about such a complex and controversial subject as economic policy, two other aspects of their letter also merit attention, both of which were derived from the experiences of writing their 1983 pastoral letter, "The Challenge of Peace." First, the process of preparing the letter involved consultation, both inside and outside the church, with a wide range of experts and representatives of groups whose interests would be affected by what the bishops said. The bishops' committee charged with drafting the letter drew on the opinion of over 200 theologians, philosophers, economists, sociologists, social policy theorists and social activists, corporate business executives, labor union leaders, government officials and assorted intellectuals and journalists. This consultation continued for two years as the bishops continued to receive criticism and suggestions on two published drafts of their letter, the first in November 1984, the second in October 1985. Thus, the final letter, approved by the full membership of the National Catholic Conference of Bishops in November 1986, is not the product of a series of closed-door meetings, but of an open process in which all sides are heard and the bishops are seen to struggle with complex issues.

Second, the letter is addressed to a dual audience—those both inside and outside the church. As the bishops observe:

> We write, then, first of all to provide guidance for members of our church as they seek to form their consciences about economic matters. . . . At the same time, we want to add our voice to the public debate about the directions in which the U.S. economy should be moving. We seek the cooperation and support of those who do not share our faith or tradition. The common bond of humanity that links all persons is the source of our belief that the country can attain a renewed public moral vision.[6]

These two aspects of the letter ensure that the document will be judged as an extension and application of Catholic teaching and as a contribution to a public moral debate on the whole array of American economic and social institutions. The process of open consultation and revision also contributes to establishing credibility with an American audience and to safeguarding the bishops' claim to be heard on a complex issue on which their expertise is obviously limited. Like their earlier statement on war and peace, the pastoral letter on the U.S. economy represents another important step in redefining the public role of the nation's largest and most powerful religious group.

At first sight, such an undertaking might appear somewhat removed from the church's main task of preaching the Gospel. Nevertheless, the Roman Catholic tradition has always maintained that, given the close relationship between the character of the social order and the personal virtue of individuals, any contribution the church can make to promote that order constitutes an essential contribution to its overall mission of evangelization. As John Paul II observed in 1981, "evangelization, the raison d'etre of any ecclesial community, would not be complete if it did not keep in mind the relations existing between the message of the Gospel and man's personal and social life, between the commandment of love for one's suffering neighbor and the concrete situations of injustice to be combatted and of justice and peace to be established."[7]

Yet, even though evangelization and the pursuit of justice are closely related, they are not identical; nor can one be reduced to the other. Their innate distinctiveness, coupled with the bishops' primary responsibility to preach the Gospel, impose limitations on the manner in which the church can address the special concerns of the time. The chief limitation is that the bishops cannot present their particular recommendations as the only feasible solutions to practical problems. "The principles of revelation," they concede, "do not provide specific solutions to many social problems, nor do they constitute a blueprint for organizing society. In proposing concrete policies in the social order, the church is aware that the more specific a proposal or program, the more room there may be for persons of sincere faith to disagree."[8] Specific policy recommendations, therefore, offer both a problem and an opportunity: a problem because specificity itself invites greater dissent; an opportunity because it provides proposals that stimulate scholars and all people of good will to reflect on the shape of the American economy and on its consequences on the lives of those who participate in it.

The basis for all that the church believes about the moral dimensions of economic life is its vision of the transcendent worth—the sacredness and dignity—of human beings. To quote again from John Paul II:

In its social doctrine, the church does not propose a concrete political or economic model, but indicates the way, presents principles. And it does so in accordance with its evangelizing mission, in accordance with its evangelical message, which has as its aim man in his eschatological dimension, but also in the concrete context of his historical contemporary situation. It does so because it believes in the dignity of man, created in the image of God: a dignity which is intrinsic in every man, every woman, every child, whatever may be his place in society.[9]

This volume is conceived in that same spirit. Its aim is both to continue and contribute to the public debate on the moral and religious dimensions of the American economy initiated by the bishops' pastoral letter. It is guided by the conviction that public reflection on the themes and issues of the letter will benefit from an informed, independent, and ecumenical discussion by theologians, ethicists, social scientists, and those actively involved in business, finance, labor and government. The book is sponsored by the Woodstock Theological Center, a Catholic and Jesuit research institute at Georgetown University, which seeks to explore contemporary issues in areas where the social sciences, ethics, public policy and theology intersect.

The essays of the book have been organized into three sections. The first focuses on the major themes of the pastoral letter and considers them in terms of their religious and moral perspective, the history of Catholic social teaching and American Catholic social thought. The essays in the second section examine specific and concrete areas of economic problems and policy: unemployment, poverty, agriculture and international trade. The concern here is to assess these issues and the bishops' treatment of them in light of economic theory and practice. The concluding section provides a series of reflections about the societal and political implications of the perspectives articulated in the bishops' letter from the viewpoint of social theory, business management, labor and politics. The reference for all of these essays has been the second draft of the bishops' letter.

Special thanks are due to John P. Langan, S.J., Senior Fellow of the Woodstock Theological Center, and Ashley J. Tellis, research associate of the Center, who served as editorial and steering committee for this project, and to Jude Howard and Eileen Phillips, who helped prepare the manuscript for publication.

Contributors

ROBERT BENNE is Jordan-Trexler Professor of Religion, chairman of the Religion and Philosophy Department and director of the Center for Church and Society at Roanoke College, Salem, Virginia. He received his Ph.D. in Ethics and Society from the University of Chicago Divinity School, and was formerly professor of church and society at the Lutheran School of Theology in Chicago. Professor Benne is author of *The Ethic of Democratic Capitalism*.

KURT H. BIEDENKOPF is a member of the Parliament of North Rhine Westphalia (West Germany), member of the governing board of the Christian Democratic Party and chairman of the party's state organization in North Rhine Westphalia. Formerly a professor of commercial and labor law at the Ruhr University in Bochum and rector of that university from 1976 to 1979, he served as secretary general of the Christian Democratic Union from 1973 to 1977 and was a member of the West German Bundestag from 1976 to 1980. He holds a master's degree in law and an honorary doctorate in law from Georgetown University, Washington, D.C., and has published widely in the areas of law and economic and security policy.

NORMAN BIRNBAUM is a university professor at Georgetown University Law Center. He was educated at Williams College and Harvard University, where he received his Ph.D. in sociology in 1958. He has taught at the London School of Economics, Oxford University, the University of Strasbourg and Amherst College. He has been an editorial consultant to *Partisan Review* and is on the editorial board of *The Nation;* he was also a founding editor of *New Left Review*. His major books include *The Crisis of Industrial Society* and *Social Structure and the German Reformation*. In addition to his academic activities, he is active in the politics of the Democratic Party and works closely with a number of European political parties and unions. Professor Birnbaum's chapter is part of a project conducted under the Humanities and Law program of the Georgetown University Law Center, supported by the Exxon Educational Foundation, and was completed during his visit as Guest Scholar, International Institute of Environment and Society, Berlin.

JAMES E. BURKE is chairman of the board and chief executive officer of Johnson & Johnson, the international health care company. He joined Johnson & Johnson in 1953, was elected to the board of directors in 1965, and in

1973, became president and chairman of the Executive Committee. Three years later, he assumed his current position. A native of Rutland, Vermont, Mr. Burke graduated from Holy Cross College and received an MBA from Harvard Business School. He is a member of the Policy and Planning Committees of the Business Roundtable and is chairman of its Employment Policy Task Force. He is chairman of the President's Commission on Executive Exchange and is a director of IBM. Mr. Burke received the Advertising Council's Public Service Award in 1983.

WILLIAM J. BYRON, S.J. is president of The Catholic University of America and a former president of the University of Scranton. He earned a doctorate degree in economics from the University of Maryland and a licentiate in theology from Woodstock College, Maryland. Fr. Byron is author of *Toward Stewardship,* editor of *The Causes of World Hunger,* and a founding director of Bread for the World.

JEAN-YVES CALVEZ, S.J. is best known as the author of a major study on the thought of Karl Marx. He is currently a member of CERAS (Centre de Recherche et d'Action Sociales) of the French Jesuits, Paris, and teaches at the Institut d'Etudes Politiques and several other Paris institutions of higher education. His main current interests are international relations of the Third World and trends in Catholic thought about society and the state. From 1971 to 1983, he was in Rome as advisor to Fr. Pedro Arrupe, superior general of the Jesuits. Two works of his translated into English are *The Church and Social Justice* and *Politics and Society in the Third World.*

CARL F. CHRIST received his bachelor's degree in physics at the University of Chicago in 1943 and his doctorate in economics there in 1950. He has taught and written on econometrics and macroeconomics at the University of Chicago (1955–1961) and at the Johns Hopkins University (1950–1955, and from 1961 to the present). He has been a visiting professor or research scholar at the Universities of Cambridge and Essex in England, the University of Tokyo, the Center for Advanced Study in the Behavioral Sciences in Stanford, California, and the Bank of Japan.

CHARLES E. CURRAN is professor of moral theology at The Catholic University of America and former president of the Society of Christian Ethics and of the Catholic Theological Society of America. His most recent books are *Directions in Catholic Social Ethics* and *Directions in Fundamental Moral Theology.*

THOMAS R. DONAHUE is secretary-treasurer of the AFL-CIO. He has served the trade union movement in a wide variety of positions ranging from part-time organizer and business agent to first vice president of a major AFL–CIO affiliate and executive assistant to former AFL–CIO President George Meany. He has served in the government as Assistant Secretary of Labor for Labor–Management Relations during the Johnson administration. He was elected secretary–treasurer of the AFL–CIO in November 1979 and has since been reelected every two years.

KENNETH R. FARRELL is director of the National Center for Food and Agriculture Policy. He holds a Ph.D. in agricultural economics from Iowa State University and is author of over 100 technical and semitechnical reports dealing with issues in food, nutrition, agriculture, international trade and the environment. Before joining the research institute Resources for the Future, Dr. Farrell was administrator of the Economics and Statistics Service of the United States Department of Agriculture, and associate director of the Giannini Foundation of Agricultural Economics at the University of California, Berkeley. He is also a Fellow and past president of the American Agriculture Economics Association.

MILTON FRIEDMAN, Nobel prizewinner for excellence in economics, is a Senior Research Fellow at the Hoover Institution, Stanford University. He is also Paul Snowden Russell Distinguished Service Professor Emeritus of Economics at the University of Chicago, where he taught from 1946 to 1976, and was a member of the research staff of the National Bureau of Economic Research from 1937 to 1981. He has published many books and articles, most notably *A Theory of the Consumption Function, The Optimum Quantity of Money and Other Essays* and (with A. J. Schwartz) *A Monetary History of the United States, Monetary Statistics of the United States, and Monetary Trends in the United States and the United Kingdom.*

THOMAS M. GANNON, S.J. is currently a visiting fellow at St. Edmund's College, Cambridge University; since 1983 he has been director of the Woodstock Theological Center and professor of sociology at Georgetown University. He received his Ph.D. in sociology from the University of Chicago and holds advanced graduate degrees in philosophy and theology. He has been president of both the Association for the Sociology of Religion and the Religious Research Association. In addition to several books and numerous scholarly articles on issues related to religion and social change, Fr. Gannon has been visiting professor at universities in England, Germany, Austria, Japan, India and China.

ALBERT GORE, JR. was elected to the U.S. Senate in November 1984 after serving eight years in the U.S. House of Representatives. He is active in numerous economic, health, environmental and consumer issues. As senator, he has also continued to specialize in nuclear arms control and nonproliferation issues. He was chosen by the Senate leadership to serve on a panel of ten Senate observers attending arms control talks in Geneva. He is a member of the Rules; Governmental Affairs; and Commerce, Science and Technology Committees in the Senate. *Washington Monthly* magazine named him one of the six most effective members of Congress in 1984.

RONALD M. GREEN is John Philips Professor of Religion and chairman of the Department of Religion at Dartmouth College. Trained in moral philosophy at Harvard, he has written widely in the fields of applied ethics, comparative religious ethics and Jewish ethics. His books include *Population Growth and Justice* (1975) and *Religious Reason* (1978).

THOMAS S. JOHNSON is president and director of the Chemical New York Corporation and Chemical Bank. His chief responsibilities involve managing Chemical's Capital Markets Group, which includes treasury, investment banking and foreign exchange activities. Mr. Johnson came to Chemical in 1969 from the United States Department of Defense, where he was special assistant to the comptroller. A graduate of Trinity College and Harvard University's Graduate School of Business Administration, Mr. Johnson has also taught finance and control subjects at the Graduate School of Business at

Ateneo de Manila University in the Philippines, and is currently chairman of the board of directors of Union Theological Seminary in New York City.

JOHN LANGAN, S.J. has been a fellow of the Woodstock Theological Center since 1975 and is currently its acting director. He holds a Ph.D. in philosophy from the University of Michigan and has taught in the theology and philosophy departments at Georgetown University. In 1983, he served as visiting professor of social ethics at the Yale Divinity School. Since 1982, he has served as a consultant on ethics and social policy for the Chemical Bank of New York. He has edited two volumes of essays, *Human Rights in the Americas* and *The Nuclear Dilemma and Just War Theory*, and his articles have appeared in *Theological Studies, Harvard Theological Review, Journal of Religious Ethics, Commonweal, Etudes* and the *Naval War College Review*.

PAUL D. MCNELIS, S.J. is associate professor in the Department of Economics at Georgetown University. He received a Ph.D. in economics from Johns Hopkins University in 1974 and a M.Div. from Weston School of Theology in 1977. He was a Fulbright Fellow on Latin American inflation and stabilization policy at the Central Bank of Peru in 1984 and a Brazilian National Research Council Guest Scholar at the Getulio Vargas Foundation in Rio de Janeiro in 1985. He is a technical consultant to the Interamerican Development Bank, and during the 1986–1987 academic year is visiting professor in the Department of Economics at Trinity College, Dublin.

WILLIAM B. NEENAN, S.J. was a professor in the Economics Department at the University of Michigan from 1966 until 1980. He left there to go to Boston College, where he is currently a professor of economics and dean of the College of Arts and Sciences. Among his numerous articles and several books is *Urban Public Economics*.

DAVID J. O'BRIEN is associate professor of history at Holy Cross College. He has served as a consultant to the National Conference of Catholic Bishops and is a member of the board of directors of the *National Catholic Reporter*. His books include *American Catholics and Social Reform: The New Deal Years* (1968), *The Renewal of American Catholicism* (1972) and, with Thomas A. Shannon, *Renewing the Earth: Catholic Documents on Justice, Peace and Liberation* (1978).

RUDOLPH A. OSWALD has been the director of the AFL-CIO's Department of Economic Research since 1976. He is a member of the Advisory Committee on Trade Negotiations and the Services Policy Advisory Committee to the U.S. Special Trade Representative, and a member of the Labor Research Advisory Council to the Bureau of Labor Statistics of the U.S. Department of Labor. He serves on the board of directors of the National Bureau of Economic Research, the Joint Council on Economic Education, the Consumer Energy Council of America and the Industrial and Labor Relations Advisory Council of Cornell University. He is also a past president of the Industrial Relations Research Association (IRRA).

MANUEL G. VELASQUEZ received his doctorate in social ethics in 1975 from the Philosophy Department of the University of California at Berkeley. Since 1977, he has taught philosophy at Santa Clara University, where he served as department chairman from 1980 to 1985. The author of several articles on applied ethics, particularly on topics in business ethics, he has also written on Catholic social teaching and has authored two books, including *Business Ethics: Concepts and Cases.* He is currently the president of the Society for Business Ethics and a member of the Executive Council of the American Catholic Philosophical Association. In 1985, Professor Velasquez testified on "Catholic Social Teaching and the U.S. Economy" at hearings held before the Committee of American Bishops on the pastoral letter.

THEOLOGICAL RESOURCES FOR EVALUATING ECONOMIC POLICY

Economic Policy Issues in Roman Catholic Social Teaching

AN INTERNATIONAL PERSPECTIVE

Jean-Yves Calvez, S.J.

The U.S. Catholic bishops' statement on "Catholic Social Teaching and the U.S. Economy" has a history of its own, stretching over a period of four years. This history has mainly involved intense and prolonged consultation and discussion with many in the Catholic community and outside its boundaries, which gives the letter a very special character. An official church document probably never has been so widely and democratically prepared. At the same time, there can be no doubt that the bishops take the full responsibility that belongs to them for what appears in their statement.

What will be examined in this chapter is the much longer history to which the writing of the U.S. Catholic bishops' statement relates. It is the history of what has been termed "Catholic social teaching." The question here, then, is how, up until now, has Catholic social teaching dealt with issues of economic policy? Answering this query will give an opportunity to evaluate the new positions taken by the American bishops against the background of the treatment of similar issues in the longer tradition of the whole church's teaching.

A CENTURY OF PAPAL PRONOUNCEMENTS

Within the context of an episcopal letter, Catholic social teaching must be understood as the pronouncements of the official hierarchy of the Roman Catholic church in the social field (for example, the family, government, peace and war, the economy). Obviously, a broader meaning exists for the term Catholic social teaching, not to speak of Catholic social thought in general.

15

In this sense, Catholic social teaching includes all that has been or is being taught today in Catholic schools or Catholic associations regarding social questions. Catholic social thought would include the private views of those Catholic theologians, scholars and ordinary believers who have written or spoken about their faith in relation to social, economic and political life. For a comparison with an episcopal letter, however, our primary reference should be similar hierarchical statements. The social teaching of national and regional episcopal conferences has been a comparatively recent development in the years since the Second Vatican Council (1962–1965).

All episcopal conferences, however, recognize a need to base themselves on the major teachings of the popes since Leo XIII and on the declarations of Vatican II, which expressed the whole Catholic church in a special way. These papal (and conciliar) pronouncements comprise more or less a century of Catholic social teaching, beginning with Pope Leo XIII's 1891 encyclical *Rerum Novarum,* which can indeed be considered the beginning of modern papal social teaching. *Rerum Novarum* is a landmark, and those who have read the famous French Catholic novel of the 1930s, *The Diary of a Country Priest,* will recall Bernanos' description of what a "clap of thunder" the publication of this encyclical represented.

Considering the whole range of papal teaching about the economy, two points may be made at the outset. First, a papal pronouncement never takes the form of a general treatise. Even if it articulates principles and expresses general perspectives, this teaching is mostly concerned with particular questions arising from difficult situations facing mankind or a major portion of it. Second, not all economic issues of concern to the church are, strictly speaking, issues of policy. After World War II, for example, the church expressed considerable concern with matters of economic organization, whether it involved Marxist collectivism, expressed in nationalization, or the movement toward a welfare state, which could endanger personal freedom and diminish or crush personal responsibility. It was not so much matters of economic policy that engaged the church's attention as the preservation of two general and fundamental values—human freedom and responsibility—that was seen to be essential for the good of the human person. These same values were reaffirmed in the 1960s, when the church advocated the maximum possible participation in economic decision making, but by then, the climate had changed and the church looked more positively toward the phenomenon of increasingly global interdependence among human beings.

Nevertheless, a whole range of questions existed that called for the development of a Catholic social teaching over the last century, questions that were also looked on as specific issues of economic policy. These included the plight of workers at the end of the nineteenth century (which, in contrast with the liberalism then fashionable, Leo XIII judged could at least partly be remedied by new legislative and economic policies); the world economic crisis in the early 1930s, particularly the problem of massive unemployment; farm policy at the time of the radical transformation of European agriculture after World War II; social development and the international economic order, with the emergence of the new nation-states in the 1960s; and, at the end of the 1970s and early in the 1980s, the returning economic crisis of inflation and unemployment. This cursory listing of issues demonstrates the widening horizon of Catholic social teaching, especially a growing sensitivity to international economic questions. This progressively global perspective may be partly explained by the absence of any worldwide secular authority to implement needed economic policies, a fact that has been of special concern to the Catholic church for some time.

A more detailed consideration follows of the various stages in the development of Catholic social teaching that correspond to the range of policy issues listed.

The Economic Policy Issues of *Rerum Novarum.* Certainly, *Rerum Novarum* (1891) constitutes the first important pronouncement of the modern Catholic church on economic and social matters. Its main concern was with the condition of workers at the end of the nineteenth century. This condition was no longer quite so appalling as when Karl Marx wrote the *Communist Manifesto* (1848) and began writing *Capital,* or at the time of the famous surveys conducted in Great Britain and France that documented the misery and exploitation of factory workers in the early industrial age. In most industrial countries, however, the workers' plight continued. It also seemed rather hopeless in view of the insistence of liberal economic thinkers that this situation represented the natural course of things according to economic laws against which the state should not be allowed to interfere.

Not everyone, of course, subscribed to the views of economic liberalism. In Bismarck's Germany, for instance, the idea of social legislation to remedy the worst conditions of the workers was making strong progress. Thus, *Rerum Novarum* was written not only in the context of the inhuman condition of workers that "cried to heaven" for remedy, but also against the background of a fierce debate between liberal and interventionist economic thinkers. This debate was also carried on within the church, especially among various schools of social thinking (for example, Angers, Liege, Vienna) that represented contradictory positions.

After denouncing the situation of workers as a violation of human dignity as expressed in "Christian philosophy" and in the scriptures and disputing the validity of revolutionary socialist solutions that were then being presented in circles profoundly hostile to the church and to religion, Leo XIII offered two basic remedies: legislation and other state interventions to ensure a just wage, decent working conditions and an atmosphere more conducive to wage bargaining, and the formation of voluntary associations as a means of overcoming the individualist patterns of social relations that had replaced the guilds and corporations of the ancient regime. The encyclical is not entirely clear about what kinds of association the pope favored. At times, he seems to mean associations of employers and workers, that is, some kind of corporation styled on the ones that existed before 1789. The encyclical, though, also leaves room for associations of workers alone. Although much stress was put on the need for a dimension of explicitly spiritual activity in Catholic workers' associations, Leo's suggestions paved the way for strong support of trade unionism throughout the Catholic population.

With regard to Catholic social teaching, the most decisive step taken by

Rerum Novarum was to establish firmly the legitimacy of some amount of state intervention in the economy in order to remedy major social evils, and more generally, to require that the economy be judged in terms of how it fosters the common good. In some circles, these propositions were sufficient to label the pope a socialist. He definitely appeared to be a progressive social thinker, even though he had made no concession to socialist views about private property. In fact, not only did he strongly defend the right to private property, he did not give it a subordinate position as was done in earlier church teaching, which maintained that the goods and wealth of the earth were destined for all people, who therefore had the right always to have sufficient access to them.

The World Crisis and *Quadragesimo Anno.* Forty years later, the international economy and world trade were experiencing the worst crisis that had ever hit the capitalist system. In many countries, unemployment was massive. The crisis, in fact, was so severe that for several years, many felt it was not possible to propose even partial remedies; for example, to devise policies that would attack unemployment, which, of course, is precisely what Schacht and Keynes would do a few years later. At the time, however, attention focused on the question of economic "systems" themselves. Capitalism was in shambles—a fact Pope Pius XI clearly acknowledged without qualification in his encyclical *Quadragesimo Anno* (1931). Another system, a socialist one, had emerged in the Soviet Union following the lines of communist doctrine, but *Quadragesimo Anno* found no hope in it because of its collectivist orientation, its materialistic system of values and the fundamentally atheistic philosophy in which it was embedded. Even more moderate Western-style socialism, in Pius XI's view, did not offer a safe way out. It was too infected by a materialistic, secular view of human nature and society, it overemphasized society against individual freedom, and it provided little justification for social authority.

In the face of such serious economic policy issues, and indeed, the collapse of an entire economic system, the pope's principal proposal was not an alternate organization of the economy, but the articulation of principles according to which a new system could be built. These principles rest on a solidaristic perspective, which was intended to overcome both excessive individualism and the rift between capital and labor. The pope explicitly alluded to Mussolini's version of corporativism, criticizing it strongly for being too favorable to state intervention and hostile to free trade unions. It is no exaggeration to admit, however, that he also invited people to search for a kind of revised, more balanced corporativism as a solution to the massive deficiencies he had observed in both liberal capitalism and socialism. The central concern of *Quadragesimo Anno,* then, was not a limited economic issue (even though Pius XI certainly addressed particular matters related to unemployment), but the problem of economic systems themselves, and Catholic social teaching moved in the direction of designing a fundamentally new type of economic organization even while it kept a critical eye on the system that was then emerging in fascist Italy.

This development is not easy to judge, since whatever experiments might have been attempted were soon buried in the war economies. Only after

World War II, especially in the years immediately following it, could the issue of reconstructing the economic system in Europe be considered. By then, however, the larger context had changed dramatically. The free economy and capitalism began a new career. The war victory of the Soviet Union contributed to the attractiveness of the collectivist communist model of organization. In some sectors of British, French and Italian opinion was a strong belief in the value of nationalization. The idea of the welfare state gained many adherents, since it responded to a desire to guarantee social security, which would prevent any recurrence of the kind of suffering, especially through unemployment, so many people had experienced during the Great Depression. All these latter developments assumed a higher degree of organization in economic and social life and some lessening of the scope for economic initiative, personal freedom and individual responsibility.

Pius XII was pope throughout the war and more than a decade thereafter, from 1939 until 1958. During the war, he stressed the importance of democracy and of providing access for all peoples and nations to the wealth of the earth; social injustice often lay at the root of war. In his many pronouncements after the war, he was principally concerned with preserving the values of personal freedom, initiative and responsibility; he pleaded for limiting nationalization (a policy, he felt, that should be used only in truly exceptional cases), and for retaining a high level of personal initiative and responsibility even within the new institutions of social security that were being established. The question of corporativism as a third alternative economic system never resurfaced in these discussions.

The Question of Development in the 1960s and 1970s. Pope John XIII, who succeeded Pius XII in 1958, brought some correction to the postwar line of Catholic social teaching. In 1961, the new pope published a new social encyclical—the third major teaching statement after *Rerum Novarum* and *Quadragesimo Anno*. It bore the title *Mater et Magistra* and was widely publicized and discussed. In one sense, *Mater et Magistra* did not address any new, burning economic issue. The world economy was in the midst of its best postwar years, although some new questions had begun to emerge about models of economic development and the related problems of the many nations, particularly in Asia and Africa, that had become newly independent. Pope John's intention was to offer a comprehensive review of the whole of Catholic social teaching, particularly its pronouncements about private property and the increasing social interdependence throughout the world (a phenomenon he termed, following French usage, "socialization"). Although John did not sharply deviate from the teaching of his predecessors, in comparison with Pius XII, he did take a more positive attitude toward "socialization" which, he judged, appeared every day to be more inevitable. At the same time, he remained a partisan of personal freedom, initiative and responsibility and urged that these must be preserved as much as possible, even under the constraints of a more "socialized" type of economic and social life.

With regard to private property, Pope John showed less reluctance than his predecessor in admitting there were situations in which public property had to be utilized for the common good and in the common interest. However, he also formulated in the same way as Pius XII the traditional Catholic teaching about the universal destination of the earth's goods, insisting that the basic human right of access to material resources is primary regardless of what institutions of private property exist in given societies. Also, never before had Catholic social teaching presented the case for private property with such clarity and forcefulness. In brief, this argument is that private property helps each person to be independent; people take better care of things they own; private property facilitates political liberty. (How far this last point applies to property in the large corporation is questionable.)

The topic of economic development in the new nations and the related questions about the international economic order were only touched on in *Mater et Magistra*. By the time of the Second Vatican Council (1962–1965), however, these issues had become a major concern. In 1961, many African states achieved independence; in 1964, the first United Nations Conference on Trade and Development (UNCTAD) took place. In 1967, two years after the end of Vatican II, Pope Paul VI issued his own document on development, *Populorum Progressio*. This encyclical as well as the council's statements rest on the conviction that the most pressing issue of the day was the plight of the many poor nations that lagged dramatically behind modern standards of development—a plight similar, on the world scale, to what confronted workers in Europe at the time of Leo XIII's *Rerum Novarum*. "The poor nations remain ever poor while the rich ones become still richer."[1]

Paul VI analyzed not only the poverty and weak bargaining power of the developing nations, but also their dependency even after political independence. He strongly indicted the existing system of international economic relations: "The rule of free trade, taken by itself, is no longer able to govern international relations"; and he questioned "the fundamental principle of liberalism, as the rule for commercial exchange."[2] There must be, he observed, "bold transformations, innovations that go deep"[3], by which the present order of things will be entirely renewed or rebuilt. It is not a question of entirely eliminating competition, but of working toward a fair equality of opportunity:

> *Without abolishing the competitive market, it should be kept within the limits which make it just and moral, and therefore human. In trade between developed and underdeveloped economies, conditions are too disparate and the degrees of genuine freedom available are too unequal. In order that international trade be human and moral, social justice requires that it restore to the participants a certain equality of opportunity. This equality is a long-term objective, but to reach it we must begin now to create true equality in discussions and negotiations.*[4]

This statement was preceded by a reference to the protective measures not infrequently used in the national economies:

> *What was true of the just wage for the individual is also true of* international contracts: *An economy of exchange can no longer be based solely on the law of free competition, a law which, in its turn, too often creates an economic dictatorship. Freedom of trade is fair only if it is subject to the demands of social justice. Moreover, this has been under-*

stood by the developed nations themselves, which are striving, by means of appropriate measures, to reestablish within their own economies a balance, which competition, if left to itself, tends to compromise. Thus, it happens that these nations often support their agriculture, at the price of sacrifices imposed on economically more favored sectors. Similarly, to maintain the commercial relations which are developing, among themselves, especially within a common market, the financial, fiscal and social policy of these nations tries to restore comparable opportunities to competing industries which are not equally prospering. In this area, one cannot employ two systems of weights and measures. What holds for a national economy or among developed countries is valid also in commercial relations between rich nations and poor nations.[5]

One of the fundamental aspects of the problem of development, according to Paul VI, is the need to allow poorer or weaker nations to be the main artisans of their progress. Again, here is a direct quote from *Populorum Progressio;* the document is often an object of controversy and it is useful to look carefully at the text itself.

World unity, ever more affective, should allow all peoples to become the artisans of their destiny. The past has too often been characterized by relationships of violence between nations. May the day dawn when international relations will be marked with the stamp of mutual respect and friendship, of interdependence in collaboration, and when the betterment of all will be seen as the responsibility of each individual. The younger or weaker nations ask to assume their active part in the construction of a better world, one which shows deeper respect for the rights and the vocation of the individual. This is a legitimate appeal.[6]

Liberation and Revolution. Very soon after the publication of *Populorum Progressio,* in fact, by the end of the 1960s, the issue of liberation and revolution began to attract attention. The issue is not only political but economic, since it arises from a doubt that there can be successful economic development similar to what the industrialized nations have experienced as long as a situation of dependency persists between the Third and First Worlds. Liberation itself cannot be achieved without revolution because those who hold power in developing countries have no interest in shaking an international dependency on which they thrive. Thus, from the time of the Second Conference of Latin American Bishops in Medellin, Colombia, in 1968 until the 1984 "Instruction" of the Vatican's Congregation for the Doctrine of the Faith "On Some Aspects of Liberation Theology," Catholic social teaching has had to wrestle with the question of social revolution, since some have presented it as the Third World's only way out of the plight of economic dependence.

Even before Medellin, Paul VI touched on this problem, showing great understanding for the kind of social situation that may lead to a popular uprising. As he commented in *Populorum Progressio,* "When whole populations destitute of necessities live in a state of subjection barring them from all initiative and responsibility, and from all opportunity to advance culturally and to share in social and political life, men are easily led to have recourse to violence as a means to right these wrongs to human dignity."[7] At the same time, the pope was already suspicious of the kind of analysis underlying the theory of social revolution in the Third World. Even though he never discarded traditional Catholic teaching about the extreme case in which overthrowing a government by force may be accepted, he nonetheless feared the possible outcome of such revolutions: "A revolutionary uprising—save where there is manifest, long-standing tyranny which would do great damage to fundamental personal rights and dangerous harm to the common good of the country—produces new injustices . . . and brings on new disasters."[8] Moreover, in the 1974 Apostolic Exhortation *Evangelii Nuntiandi,* which followed the 1971 and 1974 meetings of the Synod of Bishops in Rome, Paul extended a favorable ear to the *theological* idea of liberation, provided this idea does not reduce salvation merely to human liberation; but again, he clearly cautioned about recourse to violent rebellion against unjust regimes.

John Paul II, who became pope in 1978, strictly adheres to the same view as Paul VI. He strongly supports solidarity and solidarity movements among those who are oppressed in order to struggle for justice. He also believes there should be efforts to establish international economic institutions that can better ensure the rights of nations that have too little bargaining power in a world of free trade. At the same time, he seems less persuaded than Paul VI by the analysis underlying the theory of violent revolution, which sees violence as the only effective instrument to correct the plight of the poor in Latin America and other Third World nations. In all likelihood, John Paul II earnestly believes that applying the traditional principles of proportionality and of sufficient chance of success cautions against resorting to revolution in the present circumstances. Indeed, one should not forget how in much of Latin America, Che Guevara's rebellions in the 1960s were followed by the cruel military regimes of the 1970s. This succession of events certainly influenced the evolution of Paul VI's statements. For John Paul II, this same position was very likely reinforced by the dramatic events in Poland in which he himself took part. The history of Catholic social teaching on the world level ends with this very acute question unresolved—an issue at least as severe as the condition of European workers at the time of Leo XIII.

GENERAL CONCLUSIONS

What general lessons can be drawn from this review of the main economic and related policy issues that the highest teaching authority of the Catholic church has treated over the last century?

First, one learns something about the kind of social pronouncement the church's hierarchy can make. The binding force of such statements is highest when the hierarchy articulates principles drawn either from the Gospel or from the later tradition of the church; it is proportionately less binding when the hierarchy criticizes some particular situations as contrary to human dignity and brotherhood or when practical applications are drawn from a principle. As we have seen, Catholic social teaching can at times be very specific in both its criticisms and proposals. Leo XIII was quite explicit in condemning the wage system of his time. Many answered that these wages could not be unfair since they had been agreed on by both employer and employee. Leo bluntly replied that this agreement was not sufficient to ensure justice. Pius XI was also explicit about the impossibility for Christians to confess themselves even moderate socialists in the context of the 1930s. John Paul II has again been specific in affirming the right of workers to associate even under a communist regime, as well as denying the validity of revolution in contemporary Latin America.

At least in the case of Pius XI's corporativistic proposal in *Quadragesimo Anno,* one wonders if such specificity was wise. One can also maintain that the difficulties with this proposal came more from its lack of definition than its specificity. Pius XI had argued forcefully that there would be no solution to our economic problems without basic collaboration across social classes, but it was never made clear how this collaboration would encompass either the position of each social class or the relative position of all classes in the labor market. Hence, his successor, Pius XII, concluded that corporativism essentially means cooperation.

A second conclusion concerns the concept of justice in the tradition of Catholic social teaching. Strictly speaking, this tradition is not egalitarian. There was even a time when it was anti-egalitarian. However, Catholic teaching has persistently linked justice with a demand that society provide at least minimum living standards for those left out or crushed by the economic system. In other words, even before assessing other aspects of an economy, the church insists that all members of a society must be ensured a decent standard of living. Its underlying assumption is that without such a minimum standard, no genuine society can be formed. Even when one takes into account the various circumstances that prevail in different societies, the church will always press for correcting or eliminating any conditions that force individuals or groups to exist in situations unworthy of human beings. Finally, the church's concept of justice leads it to favor measures that will establish the highest possible equality of opportunity for all people in a society.

Third, the church might like to trust systems of free competition and free trade, but cannot fully, given the conditions in which they operate and also the characteristics of human nature. Pius XI felt that free competition in fact destroys itself, and that it gives the powerful and unscrupulous a chance to act only for their own advantage, doing a genuine wrong to others. Nevertheless, Catholic social teaching has not shown much confidence in planning institutions and economic control organizations, even though it recognizes the necessity. In Leo XIII's time, the church certainly made a strong case for state intervention, because in that environment of early capitalism, free trade and free competition were presented as an absolute and radical ideal, but its endorsement of intervention was never unqualified. Its consistent position has been to advocate a system of checks and balances as necessary for preserving human values in economic life.

Fourth, the church is never content with economic solutions that simply increase the level of production or even distribution. Its basic interest is for any form of economic organization to permit, at the same time, advantages of a more personal kind to be achieved by as many people as possible. More specifically, the church's economic policy recommendations in the 1950s and

1960s stressed *participation* in the various aspects of the economy, including participation in decision making. The church also insisted that initiative possess a high value, but the chance to exercise initiative should not be available only to those capable of becoming entrepreneurs. There should be scope for some kind of initiative for everyone taking part in economic life, especially for those involved in corporate enterprise. In this regard, the recommendations in the recent pastoral letter of the U.S. Catholic bishops for new experiments in participation are most interesting.

Fifth, Catholic social teaching has always placed importance on association among people who share some common interest, and even more, among people who suffer under the same conditions. At the time of the French Revolution as well as in early nineteenth century Britain, there were those who strongly opposed and even feared such association and "coalition." The church, however, has always favored the principle of association and, at times, has asserted the obligation to form certain kinds of association, such as labor unions, although at the beginning, it was quite critical of the revolutionary socialist tendencies prevailing in some unions. Even today, while the church admits that associations sometimes misuse their formidable power, the more common problem is that these associations possess insufficient power because of a lack of interest among people who should join them. Solidarity has been a fundamental theme for John Paul II. Typically, the church continues to feel there is seldom enough of it.

Sixth, from the beginning, Catholic social teaching has emphasized an international perspective. This world dimension is not always easy for people to keep in mind or feel responsible for, absorbed as they are by their own immediate domestic problems. The church's emphasis in this regard undoubtedly springs from the international character of the church itself, in addition to the unrestricted nature of Christian love, which the church has a duty to promote. As a result, some distance is always between the church's appraisal of economic issues and the assessments of citizens who do not share the Catholic faith. Viewing these problems with a global vision, though, helps one realize how important it is to have an international religious agency like the Catholic church to point out the worldwide dimension to which many people would otherwise remain blind.

A seventh conclusion touches on a frequent criticism of the manner in which the church deals with issues of economic policy; namely, that the church's recommendations for promoting social justice or meeting minimum standards of living are unduly sensitive to the distribution of goods and income, while insufficiently sensitive to the kind of efforts required to increase production or create more wealth to satisfy human needs better. There have been times when this criticism was justified, but more recently, the church itself has also reacted against this tendency in its approach. As the Vatican II's document *Gaudium et spes* observes, "Today more than ever before, there is an increase in the production of agricultural and industrial goods and in the number of services available, and this is as it should be in view of the population expansion and growing human aspirations. ... We must encourage technical progress and the spirit of enterprise, we must foster an eagerness for creativity and improvement, and we must promote adaptation of production methods and all serious efforts of people engaged in production."[9] This same concern continues today and has been explicitly endorsed by many national bishops' conferences. As a result, it is difficult to accept this criticism now as an excuse for failing to pay attention to the other side of the church's message about participation, especially participation in initiative, responsibility and decision making.

My eighth conclusion takes the form of a question: Has it been useful for the Catholic church to speak out on economic policy issues? Certainly, this has occasionally strained the church's relationship with the world around it as well as relationships among Catholics or between some Catholics and the hierarchy. Such activity, however, has also kept the church close to the center of public debate over the last century, demonstrating that Christianity is a religion with a developed ethical dimension and a concern about the affairs of this world. Thus, the world and its apparently profane concerns are not deprived of religious meaning, and the basic human dynamics that express themselves in economic life are not unrelated to those that orient human beings to God. Moreover, this involvement of the Catholic church—and, more generally, of all Christian churches—has probably exerted real influence on economic and social history. In many nations, it may have helped preserve a balance between excessive capitalist liberalism and imprudent confidence in state intervention. Also likely is that the church has played a considerable role in pressing for wider participation of more people in the economy and in raising our awareness of the poorer economies around the world.

Finally, does not official Catholic social teaching have a distinctly *European* character? Admittedly it does, since prior to the Second Vatican Council, hardly any other voices were heard at the center of the Catholic church. The only exception to this pattern probably was the influence of the U.S. Catholic church in preparing Leo XIII's *Rerum Novarum,* but even with regard to questions of social development at the time of Vatican II, the whole context of the argument was shaped by Europeans, not Africans, Asians, or Latin Americans; those most active in preparing the documents of the council were European experts. A few Latin American bishops, like Manuel Larrain of Chile and Helder Camara of Brazil, made important contributions, but they were exceptions.

Today, however, the situation has dramatically changed. As we have seen, the most burning questions before the church pertain to liberation and revolution, and these are Latin American questions. At the same time, the most decisive questions about developed economies, especially those of "neoconservatism" and more liberal economic trends, are now being raised primarily in the United States, though also in Europe.

Can discussion of these new questions arising from such an advanced industrial economy as the United States still draw on the tradition of Catholic social teaching? In spite of some differences, the answer could very well be yes. The basic concerns are indeed common; for example, the importance Catholic social teaching has long given to active participation by all in the economy, including participation in decision making. This emphasis seems to lie at the very core of the American bishops' pastoral letter on the economy. The same may be said about concern with the international dimensions of the economy, especially about relations between the First and Third worlds.

Here again, the basic thrust of Catholic social teaching since World War II, repeated in the letter, is quite the same. Therefore, one can speak of a harmonious development in the tradition of Catholic social teaching embodied in this letter. At the same time, it becomes clear that the various churches all over the world have strongly influenced each other in an effort to expand and further develop this tradition.

The Economic Thought of the American Hierarchy

David J. O'Brien

The proposed pastoral letter of the American Bishops, "Catholic Social Teaching and the United States Economy," stands within a relatively short but well-established tradition of commentary by the American bishops on problems in American public life. Since 1919, the American hierarchy has discussed with increasing frequency a range of public problems, none more consistently than the existence of poverty and the means to its elimination. Even longer and richer is a tradition of social action. The American Roman Catholic church was composed of working-class immigrants and their children, many of whom remained relatively untouched by the church's remarkable pastoral and educational institutions, in part because of the problems of personal and family life that always accompanied insecure employment, low income and inadequate housing and social services.

American Catholic tradition of thought and action has not been totally consistent; indeed, it has contained elements of ambiguity and even contradiction, reflecting the unresolved problems posed for Catholicism by religious freedom, cultural pluralism and the segmentation of modern society that relegates religion to personal and family life. Knowledge of that tradition, and reflection on the problems it poses, may serve as a useful background for reception of the proposed pastoral letter on economic justice, and perhaps provide as well some clues to how its teachings can be effectively carried out.[1]

THE SOCIAL THOUGHT OF A MISSIONARY CHURCH

The earliest American Catholics were English settlers, many highly successful planters, in the Chesapeake Bay area. In Maryland, they found opportunities for economic advancement unavailable at home, where, by the end of the seventeenth century, Catholics were excluded from public life and suffered a variety of civil disabilities. Lord Baltimore's Maryland project was economic in origin, but it offered the added benefit of religious freedom until the outcome of the religious struggle in England left the colony in Protestant hands. By that time, however, Catholic planter families were well-established; many of the penal laws remained unenforced, although Catholics had to struggle to maintain the faith of their children. Socially, however, they were relatively secure. Almost all joined in the revolution and rejoiced in its outcome, their enthusiasm heightened by the fact that new constitutions guaranteed their religious and civil rights. In 1789, John Carroll, from one of the state's most prominent families, took charge of a new Roman Catholic diocese that embraced the whole country. Later, new dioceses were added as the English stock population was supplemented by refugees from the French Revolution, a scattering of German, Austrian and Hispanic families, and a steady stream of Irish immigrants.

For half a century, the American church enjoyed a "republican interlude," reflecting Carroll's enlightened views and the church's new-found status.[2] Religion was private and personal, and Catholics tended to share the economic and social attitudes of others of their rank and class. Lay editors and publishers Henry and Matthew Carey of Philadelphia helped forge the economic platform of the Whig party of Henry Clay, advocating protectionism, internal improvements and a vigorous role for the national government, but their views had little relationship to their religious faith. Orestes Brownson, one of the nation's best-known intellectuals, offered a scathing critique of the emerging industrial order during the 1840 election; his words echoed the later writings of Karl Marx in their fervent denunciation of the exploitation, greed and alienation associated with the rising factory system. A few years later, Brownson became a Catholic, but he left behind his social and economic radicalism. A vigorous and controversial Catholic, Brownson rarely commented on economic affairs and, when he did, usually expressed highly conservative views and deep suspicion of working-class protests.

The bishops, who met regularly in provincial and national councils from 1829 to 1884, studiously avoided comments on political issues and expressed few reservations about the basic structure of the American political economy, emphasizing instead doctrine, discipline, religious practice, the need for vocations and the obligation to provide Catholic education. In 1829 and again in 1844, the bishops urged Catholics to participate in civic affairs with a disinterested concern for the public good. Occasionally, the bishops noted the fact that their people were for the most part poor, but their characteristic prescription for poverty was support for charity at the parish and diocesan level.[3]

One feature of the American church was that it depended entirely on the free support of its members. In his first pastoral letter in 1792, Carroll warned that those who "refuse to contribute for the ministry of salvation, according to the measure of worldly fortune given to them by a beneficent God" violated "divine and ecclesiastical laws" and were "in a state of sin, unworthy of obtaining forgiveness in the tribunal of confession." To the stick he added a carrot, pointing out the benefits that came with the spread of religion:

> *I will venture to add, that even with respect to this world you will find it to be no loss to concur toward the regular support of the ministry, and services of religion. Habits of temperance and frugality are generally the effects of evangelical instruction. The lessons and duty of industry are frequently inculcated by virtuous and careful pastors. Your children and servants will be admonished perpetually to shun idleness, dishonesty, dissipation, and that train of expense which always follows them. These, by their effect on domestic economy, will make abundant compensation for the charges in support of religion.*

Unfortunately, there were relatively few wealthy Catholics to hear this message. By 1840, the American church had grown considerably through the arrival of hundreds of thousands of immigrants from Germany and Ireland. Almost all the Irish in particular were desperately poor, yet it was on such people that the church had to rely for support. As the bishops wrote in 1837, "The greater portion of our flock is in the humble, laborious, but useful occupations of life." Such bishops as John Hughes of New York turned away from the quiet accommodation of Carroll to a more militant stance designed to organize the now numerous Catholics into a united church capable of defending its rights and directing its own life. The spread of religion, and its support, still contributed to social harmony and economic advancement, but now this argument was aimed more at the ambitious, aspiring members of the Catholic working class than at elite Catholics. Catholicism would have to be a self-made and self-supporting church, and its leaders could hardly help communicating the values of that very American ideal of "the self-made man."

Leading a church of immigrants, and a Catholic church in a Protestant country, the bishops lost that sense of shared responsibility for the common life that was part of the legacy of John Carroll. Instead, the dominant attitudes were those of a minority subculture concerned fundamentally about the welfare of its own members. In addition, the bishops had learned that the voluntary support of their members and the unity of their congregations required the clergy to refrain from interference in political matters and to concentrate on religion, which had mainly to do with sacramental practice, personal morality and family life. In 1829, the bishops told their priests, "From you [the people] expect instruction in the service of God, not suggestions as to the regulation of their own temporal concerns, with which you should scrupulously avoid any entanglement."

The pastoral statements of the bishops often reflected a piety that at first glance contradicted the aspirations of ambitious immigrant leaders. In 1833, in a typical statement, the bishops posed the classic question of what it profited one "to gain the whole world if he lose his own soul" and commented that "the riches of the world are valueless." Historian Jay Dolan has noted that this theme was almost universal in mission sermons, challenged only in temperance sermons that associated restraint with worldly advancement.[4]

Yet, the otherworldly stress on religion as a route to eternal salvation was almost always associated with other themes conducive to self-help. Individuals were responsible for their own salvation; people could choose the path to heaven. When they did so, that choice required faithful attendance at Mass and the sacraments, support for the parish and its pastor and careful attention to the moral law, almost always presented in terms of sobriety, industry, family responsibility and restraint. In 1843, the bishops included among the moral requirements of Catholic faith "strict integrity in the daily concerns of your life, fidelity in the fulfillment of all your engagements, your peaceful public demeanor, your obedience to the laws." The church was a source of order and authority in often disordered immigrant communities. The religious and moral message was one that called the very poor to a sense of order and responsibility; only then could more affirmative messages about economic advancement make sense.

When preachers told their immigrant flocks that their worth and value did not depend on their riches, this comforting message encouraged not passivity and resignation, but steady efforts to bring about gradual improvements in their lives and provide a foundation for the larger advances of their children. In 1840, after warning against "the prevailing temptations of our land ... pride of luxury, the speculations of avarice, the love of riches and the inordinate desire for gain," the bishops urged their people to be "content with the modest acquisitions of honest industry." To the young men of the community, however, the church in temperance lectures and parish societies offered a stronger, more energetic invitation to advancement through study, hard work and respectability. Bishop John Hughes and others regularly pointed to the economic progress of their congregations as evidence of the beneficial effects of religion.

The absence of serious, systematic criticism of American culture, of its political structure and economic system, meant that no religious barriers were placed by the church in the way of people's advancement. In much of Europe, and even in some early national parishes, one might hear that the very idea of advancement was unworthy, but that was not the language of most American sermons and pastoral letters. Nevertheless, the fact remains that the public pronouncements of American church leaders almost never touched on economic problems or controversies. Not until immigrant, working-class Catholics themselves became involved in movements for social change, either as actors seeking reform or objects of the reform movements of others, would the American church begin to reflect more critically on the American political economy.[5]

Three significant points emerge from this period. First, the American church affirmed the political and constitutional system in spite of condemnations of such liberalism in Rome. Even though popular piety may not have stirred aspirations for a better life, little was said or done to discourage the idea that economic mobility was morally acceptable and, in fact, quite useful to a church in need of money and in search of respectability. Finally, while bishops and priests were sympathetic to the plight of their working-class people, they rarely generalized their poverty into an overall criticism of the economic or political system. Instead, they encouraged moral reform through temperance and self-help, and self-discipline through acceptance of the church's sacramental ministry. In doing so, the church brought a principle of order to disordered immigrant communities and developed a cultural and social foundation for popular adjustment to industrial society.

CAUTIOUS PROGRESSIVISM

The American Catholic community was largely composed of immigrant workers who built railroads and canals and later filled the expanding factory system. In the latter half of the nineteenth century, Americans were challenged by the appearance of a large industrial working class, whose very existence called into question many of the assumptions of American democracy. From the great railroad strikes of 1877 through the Haymarket riot of 1886 to the bitter conflicts in steel, mining and textiles at the turn of the century, the existence of social classes and the bitterness of industrial conflict worried middle-class Americans and Catholic church leaders. On the one hand, the bishops still regarded their church as a minority that badly needed to win the respect of the Protestant elites. Thus, they had to present themselves as religious and moral leaders whose influence disciplined unruly immigrants and moderated the demands of labor. On the other hand, they depended on the support of working people and needed to retain their confidence and loyalty. The bishops walked a tightrope, and did so with considerable skill.

In 1886, James Cardinal Gibbons of Baltimore intervened to prevent Vatican condemnation of the Knights of Labor; his statement endorsed labor's right to organize and supported their contention that they had legitimate grievances, winning for the church a reputation as the friend of labor. Yet, Gibbons also argued that American workers were moderate and could achieve their goals without conflict. In the 1890s, a number of Catholic lay and clerical leaders supported arbitration of labor disputes, called on employers to treat their employees justly and urged voluntary action to solve the social problem.[6]

In 1891, Pope Leo XIII's *Rerum Novarum* affirmed the right of workers to a living wage, to organize on their own behalf and to demand from the government assistance to secure themselves against unemployment and illness. Although Leo's encyclical initially was not widely noticed in the United States, it did inspire a young priest in Minnesota, John A. Ryan, to devote his life to the pursuit of justice. After studying at Catholic University in Washington, Ryan published *A Living Wage* in 1906. He translated Leo's principle into concrete American terms and concluded that the right could be implemented only by minimum-wage legislation. He became a member of the faculty of Catholic University in Washington and actively joined many progressive organizations, working to win Catholic support for social legislation and to bring the bishops and Catholic organizations into the progressive movement.[7]

Ryan was a self-taught economist as well as a moral theologian. Influenced by leaders of the Protestant social gospel movement, such as Richard B. Ely, he was also drawn to the work of English economist John Hobson. Applying the philosophical principles of St. Thomas Aquinas and the teachings of *Rerum Novarum* to American problems, Ryan gave particular attention to the unequal distribution of wealth and income. Low wages and swollen fortunes, he argued, were not only morally wrong, but economically disastrous, a position that became even stronger as the United States moved toward a more consumer-oriented economy after World War I. Ryan's *Distributive Justice,* published in 1922, was the most comprehensive examination of the American economy ever written by a Catholic. As the title indicates, Ryan's major concern was with distribution. Like other American progressives fascinated by the productive achievements of the American economy, he tended to assume that the problem of production was solved. The United States could produce more than enough wealth to provide everyone with the minimum income needed to live in decency. This assumption made poverty unnecessary and even more unjust, and gave passion to the quest for justice that shaped Ryan's career.

Ryan's crusade to win Catholic support for social reform bore fruit. With Theodore Roosevelt and Woodrow Wilson in the White House and the nation's conscience stirred by numerous reformers and reform organizations, the idea of social reform became enormously popular in the early years of the century. In addition, the bishops were concerned about the threat of socialism among Catholic workers. Many, therefore, endorsed some forms of progressive legislation, particularly laws aimed at improving the wages, hours and working conditions of industrial workers.

In 1919, when they established the National Catholic Welfare Conference (NCWC), the bishops named Ryan to head its Social Action department, a post that allowed him to shape episcopal statements and improve the church's public image. At the same time, the Administrative Committee of the new organization published a document written by Ryan, the "Bishops' Program of Social Reconstruction." This was a comprehensive call for social reform, including public insurance against sickness, accident, unemployment and old age, support for producers and consumers cooperatives, stock and profit-sharing programs, copartnership schemes and government agencies to assist in finding employment and providing decent housing. The radicalism of the message was evident in the bishops' statement of the three "main defects" of the "present system," namely, "enormous inefficiency and waste in the production and distribution of commodities, insufficient incomes for the great majority of wage earners, and unnecessarily large incomes for a small minority of privileged capitalists." However, in a pastoral letter published later that same year, the bishops warned against radical remedies, arguing that the root cause of these "facts" was irreligious secularism, so that a "conversion of heart" was the only means of true reform.

During the 1920s, as the nation turned away from social reform, the bishops were preoccupied with renewed assaults on Catholic schools and the revival of interreligious conflict as well as the enormous expansion occasioned by the prosperity of the decade. Ryan continued to campaign for reform, but many bishops opposed his efforts. He argued throughout the decade that its apparent prosperity rested on shaky foundations, with continued maldistribution of income, pockets of poverty and unregulated utilities and securities markets posing grave dangers for the future.

Ryan's underconsumption interpretation of the economy provided him with a clear basis for response when the depression began in 1929. The immediate remedy, he believed, lay in increasing the purchasing power of workers and farmers, particularly by public works; the long-range solution required minimum-wage legislation, antitrust enforcement, unionization and government regulation of industry. He found support in Pius XI's *Quadragesimo Anno,* published in 1931, which denounced laissez-faire and called for "the reconstruction of the social order." Pius extended Leo XIII's support for a living wage to a "family living wage." He also outlined a plan of social reorganization based on vocational groups composed of workers and managers, joining together in industrywide councils to shape economic decisions in accord with "social justice," a new term that set as a norm for economic decisions the common good of each industry and of society as a whole. Ryan translated this corporatist ideal into a program of "economic democracy" based on the cooperation of trade unions, trade associations and government.[8]

The Great Depression shocked American Catholics and provided Ryan with a more receptive audience. His influence was evident in the pronouncements of the hierarchy and in individual diocesan efforts at social education and action. Obvious human need and the inadequacy of private and local resources for relief led the bishops to endorse federal action to relieve the plight of the unemployed and bring about reforms aimed at achieving full employment while protecting people against the damaging effects of the business cycle. They picked up Ryan's long-standing support for federal public works, sharply attacked laissez-faire and welcomed the reform proposals of Franklin Roosevelt's New Deal. Many were enthusiastic about the National Recovery Administration (NRA), which attempted to restore prosperity by balancing production and consumption through codes of fair competition. The NRA's experiment in government-labor-business cooperation bore some resemblance to Pius XI's proposals. Ryan argued that the NRA, by placing "human welfare" as the norm for economic decisions, represented a significant step toward a "Christian social order."

At the same time, the church was throwing its support behind the organization of labor, endorsing the National Labor Relation Act of 1935 and, in most localities, strongly defending the right of labor to organize and bargain collectively. The bishops were even more supportive of the New Deal's efforts to place a floor under society by providing insurance against unemployment and old age and by giving federal backing to social welfare. The Social Security Act of 1935 was endorsed by the bishops and so was the fair wages and hours law of 1938. By 1940, the Catholic church had permanently modified its reputation for conservatism; liberal and Protestant leaders expressed their admiration for the progressive position of the church's leadership on issues of economic reform.

However, the bishops, though offering general support for attempts to alleviate suffering through legislation, gave greater attention than Ryan to the need for moral and spiritual regeneration as a prerequisite for structural social reorganization. While their concern with social justice and their sense of Christian charity was evident, their statements continued to reflect the fears and doubts that were products of the church's minority status in the United States. In a 1930 statement on unemployment, for example, they argued that it arose from "lack of goodwill" and "neglect of Christ." They supported federal public works, but also emphasized private charity and ended by moralizing the issue. At their annual meeting a year later, the hierarchy reaffirmed its belief in the moral basis of the depression and called for a "crusade of charity" to meet the desperate needs of the unemployed. They did urge private charities to work with state and federal governments, whose aid was essential because of the magnitude of the problem. The bishops also called for permanent changes so that, in the future, those thrown out of work would not be deprived of sustenance. Emphasizing wage policy, they listed a number of necessary reforms:

> *We ask a living wage for the family; a proper proportion between the wages of the different kinds of workers; an ample sufficiency for all. We ask for wages that will provide employment to the greatest extent possible, and for an equitable sharing of the goods produced by industry.*

To achieve these goals, deal with the problems of the depression, instill a sense of justice and goodwill into industry and secure "equitable distribution of the income and wealth of the country and the world," the bishops called for conferences and organization of employees and employers. These were to be established with the assistance of the government, but operate independently of governmental control.

In 1933, the Administrative Committee again denounced laissez-faire, which denied the "oneness and solidarity of mankind." It was but one sign of a "false liberalism" that encouraged the divorce of religion and morality from life, seen also in secular education and birth control propaganda. The committee denounced the "materialistic" philosophy to which city life gave rise and urged a balance to be restored between the rural and urban sectors of society as necessary for the preservation of American values. The most important need was a moral revival, which would bring down universal condemnation on those who engaged in immoral economic practices.

To bring recovery and restore employment, the bishops strongly advocated wage increases coupled with drastic cuts in salaries, overhead, taxes and government spending. Echoing Pius XI, they called for diffuse ownership through cooperative and copartnership schemes, and joint industrial organizations through which capital and labor could work together for the common good. In conclusion, the bishops warned of the dangers of individualism and greed, which surpassed even the menace of communism, and they called on Catholics to manifest Christian teachings by their actions in civic and economic life.

Throughout the decade, the hierarchy endorsed the natural right of labor to organize, while urging unions to be mindful of the good of all as well as of their own particular group interests. In 1934, the Administrative Committee filed a statement with the Senate Committee on Education and Labor supporting the Wagner Labor Relations Act on the basis of the social encyclicals. "The worker's right to form labor unions and to bargain collectively," the bishops argued, "is as much his right as his right to participate through delegated representatives in the making of laws that regulate his civic conduct. Both are inherent rights." Only through unions could workers order their lives and secure equality of contractual power; interference with this right was unjust both to the workers and to the general public.

As the immediate pressures of the depression relaxed, some of the older fears of American Catholics revived. The Administrative Committee was roused to action in 1937 by the perceived growing threat of communism in the United States. The committee feared that the real weakness of the economic and fiscal structure, the growing discontent of the masses, and the strength of communist propaganda among university professors and intellectuals allowed communist agitators and ideas to infiltrate legitimate organizations. They warned labor unions against the use of coercion, force, destruction of property and class violence. The bishops, retreating from their earlier demands for positive state action, spoke out against undue reliance on the state to solve social problems, and instead urged the middle ground of *Quadragesimo Anno's* "vocational groups, ordering their own economic life under the guidance and encouragement of government." The poor and laboring classes should resist the tendency to set up an omnipotent state, but the alternative was not a return to the old order. "The traditional and ideal Christian society," the Administrative Committee concluded, "is not an individualistic but an organic society in which the individual, through the instrumentality of his group, works for himself, his group, and the entire social body."

In 1940, the most important statement issued by the hierarchy in the decade, "The Church and the Social Order," was published by the Administrative Committee. The bishops again denounced the divorce of social life from religion and set as the goal of Christian social action the defeat of secularism. "We must bring God back into government ... education ... indeed, into all life, private and public," the bishops wrote. "The truth of God, the law of God, the justice, mercy and charity of God, must, by conscious effort and willing submission, be made to permeate all our social intercourse and all our public relations." The statement described the dominant economic problems: the concentration and autonomous character of capital; the maldistribution of property and income; the lack of security from the propertyless condition of the workers and the prevalence of substandard wages. Reaffirming the encyclical teachings, the bishops called for state action to make private property serve the common good, curb the public disorder of disputes between labor and management, and make the possession of property more extensive. They urged that wage increases be taken from profits rather than higher prices and that labor's income be raised to a level permitting family maintenance and some saving. Union organization and collective bargaining were endorsed as immediate means for securing these objectives.

The bishops stressed the need for reaching a stable level of wages and prices and a balance between rural and urban income and between wage levels in various income brackets. To bring this about, they advocated the *via media* of Pius XI, stating that "there must be reestablished some form of guild or vocational groups, which will bind men together in society according to their respective occupations, thus creating a moral unity. Second, there must be a reform of morals and a profound renewal of the Christian spirit, which must precede the social reconstruction." Until "this organic nature of society" was "again recognized and reestablished," either state domination or economic distress and oppression would result. Reform of morals was "first in the logical order, but simultaneous in the order of time" and meant the reaffirmation not only of the virtue of justice, but of charity as well. Only the two together could bring about a "true and rational social order ... in which economic power would be subordinate to human welfare ... social incoherence and class conflict ... replaced by corporate unity and organic function," ruthless competition checked by reasonable state regulation and "the divine plan of a brotherhood of man under the fatherhood of God" made a reality on earth.

In the 1930s, the American hierarchy propagated the teachings of *Quadragesimo Anno* and applied them, however timidly, to American conditions. It gave general support to reform and labor organization, but always emphasized voluntary action, in contrast to Ryan's emphasis on legislation and institutional change. In particular, the bishops feared too much encroachment by the central government in local and private affairs, but they refrained from setting definite limits. When discussing social and economic matters, they were more critical of their country than ever before, but they left considerable room for interpretation.

The bishops also encouraged the continuation of the narrow group consciousness that had been characteristic of American Catholicism since the first impact of immigration in the 1840s. References to the communist sympathies of intellectuals and professors gave weight to the Catholic suspicion of American liberals and hampered the development of cooperation and dialogue between Catholics and other Americans interested in reform. The frequent calls for moral reform, for the permeation of "all our social intercourse and all our public relations" by the principles of Christianity through "conscious efforts and willing submission" were not coupled with a clear understanding of the needs of a free, pluralist society. Underlying these demands was an assumption that, in some way, America and its traditions were Christian, even Catholic, so that immoral practices, whether economic, personal, or social, were not only un-Christian, but un-American.

The 1930s also saw the appearance of a more radical challenge to the economic moderation of the bishops and the preoccupation with institutional reform of Ryan. The Catholic Worker movement, which began in New York City with the publication of the *Catholic Worker* newspaper in May, 1933, called for voluntary poverty and direct assistance to the poor while seeking to build a new social order based on a preindustrial vision of organic community. Dorothy Day and Peter Maurin argued that the root questions posed by the depression were spiritual and cultural and could be resolved only by resisting industrialization and capitalism and restoring a communal society based on handicraft production and a sharing of goods. Government action led to dependency and state power; trade unions represented a surrender to the industrial system and the struggle for power among interest groups. The Christian social order was one that recognized the value of persons, insured personal dignity by a humane setting for work, and drew on the spiritual strength of renewed individuals. The Catholic Worker's "gentle personalism" manifested itself in service to the poor, voluntary poverty, and direct action to create a "new society within the shell of the old."

Catholics, and many bishops, were impressed with the compassion and generosity of the Catholic Workers, but paid little attention to their cultural criticism of capitalism and industrialism. Not until the assumption of abundance—that the productive problem was solved and that only the problem of distribution remained—was challenged would such cultural criticism receive a hearing. The Worker's view of poverty, however, proved more influential, especially as Catholic leaders began to see the problem in a global perspective.[9]

VATICAN II

"The Church and the Social Order," like the "Bishops' Program of Social Reconstruction," did not stimulate renewed activism, but instead marked the end of such a period. With the outbreak of World War II, the bishops turned their attention elsewhere; after the war, they were preoccupied with the suffering of the church in communist Europe, the supposed spread of secularism, the needs of Catholic schools, and such moral problems as birth control. Between World War II and the opening of the Second Vatican Council in 1962, the Catholic population almost doubled, while many for the first time were moving into the middle class and to the burgeoning suburbs. No major statement on economic or social policy appeared between 1940 and 1963, when the race crisis once again spurred the bishops to speak out. During that long period, the Social Action Department of the NCWC under Raymond McGowan and George Higgins remained active; with the support of individual bishops, they backed legislation to protect trade unions and extend the New Deal's benefits to larger categories of workers. Although the church did not abandon its commitment to bread and butter liberalism, the pursuit of social justice was not a priority, despite the department's efforts.

The 1960s ushered in a new period of episcopal leadership, inspired by Vatican II, but required as well by the social issues stirring the country. In 1963, the bishops spoke out against racial discrimination, and thereafter consistently supported the civil rights movement and federal civil rights legislation. By 1966, they had associated racism with poverty and were championing the Johnson administration's programs called the "War on Poverty." In 1969, they launched their own "crusade against poverty," named the Campaign for Human Development the following year, pledging themselves to raise $50 million in 10 years to be granted to organizations of the poor working to overcome injustice. During these same years, the bishops supported the organizational efforts of the United Farm Workers under Cesar Chavez; they endorsed farm labor legislation that would extend the protections of the National Labor Relations Act to agricultural laborers; and in 1973, they threw their support behind a boycott against the Farah plants in Texas.

After Vatican II, the bishops reorganized their national offices into an episcopal conference, the National Conference of Catholic Bishops (NCCB), as mandated by the council. The NCCB established a secretariat, the United States Catholic Conference (USCC). Spurred by the council's affirmation of the social mission of the church and the dramatic problems that arose in the United States during the 1960s, the bishops spoke out far more often than ever before.[10] The pronouncements included pastoral letters, resolutions approved by the body of bishops, statements made on their behalf by their large administrative committee and statements made by NCCB or USCC committees, such as the Committee on Social Development and World Peace. An office of the same name included two divisions, one dealing with world issues and another with "domestic social development"; the officials of these agencies often testified before Congress.

The bishops' activism on public issues was evident in a stream of statements from these offices on a broad range of issues. More than ever before, the bishops spoke out strongly on international issues and U.S. foreign policy, with particular attention to world hunger. After concluding in 1971 that the Vietnam War could no longer be justified, the hierarchy gradually moved to a more critical stance on the arms race, culminating in its widely discussed 1983 pastoral letter "The Challenge of Peace: God's Promise and Our Response." At the same time, the bishops were addressing domestic issues. They spoke out on welfare reform in 1970, the environment in 1971, correctional reform in 1973, the world food crisis in 1974, domestic food policy and gun control in 1975, the aged and new immigrants in 1976, Native Americans in 1977, the handicapped in 1978 and the energy crisis in 1980. The bishops also gave consistent attention to issues that had slipped from the national agenda, regularly supporting reforms to ensure decent health care for all Americans and, in 1972 and 1975, backing strong federal efforts to extend low- and middle-income housing.

In 1976, they pulled together many of the principles of postconciliar teaching in a comprehensive statement, "The Economy: Human Dimensions." The continuity of contemporary teaching with earlier episcopal pronouncements was evident in the fact that this document began with a quotation from the bishops' statement of 1930 on "unemployment," which it called "a sign of deep failure in our country," "the great peacetime physical tragedy" and "one of the great moral tragedies of our time." Asserting that "our economic life must reflect broad values of social justice and human rights," the bishops explained their concern was "not with technical fiscal matters," but with "the moral aspects of economic policy and the impact of these policies on people." They summed up the "rich heritage of Catholic teaching" in terms of the "basic human right to useful employment, just wages and decent working conditions as well as the right of workers to organize and bargain collectively." The popes and the council, the bishops noted, condemned "unemployment, maldistribution of resources and other forms of economic injustice" and called for "the creation of useful work experiences and new forms of industrial organization enabling workers to share in decision making, increased production and even ownership."

They affirmed as principles that "should guide citizens and policymakers" that: economic activity must be governed by moral considerations; "it must serve people's needs"; everyone had the right to "a sufficient share of earthly goods for himself and his family"; work had to be provided for those able to work; and at every level, "the largest possible number of people should have an active share in directing" economic development. Furthermore, the bishops continued to insist that distribution was a more important consideration than production. Economic prosperity, they argued, is "to be assessed not so much from the sum total of goods and wealth possessed as from the distribution of goods according to norms of justice." Yet, government had a responsibility to play an "active role in the economic activity of its citizens," specifically by promoting "in a suitable manner, the production of a sufficient supply of material goods" and by safeguarding the rights of all citizens and helping them find "opportunities for employment."

On this basis, the bishops called current unemployment levels "unacceptable," they condemned the distribution of income and wealth and stated flatly that the priority accorded to fighting inflation over maintaining full employment was a policy "not grounded in justice." Under the heading of "policy directions," the bishops called for public job creation programs, equitable sharing of the burdens of economic change, a national income policy, welfare reform and more energetic efforts to promote cooperation between the private and public sectors. They then concluded with another quotation from the 1930 statement, illustrating their long-standing conviction that the United States had the resources to meet the needs of its people, so that poverty and unemployment represented a moral failure:

> *Our country needs, now and permanently, such a change of heart as will, intelligently and with determination, so organize and distribute our work and wealth that no one need lack for any long time the security of being able to earn an adequate living for himself and for those dependent upon him.*

Several things stand out about postconciliar episcopal teaching on economic matters. First, the bishops continued to base their teaching on principles of human dignity and human rights. In this sense, the American bishops had been ahead of the popes who, until Pope John XXIII, placed human rights within a framework of corporate responsibility, which suggested the overall good of society took precedence. Of course, papal teaching argued there was no necessary contradiction between human rights and the common good; in fact, a proper understanding of the common good included the fulfillment of human rights. In many Catholic countries, however, the church supported policies that subordinated such rights as to strike and to participate in economic decisions to government-imposed social objectives. After Vatican II, in contrast, human rights all but exhausted the moral principles of Catholic teaching; social justice, in popular use, came to mean the fulfillment of these rights rather than its earlier association with the common good, a development reflecting a new sense of the church's distance from other institutions.[11]

In the United States, where individual rights provided almost the only moral foundation of public dialogue, the church's emphasis on such human rights as "the right to a decent home" gave it a critical capacity, but often gave church statements a demanding, even preachy, tone. In time, this gave rise to criticism of the seeming irresponsibility of the bishops in demanding, for example, a decent home for every American while failing to indicate how that could be done. This, in turn, reflected a wider change in social theology, which argued that the church could, in the name of its creed, articulate broad principles and denounce their violation, but could not, as the church, prescribe how those principles should be implemented. The outcome of this development was a gap between the prophetic quality of church teaching and the moderation of church action, as well as a number of bitter disputes within the church between idealists and realists, with the idealists using standards from scripture while the realists drew from Catholic social philosophy.

Second, the bishops seemed uninterested in economic theory, and few trained economists participated in their formulation of policy. The cultural criticism of capitalism and industrial society so strong in papal teaching was given little prominence, while the systematic analysis common in the Latin American church made little headway among the American bishops. Indeed, American church teaching remained solidly within the framework set by John A. Ryan, and the bishops' positions on domestic issues remained very much in line with those developed in the 1930s: extended benefits for the poor, government action to compensate for the failures of the private sector, and a priority for full employment over other domestic economic objectives. Older interest in cooperatives, profit and stock sharing, a wider distribution of productive property and labor–management cooperation declined, confined to brief statements about the need for increased participation until the development of a new pastoral letter on the economy in the mid-1980s. Ryan's emphasis on distributive justice, with its presumption that the problem of production was solved, remained a central assumption of episcopal teaching.

Third, the bishops in the modern period have put aside their inhibitions about governmental intervention, in part because of the easing of the minority consciousness that was so strong earlier. Instead, they have combined a continuing, consistent concern for the poor, and thus, for rights to subsistence and participation, with a clearer sense of the public interest, expressed most forcefully in political responsibility statements during election years since 1976. The church, they argue, has as its tasks both to speak out on behalf of the powerless and to share with others the responsibility to shape public culture and government policy in such a way as to meet human needs and promote the common good. Similarly, they understand more clearly the need both to help Christians form their conscience on public issues and to help shape the public moral consensus of society at large. Gradually, they have learned to fulfill their dual roles as church leaders and public figures. If at times they lapse into sectarian self-righteousness, more often they speak in terms of shared responsibility for the public good.[12]

Finally, many of the elements most debated among Catholics today have deep roots in Catholic teaching. The American bishops have argued since 1919 that economic policy has a moral dimension the church has not only the right, but the duty, to address. They have always affirmed the basic right of every human being to the minimum needed to live a decent life. The notion of "the preferential option for the poor" in recent discourse represents a theological and pastoral development, but in practice, it amounts to the same concern to provide a decent minimum for all, which was the dominant principle of *Rerum Novarum* and has consistently informed Catholic teaching. Similarly, Catholic teaching has never accepted the notion of a passive government; instead, the church has taught that the state has the obligation to protect the rights of its citizens, including the right to life and to the means necessary to sustain life as well as to promote the common good of all its citizens. The principle of subsidiarity suggested that problems should be handled as close to the grass roots as possible; thus, the many proposals for cooperatives, profit and stock sharing and copartnership. This principle, though, never meant a sharp separation of the private and public sectors, as some contemporary critics claim. On the contrary, even in a decentralized social order, the state retained the obligation to protect rights and promote justice, while individuals still had the obligation to respect the rights of others and share responsibility for the common life. There was, and remains, room for considerable disagreement about the application of the principles of human rights and state responsibility to specific problems; for continued dialogue about the proper balance among political and civil rights; and between individual freedom and public responsibility, but the basic notions of human dignity and political responsibility seem intrinsic to an authentic Catholic social ethic.

The teaching of the bishops has never been long on pastoral advice. The bishops supported trade unions and, for a time, assigned priests to work with unions and encouraged labor schools in their dioceses. Similarly, in recent years, they have combined support for unorganized workers with financial and institutional assistance to organizing efforts. However, education and organization around the social teaching of the church has remained to a large extent the product of the voluntary efforts of individual Catholics. The social encyclicals were sometimes taken up by such Catholic groups as the Knights of Columbus and such movements as the *Catholic Worker*. The bishops' commitment to relieving human need was evident in Catholic charities, but neither social action nor education on social and political problems ever became central to church policy and programming; indeed, both often operated on the fringe of parish and diocesan life. Episcopal pronouncements gave legitimacy to reform, they may have made social legislation more acceptable, but they rarely stirred Catholics to act. Even after Vatican II, when papal teaching made the pursuit of justice and the defense of human dignity more central to the life and mission of the church, the American hierarchy made few efforts to incorporate social responsibility into Catholic pastoral and educational work. When most Catholics were members of the working class, they undoubtedly found in church teaching encouragement for their efforts to form unions and to secure protective legislation. Today, Catholic minorities and poor are able to call on local churches to support their struggle for justice on the basis of church teaching. Since 1919, however, the bishops have argued that Catholics also have a responsibility to help shape institutions and policies that will promote the welfare of the entire community, to pursue justice not only from corporations and governments, but within those institutions as well. As Catholics find themselves inside the corridors of power, responsible for the common life, they may discover in this tradition of church teaching the resources to overcome what today's bishops call a "schizophrenic existence" in which values of human dignity and social justice are confined to private life. The pastoral task remains.

Relating Religious–
Ethical Inquiry to
Economic Policy

Charles E. Curran

This essay will discuss the question of how the pastoral letter of the United States bishops relates religious-ethical inquiry to economic policy. In other words, this study will deal primarily with the moral-theological methodology employed in the letter. A proper evaluation must consider the methodology in this letter in the light of recent developments in Catholic moral theology and social ethics. The question of theological ethical methodology will be examined in four of its aspects: presuppositions, theological contexts, the different levels of ethical discourse and an unresolved tension.

PRESUPPOSITIONS

The first presupposition concerns the justification of the church's involvement in the discussion of the economy. Many people object that the church and theology should not be involved in economic matters, that the church has no competency in this area and therefore should stay out of it.

Throughout its history, the Roman Catholic church in one way or another has addressed the problems involved in life in this world, including the economic aspects of human existence. Beginning with the encyclical *Rerum Novarum* of Pope Leo XIII in 1891, a body of official church teachings on social and economic questions has come into existence. The economic situation of the late nineteenth century, with the spread of laissez-faire capitalism and the rise of Marxism, called for the churches to respond. In Protestantism, the social gospel approach came into existence at this time. Official Catholic social teaching has continued to be developed and proposed by subsequent popes, the Second Vatican Council, and the Synod of Bishops. Despite this continuing involvement in social and economic issues, the reason for such church involvement in the Roman Catholic perspective has recently undergone a significant shift. Before the Second Vatican Council (1965), two reasons were usually proposed to justify the church's involvement. The church was interested in the material world because a sufficiency of the goods of this world was necessary in order for people to live a spiritual life. In addition, the church has the mission to teach its members to live properly in this world and to obey God's law in order to obtain their eternal salvation.[1]

Before Vatican II, Catholic theology generally accepted the basic goodness and importance of the natural realm involving life in this world, but saw this as the bottom floor of a two-story universe, with the supernatural order on top. There was a duality or even dichotomy between the supernatural, where grace and the gospel primarily operated, and the natural, where reason and natural law pointed out how human beings should live. In this understanding, the church itself had a twofold mission—divinization in the supernatural order and humanization in the natural order.

At Vatican II and later, there was a studied attempt to overcome this duality and to relate the gospel, faith and grace directly to life in this world and the so-called natural order. "This split between the faith which many profess and their daily lives deserves to be counted among the more serious errors of our age."[2] The Pastoral Constitution on the Church in the Modern World also employed a methodology that tried to relate the gospel and faith more directly to the problems of life in the modern world. The earlier papal social encyclicals (even Pope John XXIII's *Pacem in Terris* in 1963) employed a natural law methodology, which discussed how Christians are to act on the basis of the laws governing human relationships, which God the creator has written in human nature. The earlier approach saw all of social, political and economic life in the light of the natural law and did not appeal directly and explicitly to the gospel, redemption, grace, or Jesus Christ.[3]

Since Vatican II, official Catholic social teaching has continued and extended the effort to relate the gospel and faith directly to the daily life of Christians. The gospel must penetrate and affect every aspect of human existence. The 1971 Synod of Bishops succinctly summarized the new approach: "Action on behalf of justice and participation in the transformation of the world fully appear to us as a constitutive dimension of the preaching of the gospel, or, in other words, of the church's mission for the redemption of the human race and its liberation from every oppressive situation."[4]

These commentators maintain there can now be only one mission of the church—the mission of evangelization, which includes as a constitutive dimension action on behalf of justice and the transformation of the world. There have been attempts to back down from this statement, but no sentence from a recent church document has been quoted more frequently than this passage. One can have magnificent liturgy, great preaching, and a marvelous internal community life, but without a social mission, one does not have church or the Gospel. This changed understanding explains the strong commitment of the contemporary Roman Catholic church in general, and for our purposes, the United States Catholic church in particular, to the work of social justice. If the church does not become involved in social transformation, it has betrayed the gospel and its own redemptive mission.

A further question, then, immediately arises: How do the gospel, faith and grace relate to the complex social and economic realities of the modern world? The most characteristic aspect of Catholic theology in general and moral theology in particular is often thought to be the acceptance of mediation. Revelation is mediated through scripture and tradition. The mystery of God is mediated through Jesus, the visible institution of the church and the human realities of the sacramental liturgical system. In morality, even the older Catholic approach did not appeal directly to God because God's plan was mediated in and through the natural law understood as human reason directing human beings to their end in accord with their nature.

In the present context, mediation means that the gospel, faith and grace cannot deny or go around the human, but are mediated in and through the human. The gospel does not provide a shortcut that avoids the human and supplies direct and easy answers to complex social problems. The gospel must be mediated in and through the human, human experience and the human sciences. One cannot address these complex issues without knowledge of the social sciences, human experience and all the other data involved in the situation itself. One cannot go directly from the gospel or from one scripture quotation to a specific ethical conclusion on a complex economic issue. Thus, for example, one cannot immediately conclude from the gospel imperative to come to the assistance of the poor that multinational corporations are immoral.

The proper understanding of mediation avoids two opposite errors. On the one hand, some maintain that church teaching and theology have no competency in making judgments about economic issues. The Christian church and Christian theology can go only as far as their uniquely Christian warrants will take them, which is often described as the principles expressing Christian love. Christian love, however, has no specific competency to solve complex economic issues. The opposite stance maintains that on the basis of the gospel and faith, one can with ease and great certitude arrive at concrete solutions to complex ethical problems. Through some type of ethical or theological intuition, the Christian can readily discern what is the will and the concrete act of God in these specific circumstances.

Christian love and the Gospel can and should become incarnate in the complex issues of economic structures and policies, but only in and through the human, with all the limitations of the human as such. The Gospel and faith should extend to the specific and the concrete, but in so doing, the faith perspectives cannot claim to arrive at a certitude that is beyond human possibility. Faith and gospel values should affect specific decisions in the economic realm, but these decisions also depend heavily on the complex data and the scientific theories involved. Specifically, Christian ideals and values must be brought to bear, but the final decision must mediate these aspects in and through all the relevant data and theories.

In this view, the final specific judgment is truly a Christian, a human and an ethical decision, but with heavy reliance on data from economics and the other relevant sciences. However, it is not merely a technical economic decision. The Christian and human ethical decision must take into consideration all the other aspects that enter into such a decision—the psychological, sociological, hygienic, economic and political, among others, but the final decision is truly a Christian, human and ethical one, not just a sociological or economic judgment.

Without explicitly adverting to the characteristic Catholic acceptance of mediation, the United States bishops' pastoral letter on the economy as well as the preceding one on peace illustrate this basic approach. The bishops not only talk about the principles to govern social questions, but they descend to the level of particular and specific judgments. In making these judgments, they have attempted to evaluate all the data, and they recognize that these judgments cannot claim a certitude that excludes the possibility of error. Other believing Christians can arrive at different judgments and still belong to the same church. The church in fidelity to its own Gospel vision must speak and work for justice in the economic realm, but on specific issues and policies there exists a legitimate pluralism of approaches. The very justification of the church's involvement in such issues leads to the question of the methodology used by the church in addressing these issues.

A second presupposition of the pastoral letter that also has significant methodological ramifications concerns the audience to be addressed by the bishops. Here again, the letter on the economy follows the approach of the earlier letter on peace. The bishops address two audiences. They seek to furnish guidance for members of their own church and at the same time add their voice to the public policy debate about the directions the United States economy should take. The letter recognizes that in speaking to one's fellow believers, appeals will be made to specifically Christian warrants, whereas often in addressing the public-policy aspect, the letter refrains from invoking specifically Christian warrants and appeals to common humanity, experience and reason, which are shared by all. The letter thus adopts the practical approach of addressing both audiences, but it leaves open the deeper and more theoretical question about the relationship between the Christian moral order and the human moral order. Are these two different moral orders, or is there just one moral order? The letter properly avoids dealing with the more theoretical question, but some short discussion of this important issue is called for here.

In the older understanding prevalent before Vatican II, the question as such never arose. In that perspective, all of social life was governed by natural law, which was the same for all human beings whether they were Christian or not. The question arose once great emphasis was put on the need for a distinctively Christian approach to social issues. What is the relationship between the distinctively Christian approach and the purely human approach? Perhaps the most adequate way to phrase the question for our present purposes is as follows: "Is there one social moral order for Christians and another for those who are not Christian?" One response to this question has been to affirm that there is only one social moral order, which is the same for Christians and non-Christians. Such an answer is grounded in the fact that there is only one de facto historical order, in which God wills to call all humankind to share in God's own love and life. The traditional Catholic understanding that grace brings the human to the fullness of human perfection supports this same conclusion.

The discussion began in this country with the question of the existence of a distinctively Christian ethic. Subsequent debate has helped to clarify the real question: Is there a unique Christian moral order that differs from the human moral order existing for all others who are not Christian? Many people deny the existence of a unique Christian morality. Notice that the discussion is limited to the morality required of all Christians or of all humans as such and not to specific calls or vocations within a particular community. It is not necessary to go further into the discussion at the present time.[5]

The thesis that there is only one social moral order common to Christians and all others furnishes a strong theoretical basis for the fact that the pastoral letter can address two different audiences at the same time without involving itself in any inherent contradictions. The letter itself properly avoids the more theoretical issue and merely recognizes that it is speaking to two different audiences. Such a practice, however, is much more intelligible in light of the theory proposed here.

THEOLOGICAL CONTEXTS

Two very important theological contexts are necessary to understand both the methodology and some of the conclusions of the pastoral letter on the economy—eschatology and ecclesiology. It might be only sheer coincidence, but the second draft of the earlier pastoral letter on peace and of the later pastoral on the economy both gave more importance to eschatology than the first draft.[6] Eschatology refers to the relationship of the present to the future of God's reign. The pastoral letter on the economy recognizes that the Christian lives in the tension between the presence of the reign of God here and now begun and its fulfillment, which will come only at the end of time. God's designs for human life have been revealed throughout salvation history and uniquely in the life, death and resurrection of Jesus; but the full realization of the reign of God will come only at the end of time.

The question of eschatology, or the relationship between the reign of God and the present world, can be understood in terms of the five types relating Christ and culture proposed by H. Richard Niebuhr.[7] The Christ-against-culture model sees the reign of God in opposition to what exists at the present and serves as the basis for a radical opposition between the reign of God and existing institutions and realities. The Christ-of-culture model tends to identify the reign of God with present culture and grounds a Christian ethic of strong support for what exists at the present. Niebuhr then mentions three models in the middle ground between these two extremes. If Niebuhr's Christ-above-culture model fits the pre-Vatican II theology already described, then the eschatology proposed in the bishops' letter corresponds to Niebuhr's centrist model of Christ transforming culture. This approach calls, in general, for transformation and change of the present, but cautions against expecting any naive utopias to come into existence in this world. Within such an eschatological perspective, the bishops are critical of the present structures, not radically opposed to them, and propose ways to change and modify existing policies and structures. The bishops recognize that their approach is one of pragmatic reform. There is a definite coherence between the eschatology briefly mentioned in the letter and the substantive positions taken on the American economy.

There are three important ramifications of ecclesiology for social ethics and the teaching developed in the pastoral letter. The first aspect is intimately connected with eschatology and involves the understanding of Catholicism as a church and not a sect in the typology developed by Max Weber. The sect type is distinguished by the fact that it is a relatively small group of believers striving to live the fullness of the gospel in a radical way in opposition to the world around them. The church type is more open to a wider membership, is less radical and rigorous in its ethic and does not see itself in total opposition to the world around it. Whereas the sect type often accepts the Christ-against-culture model, the church type cannot exist in such radical opposition with the existing culture.

The Roman Catholic church not only belongs to the church type, but it might be the perfect illustration of such a type. The Catholic church claims to have a universal mission and calls all to itself. It wants to embrace all peoples, all cultures, all languages, all continents. A church aspiring to such universality must recognize pluralism and diversity on a number of levels. The Catholic church has insisted on doctrinal agreement, but historically it has been open to great diversity in the political, social and economic orders. In fact, until the time of Pius XII, it was generally accepted that Catholic thought was indifferent to the type of political form of government. The form of government was secondary to the requirements for justice within any and all forms of government.[8] The pastoral letter on the economy recognizes that the church is not bound to any particular economic, political, or social system or ideology. It has been reiterated in church documents that there is room for diversity and pluralism in the church with regard to specific economic policies and institutions. However, some movements such as atheistic communism have been looked on as inherently evil. Historically, Roman Catholicism has embraced a wide range of opinions on social and economic questions and still continues to do so. The United States bishops in their two pastoral letters are very careful to point out the continuing place of pluralism and diversity in the church in judgments about complex, specific economic or political problems.

The understanding of mediation proposed earlier means that as one descends to the specific and the complex, one cannot claim to arrive at a certitude that excludes the possibility of error. The Gospel-inspired approach mediated through reason and the empirical sciences and cognizant of all the relevant data cannot claim to be the only possible Gospel-inspired answer on specifics. Thus, the pastoral letter distinguishes between the level of universal moral principles or formal church teaching and prudential judgments about specific policies. Prudential judgments do not carry the same moral authority as do universal moral principles, and on this level of specific judgments and applications there is a rightful diversity of opinion that can exist within the church. The bishops propose their judgments on these practical and specific issues and policies as being true and consistent with the Gospel, but they recognize the possibility of disagreement on these judgments within the Christian community. Thus, the acceptance of mediation confirms the Catholic approach to ecclesiology, which recognizes the diversity of positions on specific complex issues in the social and economic areas.

Perhaps the most significant ecclesiological aspect of the two United States bishops' letters has been the manner in which these teaching documents have been prepared. There has been wide-ranging dialogue with all those who might have something to contribute to the documents: activists, academicians, businesspersons, labor leaders, economists, philosophers, theologians, scripture scholars, social scientists, politicians, government officials and others. Symposia and conferences have been held at various Catholic and non-Catholic institutions of learning throughout the country. The drafts of the pastoral letter have been circulated publicly and criticism has been welcomed from every conceivable approach. The very process itself has been a great teaching tool in terms of awakening consciousness both within the church and in the society to the moral issues involved in the United States economy. The dialogical and collegial teaching style of writing this document contrasts with the approach still used in most Catholic documents, especially those emanating from Rome. It will be increasingly difficult for church authorities to propose future documents that have not been prepared with this same wide-ranging and public dialogue.

DIFFERENT LEVELS OF ETHICAL DISCOURSE

Perhaps the most significant methodological aspect of the moral teaching proposed in the pastoral letter on the economy is the explicit recognition of the different levels of moral discourse. This recognition rests on an acceptance of mediation and the need to distinguish between different levels of authoritative teaching in the document. The systematic structure of the letter's ethical methodology goes from the more general to the more specific. This structure has basically stayed the same throughout the drafts, with one significant modification in the second draft.

In the last few decades within Roman Catholicism, there has been a shift in theology from classicism to historical consciousness, with a corresponding shift from a static and deductive methodology to one more inductive. The Pastoral Constitution on the Church in the Modern World illustrates this newer approach by beginning the discussion of particular moral problems with an analysis of the signs of the times. The drafters of the pastoral letter feared that the move from the more general to the more specific as developed in the first draft gave the impression of being a totally deductive approach. At the same time, this approach did not attract the average reader.[9] The solution in the second draft was to keep the approach of different levels moving from the more general to the more specific, but to add a first chapter on the signs of the times, pointing out the problems existing at the present and the need for a moral approach to these questions. The problem experienced by the drafters was certainly compounded by the fact that one document tries to do so many different things. The letter wants to be sound from the viewpoint of systematic Catholic ethics, but at the same time, it wants to capture the interest and enthusiasm of the general reader. These two goals are not always easily reconcilable in the same document.

In general, it is important that the letter does recognize the different levels of moral discourse, especially in light of the acceptance of mediation and the need to distinguish different levels of unity and diversity within the church. Such a reflective, systematic approach does not have to be static and totally deductive, but this more scientific approach will not necessarily make exciting reading for everyone.

What are the different levels of ethical discourse distinguished and elaborated on in the letter? As described in the terminology of the letter itself, the different levels are as follows: perspectives, the Christian vocation, ethical norms and principles, and finally, specific judgments and policies on economic matters made in the light of the principles and other levels of ethical discourse. These correspond to four very significant levels of ethical discourse: a basic perspective, the person as subject and agent, the principles and norms governing human existence, and concrete judgments. These four are similar to the four levels of moral discourse proposed by University of Chicago Professor James Gustafson in his earlier work, *Christ and the Moral Life,*[10] and will now be discussed.[11]

Fundamental Perspective. The level of fundamental perspective is developed in the pastoral letter in terms of biblical perspectives with emphasis on the focal points of the faith of Israel and of the disciples of Jesus—creation, covenant and saving history. This biblical approach should inform the way in which Christians and the church approach all the issues in the economic order. There has been comparatively little discussion in contemporary Christian ethics itself about this fundamental level of ethical discourse, which can go under such different names as perspective, posture, stance, or horizon. In the pastoral letter, this level also seems to include the more general values, ideals and goals that should influence economic policies and structures.

After the first draft of the letter, there was a comparatively slight but significant shift. The first draft developed a biblical vision or perspective for economic life, but for all practical purposes, the use of the scripture is only on this first level and not incorporated into the other levels of ethical discourse. The second draft made some small attempts to employ the scriptures on the other levels of ethical discourse and did not completely limit the scriptural influence to a basic perspective. However, the basic perspective is developed exclusively in terms of scripture.

The use of scripture in moral theology is a question that has recently received much attention, but there is no general agreement on exactly how the scriptures should be employed. Catholic theology has rightly insisted that scripture is not the only source of ethical wisdom and knowledge for the Christian. In fact, as mentioned earlier, it was only after the Second Vatican Council that Catholic moral theology gave greater importance to the role and use of the scriptures within it. Given the many sources of ethical wisdom and knowledge for the Christian and the hermeneutic problem of moving from biblical times to contemporary times, the role of the scripture will be greater and more significant in the broader and more general levels of ethical discourse and less controlling and significant as one descends to the more specific. Thus, for example, one cannot prove the truth of a very concrete norm for the economy today because this was proposed as a concrete norm in very different circumstances in a particular biblical situation. However, the general scriptural warning about the dangers connected with wealth and riches has a permanent validity for Christians in all ages.

On the level of basic perspective or stance, there should be a very great contribution from the scriptures, but the basic perspective should be a systematically developed Christian one and not based only on the bible. Such a Christian perspective is heavily dependent on biblical material, but in light of all the sources of moral theology, it must go beyond merely the biblical to involve the totality of the Christian perspective. In addition, some fundamental questions can be raised about the very enterprise of trying to construct a biblical theology. Such approaches are truly human constructs made by contemporary persons and hence, by their very nature, move beyond the biblical texts themselves.

The Person. The second level of ethical discourse is the level of the person, with all one's dispositions, virtues and attitudes. This level is not explicitly mentioned in the first draft of the pastoral letter. In the second draft, this level appears under the rubric, "The Christian Vocation in the World Today," but still remains comparatively underdeveloped.[12]

No one can deny the importance and significance of this level of ethical discourse. The biblical metaphor teaches that the good tree brings forth good fruit while the bad tree brings forth bad fruit. Good actions come from good persons. Philosophical reflection reminds us that the person is both subject and agent who by one's own actions contributes to what one is as a person and at the same time expresses one's personal reality in and through action.

The fact that this level of ethical discourse is so underdeveloped is consistent with the entire approach taken in the letter. For all practical purposes, the letter deals with the changes that should be made in the existing economic structures and institutions so that they can better serve all human beings. These changes are primarily brought about in and through the political order in all its different ramifications. Comparatively little is said about the day-to-day life of the people who are working in various capacities in the economic institutions and structures, and little is also said about such institutions themselves as the corporation or business.

One of the most significant constraints facing the drafters of the pastoral letter was the fear of making the document too long. Excessive length was the primary complaint after the first draft of the letter. As a result, the drafters could not include many things. The small section dealing explicitly with the level of the person did appear in the second draft (pars. 63–66). However, it remains unfortunate that this whole aspect could not be brought out in greater detail. Not only is this an important level of ethical discourse and of moral living, but emphasis on this level shows the important role played by the laity and all the people of God in the economic realm. The day-to-day life of people in the economic order does not receive as much attention as it should.

These remarks should not be misinterpreted. Some critics in the United States have maintained that responsibility for involvement in economic life and in economic policies and issues belongs primarily to the laity. The bishops should teach principles, but should not get into the specifics of economic policies and judgments.[13] Others strongly disagree with this understanding. From their perspective, a letter of this type should place more importance on the day-to-day Christian existence of those who spend their lives working in the economic sector and focus less on appeals to workers, owners, and managers. Especially a document addressing itself to the members of the church and not just attempting to make a contribution to the public-policy debate should give more attention to what most of the people in the church community do in their daily lives. As it stands, the public-policy aim of the letter controls its content and development to the detriment of the role of the believing members of the church community in their everyday work.

Principles and Norms. The third level of ethical discourse concerns the principles and norms that should direct economic policy and structures. The bishops strongly emphasize this level as distinguished from that of prudential judgments and applications made in the light of these principles and norms. The letter itself highlights a number of these principles such as justice and human rights, but other important principles from the Catholic tradition are also included. This section will now briefly consider what seem to be the most important principles in the Catholic tradition's teaching on economic policies and structures—the role of the state, justice, human rights, preferential option for the poor and the universal destiny of the goods of creation to serve the needs of all.

Role of the State. The Catholic tradition understands the state as a natural society based on the social nature of humankind, uniting persons to achieve the common good. The common good is not opposed to but includes the good of the individual person. Consequently, the state is not seen as something bad or evil that restrains and coerces, but as something basically good, which contributes to the good and fulfillment of all its individual members. This understanding of the state based on the social nature of humankind avoids the two opposite dangers of laissez-faire individualism and collectivism. The state recognizes and protects the basic rights of individuals and of the lesser associations and groups that comprise the total fabric of society. The principle of subsidiarity governs the proper role and function of the state, which exists to help persons and lesser associations and groups, but in contemporary times, official Catholic teaching has recognized that the growing socialization in human relationships calls for a greater role for the state.

Justice. Corresponding to the three different types of relationships existing within society are three different types of justice. Commutative justice governs the relationship of individuals to individuals and is described as impartial and blind to personal differences, with emphasis on arithmetic equality. For example, if you were to borrow five dollars from one friend and five dollars from the richest person in the world, you would owe each person the same amount—five dollars. Distributive justice governs the relationship of society to individuals in properly distributing goods and services. Distributive justice is not blind, but must take account of persons and involves proportional, not arithmetic, equality. In distributing various burdens, society must take into account the abilities of individuals to contribute. Thus, progressively higher taxes should be paid by those who earn more, and public office should be given only to those capable of carrying out their responsibilities effectively. In distributing goods, a number of canons should govern proper distribution, but human needs constitute a basic criterion. Every human being has a right to that basic level of human goods necessary for a minimally decent existence. What is just from the viewpoint of distributive justice is not the same for all, but is proportionate to the needs and abilities of the persons involved. Note again the social aspect, and that distributive justice does not call for equal distribution for all, but only for a basic minimum for all.

Social justice governs the relationship of individuals to society and again is characterized by proportional equality and the need to take account of persons and their differences. In discussing social justice, the bishops put emphasis on participation, which has been an aspect developed only recently in the Catholic social tradition. To participate in the total life of society is a right based on social justice, with a corresponding duty of society and all others to recognize and facilitate this right of participation. Social justice governs the contribution that each makes to the good of the whole.

Human Rights. Official Catholic teaching only embraced and developed the concept of human rights in the encyclical *Pacem in Terris* of Pope John XXIII in 1963.[14] The Catholic tradition had previously emphasized duties and shied away from rights language as being too closely identified with the thought of individualistic liberalism. However, in defending against the abuses of totalitarianism, Catholic social thought gradually came to champion human rights. Human rights are ultimately based on the dignity of the human person. With its recognition of the social aspect of human nature, the recent Catholic teaching in emphasizing human rights has insisted not only on political and civil rights, which have traditionally been espoused by Western liberalism, but also economic and social rights. Economic rights converge with the traditional emphasis on distributive justice to underscore the fact that every human person has a right to those material goods that are necessary to live a minimally decent existence.

Other Principles. Recent Catholic theology with its shift to a more direct relationship of the gospel and faith to daily life has accented the preferential option for the poor. The privileged place of the poor in the reign of God is accentuated throughout the Hebrew and Christian scriptures. Liberation theology in South America has developed the concept at great length, but it is also a part of recent official Catholic social teaching. This preferential option is not exclusive and therefore is compatible with the more philosophical emphasis on distributive justice and human rights. Recent Catholic social teaching has also insisted on the traditional teaching that the goods of creation exist to serve the needs of all. All other rights, including those of private property and of free commerce, are to be subordinated to this primary finality of the goods of creation.

All these principles tend to put more emphasis on the social aspects of human existence than is generally found in the American ethos. This social emphasis is the basis for many of the concrete judgments made in the letter itself and for the need to regulate the activity of individuals and markets in order to achieve the common good of all.

Specific Judgments on Economic Policies. The fourth level of ethical discourse is that of concrete judgments about economic structures and policies in the light of the principles and other levels of ethical discourse. The letter considers four specific areas of concern: employment, poverty, food and agriculture and the relationship of the United States to the world economy. There is also a more future-oriented chapter dealing with economic policy under the rubric of a call for a new American experiment involving partnership for the public good. An investigation of the particular judgments and policies proposed in these areas lies beyond the scope of this particular study.

AN UNRESOLVED TENSION

Catholic social teaching and social ethics have generally downplayed the role of power and conflict in bringing about social justice and change. The tradition has constantly emphasized the harmonious working together of all for the common good. Society was often described in terms of organic metaphors, with all the parts working together for the good of the whole. Catholic ethics insisted on the importance and goodness of human reason and downplayed the role of sin, which could very well serve as grounds for a greater emphasis on conflict in society. Only very recently has this body of teaching begun to recognize the importance of participation by all. Catholic ecclesiology even today does not want to turn differences on specific economic policy and structures into reasons for division within the church. As a result, these differences are seen as examples of pluralism rather than as basic conflicts.

There must be a greater place for power and conflict in bringing about social change than the Catholic tradition has been willing to admit. Conflict must always be only a strategy and can never become an ultimate. Likewise, conflict and power must always be in service of the common good and not of selfish interests. However, experience and reality point to a greater role for conflict and power in bringing about social justice and change than the Catholic tradition in general and the bishops' letter in particular are willing to admit explicitly.

The letter contains some emphases, though, that open the door to recognizing a greater role for conflict. The letter stresses the importance of participation of all in the life of society. The bishops freely talk about the need to overcome the powerlessness and the marginalization of many people in our society. There are also frequent references to power itself. All these indications support the view that the letter should explicitly acknowledge a greater role for power and conflict in bringing about social change than now appears in the letter.

CONCLUSION

This essay has explained and analyzed the Christian social ethical methodology as found in the pastoral letter on the economy and in the Catholic tradition in general. Presuppositions, theological contexts, the different levels of ethical discourse and an unresolved tension have been examined in an attempt to analyze and explain how religious-ethical inquiry is related to economic policy, in this letter in particular and in the contemporary Catholic social ethics in general.

In many ways, the pastoral letter on the economy can serve as a paradigm for relating religious–ethical inquiry to economic policy. The letter correctly recognizes the need to mediate faith and the gospel message through human experience and the human sciences. The different levels of ethical discourse found in the letter not only underscore a very important distinction from the perspective of moral theology, but also serve to indicate the parameters of unity and diversity within the church or the faith community. The process of writing the letter, with its broad consultation and its public criticism of the various drafts, is a model for church statements dealing with the political and social orders.

Ethics, Religion and the Modern Business Corporation

Manuel G. Velasquez

Even before the American bishops issued the first draft of "Catholic Social Teaching and the U.S. Economy," it had already attracted an astonishing degree of attention from the business press. In surprisingly angry editorials, *Business Week* and *Fortune* magazines and *The Wall Street Journal* excoriated the bishops for daring to address economic issues.

The attention of the business press was astonishing for several reasons. First, because it focused on an event that had not yet taken place; it was editorializing on a nonexistent event. This was an unusual stance for an institution whose characteristic purpose is to report and respond to past history, not to anticipate the future. Second, because its negative tone was so extreme as to verge on the abusive. Indeed, in journals noted for their balanced prose, these vitriolic editorials seemed oddly out of place.

The anticipatory reaction of the business press should not be set aside as a quirk. The reaction was indicative of a deep, underlying fear of the coming event on the part of the business community and an attempt to protect itself through a proactive strategy. This fear was based on two assumptions concerning what the bishops would say. First, since the bishops were going to write on the U.S. economy, they were certain to address the institution that dominates that economy—American business. Second, whatever the bishops had to say about American business, it was certain to be critical, as if religion and business are necessarily at odds with each other.

Strangely, the statement of the bishops in its various drafts virtually ignored business organizations. Although acknowledging the importance of business at several crucial points,[1] the various drafts of the bishops' letter proceed as if the economy is constituted mainly of citizens and their government. Calls for reform are almost wholly concentrated on government policy and assume that reform will be brought about through citizen action. The letter consequently reads as if businesses are but a sidelight of modern economic activity. Where business had feared the bishops would confront them with criticism, the bishops instead gave an odd silence.

This was a mistake for several reasons. First, by ignoring the pervasive presence of business in American life, the bishops failed to see the crucial importance of articulating a spirituality that is relevant to the pervasive daily concerns of the bulk of the American population. They failed, that is, to impart religious meaning and significance to the life that so many Americans lead as members of large-scale business organizations.

Second, by ignoring the large-scale business corporation, the bishops necessarily ignored the issue that today lies at the heart of economic reform: the issue of power. For a number of reasons that are about to be articulated, economic, political and social power today is concentrated in the large-scale business corporation. Any realistic assessment of the American economy must address this concentration of power. Because the bishops ignored the corporation, they ignored the realities of power, and their calls for reform sounded naive.

Third, by ignoring the large-scale corporation, the bishops ignored the agency that more than any other is responsible for the tremendous prosperity Americans enjoy relative to the rest of the world. Instead, the statement of the bishops emerged as largely negative, focusing on problems government traditionally handles—those of distribution. The bishops therefore largely ignored the positive moral aspect of the economy, the aspect with which government has nothing to do, and which is "the bottom line" of the business corporation—productivity.

This essay elaborates on what the bishops ignored in the various drafts of their letter—the moral role of the business corporation in the American economy. The aim is not merely to criticize the bishops, but also to indicate the positive contributions the bishops made in their letter and to outline in a positive way what yet remains to be done if the moral role of the corporation is to make its way into Catholic social teaching.

MORALITY AND ECONOMICS

Moral evaluations necessarily presuppose an underlying set of moral standards on which these evaluations are based. On what kinds of moral standards must economic evaluations be based? That question can be answered only by adverting to what an economy is. As a standard, economies are viewed as institutional mechanisms that determine the goods a society will produce, how they will be produced, and to whom they will be distributed. At a minimum, therefore, an ethical theory capable of providing an adequate basis for evaluating the morality of an economy must include three kinds of ethical principles.[2] First, the theory must incorporate the proper moral criteria for evaluating what is produced; that is, for evaluating the moral value of what economists call "productivity." Second, because an economy must distribute what it produces, adequate moral standards for economic activities must include principles of justice that can illuminate the morality of the way in which society's goods are distributed among its members. Third, because goods that may be legitimately produced and distributed can be produced by means that themselves may be evil, a moral theory capable of evaluating economic activity must also identify those human rights that the process of economic production must respect.

What follows are comments on what each of these three kinds of moral criteria should be like from the perspective of Catholic social teaching. The remainder of this chapter examines the extent to which the bishops' letter adequately recognizes these three kinds of moral criteria, and the extent to which our corporate economy lives up to them.

First, since an economy is fundamentally aimed at the production of goods and services, an economic morality has to address the moral nature of productivity. The most basic and most universally accepted criterion for evaluating economic performance always has been and will always continue to be productivity. If religion is to speak to economists and others who hold that economic systems must be evaluated primarily by their productivity, it must address these fundamental questions: What moral criteria should be used to measure productivity? Are there such goods as military weapons whose production is not a measure of productivity? How does the American economy measure up to these standards of productivity?

Our religious tradition is not silent on the importance of productivity. Productivity is the subject of the first command of God in the book of Genesis: "Be fruitful and multiply, fill the earth and subdue it."[3] The Old Testament call to subdue the earth is a call to produce from the earth's resources the goods that can meet human needs, those goods that can feed, clothe, house, nourish and keep human beings healthy.[4] The command to bring forth fruit is echoed in the New Testament, when Jesus condemns the man who buries his talent without allowing it to bear fruit.[5] Humans are to make what they have increase. In short, they are to be productive, but not just for the sake of productivity. The New Testament is also harsh on those who accumulate goods without meeting real human needs or without taking due account of the real ends of human life.[6] Immediately after the parable of the talents, the Gospel inserts the command to feed the hungry, to care for the thirsty and to clothe the naked.[7] Thus, productivity must be aimed at fulfilling real human needs and at achieving real human fulfillment.

Recent Catholic social teaching has been highly suggestive on this aspect of economic activity,[8] especially in the brilliant and ground-breaking encyclical of Pope John Paul II, *Laborem Exercens*. The key lines of the encyclical are stated in section four: "Man is the image of God partly through the mandate received from his creator to subdue, to dominate the earth. In carrying out this mandate, man, every human being, reflects the very action of the creator of the universe." The encyclical, which is a prolonged meditation on the significance of these lines,[9] identifies the process of "subduing" and "dominating" the earth with the process of work, the process of being productive with the earth's resources. This process is twofold, "objective" and "subjective." In its "objective" aspect, "work" refers to the productive process insofar as it is directed at an "external object"; that is, insofar as it is directed at producing external goods. In its "subjective" aspect, "work" refers to the productive process insofar as it is a process through which man realizes himself as a "conscious and free subject, that is to say, a subject that decides about himself." Work, or productivity, thus has a twofold "purpose": its "objective" purpose is to produce external goods from the earth's resources; its "subjective" purpose is to enable humans to realize their identity as free beings capable of determining themselves. Work becomes distorted and evil when its subjective purpose is lost, diminished, or subordinated to its "objective" purpose.[10]

Work, insofar as it is the process through which man produces external goods and realizes himself as self-determining, is the process through which man participates in God's creativity: "Man, created in the image of God, shares by his work in the activity of the Creator, ... man in a sense continues to develop that activity and perfects it as he advances further and further in the discovery of the resources and values contained in the whole of creation."[11] Economic productivity is a participation in God's own activity, the process in which humanity becomes like God[12] as it transforms the world of nature and realizes its own freedom.

Thus, the first criterion for evaluating the performance of the American corporate economy is this: Is it productive in the sense of being creative and is it creative precisely of those goods needed to enable human beings to realize their identity as self-determining images of God?

Second, a moral evaluation of economic arrangements requires distributional criteria. For what an economy produces it must also distribute, allocating benefits and burdens among the humans it affects. Thus, an ethical theory for measuring the morality of economic activity will have to provide moral criteria for evaluating the distributive effects of various economic arrangements. Does Catholic social teaching favor some economic distributive patterns over others?

A distributional analysis of the American economy must strike two notes if it is to ring true to Catholic social teaching: the poor and the needy have a privileged place, and all men and women are united in a social solidarity that implies an obligation to share one's goods. These two notes are clearly part of Catholic traditional teaching. In both the Old and New Testaments, God is seen as the God of the poor. In the Old Testament, He is the God of the orphan and the widow, of the stranger and the oppressed.[13] In the Gospels, He is the God who sides with Lazarus and condemns the rich man, even as Jesus identifies himself with the poor, saying, "When you did it to one of these, you did it to me."[14] In the epistles, He is the God who chooses the poor and makes the rich "weep and howl."[15] Thus, the poor must have a special and privileged position in the moral criteria to which the Christian appeals.

Moreover, the New Testament teaching that God is our Father implies a radical solidarity: All men and women are fundamentally brothers and sisters in a single human family. In the ideal community, "All things are held in common ... and distributed to each according to his needs."[16] This community solidarity, rooted in the new covenant forged by Jesus' death and resurrection, is the perfection of the Old Testament covenant community, whereby all are required to share their goods with the poor in the radical sharing of the Jubilee year.[17] There is no way of avoiding the conclusion that Christian solidarity means that the goods we produce together must be shared with each other, especially with the poor.

In one way or another, the obligation to share one's goods with the poor has been part of the enduring tradition of the church, whether couched in medieval notions of the "common use" of private property[18] (which surfaced briefly in *Rerum Novarum*,[19] more explicitly in *Quadragesimo Anno*,[20] and full-blown in Vatican II[21]), or in the "constructive revision" of *Laborem Exercens*, which insists that ownership of the means of production must be "socialized" by making each worker "a part owner" of these means.[22]

Equally enduring is the tradition that since the needs of the poor are more urgent than those of the rest of the community, justice implies that the poor have a greater moral claim on the community's goods.[23] Building on the patristic tradition, medieval theology expressed this notion in the idea that the use of "superfluous" goods belongs by right to the poor.[24] The early encyclical tradition understandably treated this radical idea much more gingerly than the idea of the "common use" of property. The idea, though, that the poor have special claim on society's goods emerges clearly in *Pacem in Terris* in the modern language of basic human rights,[25] and is even more strongly enunciated in the Vatican Council's "The Church in the Modern World": "Men are obliged to come to the relief of the poor, and to do so not merely out of their superflous goods."[26]

These two notions—the priority of the poor and the obligations of social solidarity—together embody the fundamental distributional criteria implicit in Catholic tradition, criteria that can be put in the form of a question: To what extent does the corporate economy embody a solidarity that generates a sharing of our goods with the poor, the disadvantaged, the dispossessed, the powerless?

A third kind of moral principle that must be invoked when evaluating economic arrangements is the kind that focuses on the personal rights that economic arrangements must respect. Goods can be produced and distributed by methods that violate the humanity of those individuals who are caught up in the processes of economic production. Slavery and child labor are historical examples of economic institutions that once were part of our own processes of production, but which clearly violated the humanity of the slave and the child. Both were founded on forms of coercion and exploitation that are now outlawed. Some modern forms of production, too, can degrade and exploit the individual, while others can rob the individual of all autonomy, and still others can treat the individual as a mere means of production. Thus, economic moral principles must provide criteria for assessing how the individual is treated by society's productive processes. That is, they have to say something about the rights that protect human beings against economic exploitation.

On this topic, also, our religious tradition provides a rich patrimony in the New Testament teaching that the individual person is a creature for whom Christ suffered and died and whose freedom was secured by Christ's work, especially His death and resurrection.[27] St. Paul, in summarizing the New Creation that Christ's death and resurrection brought about, says that in being redeemed by Christ, we have become free, adopted sons and daughters of God.[28] Because we are free sons and daughters of God, we must each be treated with a respect that places us above all material things, a respect for our freedom and dignity that only God's progeny could merit. However, "respect" for our "freedom and dignity" should not be interpreted negatively as merely that we must leave each other alone—to starve, perhaps. The New Testament is clear enough that it does not have this "libertarian" notion of freedom in mind: "If a brother or sister is ill clad and in lack of daily food, and one of you says to them, 'Go in peace, be warmed and filled,' without giving them the things needed for the body, what does it profit?"[29] Rather, it means that in addition to ensuring that each and every one of us are left free to pursue our own human self-fulfillment, we must also promote each other's capacities for freedom and self-determination.[30]

This idea, that the human person possesses a right to free self-determination that all must respect, is the root of the human rights views that have become an integral part of the church's encyclical tradition. The right to self-determination is the central moral concept in *Laborem Exercens'* appeal to the idea that work must respect the fact that man "as the 'image of God' is a person, that is to say, a subjective being capable of acting in a planned and rational way, capable of deciding about himself and with a tendency to self-realization."[31] It is also the foundational moral idea in Vatican II's "The Church in the Modern World": "Man's dignity demands that he act according to a knowing and free choice."[32]

Thus, there is the third kind of principle that a religious ethic must incorporate if it is to measure the morality of the economy: Does the corporate economy embody a positive respect for the freedom and dignity of the individual redeemed by Christ and adopted by God? Does the economy, that is, respect the basic right of self-determination?

There are, then, three kinds of ethical criteria that an adequate treatment of Catholic social teaching must make explicit in examining the American economy: economic productivity, just distribution of goods, especially to the poor, and the right to self-determination.

To what extent does the bishops' letter take these three crucial criteria into account? What follows argues that while the bishops provide a superb treatment of the extent to which the U.S. economy lives up to the distributive norms implicit in Catholic social teaching, they failed to provide an equally useful treatment of the extent to which the U.S. economy respects the right to self-determination and of the extent to which it satisfies the norms of productivity.

These failures are unfortunate and significant. More than anything else, the absence of an adequate treatment of economic productivity is responsible for the negative tone of the bishops' letter in all its drafts. An understanding of productivity would have enabled the bishops to analyze in depth the positive aspects of the American economy. It also would have led them naturally to a discussion of a spirituality for the modern corporate member, a spirituality that could enable the corporate member to find meaning and hope in the corporate tasks with which the working day is filled. The bishops failed to face either of these issues.

Moreover, by dealing so gingerly with the notion of respect for self-determination, the bishops avoid the core issue of every major economic problem—power. Power is the ability of one agent to impose its will on another. It is, in short, the ability of one agent to determine another. The right of self-determination, if it implies anything, therefore, implies a transformation of the power relations in our economic institutions, and this implication the bishops utterly fail to grasp.

In order to see clearly the importance of dealing with the two issues of productivity and power in the American economy, there must first be a clearer picture of that economy. This means the central institution of that economy must be examined: the American corporation. If the bishops' letter failed to see the importance of dealing with productivity and power, it is because they failed to understand the dominant role of the corporation in American economic life. It is that role that must be examined now before turning to assess the economy from a moral point of view.

THE ROLE OF THE MODERN AMERICAN CORPORATION

If only the industrial sector of the American economy is examined, then over 200,000 manufacturing firms will be found operating today in the United States. Yet, only 500 of these—less than one half of one percent—account for 80 percent of the nation's industrial profits, 80 percent of our industrial assets and 80 percent of all industrial employees. If all sectors of the economy are considered and not only manufacturing, one can count about 2.5 million companies operating in the United States. However, the 500 largest of these—those with revenues of at least $1 billion—have sales equal to about 80 percent of the U.S. gross national product. They employ about 20 million people. Their assets are valued at about $4 trillion. Thus, it is clear that the bulk of the economy is under the private control of a relatively small number of corporate organizations.[33]

These relatively few corporate organizations have massive dimensions. Exxon Corporation, for example, had sales in 1982 of close to $100 billion. Of the world's 160 nations, only eight have government budgets larger than this. In the same year, General Motors employed about 700,000 people; only 30 nations had more workers engaged in manufacturing. The 500 major American corporations each have annual revenues exceeding $1 billion and virtually all of them operate over the entire globe, often overshadowing the economies of their host nations.

Moreover, the American economy affects the world economy in large part through the operations of these giant multinational corporations. Today, 65 percent of the largest U.S. corporations have plants in six or more nations. U.S. private investment abroad grew from $19 billion in 1950 to a phenomenal $726.3 billion in 1982.[34] As much as one half of the total real assets of the largest American corporations are now located abroad.[35]

The giant corporation, then, is an intrinsic and all-pervasive component of developed contemporary economies. Precisely because it is so pervasive and so massive, the large-scale corporation has large and widespread effects on its natural and social environments. Corporate layoffs can cripple small economies; corporate pollution can change a region's ecology; corporate

·bribery can upset a nation's political balance; corporate technology can alter a region's social structures. Since these giant corporations comprise the bulk of the American economy, since they are intrinsic to contemporary developed economies, and since their effects are so massive, it is clear that, in order to assess the American economy at its core and not at its periphery, first and foremost, the performance of the large-scale corporation must be assessed.

Unfortunately, today in America there are two radically opposed religious views concerning the morality of this all-pervasive institution. In one view, the corporation is essentially demonic and corruptive. In the other, it is essentially holy and salvific.

The first is the view of Christians like Michael Harrington and certain liberation theologians, who see the profit motive as necessarily corruptive and the modern corporation as a demonic institution created by a morally evil capitalism. In this view, the corporation necessarily spawns selfishness by its reliance on profit. It corrupts by concentrating immense power in the hands of a few. It oppresses by keeping large masses in abject poverty. It is uncontrollable because it incorporates a bureaucratic, multinational structure that escapes both individual and national controls. It is necessarily demonic.

On the other side are Christians like Michael Novak and George Gilder, who see the giant corporation as holy and redemptive, the embodiment of God's saving grace. Novak, for example, regularly, explicitly and fully conscious of what he is doing, equates the American corporation to the incarnation: It is the fulfillment of the messianic promises, the suffering servant of God by whose stripes we are saved, God's own incarnate presence.[36] George Gilder argues that corporate motives necessarily and always embody love of neighbor; the businessman devotes his entire life to pleasing others; he is a man driven by altruism.[37]

These two approaches to the corporation are not new; they are recurring religious reactions to dominant social institutions. The dominant social institution for the early church, for example, was the empire, and the political structures of the empire were seen by one sect (led by Tertullian) as unalterably evil and corruptive. A second party, led by Eusebius, saw the Roman empire as redeemed and essentially holy and salvific.[38] The two modern reactions to the corporation are the modern embodiment of the same dynamics that fueled the split in the early church over the nature of the empire—a recurring, twofold tendency either to flee the world as corruptive or to embrace it as redemptive.

A moral assessment of the corporation must confront these two radically opposed views of this most basic U.S. economic institution; it will have to take a stand on the moral nature of the corporation as a social institution. Can social institutions be intrinsically demonic? Can they be intrinsically holy? One belief is that the central and continuous tradition of the church (starting from St. Paul's approach to the institution of slavery in the New Testament through St. Augustine's approach to political institutions in the early Middle Ages and Aquinas' approach to the institution of private property in the late medieval period, right up to John Paul's approach to ownership in *Laborem Exercens*) is that social institutions in general and the corporation in particular are neither intrinsically demonic nor intrinsically salvific. They are merely instrumental means that we can use for good or evil. Thus, both the demonic and the holy visions of the corporation must be resisted and ultimately rejected. The modern corporation is neither holy nor evil. It is simply a form of organization that is currently used to produce the earthly necessities without which humans could not live.

Having rejected a general condemnation of the corporation's role in the economic life of the community, how then can it be assessed from a moral point of view? One suggestion is to do so by adverting to the three moral criteria just described: productivity, just distribution and the right to self-determination. Measuring the corporation against these three kinds of principles will give a much fuller view of its moral role in the economy than the flat condemnations or uncritical praise that others would give it.

DISTRIBUTIVE JUSTICE AND THE U.S. ECONOMY

No better evaluation of the distributional aspects of the American economy can be found than the bishops' superb treatment of this topic in their letter, "Catholic Social Teaching and the U.S. Economy." They have been criticized on the grounds that in their view, justice concerns itself with only one segment of society—the poor—while in reality, justice should concern itself with all members of society. Thus, according to the critics, justice is universal, but the bishops' letter distorts it into a "preference" for the poor. This criticism, however, is based on a superficial reading of the document.

In the bishops' letter, economic justice is defined as universal participation in the economic life of the community. Thus, the economy of a community is just, from a distributive point of view, when it has established "minimum levels of participation by *all* persons in the life of the human community."[39] Consequently, to the extent that some members of a community do not participate in the economic life of the community (either because their minimal needs are not met or because they are not given the means necessary to enable them to be active and productive, such as education, training, job access), the economy is unjust and justice will be reestablished only when their participation is ensured. Thus, precisely because justice requires *universal* participation, establishing justice implies that one must begin by dealing first with those groups that currently do not participate in the life of the economy—the poor and the "marginalized" (which, the bishops argue, includes both those at the bottom economic layers of society and the unemployed).

In keeping with the idea that establishing justice implies one must first focus on groups that do not participate in the life of the economy, the bishops proceed to identify who those groups are and to suggest institutional devices through which their participation can be secured. Three main groups on which they focus are the unemployed, those whose incomes fall beneath the U.S. government's official "poverty line" and the disadvantaged members of developing nations. In each case, the bishops' letter is rightly critical of economic arrangements that effectively bar these groups from participating in the economic community's activities and from sharing in its benefits, and the letter consequently takes on a negative and accusatory tone. This tone, though, is largely merited, since the defects the bishops identify are real and significant.

In each case, also, the bishops correctly suggest that the defects they identify should be remedied through institutional arrangements in which government must play the major role. Government is necessary because the defects the bishops identify are defects of *unjust distribution* and, as any economist can testify, in such a market economy as the United States', such distributional defects cannot be corrected through the unimpeded workings of markets. The defects of distribution identified by the bishops focus on groups whose needs are not met by markets precisely because these groups are blocked from participating in markets. They are blocked either because they lack salable labor (the unemployed) or they lack capital (the poor).

In a free market economy, neither can one rely on the voluntary generosity of free agents to meet the needs of such groups even if such agents want those needs to be met, for two reasons. First, in a free market, rational agents will seek to have others carry the burdens of correcting social ills, even those ills the agents want to see corrected. Thus, rational self-interest leads the reformer to look for ways of solving social ills that will impose burdens on others but not on oneself. Second, in a free market, all agents who divert part of their resources to correcting social ills will find themselves at a disadvantage when competing with those who do not. Thus, a free market pressures its agents to devote all of their resources to competing with other market agents.

The bishops, therefore, correctly see that the distributional defects they identify can be solved only by the imposition of government constraints. Government and only government can correct these distributional effects through transfers of income and wealth, tax and interest incentives and simple regulation. Even the "collaboration" of business interests that the bishops advocate will take place only in the presence of incentives provided by government.

The bishops' letter, then, insofar as it focuses on the distributional aspects of economic life, is superb. It correctly identifies the groups that must be helped in modern economies (those without salable labor and those without capital), it correctly links these groups to the "preferential option for the poor" that is the core idea of distributive justice in scripture and tradition, and it correctly identifies the fundamental institution on which modern societies must rely in meeting the needs of these groups—government.

The bishops' treatment of distributive justice, then, is by and large incisive and well-informed. Their treatment of economic productivity and of economic rights, however, both leave a great deal to be desired. These topics are discussed next.

PRODUCTIVITY AND THE CORPORATION

Although distributive issues underlie most of the bishops' letter, they do not constitute the foundations of economic activity. For before there is anything to distribute, goods must be produced. Production is prior to distribution. Hence, the most basic moral question we can put to an economy is this: How productive is it? Or, more specifically, how productive is it of those goods that meet real human needs? And since, as has been argued, the corporation stands at the heart of the economy, how well does the corporate economy succeed in dealing with the fundamental moral issue of productivity?

Since Adam Smith published his *Wealth of Nations* and pointed out the increases in production when men combine in a division of labor to produce the goods that earlier each produced separately, it has been commonplace to remark that increased productivity is directly related to increased corporate organization.[40] Economic productivity, that is, has a social basis.[41] To be sure, the idea did not originate with Adam Smith. Medieval thought alluded to the importance of organization in economic life,[42] and the medieval idea that economic productivity has a social basis has always been part of Catholic social teaching.[43] It was certainly Adam Smith, though, who highlighted the core idea that economic enterprise is a corporate activity and that increased productivity derives in part from the division of labor, around which the modern corporation is constructed.[44]

The division of labor, however, is only one aspect of a more general phenomenon on which increased productivity rests.[45] The increased productivity that large enterprises make possible ultimately derives from the exploitation of economies of scale: the ability to reduce the average costs of manufacturing each unit of a commodity by spreading the fixed costs of production over an ever-larger number of units. The division of labor on which Adam Smith focused is merely a special kind of economy of scale: Fixed labor costs can be spread over more units by having each laborer specialize in one aspect of the production process. However, economies of scale can operate on every kind of input whose costs are fixed in whole or in part—including labor, land, machinery and administration—as long as methods can be found to spread those costs over ever more units. Thus, the key to forcing more productivity out of society's resources is increased size—large-scale enterprises that can take maximum advantage of economies of scale.

The United States, along with the rest of the Western world, has reaped the benefits of large-scale economic organizations.[46] During the first phase of expansion of corporate enterprises, the half century preceding World War I, the American real per-capita gross national product more than tripled until, on the eve of the war, Americans had attained the highest standard of living in the world. For decades, it retained this position, challenged only by other similarly industrialized nations. Today, along with the Western nations, the United States continues to rank among the top 10 percent of the world's nations in per-capita consumer expenditures[47]; it ranks among the top 10 percent of the world's nations in standard "quality of life" measures[48]; and for decades, it has far outranked all other nations in standard measures of economic standing.[49] America's gross national product today ($2.58 trillion) is more than double that of its nearest competitor, the Soviet Union ($1.21 trillion),[50] and real per-capita gross domestic product in the United States places it at the top of the list of the world's nations (excluding the oil-based economy of Kuwait).[51]

Moreover, American productivity, measured as output per man-hours, has long been among the highest in the world. In the decade between 1950 and

1960, productivity rose 2 percent annually; between 1960 and 1970, productivity continued to rise an annual average of 2.4 percent; during the recession-plagued decade of the 1970s, the average increase was a modest 1.3 percent; since the 1983 economic recovery, it has averaged 3.3 percent. These rates compare favorably with other nations, although other Western countries have begun to do better than the United States during the last decade.[52] By virtually any measure, then, the corporate economies of the United States and the industrialized world are fabulously productive.

The modern, large-scale corporation is one of the linchpins that enabled the vast numbers of people living in the West to achieve the standard of living that otherwise would have been available only to the very wealthy. This point is important to emphasize. The higher standard of living that characterizes the lives of many in the West today derives directly from the fact that mass production introduces economies of scale that effectively lower the cost of goods. Because economies of scale render mass-produced goods cheaper to produce, they can be afforded and consumed by a vastly larger number of people than could afford the individually crafted goods of an earlier era. Whereas only an emperor could earlier afford several changes of clothing, long-distance transportation and ice cream in summer, these are affordable today to large masses of Western workers. Mass production, though, requires large-scale organizations capable of coordinating and controlling the myriad and far-flung activities of hundreds of workers operating thousands of machines in dozens of locations; it requires large-scale organizations capable of administering mass-transportation systems that can carry materials and goods to markets extensive enough to generate mass demand; it requires large-scale organizations capable of coordinating the activities of numerous retail outlets needed to make the goods available to consumers; and it requires large-scale financial institutions capable of providing the capital such large-scale enterprises need.

Thus, the large-scale corporation is the necessary concomitant to the phenomenal productivity modern societies have achieved, and it is therefore the crucial instrument for responding to God's call to be productive.[53] For a corporation is essentially an association in which society's technology, natural resources and the work of individuals are linked and concentrated in ways that continuously multiply productivity through economies of scale. The corporate organization is thus the institution through which modern man and woman continuously and abundantly respond to the command of God to be productive; to produce from the earth's resources the goods that can meet human needs, the goods that feed, clothe, house, culture, transport and promote health. Thus, by bringing people together in socially based forms of work, the modern corporation enables men and women to multiply their creativity and mirror the prolific creative activity of God the maker of the universe.

Although the sheer size of the corporation has been the key to productivity, the benefits of size are not unequivocal. For one thing, as the next section will show, the exigencies of productivity are often at war with the rights of individual workers. More important at this juncture, however, is the fact that increased size does not always imply increased productivity. On the contrary, when it expands beyond a certain size, the large-scale corporation embarks on a road of declining productivity. The declining productivity of the ever-expanding large-scale corporation derives from two sources: diseconomies of scale, and the inefficiencies of monopolistic enterprise.

Diseconomies of scale occur when an enterprise grows so large that the costs of coordinating its various parts and processes begin to climb faster than the savings derived from expanded production. For example, transportation (both internal and external) costs climb, needed information gets lost, controls atrophy, production snafus increase and administrative ability becomes unequal to the gargantuan tasks of coordination. Although the issue is contested, empirical studies indicate that most U.S. industries are dominated by firms that have increased beyond the size where economies of scale operate.[54]

Monopolistic inefficiencies, the second source of declining productivity, result when one or a handful of producers (constituting an oligopoly and not, strictly speaking, a monopoly) controls a sufficiently large portion of a market so that it can set prices and production in order to yield profits above the "average" rate of return (that is, the average for industries with similar risk and capitalization requirements). The result is a drain on consumer welfare, the appearance of internal "slack" that allows waste (the so-called "x-inefficiency"), and a decline in technological innovation. Researchers have estimated that the loss due to monopolistic production in the United States totals 2–3 percent of gross national product, or somewhere in the neighborhood of $40–$60 billion per year.[55] Since ownership of corporate stock is highly concentrated (2.4 percent of all households own 40 percent of the nation's wealth), the largest share of monopolistic profits go to this small group of owners, and this continually exacerbates the uneven distribution of wealth in the United States.[56]

Also crucial to note is that not all corporate productivity is aimed at the creation of goods that meet real human needs. In various ways, the very size of the large corporation encourages investment in the production of goods that do not meet any real human needs. First, there is the fact that the massive amounts of goods produced by the large corporation must be sold in mass consumer markets, and this, in turn, implies heavy advertising expenditures. In 1982, $66.6 billion was spent on advertising, triple the $23.2 billion expended 10 years earlier in 1972.[57] Much of this advertising is socially wasteful because it consumes social resources but provides no benefits to consumers, serving merely to shift demand from one seller to another.[58] In addition, a substantial amount is uninformative or deceptive.[59] Much of it even serves as the basis of product differentiation, which allows sellers of heavily advertised brand names to charge higher prices for products that are not of higher quality.[60]

Second, sheer size gives large corporations access to government that enables them to capture public monies to produce commodities that meet no human needs.[61] The prime example is the weapons industry, which has become a large sector of the American economy.[62] In 1982, the United States spent about $200 billion on military expenditures—about $855 per person—while world military expenditures were estimated at $660 billion.[63] Military expenditures are a substantial drain on the resources of nations, including the United States, which have large social needs.[64] Not only is it difficult to see how the production of weapons increases the welfare of human beings, but on purely economic criteria, weapons production is performed in a manner that is inefficient, wasteful and chronically subject to monopoly profits.[65] Thus, the size of the large-scale corporation carries built-in liabilities to produce commodities that are not socially beneficial.

Moreover, although the ever-increasing division of labor on which the modern large-scale corporation rests has dramatically raised the material standard of living of the average consumer, it has not had entirely beneficial effects on the quality of work life led by the average worker within the modern corporation. The division of labor required by large-scale production has led to job design, of which the long assembly line is the most familiar example, which fragments work and requires high levels of supervisory control.[66] The result is the worker's experience of alienation, nicely described by Herbert Gintis as "powerlessness, meaninglessness, isolation, and self-estrangement."[67] In spite of claims to the contrary,[68] empirical studies indicate that current job design in the large corporation continues to emphasize a division of labor that minimizes time, space, skill, equipment, training and other cost requirements, and that takes little account of worker frustration, job satisfaction, worker safety, worker autonomy, or work variety.[69] The fragmentation and monotonous repetition of tasks is correlated with high levels of worker dissatisfaction, lower job involvement leading to absenteeism and lower psychological well-being.[70] Studies of job enrichment and increasing worker control over tasks, while not altogether definitive, have tended to indicate that job enrichment and increased worker control "lead to improved performance and human satisfaction."[71]

The large-scale corporation is thus a double-edged instrument, one edge serving as a remarkably productive harvester, the other cutting the hand of the society and workers who wield it. For the very size and division of labor that enable the corporation to multiply its productivity are also the bases of its tendency to waste resources, to produce socially useless commodities and to punish the worker. Thus, it is naive to think that the large corporation with its remarkable productivity is an unalloyed blessing. It is both blessing and curse.

Nevertheless, on balance, the large-scale corporation fares remarkably well when measured against the criterion of productivity. Although monopolistic industry, the production of nonbeneficial goods and worker dissatisfaction are all major defects of the corporate economy, they are far outweighed by the astonishingly high standard of living that the large-scale corporation has made possible almost universally in the industrialized nations. Indeed, if there is one point on which every comparative analysis of economic systems agrees, it is that the corporate economy ranks first on the criterion of productivity.

Consequently, it is incredible that the bishops' letter failed to address the productivity of the U.S. economy at any great length in any of its drafts.[72] For productivity provides the most positive aspect of the American economy and enables one to see why the economy continues to enjoy widespread, even proud, support among American citizens in spite of its large defects. Indeed, the negative tone of the bishops' letter, on which many have remarked,[73] is due entirely to the fact that the bishops ignore the morally positive side of the economy—its rich productivity. Because they fail to address American productivity directly (although in a summary introduction added to later drafts, they rather briefly acknowledge its presence) and focus wholly on the economy's distributive defects, they necessarily adopt a harshly critical analysis. Their distributive analysis is negative (for the most part correctly so), but distribution is only part of the economic picture. Another part, the missing part, is productivity, and a positive moral analysis of it would have yielded a more balanced letter.

Why did the bishops ignore productivity? One reason—perhaps the fundamental reason—is because their letter assumes that government is the basic economic institution instead of business. Once government is assumed to be the major economic actor, then distribution becomes the major economic issue. For government does not produce in the U.S. system—it can only distribute and redistribute.[74] It is business that produces, and in modern Western economies, the basic business institution is the large-scale corporation. Thus, by failing to see the crucial role of the corporation in the American economy, the bishops were led inexorably to focus on the economy's negative aspects and to ignore its positive sides.

A more positive analysis of the economy was not the only casualty of ignoring the corporation. In failing to see the importance of corporate productivity, the bishops also failed to see that productivity provides an obvious basis for the development of a contemporary spirituality for modern working men and women. For modern workers spend their productive lifetimes in the context of the corporation. If these aspects of their lives are to have meaning, that meaning must be derived from the positive contribution to human life that the corporation makes possible, and, as has been argued, that positive contribution is the immensely fruitful creativity that the socialized production of the corporation makes possible.

The creativity of modern men and women in the socialized production of the corporation, even in its most alienated forms, is their response to the command of God to "dominate" the world and to be cocreators with God. Through their corporate work, men and women continue God's activity and "perfect it as [they] advance further and further in the discovery of the resources and values contained in the whole of creation."[75] Through the socialized productivity that corporate work embodies, humanity today becomes like God and realizes its dominion over the world of nature. Instead of being at the mercy of nature, humanity transforms nature and thereby realizes its own freedom over nature, a freedom that is possible only by joining together with others in corporate production. Thus, corporate productivity, suitably interpreted, provides the key to developing a "corporate spirituality" based on cocreation.

It is important, however, to resist developing such a "corporate spirituality" in an uncritically ideological manner. While it is true that the corporation is the institution through which modern men and women answer the call of God to be productive and creative in their work, it is also the institution through which modern men and women waste much of God's creation through monopolistic production, through the production of nonbeneficial and even harmful commodities and through job arrangements that dissatisfy and dehumanize the worker. This negative aspect of corporate productivity must be consciously acknowledged in the development of an adequate corporate spirituality. That is, an authentic spirituality of corporate life must not only make corporate life meaningful by revealing its relation to God's creativity in the world, but it must also show how corporate life must be transformed and restructured when it becomes destructive of that world. An authentic corporate spirituality would also have a sharply critical side that continually demanded conversion and a change of heart, a conversion that would require reform of, and even disengagement from, those forms of corporate production that were in reality forms of corporate destruction.

Little of this is to be found in the bishops' letter on the economy. Instead of moving toward developing an authentic spirituality for modern corporate men and women, the bishops devote several pages to developing what is in effect a spirituality of citizen charity. They describe the demand of God to ensure that all people are enabled to participate in the economic life of the community, and they eloquently argue that this economic task is in fact a religious one. In the end, though, this is a distributive issue, and the spirituality it involves remains unconnected to the productive activity in which the corporate worker is engaged.

POWER AND THE CORPORATION

The third criterion against which an economy must be measured is the right of self-determination. To what extent does the corporate economy embody methods of production that respect the right to self-determination? To answer this question, attention must be paid to a fact alluded to earlier: The issue of self-determination is essentially tied to the issue of power because power is the ability of one agent to impose its will on another and thereby determine the other. To what extent, then, do the institutions of the corporate economy embody forms of power that limit or violate self-determination?

Corporate power has two aspects, one external and the other internal. The external power of a corporation consists of its ability to impose its will on its external economic, political and social environments. The external power of the corporation rests on the fact of economic concentration: Since tremendous amounts of capital, labor and technology are concentrated in the corporation, it can use these resources against other, weaker economic, political and social agents.

The internal aspects of corporate power consist of the ability of some of its internal constituencies to impose their will on other members of the corporation, and to determine whose interests corporate resources will serve. The internal corporate power that certain members of the corporation possess, in particular, its top managers, rests on a network of legal, technological and customary prerogatives, which that class of corporate members has gradually forged and now enable it both to control the corporation and to maintain its position of control. Internal corporate power thus has a class basis.

The inquiry into the nature of corporate power can begin by examining the external power of the large-scale corporation, the best-studied aspect of which is the corporation's power over markets.[76] A large portion of manufacturing corporations operate in markets they dominate either because they are the only seller (monopolies) or because the number of sellers is so small (oligopolies) they can coordinate their activities to act in concert.[77] In either case, the large-scale corporation has the power to engage in various forms of collusion (price fixing, market sharing, profit pooling), it can discriminate by setting different prices for different groups of buyers, and it can effectively exclude competitors by enforcing exclusive contracts.[78] In addition, the large-scale manufacturer of consumer products can monopolize a consumer market by differentiating its products on the basis of superficial brand qualities (for example, packaging), exploiting consumer ignorance and exercising its ability to shape consumer preferences through large advertising expenditures.[79] The net result is that, within limits, the large-scale corporation can manipulate consumers, extract high prices and excessive profits out of consumers, and can force consumers to underwrite waste and inefficiency.[80]

Traditional free market ideologies emphasize the extent to which the consumer as "sovereign" of the market is a "free agent" whose uncoerced choices determine the behavior of the firm. The facts do not confirm the ideology. In reality, the large-scale corporation has tremendous market power and, within limits, is able to manipulate the consumer through its domination of markets and ability to influence consumer knowledge through advertising. Market power enables the large corporation to limit the self-determination of the consumer.

Another well-documented arena is the corporation's power over the political process.[81] Evidence is plentiful. Large firms have large financial resources available that they can bring to bear on the political process, and they control information on which government regulators must rely.[82] The history of government regulatory agencies typically moves toward a "mature" stage in which agency staffs are "captured" by persons who are either members of the industries the agencies are supposed to supervise, or who hope to get future jobs in those industries, or who otherwise reflect the interests of the regulated industries.[83] Empirical studies have demonstrated that the size of the firm is directly related to its ability to influence the federal corporate tax process,[84] and that concentration ratios of corporations that regularly deal with government (for example, firms that are subject to high levels of government regulation or are large suppliers to government, such as military producers) are directly related to levels of political contributions.[85] Studies have also revealed the key role that life insurance companies,[86] oil companies,[87] tobacco companies,[88] the health industry,[89] auto companies[90] and coffee manufacturers[91] have played in determining critical government policies. Large corporations can also influence government policies through the influence they can exert on citizens by their access to the media.[92] Thus, it is unarguable that the large corporation exerts a correspondingly large power over the political process. Antitrust law, in fact, has been heavily influenced by the realization that large firms exert undue political power.[93]

Corporate power is not limited to its effects on external agents, however; it is also highly focused internally. The corporation is itself under the control of a sharply defined internal group, a group that has the power to impose its will on other members of the corporation.

Who are the people who control the corporation? In legal theory, ultimate control of the corporation is supposed to rest with its putative owners, the shareholders.[94] They elect the directors and vote on major corporate policy issues. The directors, in turn, choose the managers who are to administer the everyday activities of the corporation, supervise the activities of these managers and formulate policy for the corporation. The managers, serving as agents of the corporation, execute the policies set by the directors and shareholders.[95]

The reality, however, differs sharply from theory:[96] Virtually every large-scale corporation is controlled by its top managers.[97] Corporate directors do not choose their managers, nor can they effectively supervise their activities. Instead, the directors are chosen by the corporation's top managers through management's control of the shareholder proxy election process, and once chosen, directors usually rubber-stamp the decisions of their managers.[98]

Managerial control of the large corporation emerged during the late nineteenth and early twentieth centuries through a process that paralleled the growth of the corporation. As the corporation grew, control of it was gradually taken out of the hands of its owners and increasingly placed into the hands of the professional managers whom the owners hired to administer the complex affairs of their growing enterprises. This separation of "ownership" from "control" of corporate property was the result of several factors, including the diffusion of stock ownership created by the need to raise capital through the sale of stock, the need to rely on professional management expertise to run the complex bureaucratic giant corporation, and the strategic positions that professional managers gradually came to occupy by virtue of their access to corporate resources and information.[99] By the 1930s, managers were in firm control of the corporation and they possessed large, although not unlimited, discretionary powers over it and its constituencies.

The managers who control the corporation are a surprisingly homogeneous group. Most of today's senior executives began their careers in finance, accounting, or in some other professional or technical position, and few emerged from the production or labor management segments. Of today's senior executives, 99 percent are white males; 70 percent are Republicans, although 75 percent describe themselves as "conservative" on economic issues and 90 percent describe themselves as "conservative" on social issues. Virtually all have a college education and about half hold graduate degrees, for the most part in business or law.[100] Managers thus constitute a rather rigidly defined economic and social class. That is, they are a group of people with common interests, common economic functions, a common economic basis of power and a common ideology.

What drives the corporate manager? Observers of the separation of ownership from control of corporate resources have suggested that the managers who now *control* the corporation do not seek the same objectives as the shareholders who *own* the corporation. Whereas owners seek increased earnings in the form of profit and growth, the theory goes, managers have large discretionary power that liberates them to seek such other objectives as status, salary increases, expense perquisites and "social responsibility."[101]

However, there is no empirical evidence that managerial objectives are different from those traditionally attributed to owners—an increase in the value of stock holdings through profit and capital growth.[102] A large body of research has established that a number of factors, in fact, guarantee that managers' objectives will be identified with those of owners, including: the pressures exerted by owners through representation on boards; the pressures exerted by creditors and other financial investors (including brokers and security analysts); compensation plans that reward managers with stock options whose value is proportional to the increase in the value of the stock held by owners; the owner-oriented ideology inculcated as the manager advances through the organization and is socialized into accepting profit and growth as the only legitimate objectives; the threat of takeovers; and legal constraints that protect the interests of stockholders.[103] There is little evidence, therefore, that managers seek anything other than the traditional objectives sought by owners: profits and growth. Thus, although managers have a great deal of power in the corporation, they put this power at the service of profit and growth because doing so is in their self-interest.

Given the profit and growth orientation of managers and their power over the corporation and its resources, the effects of their decisions on other constituencies are not surprising. Their corporate decisions are not designed to serve the interests or needs of workers or of the communities where they are located. Indeed, corporate managers impose their will in ways that, while designed to ensure increasing profits and growth, ignore the interests and wishes of both workers and communities.

Perhaps the most obvious modern imposition of the managerial will is the phenomenon of plant closings and disinvestment. Between 1969 and 1976, about 30 percent of all large manufacturing plants (those with more than 100 workers) have been closed down.[104] This means that approximately 3.2 million workers involuntarily lose their jobs each year as a result of managerial decisions to shrink or close a plant. During the late 1970s, plant closures have been concentrated in the auto industry and its associated suppliers as well as in the steel industry. Much of this plant-closure activity has been motivated by managerial decisions to shift capital to geographical areas that have lower labor costs, either within the United States or in Third World countries. American automakers, for example, have increasingly internationalized their production, as have firms in electronics, textiles, shoes and rubber. Plant closures have also resulted from managerial decisions to diversify capital out of low-profit industries into ones with higher profit margins. During the 1970s, for example, American steel companies cut capital outlays for upgrading their steel plants and equipment and simultaneously invested in real estate, cement, coal, natural gas, oil, shipping and container manufacturing.[105]

The impact of plant closures on workers has been disastrous. The period of unemployment after workers have been laid off has been prolonged; their lifetime savings have been exhausted; they have been forced to accept jobs with lower salaries and status; many have lost homes to foreclosure; all or partial pension rights often have been forfeited; most have suffered acute mental distress, experiencing loss of confidence, feelings of worthlessness, suicide, psychosomatic illnesses, alcoholism and child and spouse abuse.[106]

The critical point, of course, is that plant closures are determined by the unilateral decision-making power of corporate managers as they seek their own self-interest through increased profits and growth. Workers have no voice in these decisions, which, more than any others, determine their present and future lives. Indeed, workers are rarely notified of an impending layoff and are often discharged with neither severance pay nor job replacement training; they consequently have no opportunity to plan for their future jobless status. Of all workers, 25 percent are covered by union agreements, but only three quarters of these require notification of layoffs, and in 80 percent of such contracts, the prenotification period is one week or less; only 50 percent of all negotiated contracts provide for severance pay.[107] Thus, for millions of workers each year, self-determination is drastically diminished by the unilateral power corporate managers have over their lives.

Managerial power infringes on the self-determination of workers in other, less dramatic but no less pervasive areas. The United States today is "the only industrialized country without some form of comprehensive protection against wrongful discharge."[108] American courts today continue to adhere to the common law doctrine of "employment at will": the principle that, with the exception of certain protected classes (for example, union organizers and minorities), employers may legitimately dismiss their employees at will "for good cause, for no cause, or even for causes morally wrong, without being thereby guilty of legal wrong."[109] American law thus empowers managers to fire individuals for arbitrary reasons. This power, in turn, enables managers to use the threat of discharge to coerce employees into abdicating their rights to privacy, to freedom of speech, to safe working conditions and to due process.[110] Reformers have urged adoption of a workers' "Bill of Rights" that would extend the protections citizens have against the power of government to protect workers against the power of corporate management.[111] Although some inroads have been made on diminishing the power of corporate management, no such blanket proposals have been adopted.

Yet another area of the loss of self-determination for workers involves the loss of control over immediate work processes. Social theorists sometimes wax eloquent on the "communitarian" aspects of corporate work.[112] In reality, however, the corporation is designed as a hierarchical control mechanism in which tasks are minutely controlled, leaving little room for the free play of spontaneity and self-expression that is crucial to community. The "alienating" effects of this loss of worker control have already been noted; here, alienation does not merely lead to a loss of welfare (a decline of "productivity"), but, more important, is an indication of a loss of self-determination.

The corporate economy, then, does not fare well when measured against the criterion of the right to self-determination. In myriad ways, the economy's core institution—the large-scale corporation—uses its considerable power to determine the behavior of consumers and to manipulate the political process. Within the corporation, a well-defined class—the managerial class—controls the corporation and puts its assets at the service of profit and growth, even to the detriment of the interests of other corporate constituencies. Workers in particular can be at the mercy of the unilateral decision-making power of the managerial class, as the recent spate of plant closures has revealed.

CONCLUSION

What is the picture that emerges overall from this attempt to measure the modern American economy against the three moral criteria of productivity, distributive justice and the right to self-determination? If we assume that the fundamental purpose of an economy is to produce the economic goods a society must have, then the American economy fulfills its fundamental moral purpose with great success: It is spectacularly productive. As has been argued, this productivity is the fulfillment of the fundamental religious imperative of *Genesis:* "Fill the earth and subdue it."

This productivity, though, is linked to deep failures of justice and widespread violations of the right to self-determination. Those who reject the corporation as demonic would say that the linkage is a necessary one, that capitalist production necessarily spawns injustice and exploitation. On the other hand, those who embrace the corporation as salvific insist that the injustices are not deep and the violations are not widespread, that capitalist production is the best of all possible economic worlds.

Both of these positions must be resisted. The failures of distributive justice and the violations of self-determination are indeed serious defects, but they are not necessary concomitants of corporate production. At bottom, both arise from the way in which ownership and control of corporate assets are distributed in our society, and current patterns of ownership and control are not necessary aspects of the socialized production that the corporation makes possible. They are, instead, social patterns that are amenable to change.

In *Laborem Exercens,* John Paul II suggests that the means of production of Western economies should be "socialized" by making each worker "a part owner of these means." That suggestion expresses exactly the kind of changes in ownership and control that are needed if the wonderful productivity of the modern, large-scale corporation is to be preserved and simultaneously rid of its serious moral defects. Whether we will have sufficient will and intellect to devise and implement such changes only the future will tell.

The Bishops' Letter—
A Protestant Reading

Robert Benne

The bishops have kept their promise that their reflections on the American economy would be open to ongoing dialogue with their readers. Though they have not changed their minds about the basic thrust of their document, which in itself does not call into doubt the authenticity of the conversation, they have clearly responded to the criticism leveled by thousands of voices who have participated in the dialogue.

The second version shows marked improvements, among them, the bishops have: conveyed a more balanced view of American economic performance; learned more from the American pragmatic and reformist tradition than earlier; appreciated more readily the "market virtues" of economic freedom, initiative and productivity; emphasized more vigorously the need for economic activism among persons in the economy, including the poor (the economy is measured not only by what it does *to* and *for* people, but also by how people *participate* in it); attempted to refute the charge of statism by underscoring their commitment to cooperation among economic actors; and, most welcomed, toned down the shrill "prophetic denunciations" of the United States and its people, perhaps because of a new respect for the complexity and intractability of many serious economic issues as well as for the variety of opinions about such matters held by persons of goodwill and intelligence. They have made good their pledge that feedback would be taken seriously.

Nevertheless, the main argument is unchanged. Their fundamental ethical principle—the dignity of the human person realized in community with others—is combined with its indispensable corollary, the "preferential option for the poor," which addresses the sorry fact that too many people do not participate in that dignity in community. Standing on that principle, which they believe is a summation of the Christian moral vision, the bishops derive more specific norms for economic life and then argue that those must lead to the extension of economic democracy in America.

Economic democracy seems to mean two basic things: an elaboration of certain fundamental economic rights that will ensure that all have access to a dignified level of life, and participation in decision making in the economic process by all. This realization of economic democracy will bring closer to fruition the American commitment to democracy, which has thus far been focused on the achievement of political democracy. As the bishops put it, "These economic rights are as essential to human dignity as are the political and civil freedoms granted pride of place in the Bill of Rights of the U.S. Constitution."

In spite of the several changes that have been made in the second draft, some people are still uncomfortable about document, although they share the bishops' fundamental moral principle. Part of the discomfort is warranted, for the bishops have succeeded in drawing attention repeatedly to the serious human problems facing society—there is simply too much misery and suffering. Certainly, we ought to do more to alleviate that suffering and to move toward a more just society in which ever more people have the opportunity to participate with dignity. If the bishops can continue to make us uncomfortable by pointing to that suffering and insisting on some sort of constructive approach, their efforts will not have been in vain.

However, part of the discomfort has to do with disagreement about the specific argument of the letter, which this essay will discuss. First will be addressed questions about how one of the normative sections of the paper is handled, particularly, "Ethical Norms for Economic Life." That section contains the detailed specification of what human dignity in community really means, especially for economic life. Second will be critical rejections on the selected policy proposals made in chapters 3 and 4. Third, some disagreements will be registered with the general approach of the document; for example, its partisanship, its handling of critics and its hesitation to apply its principles to the church.

NORMATIVE CONSIDERATIONS

Although it is true that economic growth is recognized in the policy-issues section as indispensable for the alleviation of unemployment and poverty, one searches in vain for any discussion of economic growth in the normative sections of the document. In short, the document seems to avoid completely the issue of primarily what an economy is *for.* The letter certainly has a plethora of moral principles that hold economic actors accountable. They are to be imbued with civic friendship, they have duties to be commutatively, socially and distributively just, and they are called to overcome the marginalization and powerlessness of the poor. On the other hand, all persons, whether or not they are capable of contributing economically, have economic rights to life, food, clothing, shelter, rest, medical care and social security. Those who can contribute have rights to employment at an adequate wage for human dignity as well as healthful working conditions.

Besides ensuring that economic actors adhere to these rights and duties, the nation is called to moral priorities of fulfilling the basic needs of the poor, increasing active participation in economic life by those who are excluded or vulnerable, and investing wealth, talent and human energy in ways that directly benefit the poor and economically insecure.

Conversely, in the introductory section of the letter, unequal economic outcomes—employment falling on some and not others, disparities among nations, differentials between male and female incomes and poverty amid plenty—are attributed to moral failure in the economy. Inequalities are consistently attributed to injustice.

Indeed, on reading the normative sections of the letter, one would conclude that economic life is almost exclusively a moral activity. Economics *is* ethics. No doubt it is true that moral failures are present in all the problems just mentioned. It is also true that economic life as a thoroughly human activity has many moral interstices. The bishops are right in arguing that economic life has an inescapable moral dimension, especially in the face of a good deal of economic writing and business practice that tries to rule it out, mistakenly assuming that economics is exclusively a technical endeavor. However, in almost completely ignoring the technical and nonmoral values connected with the adequate working of an economy, the letter appears naive.

These weaknesses are starkly revealed in what has to be one of the most foolish statements in the letter: "They [all economic decisions, policies and institutions] must be at the service of all people, especially the poor." What does such a statement mean? When the local grocery store manager decides to purchase wholesale some fish in order to sell them to customers, how can such a decision possibly be assured to serve *all* people, especially the poor? The store manager has to serve only some people, for example, wholesalers, customers and employees. It is impossible for the manager to make an economic decision that benefits all people but especially the poor because it is only a small, limited part in an impersonal, unconsciously coordinated market system that requires the manager to be accountable to specific people in specific ways. These discrete economic decisions cannot be based on the common good, universal benevolence, or the preferential option for the poor because, if they were, the particular service to supplier, customer and employee would soon end, for the manager would have neglected sober consideration of prices and marketing and thereby bankrupted the store by failing to make an adequate profit. In a very indirect way, however, the manager is serving many people, including many of the poor, by effectively participating in a market system that in its own impersonal and broadly utilitarian way lifts the living standard of the majority.

This vast and dynamic American market system, operating in a relatively free and competitive way, hands out rewards and losses according to how well enterprises and persons respond to its demands. This process involves what Joseph Schumpeter called "creative destruction," whereby new products and services as well as new ways of producing them come to the fore while older ones are sloughed off. This process, Schumpeter avers, leads to revolutions in the means of production, which in turn, bring more and more products within reach of ordinary people, thus lifting the living standards of the majority.[1] The American economy seems to be very adept at doing what economies are fundamentally *for*—the efficient and creative combination of factors of production so that wealth is generated.

By neglecting the nonmoral, technical and instrumental values of efficiency and productivity, the bishops imply that economic activity is primarily moral and political. This has several harmful effects on the letter.

First, the letter fails to distinguish between economics and politics. The bishops are actually addressing the American political economy; they are making mostly public policy recommendations, giving very little attention to economic values and processes per se. They foster an idealistic illusion that the moral and political enterprise, mainly devoted to distribution and participation, could go on without the economic expertise and vitality that logically and chronologically take precedence.

Second, distortions in their normative approach lead them to expect too much morally of economic life. Certainly, we should expect more just outcomes in economic life, but by dissolving the inevitable tension between efficiency and equality through their failure to consider the requirements of efficiency, the bishops proliferate the moral and political demands on economic life in such a way that the goose that lays the golden egg would indeed be throttled. The letter seems to suppose that the problems of efficiency and production have been solved—all we have to do is make the process more just.

Third, this imbalance toward moralism leads to the unwise use of such concepts as "economic democracy" and "new experiments in democratic, economic decision making." Friend and foe alike have remarked how similar the bishops' proposal sounds to the platforms of European social democratic parties. While the bishops say they wish to avoid assessments of economic systems, their very list of questions to be put to economic systems exhibits a serious distrust of free market arrangements, and their commitment to economic democracy suggests a strong affinity for a moderate democratic socialism.

Clearly, Christians of goodwill and intelligence can opt for such an approach, but perhaps such partisanship is unwise in view of the difficulty those social democratic approaches have had in economic growth and job creation. That partisanship is also unnecessary because many of the letter's more specific proposals on unemployment, poverty, agriculture and the world economy need not flow from those particular ideological commitments. Many Christians will be able to affirm a good number of the specific policy proposals out of a democratic capitalist persuasion, but the socialist rhetoric could put them off.

Fourth, the rather heavy moralistic overlay at the expense of technical, practical, economic "excellence" leads to an unduly heroic ethic for lay people. There is little mention of the laity's obligation to perform cheerfully and well their daily work and thereby serve others in mundane ways. Rather, the laity are summoned to imitate the pattern of Jesus' life, take up the way of the cross, empty the self and "leave all" to follow Jesus. Now, interpreted rightly, all those injunctions have authentic Christian meaning. Further, the bishops do affirm the role of the laity in their worldly callings in the section on Christian vocation: "The vocation of all Christians is rather to draw faith and life into a vital synthesis which proclaims God's glory." The normative images, though, do not emphasize ordinary worldly excellence as a way to serve God and others.

The bishops also tend to overemphasize the amount of leeway lay economic actors have in their decision making. Lay people are more constrained by their particular place in the economic system than the bishops imply with their somewhat heroic ethic. Moreover, little Gospel comfort is given to those who are caught in the inevitable tensions between particular necessities and more universal moral aspirations, a tension that all Christians frequently experience.

In sum, the more specific, normative section of the document is flawed because it tends only to moral values and neglects the nonmoral values with which economics inescapably deals. This leads to the aforementioned unfortunate results. If one tried to keep moral and nonmoral values in a more realistic tension, different concepts than "economic democracy" and "cooperation" would be more appropriate. Also, different specific proposals would take shape. Both concepts and proposals are likely to be more consonant with American experience and ideology, and perhaps they might also be specific embodiments of the bishops' indisputable fundamental principle— the dignity of the person in community.

POLICY PROPOSALS

The policy proposals the letter makes on poverty, employment, agriculture, and the U.S. role in the world economy seem, on the whole, to be moderate and measured, especially in comparison with the normative section of the document. This is quite possibly the case because the writers are forced to take into account considerations of efficiency and practicality. The proposals are basically pragmatic and reformist, and many persons of various political philosophies can agree with at least some of them. However, there are a number of areas in which critical questions can be raised.

One wonders, for example, what all that the bishops propose would cost. The mention of dramatic increases in welfare benefits, job retraining, child care, public employment, loans for threatened farmers and development assistance, to name but a few items, raises serious questions of feasibility, especially in the light of booming federal deficits and a general loss of confidence in the government's ability to attack problems effectively. The letter can be regarded as a vision of all the things that should be done, but then the bishops have stopped with an elaboration of principles and goals. When the letter tackles practical policy, the bishops owe some estimate of the feasibility of all of these programs, or at least, they owe us a calculation of costs and of from where the additional money is to come. Without that, the letter shares the characteristic of too many church documents, that is, no realistic sense of limits.

Another worrisome problem is the letter's vagueness about whether its proposals are to be legally mandated or taken as a moral summons for all economic actors. Some proposals, such as reform of the welfare system and lessening of the tax burden on the poor, are obviously meant to entail a change in laws. How about upgrading jobs, though, and the exhortation for comparable worth, the inveighing against luxury goods (word processors, for example?) and above all, the grand proposal for a new American experiment in economic cooperation and participation? In introducing chapter IV,

"A New American Experiment: Partnership for the Common Good," the bishops say that as the nation's founders took daring steps to create structures of mutual accountability within the political system, so "we believe that similar institutional steps are needed today to expand the sharing of economic power and to relate the economic system more accountably to the common good." That would suggest that their vision of partnership among all involved in the productive process, as well as those affected by it, should be legally imposed on economic enterprises.

This is a very disturbing thought because it would mandate a specific model of ownership and decision making on a highly dynamic and experimental system, and would introduce rigidity and inflexibility into that system. The exciting experiments with Japanese models, with employee ownership and management and with other schemes for making workplaces more humane are endorsed by a range of theorists, from left-wing supply-siders like Robert Reich to hard-nosed capitalists like Louis Kelso.[2] Many true believers have great faith in these efforts to enhance human values and productivity at the same time. Conclusive evidence, however, is not yet available. The American economy is characterized by a variety of ownership and management styles, all of which compete with each other in a grand experiment about which ones shall prevail.

It is wisest to allow a thousand flowers to bloom. The many different styles of ownership and management will probably survive. We should not foreclose on the experiment as the bishops tend to suggest; the secrets of economic vitality are not known fully by anyone, nor are they fully captured by any one model. Perhaps the bishops think they know too much about "true" models.

The bishops enthusiasm for partnership and participation also is too uncritical. They seem to suggest that the introduction of participatory practices will suddenly do away with conflicts of interest within firms and within industries and communities. This probably is not so. Further, in affirming a cooperative model over a competitive one, they seem unaware of the capacity for cooperating groups to exert their self-interest in powerful ways that border on monopoly. For example, auto manufacturers, their workers and their political representatives *do* cooperate in pressing for protectionist measures. In fact, Mancur Olson has argued in his *The Rise and Decline of Nations* that collusive efforts by special interests tend to substitute political favors and protection for economic performance, thus harming the overall competitive position of the nation.[3]

The suggestion here is not that these new experiments in the "pursuit of excellence" are unworthy of the bishops' interest, but rather, that too many eggs have been put in one basket, that if these experiments were to be mandated legally, they could produce a disaster for the American economy. The present experimental system, held accountable by competition, is likelier to come up with viable models.

Perhaps the bishops think that their pastoral letter on peace has solved all the debates on defense spending and foreign policy. They imply that the United States has exaggerated East–West conflicts, that the need to address domestic ills and to participate more generally in Third World economic development obviously outweighs the need to build up the military, and that political–strategic considerations in the use of foreign aid should simply stand aside before the basic needs of developing countries. All of that may be true, but it certainly is not argued in this document. Readers of the document then can find themselves asking these questions: So what if there is a real Marxist–Leninist threat in Nicaragua and El Salvador? Are only North–South dynamics going on there? So what if the Soviet Union is involved in a gigantic military buildup? Even allowing for unjustifiable waste, has not the bulk of the U.S. buildup been necessary? Ought we really to devote money to develop Cuba or Vietnam without regard to political or strategic interests? Since the bishops would draw a good deal of their money for the costs of domestic and international economic reforms from the defense budget, they perhaps owe us more reflection on priorities than they have given us within this letter.

While most of the letter's policy proposals are levelheaded and moderate, it seems clear that they generally come from the liberal side of American political philosophy. They exhibit something of the grand old tradition of New Deal liberalism: the expansion and refinement of economic rights, increased welfare, economic planning and cooperation and interventions into markets through income policy. Except for one bow to Milton Friedman's negative income tax, little attention is given to analyses and proposals from other movements of political philosophy and action such as the neoliberal, conservative and libertarian groups.

The bishops ignore those movements at their own peril, because many of the more interesting proposals for extending justice and opportunity are coming from those sources. For example, the proposal for school vouchers is fascinating. The bishops do not take it up as a means of dramatically improving access to excellent education by the poor, no doubt because they would appear to be involved in special pleading for Catholic schools. That is unfortunate, because a voucher system biased toward the poor could be an extremely important way to extend a fairer shake to them.

Widely known is that Milton Friedman (followed by a number of libertarians) has been keenly interested in eroding the near-monopoly on primary and secondary education held by the public school system. His idea is for the state to give a voucher worth a year of education to parents for each of their school-age children. The vouchers would be nontransferable, but usable in public or private schools. This would expand parents' choice and force public schools to compete on equal footing with private schools.[4]

Many telling criticisms of this proposal have been made by persons who are not simply defensive proponents of the present system. Chief among these reservations is that middle-class parents would quickly move their children into private and parochial schools on their vouchers, those schools would fill up, and then the children of disadvantaged families would be left with the public schools, which would become dumping grounds for the worst cases. That is a convincing criticism. However, what if the families of disadvantaged children (children of one-parent families below a very low income level) were given vouchers worth 150% of the cost of a year of education? Private and public schools would arrange education to help those children and appeal to their parents because they would have an incentive to do it. Catholic and other church-related schools would have an advantage because they have had a lot of practice in these kinds of arrangements. Many poor families could then afford such an education, and the schools could afford to give it to them. Church schools would offer a more disciplined context that would emphasize moral values. They could tap the idealism of many young persons who would choose to become teachers of the disadvantaged if only they could make a living at it and work in healthy and effective environments. Meanwhile, the public schools would have to compete for their students, and poor parents would have a choice.

The worth of vouchers for private education would decline as one went up the socioeconomic scale, while all families would have vouchers worth the full amount for use in public schools. This would give incentives for middle-class families to keep their children in public schools. All across the board, the choice would be real and effective. This would not only break down the monopolies that currently help to block improvements in urban education, but would open important educational channels for the poor.

In many small town and suburban areas, these schemes would not be necessary, since disadvantaged children already have access to the same schools that more advantaged children attend. Such an approach might be tried, though, in areas where the poor have miserable opportunities. Several state legislatures such as that of Minnesota have similar plans before them. This idea illustrates an important point. Some of the most creative social policy thought is coming from conservative and even libertarian sources. Such economists as Walter Williams have many proposals that would open up access for the poor to work that are currently closed off by collusive regulation. Licensure is a key way special interest groups can cooperate to maintain monopoly conditions and freeze out unwanted entrants.[5]

Also, many economists argue that the best way to support the poor at a decent level is through direct subsidy (vouchers for fuel, medical insurance, rent) rather than trying to fix the pricing system of the market. These examples are given in order to suggest that other mechanisms are available for extending justice, ways that may be more efficient and decentralized than the kind of interventions the bishops suggest. This is to say that "economic democracy" may be related more to the expansion and power of choice than to direct participation in the economic decision-making process. While the importance of direct participation is not to be underplayed, it is even more important for the poor to have a choice of opportunities in work and in the crucial services that enhance their lives. Conservative and libertarian economists have been creative in proposing schemes that in fact support those kinds of choices. The bishops do not have to accept the philosophical underpinnings of those economists in order to accept, or at least take seriously, many of their proposals.

GENERAL APPROACH

The tendency to entertain only liberal analyses and policy proposals in the Catholic bishops' letter, as well as in most other mainline church statements, raises a serious question of basic approach. How helpful is it for the church to commend particular public policy options? The churches have been infatuated with this kind of witness, but it is not clear that such an approach is the wisest and most helpful to both members and nonmembers as well as the church itself. Church statements often alienate large numbers of the laity, not only because the people disagree with the positions taken by their church, but because they observe their views are often not considered by church leaders. In this regard, it seems rather ungracious of the bishops not even to mention the Lay Commission or its letter. Further, they do not consider the arguments of such writers as Murray, Auletta, Williams and Sowell.[6] They never mention Michael Novak's writing, although the bishops' committee did hear testimony from him and several other conservatives. It is as if the bishops do not want to say anything nice or even recognize the existence of their "enemies"—but the laity do in fact read such analyses. When the church does not even recognize their existence, many people become suspicious that the writers of church statements are not playing fair.

The churches might be wiser to adapt another approach in their address to most social issues, that is, "most" and not "all," because there are some issues to which the church has long-held, settled commitments. Its clarity on apartheid, for example, cannot be challenged. However, the church should maintain flexibility on how Christians might resist apartheid in South Africa; there seem to be a number of morally viable options.

Wiser and more helpful would be for the church to encourage fair moral discourse on the great issues facing us. At the outset, the church could attempt to discern the limits of permissible Christian options by identifying those positions and actions that are clearly beyond the pale of Christian moral possibility. Then, it would be helpful to identify the key analyses and policy proposals, perhaps including its own if it thinks it really has something unique to add to the discussion at that level. The church could follow up by carefully critiquing the major analyses and proposals, lifting up weaknesses and strengths. In a few cases of authentic urgency and churchly clarity, it could come out for a specific option, but this would be done relatively infrequently. In most cases, the laity could be left to make up its own mind within the range of possibilities.

Moreover, the church could become much more of a mediator of divergent opinions and interests than it has been. Like the Evangelical and Catholic academies in Germany, the American churches could spend more time and energy providing a gracious context for bringing together divergent groups and interests to facilitate conversation. These efforts might lead to the kind of partnership, cooperation and accommodation the bishops call for in their "New American Experiment" chapter, and could be more helpful than constantly taking positions on issues. Further, it would honor and support the laity in its rightful role in the practical affairs of the world.

Although clearly, the bishops have tried to apply their own moral principles to the life of the Catholic church, that effort is still unsatisfactory in regard to two important issues. The bishops insist that economic life should be characterized by democracy. They actually give very few reasons for this—they just think it would be a good thing. They also insist that economic life should be free of sexual discrimination. The reasons they give here are fairly compelling. In neither case, however, do they consider whether these challenges should be addressed to the decision-making and leadership practices of the Catholic church. There may be good reasons why these challenges should not be heeded, but there may also be good reasons why all economic decision-making cannot be democratic. In neither case have they made compelling arguments. If the bishops want to commend strongly certain principles to worldly spheres of activity, they owe us reasons why they should not as well apply to the religious.

Finally, there leaves one nagging concern. Though this chapter has referred to the letter as the bishops' letter, some people believe that it is actually their staff's letter. The bishops approve its final form, of course, but the flavor of its argument is decidedly academic rather than ecclesiastic. Such is the case with the lion's share of church statements. Without resorting to nefarious, "new class" theories it has been suggested that the domination of statements by church staffs is not unnoticed by the lay constituencies of the various churches. The bishops lose some credibility as pastoral leaders when they shift the responsibility in drafting statements to their staffs.

CONCLUSION

This chapter concludes with a word of praise and caution. The praise comes for the service the bishops have provided in keeping before us as Christians and as a nation the issue of deprivation in our land of plenty. This is not terribly fashionable to do, but the bishops, shrewdly drawing out the discussion through several drafts after the election of a conservative U.S. president, have succeeded in keeping a public debate going. Moreover, considering the possibilities for real disaster, the bishops have done rather well. Protestants can learn much from their seriousness and thoroughness.

Concerning the word of caution, it can be suggested that all religious communities, particularly those of the Protestant and Catholic mainstream, become more "intentional" and disciplined about the primary reason for their existence: the formation of their members into the religious and moral vision they bear. That process of formation seems to become weaker as time goes by, especially for the young. The *substance* of both Catholic and Protestant traditions is becoming fainter. Meanwhile, those communities seem increasingly focused on the *implications* of their religious and moral vision, implications that can and ought to be open to a variety of interpretations. Is the attention of the bishops and the religious professions too bound up with implications and too little with fundamental formation? If so, the moral weight of what they propose will soon dissolve because they will have too few troops for them to be taken seriously.

6

The Bishops' Letter— A Jewish Reading

Ronald Green

The bishops' pastoral letter on the U.S. economy appears at a peculiarly uncertain moment in the history of American Jewish thinking about social and
economic issues. For many decades, American Jews have strongly supported
progressive initiatives in the economic and social sphere. Indeed, Jews have
so often been identified with the ideals of the welfare state that, in the words
of one writer, "Jewish liberalism" has been almost a redundant term.[1] Nevertheless, on several fronts, this traditional identification of Jews with progressive
social and economic causes has recently been called into question.

Although Jewish voters continue to support Democratic party candidates
at substantially higher rates than the other immigrant religious groups that
once formed the New Deal coalition, there has been some movement among
Jewish voters toward moderate Democratic, Republican and even conservative
candidates.[2] More important, perhaps, is the fact that some of the most important Jewish intellectuals and activists involved in shaping both Jewish and
non-Jewish thinking about economic matters are now to be found on the
conservative rather than the liberal side of public debate. Such thinkers as
Robert Nozick, Irving Kristol, or Milton Friedman appear to have partly replaced the Herbert Marcuses or Allard Lowensteins of a previous era.

In many ways, of course, this transformation is to be expected. As Jews
have attained middle- and upper-middle-class affluence and nearly full social
acceptance, some have naturally been attracted to doctrines of economic individualism and success. This transformation, however, has also created a
sense of puzzlement about the Jewish past and the traditions with which many
Jews have identified themselves. Recently, for example, voices have been heard
saying that Jewish liberalism, especially Jewish concern for the economically
disadvantaged and socially marginal, is a very recent and peripheral aspect
of Jewish life and thought; that it is the product of nineteenth century European
experience and Jews' opposition to the alliance of economically conservative

and anti-Semitic forces arrayed against them; and that it was reinforced in America by an encounter with the nativist, isolationist and conservative economic interests that opposed the New Deal and forced Jews to the left. This Jewish liberalism, it is said, is as ephemeral as the New Deal coalition itself, a short-lived "marriage of convenience" between an embattled ethnic group and a social ideology. If this marriage is now coming to an end, it is because changing circumstances have permitted Jews to return to the attitudes they have historically possessed: a preference for unfettered capitalistic activity, individual economic initiative and self-reliance.[3]

The remarks that follow will challenge this view. "Jewish liberalism," it will be suggested, is not a novel phenomenon, but an enduring, and indeed, almost defining, aspect of this ancient tradition. Moral concern for the poor and disadvantaged has its deepest roots in the Hebrew bible, but also is reiterated in the normative sources of Jewish thinking—the Talmud, and the writings of its great medieval codifiers. More important, this concern was expressed in the daily practice and institutions of Jewish communities over many centuries.

Another way of saying this is to observe that many of the most basic themes of Jewish social thought are deeply congruent with those emphasized in the bishops' letter. Proceeding from a common foundation in biblical teaching about social justice, both traditions elaborated a rich series of shared understandings of the nature and limits of economic life, and both sought to embody these understandings in the lives of their respective communities. For this reason, a brief review of some of the major themes enunciated in the bishops' letter is a useful way of beginning a survey of Jewish teaching on these issues. Although there are some important differences in nuance between Jewish and Catholic economic ethics, the major themes announced by the bishops have corresponding importance and saliency in the traditional Jewish sources. Apart from its value to Catholics and Americans in general, the pastoral letter, therefore, performs a special service for Jewish Americans: It reminds them of some of the major ethical themes their own tradition has contributed to Western thinking in the area of social and economic life.

THEMES IN THE PASTORAL LETTER

Four themes appear to predominate in the bishops' letter. These are not always singled out as such, nor are they entirely distinguishable, but they appear frequently enough to merit independent identification.

They include, first, an emphasis on human dignity, and the resulting test of an economic system in terms of what it does *for* people and what it does *to* people.[4] This theme underlies the letter's stress on the importance of individuals' participation in the economic system and on the value of labor, not merely as a way of meeting material needs, but as a mode of self-realization.[5]

Second, there is the theme that the right to private property is not unqualified. This view, rooted in centuries of church teaching, holds that the goods of the earth are ordained by God as the common property of all human beings. Although private possession has penultimate legitimacy as a way of ordering use of these goods, such possession is always to be regarded as a form of "stewardship" of resources for the common good and can be limited by urgent social needs.[6]

The third theme follows directly from this—the special obligation that exists to sustain and aid the poor. Precisely because the goods of the earth are divinely ordained to *all* human beings, the poor have a right of access to the goods and opportunities needed to sustain life in dignity. Assistance to the poor is not merely an obligation of charity and private giving, but a strict demand of justice, and the test of a social system is partly how well it serves the needs of the disadvantaged. This understanding, along with other motifs drawn from the biblical and later Christian tradition, help form the "preferential option for the poor" espoused by the letter.[7]

Finally is the theme that these attitudes and obligations are not confined to only the local or even national community, but extend to humankind as a whole. Allowing for the enormous complexities that bear on economic sharing beyond the national level, the letter affirms the oneness of human moral community and the requirement of global responsibility in the economic domain.[8]

BIBLICAL FOUNDATIONS

The deep congruence between Jewish teaching and the themes of the bishops' letter has its origin in a shared heritage of biblical faith. Here are found the essential ideas and norms that shape all subsequent Jewish thinking about economic life.

The emphasis on social justice is, of course, a hallmark of prophetic faith. The beginnings of Israel as a nation stem from a battle against economic oppression at the hands of Egyptian masters, and the memory of this is reflected in the many specific covenantal requirements of justice imposed on the nation. Under the constant reminder that they were once themselves bondsmen in Egypt (Exod. 23:9; Deut. 15:15, 16:12), the Israelites were required to show special solicitude for the economically and socially "marginalized" in their midst: the poor, the slave, the orphan, the widow and the sojourner.

This concern was embodied in a series of commandments that furnish the basis for what subsequently becomes Jewish law *(halakhah)*. Among other things, these commandments include: the provision for the cancellation of debts, return of alienated property and the emancipation of slaves in the Jubilee year; the requirement that the spontaneous growths of the field and garden during the Sabbatical year be left free to the poor (Exod. 23:11); that every third year a tithe—one tenth—of all products be given to the needy (Deut. 14:28–29); that at every harvest, a corner of all grain fields (Lev. 19:9, 23:22)—later interpreted as amounting to one sixtieth of the crop—as well as the gleanings, the forgotten sheaves and the imperfect and topmost clusters of grapes, be left to the poor and the stranger (Lev. 19:10). In connection with the three pilgrim festivals (Passover, Weeks and Tabernacles), when attendance at the capital was required of all families, it was ordained that the stranger, the widow and the orphan be invited to share the food of the pilgrims (Deut. 16:11–14). Special care was enjoined for the weak: The stranger was not to be oppressed, the widow and the orphan were not to be dealt with harshly (Exod. 22:20–23, 23:9; Lev. 19:23–34); a borrower was to be given loans without interest (Deut. 15:7–11) and the borrower's garment, taken in pledge, was to be returned by nightfall (Exod. 22:24–26; Lev. 25:35–38).

Connected with these specific enactments and underlying them are several fundamental ideas that form part of the permanent legacy of biblical thinking about economic life. One is the idea that the most basic productive resource and most valued possession, land, belongs to God. The refrain, "The earth is the Lord's, and the fullness thereof" (Psalms 24:1) was taken literally by this tradition. While members of the community are entitled to a patrimony, this proceeds as a gift from God's hand, and in the most basic sense, God remains its owner. As Roger Brooks has observed, only this understanding explains the panoply of covenantal requirements for the distribution of the land's produce to the two landless groups: the priests and the poor. Within the biblical and later Talmudic conception, Brooks says, the ordinary Israelite is, in a sense, a "tenant farmer" for God:

> [He] works God's land and enjoys its yield, with the result that a portion of all he produces belongs to God. In order to pay this obligation, Israelites render to the priests grain as heave offering, tithes and other priestly rations. Similarly, a specific portion of the Land's yield is set aside, by chance alone, for the poor. So underlying the designation of both priestly rations is a single theory: God owns the entire Land of Israel and, because of this ownership, a portion of each crop must be paid to him as a sort of sacred tax.[9]

By attributing ownership of essential property to God, therefore, Hebrew thought essentially undermines any property claims of individual owners that run counter to social need and it provides the conceptual basis for an insistence on economic interrelatedness and obligation. Although there are small differences in the way the individual right to property is qualified in Hebrew and later Catholic thinking—the Hebrew tradition tends to stress God's ownership while Christian thinking tends to stress God's primordial establishment of common human ownership[10]—the practical implications for economic life are the same in both cases: Human owners are regarded as holding their possessions in trust and subject to the conditions of righteous stewardship.

Another key idea follows. Within this context, assistance to the poor and the marginal is not requested or encouraged, but is required. Benevolence, as Ephraim Frisch has put it, "is viewed, not as a matter of grace, but as an imperative duty."[11] It follows that the poor have a religiously grounded "right" to sustenance and support. Furthermore, whenever serious economic misery occurs, it is regarded not as the fault of the poor themselves, but as the result of a failure of moral obligation by the more fortunate. Within the prophetic world view, the belief that the poor merit their fate, a view found in some Hindu and Buddhist as well as in some later Protestant thinking, has no place. On the contrary, within the Pentateuch and prophetic writings, destitution is almost always attributed to social and economic exploitation of the weak by the strong.

TALMUDIC ELABORATIONS

With the enduring shift in Jewish communal life from Israel to the communities of the diaspora following the Roman War in the year 70 a need developed to expand the Pentateuch's structure of legal regulation to cover the new circumstances of life in exile. This stimulated a process of biblical commentary and legal expansion already begun during the intertestamental "Mishnaic" period. The result was the body of legal interpretation and quasilegislation represented by the Talmud. Completed by roughly the middle of the first millennium in its extensive Babylonian version, this multivolume work itself became subject to interpretation and to a more systematic codification at the hands of such medieval commentators as Rashi, Moses Maimonides, Jacob ben Asher and Joseph Caro. By means of this vast corpus of material, the biblically established norms of social justice were systematically elaborated and implemented in the daily life of Jewish communities.[12]

On the institutional level, a considerable task faced the rabbinic sages. They had to take a body of social welfare legislation developed in what was essentially an agricultural setting and adapt it to the increasingly urban and commercial life of medieval Jewry. Had obligations to the poor been taken lightly, this transition might have permitted Jews to abandon the older requirements merely by allowing them to become irrelevant and obsolete. Instead, this older agricultural law was thoroughly adapted and reinterpreted to suit the new situation, and commandments were sometimes made even more demanding.

The practical rules elaborated in the Talmud pertaining to responsibility to the poor came under two headings: *Zedakah* and *Gemilut Hasadim*. The root meaning of *Zedakah* is "right" or "justice," and although it is sometimes translated as charity, it refers to the religiously mandated giving and support of the poor established within each autonomous Jewish community. *Gemilut Hasadim*, sometimes translated as "loving kindness," is more properly thought of as "charity" in our common, contemporary sense of the term, since it refers to those forms of voluntary almsgiving and personal service—for example, the provision of dowries for poor maidens or visitation of the sick— that go beyond the letter of legal requirement.

In the Talmud and rabbinic rulings, *Zedakah* was given complex legal embodiment. The traditional obligations of landowners were not forgotten, but were supplemented by a series of institutions and practices more suited to urban or village life in the diaspora. In the words of Isadore Twersky, each Talmudicly governed community "appears as a modified welfare city–state, with its special functionaries who collect the compulsory levy and act as trustees for the poor and the needy."[13] Each city, town or village, for example, was required to set up two basic funds for relief of the poor. One, the Tamchui or "plate," was designated for emergency relief and was available to transients and local poor with less than two days food at their disposal. The second, the Kuppah or "chest," was designated for the ongoing support of the community's indigent.[14] The near-universality of these institutions is suggested by Maimonides' comment that he had "never seen or heard of an Israelite community that does not have an alms fund."[15]

The collection and distribution of these funds were governed by a series of carefully detailed regulations. For example, this work was the responsibility of special administrators of charity *(Gabba'ei Zedakah)*, individuals of outstanding integrity who served without remuneration.[16] The amount owed by each household was carefully stipulated—usually as the *Ma'aser* or tenth of annual income[17]—and none but orphans or nonresidents were exempt from contributing. Criteria were established that, even by modern standards, are relatively generous for determining who could receive assistance and how much they might receive. For example, a family did not have to relinquish its home or utensils to be eligible for aid.[18] Individuals who were accustomed to a higher standard of living might be given more from the fund.[19] Begging was strongly discouraged—in the effort to direct all support of the needy through the well-regulated public agency[20]—requests for aid from the plate or fund were almost always respected and not subject to rigorous scrutiny. In all cases, the governing rule was, "We must show charity even to the deceivers."[21]

Behind this extensive structure of social welfare legislation were a series of fundamental ethical conceptions that reached back to the bible. Foremost among these is the idea that material resources are not the exclusive possession of any human owner, but are goods bestowed by God and held in trust for him.[22] One consequence of this belief was the conviction that those needy persons who call on the community's assistance do so not as an appeal to others' charity, but as a right. This understanding is demonstrably exhibited by a famed Talmudic story concerning a poor man who had visited Raba. The sage asked the poor man what he usually had for dinner and the poor man replied, "Fatted chicken and old wine." "But," said Raba, "do you not feel worried that you are a burden to the community?" To which the man replied, "Do I eat what is theirs? I eat what is God's." The story concludes as Raba's sister arrives bearing a gift of fatted chicken and old wine for her brother, which the sage then offers to the poor man with apologies for his questions.[23]

A further consequence of the idea that material goods are God's possession was the view that *Zedakah* does not represent a favor that might be withheld but, as Frisch puts it, "an imperative obligation springing from elementary considerations of justice."[24] If, from the standpoint of the poor, assistance is a right, from the standpoint of the giver, it is a religious and legal duty. In the words of Maimonides, "Gifts to the poor are not benevolence, but debts."[25] It follows that all people (except orphans) are required to give charity. Even the poor who themselves are supported by charity are required to give a portion of what they receive.[26] The fact that we are here in a realm, not merely of voluntary and private benevolence, but of socially mandated giving, is evidenced by the fact that any who refuse to pay their legally stipulated minimum contribution to the community fund or give less than what is proper should be compelled by the court (Bet Din) to give what the court designates, and the authorities may seize their goods for this purpose.[27]

Once again, notice how similar these Jewish conceptions are to traditional

Catholic teaching. As in the Catholic view, obligations to the poor belong to the domain of justice and right. Precisely because all owners of property hold their possessions as conditional grants from God, private possession has no ultimate sanctity; property rights may be overridden to meet the needs of the less fortunate of God's creatures, who just as validly receive his graciousness as do the more-fortunate property owners themselves. As in Catholic thinking, the final responsibility for effecting these rights falls on society in its collective institutions. Although Jews rarely had full political authority, their communal religious institutions were for all intents their government, and *Zedakah* was institutionally organized and enforced.

Finally, as in Catholic thinking, these socially mandated obligations did not exhaust the moral and religious responsibilities of individuals to their less-fortunate brothers and sisters. *Gemilut Hasadim,* private giving and purely voluntary service to others, began where legal obligation ended and its expression might be unlimited. According to the Talmud, *Gemilut Hasadim* comprises a wider range of human kindness than does *Zedakah. Zedakah* can be given only with money, while *Gemilut Hasadim* may include personal service; *Zedakah* can be given only to the poor, while *Gemilut Hasadim* both to the poor and the rich; *Zedakah* only to the living, and *Gemilut Hasadim* to the living and the dead (through service during mourning or in the preparation of the deceased for burial).[28] In rabbinic thinking, *Gemilut Hasadim* was the subject of numerous treatises and lyrical expressions of praise, regarded as one of the loftiest expressions of human compassion.[29]

Although Jewish thinking did not articulate the formal Catholic principle of subsidiarity, there was, in other words, a strong conviction that impersonal social institutions must not be entirely allowed to replace forms of personal giving and neighborly concern that both express and stimulate compassion among human beings. Halakhah thus walked a fine line between the twin requirements of individual and collective responsibility. "Although the balance may be delicate and tense," Isadore Twersky observes, in the thinking of the rabbis, "corporate responsibility does not eclipse individual awareness and should not dull individual sensitiveness."[30]

Mention of private giving introduces another theme in Jewish thought that has corresponding importance in Catholic teaching: the theme of human dignity as the basis of all thinking about economic life. In the bishops' letter, this theme undergirds the emphasis on participation in economic systems and the importance of work in human activity. These emphases also have resonance in Jewish thinking, as will be discussed shortly. However, the emphasis on human dignity has another, more immediate, expression in Jewish thought. It produces an intense concern with the suffering and humiliation associated with poverty or dependency and it leads to sustained efforts to minimize the humiliation associated with the acceptance of charity or "relief." In this connection, certain forms of private giving come under critical scrutiny.

Two aspects of Jewish thought contribute to these concerns. One is the sense that poverty represents a great evil. "There is no lot which is harder than poverty," says one rabbinic commentary, and it adds, "If all troubles were assembled on one side, and poverty on the other, poverty would outweigh them all."[31] This is a somewhat typical example of rabbinic hyperbole, though it reflects the deep valuation of material well-being in a faith in which the disempowerment and low status associated with poverty are regarded as unmitigated evils, and that has no significant tradition of asceticism.[32]

A second aspect contributing to a concern for the psychological state of the poor is the almost exquisite attention Jewish thinking gives to the avoidance of inflicting shame or humiliation on another person. Recognizing that self-respect is an individual's most precious possession, the rabbis repeatedly affirmed that any conduct that publicly shames another person represents a very serious moral wrong. For example, the Talmud records R. Simeon ben Yochai as saying, "Better had a man thrown himself into a fiery furnace than publicly put his neighbor to shame."[33] In a related teaching, one who publicly humiliates another is likened to a murderer: If the second sheds blood, the first causes blood to rise to the face of a fellow human being.

This concern about protecting the poor from humiliation was reflected in the rabbis' discomfort with certain forms of direct, person-to-person charity. One commentary, for example, records the remark of R. Jannai to an individual whom he saw giving money to a poor man publicly: "It had been better that you had not given him, than now that you have given him publicly and put him to shame."[34] Commenting on Psalm 41.2, the rabbis remarked that the words are not "Happy is he who gives to the poor," but "Happy is he who considers the poor," that is, the person who takes into account the feelings and self-respect of the charity recipient.[35]

To prevent the possibility of humiliation, the rabbis insisted on the primacy of the kind of "impersonal altruism"[36] represented by the community fund. When private benefaction was unavoidable, they recommended secret giving as the model of charitable endeavor.[37] One Talmudic passage gives this idea whimsical expression by speculating on the forms of the letters Gimmel and Dalet. Since the two letters together can signify "Gemol Dallim," or "Show kindness to the poor," the question is: Why is the foot of the Dalet turned toward the Gimmel? The answer offered is that the Dalet (that is, the poor) should be on hand (they should not make it necessary for the benevolent to run after them). Why is the face of the Dalet turned away from the Gimmel? So that the help should be given to him secretly, sparing him blushes.[38]

To avoid further humiliation, the rabbis always emphasized the value of loans or offers of employment over outright gifts to the needy. Indeed, Moses Maimonides codified this teaching in his listing of the "eight degrees of charity" that appears as part of his treatise on the "Portions of the Poor" in his famous code of Jewish law, the Mishneh Torah. This listing expresses many concerns. For example, spontaneous and unsolicited giving is ranked higher than mere responses to requests for aid. Secret giving is commended over public display. Maimonides, though, reserves the highest degree for the kind of aid that not only spares the feelings of the recipient, but strengthens the individual's self-respect. This is the degree of "one who upholds the hand of an Israelite reduced to poverty by handing him a gift, or entering into a partnership with him, or finds work for him, in order to strengthen his hand, so that he would have no need to beg from other people."[39] Maimonides and other commentators become active, productive members of the community. Nevertheless, they still recommended this procedure of offering loans—and sometimes even requiring modest collateral to secure them—as a humane ruse to preserve the recipient's self-respect.[40]

As in Catholic teaching, these concerns also led Jewish commentators to insist repeatedly on the importance and value of work. Although the poor have a right to support, one should make every effort to avoid dependency. According to the Talmud, for example, a father had the responsibility to teach his son a trade, and one who failed in this duty was regarded as making his son a robber.[41] Work, however menial, is superior to dependency. "Flay carcasses in the marketplace and earn wages and do not say, 'I am a priest and a great man and it is beneath my dignity,'" admonishes one Talmudic text.[42]

In sum, with respect to human dignity and human need, traditional Judaism, like Catholicism, traces a course through a tensely related series of issues. Recognizing the evils created by dependency, it stresses the value of work and discourages, for giver and receiver alike, perpetuating a status of charity recipient. Nevertheless, it does not allow these admonitions against dependency to become a reason for disparaging the poor or the state of poverty itself, and it never allows these admonitions to undermine the welfare rights of those in need. Disesteeming poverty, it stresses both the right of every human being in circumstances of hardship to call on the community for assistance, and the corresponding duty of the community to make this aid available without prejudice or disdain. Unifying these seemingly disparate insistences is the theme of human dignity. Above all, the moral aim of an economic system is to sustain dignity by furnishing the work and participation for self-support and, where this is not possible, the means to sustain life without damage to the self-respect of the recipient.

A final theme in the bishops' letter with which classical Jewish thinking displays important affinities concerns the scope of the obligations of justice. The bishops strongly affirmed the global extent of justice. The individual's and the community's responsibility to alleviate misery and injustice does not stop at national frontiers, but extends, in principle, to human beings everywhere. In the words of the pastoral letter, traditional Catholic teaching emphasizes "the unity of the human family, the universally beneficial purpose of the goods of the earth, the need to pursue the international common good," and the imperative to pursue justice to eliminate the "shocking inequality" between rich and poor."[43]

In two respects, this breadth of responsibility would seem alien to classical Jewish thought: First, because under the constrained circumstances of life, there would seem to be few occasions to be concerned about the welfare of individuals beyond the boundaries of one's local community, and second, because whatever forms of assistance existed were religiously oriented and would naturally be directed first to one's coreligionists. This tendency would seem to be accentuated by what Max Weber has termed the "pariah" status of classical Judaism: As members of a persecuted and despised minority, Jews might be expected to place priority on their duties to coreligionists and minimize ethical responsibilities to members of the larger, and often persecuting, communities around them.[44]

Even though these and other factors play a role in limiting the scope of justice in classical Jewish thought and practice, powerful tendencies are also on the other side impelling Jews to a wider, and even universal, perspective.

One is the international nature of the Jewish community itself. From the earliest date, Jews recognized themselves as part of a community of persons whose membership transcended national borders. A common culture and, perhaps even more important, a common experience of persecution and suffering, bound the members of this community to one another. In times of pogrom, Jewish communities far removed from the events could be called on to lend financial assistance to their coreligionists or to receive refugees from the centers of persecution. During the medieval period, when piracy and the holding of hostages imperiled every Jewish traveler, the ransom of captives became a preoccupation of Jewish communities everywhere.[45] Indeed, the importance of this activity was expressed in the priorities established by the rabbis for handling cases of distress: The ransom of captives received the highest priority, followed in order by the alleviation of hunger, the provision of clothes, relief of extraphysical wants and the supplying of means for poor brides to marry.[46]

Finally, from the earliest date, Jews everywhere felt an obligation to assist the small and usually impoverished community of Jews who continued to live in Israel.[47] Although the general rule was that "The poor of your own town come before the poor of any other town,"[48] this was suspended for the poor of Israel, who took precedence over all other needy persons.[49] In the ongoing and institutionalized collections for these coreligionists, a basis was established for the unprecedented support diaspora Jewry has given to the modern state of Israel.

Charitable exertions, however, were not confined to coreligionists. On the local level, obligations extended beyond the confines of the religious community. The rule was "to give to everyone who stretched out his hand."[50] From the earliest date, and with a view to harmonious relations among neighbors, Gentiles were helped from the public benevolent fund. "In a city where there are both Jews and Gentiles," the Jerusalem Talmud says, "the collectors of alms collect both from Jews and Gentiles; they feed the poor of both, bury both, comfort the mourners whether Jews or Gentiles, and they restore the lost goods of both—for the sake of peace."[51]

This is not to say that in cases of conflict, Jews did not often favor their coreligionists above others. Not only was this partly permitted by tradition, which for such specific economic obligations as the prohibition of usury imposed stricter requirements for the treatment of the fellow Jew than for the non-Jew, but it was a natural response to the conditions of persecution Jews so often faced. Nevertheless, within the sphere of economic ethics, as elsewhere, classical Jewish thought possessed a strong sense that human beings are their brothers' and sisters' keepers, that neither geographic, cultural, or religious boundaries permit standing by while another human being faces alleviable distress.

CONCLUSION

The correspondences between classical Jewish and Roman Catholic thinking should not be surprising. Both traditions spring from a common biblical foundation, and both have sought to mold their societies, not just religiously, but socially and economically, recognizing that religious faith goes beyond private spirituality to touch all dimensions of life in community. Nevertheless, these correspondences are worth stressing.

In many of its key themes, especially in its emphasis on the preferential option for the poor and the human purpose of economic systems, the bishops' letter has come under attack from within and without the Catholic community. Some of these criticisms have related to technical matters and have disagreed with aspects of the bishops' proposals for implementing these moral values, but other criticisms, sometimes presented under a guise of technical disagreement, have called into question the bishops' basic moral priorities. Here, the history of Jewish thinking about economic life becomes relevant. What we have seen is that Jewish thinking profoundly agrees with the priorities articulated in the bishops' letter. Not economic efficiency, but concern with the dignity of individual human beings, especially the needy and disadvantaged, has always been to the fore in Jewish thinking. The paramount moral theme has not been the right to the ownership and use of one's own property, but one's responsibility for the just stewardship of that property.

Behind all this lay a spiritual perception shared by Catholic thinking that all good fortune, whether personal or material, proceeds from God's hands. Those who have been blessed in this way, whether by health, strength, ability, or wealth, have a corresponding duty to use their resources to aid those less fortunate, and they subvert this understanding when they turn their blessings into "merited" possessions they can use to the neglect or detriment of others. In this most basic theme of all, Jewish teaching lends its voice to the deep moral and spiritual message conveyed by the pastoral letter.

If Catholic teachers can take heart from the support afforded by the heritage of Jewish teaching, then Jews, too, can learn from the bishops' letter. As indicated at the outset, the American Jewish community understandably faces a period of moral and spiritual confusion. As the prophets recognized long ago, material prosperity and social status make it difficult to call to mind the plight of one's less-fortunate neighbors. This may be a reason the *Haggadah* or liturgy for the Passover ritual to this day asks Jews to distance themselves from their good fortune and to regard themselves, even momentarily, as though they were members of the generation just saved from slavery and oppression.[52] In this respect, the pastoral letter serves as a modern *Haggadah*. It reminds Jews of the deepest themes of their own tradition, and it presents to them the model of a daughter tradition whose leadership, at least, is willing to remember these themes at a time in the life of both religious communities when it may be less popular or convenient to do so.

CENTRAL ISSUES

Good Ends, Bad Means
Milton Friedman

The basic objectives that the bishops set forth in the draft of their pastoral letter are highly commendable. At the same time, the means they propose to attain those objectives would have precisely the opposite effect by making matters worse, not better. In addition, the collectivist moral strain that pervades the document is repellant.

This discussion of the draft letter will list the bishops' objectives, examine the means they propose and why it is that those means would be counterproductive, and finally, comment on the moral vision that pervades the document.

OBJECTIVES

The bishops specify four major objectives. The first is to reduce unemployment, particularly among the young, an objective that is wholly agreeable. It is a disgrace that unemployment among young black teenagers is over 40 percent. Popular discussion tends to lump all the unemployed together, to regard them as a single homogeneous class. That is a serious mistake. A student who is looking for a part-time job for supplemental income is counted as one unemployed person, while the unemployed father of a family in which he is the sole earner is also counted as one unemployed person. It is adding horses and apples simply to record two unemployed persons. In order to discuss the problem of unemployment intelligently, it is important to break down its components, and the component of most concern is unemployment among the young, particularly among the black young.

The second objective of the bishops is to foster greater opportunities for the poor. Again, that is an objective every person of goodwill accepts, but it should be broadened. We want greater opportunities for everybody. It is a mistake to regard the so-called poor as a special class. Not only are the poor at any time human beings like the rest of us, but the poor at one time are not the same as the poor at other times, and the very concept of who are "the poor" is a matter of perception, not of fact.[1] We want opportunity for everyone, though obviously the need is greater for some than for others.

The bishops' third objective, treated by them in the second draft as part of the second objective, is to reform the welfare system. Our present welfare system is a disgrace and a scandal. It can also be agreed "that the middle classes receive far more from the federal government than do the poor" (first draft), the bishops' complaint explicit in the first draft and implicit in the second. If we cumulate all government spending on programs that are labeled as directed at the poor and divide the total by the number of people who are said to be poor, the result is higher than the average income of all the people in the country. If that money were really going to the poor, there would be no poor. The label on the bottle is welfare for the poor; the content is welfare for us. We are fond of pointing our finger at "special interests"; we can find those special interests by looking in the mirror. That is especially clear for students at a state university. There is almost surely no government program in the United States that so clearly uses taxes collected from persons with relatively low incomes to help persons with relatively high incomes as our state system of higher education.

The bishops' fourth objective is to contribute to improvement in the conditions of the poor in the low-income countries of the world and, once again, that is an objective that all of us must share.

The bishops include in their second draft a major section on agriculture, but it is hard to find in it any major objective on a par with the four here listed. Its inclusion presumably was a response to the current U.S. farm crisis. The discussion reflects accurately the conflicting objectives of operators of small and large farms, consumers, taxpayers and politicians. However, it offers little else but bromides as "guidelines for action."

MEANS

Why, then, the sharp disagreement with the means the bishops propose to promote these objectives? The reason is because those means are warmed-over proposals that have been discredited by experience. All of them have been tried and all of them have proved to be counterproductive.

The key to the bishops' approach is reliance on government and distrust of voluntary arrangements. They put their faith in compulsion, not in voluntary cooperation among individuals. They see the answer to each and every problem in a greater role for government and particularly for central government. The entire document shows a lack of understanding of how free cooperation among individuals through a market can achieve coordination on a large scale. To illustrate this point in a simple way: Though the bishops' draft supposedly deals with economic problems, it pays no attention whatsoever to relative prices. Indeed, the term "relative price" does not appear to occur in the document.[2] To an economist, that is as shocking an omission in a discussion of economic problems as it would be to a theologian to find no mention of God or Christ in a discussion of theological problems.[3]

The document neglects the vast amount of empirical evidence that has accumulated over the years on the consequences of the policies the bishops propose. Consider each of their major recommendations.

With respect to the first, employment, "We recommend," they say, "that the nation make a major new commitment to achieve full employment. . . . Toleration of present unemployment rates . . . should be regarded as unacceptable today." Essentially, every country in Europe, beginning with Great Britain, adopted after World War II precisely such a commitment to full employment. All of them defined it initially in line with the bishops' recommendations (implicit in the second draft, explicit as "in the range of three percent or four percent" in the first), yet suppose you compare unemployment in the United States and in Europe. At the depth of the recent recession, unemployment in the United States was 10.7 percent. It is currently (September 1985) 7.1 percent. Both levels are much too high. Yet, in Great Britain, which pioneered adopting the precise policy that the bishops recommend, unemployment is 13.1 percent; in France, 9.9 percent; in Italy, 12.6 percent; in the Netherlands, 15.4 percent; in Belgium, 13.7 percent; in West Germany, 9.2 percent (August or September 1985).[4] If the way to lower unemployment is for government to adopt a policy of full employment and set a goal of three or four percent, how is it that most countries to have done so have failed to achieve their objective? On the contrary, their attempts in the 1960s and 1970s led to the "stagflation" of the 1970s marked by rising inflation and rising unemployment, rather than by the lower unemployment that was their objective.[5]

Compare the experience of the European countries with the United States over the past 15 years. U.S. employment has gone up more than 25 million persons. In the Common Market countries, employment is lower today than it was 15 years ago. That is equally true for the past two years. Or, suppose we look not at unemployment, but at employment, not at how empty the glass is, but how full. The fraction of the American people who are employed today is the highest it has ever been in history. Experience clearly provides no support for the idea that a government declaration of a policy of full employment is an effective device for eliminating unemployment.

The second major objective of the bishops, to foster greater economic opportunities for the poor, again involve direct government intervention according to their proposals. All of them have been tried in one country or another: fiscal and monetary policies; job training; apprenticeship and job creation programs; central economic planning; trying to organize the economy. History speaks with one voice on this issue: The most effective engine for improving the lot of the poor, the one method that has enabled low-income people to rise on the scale to become middle-income people, has been a free capitalist system and a free market.

Consider our own history. Most of the people reading this chapter are descendants of people who came to this country with two hands and very little else. They came to the United States poor, they had an opportunity to improve their lot, and the nineteenth and early twentieth centuries, were periods of enormous progress in which millions of people were able to provide a better life for themselves and their children without any government programs. On the contrary, if today's government programs had existed, it would have been impossible for many of our forebears to have emigrated to the United States. We are the products of what people seeking to improve their lot can achieve themselves through voluntary cooperation in a free market. It is not an accident that no country in the world has so large a fraction of its population in the middle and upper classes as the United States.

We need not go back to the nineteenth century, however. Look at the situation today. Compare East Germany with West Germany. Here are two countries with people of the same background, the same culture, the same tradition. Which country had to build a wall to keep its people from trying to get out? In which country are the ordinary people, the poor people, better off? Or again, it is not Red China that has to police its border with Hong Kong to keep out people from Hong Kong who are trying to get in—it is Hong Kong that has to police its border to keep out people from Red China. In the whole Far Eastern crescent, from Japan through Taiwan through Hong Kong to Singapore, the condition of the poor has improved tremendously. Why? Because those countries have relied primarily on free markets and capitalism and not on central economic planning. In the main, those governments have been willing to let markets work.

The bishops quite rightly deplore the residual extent of poverty in the United States. However, it is worth noting that the level of income that the U.S. government regards as marking the difference between the poor and the rest of us is well above the average income of the rest of the people of the world, including the residents of such affluent areas as Europe and Japan. The official poverty level of income is a multiple of the average income of the people in the low-income countries of the world; it would be affluence in those countries. Of course, poverty is a relative matter. It is right and proper that a such prosperous people as we should regard as poverty levels of living that would be considered affluence in many parts of the world, and should be seeking to reduce the number of persons living at these levels. One ought, however, to have a sense of proportion and to compare what is true here with what is true elsewhere.

Moreover, what is the source of the residual poverty in the United States? The implicit assumption in the bishops' letter is that the residual poverty reflects a failure of the market system and can only be cured by government intervention. The situation is precisely the reverse. Government policies are the major source of the residual poverty in the United States. Why, for example, is the unemployment rate among black youngsters 40 percent? In the first place, because the schooling available for them has been so defective. Who has provided that bad schooling? Not the Catholic church. Where the Catholic church has operated schools, they have attracted the children of the disadvantaged in the slums. The poor schooling has been provided by governments that have been unwilling to adopt voucher plans that would enable parents to exercise greater control over the kind of schooling their children get.

Consider some of the other governmental policies that have been responsible for the residual poverty. We first handicap black teenagers by making it nearly impossible for them to get decent schooling. This then becomes a double whammy when we impose a minimum-wage law that makes it difficult if not impossible for them to get entry-level jobs that would provide on-the-job training as something of a substitute for the schooling they lack. Numerous studies have demonstrated that rises in minimum-wage rates have been a major source of the increase in teenage unemployment by reducing the number of jobs available to teenagers. Before the minimum wage was raised to anything like its present level, unemployment rates of teenagers were about double that of the population as a whole, which is understandable because they are just entering the labor market. More significant yet, the unemployment rates of black and white teenagers were almost exactly the same. In the late 1940s and the early 1950s, the rate was about 10 percent for each. As the minimum wage took effect and was raised higher and higher relative to the average wage, unemployment went up for both whites and blacks. It went up much more sharply, however, for blacks than whites, so that today, the teenage unemployment rate among black youths is over twice as high as the teenage unemployment rate among white youths. The people who are most hurt by the minimum wage are precisely the people the bishops would most like to help.[6]

Urban renewal and public housing deserve much of the blame for the slums that disgrace some areas of our major cities.[7] A visit to the Watts area of Los Angeles some years ago, not long after the infamous Watts riots, illustrates this point. A number of members of the UCLA faculty were being shown around by a very able black man who was in charge of a voluntary program to help the young people in the community. In view of his office was what looked like a rather nice building across the road. When the man was asked, "There's a pretty good building. What's wrong with that?" he replied, "That's the worst thing that ever happened to Watts. That's public housing. How do you suppose we are going to provide our children with good role models if we take all the poor people, all the families deserted by fathers, just mothers and children, and put them all together in one building where almost all the residents are entirely on relief?"

Government support of trade unions has reduced the opportunities available to the disadvantaged. The Davis-Bacon Act is a government program to make sure that building unions are able to enforce wages that are very high, wages that blacks and others would be delighted to have an opportunity to earn. It is not often realized that in the late nineteenth century, blacks constituted the majority of carpenters, painters and other craftsmen, whereas now they are scarce. Why? Because trade unions have kept them out in the self-interest of the people who are members.

There are demonstrations on campuses and elsewhere about apartheid in South Africa. The demonstrators should read a splendid book about the sources of apartheid in South Africa by W. H. Hutt on *The Economics of the Colour Bar.*[8] He attributes the origin of many of the apartheid policies there to white trade unions insisting on equal pay for equal work. Things are not always as simple as they seem, and in particular, intentions are one thing, but results can be very different.

In a recent remarkable book, *Losing Ground,*[9] Charles Murray points out that before the Great Society programs started in the 1960s, the rate of poverty in the United States had been declining sharply and other indicators of the condition of lower-income groups had been showing rapid improvement. Surprisingly, it may seem, as the Great Society programs took over, as the amount of money spent on them multiplied, the rate of poverty stopped declining and started to rise, and the various indicators of the condition of the lower-income groups—broken families, families headed by single persons, the rate of crime, and so on—started to deteriorate.[10]

The third major recommendation of the bishops is a major reform of the welfare system. The bishops mention in their second draft an alternative to the welfare system—a negative income tax—as one "that deserves continued discussion." A negative income tax would achieve all of the bishops' objectives. The particular proposals they make may not do so, although in this area, the bishops concentrate much more on outlining the difficulties than on providing specific alternative policies.

The bishops' final objective is to contribute to improving the conditions of the poor in low-income countries. Here, they praise foreign aid, particularly in multilateral form, and denigrate foreign investment. They believe that foreign investment can harm rather than benefit, "can sustain, or even worsen, inequities in a developing country." They believe that the way to help poor nations is to transfer funds through foreign aid. The facts appear to indicate precisely the reverse. The countries that have received the largest amount of foreign aid have had the least success in improving the lot of their people. Simply look at such countries as Tanzania in Africa that have received massive amounts of foreign aid yet the state of the people has become steadily worse. Why? It is not an accident. The reason is very simple: Foreign aid given to governments strengthens governments. Yet, the problem in almost every underdeveloped country is the tyrannical governments that are running them in the interest of the governing class and not of the people. Experience in countries around the world has borne this out, and this has been documented in a number of excellent books by Peter Bauer and Melvyn Krauss.[11]

The most effective device for promoting development in underdeveloped countries is to open their markets to foreign investment and to encourage free markets at home. Countries already cited as doing well—Singapore, Hong Kong, Taiwan, Korea—have been relatively open to foreign investment; all of them have relied extensively on private markets rather than on central planning. The countries that have done badly with respect to economic development—India, Tanzania and other African nations, some in South America—each and every one of them has relied on central planning and collectivist controls.

Given the bishops' proposals, the challenge would be to find one government social-welfare program that has achieved the objectives of the well-intentioned people who supported it. Otherwise, the generalization to which experience leads us is that the most effective way to achieve the objectives of the bishops is to take each of their policy recommendations and reverse it. There is a famous phrase of Adam Smith's about how people who intend to pursue only their own good are led by an invisible hand to promote the public good. Perhaps the right title here is "The Invisible Foot of Government."

MORAL VISION

Finally, there is what can be regarded as the most serious problem with the bishops' letter—a collectivist moral vision that pervaded the first draft and intrudes excessively in the much-improved second draft. This does not refer to the objectives, which are to be commended, but to a moral vision. The bishops write, "A country ... has a moral obligation"; "Society has a duty"; "Government has a moral function"; "What does the economy do *for* people? What does it do *to* people?"

There is another moral view that suggests something wholly different: that "a country" or a "society" is a collection of individuals; that the basic entity is the individual or, more fundamentally, the family, and that only individuals can have moral obligations. According to this view, a building cannot have a moral obligation; a "country" cannot have a moral obligation, and a "society" cannot have a duty. The people who constitute the country or society have moral obligations and duties, and government is a means whereby individuals cooperate with one another to achieve common ends. Those who hold this view do not want to see the country or society or government viewed as an organismic entity with moral obligations in and of itself.

People are responsible in their individual capacities and through those organizations that they individually form. An obligation imposed on oneself cannot be discharged by imposing it on someone else. One cannot be compassionate by spending somebody else's money (Congressionally speaking). People are compassionate when they spend their own money, when they put themselves out for someone else's benefit. The economy cannot do anything for or to people; it is a means whereby people do things for themselves or to or for one another. Only people can do things to people; only people can do things for people.

Moreover, the bishops' draft shows something of a split personality with respect to its moral vision. How can the collectivist statements just quoted be reconciled with such other laudable statements in the letter as "The dignity of the human person, realized in community with others, is the criterion against which all aspects of economic life must be measured"? Or, "The church's teaching opposes collectivist and statist economic approaches"; "The primary norm for determining the scope and limits of governmental intervention is the 'principle of subsidiarity.' ... This principle states that government should undertake only those initiatives necessary for protecting basic justice which exceed the capacity of individuals or private groups acting independently"; that is, functions should be performed at the lowest possible level in the social hierarchy. Yet, almost every specific proposal in this document is directed to the federal government.

A final point illustrates the problem of moral vision in another way, in terms of the notion of economic rights. The second draft refers to "the rights to employment, to healthful working conditions, to wages and other benefits sufficient to provide individuals and their families with a standard of living in keeping with human dignity, and to the possibility of property ownership" as "economic rights" that "should be granted a status ... analogous to that held by the civil and political rights to freedom of religion, speech and assembly." However, except for "the possibility of property ownership," these so-called "economic rights" are not at all "analogous" to the civil and political rights listed.

A specific example may clarify the difference. Father Byron, commenting on the bishops' letter, referred to economic rights as including, for example, an economic right to adequate nutrition. It is, of course, desirable that people get adequate nutrition, but a *right* to adequate nutrition is not a right of the same character or of the same kind as the right to free speech. Free speech is something that everyone can enjoy simultaneously. The only obligation it imposes on other people is not to interfere with it. Freedom of religion is similar. All are free to exercise their own religion. The right to free speech, freedom of religion, freedom of assembly—those are all rights everyone can enjoy simultaneously.

The situation is very different with a right to adequate nutrition. Everyone cannot simultaneously have the right to adequate food unless there is some cornucopia from which the food comes. If person A has the right to have food, then person B somewhere else must have an obligation to grow the food and provide it—the relation is one of master and slave, not mutual freedom. It is a desirable objective for people to have adequate nutrition, but to label it a right and to call it an economic right on the same basis as the right to free speech or religion obfuscates the issue.

There are true economic rights; for example, the "possibility of property ownership" listed by the bishops, which everyone can enjoy simultaneously. Or, to take a different example, it is an economic right on a par with freedom of speech for individuals to be free to make whatever voluntary transactions they wish as long as they do not interfere with third parties. As an aside, this right of "voluntary transactions" is violated by a great many laws now on the books. For example, tariffs violate that freedom—they are an interference with our human rights. Similarly, the minimum-wage rate is another inter-ference.[12] The designation of a "right" to food, housing, adequate nutrition and the like to be on a par with the rights of free speech, religion and assembly reflects a collectivist moral vision, a vision that is wholly inconsistent with designating "the dignity of the human person, realized in community with others" as "the criterion against which all aspects of economic life must be measured."

Poverty

MEASUREMENT, TRENDS AND CAUSES

William B. Neenan, S.J.

In Charles Dickens' *David Copperfield*, Mr. Micawber offers a simple economic equation. Although intended to demonstrate the importance of balancing a budget, it can be applied to distinguish between economic sufficiency and penury: "Annual income 20 pounds, annual expenditure 20 pounds ought and six, result: misery." For some purposes of economic analysis and policy discussion, this application of Micawber's viewpoint—defining a somewhat arbitrary quantitative benchmark that divides the "nonpoor" from the "poor"— has considerable usefulness.

The American bishops' perspective in their pastoral letter is somewhat broader than that of Micawber and broader also than the approach that will be followed in this chapter.[1] The bishops call for a "new cultural consensus that all persons really do have rights in the economic sphere and that society has a moral obligation to take the necessary steps to insure that no one among us is hungry, homeless, unemployed, or otherwise denied what is necessary to live with dignity." The bishops point out that inadequate income and uncertain employment are associated with substandard housing and poor nutrition, which in turn, generate feelings of powerlessness and dependency, which undercut both individuals' sense of dignity and the common good of society.

In their capacity as religious and ethical teachers, the bishops adopt this broader perspective relating income, poverty and the loss of human dignity in contrast to economists who, by profession, typically view poverty only in its narrower economic dimension. Thus, the bishops view the economy as "men and women working together, developing the gifts of God's creation and building a world fitter for human living. All this work must serve the material and spiritual well-being of people. It influences what people hope and believe about their destiny. It affects the way they live together. It touches their very faith in God."

Even though the primary focus of this chapter is poverty conceived in the relatively narrow terms of income poverty, there will be some allusions to the broader approach taken in the pastoral letter. There are four sections: definition and measurement of income poverty; historical poverty trends in the United States; identification of general causes of poverty; and some observations on the question of the bishops' "preferential option for the poor" in the light of the previous discussion of income poverty. The perspective employed in this chapter, though indeed inadequate for a total understanding of the multiple spiritual and material privations that beset human beings, is useful for policy considerations because it allows a somewhat objective measure of poverty. Income data are available to provide a continuous series for making intertemporal comparisons of poverty, and many personal and social privations do result directly from income poverty.

DEFINITION AND MEASUREMENT OF INCOME

In the 1960s, the federal government officially adopted a measure of poverty defined in terms of annual household monetary income. Poverty rates thus defined have been calculated for every year since 1959. The income concept used in estimating these official poverty statistics includes wages, salaries, net income from self-employment, property income, cash transfers from Social Security and other government programs and other such forms of regular cash income as private pensions and alimony. Some economists call this concept *posttransfer income.*

Other income concepts can be used to illuminate various aspects of the problem of poverty. For example, *pretransfer income,* which distinguishes market income from government transfers, allows us to measure the income received from market sources alone. *Prewelfare income* includes market income plus such social insurance transfers as Social Security and unemployment insurance, but excludes income received from public assistance programs. Since social insurance benefits are perceived by many in society as "earned," some might consider the "real" poverty population as those who are poor only in terms of prewelfare income. Finally, a fourth concept, *adjusted income,* includes posttransfer income plus the value of in-kind benefits from food stamps, Medicare and Medicaid, less federal income and Social Security taxes and corrected for underreporting of income. Although each of these concepts has some relevance for policy discussions, the analysis here will be based on posttransfer income, the concept used to calculate the official poverty rates of the federal government.

With a definition of income established, there must then be chosen a threshold income, or poverty line, that divides the population into the "poor" and "nonpoor." An initial choice must be made between a threshold that establishes categories of those who are "relatively" poor and "absolutely" poor. "Who are the wretched of the earth?" Michael Harrington asks. They are the more than 2 billion human beings—54 percent of mankind—who live in countries where the per capita gross national product in 1973 was under $200.[2] In comparison with this degree of privation, few Americans are poor.

Many Americans, however, who are well off by historical or international comparisons, are certainly deprived relative to their fellow affluent citizens. Thus, two contrary judgments emerge even from a relative perspective, depending on whether the relative income criterion is global or domestic: first, that few Americans are "poor" when compared with people in the Third and Fourth Worlds, the vast majority of whom live barely at the subsistence level, and second, that Americans with incomes at the lower end of the U.S. distribution scale are deprived in the context of their own society.

The definition of poverty to be discussed in this chapter, however, is not based on a relative concept, as useful as that may be for many purposes. Here, we will focus on the absolute definition of poverty employed in the federal calculation of poverty statistics. The poverty dividing line for this purpose is equal to the annual cost of the Department of Agriculture's "economy diet" for a family, multiplied by three, under the assumption that food constitutes one third of the expenditures of a typical household. Therefore, three times the dollar value of the "economy diet" is the income benchmark separating the "poor" from the "nonpoor." The value of this dividing line is adjusted to allow for family size, the age and sex of the family head and the number of children under 18 years old. These absolute poverty lines are in turn adjusted annually for changes in the consumer price index. Hence, the official poverty lines provide absolute measures of poverty for families in different circumstances, quite independent of their relative position in society. "Poverty" on this basis would be eliminated if all families or unrelated individuals would receive an annual income greater than these absolute poverty thresholds. The poverty threshold for a family of four in 1984 was $10,609.

It must be emphasized that the poverty rates that emerge from the federal government's definitions and assumptions possess no intrinsic ethical value superior to other measurements of poverty based on other income definitions or poverty thresholds. Poverty statistics were developed "to direct our attention to the lower part of the income distribution . . ."[3] to help us see the people who live in Harrington's "other America." Significant debate continues, for example, whether and to what extent in-kind payments should be included in the measurement of income, whether minimum needs are adequately reflected by basing the poverty threshold on the value of the "economy diet" and whether a relative rather than an absolute index of poverty is the more valid measure of economic distress in the United States.

POVERTY TRENDS

Data summarizing the extent of poverty as defined by the official statistics are shown in Table 8.1 for the years 1959, 1973, 1979 and 1984. These years were chosen because 1959 is the first year for which such data are available, 1973 is the year in which the overall incidence of measured poverty has been lowest, 1979 is the last year before the beginning of the most recent severe recession, and 1984 is the year for which the most recent data are available.

TABLE 8.1
Persons below the poverty level and poverty rates by race, Spanish origin, family status and age for 1959, 1973, 1979 and 1984

CHARACTERISTICS:		POOR PERSONS (thousands)				POVERTY RATES (percentages)			
		1959	1973	1979	1984	1959	1973	1979	1984
All persons (all races)		39,490	22,973	26,072	33,700	22.4	11.1	11.7	14.4
Whites									
In Husband/Wife: Families		20,211	7,409	8,120	11,434	14.7	4.9	5.4	7.5
Children		8,966	3,001	3,279	4,709	17.4	6.0	7.3	11.0
In No Husband: Families		4,232	4,003	4,375	5,866	40.2	28.0	25.2	29.7
Children		2,420	2,461	2,629	3,377	64.6	42.1	38.6	45.9
Age 65 and Over		4,744	2,698	2,911	2,579	33.1	14.4	13.3	10.7
Unrelated Individuals		4,041	3,730	4,452	5,181	44.1	23.7	19.7	19.9
Blacks									
In Husband/Wife: Families		6,696	2,496	1,984	2,438	50.9	17.7	14.6	17.4
Children		3,547	1,188	858	1,085	60.6	21.7	18.7	24.3
In No Husband: Families		2,416	4,064	4,816	5,666	70.6	56.5	53.1	54.6
Children		1,475	2,635	2,887	3,234	81.6	67.2	63.1	66.2
Age 65 and Over		711	620	740	710	62.5	37.1	36.2	31.7
Unrelated Individuals		815	828	1,168	1,255	57.0	37.9	37.3	35.8
Spanish Origin *									
In Husband/Wife: Families		-	1.328	1,546	2,428	-	15.2	15.1	20.0
Children		-	758	837	1,223	-	18.8	19.2	27.5
In No Husband: Families		-	811	1,053	1,764	-	57.4	51.2	56.2
Children		-	606	668	1,093	-	68.7	62.2	71.0
Age 65 and Over		-	95	154	176	-	24.9	26.8	21.5
Unrelated Individuals		-	157	286	545	-	29.9	28.8	36.8

*Persons of Spanish origin may be of any race.
Sources: U.S. Bureau of Census, Current Population Reports, Series P-60, No. 149, *Money Income and Poverty Status of Families and Persons in the United States: 1984* (Advanced Data from the March 1985 *Current Population Survey*), U.S. Government Printing Office, Washington, D.C., 1985, Table 15.

From Table 8.1 can be identified a number of salient factors concerning the dynamics of poverty over the past quarter century. First, there has been a decline in the overall poverty rate from 22.4 percent of the nation's population in 1959 to a historic low of 11.1 percent in 1973 followed by a drift of the rate until 1979 and a displacement upward during the severe recession of the early 1980s. The principal factor determining these overall changes in the poverty rate has been the level of economic activity. When the economy is growing faster than the number of new entrants into the labor force, the poverty rate tends to fall. When growth is sluggish, income is depressed, unemployment rises and the poverty rate rises for those whose primary sources of monetary income are wages and salaries. This association among income levels, unemployment and poverty can be seen from an examination of Table 8.2, which reports poverty rates, median family income and unemployment rates during selected years since 1959.

The poverty rates for blacks and those of Spanish origin are several times higher than the rate for whites even though the majority of poor people are white. Thus, in 1984, 11.5 percent, or nearly 23 million, of the white population were poor according to the federal poverty criteria, whereas 33.8 percent, or 9.5 million, of the blacks and 28.4 percent, or 4.8 million, of those of Spanish origin were poor. The relationships among these groups have remained fairly constant over the past 25 years; however, blacks living in husband-wife households experienced a greater percentage reduction in the poverty rate between 1959 and 1984 than have whites in similar households (Table 8.1). This reduction, though, has been offset by the relatively larger

TABLE 8.2
Poverty and Unemployment Rates, Selected Years

YEAR	POVERTY RATE ALL PERSONS	MEDIAN FAMILY INCOME (in 1983 dollars)	UNEMPLOYMENT RATE CIVILIAN WORKERS
1984	14.4	25,391	7.5
1983	15.3	24,580	9.6
1982	15.0	24,187	9.7
1981	14.0	24,525	7.6
1980	13.0	25,418	7.1
1979	11.7	26,885	5.8
1978	11.4	26,939	6.1
1977	11.6	26,320	7.1
1076	11.8	26,179	7.7
1975	12.3	25,396	8.5
1974	11.2	26,066	5.6
1973	11.1	27,017	4.9
1972	11.9	26,473	5.6
1971	12.5	25,301	5.9
1970	12.6	25,317	4.9
1969	12.1	25,636	3.5
1966	14.7	23,123	3.8
1965	17.3	21,968	4.5
1960	22.2	18,907	5.5
1959	22.4	n.a.	5.5

Sources: U.S. Bureau of the Census, Current Population Reports, Series P-60, No. 149, *Money, Income and Poverty, Status of Families and Persons in the United States:* 1984 (Advanced Data from the March 1985 Current Population Survey), U.S. Government Printing Office, Washington, D.C., 1985, Table 15; and Council of Economic Advisors, *Annual Report* (Washington, D.C.: U.S. Government Printing Office, 1985), Tables B-27 and B-33.

percentage of blacks than whites living in no-husband families, for which the poverty rates for all groups have lagged behind the general reduction in poverty. In 1984, 52.9 percent of all persons living in no-husband families received annual income below the poverty threshold.

The increase in both the number of divorces and the number of children born to unwed parents in the past several decades has resulted not only in the "feminization of poverty," but what also might be called the "childrenization of poverty." Whereas the poverty rate for all people declined nearly 36 percent between 1959 and 1985, it declined only 22 percent for children, primarily because the number of children in no-husband families, especially black no-husband families, increased significantly during this period (Table 8.1). Evidence supports the judgment that in the U.S. society, contrary to previous experience, black and Hispanic children face lower prospects than their parents.

The only major group that has experienced a significant decline in the incidence of poverty since 1970 has been those 65 years of age and over. This reduction is attributable primarily to the increase in Social Security and Supplementary Security Income benefits that occurred between 1970 and 1974. Since that time, the indexing of these benefits has allowed recipients to improve their position slightly related to other groups, especially during recessions. In fact, in 1982, the poverty rate for those 65 years of age and over dropped below the rate for the rest of the population for the first time (Table 8.1). Hence, there is an example of income-transfer programs reducing the incidence of poverty within a targeted group. Effective as the Social Security program has been, there remains the important and controversial question of how it is to be financed in the 1990s and beyond.

Three factors are closely associated with poverty in the United States, and therefore, to be given primary attention in designing antipoverty policies: low labor productivity; nonparticipation in the labor market; distortions of the labor market due to discrimination and minimum-wage legislation. These problems are by no means independent of one another. Some people, for example, may have low skills, be subject to discrimination and drop out of the labor market because of discouragement over job prospects.

Inadequate schooling and training as well as poor health limit one's human capital and reduce one's productivity, resulting in a negative circular relationship among education, health and earnings. Inadequate education leads to low earnings, which in turn may be associated with the educational deprivation of one's children. People with minimal training find their way to low-paying jobs that typically have less on-the-job training than do higher-paying positions. Likewise, poor health leads to absenteeism and lower earnings, which in turn are associated with deficient nutrition and medical care.

The traditional American judgment that education is the key to economic betterment is often based on raw data that show income levels rising with education levels. It would be very misleading, however, simply to look at these data and conclude that poverty could be eliminated merely by extending the years of education for the poor. The additional income associated with increased education may be due to a number of factors, such as greater ability and motivation and a screening process that rewards factors independent of education itself. If, after all, the number of college graduates were to be doubled overnight, the return on a college education would certainly fall.

Perhaps of greater importance in overcoming poverty than simply increasing the average years of education is the quality of primary and secondary education currently available low-income families in large cities. Although national attention has recently been directed toward the quality of primary and secondary education, dropout rates continue to be high in urban schools and the quality of education uneven.

There are three groups whose attachment to the labor force is necessarily weak and who are likely to have below-average earnings: the elderly, single women who head families and teenagers. The labor force participation rate for those 65 and over has generally been declining for decades, in large measure because of the impact of Social Security and Supplemental Security Income transfers. In 1948, 27 percent of those 65 and older were in the labor force, but by 1984, this rate had fallen to 11.1 percent. As we have seen, however, the incidence of poverty among those 65 years and over is now lower than for those under 65, despite their lower participation in the labor force.

A similar reduction in poverty has not been enjoyed by female heads of households and by teenagers. As a consequence of family responsibilities and the often scant prospects for employment in other than low-paying occupations because of inadequate education, only 37 percent of female heads of households were employed full-time in 1984. In addition, whereas Social Security payments have contributed to a reduction in poverty among those 65 and over who have retired from the labor force, Aid to Families with Dependent Children (AFDC) payments to female heads of households outside the work force have declined in real value in recent years.

Since World War II, the teenage unemployment rate has consistently ranged from two to three times the national average. There was a dramatic rise in the rate of increase in the teenage population during the 1960s, which has been reversed in recent years as the baby-boom cohort moves into middle age. During this period, the labor market has been relatively successful in absorbing large numbers of white teenagers, and consequently, the white teenage unemployment rate has remained fairly constant. The black teenage unemployment rate, however, increased to 42.7 percent in 1984 from 19.4 percent in 1970. Furthermore, reported unemployment understates the actual problem facing black teenagers because labor force participation rates of black youths have fallen during this time while the rates for white youths have risen. This withdrawal of black teenagers from the market economy is primarily explained by discouragement at job prospects and constitutes one of the most intractable, long-run problems facing the nation.

Labor market discrimination against minorities, women and other groups continues to exist in the United States. Less definite is its magnitude and impact on the incidence of measured poverty. Discrimination leads to reduced earnings and diminished opportunities for professional advancement for those affected. Though these consequences are serious social problems, it is difficult to determine their impact on the annual measured incidence of poverty as indicated in the official statistics. Obviously, discrimination reduces the level of income received by the affected group.

There has been a long-standing controversy among economists and policymakers whether minimum-wage laws, by attempting to alter the relative wage structure, actually increase the welfare of low-wage workers. Do increased wages for those employed in jobs covered by such legislation offset the unemployment that results from maintaining above-market wage rates, so that it can be said the overall welfare of low-wage workers as a group is improved? Will there be a general upgrading of occupations as a consequence of the legislation, so that over time, low-wage jobs will be eliminated without a large increase in unemployment? Or will upgrading result in greater unemployment, as workers with low skill levels are simply not hired? Evidence suggests that as the legal minimum wage is raised, employers tend to hire adults in place of teenagers. Consequently, unemployment among teenagers is higher than it would be in the absence of minimum-wage legislation.

The dramatic rise in the number of families with a female head of household and one or more young children, the persistence of higher unemployment among black teenagers, the high dropout rate in urban public schools—these are signs that have led some to posit the creation of an American underclass. This underclass, according to this viewpoint, existing in a "culture of poverty" and supported by the welfare economy, is developing a distinct set of values and aspirations that isolate it from the central values of the nation. According to this hypothesis, the welfare dependency of one generation is transmitted to children, thus perpetuating a group in society with values in conflict with the traditional work ethic.

Despite anecdotal support for this "culture of poverty" hypothesis, there is compelling evidence that a large, dependent underclass is not emerging in the United States. An analysis of a nationally representative sample of American families for the years 1969–1978 indicates that even though the experience of poverty is widespread (one quarter of the U.S. population is estimated to have been poor in some year between 1969 and 1978), only 2.2 percent of the entire population were poor during eight or more of those ten years.[4] Thus, even if one were to find that all those experiencing persistent poverty conformed to the "culture of poverty" stereotypes, only a small portion of the poor would constitute an underclass.

In point of fact, those who are persistently poor do not fit the description of being welfare dependent and alienated from the values of society. One third of the persistent poor are elderly or live in a household with an elderly head; two fifths live in a household with a disabled head; two thirds live in the South; and only one fifth live in large cities.[5]

What policies offer the best hope for addressing the problem of poverty in the United States? The major causes seem to be labor-market related, such as job loss and low earnings, and such changes in family composition as death, divorce, or having children outside the traditional family. Programs to reduce poverty stemming from these factors should focus on maintaining high levels of employment, providing income support for those whose family situation has exposed them to poverty, and promoting the stability of the traditional family. The bishops' emphasis on such programs, therefore, quite appropriately addresses the principal causes of poverty. However, as experience has shown, it is difficult to design such programs so that their full effectiveness can be guaranteed.

Statistical discussions of poverty, though necessary for formulating effective policy, can also distract attention from the shattered lives and broken hopes of the millions of our fellow citizens who are poor. To the extent that this happens, a sense of urgency is deadened and resolve to act weakened. A principal strength of the bishops' contribution is that they speak movingly of the homeless sleeping in church basements and standing in soup lines; of farmers losing not only a living, but a way of life. In addition to understanding the causes and extent of poverty, the nation must be inspired by a common social purpose if the problem of poverty is to be addressed forcefully and successfully. What has been lacking for some time is precisely a national consensus that the widespread privation in our midst is a scandal that prods us to devise and implement an appropriate mix of market activity, private and corporate action and government initiative.

An excellent place to begin is where the bishops began: "The dignity of the human person realized in community with others is the criterion against which all aspects of economic life must be measured." It is also an inspiring place to end.

Unemployment and Macroeconomics

Carl Christ

The U.S. Catholic bishops have brought forth a thoughtful document that challenges all who think and act in the economic sphere. It is their pastoral letter on "Catholic Social Teaching and the U.S. Economy." The aims of the letter are admirable. They are consistent with the tenets of many of the great religions and ethical systems of the world. They include respecting the dignity of the human person and achieving economic justice, and they reach beyond the borders of our land, voicing a concern for all who live on this globe.

The letter avows two purposes: to guide Catholics, and to influence public policies of the United States. This chapter will deal with the second purpose, from the point of view of an economist, a citizen and a non-Catholic. It will deal mainly with the letter's treatment of two topics: unemployment and economic inequality. The bishops are deeply concerned about severe inequality, and this concern underlies much of their discussion of the economy in general and unemployment in particular.

The bishops state their fundamental moral criterion for the economy thus: It must be at the service of all people, but especially the poor. It must be judged in the light of what it does to and for the poor, and what it enables the poor to do for themselves. The bishops recognize that the United States is one of the most economically successful nations on earth, and that it has quickly grown to provide a very high standard of living for most of its people. They acknowledge that economic freedom, including the right of private property ownership, is an important ingredient in this success. Yet, they point to poverty and unemployment, not only in this country, but abroad, especially in the developing countries, and they urge action to remedy these ills.

The action urged by the letter is both private and public, but primarily public: All who have more than they need must come to the aid of the poor. Government, however, has a moral obligation to secure basic justice for all— that is, proper treatment of the powerless, and minimum standards for all social and economic life—and to protect human rights to life, food, clothing, shelter, rest and medical care, and to security in adversity and old age. This obligation is tempered by the principle of subsidiarity: Of the things necessary for basic justice, government should do only those that cannot be done by private agents acting independently. Thus, the letter advocates neither an un-fettered free market economy nor a socialist one. The view that laissez-faire leads to justice and equity is rejected. Collectivist and statist approaches are opposed in general, though socialization of the means of production is not ruled out under suitable (unspecified) conditions.

The pastoral letter may be compared with the lay letter entitled, "Toward the Future." One of the principal differences between the two is that the lay letter puts more emphasis on individual responsibility and less on govern-mental responsibility than does the pastoral letter.

Admirable though the aims of the pastoral letter are, they are sometimes (perhaps deliberately) stated in imprecise terms and hence give little quan-titative guidance. Here are some examples: Minimum standards are required for basic justice. Pay should be adequate. A floor of material well-being for all is called for by distributive justice. A basic level of access to goods and services must be made available to all. Wages should be sufficient to provide a standard of living in keeping with human dignity. Minimum necessities of nutrition, housing, education and health care should be provided. New jobs with decent working conditions are an urgent priority. Employment oppor-tunities at decent wages must be provided. Full employment is the foundation of a just economy. These goals are inspiring, but not specific enough for an observer to tell whether they have been met.

The bishops temper their goals with considerations of realism. They rec-ognize that moral principles interact with empirical data and competing de-mands for limited resources, and that the soundness of their practical rec-ommendations must depend on the accuracy of their facts and the validity of their assumptions. This is most welcome. Unfortunately, the letter's principal recommendation on unemployment falls short in this respect.

UNEMPLOYMENT

The bishops advocate the use of fiscal and monetary policies to pursue full employment as the number one goal. They do not define their concept of full employment in precise, quantitative terms. However, one can see that they think it is well below 6 percent of the labor force, and possibly as low as 3 or 4 percent, since they offer the following statements (all of which, except the last, are factual): At business cycle peaks during the first 25 years after World War II, the unemployment rate was down to the 3 and 4 percent range. It has been rising in recent years. Since 1979, it has not been below 7 percent. Unemployment rates of 6 to 7 percent are neither inevitable nor morally acceptable.

It can be said that the letter fails to respect empirical data and reality when it calls for the use of monetary and fiscal policy to pursue full employment as the number one goal. The best available evidence shows that monetary and fiscal policy in the United States cannot bring about a permanent reduction in the unemployment rate. Furthermore, if fiscal and monetary policy are used for this purpose, this alone will not only fail—so will another important goal, namely, price-level stability. The letter voices concern for price stability, but only as a goal secondary to full employment. Clearly, public opinion places a high value on price stability, and with good reason.

From 1970 to the present, there has been no year in which the annual unemployment rate has been lower than 4.9 percent. From 1980 to the present, the rate has never been below 7 percent. In the 55 years since 1929 (when reasonably reliable estimates of unemployment begin), there have been only three instances in which the rate fell to 4 percent or less. Each was associated with a war. The first was 1943–1948 (six years), the second was 1951–1953 (three years) and the third was 1966–1969 (four years). Other than those three instances, after 1929, there has not been any year whose unemployment rate was as low as 4 percent. More detail appears later.[2]

It is true that monetary and fiscal policies were highly expansionary during those three periods when unemployment was 4 percent or less. It is highly significant that in no case was the improvement in unemployment a permanent one. Each of these periods was followed by increased inflation as well as a relapse in unemployment. The experience since the early 1960s is especially instructive: Continued expansionary policy since then has given more inflation but not less unemployment. The Phillips curve, which was once thought by many to offer a stable tradeoff between unemployment and inflation, has turned out to offer no permanent gain in employment in return for increased inflation.[3]

The United States is not the only country to have found that a persistent expansionary fiscal and monetary policy produces a merely temporary improvement in unemployment, and is followed by a more permanent increase in the rate of inflation. Canada, Britain, France, Germany, Italy, Sweden, the Netherlands and Japan all had similar experiences in the period after World War II.

Not only did our unemployment rate fail to show a permanent improvement following our expansionary policies of the 1960s and early 1970s, the unemployment rate since 1975 has actually been higher than it was before the expansionary policies of the Vietnam War era. In Table 9.1 are the figures for the average civilian unemployment rate and the highest and lowest annual rates during several periods. Each of these periods has been chosen to end approximately at a business cycle peak when unemployment was low (except for 1929–1941 and 1942–1945).[5] The increase in the average unemployment rate through time since World War II is evident. It was unbroken except for the 1958–1960 cycle, and it accelerated after 1973. However, there is no marked trend in the size of the fluctuations in unemployment from trough to peak: For cycles since 1948, they have been between about one and three percentage points.

In order to speak sensibly about unemployment and how to deal with it, there must be some understanding of why it has risen as it has since World War II, and especially since the business cycle peak year of 1973. There appear to be several contributing causes, and not only because of the expansionary policies of the 1960s and early 1970s.

First, the proportion of women in the labor force (especially married

TABLE 9.1
Annual Unemployment Rates

Period	Average	Highest	Lowest	
1929–1941, 13 years	16.2%	24.9%	3.2%	(Great Depression)
1942–1945, 4 years	2.4	4.7	1.2	(World War II)
1946–1948, 3 years	3.9	3.9	3.8	
1949–1953, 5 years	4.1	5.9	2.9	(Korean War)
1954–1957, 4 years	4.6	5.5	4.1	
1958–1960, 3 years	5.9	6.8	5.5	
1961–1969, 9 years	4.7	6.7	3.5	(Vietnam buildup)
1970–1973, 4 years	5.3	5.9	4.9	
1974–1979, 6 years	6.8	8.5	5.6	
1980–1984, 5 years	8.3	9.7	7.1	

women) has increased substantially. The unemployment rate for women has typically been one to two percentage points higher than that for men (though the difference has declined in the 1980s). This difference appears to be due to at least two factors. First, women on average have a lower degree of training than men, and unemployment is inversely related to training. Second, married women leave and reenter the labor force more frequently than men do, presumably in part in connection with the bearing of children. The result is that the average unemployment rate for the whole economy, being a weighted average of the rates for men and women, rises when the relative weight of women in the labor force rises. It has been estimated that this factor may have added a bit less than one percentage point to the unemployment rate in the last decade.

Second, the proportion of young people in the labor force reached a peak in the 1970s as the children born in the baby boom after World War II came of working age. The unemployment rate among teenagers (age 16–19) is typically about ten percentage points higher than the average for the population as a whole, and that for age 20–24 is about five points higher than the average. As the baby boom cohort has matured and gained experience, it has seen a decline in its unemployment rate, just as other cohorts have done. This has now begun to exert a downward effect on the average unemployment rate, which can be expected to continue in the future, other things being equal.

Third, the drastic increase in the price of energy relative to other items since 1973 has meant that the optimal design of plant and equipment is now different from what it was before, when energy was cheap. That is, plant and equipment designed to use small amounts of energy is now highly desirable. Hence, some plant and equipment, the kind that uses energy in large amounts, has been rendered inefficient or obsolete. Correspondingly, workers whose skills are particularly adapted to such equipment are not as productive as before, at least not without some retraining, and hence, are likelier to be unemployed than before.

Fourth, as we have increased the benefits from unemployment compensation programs, we have reduced the urgency felt by the unemployed to look for new jobs, by giving them the means to look longer for a satisfying job instead of having to take the first one that comes along. Thus, we have brought about some increase in the unemployment rate. There is evidence from Britain that the dramatic rise in its unemployment rate from the 1950s to the 1970s is in part due to a substantial increase in the level of unemployment compensation offered. In the early postwar years, Britain offered each unemployed person roughly the same payment, an amount less than the normal income of an unskilled worker. The unemployment rate was then typically in the range of 1–2 percent. The system was changed to provide more generous benefits, roughly in proportion to the previous earnings of each unemployed person. Thus, a skilled high-income person who lost a job could receive a much higher payment than under the old system. Over the next few years, there was a substantial increase in British unemployment rates.[6-9]

Fifth, the coverage of the minimum-wage law has been increased over the years so that it now covers most of the labor force. The result has been to make it illegal to hire people who are ready, willing and able to work at or below the minimum wage. This has contributed to higher unemployment rates, especially among unskilled or young workers whose productivity does not warrant their being offered jobs at the minimum wage or above. Until 1968, the effect was growing because the minimum wage itself was increased faster than the average of all wages, so that the relative value of the minimum wage rose (for example, to over half the average of all manufacturing wages). Since then, the relative value of the minimum wage has fallen, and since 1981, there has been no further increase in it, so that its real purchasing power has now declined. Thus, since 1968, the effect of the level of the minimum wage has been declining while the effect of the breadth of its coverage has continued to grow somewhat. Many believe the minimum-wage law should be repealed, although perhaps it could be justified in the case of workers tied to a single labor market that has only one employer, who can therefore exploit the market power over them by paying a lower wage than would prevail in the presence of competition for labor. However, a uniform minimum wage is a very blunt instrument for such a purpose.

Sixth, beginning in 1972, in order to be eligible for food stamps and Aid to Families with Dependent Children (welfare), candidates were required to register with the U.S. Employment Service for work. Following this change, the published unemployment rates moved upward. It is quite likely that this increase is due at least in part to the new requirement. Why? Consider what happens when the unemployment survey-taker questions a person who has no job and who is receiving food stamps or welfare. The survey-taker asks, "Are you looking for work?" Being registered with the U.S. Employment Service for work, the person is virtually certain to say "Yes," whereas before the registration requirement was imposed, the answer in many cases might have been "No."[10]

Seventh, it is tempting to speculate that the decline of the quality of education in public schools may have contributed to the increase in the unemployment rate among young people, particularly black young people. This is, however, a subject that needs further research.

Clearly, when a willing worker is fired or laid off, that worker bears a personal cost. Has the personal cost of unemployment increased as the published rates of unemployment have risen, and if so, how much? One consideration, already mentioned, concerns the effect of unemployment compensation. Consider an unemployed person who is receiving unemployment compensation and who is offered a job that would have been accepted in the absence of unemployment compensation. When such a person chooses to decline an offer, preferring to continue to draw unemployment compensation and keep looking for a better job, the resulting additional days of unemployment do not represent an additional hardship; rather, they represent a choice made by the unemployed person in the expectation of an improved position in life. If we were to regard all unemployment as a hardship, even the type under discussion here, we might conclude that unemployment compensation programs are bad and should be abolished because they contribute to higher unemployment rates. Such a conclusion, however, would be quite unwarranted.

Competent and willing workers sometimes do lose their jobs for unforeseeable causes through no fault of their own. It is quite justified for the body politic to provide some degree of compensation to tide over these people while they seek new jobs, even though it does raise the unemployment rate. (Unemployment compensation for workers laid off in predictably seasonal jobs is another matter, and less justified. Those who enter these jobs know that seasonality is involved, and can be expected to accept them only if employers offer suitable terms.)

A related consideration concerns a different measure of employment, the so-called employment ratio. It is the fraction of the working-age population (age 16–64) who is employed, and it is equal to the product of (1 minus the unemployment rate) times the labor force participation rate, as follows:

Employment Ratio = (Number Employed)/(Working-age Population)
= [(Number Employed)/(Labor Force)]
× [(Labor Force)/(Working-age Population)]
= [1 minus the Unemployment Rate]
× [Labor Force Participation Rate]

This employment ratio has been rising rather steadily and is now almost at an all-time high. In Table 9.2 are figures for civilians for several business cycle peak years, beginning with 1948 (the first normal postwar peak year)[11]:

TABLE 9.2
The Unemployment Rate and the Employment Ratio

(a) Year	(b) Unemployment Rate	(c) = 1 − (b) 1 minus Unemployment Rate	(d) Labor Force Participation Rate	(e) = (c) × (d) Employment Ratio
1948	.038	.962	.588	.566
1953	.029	.971	.589	.572
1956	.041	.959	.600	.575
1969	.035	.965	.601	.580
1973	.049	.951	.608	.578
1979	.058	.942	.637	.600
1984	.075	.925	.644	.596

Thus, even though the unemployment rate has been rising since World War II, the employment ratio has been rising. If the success of the economy in providing jobs is measured by the fraction of the working-age population (rather than the fraction of the labor force) who is employed, then that success has been growing, not deteriorating. This is suggestive, but it is by no means conclusive. Note that a high employment ratio is no consolation to an unemployed person who happens to belong to a family that has no employed members. Further, those who believe that the unemployment problem is getting worse often point to the discouraged-worker effect: When unemployment is high, some people who would like to have a job do not look because they are so discouraged about the prospects of finding one. Undoubtedly, this happens, but it is hard to measure its frequency. Table 9.2 makes clear that however great it is, the discouraged-worker effect has not grown enough to offset other influences that have raised the employment ratio.

The bishops' letter discusses the costs of unemployment at some length, but says relatively little about the costs of inflation. As noted earlier, the effort by many nations to reduce unemployment by means of expansive monetary and fiscal policy in the 1960s and 1970s was a failure (after a brief, temporary success) and worse, it resulted in increased inflation. There are substantial costs associated with changes in the inflation rate. When inflation accelerates, it erodes the value of money, transferring real wealth away from those who have previously agreed to receive money in the future and to those who have agreed to pay it. The losers are those who have lent money, or have leased their property, or have joined pension plans, or have bought life insurance. When inflation slows down, real wealth is transferred in the opposite direction. The inflation rate rises and falls repeatedly when monetary policy alternates between expansion, to try to reduce unemployment, and tight money, to try to stop the inflation that resulted from the monetary expansion. Such variation in the inflation rate makes it very difficult to predict the consequences of long-term investments and contracts. This disrupts the ability of everyone to make the wisest and most productive decisions for the future, imposing a severe cost on the economy. This cost can be avoided without long-run damage to employment, by a steady monetary and fiscal policy that stabilizes the price level.

Suppose it is granted that monetary and fiscal policies designed to stabilize the price level cannot reduce the average unemployment rate. Can they reduce the size of the fluctuations in unemployment between business cycle peaks and troughs? In principle, yes. This requires expansionary policy to attenuate oncoming recessions, and contractionary policy to attenuate oncoming booms. In practice, time is required for policy changes to be enacted and to exert their effects. Hence, it is important to be able to predict the onset of a recession far enough in advance so that the effect of a deliberate expansionary policy change will be felt during the recession when it is needed, rather than later during the subsequent upswing when it would be destabilizing. A corresponding statement holds for contractionary policies. Thus far, our predictive ability has not been good enough to allow successful timing of discretionary countercyclical policy. Built in, automatic fiscal stabilizers, however, work much better in this regard. Tax revenues fall in recessions and rise in booms. Government expenditures for transfer payments do the opposite. This makes the federal budget deficit bigger in recessions and smaller in booms, which exerts an automatic stabilizing effect. If the budget were balanced every year, as advocated by some, this stabilizing effect would not be available.

It is useful to distinguish two types of policy that affect the unemployment rate. The first type attempts to reduce unemployment by expansionary fiscal and monetary policy. We have seen that this type cannot be recommended on a permanent basis because of its inflationary effects, though it may be used countercyclically to reduce the magnitude of business fluctuations.

Is there nothing more that can be done? Far from it. The second type of policy affects the average level of unemployment that is consistent with a constant rate of inflation (and thus, consistent with a zero rate of inflation, that is, price stability). Labor is far from homogeneous; therefore, employment equilibrium requires more than merely a matching of the total quantity of labor demanded against the total quantity supplied. It requires a matching of the amount of each kind of labor demanded in each market against the amount of that kind of labor supplied in that market. In this vein, the letter properly advocates the expansion of apprenticeship and job-training programs. It also urges the improvement of the quality of education, but gives insufficient emphasis to this point and to public health measures for maternal and child care. These are steps that can increase people's ability to be productive and thus increase their value to employers and their ability to provide for themselves. The letter also advocates other measures aimed at such especially intractable unemployment as public service jobs and public subsidies to private employment.

INEQUALITY

The question of equality versus inequality underlies much of the bishops' discussion. Their letter does not go to the extreme of calling for absolute equality in the distribution of income and wealth, nor does it endorse the view of Rawls that income inequality is justified only if the poorest person benefits by it.[12] Rather, the letter takes a less-stringent view. Some degree of inequality is not only acceptable, but may be considered desirable for economic and social reasons (presumably, though the letter does not say so, these reasons include the encouragement of the productive activity that the letter calls for). The freedom of entrepreneurship, business and finance should be protected; however, no one can own or control capital resources without regard for others. No one has the right to unlimited accumulation of wealth. There must be a "preferential option for the poor": The basic needs of the poor must precede the desires of the fortunate. There is a strong presumption against extreme inequality of income and wealth as long as there are poor, hungry and homeless people in our midst. The letter finds the disparities of income and wealth in the United States to be unacceptable.

The letter expresses concern not only about inequality within the United States, but about inequality in the world. It refers to a $13-trillion world economy in which the U.S. economy alone accounts for over a fourth. (This is approximately true: Gross national product in the United States in 1984 was about $3.7 trillion.) The letter deplores the disparities between poor nations and rich ones and urges that U.S. policy should reduce them. In this connection, consider some simple and rough calculations. The world population is about 4 billion, and the U.S. population is about 240 million. Hence, the average gross product per person is about $3,000 for the world as a whole, about $15,000 for the United States alone and about $2,000 for the rest of the world. If the world's output were to be redistributed among the world's population to bring the rest of the world's average income up to $3,000 and ours down to $3,000, it would require that the American standard of living be cut to about one fifth of its present level. Is it likely that Americans will unilaterally make resource transfers approaching this? Without a world government, there is no authority that can require redistribution among nations. The problem is centuries old and is likely to remain for a long time.

Consider what kinds of public policy are available to increase the degree of equality of income and wealth within a nation. An obvious one is progressive taxation, which the letter supports. A progressive income tax is one that takes a larger percentage of a high income than it does of a low income. A progressive wealth tax does the same with wealth. A proportional tax takes the same proportion from everyone, rich or poor (the tax rate is constant and is the same for everyone). For simplicity, consider income taxation; much of what is said about it applies to wealth taxation. Most modern economies have at least some form of progressive income taxation. It makes the distribution of income after taxes more nearly equal than it was before taxes. In principle, the tax rate for the lowest income groups can be negative, in which case the effect is to redistribute income from the higher income groups to the lower.

Could such a progressive tax system be used to create complete equality of income after taxes? There is general agreement that it could not. The reason is that a tax rate of 100 percent would be required on all income that exceeded the average, and a negative rate would be required on all income below the average. Thus, anyone capable of earning more than the average would have little incentive to do so, because 100 percent of the excess above the average would be taxed away. Also, anyone incapable of producing as much as the average would have little incentive to produce anything at all, because 100 percent of the deficiency below the average would be made up by the tax system. The result would be a reduction in taxable productive activity, except by purely altruistic persons or persons who enjoyed taxable activity for its own sake. Even the poor would be harmed. This amounts to killing the goose that lays the golden egg. No nation has adopted it, and no nation is likely to adopt it.

The more progressive a tax system is, the greater the risk it will discourage productive activity. However, no evidence is known that the U.S. tax system is reducing output so much as to harm even the poor.[13] Nevertheless, it is prudent to consider not only the tax system's redistributive effects, but also its incentive effects, especially in the higher brackets where they are likeliest to be significant.

The question of whether to have a progressive tax at all, and if so, how steep the progression in rates should be as one goes up the economic scale, is controversial. It is and should be settled in the political arena. One option is a modest degree of progression in both income and estate taxation, with a top rate of 50 percent or less. Why so modest? First, the incentive effects just discussed begin to be significant at high tax rates. A second reason is rooted in American experience of the past half century: If the rate structure is made highly progressive, then special interest groups will attempt to get special provisions (loopholes) written into the tax law, and many of them will succeed. For many years the U.S. income tax structure has been a monster of unfairness, riddled with loopholes. It has permited some millionaires to pay no income tax at all while taxing propertyless wage and salary earners at rates of 11 percent to 50 percent or more. At this writing, the prospects appear good for a major tax reform that would retain some progressivity, and would tax persons with equal incomes more nearly equally than before.[14]

A second way of influencing the distribution of income is through a system of transfer payments to poor people. In principle, it is similar to a progressive tax system except that it works on the expenditure side instead of the tax side. The letter advocates changes in the welfare program, with several goals in mind. One is to provide adequate support to the poor in a manner that respects their dignity. Another is to establish national eligibility requirements and a national minimum level of benefits. Another is to make welfare available to two-parent as well as one-parent families. Another is to encourage employment rather than penalize it. Another might well be to keep the cost low enough so that the electorate is willing to pay it. These goals are all laudable, but they are incompatible. Some choice among them must be made. Assistance based on income only, with no other eligibility conditions, is very expensive. Cost can be reduced by imposing stringent eligibility conditions, such as work requirements, but the enforcement procedures needed to verify conditions are regarded by many as disrespectful of personal dignity.

Transfer payment programs can be more or less efficient in achieving their stated goals. Some programs are designed to influence the allocation of expenditures by poor families toward items that are regarded as beneficial and away from items that are not. School lunch programs and food stamps are sometimes regarded by donors as preferable to outright such cash grants as welfare payments on the ground that they encourage spending for beneficial purpose, nutrition. However, it is relatively easy for a family to shift its expenditures around to use the nutrition subsidy for whatever it wishes, which may or may not be for nutrition. Public expenditures for education and public health are less subject to private reallocation, and are likely to result in improved productivity of individuals. Hence, they are likely to lead to a lasting rather than a temporary increase in equality.

Many federal aid programs benefit the fortunate more than the poor. The farm subsidy program is a conspicuous example. Much of the expenditure goes to the owners of large farms rather than to poor small farmers. The student loan program is another example. Many loans go to students from well-to-do families.

A third way of trying to reduce the inequality of the income distribution is by prohibiting activity that might increase inequality. Wisely, the letter does not advocate this. Economic activity has direct effects, and it also has indirect effects, some of which reach far and take long. The direct effects of the invention of the transistor include more reliable and cheaper phonographs, radios, televisions and computers, as well as higher incomes for producers. The indirect effects include lower incomes for the former manufacturers of radio tubes unless they could adapt to the new technology. It is very difficult to determine whether any poor people became worse off by the invention of the transistor. In general, the effects of new discoveries, changes in tastes, exhaustion of natural resources, government policies and anything that affects the economy, on the welfare of every particular group of people, are very hard to determine. Supposing that the invention of the transistor, which has been of such great benefit to so many, did somewhat reduce the economic welfare of some poor people. Should it then have been prohibited? Surely no one would say so.

With very few exceptions, today's poor in America have a higher material standard of living than did the poor of yesteryear. This suggests that the changes attendant on improved technology, capital equipment and skills have more often benefited the poor than harmed them. If this continues to be true, then there is no need to try to compensate every poor person who may be damaged by any single forward step of economic progress, for subsequent steps will more than make up for the damage.

The key to the controversy over inequality lies in the distinction between two kinds of inequality. Let us distinguish inequality of opportunity from inequality of income or wealth. Inequality of opportunity is unfair, whereas inequality of income or wealth need not be. This is because different people choose to act in different ways even when faced with equal opportunities. For example, a person who puts forth great effort or takes great risk in order to produce something is usually regarded in fairness as being entitled to greater rewards than another person faced with the same opportunities who does not. Therefore, inequality of income or wealth, to the extent that it arises from different behavior and not from inequality of opportunity, is not something that requires redress by public policy.

The definition of equality of opportunity is not easy to agree on. We may agree that it requires publicly financed education, up to a certain age, for all American children. (One can already see potential controversy over how to define an American child: Are the children of illegal immigrants included?) We may agree that it includes certain public health measures. We may agree that it excludes job and housing discrimination on the basis of race, sex, or religion. It is harder to reach agreement about what it means with respect to differences in native abilities to sing, play baseball, invent new technology, manage complex organizations, or do anything else that influences income and wealth. It is also hard to agree on the extent to which people who have accumulated wealth should be free to provide material advantages (opportunities!) to their children that are not available to the children of poorer parents. The consensus in these matters, judged by what modern societies do, appears to be a political compromise. Societies recognize a right of people to spend their income for the benefit of themselves and their children. However, there are progressive taxes on income and on inheritance, and there are publicly financed programs of transfer payments to the unfortunate, which limit the degree of inequality of income and wealth that results from all causes, including inequality of both effort and opportunity.

There is a major problem in using public programs to assist the economically unfortunate, involving both efficiency and fairness, and has been alluded to earlier. The problem is how to design a program that aids those who are unfortunate now, without at the same time interfering with the efficiency of the market mechanism and encouraging others to behave in a way that increases the chance they will become unfortunate in the future. The further a program goes in trying to raise the unfortunate to a higher economic level, the more severe the side effects on efficiency and fairness. A series of compromises forged in the political arena, giving some weight to the view that people are entitled to enjoy the fruit of their own efforts and some weight to the view that the unfortunate should be assisted may be the best solution we can find.

10

Policy Issues and Options For Agriculture and Rural America

Kenneth R. Farrell

The Catholic bishops' pastoral letter on the American economy raises a series of fundamental moral, ethical and economic issues about the current state and direction of American agriculture and rural communities. Both policies and performance are found wanting in several respects. Market-driven, low-food-price policies in concert with science-driven technologies are leading to a loss of a valued way of life and the decline of many rural communities. Economic concentration in ownership of natural resources and in agricultural production is limiting participation of people in agriculture and rural communities. Institutional pluralism and diversity are being eroded. "The continuation of current practices . . . constitutes a danger to future food production."

As guidelines for policy action, three elements are proposed. First, moderate-size farms operated by families full-time should be preserved and their economic viability protected. Second, the opportunity to engage in farming should be protected as a valuable form of work. Finally, effective stewardship of our natural resources should be a central consideration in any measures regarding U.S. agriculture.

Several prescriptions for policy action are offered: effect special measures to deal with the immediate credit and financial crisis; target commodity program benefits to producers who genuinely need assistance; reform tax policies to slow the growth of large farms and tax-sheltered investments in agriculture; redirect efforts of the land-grant colleges and universities toward improving the productivity of small- and medium-size farms; encourage farmers to adopt more conservation practices and distribute the costs of this conservation broadly; extend minimum wages and benefits and unemployment compensation to hired farm workers on the same basis as all other workers.

Little has changed in agriculture and rural communities since the first draft of the bishops' letter in October 1985. Domestic and foreign demand for U.S. farm products remains stagnant or in decline. Farm income continues to be weak; land prices continue to fall over a broad cross-section of agriculture; supplies of commodities remain large in the United States and abroad; close to a third of commercial farms are experiencing substantial-to-severe financial stress; rural businesses related to agriculture are feeling the pangs of the five-year recession in agriculture; the financial base of local governments continues to erode. Positive indicators are declining interest rates, low rates of inflation, declining value of the dollar and evidence of recovery of growth rates in some foreign economies. However, most analysts conclude that substantial recovery in farm prices and income are at least a year away.

After prolonged debate, new five-year agricultural legislation, the Food Security Act, was enacted late in 1985. Although the new legislation contains some significant innovations it is, by and large, a continuation of a succession of legislation dating to the New Deal. Very few policy analysts, policymakers, or farmers believe the new legislation is more than a palliative in dealing with the underlying economic problems and fundamental policy issues confronting American agriculture. None expect the new law to resolve, by itself, the immediate, pressing financial problems confronting commercial family farms. Some regard it as a costly irrelevancy to resolution of economic problems rooted largely outside the sector in macroeconomic policies and in the international economy. Even fewer regard the new law as a sustainable framework for longer-term agricultural policies. The bishops' concerns will scarcely be allayed by the new bill or by subsequent legislation focused more specifically on the financial problems of the sector.

The symptoms of malaise and policy failures related to agriculture and rural communities abound, and there is no paucity of short-term prescriptions: the Food Security Act contains an extensive array. If public policy is to be formulated to guide future development of agriculture and rural communities, careful diagnosis of the underlying causes of the malaise and past policy failures is required.

FORCES SHAPING THE POLICY ENVIRONMENT

Since the early 1930s, when government first began to play a major role in agriculture and rural America, policy has been evolutionary.[1] Each major bill has been built on the legislation that preceded it, modified to reflect changing circumstances. The basic goals and methods of government intervention have changed very little.

The patchwork of policies emerging from this process has become increasingly antiquated. Agriculture and rural communities have become so vastly different in structure and in their relationships to the domestic and world economies that some of the very premises of long-standing policies are at issue. The clash between current policies and the economic, social and political realities is leading inexorably to basic reappraisal and realignment of these policies. Seven underlying forces are especially significant.

The Changing Role of Agriculture. The first of these forces concerns farming's place in the rural setting and the total food system. Farm commodity price and income programs began in the mid 1930s, at a time when 44 percent of the nation's total population was classified as rural. Farm people alone made up 25 percent (and 56 percent of the rural population), and the nation still was very much rural and based on agriculture. Today, the rural population is a few million larger than in the 1930s, but it is only 26 percent of the total (Table 10.1). The farm population is only 9 percent of the rural population. Nearly 25 million fewer people live on farms today than in the 1930s.

Farming's importance in the rural economic base also has changed. As recently as 1950, farming accounted for at least 20 percent of the economic activity in 66 percent of the nation's more than 3,000 counties. Today, that is true only for one fifth of the counties, not necessarily because agriculture has declined, but because of much more rapid growth in nonagricultural economic activities.

In the 1930s and later, farm and rural people were relatively isolated, lacking access to many of the services that urban people enjoyed, such as education, transportation, health care and communications. Those differences essentially are gone today, in large part because of federal programs.

Changes have occurred on the farm itself. Once relatively self-contained, farms today are much more closely integrated into the national economy. They depend heavily on industrial inputs, are highly capital-intensive, larger and more specialized. Many of the functions once performed on the farm have been shifted backward to the input supply and service industries and forward to the food processing and distribution industry.

As the nature of the farming operation changed, it became more common to view it as one component of a total food system embracing all activities from provision of farm inputs through commodity production and on to final consumption. Defined in this manner, the food and agricultural system accounts for slightly over one fifth of the nation's gross national product (GNP)

TABLE 10.1
Total, Rural and Farm Populations of the United States (millions)

Year	Total	Rural	Farm	Farm as a Percentage of Total
1920	106.5	51.6	32.0	30.0%
1930	123.1	54.0	30.5	24.8
1940	132.5	57.5	30.5	23.0
1950	151.9	54.5	23.0	15.1
1960	180.0	54.1	15.6	8.7
1970	204.0	53.9	9.7	4.8
1980	227.2	59.5	6.1(a)	2.7
1982	231.5	60.0	5.6	2.4

(a)Reflects the change in farm definition adopted in 1974.
Source: Economic Development Division, Economic Research Service, U.S. Department of Agriculture.

and 21.5 percent of total labor force employment. The system, thus, is responsible for about one fifth of overall economic activity. Farming accounted for about 11 percent of the food and agricultural system's contribution to GNP and about 12.5 percent of the employment.

An important policy implication of these changes is that the case for special treatment of agriculture and rural communities has diminished significantly in the past 50 years. Furthermore, agriculture can no longer be equated to rural America, nor can agricultural policies be equated with rural community policies in many parts of the country.

Structural Change. A second category concerns the structural evolution of the farm sector itself. Today, there are 2.4 million farms, which are very difficult to characterize broadly because of their high diversity. One of the most striking features is the concentration of production among them. Only 28 percent of the farms—those selling more than $40,000 of agricultural products annually—account for 86.8 percent of all agricultural output. The largest 1 percent of the farms (about 25,000) sells at least $500,000 of products annually and account for 29 percent of all agricultural product sales. The largest 4 percent claim almost 50 percent of the sales. The remaining 72 percent of all the places counted as farms—1.7 million of the 2.4 million—sell less than $40,000 of agricultural products annually. Together, they sell only 13.2 percent of the agricultural output.

Raising farm incomes closer to incomes in the nonfarm sector has been the overriding policy objective since farm programs began in the 1930s. Indeed, average incomes of farm people now do compare favorably to those of the rest of the population. Although pockets of poverty persist, widespread poverty is no longer the chronic, pervasive problem it once was in agriculture, largely because of income earned off the farm by residents of smaller farms. Off-farm income now accounts for 60 percent of the total income of farm people. The 72 percent of the farms with less than $40,000 gross sales earned 80 percent of the off-farm income in 1983. These same farms registered no net farm income, excluding government payments; in fact, they incurred losses of $1.7 billion.

Off-farm employment opportunities and earnings not only have improved the overall financial situation of farm people relative to others, but also have narrowed the income gap between large and small farms. Average incomes are lowest on intermediate-size farms ($20,000–$100,000 of gross sales), which rely heavily on farming alone for family income.

The distribution of government payments remains based on volume of production. Thus, they are skewed toward the larger farms, but payments make up a significant proportion of the total income of the midsize farm. Direct payments, which include deficiency, land diversion, conservation, wool program and other minor ones, were distributed among farms in 1983 as presented in Table 10.2.

The balance sheet of the farm sector reveals that assets now approximate $850 billion, with a total debt of about $200 billion—a debt-to-asset ratio of almost 23 percent. This ratio is not particularly high compared to other industries in the economy and suggests a fundamentally sound farm economy,

TABLE 10.2
Distribution of Direct Payments to Farms

Sales Size	% of Farms	% of Output	% of Payments
Less than $40,000	72%	13.2%	22%
$40,000 to $100,000	16	20.0	33
Over $100,000	12	66.8	44

but the situation within the sector is highly varied. Average debt-to-asset ratios increase as farms become larger. For the smallest farms, the ratio averages about 15 percent, but it rises to nearly 37 percent for the very largest farms.

Another indicator of economic status of the farm sector is returns on investment. Over the 40 years beginning with 1940, total returns have compared relatively favorably to returns on investment in the nonfarm economy. Returns in agriculture were especially favorable in the 1970s, averaging about 12 percent after adjustment for inflation. Since 1980, returns have been much less attractive, reflecting declining land values and lower incomes, and indeed, have usually been negative since 1981.

Dependence on Foreign Trade. A third significant change for agriculture, and one especially important for policy, has been the extent to which the United States has come to depend on trade. In 1970, agricultural exports were $7.3 billion and imports were $5.8 billion, resulting in a trade surplus of $1.5 billion. Exports were only 14 percent of farm cash receipts. Export growth was phenomenal in the 1970s, however, peaking in 1981 at $43.3 billion, while imports were $16.8 billion. The trade surplus of $26.6 billion was almost 18 times greater than just 12 years earlier. Although exports have dropped precipitously from 1981 to less than $30 billion in 1985–1986, in the aggregate, they still account for nearly one fourth of farm cash receipts.

The economic status of the farm sector, indeed the entire food and agricultural system, has become geared to the strength of foreign markets and factors that drive those markets. This has been vividly illustrated by the boom–bust cycle of the past 13 years. The 1970s boom was made possible by devaluation of the dollar, global economic progress, gradual lowering of price supports across the later 1960s and other factors. The bust of the 1980s was strongly influenced by global recession, a sharply strengthening dollar and high interest rates. Clearly, the farm sector is no longer isolated from fundamental economic trends at home or abroad. It has a large stake in the pace at which developing countries grow, how the Third World manages its debt, the size of the U.S. budget deficit and the value of the dollar, among other things.

Importance of Macroeconomic Policy. This leads into and overlaps with the fourth major change affecting agriculture—the overriding importance of macroeconomic policy to the health of the farm sector, indeed the entire food system, and rural America. This results from greater integration of the farm sector into the national economy—the heavy use of industrial-origin inputs, large debt-capital requirements, a high degree of specialization—and dependence on foreign markets, in which U.S. access and competitiveness are determined largely by macro policy. The farm sector is directly affected by the influence of macroeconomic policy on demand growth through income growth in the developing countries (the fastest-growing markets), competitiveness of U.S. products through the value of the dollar, and the cost and availability of investment and operating capital.

The increasingly pervasive influence of macro policy greatly alters what farm commodity programs can and cannot do, and consequently how they should be structured, to the point where many believe that macroeconomic policies probably are more critical to the health of the farm sector than traditional farm and commodity policies.

Expanding Productive Capacity. By conventional measures, productivity and output of U.S. agriculture have increased dramatically since World War II. Based on our recent research, total factor productivity grew at an average annual rate of 2.2 percent in the 15 years immediately after World War II, 1.0 percent in the 1960s and 1.7 percent in the 1970s.

A large part of the growth stemmed from development and application of land- and labor-saving technologies: new and improved mechanical power, improved seeds and animal genetic stock, hydroelectric and fossil fuel-based energy, fossil fuel-based fertilizers, pesticides, herbicides, fungicides and other chemicals to aid livestock and crop production. Pesticide and fertilizer use, for example, increased annually at more than 6 percent between 1948 and 1978. Several major publicly financed water development projects became operational in the 1950s and 1960s. Irrigation, in response to low water and energy prices and new water-application technologies, expanded rapidly from both surface and underground sources to 50 million acres in 1980, almost double that of 1950.

Productivity of land, as measured by yield per acre, grew nearly 50 percent between 1948 and 1978. Although the harvested cropland area was variable, acreage in 1982 was virtually identical to that in 1950, but crop production nearly doubled in that period. Labor inputs declined nearly 70 percent; labor productivity grew at an annual average rate of 4.8 percent during 1948–1978.

During the past 30 years, U.S. agricultural output has expanded at an average annual rate of more than 2.0 percent. There are no inherent technical reasons why that rate could not be maintained well into the twenty-first century. The sources of that growth will be essentially the same as those of the past several decades: productivity-enhancing technology, more intensive use of resources, more effective management, interregional shifts in production patterns and, if necessary, a modest net increase in harvested cropland. Important is that the technical production frontier can be expanded substantially for both crops and livestock with "off-the-shelf" technology. In addition, we are only beginning to glimpse the productivity-enhancing effects of biotechnologies applicable after the turn of the century.

The growth in productive capacity in the United States and in other countries in the next decade or two may well perpetuate the long-term decline in real prices of agricultural commodities, a trend characteristic of much of the past 75 years. If these perceptions prove to be correct, the need to adjust an expanding productive capacity to effective demand for farm products will continue to be a central policy issue, as has been the case during much of the past 50 years.

The Natural Resource Base and Environmental Quality. U.S. agriculture has a richly endowed natural resource base. Coupled with favorable climate, productivity-enhancing technology and the increased managerial capabilities of farm operators, the system yields a cornucopia of relatively low-cost food and fiber products beyond the imagination of even the optimists of a generation ago.

A recent comprehensive assessment of the resource and environmental effects of agriculture in the United States suggests that the major environmental threat emanating from agriculture is that of soil erosion and its associated effects on water quality.[2] Sheet and rill erosion now exceeds the level that permits crop yields to be maintained economically and indefinitely on some 27 percent of U.S. cropland. Sediment delivered to the nation's waterways is projected to nearly double by 2010 under economic and technological assumptions of the study. These estimates derive in large part from a 60–70 million-acre increase in cropland to meet projected domestic and foreign demand for U.S. agricultural products. This expansion in cropland would further induce agricultural production on erosion-prone land and thus cause a significant decline in marginal agricultural productivity growth rates. A more recent assessment of global food prospects suggests a lesser but still substantial increase in cropland by 2010, given no major breakthroughs in technology.[3] In either case, the pressure could be high on natural resources and environmental quality.

For most of the last half-century, U.S. agriculture had access to low-cost energy and publicly subsidized low-cost water for irrigation. As a result, farmers have made profligate use of both. Current irrigation levels with average precipitation result in the "mining" of over 22 million acre-feet of water from aquifers in the western United States. Nationally, nearly a quarter of the groundwater used by agriculture is not replenished. Falling groundwater levels coupled with higher energy costs are forcing major adjustments in agricultural production in a multimillion-acre area in the central and southern Plains states.

Beyond these physical and economic dimensions of water resources are major problems of water quality. Groundwater contamination from agricultural as well as nonagricultural sources has become serious in many parts of the country. Western irrigation practices have raised groundwater salinity. Perhaps one quarter of the lands currently under irrigation in the West are heavily dependent on nonrenewable water supplies, and the productivity of several million additional acres is threatened by rising salt levels.

Other water-quality problems—dissolved oxygen; suspended solids carrying bacteria, nutrients, and pesticides; excessive phosphoric and nitrogenic nutrients—derive in part, occasionally in major part, from agricultural production practices and runoff into streams and lakes. Growing public pressure to control nonpoint pollution (nonsite-specific pollution) could significantly increase agriculture's future production costs.

About 1,000 new chemicals are introduced each year in the United States. Some 55,000–60,000 chemicals are marketed annually. Comparatively little is known about the potential toxicity of many of these chemicals, about precisely how they are used, whether and how they enter the food chain and other ecosystems and their ultimate effects on human health and other species. Controls on use of pesticides in agriculture and forestry have become more stringent, and progress has been made in developing less-toxic but effective pesticides and integrated pest management systems that reduce application rates. Nonetheless, pesticide use remains pervasive in the production of major field crops.

Agricultural development in the United States must now be viewed in the context of its interdependence in larger, highly complex environmental and ecological systems as well as economic systems.[4] The goals of enhancing agricultural productivity and output per se are coming increasingly into question. This suggests possible tradeoffs between agricultural productivity growth as currently measured in favor of greater protection of the natural resource base and reduced levels of environmental pollution. The tradeoffs need to be defined and measured more fully and accurately so that more informed choices can be made, and there is need for new or improved institutional designs to facilitate effective expression of those choices.

The Budget Deficit. The long-term consequences of America's huge current and prospective federal budget deficits are difficult to exaggerate, among them that spending on agricultural programs will be under severe pressure for years to come. Projections for the forthcoming five fiscal years under the Food Security Act are for outlays of roughly $15–$20 billion annually for commodity programs alone. These amount to a small share of the total federal budget, but they are highly visible and likely to be attractive targets in any serious effort to reduce the deficit.

Even under the most farsighted political leadership, correction of chronic deficits is years away. No easy solutions are in sight, Gramm-Rudman-Hollings notwithstanding. Agriculture will not, nor should it, escape the impact of deficit reduction. Indeed, agriculture stands to benefit from overall deficit reductions to the extent that lower interest rates would reduce production costs, ease financial stress and result in a cheaper dollar that would encourage exports.

POLICY IMPLICATIONS

The picture that emerges from the preceding overview is that of a diverse, science-driven, highly productive agriculture, a sector marked by increasing economic concentration, ever-closer links to other sectors of the domestic and world economy and growing dependence on export markets to absorb its products. Moreover, it remains, as agriculture always has, an industry marked by short-term and cyclical instability as a result of the vagaries of weather, biological processes and economic policies, domestic and foreign.

Overlaying the sector is a mosaic of pervasive market-intervention policies derived from a different era, policies that induce rigidity in resource use, contribute to environmental externalities and distribute benefits in a highly skewed manner, with the major beneficiaries being large-scale operators and landowners.

The bishops correctly emphasize that as a society, we face choices concerning the future of agriculture and rural America—what it does for and to people and how people participate in it. As they forcefully assert, there are moral and ethical standards by which policies by the people and for the people should be formulated in addition to the economic criteria this chapter has emphasized. However, we should not lose sight of the fact that the agricultural system that has evolved over the past century has been, in many respects, highly successful and has contributed immensely to improved standards of living and the economic welfare of most citizens: an abundance of low-cost food for domestic and foreign consumers and release of resources for production of other goods and services, for example. The pragmatic issue is what types of policies we want for the future that preserve the benefits of the current system, are sustainable in the long run, avoid the excesses and distortions of current policies and yet are consistent with equity goals and Christian teachings. In addition, these lofty goals must be sought in realization that as a society, we possess finite resources by which to achieve them.

Any major recasting of current policies should be preceded by the review and clarification of goals.[5] Current policies as a result of 50 years of amendments and tinkering are rife with inconsistencies. Some are predicated on a structure of agriculture that no longer exists. Some are built on the premise of a "closed," insular agricultural sector, the circumstances of which have long since ceased to exist. Who are the intended beneficiaries of public policies—consumers, midsize producers, farm workers? Is the goal of policy to stabilize supplies of food or to raise farm prices above market equilibrium levels and transfer income? Only when long-term goals of policies for agriculture and rural areas have been clarified and made more consistent can we expect to avoid the types of policy failures prevalent in the past several decades. The bishops' letter is a constructive beginning of a much-needed dialogue on policy goals.

The forces leading to change in the policy environment identified in the preceding section suggest several elements of long-term policies. The significance of macroeconomic policies and conditions in determining economic performance in agriculture suggests the need for flexible agricultural policies. The inherent instability of agricultural production in markets that have become increasingly interdependent implies the continued need for public food reserves. Price and income instability suggests the possible need for more effective insurance programs to cope with risks. Experience with commodity price programs has demonstrated that they are an imprecise, costly means of transferring income to the farm sector. How might they be more effectively "targeted" to intended beneficiaries? Or, should commodity programs be scrapped and some form of means-tested income transfer substituted? The targeting of conservation payments and provisions to ensure that recipients of income transfers comply with accepted conservation practices has been suggested as a means of achieving greater coherence between agricultural production and natural resource policies.

Major restructuring of current policies will not come easily. Powerful political constituencies surround virtually every major component of current policies. Dissatisfaction, however, with current policies and their administration is pervasive and growing as a result of past failures, high public costs, uneven distributive effects and growing recognition that the resolution of economic problems in agriculture and rural areas rests less with agricultural policies than on macroeconomic and international economic policies. In combination, these circumstances will lead inexorably to the reorientation of current policies. The bishops' letter broadens public perspectives on the issues and options and thus is an important contribution to the continuing dialogue that will be needed to bring about change.

The Preferential Option for the Poor and the Evolution of Latin American Macroeconomic Orthodoxies

Paul D. McNelis, S.J.

In their pastoral letter "Catholic Social Teaching and the U.S. Economy," the American Conference of Catholic Bishops has affirmed the preferential option for the poor of the Latin American Bishops' Conference as a fundamental criterion for making moral judgments about economic policy. This affirmation is welcome and challenging to those with experience in Latin America.

In Latin America during the past 10 years, there have been dramatic switches in the design of macroeconomic stabilization policy, which reflect a shift in fundamental assumptions about the structural relationships and constraints facing householders, firms and financial institutions in various sectors of the economy. During the late 1970s, in particular, there was a turning away from the fundamental assumptions of the Keynesian "old orthodoxy" to the "new orthodoxy" of monetarism and liberalization through tariff reduction, decontrol of administered prices and interest rates and removal of controls on foreign investment. This shift from the old orthodoxy or "old style" stabilization program of Keynesian stabilization policy to the "new style" program of monetarism and liberalization produced higher inflation in Argentina and Uruguay and a deep depression in Chile, as well as a deterioration of the distribution of income in these countries. Brazil, which followed some tenets of the "new orthodoxy," experienced recession and a rigidity and inertia in its inflationary process despite strong reductions in overall demand. The preferential option for the poor can be seen as a call for a critical analysis of the fundamental assumptions or orthodoxies implicit in the design of stabilization policies. It is also a call for a return to the old style policy of Keynes' macroeconomics, with special concern for the welfare burdens of austerity programs and the welfare benefits of longer-term investment in basic needs.

The first part of this study will sketch out the background of the old and new orthodoxies in macroeconomic stabilization policy. The second part is a review of the track record of the new style policies in South America, and the third part proposes a return to the old style policies with emphasis on the longer-term welfare burdens and benefits. The last part is a conclusion, which contains an agenda for building a political coalition and partnership for a new economic policy in the United States based on the preferential option for the poor, both of the United States and of the Third World, particularly the Latin American debtor nations.

BACKGROUND OF THE "NEW STYLE" STABILIZATION POLICIES

After a number of years of economic populism, hyperinflation and huge balance-of-payments deficits, authoritarian regimes seized power in Argentina, Chile and Uruguay. The reduction of inflation, the elimination of balance-of-payments deficits and the restoration of "rationality" through a return to a "free-market" pricing system characterize the main economic goals of the new authoritarian regimes in the Southern Cone. Broadly speaking, the first two of these goals fall in the realm of open-economy macroeconomics. Policies designed to eliminate the balance-of-payments deficit and to reduce inflation are called "stabilization policies." The third goal falls in the realm of public policy microeconomics. This chapter will concentrate on macroeconomic stabilization policies and will discuss the microeconomic aspects only insofar as they interact with Southern Cone macroeconomic policy-making.[1]

The theory of macroeconomic stabilization in the open economy is based on the "target/instrument" approach of Tinbergen, Meade and Mundell. This approach simply states that the number of policy instruments available to policymakers must at least be equal to the number of policy targets or goals. In open-economy stabilization policy, there are two targets: an internal one, domestic inflation reduction, and an external one, the elimination of the balance-of-payments deficit. Policymakers typically rely on three instruments: fiscal policy, monetary policy and exchange-rate policy. From this perspective, the problem of policy-making reduces to the "optimal match" of particular policy instruments with policy goals. The idea of the "optimal match" of targets with instruments is simple, and for this reason easily overlooked or forgotten. Considerable confusion in policy debates could be avoided if one approaches the policy-making problem from this perspective. "Old style" and "new style" programs, for example, are just alternative solutions to the optimal matching problem of targets and instruments.[2]

What are these policy instruments, and how do they work? *Fiscal policy* involves changes in government spending and taxation. Government spending and taxation have direct effects on current income, on which current consumption decisions are made. With higher or lower consumption, there is higher or lower demand in the economy. This, in turn, affects inflation. *Monetary policy* affects the economy through another channel. The Central Bank regulates the amount of reserves that private banks must keep on deposits. With a required reserve rate of 20 percent, for example, a private bank must retain $2,000 on a deposit of $10,000. With this reserve requirement, the bank may lend only $8,000 in the form of new credit. The focus of monetary policy is this process of credit expansion: If the central bank raises the required reserve rate to 30 percent, for example, then the private bank must retain $3,000 in reserves. Thus, it can lend out only $7,000. The supply of credit is effectively reduced, and interest rates rise, since it is now harder for a bank customer to get a loan. The higher interest rates, in turn, affect new investment in the economy, and thus reduce spending and overall demand. Finally, *exchange-rate policy* changes the price of foreign money. Currency depreciation is simply an increase in the exchange rate or the price of foreign money. With a depreciation, foreign money is more expensive, and ultimately, domestic residents have to pay more money to buy foreign goods. Thus, a depreciation raises the price of imports and thereby cuts demand. By the same process, a depreciation makes the home currency cheaper. If it takes more pesos to buy one dollar, then it takes fewer dollars to buy one peso. Thus, a depreciation allows foreigners to buy home-produced goods with less of their own money, so the price of exports falls in foreign markets and demand increases. This leads to new activity in the export industry in the home country.[3]

As every college-educated veteran of a course in Principles of Economics should know, the Keynesian and by now old style stabilization program for dealing with balance-of-payments deficits and inflation is a combination of currency depreciation and tight fiscal policy, through spending cuts, tax increases, or both. Thus, the old style solution for the target/instrument "match" is to tie exchange-rate policy to balance-of-payments deficits and fiscal policy to inflation. The policy team can be subdivided into those who manage the exchange rate, sufficiently depreciating the currency to cut import demand and raise exports, and those who control the federal budget, sufficiently cutting spending and raising taxes to lower inflationary pressures. Monetary policy is not part of the package.

Australian economist W. M. Corden calls the old style program of currency depreciation and fiscal stringency a program of "expenditure switching" and "expenditure reducing." The currency depreciation switches demand away from imports (which are now more expensive) toward home-produced goods, which in turn helps the balance-of-payments situation. The expenditure-reducing program of tax increases and spending cuts lowers overall demand in the economy and thus cools off the inflationary process. Thus, under this expenditure switching-and-reducing policy of depreciation and austerity, there is no need to impose tight monetary policy lending rates. Credit may remain loose and interest rates low in order to promote a normal rate of investment. The continued investment will ensure continuing expansion in employment opportunities at a time when overall consumption demand is falling. The unemployment effects of the stabilization program will thus be mitigated.

Of course, the old style programs of expenditure switching and reducing entail real hardships. The expenditure-reducing policy of fiscal austerity falls primarily on consumption spending. Why? Tax increases or government spending cuts have their first effects on current disposable income, on which current consumption decisions depend. A reduction of current disposable income, therefore, means a reduction of consumption spending. Since interest rates remain low during the stabilization program, there is little fall in investment. Consumers, then, and not investors, bear the burden of the stabilization program. Similarly, the expenditure switching makes imported goods, foreign travel and tourism more expensive. This implies a reduced standard of living or lower style of life for a segment of the population. The real question raised by the implementation of the old style stabilization program is *whose* consumption and *whose* standard of living are most affected.[4]

There are a number of reasons why the new authoritarian states in the Southern Cone did not opt for old style programs. First is the unpopularity of tax increases among the more powerful and elite constituencies of the regime. Second, the need to maintain national security calls for more centralization and military support, making it difficult to reduce government spending. Third, the prospect of a sudden change and large jump in the exchange rate, as a result of an expenditure switching policy, may undermine the appearance of political and social stability that the new authoritarian regimes hope to create.

The new style stabilization program that the Southern Cone policymakers opted for rests on the monetary approach to the balance-of-payments, revived by the late Harry Johnson at the University of Chicago in the late 1960s. It should not be surprising that the principle policymakers behind the implementation of the new style programs happen to be economists educated at the University of Chicago. The new style program solves the policy match or "assignment problem" in a different way: Monetary policy has the job of correcting the balance-of-payments problem, and exchange-rate policy the job of reducing inflation. In the new style program, fiscal policy is put on the shelf, and the exchange-rate policy calls for an appreciation or a controlled depreciation, not a free depreciation geared to the balance-of-payments problem as in the old style program. How does this new style stabilization program work?

First, one must remember that the overall balance of payments consists not only of exports less imports (this is the balance of trade), but also includes net interest payments on outstanding debt (this component is especially important for Brazil—$14 billion in 1982). The balance of trade and the interest account add up to the current account. However, the overall balance also includes the capital account, which is simply capital inflows into the country (in the form of foreign loans or investments) less capital outflows (in the form of domestic loans or investments in foreign countries). The capital account and current account add up to the overall balance of payments.

The monetary approach to the balance of payments discounts the effects of exchange-rate changes on the balance of trade, since the demand for such specific import items as oil may not be quickly affected by exchange-rate changes anyway. Instead, it highlights the effects of domestic interest rates on the capital account: In a tightly linked international financial system, an increase of domestic interest rates above world levels may induce a large inflow of foreign finance anxious to take advantage of the higher interest rates. Thus, if there is a serious balance-of-payments deficit, policymakers need not let the currency depreciate. Instead, they should opt for higher interest rates through restrictive monetary policy. The higher interest rates will induce foreign portfolio managers and international lending institutions to send dollars into the country to purchase the high-yield domestic assets. It does not matter immediately to the balance-of-payments issue if dollars come into the country for the purchase of export goods or for the purchase of high-yield domestic assets. The effect is the same—an improved balance-of-payments position—and it is in this sector that new style programs have been most successful.

Many of these high-yield assets purchased by international lending institutions, especially London-based branches of American banks, were high-risk loans, and eventually, the Southern Cone countries, especially Brazil, will have to face repayment of these loans. Thus, the roots of the present debt crisis may be traced to the monetary approach to the balance of payments. Brazil in particular was all too eager to receive loans in dollars to cure its immediate balance-of-payments difficulties, and international lending institutions, especially the newly established American branch banks in London (the Eurodollar banks) were all too "bullish" to take the higher risks.

The new style program assigns exchange-rate policy the job of slowing domestic inflation—the new style model of inflation is radically different from the old style model. In the new style model, the exchange rate is the driving force of domestic inflation since, as stated earlier, a depreciation increases the cost of foreign currency and thereby raises the price of imports at home. Thus, a depreciation leads to a jump in the price of imported final goods (such as cars or cameras) and imported intermediate goods (such as steel). The increased price of imported cameras, for example, enables domestic producers of cameras to raise their prices and still remain competitive. The increased price of steel and other imported intermediate goods forces producers to pass this basic cost increase on to consumers in the form of higher prices. The depreciation, then, leads to higher inflation in the domestic economy by raising the price of imported final goods and imported intermediate goods.

Which inflation models form the basis of the old style and new style policies? In the old style view, inflation is determined by demand, a result of too much domestic spending, and tax increases or spending cuts (or both) are necessary to cool off inflationary pressures. In the new style view, inflation is determined by exchange-rate changes. A depreciation of the currency is rapidly transmitted to the domestic market in the form of higher import prices, higher prices of domestic goods that "compete" with imports, and higher prices of domestic goods that are made with imported intermediate goods.

In a sense, both the old style and new style models of inflation are appropriate. However, the old style model may be more applicable in a relatively large, independent economy, such as the United States, in which imported final goods and imported intermediate goods have a relatively small share of total sales. On the other hand, the new style model would be more applicable to a relatively small, dependent economy, such as one of the BENELUX countries (Belgium, the Netherlands and Luxembourg), in which imported goods constitute a significant share of total sales. In any of these countries, a sudden depreciation of the currency would quickly generate new domestic inflation.[5] Unfortunately, the Southern Cone countries are between and betwixt, not quite as independent as the United States and not as highly dependent as the BENELUX countries for imported goods.

How about balance-of-payments adjustment—which models underlie the old style and new style remedies? The old style emphasis is on current-account conditions, and the cure is export promotion and import reduction. The new style emphasis is on the capital account, and the cure is high interest rates through restrictive monetary policy. Clearly, the new style cure cannot last in the long run unless exports become competitive enough and earn enough to repay the foreign loans.

In conjunction with its anti-inflation program, Brazil opted for a widespread system of indexing wages, interest rates, rents and tax rates in order to remove the uncertainty of high inflation on long-term contracts. However, the official inflationary "correction index" for wages seldom kept pace with actual inflation rates. The Chilean stabilization program also followed a similar indexing procedure. The indexing system, especially in the earlier stages of the stabilization program, appears not as a corrective device against long-term inflationary uncertainty on long-term contracts, but as a weapon of the government for squeezing wages. Despite the calls for a free market and a return to an uncontrolled pricing system in all sectors of the economy, there has been little hesitancy to interfere in the labor market during Southern Cone stabilization programs. Although a wage squeeze may pay off in a short-term inflationary slowdown, it can hardly be the basis of a longer-term stabilization program based on a free market and an uncontrolled pricing system.[6]

One final point about new style programs. In the monetary approach to the balance of payments, the rate of inflation and the balance-of-payments deficit are monetary variables by assumption. Thus, a reduction in the rate of inflation and the payments deficit need not generate such real effects as rising unemployment or falling production. The disinflation process can be recession-free. Unemployment side effects appear only as a result of sector rigidities in the economy or other such market imperfections as trade union contracts, minimum-wage laws and regulated prices.

THE TRACK RECORD OF THE "NEW STYLE" PROGRAMS

"Overkill" accurately describes the effects of Southern Cone new style stabilization programs, both in credit-tightening and exchange-rate policies. This overkill brought only temporary gains in the fight against inflation, with a cost of rising unemployment and the prospect of more trouble down the road.[7]

The implementation of new style programs is usually followed by a burst of "corrective inflation" brought on by the removal of price controls and other nonrational interference in the industrial sector during the previous populist regimes. During the first two years of the Argentinian program, 1976–

1978, for example, price controls were removed and guidelines on minimum wages became nonbinding. After this initial inflationary surge, inflation will dampen because of the squeeze in wages from the official indexing of contracts at rates considerably lower than the actual rate of inflation. With lower wage increases relative to inflation, the costs of production decrease and producers can translate these lower costs into lower price increases.

Balance-of-payments targets appear to be the major victories for the Southern Cone new style policies in the initial stages. The high domestic interest rates brought massive inflows of dollars into the Southern Cone countries. In order to purchase the high-yield assets denominated in local currency, international portfolio managers, of course, had to switch these dollars into cruzeiros or pesos. Once these dollars were switched into the local currency, they became the international reserves of the Southern Cone central banks. In Argentina, for example, international reserves increased more than seven times from April 1976 to April 1978. The reserve holdings of Brazil jumped from a deficit of $4.5 billion in early 1978 to a surplus of $9.7 billion in December 1979.[8]

The rapid accumulation of these dollar-foreign-exchange reserves ultimately became a curse because, at an official exchange rate of 300 cruzeiros for one U.S. dollar, for example, the central bank must print and pay 300 cruzeiros for each one dollar it accumulates in reserves. Thus, the new reserves lead to a rapid increase in domestic money, which in turn, causes a loosening of credit and lowering of interest rates.

To counter the rapid buildup of the domestic money supply induced by the international reserve increase, the central bank must adopt a sterilization policy. That is, at the same time the central bank is issuing domestic money in exchange for the new dollar reserves, it adopts a policy of issuing new interest-bearing assets to the public with higher rates of return. With these higher yields, the public will be induced to buy these assets with the newly issued domestic currency. Thus, the "sterilization" process effectively takes out of circulation the new domestic money induced by the reserve buildup. The trouble with this is that it does the job at higher and higher interest rates. Should it be surprising that real interest rates, corrected for inflation, were upward of 35 percent in Chile, 50 percent in Brazil and 135 percent in Argentina in recent years?

The sterilization process in the Southern Cone could not completely absorb the expansionary effects of the new reserves on domestic money. The reason is because the domestic market for assets denominated in local currency is not wide enough, in terms of large numbers of buyers and sellers, or deep enough, in terms of variety of maturity options, to handle the enormous sterilization job. The central banks could not sell off enough new high-interest assets to take all of the new money out of circulation. As a result, a huge domestic buildup of currency took place, and the central banks, despite their efforts to sterilize, effectively lost control of the money supply. In Brazil, for example, between 1979 and 1980, the outstanding amount of assets issued by the government to the public more than doubled, and so did the money supply. The increase in domestic money, in turn, generated new inflationary pressures by increasing spending, while the high domestic interest rates choked off new investment. Recession-with-inflation is not so surprising after all when one couples massive dollar inflows with partial sterilization efforts leading to high interest rates.

The recession-with-inflation consequence of the balance-of-payments victories in the Southern Cone were further aggravated by the controlled depreciation of the currency, or even controlled appreciation, set by the crawling peg. In Argentina, for example, between 1976 and 1979, the rate of depreciation fell from 117 percent before the stabilization program to 27 percent after the stabilization program. This lower rate of depreciation proved politically very attractive. With this lower rate, imports became relatively less expensive, along with foreign travel and tourism, generating a higher style of life and an unexpected feeling of euphoria among the upper and middle classes in the wake of stabilization. This was especially true in Argentina through 1980: The middle class had never been in such a prosperous position as when the peso reached unprecedented purchasing power over imports and Argentine tourists flocked to Rio de Janeiro for cheap vacations. This type of situation cannot last. With cheaper imports and more expensive exports, the balance-of-payments will deteriorate and ultimately need correction. The fall in exports also adds to the unemployment total as export production declines.

Eventually, the government will have to depreciate the currency at the faster rate through a "maxidevaluation." Thus, the recent maxidevaluations in Brazil should be seen as eclectic Delfim Neto fixes and not as ingredients to new style programs. Unfortunately, the maxidevaluation will only feed back into further inflationary impulses, since imported final goods (such as cameras and cars) and imported intermediate goods (such as steel) become more expensive. The initial crawling-peg policy cannot help but contribute to the inflationary problems of the economy.[9]

So far, the consequence of the new style programs appears to be higher interest rates, rising unemployment and new inflationary impulses. There is more trouble, however, on the horizon. The massive buildup of debt from international lending institutions and the Eurodollar banks will ultimately have to be paid back, and the prospects of meeting the repayment schedules become progressively more bleak in the midst of recession, inflation and high interest rates. These repayment schedules can be renegotiated, but how long can renegotiation be a way of life without some drastic action by the borrowing countries, such as a moratorium, or by the international banks, such as a declaration of default? The eclectic program of Delfim Neto in Brazil had all but abandoned inflation as a stabilization goal in favor of massive subsidies of export industries in order to maintain debt repayment through export revenues. Thus, the massive inflow of dollars, a consequence of new style programs, eventually gives way to a one-sided export-promotion strategy under the threat of debt moratorium or default.[10]

The burden of the Southern Cone new style programs, with their high borrowing rates, falls most heavily on the lower income groups, who do not have the immediate cash and must borrow at high interest rates for meeting expenditures on housing or consumer durables. The unemployment overkill also hits the lowest income groups the hardest. In the recession, the first to go are the workers with the lowest skills or education whose jobs can be mechanized with few new expenditures or reassigned to other workers in an "efficiency move." The cost distribution of the new style program, then, is decidedly regressive: Those with the lowest incomes bear the largest share of the burden. One-sided export-promotion policies only aggravate the regressive effects of the new style programs, public funds for investment are diverted to export industries, and little is left over for investment in such basic human needs as education, water purification, or famine prevention (as in the northeast of Brazil). The lowest income groups also bear the largest burdens of public investment policies, for the sake of facilitating continuous debt repayment or forestalling moratorium or default.[11]

ALTERNATIVES TO THE NEW ORTHODOXY

Are there any alternatives to these new style programs, which may be more successful in reducing inflation, less costly in terms of recession and unemployment and more equitable in the cost distribution of the disinflation process—less regressive, less burdensome, on the lowest income groups? There are.

The preceding analysis suggests that tight money and high interest rates do more harm than good by leading to overkill in unemployment, a falloff in investment and a Pyrrhic victory in the balance-of-payments capital account. The twin goals of slowing down inflation and reducing the balance-of-payments deficit call for current-account measures: an effort to reduce the fiscal deficit through tax increases and expenditure cuts, and an effort to lower imports and stimulate exports. This is surely old style talk, but all deficits, whether in the forms of too much government spending with too little tax revenue or too many imports with too few exports, have to be paid for, and cannot be postponed forever. This means fiscal austerity and currency depreciation. However, if the program is coupled with a loose monetary policy of low interest rates, it need not generate a fall in investment. With continuing investment, expansion will continue in new employment opportunities.[12] Private investment should also be coupled with a wise policy of public investment. Too often in public investment policies, economic efficiency has been confused with technological efficiency. What may be most efficient for the engineer, such as the latest electronically controlled rice-processing plant, may not be the most efficient investment for an economist in a country of high unemployment. The economically efficient investment would call for a labor-intensive technology in the rice-processing plant even though this type of technology is not the latest, because in good decision making, investment is based not on technology, but on the relative abundance or scarcity of resources. In a labor-abundant economy, public investment should be in relatively labor-intensive or labor-absorbing technology and not in the latest, most up-to-date technology imported from countries where labor is relatively scarce. One of the great tragedies of so many semi-industrialized countries, not only in the Southern Cone, is the emphasis on copycat investment projects that will have negligible impact on the massive unemployment problems both during and after the stabilization program.

Inflation stabilization also involves recognizing the systematic inertia that keeps inflation going independently of the "original sin" that may have triggered the inflationary process, such as a change in the exchange rate or too much spending. Whichever models of inflation may be appropriate for the start of inflation, either the old style or new style, inflation keeps going because of profit-motivated pricing by firms. If wages go up 50 percent, for example, firms can be expected to mark up their prices at least 50 percent in order to maintain or increase profits, even if demand for the product is falling, and prices would be expected to fall. To slow up inflation, then, policymakers must slow up wage increases through wage controls. However, wage controls can be successful only if there is a guarantee to workers that prices will also slow down, that producers will not continue to increase prices after workers have agreed to moderate their wage demands. Outright price control in the private sector has not been a success story either in the industrialized or semi-industrialized countries. One way policymakers can discourage price increases that exceed moderated wage demands is through an excess profits tax. The fixing of such public-sector prices as utility rates, in line with wage demands, can also provide some discipline to firms.[13]

The crisis mentality over debt repayment has led to a one-sided program of export promotion through maxidevaluation and investment in export industries. This strategy has led to the neglect of the nontraded goods sector of the economy in such public investment as basic agricultural foodstuffs (beans and rice, for example), but also in water purification, health care and domestic transportation. The neglect of investment in this nontraded (and in basic human needs) sector of the economy has been an important source of scarcity and "homegrown" inflation. Thus, the crisis mentality has led to an unbalanced-growth policy (exports first, then the nontraded sector), a policy that will contribute only to more inflation and more hardship among the lowest income groups. A balanced-growth strategy of public investment in both the traded and the nontraded, basic-human-need sectors is the only viable policy for reducing inflation and alleviating the hardships of the least powerful groups.

Of course, the crisis mentality that underlies the unbalanced-growth policies in the Southern Cone can be calmed by a more realistic policy of the International Monetary Fund (IMF) toward the major debtor countries. Too often, the IMF has come to the aid of semi-industrialized countries facing difficulties with harsh macroeconomic "strings," requiring drastic monetary policies and extremely high interest rates. For this reason, Southern Cone policy teams have opted for eclectic unbalanced-growth policies instead of seeking IMF help. If, as the late Carlos Diaz-Alejandro has suggested, the IMF would shed its "Gothic" image and approach the international repayment problem with more realistic longer-term, low-interest financing, then the crisis mentality will be calmed and policy teams would have greater scope for pursuing balanced stabilization policies.

Many of these alternatives to the new style policies are being implemented in the package deals engineered by the Alphonsin government in Argentina and the Garcia government in Peru, which involve collective agreements among the government, unions and industrialists. If the stabilization measures of these democratic regimes succeed in reducing inflation and promoting growth and welfare among all classes of society, then similar programs may follow throughout Latin America. The challenge for the United States and international lending institutions is to give these alternative macroeconomic stabilization experiments time to work.

AGENDA FOR THE UNITED STATES

When the Carter administration left office, there was a general disenchantment with old style fiscal measures and the gradualism in conducting stabilization policy. The Reagan administration took office with a popular mandate for "shock treatment" in the fight against inflation. Like their Southern Cone counterparts, the present U.S. policy team relied on tight monetary policy and a stronger home currency. Interest rates increased, but the middle-class importers and tourists never had it so good with the dollar. The Regan Administration effectively put fiscal policy on the shelf as a stabilization instrument. Tax cuts and new military expenditures actually widened the budget deficit of the federal government, but were justified on the basis of supply-side economics (cutting taxes to stimulate long-run productivity) and national security. As in the Southern Cone, there has been a quick victory in the fight against inflation, a drop from a double-digit level to 4%, but there has also been unemployment overkill. For the first time in U.S. history since the Great Depression, the unemployment rate reached double-digit levels. The strong dollar has also brought a slowdown in export competitiveness and a slump in these industries, further aggravating the unemployment hardships. Even though the recovery since 1983 has reduced the unemployment rate from its double-digit level in 1982, the current regime appears to show little interest in taking specific steps to reduce unemployment through monetary ease and lower interest rates.

The shift from the old style policies of the Carter administration to the new style policies of the Reagan administration began with the appointment of Paul Volker as chairman of the board of governors of the Federal Reserve System by President Carter in October 1979. Volker has followed a "monetary target" rather than "interest target" approach to monetary control as part of an overall shift to a monetarist stabilization program. This shift from the Keynesian approach with low interest rates and monetary ease reflected a disenchantment among Democrats and Republicans alike with old style programs, which proved ineffective in reducing inflation or unemployment after the oil shocks of 1973 and 1979.

The high interest rates and the strong dollar pose problems for employment in the United States, but they also pose problems for longer-term growth and stability in Latin America. The high interest payments on Latin American debt (due to the high U.S. interest rates) and the collapse of the terms-of-trade and commodity prices of Latin American debtor countries (due to the strength of the dollar in world markets) have produced continuing hardships in Latin America during the time of the post-1983 world recovery. The drying up of new loans from U.S. financial institutions to Latin America has meant that for the first time in recent history, there has been a net transfer of resources from Third World countries to the First World creditor nations.

The preferential option for the poor, then, has implications for macro-economic policy in the United States. The United States cannot simultaneously be a good neighbor to Latin America, stick with its new style macroeconomic policy, protect domestic jobs and help financial institutions recover the interest and principal on their loans to Latin America. A turning away from the new style program to a Keynesian program of monetary ease, lower interest rates and a weaker, but more realistic, place of the dollar in world money markets will alleviate the debt burdens on Latin American economic planning and lead to lower U.S. unemployment rates. This alternative program need not render the United States more vulnerable to oil shocks, since policymakers have a variety of policy instruments, including monetary contraction and tax increases, for reducing demand in the aftermath of an oil shock.

In their pastoral letter, the bishops have called for a "new partnership" in the setting of economic policy at the local, national and international levels. In order to forge this coalition based on the preferential option for the poor, three agenda items could follow up this pastoral letter. First, a systematic theoretical basis for an alternative economic regime could be spelled out, using the logic of economic analysis of structural relationships and the moral aims of the pastoral letter. Second, data could be compiled that would give a more precise meaning to the problems cited in the pastoral letter, and provide a basis for agreement among "reasonable men and women of good-will." Finally, transition policies could be elaborated that would carry us from the present situation to long-term policy setting based on the preferential option for the poor.

Just as Keynesian economic analysis provided a theoretical basis for the New Deal political coalition, and the monetarist doctrine provided one basis for the Reagan policies, so there is the need to formulate a theoretical basis for a return to the old orthodoxy based on the longer-term welfare goals of the preferential option for the poor. This chapter has attempted to sort out some of the critical assumptions behind the old and new orthodoxies in recent Latin American macroeconomic policy. Beyond stressing the need for lower interest rates and a lower value of the dollar in world markets, there is need to spell out more rigorously the structural interrelationships among export and domestic industries in the United States, domestic unemployment and the welfare of Latin American debtor countries, so that proper policy tradeoffs may be clearly known and moral judgments made in the light of these ines-capable tradeoffs. Succeeding drafts of the pastoral letter have not adequately touched on this issue; this must be a priority if follow-up to this letter is to bear policy fruit.

There is also the need to compile a more precise data base on key variables that serve as indicators of changes in economic welfare and economic policy if the bishops wish to convince people to join in their new partnership for an alternative economic policy. Two examples show the need for a more precise use of data in making welfare judgments and arguing for changes in economic policy. One is unemployment, the other is the value of budget deficits. Although the unemployment rate of 7 percent in the 1980s is often compared unfavorably with the 3 percent unemployment rates of the 1960s, the changes in the demographic composition of the labor force as well as the differences in frequency and duration of unemployment in the 1960s and 1980s make comparisons of raw unemployment statistics less reliable indicators of changes in economic welfare. Christina Romer has shown, for example, that it is not even certain if the post-World War II economic climate in the United States is stabler than the pre-World War II economic climate because of the different ways economic statistics were gathered and the different welfare implications of these statistics in particular historical episodes.[14] As for budget deficits, the Gramm-Rudman-Hollings bill is a telling example of statistical illusion. The raw federal budget deficit includes capital as well as current operating expenditures. What matters for macroeconomic activity and long-term interest rate adjustment is the balancing of current operating accounts of the budget. There is no need for the federal government to cover capital expenditures, whether on buildings, roads, or space stations, out of current tax revenues, any more than individuals need to cover housing expenditures out of current income. Focusing on the raw fiscal deficit as an instrument or indicator of macroeconomic policy is wrong. Thus, the bishops, if they are to avoid the errors of Gramm-Rudman-Hollings supporters, must present their welfare arguments in terms of more precise welfare indicators, and formulate policy proposals in terms of more precise economic policy indicators. This is a big order, and involves the tedious task of evaluating sampling techniques and assumptions as well as econometric adjustments of data, but it is essential if the bishops wish to make a case for a new partnership and an alternative economic policy to a broad spectrum of people.

Finally, it is necessary to formulate transition policies from the present economic setting of policy to a new, long-term one based on the preferential option for the poor. One example illustrates this point. For the United States to move to lower interest rates and a lower value of the dollar, coordination with European and Japanese central banks is essential. With this coordination, lower interest rates will simply trigger an outflow of dollars from the United States to Europe and Japan. U.S. monetary ease must go hand-in-hand with monetary ease in the industrialized world, and exchange rate targets for the dollar must be agreed on by major trading partners of the United States if later fluctuations are to be avoided. While the bishops' call for a global central bank is a worthy long-term goal, a realistic transition strategy of greater policy coordination should be promoted if there is to be a smooth transition to a new setting of policy based on partnership for the public good and preference for the needs of the poor. In this case, partnership means international partnership among central bankers for the welfare of the poor in Third World debtor countries.

In conclusion, the bishops have urged us to look more critically at economic policy on a local, national and global level. They have called for a new partnership to reformulate economic policy. Doing this involves the theoretical task of developing logical propositions about structural relationships among key welfare groups, the compiling of reliable data bases as indicators of economic welfare and economic policy, and the design of transition policies to bring the United States out of its current method of setting policy and to an alternative long-run policy regime. This is a challenging, but welcome task for economists and all men and women of goodwill.

COLLABORATING TO SHAPE THE ECONOMY

The Bishops in the Iron Cage

THE DILEMMAS OF ADVANCED INDUSTRIAL SOCIETY

Norman Birnbaum

The American Catholic bishops' new pastoral letter, "Catholic Social Teaching and the U.S. Economy," is instructive in many ways. Two themes, however, are particularly salient. One is the response of the church to an especially opaque and troubled period of our history. The other is continuous with the first, but gives general significance to the specifically Catholic aspects of the letter. It is the question of the relationship of human moral purpose to economic and social mechanism. The bishops have served not only Catholics but the rest of us very well by dealing with our institutions critically. Had they contented themselves with calling on everyone in general and no one in particular to make sacrifices, or portrayed our society as a heaven on earth, no doubt they would have had the benefits of sententious praise from *The Wall Street Journal* and an invitation to be photographed with the President at the White House. In the event, their attempt to look at our society from higher moral ground has evoked large anxieties from those who have good reason—or, rather, effective reason—to insist that the moral development of humanity has culminated with and in themselves. In the ensuing round of criticism, no argument has been too crude or vulgar if it were thought likely to denigrate the bishops and their work. The analysis that follows is, indeed, critical. It expresses, however, a moral solidarity with the bishops' enterprise and is intended as the highest form of tribute among friends—frankness.

Modern Catholic social teaching had its origins in the response to industrial capitalism (and modern culture and society, generally) of a church with deep roots in and profound attachments to preindustrial institutions. In the lands of the Counter-Reformation, France and Italy, the ideas of the French Revolution constituted the original modern threat to the values espoused by Roman

Catholicism. In industrial England, liberalism (correctly intuited by Catholic thinkers as a derivative of Protestantism) was a major problem. In Germany, the church had to struggle against three fronts: an authoritarian Protestant state, an imperial or pseudoliberal capitalism allied to it, and a socialist movement that threatened each confession's hold on its believers. The general ideas in the successive papal social encyclicals (and their elaboration in the work of theologians and concretization in Catholic social movements and parties) always took particular national forms. The United States, of course, had a preindustrial culture but, unlike Western Europe, hardly a prebourgeois society. In our nation, Catholicism could draw on a European heritage for distinctly American tasks.

The United States is a Protestant foundation. Max Weber had the inspiration for his work on capitalism and Protestantism (more specifically, inner worldly asceticism) in Rome, but he did much of the research in the United States. American Protestantism has now fragmented. It has fused in myriad ways with both fundamentalism and its secularist antithesis. Catholicism has long since ceased to function as a church of immigrants. The Roman Catholic church, the Roman Catholic community, has *le droit de la cité*. This was earned, not least, in the church's support of the immigrant workers in late nineteenth and early twentieth century class conflicts, in the alliance it contracted with the Democratic Party to develop an American welfare state. The differences between the social histories of Catholicism and Protestantism in our nation were, for a period of some decades, obscured. They were apparently replaced by an economic and political consensus extending from the later terms of Roosevelt into the presidencies of Nixon, Ford and Carter. That consensus rested on the extension of empire abroad and the consolidation of a welfare state through a social contract at home. We need only recall the roles of the first Catholic U.S. president, John F. Kennedy, and Catholic labor leader George Meany, to measure the contribution of this American community to that consensus. (John Courtney Murray's theology of pluralism was, perhaps, in this period a Catholic counterpart to Reinhold Niebuhr's theology for our new empire.)

That consensus is now at an end and every American community is divided. Protestantism has split into a fundamentalist wing, espousing a new American tribalism, and a numerically dominant but politically confused liberal segment. An articulate part of American Jewry has been so traumatized by the Holocaust, is so uncertain of its integration in our society, that it has (frequently in quite explicit terms) abandoned the Enlightenment. Most Jewish voters, it is true, remain with the (disoriented) Democratic Party, possibly less because of enthusiasm for its ideas than fear and loathing of its fundamentalist opponents. That Catholics are divided is obvious. Think of the differences between the Honorable William Casey and Senator Edward Kennedy, or between William Simon and Monsignor George Higgins. It is against this ideological background that the bishops have conceived their letter. The letter is honest; it is does not pretend to satisfy everyone, to promulgate a rhetorical synthesis that would leave real conflicts of value and opposing views of society utterly untouched. Its difficulties, nevertheless, arise from the situation that has generated the prevailing disorientation: Our economy, indeed our culture and society, are changing so drastically that the models of analysis that but 20 years ago were effective no longer work.

The quantitative importance of industrial production in our economy has declined in favor of a curiously skewed distribution in the tertiary sector. There, highly renumerated financial, professional and technical activities co-exist with (quantitatively far larger) routinized processes that pay the labor force far less than industrial jobs. The role of the state in the economy has increased; the ideology of deregulation does not preclude military investments in particular, political steering in general (as in the Federal Reserve's omnipresence). The internationalization of the economy proceeds apace, from the transfer of production abroad to the nation's emergence as an international debtor.

The bishops, unfortunately, tend to think in terms that were appropriate three decades ago when a social contract was possible (since a much higher proportion of workers were in unionized industry), when our domination of the world market was evident, and when full employment and a rising standard of living rendered the problem of poverty apparently soluble with our existing social technology. Now, real living standards are in decline in the United States, full employment or anything like it seems impossible to attain and our political control of the world market is but partial. This situation has been accompanied by, when indeed it has not produced, discernible and perhaps profound changes in our society's attitudes to work, to the distribution of the national product and to the American welfare state. These changes are by no means uniform. Contradictory and uneven, they reflect differences of experience and interest within our society. What renders the situation especially opaque is the apparent inability of the social sciences to perform their tasks of public enlightenment. That formulation requires correction; the social sciences are themselves protagonists in the ideological conflicts ensuing from these institutional changes. The bishops refer to their recourse to the social sciences, but the adumbration of fact in these matters follows the assertion of value. We will have to ask, to what extent do the bishops' moral and political intentions lead them to a truer depiction of our historical situation?

The bishops' letter is, in fact, a study of the generic human process, since the question of the relationship of value to fact entails the problems of the connection of constraint and intention, social mechanism and spirit. The changes proposed by the bishops in the U.S. economy and society would alter the workings of what are usually depicted as immutable economic laws or intractable social processes. (Many exhausted social reformers use the term "intractable" to refer to problems they have been unable to solve and to justify an attitude of irritated passivity before demands that we, and they, think of new solutions.) The bishops raise beyond the question of political strategy that of our moral autonomy. They do so in a society that is well able, for all of its claims of enlightenment, to shape the spirit to its institutional ends.

Let us examine the bishops' values, then, not only for their moral properties, but for the possibility that they can be realized in this and not some other world. The reproach of utopianism or irrealism raised against social reformers or revolutionaries of any kind is usually a device for their enemies to espouse the values of their own social order without taking moral responsibility for doing so. It expresses the familiar Philistine conceit: The world being the way it is, it cannot be otherwise. The bishops' values are, indeed, worthy of respect (if, as we shall see, at times contradictory). If our society is so resistant that these values cannot be realized, that does not necessarily constitute an argument for renouncing them. However, we ought to know whether the bishops' view of social possibility is plausible and how that view influences the articulation of their values as well as being influenced by it.

The bishops' own beginning anticipates much of what follows in their letter. "What does the economy do for people? What does it do to people? And how do people participate in it? The economy is a human reality, formed by human decisions and associations." Behind the impersonal structures of the economy, behind the regular functioning of the economic system, they discern human beings. In a tradition of social discourse that goes back to Aristotle rather than beginning with Locke, they propose to scrutinize institutions for their purposive intent and unintended effect. Another heir of Aristotle, Marx, also made it his business to dissolve the conceptual reification of what he described as bourgeois political economy as an indispensable precondition of the reintroduction of moral purpose into it. It should not be supposed, the narrowness of some its practitioners notwithstanding, that the doctrine of bourgeois political economy was in its beginnings so devoid of moral purpose. Adam Smith wrote a treatise on the moral sentiments, and the Calvinists who according to Weber fathered modern capitalism were convinced they were doing the work of the Lord. The bishops, of course, draw on the traditions of modern Catholic social thought, with their emphases on the importance of community, family and person as categories of both descriptive and moral discourse that are prior to cost-benefit analysis.

One difficulty with the bishops' beginning is that people are not constants. Human character is mutable, even if the changes induced by cultural and social processes may take as long as generations to become evident. American culture has developed its own variant of industrial capitalism. In one way or another we, even if children of a recent immigration, are all children of the market. Our patterned drives, our sensibilities, bear the mark of our nation's economic history. The bishops call for major revisions in our ideas of common life in order to allow us to become different, fuller human beings. They alternate, as we shall see, between a strategy of institutional change and one that rests essentially on moral conviction. They have made matters conceptually too easy, however, and politically, alas, too hard for themselves. Are humans infused with market values suddenly to set these aside, to invent newer, more generous institutions? How are persons who in their souls are often desperately identified with market institutions to develop, in the deepest reaches of themselves, alternative moral convictions? The culture of capitalism cannot be thrown off or significantly altered so quickly.

The bishops' recourse to moral injunction is nonetheless politically comprehensible: Only strong moral convictions can overcome the barriers of habit, spirit and structure that make our history seem an eternal repetition of harshness, our society less than a human home. Where the bishops' argument is incomplete is in the connection of moral discourse to political interests and to material ones. Occasionally, too, moral and theological conviction involves the bishops in ambiguities. If the impoverished, free of the burdens of acquisitiveness and wealth, are indeed blessed, should we not seek a society in which an asceticised equality would prevail, rather like one or another of the Protestant communal experiments of the nineteenth century? The bishops hesitate between their insistence that the material goods of the world be more equitably shared and their hardly concealed suspicion that they are dross.

The discussion that follows seeks to apprehend the bishops' thought under the rubrics, successively, of their ethos, their conception of human nature and society, their depiction of the economy, their notion of rights (especially their suggestion for the addition of economic rights to the structure of basic human and political rights) and their political strategy.

ETHOS

The bishops proceed from a religious conception of human reality and human potential to the formulation of a social ethos. They are quite clear about the discontinuities in the path they trace. There is an order of stringency in their thought in which basic theological positions are fixed, but the political philosophical consequences are far more open. Theology, they declare, has drawn on "philosophy and empirical analysis" to give us "a deeper understanding of the human person, the rights and duties of different groups and of the nature of communal life." The bishops are a good deal less stringent about the philosophical, or even the theological, presuppositions of much that claims to be "empirical analysis." They assume the existence of an epistemological difference, but do not attempt to specify in a formal way their own movement from one to another sort of discourse.

The casualness of the bishops is only apparent. In the end, it frees them to sketch the outlines of a social project that few social scientists, whatever their values, would attempt. Sicklied over by the pale cast of thought, most social scientists prefer to remain within the confines of one or another discipline, leaving to some intellectual enactments of the Greek Kalends (or to that peculiar class of specialists in nonspecialized work resident in the interstices of our academy) a purposive synthesis of critical reflection, empirical analysis and prescriptive political philosophy. It was, however, the effort to construct that synthesis that originally motivated social inquiry.

The bishops commence with creation, which in their view gives us "an unalienable dignity which stamps human existence prior to any division into races or nations and prior to human labor and human achievement." No larger challenge to the vulgar Protestantism (and quietistic Catholicism), which sees humanity as perpetually beset by the curse of labor, could be imagined. A historic substratum of humanity is identical with our history. We do not earn the right to think ourselves human, we possess it. The bishops will not be offended if we term this a sociological preredemption.

The bishops' task is to find an American argument for this assumption in a society in which class, confession, race and region account for very sharp differences and conflicts among its citizens. More, they have to demonstrate that their vision engenders a limited set of economic ideas. To begin with, they are bound by their starting point to refuse the insistence of many economists on the analytic or conceptual autonomy of the market, much less that of many philosophers on the market as an institution that guarantees liberty where it does not exemplify or incorporate it. No doubt, a historical and subtle intelligence like Joseph Schumpeter would concede the point. For him, the market in general was a conceptual model and markets in particular were historical structures. Hayek (in positivist reaction to European social Catholicism) thought of the market as both ideal and real. Even he, however, presumably experiences spiritual discomfort in the face of reductionists like Gary Becker or Richard Posner, for whom all of human action is translatable into exchange transactions.

The bishops make clear, too, their refusal to treat property as an absolute right. "From the patristic period to the present, the church has affirmed that misuse of the world's resources or appropriation of them by a minority of the world's population betrays the gift of creation since whatever belongs to God belongs to all." The abstract notion of common property, however, has been compatible in practice with a considerable number of variations, all of them allowing large amounts of social differentiation and inequality. The Roman Catholic church has found ample opportunity throughout its history to tolerate, indeed legitimate, the right of the propertied to exercise moral and practical judgment on their use of creation or those parts of it entrusted to them. Of course, the notion of stewardship provided an opening for an ecclesiastical critique of profane behavior. Just as often, the rich were able to use it to justify their privileges. The fact that the Calvinist elaboration and extension of the idea of stewardship is especially profound (and occasionally, especially self-righteous, even hypocritical) makes a Catholic reinterpretation of property rights especially difficult in the United States. George Fitzhugh, after all, opposed the benign patriarchy of slavery to the harsh atomization imposed on labor by the market. Given the polyvalence of the idea of appropriate use of a common inheritance, what criteria do the bishops employ to concentrate their vision?

The bishops make the case for an aesthetic of justice, a sense of moral fitness. They refer to Old Testament ideas of justice as a form of witness to "the rightness of the human condition before God and in society." True to Moses, they define sin in this context as "an attempt to overturn creation by making God in human likeness." It is idolatry that produces the quest for unrestrained power and the desire for great wealth. In the early modern period, this formulation was employed to condemn the systematic attempt to make life on earth, if not entirely paradisical, somewhat less hellish. Power and wealth may need to be used for that global redistribution the bishops espouse, more precisely, to overturn the structures that block it. The bishops imply, putting them on common ground with many who are not Catholic, indeed, not theists, that their formulation can be reversed. The phenomenon known as idolatry in the Judaeo-Christian tradition can also be understood as the pursuit of power and wealth as ends in themselves. A social contract, a common agreement on other ends for and in society, can discipline, indeed transform, this regressive human tendency. A doctrine of contract could also give us another understanding of sin, as the dissolution of the bonds of community. The bishops' own idea of a social contract is insistent in its reference to the Old Testament, presumably an expression of the intensive ecumenical currents in the church in recent decades, as well as a tribute to the Calvinist and Jewish contribution to American social thought.

The bishops intend the idea of the covenant to serve as a universal model. A true covenant for them is marked by spiritual faith and psychological hope, and these in turn are expressions of an inner authenticity in the members of the community. "The same God who came to the aid of an oppressed people and formed them into a covenant community continues to hear the cries of the oppressed and to create communities which are to hear his word. God's love and life are present when people can live in a community of faith and hope." The bishops, in other words, see exemplary power in the Messianic currents that moved Israel at the time of Jesus' prophecy, a model for both sacred redemption and secular action. "Our action on behalf of justice in the world proceeds from the conviction that, despite the power of injustice and violence, life has been fundamentally changed by the entry of the Word made flesh into human history." Social engagement, then, rests on a sense of consonance with eschatological process. As for those "surrogates for love and acceptance" offered by what the bishops describe as the consumer society, the bishops hold that the sense of nurture given in the life of a sacramental community can make these superfluous.

Discipleship, at this point in the argument, becomes important. It can open ordinary life, alter it in marketplace and workplace. The bishops, clearly, mean something other than the kind of external affiliation expressed in such practices as the Christian Yellow Pages. Membership in a spiritual community rather than in a material or visible one, whatever its name, is at issue. The bishops refer to the Apostolic age and its immediate sequel, in which Christianity spread amongst the poor of the ancient world. "In the face of poverty and persecution, these disciples continued to transform human lives and to form communities which became signs of the power and presence of God."

For the bishops, then, discipleship is the *via regis* to participation in community and to the solidarity this in turn expresses. Discipleship is the mode of Christian existence, for rich and poor, young and old, man and woman, and (on the model of initial conversion in the early Christian age) Gentile and Jew. For the bishops, further, the poor have a universal role, as a group especially open to discipleship and as a model for the rest of society. The bishops refer to Luke, who depicts Jesus as a prophetic critic of the rich and an advocate of the poor and powerless. The poor, "not blinded by wealth," are free to accept the Gospel, since "human powerlessness makes them a model of those who trust in God alone." The bishops note that the early Christian communities were organized for the welfare of their members and practiced sharing. What impresses them, however, is the emergence in the New Testament of the "righteous poor" and the power of witness of Evangelical poverty.

The poor, unblinded by the temptations of property and wealth, see more clearly. The offer of salvation "calls for an emptying of self, both individually and corporately, that allows the church to experience the power of God in the midst of poverty and powerlessness."

The bishops transmute poverty and powerlessness into themes familiar to us from the contemporary discussion of alienation which, to be sure, has religious components and origins. They argue that even as we live in a very wealthy society, we have every reason to be disturbed not only by the obvious economic disparities between prosperous Americans and those who are obviously not, but by the inner poverty caused by our integration in the American economy. "The image of disciples who 'left all' to follow Jesus is difficult to reconcile with a contemporary ethos that encourages amassing as much as possible." The letter is suffused by the intimation that the psychological and spiritual traits required for survival in middle-class America are far from sublime, but the bishops do not quite address the issue directly. It is possible, after all, that our own structures (incidence and rates) of familial and sexual pathologies, psychosomatic disorders and generalized malaise have less to do with a hypothetical human condition and more with the specific ways in which we have to labor and live.

Perhaps the bishops are, not quite subliminally, aware of a major ambiguity in their letter. If a materially ascetic ideal is the precondition of spiritual plentitude, why their emphasis on redistribution? Would it not be more appropriate to concentrate on the development of new institutions that would facilitate the experience of new qualities in our common life, in our individualized ones, too? The bishops might well reply, with perfect reason, that a certain form of spiritual critique of a materialist civilization ought not to be the exclusive property of those who are well off. If there is a material substratum to reflection on the possibilities of a new spirituality, it ought to be accessible to those who are now poor as well.

In any event, their ethos exhibits at this point a sharp and striking discontinuity. They verge from the question of the spiritual content of our society to the problem of allocation, to the "preferential option for the poor," which they see as an irreducible fundament of any decent politics. "The obligation to provide justice for all means that the poor have the single most urgent claim on the conscience of the nation." No doubt, the bishops see this demand as part of a larger context. The kind of spiritual qualities they seek in society cannot be attained in the absence of justice, which in turn entails solidarity. In placing redistribution at the center of their project, however, the bishops oblige us to confront an entire series of questions; for the moment, two. One is whether our society can be altered in this way, whether it may not engender poverty by virtue of its organization. The other is whether human beings, as constituted in our society, can be persuaded (by religious conviction or otherwise) to elect the option for the poor. Let us begin with human nature in its American form (or, rather, forms) with the discussion of society, which is in fact inseparable from the immediately following discussion of the economy.

HUMAN NATURE AND SOCIETY

To what extent are human beings capable of actualizing in their daily lives the values of community, justice and solidarity espoused by the bishops? The question may be put in a different way: Have the institutions the bishops seek to change so shaped humans to their measure that their moral and factual identification with capitalism precludes major changes?

To a large degree, questions of cognition, of historical and social imagination, confront us. Thinking is supposed to be the vocation of our academy. It is remarkable, however, how much academic thought on society is routinized, stuck to the surface of events. That rather substantial segment of the citizenry without doctorates can hardly be expected, in most cases, to do better. The imagination of a different society fails us, especially in a situation in which no large and persistent social movement conceives of politics as a form of permanent education. Moreover, we know that imagination, in the sense of the ability to think of institutions as differently organized, is not only a matter of cognition; it is also one of volition, of affective engagement. We may be in a vicious circle, in which the absence of a deep demand for change in effect consecrates the institutions in which we live, endows them with spuriously permanent traits.

A fundamental question should disturb us. Recall Sigmund Freud's counterposition in *Civilization and its Discontents* of life instincts to death instincts. He suggested that Eros and Thanatos, whom he described as eternal antagonists, were historically equally balanced. Suppose that humans endure exploitation, misery and tyranny because of inwardly turned aggression? We need not compare our society, with its official if superficial optimism, which, in some respects is an unfortunate derivative of a flattened Protestantism, to such epochal systems of humiliation as Imperial China or Tsarist Russia. Still, across all boundaries, humans have often accepted social contracts on very poor terms. Sometimes, low standards of living were exchanged for protection; at others, psychological tranquility was obtained by declaring the social world immutable. Turned inward or outward, then, and combined or fused with real or imagined advantages, a permanent core of aggression in the human psyche may render the notion of a solidary community implausible. In these matters, there is also a tacit aggressiveness, which consists of doing nothing about the misfortunes of others while enjoying such benefits as one can.

Is this depiction of human nature unduly harsh? It can be softened to La Rochefoucauld's dictim that nothing is easier to bear than the misfortune of others. We may say that the human capacity for love and solidarity diminishes with social distance. That is, perhaps, a tautology; but it encompasses phenomena of particular interest to us. The bishops call for a modern version of discipleship to be effected in every institutional setting. Our own institutions, however, are characterized by the separation of home and workplace, the distinction between familial and occupational ties, or put rather crudely, between love and money. These institutions require different sorts of behavior, generate different and antithetical norms. Not alone do they legitimate lovelessness in one sector; they may well demand it in the name of love in another. The bishops criticize the accumulation of material goods, but for many of our fellow citizens, accumulation is a fulfillment of an obligation to family, a defensive pattern of behavior that seeks to create space for more positive and humane goals.

Consider the bishops' warning against the "temptation to separate the life of the faith and the realm of technical and professional activities." Much modern historical and social thought has taken that separation as its theme, depicting it as the basis of both modern social structure and our putatively rational cultural cosmos. Large-scale organization, scientific inquiry, rational technique in their modern forms (all accompanied by an increasing division of labor) have been attributed to the separation. If Max Weber emphasized the Protestant origins of what he termed the "disenchantment of the world," others before him gave different explanations of the process. Machiavelli's statecraft, indeed, entails the separation of the realm of governance and power from ecclesiastical stewardship: We have to confront a historical phenomenon of which Calvinism was but one expression.

It is perfectly possible (and morally necessary) to ask if the process contains intrinsic limits. The fragmentation of roles in modern industrial society has not quite fragmented the human psyche, but has inflicted wounds on it. How else explain occupationally induced stress and sickness in the economically most advantaged levels of our social system? Aggressiveness and implacable impersonality in the workplace as well as love in the family afford not reasonable variety but pathological alternation. The bishops place themselves on the side of wholeness; their theological beginning point has sane psychological ends. We do not find in the letter, however, much indication that the bishops have reflected deeply on the problem of the selection by modern societies of precisely those persons with highly aggressive, competitive and manipulative personalities for posts that bring the largest economic and political rewards. The values they contest, then, are doubly difficult to transform since they are incorporated in the personalities of those who also serve as role models in much of the society. To be sure, American society is not totally dominated by these values. Consider the preference of some American ethnic groups, usually Catholic, for the market-immune benefits of civil service jobs. Consider, too, the enormous and diffuse interest in psychological growth. We may regard much of the movement as exhibiting a very attenuated spirituality, but there can be little doubt about its search for a definition of self and others in terms not dictated by the market. It is true that Christopher Lasch has written of the "consumption of the self" and portrayed much of the psychological growth movement as permeated by the values it ostensibly opposes. That may be true, however, of most movements of this sort.

The bishops make no mention, additionally, of an important theme in recent inquiries into the values of industrial society—the complex of attitudes and behavior termed postmaterialist. To summarize, postmaterialist values reflect an understandable desire to work less and enjoy more. What is at issue, however, is the precise nature of that enjoyment. The bearers of these values seek intrinsic personal satisfaction, a fuller sense of self and others, and eschew rigid attachment to career goals in conflict with these extra-occupational gains. The postmaterialists who can afford their new values usually come from the managerial and professional middle classes, although some evidence suggests their spread to younger white collar and manual workers. Postmaterialism has been connected with the newer forms of social criticism found in the environment, consumer and peace movements. Its potential for privatization, however, is not small. It can also be asked whether the postmaterialists expend much of their ample energy and time worrying about the plight of those who cannot think about a better use of their leisure since they lack work, or those who have work but lack the capacity for criticism that the postmaterialists take for granted.

With regard to social perception, we live in a divided society in which allocation by price separates associations, communities, neighborhoods and workplaces. "The other America" of which Michael Harrington wrote 25 years ago and the "invisible poor" are identical. Solidarity depends on an effort of recognition. President Reagan's absurd insistence that unemployment statistics cannot be true because he reads "help wanted" advertisements in newspapers no doubt bespeaks his own intellectual limitations, but it coincides with attitudes widely distributed in the population. The effort of recognition presupposes a capacity to identify with others who are very different, and to do so in a society in which some differences are frightening because they remind us of the fragility of our own positions.

The bishops ask that Americans develop "the inner freedom to resist the temptation to seek more." Quite apart from the institutional constraints that in American society do not favor the predominance of human traits of this sort, the bishops raise larger and as yet unanswered quesions about human nature. Can humans develop the characterological flexibility, the inner strength, the independence of authoritarianism, to participate critically in decision making? It is true that human history, and indeed our own society in its present form, shows no one modal character type. It is also true that the introduction into our society of the moral dimensions sought by the bishops challenges elites whose very identities are organized around the values the bishops seek to alter. No human is an island, and the most competitive or ruthless personality no doubt has, if not a heart of gold, a twinge of doubt, a longing for some other pattern of feeling. The making of the earth into a human home is a project Christianity shares with at least one of its great secular successors, Western socialism. Readers will have no difficulty in discerning the influence of that tradition on the following analysis of the bishops' view of society.

The bishops' conception of society, it should be remembered, is not abstract or mechanistic. They conceive of it as a set of human institutions that, made by humankind, can also be remade. This is a consequence of their belief that the confinement of the Christian life to formally religious settings is too limited. The symbolic reenactment of the Eucharist in small settings is for them a call to carry the Word of God into actual human history.

The bishops begin, in effect, with the internationalization of national societies. The visible and invisible connections between nations in fact erase boundaries, render our conceptions and rhetoric out of date, enlarge our responsibilities and, alas, diminish our possibilities of action. Our awareness of the structures and processes of the new global society is confused and indistinct. Thirty-second television images of poverty and revolution, turbulence and routine, in distant and unfamiliar places, constitute no substitute for an understanding, for example, of economic problems in the poorer societies. Those who do not grasp the interconnections between their own situation and the workings of a centralized economy in the United States cannot apprehend the content of such arcane phenomena as export and import prices, currency ratios, the international commodity market, the role of the World Bank and the International Monetary Fund.

The bishops themselves seem to find the problem of dealing with the new international system difficult. Indeed, they do not approach it as a system. They refer to the fact that the United States (and, of course, the other industrial nations) are rich, the others poor. The notion of the United States as a capitalist metropolis, which leaves to other parts of the world a provincial role, is missing. So, to a large extent, is an analysis of the extreme international economic competition that sets our nation now against Japan, now against the European community, now against the new industrial nations with their cheap labor forces. Their perspective is curiously additive. On the one hand, they depict the American economy. On the other, they refer to international disparities of income and wealth. They do not systematically connect the two, however much they sense the existence of a factual connection and insist on the necessity of a moral one.

The bishops suggest that there are three actors in the international field: nations, multinational corporations and multinational institutions (such as the World Bank). The idea of "actors"—a term familiar enough from political science—is itself questionable. It entails a personalization, a reification, of complex institutional relationships that are endowed with a spurious finality and simplicity. No doubt there is an international system of exchange and power, with circuits and nodal points of concentration. The "nation" of Zaire is a loose assemblage of tribal groups united in common servitude to international capital and exploited directly by its own elite, such as it is. To a remarkable extent, we could also describe Zaire's former imperial proprietor, Belgium, as a set of quarreling ethnic groups united in common subordination to multinational capital. The "nation" of the Union of South Africa is integrated in the international economy, but this lends even more complexity to the task of analyzing the balance of class and racial organization in its social structure.

Perhaps it is the very complexity of depicting relationships of this sort that induces the bishops to revert to the rhetoric of "perception"—a term used by second-rate journalists and third-rate social scientists to avoid thinking about the structure of reality. Where all is "perception," nothing is true or false. The bishops suggest that the poor peoples of the world "perceive" themselves as dependent on the industrial nations. That "perception" may be the result of systematic political enlightenment or indoctrination, a clear sense of fundamental relationships or a confused search for a historical alibi, or a construction by analysts lacking analytical capacity. "Perception" may well be a poor man's version of the theory of ideology, but the concept of ideology has at least the advantage of relating the thought of given groups to their historical situation, and of trying to assess the functions of that thought in terms of group purpose and its validity in terms of the theorist's own view of the structure of the whole. Fortunately, for the far greater part of the letter, the bishops for better or for worse do write as if they were describing a unitary structure of reality (however complex) and relegate the rhetoric of "perception" to the obscurity it merits. It is quite clear from the balance of the text that the bishops think the poor nations are dependent on the industrialized ones. This phrase may well conceal far more than it illuminates; dependence is a relationship in which the weak are not without actual or potential strengths. It does not, however, relegate a structure of exploitation to the status of an ephemeral opinion.

The bishops also criticize the criterion of "national security" as a standard for the American evaluation of our relationship to the poorer nations. This is connected to the general (and recurrent) theme in the letter of wasteful (or at least, excess) military expenditure. The criticism is in fact a criticism of the militarization of our social thought, or more accurately, of its integration in an imperial cast of mind. Here, the bishops touch on themes found in the reports of both the Brandt and Palme Commissions, reports that seek under the rubric of "common security" to develop a realistic calculus of the mutual interdependence of global society, or rather, its component parts. The bishops imply that in the long run, our security depends on a certain pacification of the earth, the conversion of the globe into a human home for all of us. Here, however, they do not deal with the dimension of time. An increase in the standard of living of the poorer nations and the kinds of qualitative and quantitative changes in the allocation of income and property within the richer ones the bishops desire, would take time—generations rather than decades— whatever dramatic beginnings may be made now. The beneficiaries might well be our grandchildren. Even dealing with domestic reallocation, the bishops do not give much weight to the heavy problems of intergenerational relations. Edith Brown Weiss has applied the notion of a trust in common law to the idea that any given generation holds the planet in trust from past generations for future ones. She suggests that the idea may well serve as a device to ensure due attention to environmental fragility. The bishops deal with this and other structural matters in the following terms: "We believe that the ethical norms we have applied to domestic economic questions are equally valid here. As in other economic matters, the basic questions are: (a) Who benefits from the particular policy measure, and (b) how can any benefit or adverse impact be equitably shared?"

Suppose, however, that structural alterations are dealt with for which no immediate measure of benefits and costs is applicable, since the consequences will be experienced in the future. Suppose too, that those people affected have very different beginning points so that equitable sharing among them is very difficult. On a somewhat mechanical cost–benefit analysis, the bishops superimpose a set of moral injunctions. They generalize the preferential option for the poor to the international sphere. The bishops are somewhat more structural in their thought when they reflect on the many dimensions of foreign investment that may reinforce patterns of inequality in the recipient nation as well as increase them in the investing one. Their thought does not, however, adhere to a rigorously structural plane. When they envisage altering a historical system such as the United States, with its established ideological and value systems, its intricately connected system of conflict and consensus, their discourse returns to that individuation of morality that is, indeed, the bane of a version of American Protestantism.

The bishops appeal to persons rather than groups, to psychic sensibilities, without thinking about the need to alter the broader ideologies that make these coherent. They seek to change behavioral patterns rather than the jagged combinations of constraints and inducements that constitute immediate social contexts. It is surprising that these theologians, exquisitely attuned to the invisible dimensions of spiritual existence, underestimate the invisible dimensions of social existence. The accumulated historicity of institutions, the ways in which these capture or predetermine moral socialization—not least, by forming family structures—lie behind the immediate functioning of a society. Another way to describe the situation is to say that function and history are inseparable, that the past is incorporated in the present.

The bishops' view of American society is singularly static and tied to a society ruled by the consensual politics of 1945–1965, of which President Lyndon Johnson's Great Society program was the last large expression. The industrial component in our economy has declined since, bringing with it a decline in the influence of the unions and the Democratic Party. Meanwhile, the nation's position in the world market has altered as other economies have become more competitive. An increase in employment in the tertiary sector and a large increase in the number of working women have been accompanied by a decline in real income for a majority of those in the labor force. The bishops' injunctions to share ignore the fact that, however much income and property may have increased at the top of the society, there is less to share for groups that had previously counted on a rising standard of living. The new American society is more receptive to Social Darwinism because it finds itself in a global economic struggle, quite apart from the geopolitical and military aspects of the U.S. confrontation with the U.S.S.R. and assorted national liberation and revolutionary movements. The arms budget, an important immediate stabilizing element in the economy, whatever its long-term consequences for the decline and distortion of our infrastructure, refracts much of the situation, but it seems to have a self-perpetuating capacity of an autonomous kind. The bishops place their hopes for justice quite explicitly on something approaching full employment, or at least a revival of that social contract that marked the earlier or consensual phase of the postwar epoch. That, however, is the American society, which has changed fundamentally: The new structure is inextricably connected to changes in the economy.

THE ECONOMY

To begin, there is the question of psychic economy, as relevant here as in the discussion of the bishops' conception of human nature. The bishops, epistemologically and morally, oppose "pure" economic reasoning. They do not mention but no doubt can see little use in the intellectually impoverished reductionism by which a Gary Becker or a Richard Posner seek to apprehend human phenomena. Human nature and society cannot be explained in terms of a cost–benefit calculus and, let it be said, neither can the working of economic institutions. The recent prominence of this aridly improbable account of the social world, the academic equivalent of the success enjoyed by Ayn Rand, requires an explanation.

Are there periodic alternations, from one epoch to another, in the balance of attachment and narcissism, solidarity and egoism, love and selfishness? Different, even antithetical, ideologies strike virtually the same population as "right" within very short periods of time, "right" in the sense of that apprehension of aesthetic wholeness and moral fitness evoked by the bishops in their definition of justice. Paul Hazard has remarked that at the beginning of the eighteenth century in France, no cultivated person did not believe in providence, but at the end of it, no cultivated person did. Surprisingly little is known in detail about the mechanisms by which these large spiritual changes take place; not even much about the precise relationship of ideology to psychology in the matter is known. There are very penetrating studies of particular sequences and such general works as Karl Mannheim's *Ideology and Utopia,* but each sort of work sensitizes one to the kinds of forces likely to be found in new cases, no more. Given the nature of the social sciences, that is all for which one can hope. If each historical situation has its own structure, the application of general analytical and moral ideas to it must sooner rather than later encounter limits. The range of possible American responses to the new economic and social problems we face, then, is not infinitely open—it must draw on the spiritual resources and structures (one could also say, ideological and psychological currents) of our period. The bishops do not confront these matters directly, just as they do not confront the "historical accumulation" on the level of social functioning. At times, this leads them to a condensation, even a foreshortening, of perspective.

They suggest that even a short while ago, a jobless rate of 7 percent of the labor force would have been "intolerable." That was surely true of the Kennedy–Johnson period, but President Roosevelt's Committee on Economic Security, which proposed Social Security legislation, gave an 8 percent jobless rate as normal for the prosperous decade 1920–1930. Suppose the relative prosperity of the period 1945–1965 was a historical exception, given the propensity of capitalist economies to produce unemployment. Indeed, there is no reason to suppose that only capitalism produces unemployment. There is plenty of poorly disguised unemployment in the U.S.S.R., and the state socialist economies face accelerated and perhaps permanent technological unemployment, as does ours. The bishops are thoroughly American when they envisage a linear conception of economic and moral progress. Suppose, again, that history does not consist of straight lines and that the kinds of material accumulation that would easily allow the concern for others central to the bishops' morality is not now possible.

The bishops recognize that we do not begin with a new society. Unlike the self-interested humans in John Rawls' *Theory of Justice,* we do not operate behind a veil of ignorance. We live in a society with fixed interests. "The concentration of privilege that exists today results far more from institutional relationships that distribute power and wealth inequitably than from differences in talent or lack of desire to work." The bishops seek, in these circumstances, not an arithmetic equality they deem neither desirable nor necessary, but a decent minimum of income for all, a minimum demanded by our respect for persons and the claims of solidarity. Decent minima, however, are culturally and historically variable. Further, the connection of income to work poses problems in the large middle ranges of American society, where tens of millions of Americans have made the connection between work and reward a central component of their own self-respect.

The bishops suggest that work has three meanings: the satisfaction of material needs, self-expression and a contribution to society. Analytically, this may very well be so. Empirically, many Americans do not make such distinctions. Proposals for a minimal income that would separate income from work, if necessary, would not treat persons by virtue of their productivity in material terms, but as brothers and sisters in need. The resistance to welfare, to programs like Aid to Families with Dependent Children, has been manipulated by politicians (including the present president) with more cynicism than humanity. The American public is clearly not prepared to dismantle the welfare state. Nonetheless, a considerable amount of ground is to be covered before the work ethos internalized by industrializing America in the nineteenth century is transformed into something viable for the twenty-first and more constant with the demands of social solidarity.

The bishops, meanwhile, call for the triple functions of work to be made visible in the work of all, "no matter what their role in the marketplace: blue-collar workers, managers, homemakers, politicians," as well as in communities and corporations. Regarding corporations, it is true that management is often interested in job enrichment or the humanization of work. It is sometimes thought to increase productivity in a measurable way. At other times, managers wish to be thought of as socially responsible, and some indeed actually wish to think of themselves in this way. They are obliged to work through their institution, however, and that entails severe limits on departures from the criteria of profitability.

American institutions, and not least the economic ones, are functionally specific. Talcott Parsons treated this in his own vocabulary, drawing on Weber's analysis of rationalization in Western social structure. Mannheim, quite different from Parsons in his politics, also drew on Weber in his distinction between functional and substantive rationality. Functional rationality served a narrow and predetermined institutional end, while substantive rationality was the result of choice and reflection, in which institutional function was measured by a purposefully examined canon. The bishops seek to provide our economy with criteria of human wholeness. They ask "blue-collar workers, managers, homemakers, politicians" to consider the moral dimensions of their tasks, but underestimate the extent to which we are all prisoners of what Weber termed the "iron cage," the institutionally generated system of constraints that constitutes the organization of Western capitalism. The bishops follow Pope Leo XIII *(Rerum Novarum)* in declaring that workers are not merely factors of production, they are persons. They see that arguments for the welfare state that stress its functions in guaranteeing social peace and, even more, expanding the domestic market, are at times fragile. In a period of economic constraint, social peace may have to be sacrificed to maintain the profitability of capital. The weakness of the American unions, quantitatively, has obliged them to retreat in unionized industries when threatened with large-scale closures. In such a society as the German Federal Republic in which, through its allied political party, the Social Democrats, the unions are far stronger (both quantitatively and qualitatively), large-scale capital has deliberately broken the social peace by altering the law regulating the payment of unemployment assistance in the case of strikes. The bishops' argument for the welfare state (and for a social contract) rests on their insistence on the absolute moral value of the person. This insistence is immune to arguments about profitability, but may well have the function of moral resistance rather than of indicating precise institutional modes for defending that moral value.

The bishops come closer to an institutional critique in their depiction of property as held in trust. No doubt a view of trusteeship could be promulgated in which the return on capital was calculated on a different time scale and considered in light of different criteria of ultimate allocation. "The use of financial resources solely in pursuit of short-term profits can stunt the production of needed goods and services: A broader vision of managerial responsibility is needed." The bishops' criticism of the short-term vision of American managers is different from that of the kinds of critics who write for the scholarly journals published by our schools of business administration. These suggest that the long-term profitability of American enterprise is insufficiently pursued by managers under pressure to demonstrate profitability in very short runs. The bishops propose a very different notion of profitability, assenting to Pope John Paul II's approval of the propriety of socializing, in some circumstances, "certain means of production." The present disposition in our political system to entertain notions of this sort is extremely limited, except for the permanent if unacknowledged socialization of large sectors of the arms industry through the Pentagon budget. Here and there in the universities and in reflective segments of the labor movement is a readiness to consider socialization a plausible option. Elsewhere, a concatenation of circumstances works against it, from the limited success of state socialist models to the absence of a public capacity for thinking beyond the narrow limits of present political discussion.

The bishops, then, seem to be limited to appealing to the private sector to work for the common good and to asking under what conditions it can be induced to do so. It is here that they deal with the economic functions of government, taking a positive view of its potential for assisting in the attainment of a "more just economy." They seem to understand government as a mediative institution, as an "indispensable forum" for political debate on the "conflicts and tradeoffs" of a humane and reasonable economic policy. The bishops are clear, of course, that government does have enormous functions in the present economy, including those of reallocation and steering. The letter, however, does not attempt to reassess the functions of the federal government in the years in which there was a somewhat successful version of a mixed economy—a reassessment that could serve as a preliminary to a new conception of its limits and possibilities. This is all the more surprising in view of the large and insistent literature on such questions as deregulation, which would have us believe that the American economy was a fettered colossus until 1981.

In fact, of course, through politics, the American financial and industrial elite exercises larger influence on government economic policy no matter which party is in power. That pressure does not by any means take the form of demanding an end to, or serious diminuition of, government intervention. It consists, rather, in giving that intervention (Federal Reserve policy, fiscal structure, the administration of antitrust and the policies of regulating agencies) a content favorable to the private sector, and conflicting interests in the private sector regard it as normal to use government intervention against each other. The letter, then, appears to move on an intellectual plane in which a debate extending from such early figures as John Commons and Thorsten Veblen, through Adolf Berle and Gardiner Means to John Kenneth Galbraith and such more recent thinkers as Arthur Okun and James O'Connor is not fully used. The actual question is not whether we should have government intervention, but of what kind and with what end and through which instruments. The bishops know this, but hesitate unduly about proceeding to sketch alternate and fuller uses of government.

The bishops attach primary importance to the "principle of subsidiarity," which limits governments to doing what individuals and private groups cannot do independently. Cannot this principle, however, be deformed to legitimate the sovereignty of private groups usurping public functions? The bishops have anticipated the question. "The principle of subsidiarity guarantees intellectual pluralism, providing space for freedom, initiative and creativity. It does not, however, support the view that government that governs least governs best." The bishops do not quite deal with the problem that our institutional system may restrict the values they honor, that the concentration of economic power and the dispersion of political power may combine to allow the homogenization of large areas of our society. After all, elsewhere in the letter, the bishops complain about what could be crudely termed consumption as a way of life. The principle of subsidiarity assumes what it is very difficult to assert about our society—that it allows autonomous value development and its institutionalization. Instead, the industrial fabrication of a culture (in itself a large-scale segment of our industry) takes value creation out of the hands of smaller groups. The complaints of the evangelical Protestants about the allegedly liberal media are in some measure, perhaps, paranoid, but it can hardly be denied there is a problem of cultural fabrication. Finally, how would the bishops deal with a recurrent dilemma of reform? In order to create free space for pluralism, central power sometimes has to be used.

Given their views on the importance of work to the moral (and therefore psychic) economies of persons, the bishops emphasize the importance of full employment. It is also, they say, a defense against poverty in an economy in which so few can own productive property. They do not pause here to consider devices for the diffusion of property ownership, such as the Meidner plan in Sweden, by which workers through their unions would gradually acquire ownership rights in the companies for which they labor. They do not ask if European devices for joint control in industry (like codetermination in Germany) have been successful, and how these might be transposed to the United States. They do see employment as a basic right, but are apparently unconvinced that there are certain ways to guarantee it. They seek full employment without inflation, but do not refer to studies by Fritz Scharf and others that show this is most often attained when strong unions and social democratic parties can negotiate and administer national social contracts covering the critical and dominant sectors of a national economy.

The bishops favor creating public jobs as a last resort, but in noting that 80 percent of recent job creation was in the private sector, do they not open the way for the reemergence of a notion of second-class economic citizenship for those in the public sector? The point has general implications; the bishops find it difficult, however much they are in principle prepared to consider new institutions, to move away from the model of government-stimulated private economic growth of the past decades. They do seek investment in our crumbling infrastructure, the expansion of employment in the social services and the helping professions and a new housing program. They make it clear they are not offering a "technical blueprint for economic reform." To some extent, however, one must inquire if their moral energies have been matched by programmatic ones of equivalent persuasive force.

The bishops argue that arms spending seriously distorts our economy. Here, they refer to the argument of their 1983 letter, *The Challenge of Peace.* The question of these distortions is not met, however, by an appeal to a different kind of economic rationality alone. The distortions are produced by interest aggregates pursuing an explicit political strategy. Purposive elite strategies, the manipulation of public ignorance, the cultivation of public anxiety and fear are at the basis of the foreign policies that require a grotesquely swollen arms budget. Our society is organized to a considerable degree by the struggle for global hegemony and by the institutions that direct that struggle. The term "military-industrial complex" coined by Malcolm Moos for Dwight Eisenhower is too limited. To that complex must be added large parts of the academy, of our political elite. Economic gain and national security, however imprecise or systematically deformed the two sides of the equation, are conjoined in a cost–benefit analysis that was made quite explicit at the beginning of what is termed the Cold War. When Paul Nitze as a senior official in the Truman Administration drafted National Security Memorandum 68, the charter document of our foreign policy for the past four decades, he was assisted by the then Chairman of the Council of Economic Advisors Leon Keyserling. Keyserling, close to the unions and influential in the formulation of the Full Employment Act, held that a major world role for the United States was the precondition of domestic prosperity.

The subsequent policies of the Democratic Party, and especially its welfare state component, with adamant support from the AFL–CIO, are evidence that its leaders thought the welfare state at home was at the very least consonant with global engagement and a very high military budget. Indeed, a distinguished historian of recent foreign policy, John Gaddis, suggests that as the party of disinflation and fiscal restraint, the Republicans were in practice more hesitant about these budgets and foreign engagement. President Reagan has clearly broken with this Republican tendency, and his economic policy may fairly be described as military Keynesianism. Perhaps that accounts for the present retroactive approval of Eisenhower from groups and persons who 30 years ago were hardly sympathetic to his presidency. No doubt, the present president seems (sublimely or otherwise) unaware of the fact that the increased military expenditures of his administration compensate for lessened social expenditure. He can hardly be unaware of the employment and profits provided by arms expenditure, a point made by his administration to win support for its program for arms in space.

Ideologies condense or crystallize complex socioeconomic programs in ways that bespeak poetry rather than sociological discourse. The more naive (or unthinking) the poet, the more authentic the impression, which is another way of explaining Ronald Reagan's "sincerity." Many of the obstacles to the kind of new economic rationality the bishops seek are ideological and psychological. Welfare state expenditure increases the purchasing power of groups suffering from chronic underemployment or unemployment. It may avoid complete social disintegration in our cities and the poorer parts of the countryside. It may, therefore, be indispensable to maintaining or even ultimately increasing the living standard of employed workers taxed to pay for it. They, however, do not see this connection. They are so attached to notions of the connection between income and work that the thought of subsidizing those who do not work strikes them as violating some law of social nature, as well as an attack on the sources of their own self-esteem. In any event, the bishops deal insufficiently with the problem of the abstract or invisible nature of causality in these matters and with the pauperization of public discourse about them.

In dealing with the incidence of poverty, the bishops draw on familiar evidence to suggest that it falls disproportionately on women and children, on blacks and Hispanics. Still, one out of nine white Americans is poor, not an entirely invisible group, but concentrated in certain regions, states, neighborhoods and sectors of society. Men as opposed to women and whites as opposed to blacks enjoy substantial economic advantages from discrimination. The accumulated and fused ideological and psychological factors that account for racism and sexism possess a historical inertia, a substance of their own. Over 40 years ago, in *An American Dilemma,* Gunnar Myrdal proposed an economic strategy to overcome racism—a gradual increase in the economic level, and therewith social acceptability, of the blacks. Parts of the American black community are now economically integrated and as prosperous as many sectors of the white community, but racism persists. Is it because so many blacks are poor, a condition taken by racists as so threatening that they must believe it was somehow brought upon themselves by the impoverished? Sexism persists, often in the most pervasive and subtle ways. Since blacks and women (and the poor, of any color and sex) are undervalued, the bishops may in the end prove right about their moral appeal. Only the force of morality may overcome by dissolving hardened structures that serve to keep others at a moral distance in such a way as to deny or minimize their common humanity.

The bishops are aware that economic standards change, that much is relative in our judgment of economic life. Church teaching, they remind us, allows for differences of income within a generally just framework of distribution. There is a psychoanalytic phrase about the narcissism of small differences. Even these (small when viewed historically or globally) may serve as foci of invidious distinctions that can preclude solidarity or make its attainment doubly or trebly difficult (think of the England of V. S. Pritchett or E. M. Forster, the America of John O'Hara). Let us assume that national income increases, so that all the income and property groups remain in the same relative position. The effort to increase national wealth, the effort to retain acquired advantages, may divert moral and political energies from common tasks; it may indeed prevent the idea of common tasks from becoming salient. Here, the bishops' reliance on redistribution rather than on new structures of the common life causes problems. In the *Monthly Review,* the editors (who can hardly be taxed with excessive ideological service to capitalism) have just argued that the recent expansion of financial services has prevented depression. The values that expansion engenders are probably far from congenial to the bishops.

Briefly, the bishops move uncertainly from criteria of economic justice in a quantitative sense to qualitative judgments of institutions (actual or possible) on no very steady course. Enough material goods in the hands of those now without them will enable them to participate more fully in the life of our society. That life, however, is marred by its pursuit of highly instrumental values rather than by common purposes. In individualized and egotistical fashion, its members pursue material gain, and their energies are not directed to the communal and social values the bishops favor. The bishops would have done well to consider the fusion of the idea of material accumulation and spiritual enlargement in the idea of progress in its conventional form (recall Spencer's very positive reception in late nineteenth century America.) These ideas may well infuse economic thinking; consider such a title as *The Wealth of Nations,* or the term "welfare economics." Brecht was right when, in rather close imitation of Engels' graveside eulogy of Marx, he declared that first comes eating, then morality. The proposition taken alone, however, can for all of its realism lead to an arid or arrogant Social Darwinism.

The bishops wish to make more jobs available to cure poverty and its ensuing social disenfranchisement. The full integration of the poor in the economic system might turn them, however, into the kinds of persons the bishops think require a good deal of spiritual improvement. Again, the bishops are caught between their reliance on absolute increases in the quantity of goods and the standard of living, and their desire for different sorts of human institutions and relationships. They recognize, for instance, that the movement of women into the labor force is for the time being irreversible; they call for improved parental leave arrangements and day care services. What, however, about the consequences for character formation because of this new development in the labor force? It may be that closeness between child and parent is worth more, culturally and socially, than immediate income improvements, and that a mother's allowance or salary ought to be paid directly to women who remain home for the first few years of their children's lives.

The bishops favor the retention of family farms as a social form with its own values, but they also wish for the kind of high agricultural productivity usually made possible by larger units. They suggest that small farmers are not as ruthlessly market-minded as large agricultural corporations. Did not, however, small farmers burden themselves with debt to take advantage of the expected increase in land prices, and so arrive in many instances at their present financially critical state? This episode suggests that our nation is dominated by a set of social values that does not respect size, leaves few or no enclaves in society and may have to be taken (or rejected) as a whole.

As an antidote, the bishops offer the notion of stewardship, a useful Calvinist notion in its original form, but not invariably discernible in the behavior of our economic and political elites. They do not bring the idea of stewardship into direct connection with that of subsidiarity, except for the implication that if stewardship functions well, subsidiarity is made considerably more plausible. On the international plane, they have doubts, and cite Pope John XXIII on international economic structures that no longer correspond to "the objective requirements of the universal common good."

In response, the bishops ask for self-restraint and self-criticism by all parties, traits that would imply a common structure of moral discourse when precisely the problem is that arriving at one is so difficult in the light of antagonistic interests and organized inequalities. The bishops suggest that nationally and internationally, the teaching of Jesus is that "the concept of neighbor is without limit." The trouble is, the concept is so limitedly accepted.

RIGHTS AND POLITICS

Finally, there is the bishops' conception of economic rights and the question of the political strategy that could consolidate (or, indeed, bring into being) these rights. Do the bishops have a way out of the iron cage?

The notion of economic institutions at the service of a nation is a sublime one, but it ignores two major aspects of our culture. One is the identification by millions of persons with the economic institutions that confront them. They internalize their standards, measure themselves in terms set by these institutions. The other is blocked access to the means of critical reflectiveness. It has already been suggested that our professors do poorly enough in envisaging alternative social arrangements. It is not surprising that those without so many cultural resources find it difficult to escape, intellectually, the constraints of daily life. No doubt a good deal of disrespect for authority, a hard human capacity to see things in their nakedness, characterizes many Americans, and it is a legitimate source of our national pride. It generates, alas, no new social project and all too often degenerates into a bitter privatization.

The bishops, then, in insisting on the compelling power of values other than those produced by or consonant with the market, neglect to ask themselves if American society allows autonomous moral decision, or enough of it to make a transformation of values a plausible moral and political project. Solidarity is a virtue enjoined by Christianity and other major religions as well as by the tradition of secular Enlightenment. Solidarity unconnected to concrete, immediate and visible institutional roles is difficult to attain by those who are not moral virtuosos. Did not Brecht have Galileo say, "Pity the land that needs heroes?" Consider the difficulties of extending the notion of citizenship across borders. Take the case of Western Europe. The West Europeans, particularly the French and Germans, have finally reached the conclusion that neighboring nations may be human after all. They are not prepared to extend the compliment to North Africans or Turks, and in Italy, there are still difficulties for the Sicilians.

Solidarity, urged by the bishops on the larger society as a major organizing principle, seems to work best in smaller, more familiar and intimate settings. Michael Walzer dealt with this systematically in his *Spheres of Justice,* in which he argued that universalism had to be tempered by recognition of the local, nay, tribal, structure of much of our existence. The problem is especially acute in such a nation as our own, in which national identity coexists uneasily with ethnic, religious and regional differences of a profound kind. That a society so divided can move readily to dismantle and transcend class barriers is improbable, given that these barriers are constituted by a peculiar combination of aggregated interests and psychocultural values. The weight of our social historical experience bears heavily on us. Here, we may understand the bishops' letter as a contribution to an American future that still has some openness, some indeterminacy, some chance for a change for the better, despite what may be conceived as the accumulative processes of American history and their constraining character.

One of the more vulgar features of current discussion of political and social issues is a tendentious use of the term "mainstream" to fix the contours of the discourse. It is a pseudohistorical term, since the process of locating the "mainstream" extrapolates from a superficial reading of the present to a narrow prediction of the future. An unavowed ideological intent almost invariably marks the use the word; the users situate themselves, with no excess of modesty, at the center of history and relegate others to the periphery. The bishops' insistence on the force of moral argument puts them in an American tradition of swimming against the "mainstream," a tradition of prophecy with many Protestant, and for that matter, Jewish and secular exemplars. Countercyclical thought is no less real than an anxious effort to adapt to what is taken to be inevitable.

The bishops have done us a large favor by thinking countercyclically. The trouble is, they are not quite clear about the limits of what they are doing, and so insufficiently distinguish between the analytic and the prophetic dimensions of their own thought. The way prophecy enters the analytical canon, to be sure, is not linear. The bishops do not suffer from any lack of inner conviction, and in a message addressed to the rest of society, they would heighten their pedagogic effect by consistent and thorough adherence to the note of intellectual caution they themselves supply. They proceed from firm moral and theological foundations to spheres in which their thought is far more tentative. Indeed, the pedagogic effect in the best case would be larger for those who make matters too simple for themselves by insulating these spheres from one another.

Pope John XXIII in *Pacem in Terris,* they observe, asked that human rights be conceived in terms of economic rights, too. "We believe, therefore, that these economic rights should be granted a status in the cultural and legal traditions of this nation analogous to that held by the civic and political rights to freedom of religion, speech and assembly." President Franklin Roosevelt himself attempted in his idea of Four Freedoms to incorporate economic minima in a new American canon. In addition, if we think back to such figures as Wendell Phillips or John Dewey, the connection between economic and human rights has been a persistent theme in both American radicalism and social reform. Basic ideas of rights, however, are matters that require ideological and intellectual roots in society as well as formal discussion. They are not institutionalized by a grant of status, but are institutionalized when they already possess status. The desperation or fanaticism with which important groups in our nation now argue that the American regulatory and welfare state is alien to our traditions suggests that the polarization of debate on these matters is acute. It is certainly not new, and what is so helpful about the bishops' letter is the matter of fact tone with which they refuse concessions to what is a contemporary attempt to fabricate a false view of our history. That much said, one must also observe that the opponents of economic rights (except for those that attach to possession of property) have the advantage for the moment of working in alliance with major power groups in our society. The chances of another forward thrust in social reform of the sort advocated by the bishops depend on politics, in the large sense of a conception of our common life and the practice of it.

The bishops' ethical framework is strongest in stating general principles. "First are the duties all people have to each other and to the whole community: love of neighbor, the basic requirements of justice and the special obligation to those who are poor or vulnerable. Corresponding to these duties are the human rights of every person; the obligation to protect the dignity of all demands respect for these rights. Finally, these duties and rights suggest several priorities that should guide the economic choices of individuals, communities and the nation as a whole." These precepts are not linked to definite character structures, communal organizations, or economic institutions. They provide very general, possibly too general, standards by which these may be judged. Without intending to do so, have the bishops in their own thought reproduced that separation of ethics from economics and politics they so rightly deplore?

The basic requirements of justice, as well as the consonance of duties and rights, are historically variable. In the most influential of recent treatises on justice, John Rawls thought it best to revert to the intellectual device of most theorists of the social contract—to posit an initial equality of starting position. Historically, of course, the problem is how to overcome (or minimize) structural inequalities that either reproduce themselves or even tend to increase. "Dignity" is, no less than justice, a concept that requires specification. The bishops oppose to a notion of dignity derived from economic function (a notion not necessarily confined to capitalist economies), an idea of dignity dictating economic function. They attempt to make things more precise by introducing a number of dimensions into their idea of justice. They distinguish between the norm of reciprocity, attached to what they term commutative justice, and a social justice, society's obligation to enable individuals to participate. Distributive justice enters as a different sort of relationship.

Clearly, the bishops cannot and do not content themselves with abstract argument, the making of distinctions on a plane removed from the complexity and contradictions of social life. They do proceed to proposals that go beyond the preferential option for the poor. They do not, unfortunately, deal with a fundamental political difficulty in their conception of rights. If the preferential option for the poor is made the major standard of policy, an appeal to the immediate interests of the rest of society is either neglected or reduced to secondary status. A moral or moralizing politics becomes dominant. No doubt there are interests, for example, the question of social stability, the advantages to be derived from increasing the standard of living of a large segment of the population, that attach to the option for the poor. These may or may not be immediately evident to others in the society, particularly large numbers who are haunted, consciously or not, by the threat of poverty or of social degradation. Our historical experience, however, reminds us of the late Knute Rockne's response to a journalist's question about what he thought of the fact that nuns living near Notre Dame regularly prayed for the success of the football teams he coached. The prayers, he said, invariably worked better when the line was heavier. Moral appeals are often most effective when integrated with a comprehensive view of society that includes a direct statement from those appealed to of their interests. It is the fusion of factual prediction and moral prophecy, indeed, which gives compelling force to historically effective ideologies.

The bishops' own analysis insists on the inner impoverishment, the lowered quality of life, produced by the social roles imposed by market capitalism in its American form. If the analysis is correct, it can serve as the beginning of the construction of a coalition uniting the poor and the ostensibly privileged. The privileged, to be sure, are also menaced by the uncontrolled uncertainties of the business cycle, by the environmental depredation entailed by unregulated capitalism, and are subject as consumers to exploitation and fraud in a systematic way. Moreover, among those adhering most firmly to an ethos of work, the parasitic and speculative aspects of the new American capitalism can hardly evoke enthusiasm. What do the bishops propose by way of a coalition that would unite these disparate groups and themes?

Here, they begin with a citation from the present pope. "The needs of the poor take priority over the desires of the rich; the rights of workers over the maximization of profits; the preservation of the environment over uncontrolled industrial expansion; production to meet social needs over production for military purposes." The bishops recall the American experiment in promulgating civic and political rights. "We believe that the time has come for a similar experiment in securing economic rights: the creation of an order that guarantees the minimum conditions of human dignity in the economic sphere for every person." The consolidation of the rights promised by the Declaration of Independence and the Constitution took time and much conflict, including a civil war. In this case, the bishops think rather ahistorically, making suggestions that resemble an unconnected list of proposals rather than a coherent program. The reason may very well be their renunciation of the effort to construct a common economic denominator across class lines. Perhaps that should be amended. The impoverished and those who for the moment are working (even, to be sure, major parts of the managerial, professional and technical labor force) are in fact different segments of one class working for capital. There is no prevalent American political rhetoric to state that, and most academic social science is strenuously dedicated to obscuring the hierarchical structure of our society. The bishops intuit all of this, but somehow never quite manage to say so.

Instead, they make such statements as these: "The nation's founders took daring steps to create structures of mutual accountability and widely distributed power to ensure that the political system would support the rights and freedoms of all. We believe that similar institutional steps are needed today to expand the sharing of economic power and to relate the economic system more accountably to the common good." The bishops do propose experiments in cooperative ownership, worker participation in management and partnership between labor and management in general. They criticize plant closings without consultation with local communities or provision for adequate compensation for the newly unemployed. The difficulties here are many, but two may be mentioned. One is that the extreme concentration of decision in contemporary capitalism renders some of these proposals impractical without large-scale changes in, among other things, financial institutions. The other is a recurrent theme of this chapter—the want of social imagination, of the capacity to envisage alternatives.

The bishops do imagine preconditions for experiments of this sort, that we rethink our ideas of individual responsibility, reeducate the Christian community as Christians (here used in a larger sense). The bishops dislike "the many cultural manifestations around us that emphasize values and aims that are selfish, wasteful and opposed to the scriptures." These, however, are not just cultural manifestations, but ideological and psychological derivatives of a social structure organized in such a way that the bishops' practical Christianity is almost precluded.

The bishops face a very difficult problem. They propose to concentrate on the moral foundation of politics rather than on a full program of political alternatives. In modern societies, however, moral discussion is political discussion; codes of behavior, however subtly, work to uphold or alter concentrations of power. That they do so by capturing and occupying the moral imagination may make them more, not less, political. Moreover, in contemporary America, consensus is hard to find. We do not have an agreed political or social ethos. How much of our factual submission to the present structure of property is due to the fabrication of a morality for purposes of control and domination is a question, alas, the bishops did not ask. There are, to be sure, deep moral currents in our culture, often enough in the uncertain custody of the churches, immune to transient pressures and the naked force of interest. The moralists, ecclesiastical and other, are obliged to wage continuous battle against the homogenizing, nay obliterating, force of what has been termed here fabricated moralities.

The strengths of the bishops' letter, then, are found in its resolute, if somewhat unarticulated, struggle against conventional notions of social possibility. Its weaknesses reside in a certain incompleteness, on the moral as well as institutional plane. It is much to be hoped that the bishops will return to the task, this time seeking to join moral discourse much more closely to social analysis. To do so, they will have to inquire stringently into the authenticity of much that passes for morality, and of much that claims to be a social science.

The Shape of Our Destiny: America's Economic Choices

The Honorable Albert Gore, Jr.

Nations sometimes lose their way. In recent years, the shining promise of America—the chance to shape one's own destiny—has begun to slip away. For many, the American dream is collapsing even as the nation's potential reaches new heights. Our country has done much to promote justice and prosperity—but the bishops' pastoral reminds us we can do better.

Our country is not alone, of course, and we are much better off than most. Some other nations have completely lost the ability to control their economic affairs. In the world as a whole, though, more and more problems seem at times to escape our grasp, from budget deficits and the trade gap to interest rates and unemployment. Nations are struggling to fulfill their promises at a time when their citizens have come to expect more than ever before. Caught in a global squeeze, governments have to rely on one another more as events grow less dependable.

In the face of one overwhelming challenge after another, few have mustered such courage as the bishops. Some observers, including many of our current leaders, have concluded that government itself is the problem, and that all other troubles will vanish if government simply steps out of the way. Others argue that government is all that keeps matters from getting still worse.

Both sides are right—to a point. In many cases, self-defeating government policies do merely add to our burdens. On the other hand, our country's uneven economic performance in recent years suggests that many problems will persist unless government does *something*.

Obviously, we cannot afford to give up on government, as conservatives sometimes seem to suggest, or prop it up against all odds, as others counter. Like our forebears, we must be loyal to what works and not hesitate to scrap what does not. Across the political spectrum, Americans have lost faith in the government's services and patience with its demands. Our nation must find promises that people can believe in and the government can afford.

The pastoral letter leaves no doubt where government and society have failed. Unemployment remains intolerably high, while we continue to ignore the need for job creation and retraining. A nation that once pledged to wipe out poverty has almost forgotten it exists, even as more and more people become poor. Half the black children under the age of six live in poverty, along with 40 percent of the Hispanic Americans under 18. As the bishops point out, a vast segment of our population is virtually excluded from American society because they are poor, out of work and undereducated. For far too many, opportunity is just one more thing they cannot have.

For every problem government has neglected, it has aggravated another. Many social programs are well-meaning but counterproductive, standing between the people they affect and the progress they seek. By tending to favor single mothers who do not work, for example, Aid to Families with Dependent Children (AFDC) sometimes splits up families and encourages dependency. Other programs penalize employment and humiliate the people they should help.

One could hardly expect every program to work exactly as it was designed. What is more disturbing is that so many policies remain intact long after flaws become apparent. Too often, government does not pay enough attention to the human consequences of its policies. Ironically, our democracy comes up short where it should be strongest, as politicians and bureaucrats fail to see the value of local understanding and experience. In business as well as government, our country is just beginning to recognize that the person who knows a job best is the one doing it.

In order to make any lasting social progress, government must learn to listen. Businesses now use so-called quality circles, which give all employees a chance to hear others' ideas and generate their own. Government must find a similar way to encourage greater individual initiative and harvest new ideas at the local level. Fortunately, the means are already in place, for democracy is the ultimate quality circle.

Our democratic system was designed for another age, however, and it no longer works as well as it could. This nation was founded as a representative republic, in the days when genuine public participation was impractical. It may be time to move closer to a true participatory democracy, not by holding a national referendum on every Congressional resolution, but by sharing more responsibilities at a level where people feel they can make a difference.

GOVERNMENT'S MORAL FUNCTION

We must not fool ourselves: Some things government cannot do and never will. Yet, it would be a grave mistake to let government do nothing. We should strive not to shirk responsibilities and quash hopes, but to raise standards and fulfill expectations. We can do more, and we can do better.

Whatever the limits of national policy, Americans will not relinquish their obligations to society. The people of this country chose long ago to look out for one another. Through the years, cities, states, churches and charities have joined the federal government in meeting those needs. Economic triumphs only strengthened America's moral commitment. In the words of Pope John Paul II, "Freedom and riches and strength bring responsibility. We cannot leave to the poor and the disadvantaged only the crumbs from the feast. Rather, we must treat the less fortunate as guests."

For the most part, our economic system has served this country well. America remains the best place to find and build a better life. But capitalism is a clumsy tool. While the nation as a whole grows steadily richer, many individuals get left behind. Over the past two decades, the gap between rich and poor has actually widened. In the late 1960s, the richest fifth of American families had four times the income of the poorest fifth. By the early 1980s, the rich increased their share to eight times that of the poor. This nation will never stand in the way of the resourceful, but it cannot afford to neglect the needy. In pursuing economic growth, we should see that everyone benefits.

Government has a duty not to meddle in people's lives, but to enhance them. As the bishops observe, "Government has a moral function: protecting human rights and securing basic justice for all." In short, it should channel our good intentions toward our highest aims, an *enabling state* that gives people the tools to shape their own destiny.

In America, we cherish the ability to reach any goal we set for ourselves. In the complex modern world, however, hard work and determination are not always enough. Dizzying changes bewilder some and frustrate others. For many, the opportunity has vanished even if the will endures.

Confronted with similar frustrations, government cannot do everything we once hoped, but it can clear the way for each of us to reach our dreams on our own. Even though we can no longer depend on events to turn our way, together we shall make them turn out right.

That may be the kind of government we have wanted all along. Americans are the most independent people in the world. We do not like to be told what to do or how to do it. All we ask from our leaders is the chance to blaze our own trail. A government built on the pursuit of liberty must now seek to set each of us free.

Freedom begins with opportunity. If government has neither the means nor the mandate to guarantee everyone equal success, it must assure everyone an equal chance to succeed. Our society has made tremendous progress in protecting individual rights and personal security, but a safety net is not enough. We need a ladder of opportunity. Like freedom, opportunity requires constant vigilance, or it will slip away from those who need it most. As James Tobin has observed, "Today's inequality of condition is tomorrow's inequality of opportunity."

One way to promote opportunity is to give people the skills to seize it. A government that provides education, retraining and other tools for success can secure lasting prosperity for all its citizens. In the long run, government is an investment in ourselves, and our future depends on how resources are spent. Our current leaders have misunderstood the role every individual must play in this nation's economic future. By ignoring the need to build *human* capital—a relatively cheap investment with bountiful returns—we rob ourselves of our tremendous potential.

Government must strive to create opportunities. Today's economic challenges demand more than a caretaker regime. The American economy will never keep pace with global competition if our leaders tremble while others act. For the future, we need a dynamic government eager not to let things happen, but to make them happen. Strapped for resources, we must become resourceful. Instead of giving in to inertia, government can serve as the catalyst for the changes society desires. It cannot do everything we ask, but it can make sure the right things get done.

Our nation can do more to link needs with opportunities. As a matchmaker between individual skills and economic demands, government could smooth considerable hardship and inefficiency out of our economy. Every other industrial nation requires businesses to inform the government of job openings; the United States leaves unemployed workers to fend for themselves. Government could help businesses in turn by supporting small business incubators, which enable new companies to share rent, support staff and entrepreneurial expertise until they are ready to go out on their own.

Sweeping technological changes will soon give government unprecedented ability to tailor policy to individual needs. Although the federal government has always been a storehouse of information and expertise, leaders have had trouble tapping it. The current revolution in information technology could transform the nation's role. With imagination and foresight, we could design government to be fair, flexible, venturesome and effective.

We are just beginning to explore the possibilities. Consider what many businesses now can do. One clothing manufacturer waits to dye its garments until the last minute, tracking the desires of potential customers to make sure it can give them the colors they want. This flexible, customized approach cuts waste, boosts consumer satisfaction and costs the company almost nothing. By contrast, the federal government insists on hard-and-fast uniformity, with policies that offer any color you want as long as it's gray. If a tailor can enter a person's measurements into a computer program that will design and manufacture clothes with a perfect fit, the government should be able to fashion its solutions in the same way.

Government can no longer promise more of everything for everybody. Yet, it could still satisfy more while spending less, for specialization is getting cheaper. In the computer age, as Alvin Toffler once predicted, "Diversity will cost no more than uniformity." That paradox presents a welcome opportunity for government. By emphasizing flexibility and adaptation, we could design programs to deliver a variety of services as efficiently as a single one. At last, government could aspire to true fairness, giving people exactly what they need instead of what everyone else is getting.

To make the most of this country's diversity, government must once again place its faith in people, not programs. Rather than tell people what to do, it should listen and learn to help them do what they want. As long as we really trust the American people, there is no limit to how far this nation can go.

Trapped by rising public demands and diminishing federal resources, the government has left itself only one way out. People do not want fewer services, they want more for their money, so while government is bound to get smaller, it must also get better.

The federal government may shed responsibilities in those cases in which the states could offer a better deal. Smaller, more flexible and closer to local concerns, the states can experiment with promising policies. Several states have excelled, for example, in developing incentives for economic growth. The federal government should regard states as a kind of political laboratory, encouraging them to test new ideas and turning the results into a blueprint for national policy. Such decentralization is healthy, as long as states do not receive the initiative only to drop it. If we work together toward the same ideals, the whole can indeed be greater than the sum of its parts.

REBUILDING ECONOMIC JUSTICE

What can we expect from a slimmer, more versatile government? It is worth exploring how our new choices could rebuild the foundations of economic justice in America.

As the bishops have shown, the outlook for economic justice in this country depends on jobs. People need to work, not only to earn a living, but to make life worthwhile. We work to feed our minds and our spirits as well as our children. Jobs are our main link to society—without them we would feel left out. In the words of Pope John Paul II, "Human work is a key, probably the essential key, to the whole social question."

Government has no more important moral duty than to help its citizens find work. Since the New Deal, this nation has made employment one of its highest priorities. During the Great Depression, government provided jobs directly through the Civilian Conservation Corps and the Work Projects Administration. We committed ourselves to an unemployment insurance program, offering a short-term bridge to those in need. It has helped millions of Americans through hard times, and has given our economy a relatively efficient way of enduring business cycles.

Despite its remarkable record, unemployment assistance has fallen into neglect in recent years. During the first half of this decade, federal spending on employment and training programs declined 80 percent in real terms. Because of budget cutbacks and a tight job market, two thirds of the unemployed in this country go without a job long enough to exhaust their benefits. Even though raising employment would reduce the budget deficit by bringing in tax revenue and saving money on income security programs, the current administration refuses to encourage job creation.

To be sure, unemployment is becoming an increasingly stubborn problem, especially as more Americans decide to enter the labor market. We do not want nor can we afford to give everyone jobs in the public sector. At the same time, we cannot rely on the private sector to take care of full employment on its own. Government must find new ways to help companies create jobs and people fill them.

Anyone who thinks the current system is working should talk to someone who isn't. Contrary to popular assumption, most unemployed Americans want to work. Unfortunately, unemployment insurance does very little to help them get back on the job. Employment bureaus have scant resources and limited success. According to one study by the Bureau of Labor Statistics, while one of every three jobless workers consults a state employment agency, only one in twenty finds a job that way. The states, in turn, blame the federal government for giving them plenty of responsibility but little guidance.

Job creation can work if the government takes an interest in several promising state programs already under way. The Minnesota Emergency Employment Development (MEED) program, for one, created more than 25,000 new jobs in two years for workers who had exhausted their unemployment benefits. For every new job, MEED paid employers up to $5.00 an hour over six months, much of which was offset by $37.1 million in added state income tax revenue and lower welfare costs. Congress should examine the Minnesota experience to see whether a National Emergency Employment Development (NEED) program could work in other states. Another intriguing proposal would give minimum-wage summer jobs to disadvantaged teenagers who meet high academic standards. As a vocational counterpart to the immensely successful Upward Bound program, it could provide essential job experience for an estimated 700,000 youths who would otherwise have trouble getting it.

Like apprenticeship and placement, job training has become increasingly essential. Our economy is in the midst of a dramatic transformation that threatens to leave many Americans behind. In the first half of this decade, technological change and rising foreign trade put more than 5 million experienced employees out of work—and one third of them could not find another job. The demand for special skills will continue to grow. Yet, the government is spending enough to train only 5 percent of the Americans who need it. Sweden devotes 90 percent of its unemployment assistance to job creation and training; the United States spends less than 20 percent. While offering unemployed workers a few months of subsistence, we seem to have forgotten they would be better off in the long run with a few new skills.

Congress and the states will have to pool their efforts to keep America working. The federal government can offer trade adjustment assistance, using a small surcharge on imports to retrain workers who lose their jobs to foreign trade. California has launched a retraining program, supported through the state's unemployment payroll tax, for workers displaced by technological change. The jobless get to go back to work while employers receive skilled and dependable new workers.

In the future, businesses will need to assume a new responsibility for educating and retraining their employees. The Ford Motor Company and the United Auto Workers (UAW) have earmarked a nickel of each worker's hourly wages to establish the National Development and Training Center in Dearborn, Michigan. The UAW recently signed another landmark agreement with General Motors to guarantee lifetime job security for workers at the company's new Saturn plant in Spring Hill, Tennessee. More companies should follow the lead of Brown & Williamson, which opened a comprehensive job search program for workers at a Virginia plant it was planning to close. "It's part of a philosophy that people are important," one official told *The Washington Post*. "After years of allegiance and support, you can't just dump them." America's faith in that philosophy—making people feel important and giving them the tools to fend for themselves—will determine the future of economic justice in this country.

ASSISTING THE POOR

We owe the same support and encouragement to Americans who live in poverty. For so many to be poor in a nation so rich does indeed pose "an urgent moral and human challenge," as the bishops point out. Budgetary restraints have placed new pressure on government to abandon the war on poverty, but we must not retreat. In the words of John F. Kennedy, "If a free society cannot help the many who are poor, it cannot save the few who are rich."

The bishops rightly call for a more humane, efficient and effective means of providing public assistance. Instead of helping the poor to lift themselves up, our welfare system wears them down with red tape and continual abasement. We discourage recipients from working and punish them almost as if they had chosen not to be rich. A morning in any welfare office will shatter that myth and show just how far our society has left to go.

Americans must begin by reshaping the system to fit our real values—self-reliance, the family, hard work. All must take part in the effort, from churches and charities to businesses, local governments and not least, the poor themselves. Instead of blaming the troubles of the poor on society, we should join with the poor to change it. We should expect more of welfare recipients and of ourselves, for together we can all do better.

Government can give the poor two things they sorely lack—tools and choices. In this land of promise and opportunity, millions of poor Americans do not have much choice: They do what they can to survive. Although government cannot make them rich, at least it can let them choose not to stay poor.

For many, public assistance is only temporary, but for some, it can start a long slide into dependency. Half the women who receive AFDC payments remain on welfare for eight years or longer. These women have demonstrated their potential in numerous pilot projects, yet we continue to slight their needs for day care, health care and basic job skills. Those not able to work should not have to; those who can work should be given the chance.

Massachusetts has introduced a model alternative to welfare. Under a program known as Employment and Training Choices, welfare recipients can choose to trade in their check for education, training, or a job. The state offers them child care, transportation and counseling for up to six months. Thousands of beneficiaries have left the welfare rolls for permanent jobs in the private sector. Best of all, the program is entirely voluntary. No one wants to depend on the government for help; the people who deal most with the government surely like it the least. The poor would rather government got out of their lives, not by cutting their welfare, but by finding them a job so they can stand on their own. The Massachusetts program demonstrates once again the supreme principle of our democratic society: Give people a choice, and they will not disappoint.

THE NEED FOR LEADERSHIP

We choose a government to make our lives better. As our task gets harder, many long for an easy way out. In recent years, some politicians have spread cynicism, seeking to control government by promising to weaken it. Yet, even as its role changes, the federal government will become more important with each new challenge. We have the right to demand more from our government, not more programs, but more leadership. Instead of believing that "government can't do anything right," we should look for leaders who can help government do the right thing.

As individuals, we all have limitations, but our democratic society was designed to bring out the best in us. We are bound together by a common social purpose that makes the most of personal initiative and private charity. While Americans have always been rugged individualists, we recognized long ago that we must unite to survive.

The pastoral letter on the American economy can lead the way to the "new forms of cooperation and partnership" the bishops envision. Together, we can build the nation of our dreams, a community of communities, with room for all and a special place for each. In the vast global village, this country will preserve the decency of a small town.

America was not built to be a place for the rich to get richer, the big to get bigger, and the rest to get used to it. In a democracy, all must share power and opportunity equally. We have proved before that we can promote justice and prosperity with sound policy and a clear conscience. We can do it again, and this time we can do better. By giving people the tools to control their own destiny, we as a nation at last will find ours.

An Agenda For Economic Growth and Social Justice

Thomas S. Johnson

The timing of the publication of the first draft of the Catholic bishops' pastoral letter on the U.S. economy, in late 1984, was very appropriate. In the first four years of the 1980s, according to most polls and analyses, the mood of the American people had shifted from one of pessimism in the 1970s to one of greater optimism. The economy had been through two years of solid growth following a very deep recession in 1981 and 1982; inflation was much lower; new businesses were developing in areas of U.S. competitive advantage, and personal income was growing rapidly. At the same time, large segments of our population had been left out of that progress. Entrenched pockets of poverty had been untouched by the new economic growth, and major geographic regions of the country, particularly those whose industrial structure was devoted to the traditional smokestack industries, were not enjoying a share of the progress.

It was entirely right and proper for the bishops to comment on behalf of the church on the continuing problem of poverty in our society and on the obvious inequalities in distribution of income and opportunity. In both the first draft and the second draft published in late 1985, their emphasis on irreducible human rights, and particularly on the need for every individual to participate with dignity in the productive activities of society, was poignant and irresistible. Their argument that how the poorest members of society are faring is the ultimate test of the correctness of society's systems can only be ignored by those who lack sensitivity to the human condition.

Moreover, by placing their arguments in a worldwide context, including in their analysis questions relating to less developed countries, the bishops appropriately recognized an increasingly interdependent world, more and more subject to the same economic, political and technological forces.

The thesis of this chapter, which probably cannot be proved in rigorous mathematical terms, is that in the long term, greater aggregate growth will serve all groups and that policies must be designed, therefore, to facilitate both growth and social justice rather than set in terms of a tradeoff between these two goals. This argument goes beyond the bishops' assessment of the many benefits of our market-oriented economic system, and is in vivid contrast to the "trickle-down theory" or "benign neglect" because it characterizes programs to ease the burden of the poor—particularly the transitionally unemployed—not only as ethically correct, but as positive design elements in the overall system for growth and economic justice.

Many aspects of the American landscape that affect our condition are beyond the scope of this chapter. For example, the vast size of our country is both an economic advantage, in providing tremendous market scope for good products, and a problem, in making necessary economic adjustments (for example, job mobility) more difficult than they would be in a more compact setting. In addition, our multi-ethnic and multiracial makeup is both an opportunity for a cultural richness unmatched in the world and a unique challenge to a nation seeking truly to provide justice and opportunity for all.

Notwithstanding our special challenges, America has provided a great measure of prosperity, justice and opportunity to its people. The fact that large groups are subjected to conditions of poverty is unacceptable. The temptation is to see this unjust condition as a reason for fundamental change in our market-driven economic process, or alternatively to argue that a poor minority is merely an unfortunate and necessary consequence of a system that produces greater good for the majority.

Neither position is appropriate. Each is based on the presumption of an incompatibility between growth and justice, and each presumes also that we are managing the existing set of arrangements as well as possible. This paper argues that many of our recent problems result from economic and social mismanagement. It further argues that many of the compromises that have been made in our major economic premises have produced both poor economics and little or no social benefit. It also suggests an agenda for a more competitive and productive economy with a greater measure of distributive justice. It is an optimistic argument, essentially predicting there can be a "win-win" outcome not requiring us either to reject market-oriented economics or to accept as inevitable that many members of our society will not share in its fruits.

The chapter is organized into three sections. It will deal first with the most important macroeconomic policies and the desirability of having them pointed in the direction of growth of production and income. It is argued that maximizing growth is a critical element in maximizing social welfare. Second, other governmental economic policies are discussed as they relate to the promotion of economic growth. A call is made for a more competitive business economy, with a minimum of special-interest compromises. Third, a review is undertaken of the policies that deal with the needs and responsibilities of our society's different income groups. A distinction is thus made between policies primarily directed at increasing production and aggregate income and those that influence the distribution of income. Always the purpose is to search for policies and means of allocating resources that reflect the twin objectives of growth in aggregate income and production and social justice.

THE MACROECONOMIC POLICY SETTING

The tremendous income and wealth produced by the U.S. economic system has relied on many factors: abundant resources, skilled labor, a large, mostly unimpeded domestic market place and a sympathetic set of governmental structures, among other conditions. The bishops have pointed out that there have been many beneficial consequences of our prosperity. They also note correctly that there remain many problems in U.S. society that have not been dealt with adequately, particularly the persistent problem of poverty that afflicts large numbers of our people.

A central question in appraising the bishops' prescriptions is the degree to which the overall design of an economic system is to be held accountable for these problems. This chapter will argue that it is useful to separate macroeconomic policies (fiscal, monetary and trade policies) from other socioeconomic policies that are complementary to the central economic policies (for example, antitrust rules) as well as from policies that relate to problems that cannot be addressed directly through the design of the economic system, including the most difficult income-distribution challenges. It is desirable to keep clear the distinction between policies designed to foster maximum growth of production and income and those that are designed to solve problems that are better addressed in other ways.

Even relatively small differences in economic growth over time that might result from alternative overall economic policies can add up to powerful resource increments with which society can add to its well-being. For example, a 1 percent greater real growth rate in each year for the ten years ending in 1984 would have resulted in $368 billion of additional gross national product (GNP) by 1984. This would have been the equivalent of $1,555 for every man, woman and child in the United States in that year.

The present rate of aggregate taxation of total U.S. income is roughly 31 percent. The additional income resulting from 1 percent more growth could have put into the hands of federal, state and local governments an incremental $114 billion in 1984 and just under $500 billion over the last ten years, which could have been used for desirable social purposes or for reducing government debt. Moreover, given the economy's propensity to save about 7.5 percent of its GNP, this additional income could have yielded $120 billion in incremental investment capital over the same ten-year period to propel still further income and productivity growth.

These numbers dramatize the importance of economic growth. Arguments that restrict growth for the sake of worthy social objectives must meet the test of whether the compromise in growth is the best means of accomplishing those objectives. The bishops have insisted that large pockets of poverty are unacceptable, and there can be no disagreement with that assessment. It is helpful, however, to try to assess cause and effect in an attempt to get at policy prescriptions to solve the poverty problem. Is the problem inherent in the basic design of our economic system, or does the persistence of poverty in our nation result from imperfections in other, mostly noneconomic, aspects of our social structure?

An examination of the economic history of the United States in the postwar period suggests that the basic design of our economy may not be at the heart of the problem of persistent poverty. For the first 20 years or so after World War II, the United States experienced high growth and, on average, relatively low unemployment, as well as relatively stable price levels. From the late 1960s into the 1980s, on the other hand, the experience was much less satisfactory: Unemployment rose to unacceptable levels. Likewise, inflation became a problem and real economic growth slowed. Despite the Great Society programs, poverty persists and by many measures, those within our society who live at or below the poverty level have become much more numerous, especially since 1979.

Since our economic performance was much more satisfactory during the earlier postwar period than it was following 1965, it is helpful to question what changes may have occurred either in our economic system or other factors that can explain the deterioration in performance. There were several important developments after 1965 that distinguish this period from the earlier years. A short list would include the massive increases in oil prices, tremendous swings in agricultural production and prices throughout the world and the dramatic shift in U.S. fiscal policy that occurred during and following the Vietnam War—"guns and butter." In addition, the 1970s were marked by a long period of rapid expansion of the money supply in the United States.

These factors together should be examined carefully for clues to the unacceptable economic performance before concluding that the basic design of the economic system is causally related to the persistence of poverty. Faulty fiscal and monetary policies during this period were at the heart of increasingly unsatisfactory performance.

Fiscal Policy. Starting with the buildup for the Vietnam War, the United States entered a period of large and increasing government budget deficits. There had been deficits prior to 1965 as well, but they had been limited to a relatively low percentage of GNP. After 1975, and in an accelerating degree, deficits began to rise. More dramatic than their relationship to GNP was their relationship to savings.

By the 1980s, the deficits had grown to a level that now represents approximately two thirds of net private savings; that is, roughly two thirds of total net new capital available for investment is currently being used to finance the excess of public (government) consumption over taxation. The result of the very large budget deficits has been to raise the cost of capital for private purposes. Interest rates have risen relative to the underlying level of inflation to levels that are unprecedented in modern U.S. history. A large premium is also being extracted for lending funds for the long term rather than the short term, and many suggest that the deficits are the cause of this. The result of high interest rates and, particularly, the extremely sharp yield curve, is to make capital much more expensive for long-term investment than it otherwise would be. Thus, government deficits are inhibiting productive private investment that would lead to greater long-term production growth and higher income levels and employment. Moreover, the national debt that is being created is a massive income transfer out of future earnings derived from productive work to holders of financial assets. It is highly doubtful that present policies leading to unprecedented peacetime consumption of capital by the government will create a desirable long-term economic return.

Any consideration of economic policy and the results it creates in moral or ethical terms must start with the level of public spending relative to tax revenues. A central question is whether our current prosperity represents borrowing from the future for current consumption. This is what we are doing, and the bishops should be concerned with the ethics of leaving to future generations the need to carry the debt burden that is being created by present governmental policies. This is the reverse of investment and will produce negative returns in the future.

What government spends money for is also relevant in terms of future economic performance. Most thoughtful analysts agree, for example, that solutions to the federal budget deficit will require some moderation in defense spending. Moreover, there is a considerable body of opinion that spending on defense may have a less beneficial impact on productivity than other types of spending, for example, for education or roads, and that defense spending may be more inflationary than other spending. Great care must be taken, therefore, to ensure that defense spending does not exceed what is absolutely required for an adequate national defense.

In addition to aggregate spending in relationship to revenues, it is important to consider the way in which taxation is imposed and whether it has a beneficial or a harmful effect on future economic growth, especially the allocation of savings to productive capital investment. An important example of forms of taxation having an impact on capital allocations is the tax deductibility of interest on home mortgages. During the postwar period, the United States has devoted a large percentage of its total income to housing construction. At the same time, it has not solved the housing problems of the poor. The tax deductibility, which reduces the total real cost of borrowing for housing, together with such other governmental policies as interest rate controls that have likewise been aimed at fostering housing construction, have resulted in a larger portion of total investment in housing than would otherwise be the case. Investment capital thus deployed cannot be used in other ways that might be more effective in creating greater long-term productivity. Investment funds devoted to new productive enterprises and technologies would enhance the productivity of the existing labor force, reducing production costs and leading to greater output. Careful consideration should be given to the overall impact, from an ethical–social point of view, of our implicit subsidies to housing construction.

In these two major respects, the overall balance between revenues and expenditures and the specific ways in which they affect investment and consumption, fiscal policy should be redirected toward increasing growth of production and employment. The power inherent in even very small growth differentials that could result from more effective macroeconomic policies is so dramatic that it can be a primary vehicle for creating resources ultimately to solve our poverty problems.

Monetary Policy. Monetary policy as well deserves careful examination. During the 1970s, while fiscal deficits were rising to historically high levels, rapid creation of money beyond the level needed to finance the amount of real growth that was occurring in the economy ultimately contributed to a burst of high inflation. For the first time in recent U.S. economic history, in 1979 and 1980, consumer surveys indicated that Americans were buying goods in anticipation of future price rises. Consequently, the Federal Reserve Board imposed extremely high interest rates to wring out of the economy its inflationary bias. This caused a most severe postwar recession, from which we are now recovering. The economic and social costs of lost production as a result of that recession are enormous. In purely dollar terms, for example, the amount of lost production from 1979 to 1983 was equal to the decline in production during that period plus an assumption for "normal" growth of, say, 2.5 percent. This total is equal to $736 billion (1984 dollars)—or $3,112 per capita—a terrible cost to pay for macroeconomic policy mistakes. Moreover, the human costs were, as the bishops point out, imposed disproportionately on poor people.

The combination of fiscal and monetary policies deserves the greatest attention from those concerned with the growth of production and employment, and it is here that the ethical considerations relating to a just society should begin.

Trade Policies. The third traditional element in macroeconomic policies (after fiscal and monetary policies) relates to international trade. During the postwar period, U.S. policy has been to minimize barriers to world trade. This policy has been adhered to faithfully by Republican and Democratic administrations despite the challenges that arise at times from individual industries in the United States that are experiencing international competitive difficulties. Most economists agree that the maximum flow of world trade adds to the aggregate world wealth. Just as one of the foundations of U.S. economic strength is the size of our domestic marketplace, increasing the freedom with which goods and services travel across national boundaries creates incremental aggregate wealth for all.

In recent years, a number of traditional U.S. industries have been experiencing difficulty competing internationally. As technology and other countries' infrastructure developments enable them to get into such industries as steel, textiles and consumer goods that have traditionally been strong parts of the U.S. economy, our aging industrial base is finding it increasingly more difficult to compete on a price basis. Calls are heard for various forms of protection from this threat. The bishops have argued that we should not create barriers to imports from Third World countries because the populations of those countries have a moral right to employment. The draft letter does not address extensively, however, the other side of this problem—the displacement of American workers in industries that are no longer competitive. The model that calls for overall macroeconomic policies to foster maximum growth of production and employment includes a serious commitment to free trade as a natural extension of the other tenets of a competitive economy. The ethical consideration relating to displaced workers, thus, is whether to compromise aggregate economic growth (in this case worldwide) to preserve jobs in newly uncompetitive industrial sectors or to encourage transition from the more traditional productive enterprises to new, higher-value-added industries, with a humane set of programs and policies to alleviate the human difficulties that are caused by the changes.

The last third of the twentieth century has brought into focus perhaps the ultimate ethical dilemma posed by world trade. Even more dramatic than the problem of poverty in the United States is the plight of hundreds of millions of people in the Third World. The contrasts in wealth between U.S. workers and residents of the two thirds of the world classified as "less developed" may imply the inevitability of less relative—perhaps even absolute—income for Americans in the future.

For thoughtful, religious people, justice cannot end at national borders. This important moral question must be considered in the days ahead, but all of the economic policy prescriptions presented in this paper are aimed at higher productivity and greater aggregate production and income. At the very least, these policies are not inconsistent with ultimate solutions to worldwide poverty, they should add to the near-term employment possibilities for other nations, and they would soften any relative or absolute diminution of American workers' incomes that may ultimately occur.

The three legs of macroeconomic policy—fiscal, monetary and trade—can all be directed toward achieving maximum growth. This is not to say there is agreement on how to achieve that growth, but it is an argument that growth-oriented policies may be put in place without compromising the ethical mandates the bishops have so eloquently set forth. The major reason for advocating maximum growth is simply the amount of incremental resources and employment that can thereby be created. Those resources can contribute more quickly to solutions to the poverty problem than can most redistributive moves within a slower growth model.

During the most recent period of our postwar economic history, U.S. policies have added up to "guns and butter" in the fiscal realm, with excessive money creation until 1979, when Paul Volcker became chairman of the Federal Reserve Board and challenged our traditionally held free trade policies. In the last several years, our robust expansion has been fueled by the largest deficits in peacetime history and strong foreign investment in dollar securities. Interest rates are high, reflecting the financial market's skepticism about the longer-term inflationary consequences of the federal budget deficits, and they have added to the inflow of foreign capital, thus enabling the deficits to be financed. This implicit "beggar thy neighbor" policy cannot go on forever, and the first order of setting economic policy must be to put in place a more balanced fiscal policy. Eliminating huge fiscal deficits, and especially the expectation that these deficits will continue in the indefinite future, would bring interest rates down and thereby improve the climate for long-term investments, reduce our reliance on foreign capital and set the economy on a surer footing for future growth.

OTHER POLICIES TO PROMOTE GROWTH

In addition to the three basic legs of macroeconomic policy, there are other areas of public involvement in the functioning of the economy that can be directed toward promoting healthy growth of income—"the economic pie." The importance of growth is so great that all of our national economic policies should be examined from the perspective of what they do to help or impede growth. In the last seven or eight years, beginning with the early moves by the Carter administration to deregulate oil prices, the United States has been going through a period of deregulation of important sectors of its economy. The net benefits that have been derived from deregulation in such areas as oil prices, air transport, the trucking and railroad industries and interest rates (for depositors and investors) have been dramatic. Surely, we have had enough experience, for example, with the pricing trends that have occurred as the result of airline deregulation to understand that the real cost of air transportation today is lower than it was ten years ago, on average. Likewise, freely competitive interest rates (for example, making available market-level deposit rates at banks) have produced great benefits to savers.

At the same time, there have been difficulties associated with deregulation. For example, the impact of deregulation of airline ticket prices has not been uniform. Some routes actually cost more today, resulting in economic difficulties for those communities, and some people have lost their jobs. The challenge to public policy is twofold: First, the adjustment difficulties we have witnessed when anticompetitive regulation is removed should make us much more hesitant to adopt similar policies in the future, and second, government must accept some responsibility for alleviating the transitional difficulties that result when it changes policy.

Creation of as much growth in aggregate production and income as possible requires careful attention to where restrictions on business are impeding growth to a greater extent than they are creating a beneficial social impact. Many policies that have been created over the years for worthy objectives have had unintended consequences that are very costly to the economy. This section deals with some major areas of public policy where there are important opportunities to produce greater economic growth.

Antitrust Policy. A trend has already begun to reconsider some of the tenets of antitrust policy. The world of the 1980s, with much greater international economic competition, new technologies and freer movement of capital, is very different from the world envisioned when traditional antitrust policy was formulated. In the steel industry, for example, it is irrelevant to think in terms of a "U.S. market." Competition on an international scale has created a truly worldwide market for many products. Industry concentration policy that ignores the worldwide nature of the market creates barriers to the formation of units that are of sufficient economic size. Likewise, policy that is geared to the short-run preservation of jobs at the expense of longer-term competitiveness of the enterprises in which those jobs are held is shortsighted. An urgent review of antitrust policies, particularly relating to the definition of relevant markets, might offer very beneficial effects in terms of U.S. competitiveness that would in turn enhance the growth of the economy.

Fostering Competition. We should continue to move toward minimum interference with the free functioning of the competitive economy and the price mechanism as the main arbiter of what gets produced. Much has been accomplished in recent years to remove impediments to competition, but much remains to be done. Some areas where further deregulation should be considered: restrictive labor practices in certain businesses, including construction; further financial reform, including the removal of restrictions on interstate bank branching as well as many of the provisions of the Glass Steagall Act; and a careful review of the procedures involved in receiving approval for projects that may have an adverse affect on the environment.

A good example of when procedures took over for principle regarding the environment is the more than a decade of acrimonious deliberations on the proposed Westway highway in New York City. The cost of talking about the ultimately abandoned project for over ten years was a tremendous economic burden. An intelligent society should be able to do better than this and in many other environmental controversies.

Encourage Savings and Investment. A whole series of governmental policies should be reviewed to ensure maximum incentives to save and invest and to curb current consumption. Encouraging savings is obviously critical for creating future economic growth and greater productivity. It is a moral imperative in a world of scarce and diminishing resources. The United States is the wealthiest nation in the world, and our policies should be directed at avoiding unnecessary consumption and encouraging investment for the ultimate benefit not only of Americans, but of poor, capital-short countries.

Tax policies should be based on promoting savings to the greatest extent possible, and in this respect, the current national discussion of a broader and relatively flatter income tax system is constructive. So, too, is the effort to reduce or eliminate double taxation of corporate earnings and dividends.

Conduct of Governmental Policy. When intervention in the workings of the private economy is deemed absolutely necessary for public policy reasons, the procedures should be as direct as is possible. For example, our farm programs should be reexamined from this perspective. If it is desired from a public policy point of view to support farm incomes, the preferable way to do this would be the most overt way, that is, direct subsidies to farmers. Such indirect means as buying and storing commodities or supporting farm prices at levels otherwise unsustainable may have a higher cost than the more direct way. Another example is governmental policies to encourage oil exploration. If this is deemed desirable, then direct subsidies rather than tax incentives should be used.

It is also desirable for regulation to involve a minimum of discretionary decision making by government employees. Interpreters and monitors are expensive, and they introduce the possibility of a self-perpetuating system that begins to lose sight of the major objective.

When regulation is necessary, a maximum amount of constructive dialogue among the parties concerned, particularly on the potential long-term effects of the regulation, should be encouraged. Many countries have achieved co-operation between government and business for broad social objectives, and efforts should be made to foster a greater feeling of mutual responsibility rather than antagonism between business and government in the United States. In this respect, the bishops' draft has been quite forthright in advocating a spirit of cooperation at various levels in the economic process, and the desirability of this type of interaction between business and government should not be ignored.

Government's basic role in the business economy has often been stated as twofold. First, it should have policies that foster a maximum of healthy, constructive competition. The greatest impetus to improve cost efficiencies, production scale, distribution effectiveness and all the other aspects of business success occurs in an environment where competition strengthens and challenges individual effort, and our society's policies should be aimed at deriving the maximum benefit from that effort.

Second, government has the unique responsibility to set the overall guidelines within which competition is to occur. Standards for fair and honest business behavior, appropriate ecological concerns and employment conditions that foster freedom of choice and dignity for the individual worker are the province of the government.

The church can play an important role in maintaining the proper orientation to these and other important principles. Extremely difficult issues relating to each of these areas have arisen in recent years. Disclosures of unethical behavior on the part of business leaders have shocked the public. The damage to our ecology that has been caused by lack of concern, and the deliberate concealment in some cases of harm that is being done, have been very much in the public eye. Moreover the social costs of business decisions that cause unemployment are almost immeasurable. The church can contribute in a special way to help society evolve principles of business conduct that will improve the human condition both materially and morally.

Collaboration. The bishops have stressed in their letter the desirability of collaboration among various segments of U.S. society. Much good can result from careful dialogue among individuals and institutions on the important tradeoffs every society must make. The period since the middle 1960s in the United States has been characterized by a heavily confrontational approach to the rights and privileges of various sectors of society. Much has been written about "single-issue politics," for example, in which powerful political factions devote their efforts to a narrow interest without any mechanism for considering where there may be conflicts among legitimate interests.

The church can do much to create better understanding of the wholeness of human existence and to remind each of us that our personal and group behavior contributes to the overall human condition. It can help us to avoid behaving according to the rule of "every man for himself." The bishops call for local collaboration for these purposes, but could perhaps make their message even more powerful by constructing formulations for the same kind of collaboration between society's political and business leaders and its other members, for the same purposes of mutual betterment.

POLICIES TO PROVIDE FOR HUMAN NEEDS

The bishops have articulated their view of an economic system that has served the majority of U.S. citizens well. The aim here is to argue for a set of policies aimed at producing maximum economic growth and a complementary set of policies that ensure all members of society share in an adequate measure of material well-being and personal dignity. The bishops have argued that the well-being of the poorest members of society is the ultimate test of the acceptability of the overall system. The argument here presented is that the design of a business–economic system is only part (possibly the major part, but still only a part) of the overall social scheme. It seems useful to make a clearer distinction than the bishops have made between the positive elements that can be designed for a business economy that will foster overall growth of production and income, and other social design features to ensure minimum levels of individual participation in the fruits of that wealth.

The administration of President Ronald Reagan has coined the term "social safety net," and it is a very appropriate one. The first two sections of this chapter dealt with macroeconomic and other governmental policies toward individual business segments and enterprises that should be aimed at producing growth in the aggregate economy. The remaining sections argue for programs that, with a minimum of interference with productivity and growth, strive to achieve the kind of sharing in the fruits of the economy that the bishops advocate—the social safety net.

The bishops cited much convincing evidence on the demography of the poor in the United States. They demonstrated that large numbers of Americans are, at least for certain periods, subjected to conditions of poverty. In presenting evidence to demonstrate that the problem of poverty goes beyond the long-term subjection of certain people to poverty conditions, the bishops have done a great service, and here is made use of the distinction between long-term poverty class members and those who experience poverty temporarily. After discussing the poverty groups, some comments will be directed toward the middle class and higher-income groups.

The Long-term Poor. Since the 1960s, with the Kennedy and Johnson administrations' concern about poverty, Americans have been aware that there are segments of the population that have never participated fully in society's well-being. In the 1970s and 1980s, much frustration has been experienced because the programs put in place at great expense do not seem to have produced adequate progress. The frustration is understandable. Surely, though, correcting long-term poverty conditions will require great patience. Part of the frustration also results from some clear program failures as well as overall unsatisfactory economic performance during much of this period. Although these disappointments are understandable, it is at best naive and at worst mean spirited to assume that the problem of overspending relative to revenues by the government (guns and butter) arises from devoting resources to poverty programs.

Contrary to some political rhetoric, only a relatively small portion of so-called "social spending" programs has been devoted strictly to the poorest members of society. For example, the aggregate expenditures for Medicaid (the health program aimed specifically at poor people of all ages), food stamps, the federal part of Aid to Families with Dependent Children and other income security programs, excluding retirement and unemployment compensation, have amounted to only 9.2 percent of federal outlays over the last five years. In contrast, the amount devoted to Social Security, essentially a working- or middle-class benefit, and Medicare, which is a transfer payment to all people above a certain age irrespective of their income and wealth, added up to about 27 percent of the federal budget. The percentage growth of programs aimed at the long-term poor has exceeded that of the middle-class programs because the need-determined programs did not exist until the 1960s. However, the dollar growth of the programs oriented to the other groups has been far greater. Since 1965, programs directed at the poor have increased more than 27 times, while middle-class entitlements rose by a factor of 11. In dollar terms, however, growth in the middle-class entitlement programs far outstripped growth in programs for the poor—$234 billion to $93 billion. Any discussion on whether the poverty programs have been effective or whether the resources devoted to them have been the cause of our economic problems needs to be tempered by these facts.

This group, "the poorest of the poor," or the "structurally unemployed," requires programs designed specifically for its needs. Recognizing that its condition is the result of very long-term factors, we must accept that it may be necessary to transfer resources to this group on a very long-term basis before large numbers of its members will begin to move out into the higher-income levels and become more self-sustaining. There are educational and social barriers that prevent easy, quick solutions.

The just society, following on the bishops' principles, must therefore design programs that do two things. First, programs must provide for the minimum material needs of the poor, in ways that show respect for their human dignity, for as long as necessary. The programs must be nonpunitive and nondiscriminatory in the way they are designed and administered. If we are to move toward an even greater level of true unity in our society, this requirement—that we truly accept those members who are the long-term least fortunate among us—must be inherent in the design of the programs. The frequent need to requalify for certain types of benefits should be reconsidered. We should also move in a radical new direction in programs for the structurally unemployable members of society. Some sort of long-term minimum income maintenance—a negative income tax—would probably best serve this objective.

Second, programs must be designed that will help members of this group move into the mainstream of society and gradually become able to assume greater responsibility for their part in the productive aspects of our lives together. In combination with income maintenance, therefore, fundamental programs relating to health and education are necessary. Special efforts must be devoted, for example, to prenatal care and eradication of substance abuse within these groups. Affirmative Action programs must be maintained, and efforts aimed at encouraging employment of the poor should be emphasized.

The church has an important role to play regarding this poorest group. The poorest ones need encouragement and counseling that can best be delivered by volunteer, nongovernmental programs. If we move toward the adoption of a general income maintenance program, and away from ones directed toward specific needs, churches should assume greater responsibility for helping individuals with the decisions they will need to make on how to use the financial resources society will provide. On a very localized basis, this sensitive caring for poor people on a family-by-family basis can be the most compassionate way to help them gradually assume more responsibility for themselves.

The Transitionally Unemployed. The bishops refer to large numbers of people who pass through the condition of poverty on an occasional basis. In the policy model that is presented in this chapter, the temporary members of the poverty income level are referred to as "transitionally unemployed." They enter poverty as a result of temporary economic conditions, industry displacement, or other factors that do not presuppose their being disadvantaged in some longer-term, more fundamental way. They are capable of productive employment, but do not have adequate opportunities for employment for some period of time.

The problems of the transitionally unemployed as opposed to the long-term poor are commonly thought to be temporary in nature. Nevertheless, as we have painfully learned in the early 1980s, the length of time can be quite extended. In fact, in many industries and sections of the country, serious unemployment has persisted much longer recently than in any previous post-war economic slowdown. On the other hand, this group is basically employable except for the serious problem that the specific skills they have learned may no longer be required in the emerging industry structure.

It is the transitionally unemployed who are affected by the important debate about the direction of investment, business prerogatives with regard to opening and closing plants, and criteria for antitrust enforcement, trade policy and the like. The arguments over the allocation of scarce resources and investment direction are valid, but more important is to develop an overall set of economic and social policies to reconcile the pursuit of high growth in aggregate production and income with the need to ensure social justice.

If the discussions regarding these groups remain at the level of which industries will be favored in trade and investment policy, the arguments will forever follow the pattern, "How do we divide up a fixed-sum pie"? The "fixed-sum" approach to policy is wrong and reflects a lack of understanding of the power of a competitive economic system. Policies should be designed to promote both growth and social justice rather than set in terms of a tradeoff between these two goals.

There is much discussion of the smokestack industries and the areas of the United States that are now suffering from the decline of those industries. Ominous forecasts about the long-term stagnation of whole regions of the country are commonplace. Not enough attention is given, however, to the cases of New England and the Southeast, regions that have undergone constructive transitions to new industrial mixes and have reentered the mainstream of the American economy. There is every reason to expect that the smokestack areas will benefit from the same kind of transition. The real questions are not whether that *will* happen in a market-oriented economic system, but how quickly will it happen, as well as what will be the human costs of the transition, and are there constructive ways to alleviate these costs?

The transition discussion has to be elevated above the "competing claims" level and made part of society's overall agenda for economic growth and individual justice. The bishops argue, for example, that social justice requires that we not discriminate against accepting products from the Third World. The bishops did not go far enough. It is not only just to accept the products of the Third World when they can be delivered to our shores at a lower cost than our cost of producing the same products. It is actually desirable to accept those goods. If products ranging from rubber-soled shoes to transistors can be produced more cheaply in other parts of the world than in the United States, we should buy them and have policies at home to facilitate the transition of our economy to a mix that better reflects our emerging capabilities.

This is, of course, more easily said than done, but it is at the heart of our policy options. Of course, national security considerations may dictate that we will want to preserve certain industries even if they cannot compete effectively in world markets. However, if in general we opt to continue the struggle among marginal industries and their employees for economic favors in the form of subsidies, tariffs, or uneconomic work rules, we will be distracted from the inevitable transitions that are bound to occur over some period of time. Government should encourage the transition of our economy in more productive and competitive directions, and social policy should be aimed at alleviating the burden on the workers and their families who are adversely affected. Discussed here are criteria for policies to accomplish these objectives.

First, as argued in other parts of this chapter, we must strive to understand the changes that are occurring in our industrial mix in response to new technology, our population's set of skills and world trade patterns. Those changes that are desirable and inevitable should not be fought, but should be accepted and facilitated from an overall income growth perspective.

Second, a "no-fault" philosophy should be adopted in dealing with individuals who are adversely affected by these transitions. Our thinking must be oriented to the notion that it is not only society's responsibility, but also a very desirable feature in the design of our economic system to facilitate rapid transition in these areas.

We could perhaps learn from the Japanese, who have found ways in their economic and social system to move through transition phases without creating pariahs out of individuals who are affected adversely by trends over which they have no control. Moreover, the social cost of moving through these periods of transition with dignity and at as fast a pace as possible should be viewed against the risk that members of the transitionally unemployed might slip into the category of the long-term unemployed.

Income maintenance programs for the transitionally unemployed should be reexamined, especially the threatening aspects of cutoffs after a certain number of weeks. The inherent presumption that without these cutoffs people will not seek work and will, of their own accord, become society's wards, should be questioned. The bishops argue that the vast majority of Americans want to function as productive individuals. People want to work, and it should not be necessary to design programs for the transitionally unemployed to ferret out and "punish" those small numbers of individuals who may not be seeking to work. The cost in terms of lost dignity and self-confidence that is imposed by the ever-present threat of an end to unemployment compensation cannot be measured and should not be acceptable to a just society.

However, people should not be as well off materially if they are unemployed as if they are employed. Individual have the responsibility to contribute according to their abilities. Personal initiative to find employment that maximizes the fit between each individual's skills and desires and the needs of the economy is best served by maintaining a real economic incentive for getting back to work as fast as possible. Unemployment compensation should be redesigned to be less threatening to human dignity while preserving this incentive.

Third, policies should be geared to minimize interference in individual decision making by families. Most of the unemployed do not need help in determining how their resources should be used, and interference in their family decision making is potentially damaging to their dignity as human beings. When unemployment compensation runs out and families are forced into the welfare category, this kind of interference frequently occurs. The concept of a degree of automatic income maintenance, perhaps through a negative income tax mechanism operated on a short-term basis or by reexamining the relationship between unemployment compensation and welfare, should be considered.

Fourth, the highest priority in program initiatives to complement income maintenance should be getting people back to work. Such programs as job training, relocation assistance, tuition subsidies and government job information and referral services to assist in reemployment should be emphasized. Individual freedom to choose among these programs should be preserved to the maximum extent possible. A test of the effectiveness of the programs should be whether they have succeeded in moving people quickly to reemployment. If individuals are not motivated to participate in the programs, that should be taken at least in part as an indictment of the program rather than an indictment of the individuals.

Transitional unemployment is a consequence of changes in the overall economy, and the transitionally unemployed should be dealt with in a constructive rather than a punitive way. Specific policies toward businesses should encourage them to respond to evolving technologies and product demands and should not discourage transitions out of industries whose products are either no longer desired or competitive. The workers who are adversely affected by these transitions should be regarded, in a sense, as providing an opportunity for our society to move toward greater support for individual dignity and development. Programs to foster a dignified transition for these individuals should contribute to the overall growth of income and production.

The discussion in this section has concentrated on unavoidable and desirable changes in the economy that cause transitional problems. There is no justification, however, for periods of difficulty induced by irresponsible governmental economic policy. Recently, problems associated with inevitable economic change have been compounded by an unacceptable macroeconomic policy formulation. The bishops point out the costs of these policies in human terms, and society should not accept this kind of mismanagement by its political leaders.

The Middle-income Segment. Most Americans consider themselves members of the middle-income class. The middle class may be defined as those who are neither among the structurally poor, nor at high risk of transitional unemployment, nor rich. The middle-income group is by far the largest category in terms of population as well as in aggregate income, personal expenditures and taxes paid. The overall fiscal posture vis-à-vis this group, therefore, is terribly important, and it is worthwhile discussing principles that ought to guide society's attitudes toward the middle class.

If our nation is to provide adequately for the material needs and the human dignity of poor people, the middle-income group will obviously need to be net contributors to the support of government's programs. The suggestions made in this chapter are meant to be policy guides rather than a carefully priced-out program. However, an acceptable level of economic justice may well require a larger net contribution from the middle class.

How overall tax and benefit programs affect the middle class is at the heart of our present dialogue about taxation and the so-called entitlement programs. Rhetorically, our leaders sometimes tend to equate the federal government's income transfer programs with its poverty programs but, as discussed earlier, the largest income transfers occur among the working or middle classes. The chief examples are Social Security and Medicare. In addition, there are many other programs whose major beneficiaries are the middle class. Some examples: the student loan program; subsidized student lunches; free or subsidized Coast Guard and airport services; veterans' programs and a host of benefits that are effected through tax deductions. The most important of these are the tax deductions for interest paid on home loans and for state and local taxes.

No magic arithmetic dictates how an overall fiscal program should add up in terms of the aggregate amount of production that is channeled through government programs. In the United States, the aggregate of federal, state and local government expenditures is roughly 35 percent of GNP, and it is desirable to keep government spending as low as possible relative to total production.

Whether meeting society's critical needs may ultimately require higher aggregate spending is beyond the scope of this paper. Clear, however, is that the huge federal government deficits of the last few years compound the problem of meeting the needs discussed in this chapter. Revenues and expenditures must be brought into closer balance. There are many different opinions on how to move toward a more responsible fiscal policy, but most careful analysts would argue that, given the size of the problem, a combination of further expenditure cuts in the federal budget and some tax increases will be necessary. Both middle-class entitlements and military spending will probably need to share in the expenditure cuts, simply because, together with net interest paid, they now constitute the lion's share of the federal budget.

If this prescription is accepted, the middle class will likely need to contribute more, through somewhat lower entitlement benefits and somewhat higher taxes. Several suggestions might serve as guiding principles in this most difficult political equation. First, we need to call into question our ability to afford programs for the middle class that are not needs-tested. The political dialogue from the late 1930s up to the present regarding needs tests should be reopened. The question is not so much whether society can continue to afford undifferentiated health and retirement programs for the middle class irrespective of their need, but whether it is right from an ethical standpoint to make this tradeoff if it implies less than a decent minimum of support for the poor. The bishops know that the answer is that the poor's needs must be considered a high priority, and a key measure of how well our nation performs in the future will be our ability to adjust to that priority.

Previous assumptions regarding middle-class entitlements and taxes must be questioned if we are to accomplish the economic and moral objectives the bishops address. Specifically, subsidization of retirement benefits for all through the Social Security system, particularly when benefits are received even by those who do not need them, must be questioned. Nonneeds-tested receipt of Medicare benefits by the elderly must likewise be reexamined.

Second, we must question the unlimited tax deductibility of interest on home mortgages. The tax changes now being enacted include some limitations on interest deductibility, but not for interest payments on mortgage loans. If necessary, even the deductibility of interest on home loans, especially second residences, may have to be reconsidered. In effect, this deductibility, if without any limit, is a subsidy to the middle class, perhaps at the expense of critical programs for the poor that are necessary to meet the bishops' tests of fairness.

Third, careful attention should be devoted to the fairness of taxes imposed on the middle class. Because this is the largest group in our population and it pays the lion's share of personal income taxes, great care must be taken not to undermine their willingness to support programs with their tax dollars. The current tax reform effort is a worthy objective if it creates a greater underpinning of support among the population for the way taxes are levied.

Fourth, we must winnow out special interest programs that support one group against others within the middle class, groups that in general should be left to their own self-sufficiency. We should reassess carefully such areas as the farm program, industry regulation, specialized education and other social services, with a view toward avoiding doing for people what they can do for themselves, or what they can as well do without. The just society's highest commitment must be to what is necessary for the long-term poor and the transitionally unemployed.

The Upper-income Group. The bishops comment on the concentration of wealth and income among the wealthiest few individuals and families in our society. Their measure of fairness of the overall system—how the poorest members of society are faring—was a nonradical one, and the bishops do not advocate punitive or severe measures regarding the wealthiest in society. There are important contributions to be made by the wealthy, particularly since they control a disproportionate amount of the nation's savings.

First, all the points made in the section dealing with middle-income people are equally applicable in the case of the wealthy—and even more so. The wealthy should not receive advantage either through subsidization that goes beyond the basic infrastructure from which all benefit, or taxes. Many areas of the tax code that have grown up over the years are nominally aimed at directing investment in certain ways, and great care must be taken, particularly in the current reassessment of the tax system, to eliminate provisions that create unfair advantage for the wealthy. Ideally, investment direction should not be governed at all through the tax code, and desirable social investment should probably be made openly and directly by government. Short of that ideal, however, every part of the tax code designed to foster investment in areas deemed socially desirable, for example, energy exploration, should be reassessed to determine whether that means of promoting the social objective is the best way to accomplish it. Moreover, these programs should not provide benefits to the owners of wealth beyond the absolute minimum cost required for society to accomplish its objective.

Second, tax programs should be designed to promote savings and investment by the upper-income groups. Our nation has great wealth and our ability to create added production and income for the benefit of all, as well as to conserve resources for future generations, depends greatly on how we make decisions regarding current consumption versus savings and investment. Those who have high income and wealth have a special responsibility to save and invest wisely, and the tax system should be designed to encourage savings.

Third, it is a principle that has long been accepted in our society that the upper-income groups should pay a higher share of their income to support governmental programs than should the rest of the population. This principle should remain in effect. It is true, of course, that higher taxation in percentage terms of the wealthiest members of society will not yield dramatically higher aggregate tax revenues. Nevertheless, the concept of a graduated income tax is accepted by Americans and is, of course, advocated by the bishops.

In the current discussion of tax reform, a central theme is to eliminate many tax preferences and bring tax rates down as well as to narrow the range of income taxation between the lowest and the highest levels. The important income tax rate from the viewpoint of stimulating additional savings and investment is the marginal, or highest, tax rate, and it is therefore desirable for that rate to be as low as possible.

Perhaps as important as economic justice within our own society is the question of how much all Americans consume of the world's resources. As the bishops point out, Americans, representing about 5 percent of the world's population, are now consuming 25 percent of the world's annual production. Whether in absolute terms, a differential of this stark magnitude can be justified at all from a moral point of view is questionable. This statistic surely points up dramatically how desirable it is that tax measures and other elements of the economic system should act as a brake on current consumption in favor of savings and investment. Investment now will produce an increase in the world's aggregate wealth in the future, and it is inherently the responsibility not only of the wealthier members of society but of society as a whole to provide for the world's future well-being by saving as much as possible.

CONCLUSION

The bishop's call for a rethinking of the U.S. economic system and its impact on the human condition cannot be ignored. Their insistence on using the size and persistence of the poverty problem in America as a gauge of whether the system is producing acceptable results is the clearest possible challenge to our leaders and to every thoughtful citizen—and the results have not been acceptable. Change is required.

Are the basic tenets of democratic capitalism flawed? No system has produced so much wealth for so many. Our economy has been mismanaged and the principles of a competitive economy as a powerful engine for producing wealth have been compromised. Neither a totally laissez-faire approach to the economy, trusting entirely the "invisible hand" for solutions to all problems, nor a "statist" approach, rejecting the tremendous power of individual incentive, is called for. Instead, we should improve our economic management, remove unnecessary barriers to maximum performance of our private economy and adopt new approaches to social welfare programs.

In managing the economy, we should:

1. Bring the federal budget deficit down to levels that will reduce public versus private competition for needed capital.
2. Continue a responsible monetary policy.
3. Maintain our traditional free trade posture while emphasizing improved world competitiveness for American industry.
4. Continue to remove unnecessary regulation and anticompetitive rules for industry.
5. Adopt a set of trade and antitrust policies that recognizes the challenges to American businesses as they face worldwide competition, sometimes from firms that have governmental support. The emphasis should be on encouraging American business to be more competitive, not on punitive measures toward other nations.
6. Gradually eliminate special advantages and protections enjoyed by industries no longer capable of being competitive in worldwide markets.

7. Encourage the movement of capital and labor resources into emerging industries in which the United States has the potential of being competitive in the long run.

8. Redirect tax policy to encourage greater levels of savings by people of all income levels.

In our social welfare programs, we should:

1. Recognize the long period of time and large expenditures that will be necessary to alleviate the condition of poverty among the parts of our population who are unable with their present skills to be full participants in the labor force.

2. Adopt a "no-fault" attitude toward both the long-term and the transitionally unemployed, and revamp the means by which assistance is delivered to help maintain a maximum of privacy and individual dignity for people afflicted by poverty.

3. Deliver as much of the required assistance as we can in the form of a minimum-income maintenance program. The level of income should be set to guarantee a dignified minimum standard of living while preserving a real economic incentive for individuals to seek work, and the assistance should allow a maximum of individual decision making by recipients on how their income is spent.

4. Where functional programs are required (for example, in education), a pragmatic attitude should be adopted that allows experimentation with innovative approaches to problem solving, with the flexibility to drop programs that do not produce desired results.

We have a "win-win" opportunity to make our magnificently productive economy function even better and to share more equitably the fruits of our wealth. The right place to start is in a reordering of federal fiscal management to produce lower governmental deficits. This will lead to lower interest rates and easier access to capital for productive investment.

Business leaders have a special responsibility to engage in meaningful dialogue with political leaders and others, including the church, on how to make the system work better for the benefit of all. There has been, for at least 20 years or so, a failure of our elected leaders to deal effectively with the economy, and it is time for us to insist on a better job from them. The more than $200 billion in federal debt now piling up every year, borrowed from other nations and against our children's future, is the single biggest impediment to a more prosperous and just society. The specter of the world's richest nation importing capital from other nations to finance current consumption is a moral travesty in a capital-short world. Failure to manage our nation's finances the way each of us knows we must manage the finances of our businesses and our families will leave an ever-widening gap between the rich and the poor, and a diminishing claim to moral leadership in the world.

Success is more characteristic of our history. Let us commit ourselves to the challenge set forth in the bishops' letter to regain mastery over our economic future and share the fruits of our productivity willingly, happily—because it is right—with our least fortunate brothers and sisters.

15

A European
Point of View

Kurt Biedenkopf

The pastoral letter of the American Catholic bishops deserves to be called a historic document. Although the Catholic church in the United States has previously addressed questions of economic and social policy, until this letter, no comparable effort had been made to translate Catholic social teaching and thought since *Rerum Novarum* and *Quadragesimo Anno* to the specific conditions of economic life in the United States.

Traditionally thought to be an offspring of Protestant thinking, modern American capitalism was not considered by Europeans as close to the fabric of Catholic social thought or related to its basic principles. Rather, it was assumed that the manifestations of an open, dynamic, decidedly democratic organization of the economic order that developed in the United States since the Civil War were distinctly Protestant in character; they are based on individualism, personal achievement and self-reliance, private property and competition. They brought forward the modern corporation as one of their major institutional developments, which was and has remained very specifically American. This new economic order, quite different from those of European industrial nations, was strongly influenced by the openness of a continent, by the remarkable mobility that accompanied the movement west. Both these qualities have remained as American social characteristics.

All this—individualism and mobility, democratic and economic competition, self-reliance and pronounced freedom of the individual, not to mention the strict separation of church and state—are hardly expressions of Catholic social thinking; they developed with the industrialization of the Old World and in answer to the social question of the late nineteenth century. Surely the social question, pointedly posed by the conditions of life and work of factory workers in Britain and, decades later, on the continent, especially in Germany, was not strictly a European phenomenon. Poverty and hardship, exploitation of the worker and miserable working conditions also accompanied the process of industrialization in the United States, in addition to the human sufferings brought about by slavery. Yet, the social question in the traditional European sense the church first addressed in *Rerum Novarum* was never raised in quite the same way in the United States.

The tremendous surge of people entering the New World longing for freedom, determined to escape the narrowness of "enlightened absolutism" and the paternalism of the state and semifeudal social structures, were willing to move from opportunity to ever new opportunities should existing conditions prove unacceptable. This willingness, combined with the promise of opportunities held out by the expanse of the country, prevented conditions from developing in the New World similar to those that, in nineteenth century Europe, brought forth socialist movements, the birth of mass unions and the assumption of social responsibilities on the part of the state through social legislation.

That Marxist thinking and socialist movements never amounted to much in America and that industrial unions and social legislation did not develop until well into the twentieth century has a great deal to do with the basic historical differences that separate economic and social developments in Europe and the United States. In Europe, markets around the turn of the century were mostly cartels regulated by producers alone or in combination with state intervention. In continuation of mercantilistic traditions, state intervention was considered an indispensable remedy against the consequences of unchecked capitalistic competition. At the same time in the United States, the Sherman Anti-Trust Act was enacted in 1890 as a charter of economic freedom and an expression of the determination of the American people to accept neither a political dictator nor a dictator of prices in the market place. Legal protection of industrial unions in the United States had to wait until the Wagner Act of 1936 prevented courts from treating workers' associations as illegal conspiracies. In Germany, industrial unions were protected de facto since the beginning of the twentieth century and enjoyed constitutional protection since 1919. In the United States, social legislation in any meaningful way began with the New Deal as a response to the consequences of the Great Depression. In Europe, especially in Germany, the welfare state had developed its basic structures prior to World War I.

It is against this background of significant differences in economic and social development of the Old and the New Worlds that the pastoral letter now addresses the social question. In order to evaluate its message, it is important to note its purpose. The letter wants to analyze the U.S. economy and approaches this task in a pragmatic and evolutionary way. Its approach is shaped by three questions: What does the economy do *for* people, what does it do *to* people, and how do people *participate* in it? Again, it asks one single question: How does the economic system affect the lives of people—*all* people?

Thus, the pastoral letter's primary criterion in judging the economy is not adherence to particular ideologies, but the impact it has on human beings. In reflecting on the particular realities of the American economy, the bishops are aware of the need to address not only individual issues, but the larger questions of the economic system itself. These systemic questions cannot be ignored in the Catholic vision of economic justice. Some of the questions the bishops consider to be systemic are stated as examples, but they are not explored directly. Rather, the bishops prefer to address four specific topics: employment, poverty, food and agriculture and international economic concerns. These topics were chosen in view of their relevance both to the economic "signs of the times" and to the ethical norms of Catholic social teaching. They are meant to exemplify the interactions of moral values and economic issues, but do not constitute a comprehensive analysis of the U.S. economy. The letter addresses many questions that are clearly affairs of this world and have a rightful independence the bishops must respect. Within the context shaped by such respect, however, the bishops seek to uncover the moral and religious meaning of the urgent economic problems facing the United States today. In doing so, they present the church's moral and religious tradition as a framework for addressing the deeper question about the meaning of economic life; "something not well-known in our country today," as the bishops see it, "must transform the lives of individuals and our culture as a whole." For it is meaningless to seek to transform structures if the hearts of people are not changed. Thus, the twofold aim of the pastoral letter is to help U.S. Catholics form their consciences on the moral dimensions of economic decision making, and to articulate a moral perspective in the general societal and political debate that surrounds these questions.

This two-tier approach of the pastoral letter, while basic to the document, is the main source of a certain ambivalence that characterizes the bishops' approach to economic matters. At the heart of this approach lies the unresolved question of the relationship between the structures of the economic system and its structures and the economic actions of all those who live, work and operate in the framework of the economic order. The answer to this question is crucial to any policy or effort to bring about fundamental change in those social and economic structures that today "perpetuate glaring inequalities and cut off millions of citizens from full participation in the economic and social life of the nation."

The bishops are, of course, aware of the interdependence between the structures and institutions of the economy and of society at large and the actions and attitudes of people. They clearly see this interdependence when it comes to making the right use of institutions; that is, they stress the need of moral reform. Their letter is a most impressive document in appealing to a wealthy majority on whom rests the responsibility to share with the poor and care for the needy and those who cannot help themselves. In the best of Catholic tradition, the bishops arouse the consciences of all who are strong and can help. They firmly declare the disparities of income and wealth in the United States to be unacceptable. Justice, they hold, requires that society take the necessary steps to decrease these inequities. For the obligation to provide justice for all means "that the poor have the most urgent claim on the conscience of the nation." The fulfillment of their basic needs is of the highest priority. With equal determination, the bishops take their stand on unemployment. As a nation, they feel, Americans simply cannot afford to have millions of able-bodied men and women unemployed. Neither the economic cost, the social dislocation and the enormous human tragedies caused by unemployment nor, in the end, the assault on human dignity that occurs when millions are left without adequate employment are affordable. Therefore, the pastoral letter "cannot but conclude that current levels of unemployment are morally unacceptable."

These clear moral condemnations of poverty and unemployment and the resulting demands for moral reforms and fundamental changes in attitudes are, however, not accompanied by equally precise suggestions on how these changes can be brought about. Even though the bishops have little hope of altering the unacceptable conditions of poverty and unemployment through structural changes if the hearts of people are not changed, they pay surprisingly little attention to the possible influences structural conditions can have on people's hearts. As a consequence, they hardly pursue the question of which structural changes might be required in order to bring about a change in heart without which the present morally unacceptable conditions cannot be eliminated.

The bishops are, of course, aware of the need for structural change. "Whether the problem is preventing war, building peace, or addressing the needs of the poor, Catholic teaching emphasizes not only the individual conscience, but also the political, legal and economic structures through which policy is determined and issues are adjudicated. Sin can be social as well as individual. The pastoral letter, though, remains surprisingly vague when it comes to defining the political and economic structures involved and the nature of their change. A constant effort to shape decisions and institutions in ways that enhance human dignity and reflect the grandeur and glory of God is seen as a most important path to holiness."

The bishops hold that social justice includes a duty to organize economic and social institutions so that people can contribute to society in ways that respect their freedom and the dignity of their labor. Thus, social justice demands that society's institutions be ordered in a way that guarantees all persons the ability to participate actively in economic, political and cultural life. To this end, in view of the pastoral letter, the United States needs serious dialogue about the appropriate levels of private- and public-sector involvement. The key priorities stipulated by the letter are to govern both personal decisions, social policies and economic institutions. The bishops see parallels with the political challenge that confronted the founding fathers. They had to develop ways of thinking and political institutions that had not existed before in order to create a new form of political democracy. They thus launched an experiment in the protection of civil and political rights that has prospered through the efforts of those who came after them. The bishops see the need for a similar experiment in securing economic rights: "The creation of an order that guarantees the minimum conditions of human dignity in the economic sphere for every person." Through their letter, they hope to contribute to such a new venture to secure economic justice for all—a new "American experiment."

To be sure, the bishops' letter does assert certain basic principles that challenge the nature of economic and political institutions. One relates to the church's opposition to all statist and totalitarian approaches to socioeconomic questions.

Social life, the bishops point out, is richer than governmental power can encompass. However, in spite of the important roles played by social pluralism and social groups in the pursuit of economic justice, government has a moral function to protect human rights and secure basic justice for all members of the commonwealth. More specifically, government is expected to assist and empower the poor, the disadvantaged, the handicapped and the unemployed. It should assume "a positive role in generating employment. The way society responds to the needs of the poor through its public policies is the litmus test of its justice or injustice." As a consequence, the bishops recommend that the nation make a major new commitment to achieve full employment.

True to basic Catholic social teaching, the pastoral letter defines the relationship between government and society through the principal of "subsidiarity." Government should undertake only those initiatives necessary for protecting basic justice that exceed the capacity of individuals or private groups acting independently. Government interventions are called for, then, when small or intermediate groups in society are unable or unwilling to take the steps to promote basic justice. From these principles, the pastoral letter concludes that the role of government is to work in partnership with the many other groups in society, helping these groups to fulfill their tasks and responsibilities more effectively, not destroying them. It sees the need to move beyond abstract disputes about whether more or less governmental intervention is needed to considerations of creative ways to enable government and private groups to work effectively together.

To ensure this cooperation, the letter stresses the need for economic planning. Anticipating negative reaction, it points to the fact that planning already takes place on all levels of the economy and of necessity must continue. One must agree with the bishops when they insist on that reasonable condition for any functioning society, let alone a free society based primarily on the cooperation of its members and their agents in the framework of public consensus on the major objectives of society.

If the bishops' position on government and society meets with criticism, it will not be because of the application of the principle of subsidiarity, nor because of the general notion that planning is a reasonable element in society and its economic activities. It will be because of the rather open definition of government and the concept of cooperation. The bishops relate individual and group responsibility to the functions of government by presenting government as an agent through which citizens collectively carry out their moral responsibility to help the poor. This concept, taken together with the recommendation to establish a partnership between government and social groups, may reveal a lack of appreciation for the basic differences between governmental action and group action and between the power of government and individuals acting in concert or through social agents of their choice. One of the reasons for the growing uneasiness about expanding government is the continuous erosion of these basic differences. It results in a cross-penetration of government, the state and society, thus leveling traditional distinctions between society and the state that, in the bishops' view, provide the basic framework for organized public efforts to respond to the demands of justice in society.

It is difficult to determine whether this conclusion is implied in the pastoral letter or is faithful to its intentions. The bishops have chosen to remain vague on practically all questions of practical institutional arrangements to support or supplement their demands for social action beyond the responsibilities of the individual in promoting social justice. This is all the more surprising in light of what the Lay Commission on Catholic Social Teaching and the U.S. Economy has said on the subject. Contrary to the pastoral letter, the Lay Commission's statement, *Toward the Future: On Catholic Social Thought and the U.S. Economy*, places considerable emphasis on the relationship between the fundamental ordering of political, economic, moral and cultural institutions. An unsound order, this document points out, dooms even virtuous people to misery. If the United States is not today a "Third World nation," this is so, the commission holds, above all because of the fundamental ordering of its institutions.

Ordering of institutions, like ideas, has consequences. It is to these consequences, to questions of system and economic structure, that the Lay Commission directs its attention, not in order to slight the importance of the virtues of social justice, but to address what the commission calls the most disputed point of the day; namely, the paradox that virtuous people can be undermined by systems of poor design. Good systems can be made to fail by a people of inapposite or unvirtuous behavior. It is this paradox, or this interdependence of virtues and institutional arrangements, that should be the centerpiece of any effort to apply Catholic social thinking to modern industrial democracy, in the United States or elsewhere. The Lay Commission repeatedly concerns itself with this problem. It recognizes that without the practice of virtue, no institution can function well. However, although it is one thing to have valid social principles, it is another to work out the practical institutional arrangements through which these principles can be routinely embodied in the laws and habits of everyday life. In citing James Madison, who argued that the rights of Americans are defended by the habits and institutions of the American people, the Lay Commission asserts that habits and institutions are precisely what Catholic social teaching needs in order to become incarnated in everyday life. From there, it proceeds to discuss three American habits especially deserving of comment: free association, cooperation, and the underlying virtue of both, typically called by Americans "the principle of self-interest rightly understood."

It would exceed the scope of this essay to elaborate on what the Lay Commission has to say on each of these habits. For the purpose of this argument, however, it is noteworthy to cite the commission's argument on the principle of self-interest rightly understood. In this context, the commission states one of the most fundamental observations governing the relationship between virtues and institutions: A free political economy does not discourage acts of heroism and self-sacrifice. It encourages many to dream great dreams, spiritual as well as temporal. However, a free society is not constructed on the belief that humans are angels. The sound daily working of institutions depends on the practice of common virtues accessible to all, conformed to common weaknesses, checking the worst excesses and trying to inspire the common best.

This observation is of great importance. It takes notice of the fact that individuals can be expected to act basically in accordance with the common good only if the institutions support this behavior and discourage continuous neglect of what would be required by the common welfare of all. The German Jesuit social philosopher, Father Oswald von Nell-Breuning, shortly after World War II, summed up the proper relationship between virtue and institutions by stating: "Those institutional orderings most deserve to be called morally acceptable that require the least moral effort on the part of the individual members of society to function properly and promote social justice."

The pastoral letter does not advance this basic principle with a clarity equal to that of the Lay Commission. This leads to many considerable shortcomings. One is the ambivalence already noted. On more basic issues, however, the pastoral letter cannot and does not answer important questions on the nature, direction and content of the structural changes it deems imperative if social justice is to be advanced. Rather, the bishops, when faced with the criticism that their treatment of institutional questions is insufficient, seem to take refuge in appeals for moral departures, reforms and increased efforts on the part of all, which can and should advance social justice.

No doubt this quest for moral and spiritual improvement of society is laudable. Yet, it leaves two questions unanswered that are basic to the ultimate success of any political or spiritual endeavor to promote social justice; namely, which institutional arrangements can we expect to produce the incentives to solve social problems of poverty or unemployment, and how must we construct the social order to allow productive and income-generating forces and incentives to aid the poor and assure basic human rights in the economy to unfold in harmony?

When the social question arose in Europe and later in the United States, majorities could gain from governmental intervention in the distribution of income and wealth, and the minority of those who were well off stood to lose. It was the time when coalitions of groups less well off could form and hold majorities necessary to legislate redistribution of income. The demands for more social justice in distributing income and opportunities and the political majorities necessary to support these demands through governmental action coincided. What was required on the grounds of moral principle was also desired by political majorities. This was the time of advanced social legislation, the expansion of governmental intervention and the development of elaborate social systems advancing social justice.

Today, partly as a result of this very development, the situation has basically changed both in the United States and in all other advanced industrial democracies. Redistribution is no longer desired by majorities because the majority is well off. It stands to lose rather than to gain if governmental intervention continues to change the pattern of income and wealth distribution to the advantage of those who are needy. As a consequence, moral demands for the distribution of income and opportunities and the interests of the majority no longer coincide. Rather, the majority that is well off must be convinced that minorities must be helped. This, quite obviously, is a different political task. The political support of those who stand to lose must be obtained if legislation or governmental action is required to help the poor or unemployed. Legislatures will not act even on moral grounds if they cannot convince themselves that majorities are willing to support the action. For the same reasons, governmental intervention cannot substitute for the lack of willingness on the part of the majority to support those in need, since this, too, requires the support of majorities and will, therefore, not take place unless support is forthcoming. By giving prominence to appeals for moral reform and the need to face up to individual responsibility for the poor, the pastoral letter acknowledges this rather fundamental change in the political structure of present-day America.

There can be no doubt that persuading the majority of those who enjoy good incomes and hold jobs to support programs to help the underprivileged would be greatly assisted if the political process could draw on the moral support of the church and on the authority of Catholic social principles accepted by the population at large. Appeals to moral principles, though, are not enough. Modern society is, after all, not made up of angels. If the promotion of social justice and efforts to overcome poverty and unemployment are to be successful in the long run, virtues have to be supported and encouraged by institutional arrangements. This has always been true, but support and encouragement have become a *conditio sine qua non* for successful social policies ever since the political and economic self-interests of the majority and the needs of the poor no longer coincided.

Surely, one of the shortcomings of the pastoral letter is that it does not give adequate weight to this important relationship between social responsibility and the institutional support of social virtues. As a consequence, many of the policy suggestions contained in the letter seem somehow unpolitical. They have the character of rather general appeals and suggestions without the hard substance of political practicality.

A good example is the pastoral letter's treatment of unemployment. The bishops with every good reason consider the present unemployment levels as unacceptable. They demand a change. The way they formulate this objective, however, and draw conclusions for political action indicates they have not fully analyzed the causes of unemployment and have not given sufficient attention to the interdependencies between unemployment on the one hand, and the structures and institutional arrangements in the labor market and in the area of social legislation, institutions and arrangements on the other hand.

Instead, the bishops argue that if America is to move toward full employment, it must first establish the right to a job for every American who wants to work. This consequence must appear obvious if one follows the letter's statement that no economy can be considered truly healthy when so many millions of people are denied jobs by forces outside their control. At no point, however, does the pastoral letter make any effort to state more precisely who is responsible for the denial of jobs, who denies them and why. This leaves but one rather general conclusion, namely, that society or the system denies jobs to millions who want to work. Obviously, such analyses alone cannot support political answers to the question of unemployment or the institutional alternatives to existing institutional conditions. As a result, the pastoral letter remains vague on what should be done to remedy this unacceptable situation. In the opinion of the bishops, participation in the life of the community as a basic human right also calls for the protection of the rights of employment, to healthy working conditions, wages and other benefits sufficient to provide individuals and their families with a standard of living in keeping with human dignity. These fundamental personal rights are seen as the minimum condition of a society whose economic institutions respect human dignity, social solidarity and justice. They are held to be as essential to human dignity as are the political and civil freedoms granted in the Bill of Rights of the U.S. Constitution.

No one will dispute the importance of these rights. Contrary to political and civil freedoms that protect the individual from the powers of the government or from powerful social institutions, these economic rights must be served by political and economic institutions, by institutional arrangements to bring forth the desired effects. If there is to be a basic right to a job paying adequate wages to support a family, there must be someone to answer this demand by fulfilling an obligation to create the job. It is obvious that a social obligation to create jobs and hire those who want to exercise their right to work is different in kind from the protective function of political and civic freedoms from oppression or denial of free speech.

The pastoral letter does not recognize this difference sufficiently, but of course, it cannot avoid it. Thus, it must remain ambiguous when it tries to answer the question how the right to work can be accomplished. Indeed, the letter is full of ambiguity. For example, the bishops criticize policies that put large amounts of talent and capital into the production of luxury consumer goods and military technology while failing to invest in economic sectors that produce urgently needed jobs. They consider new forms of cooperation among labor, management, government and other social groups essential for solving the problems of unemployment. A broader vision of managerial responsibilities is called for. In accordance with Catholic social teaching, a social mortgage is placed on private property. (Article 14 of the Constitution of the Federal Republic of Germany, by the way, relates the protection of private property to the existence of social responsibility by the property owner, thus defining the substance as well as the limits of the right to private property.)

The bishops oppose collectivist and statist economic approaches, but they also reject the notion that the free market automatically produces justice, an idea that has long been overcome in the discussion of the structures and institutional arrangements of what is called in Germany "soziale Marktwirtschaft" (social-market-economy). Relief for the poor, the bishops feel, cannot be left to the arithmetic of the marketplace. A greater spirit of partnership is needed; competition alone will not do the job. There is no doubt of a bias against the market and competition as institutional arrangements for the participation of many in planning the economy and distributing goods and services directed by the price mechanism, which for a long time has been characteristic of Catholic social teaching and repeatedly manifests itself in the pastoral letter.

Possibly, it is this very bias that keeps the bishops from a more thorough analysis of these institutional arrangements. This deficiency is all the more surprising if one considers that it was in the United States at the turn of the century that the political implications of a competitive market economy were fully realized, while Europe remained under the control of economic structures that left little room for open competition, innovation and free market developments. In any case, the pastoral letter makes no effort to discuss or explain the kind of institutional arrangements that could bring about an economic order that would achieve both economic goals and social justice. This politically decisive task is left to the vision and imagination of those who are considered responsible for overcoming the unacceptable deficiencies of the American economic system—business, labor leaders, politics, the general public, or society at large.

Had the pastoral letter been restricted to describing general obligations of a moral and political nature resulting from economic conditions in the United States, this omission would have made sense. The bishops would have served notice to the American people that principles of Catholic social teaching must find social conditions in the country unacceptable and would therefore require changes. In that case, however, the bishops would have stopped short of giving advice as to how the desired results could be brought about. They would have considered the development of new institutional arrangements, structures and legislation as secular matters and would have respected the responsibility of those who are entrusted with respective mandates.

Many feel that this restraint would have been appropriate, but perhaps not. Catholic social teaching can produce more than the definition of moral and ethical demands on society resulting from unacceptable developments. It does supply us with the principles of justice, solidarity and subsidiarity, and a frame of reference for the ordering of institutions in such a way as to conform to these principles. In order to make adequate use of this frame of reference, though, one must first study and describe the existing institutional arrangements and the way they function. One must appreciate their complexity and interdependence, understand their consequences and the laws governing these consequences. One must also analyze the deficiencies in these arrangements that produce injustices and violations of basic economic "rights." Only then will it be possible to respond with political effectiveness to the deficiencies the pastoral letter so eloquently describes.

The Lay Commission has come considerably closer to this objective than the pastoral letter. It pays equal attention to the problem of helping the poor and to the conditions that lead to the creation of wealth, without which all efforts to better the situation of the underprivileged in society must remain futile. While the pastoral letter hardly mentions the fact that only prosperous businesses can create additional jobs and, as a consequence, conditions must be created in which businesses can be creative and prosperous, the Lay Commission devotes considerable prominence to this important aspect of the democratic order and its institutional arrangements. In doing so, the Lay Commission analyzes the basic institutions and concepts of a socially responsible market economy and their interdependencies; namely, unions, profit, self-interest, the profit motive, the market, multinational cooperation and rich and poor nations. What the Lay Commission has to say on each of these subjects and how it relates them to the principles of Catholic social teaching rank among the best reflections on and interpretations of Catholic social thought and the modern industrial democratic societies of the West.

To sum up, from a European point of view, the pastoral letter is both a historic and encouraging document, in spite of its shortcomings. It demonstrates the vitality of Catholic social thought and the creative influence it can have on the problems of our time. The bishops are to be applauded for opening the debate on the future of social justice in the modern industrial democratic societies of the West, particularly in the United States, and for assuring Catholic social teaching a prominent role in this debate. Their openness and clarity in describing existing deficiencies and unacceptable conditions and in confronting us with the religious and moral imperatives that call on us for remedy deserve praise and encouragement.

As the debate continues, however, an effort should be made to bring the pastoral letter and the Lay Commission's report more closely together. Seen as a whole, both documents offer impressive proof of the moral as well as institutional guidance Catholic social thought can give to the permanent cultural and political task of constructing an economic and social order that gives glory to God by serving the dignity of human beings.

16

Reactions from Management
MANUFACTURING
James E. Burke

The bishops have undertaken an awesome task in producing a pastoral letter on "Catholic Social Teaching and the U.S. Economy." The subject is complex, and even in these early stages of the discussion, it has generated strong intellectual and emotional responses from many diverse factions. The very fact that there is such interest on the part of so many is in itself an early reward for the bishops' efforts and a tribute to what they are trying to accomplish.

The stated fundamental aims of the letter are "to provide guidance for members of our church as they seek to form their own consciences about economic matters," and to add the bishops' collective voice "to the public debate about the direction in which the U.S. economy should be moving." Too, the consultative process used in drafting the document helps to focus and clarify the bishops' own thinking as they pursue their mission.

This chapter fully supports the bishops as they lay down principles for Catholics for the creation of a more humane society, respecting the independent rights of all its members; it is also in complete accord with the Biblical underpinnings of the text of the document. In the spirit of constructive criticism, however, some strongly dissenting views are offered.

The current very serious social problems in the United States are well articulated by the bishops, who have made a real contribution to society by sensitizing it to the need for new and more creative solutions. While it is quite appropriate for the bishops to call for solutions to these problems, their position is greatly weakened by offering recommendations about specific decisions or policies. These are extremely complicated problems and the bishops themselves seemed to question the propriety of their own efforts when they note:

> *We are aware that the movement from principle to policy is complex*
> *and difficult. We undertake this task with the firm conviction that mor-*

al values are essential in determining public policies, but with the understanding that ethical principles in themselves do not dictate specific kinds of programs or provide blueprints for action. Rather, principles must interact with empirical data, with historical, social and political realities, and with competing demands for limited resources. The soundness of our prudential judgments in this area will depend not only on the moral force of our principles, but also on the empirical accuracy of our information and the validity of our assumptions.

The "empirical accuracy" of some of the information in the document, as well as the "validity" of some of the assumptions made, are questionable. Even though the second draft is considerably less negative in tone than the first, it still improperly portrays the U.S. enterprise system as one primarily motivated by profit and lacking in any moral imperative. It continues to cast the multinational company as an institution designed to serve narrow interests rather than one that by its very nature also serves the commonweal. Consequently, the search for solutions to our social problems tends to focus on government and thus leads to the likelihood of a reincarnation of the failed programs of the past.

The bishops' pastoral letter remains unbalanced because in its concentration on the unsolved problems in our society, it neglects any serious examination of the extraordinary accomplishments that we have made in the very areas of their concern. As a result, while they reference the "principle of subsidiarity" of Pius XI's by saying, "This principle states that government should undertake only those initiatives necessary for protecting basic justice that exceed the capacity of individuals or private groups acting independently," the bishops appear to have no real understanding of what has been done, is being done, and can be done by the private sector as they call for a more active governmental role.

The bishops address four specific priorities: unemployment, poverty, food and agriculture, and international economic concerns. Although all of these are enormously important, this study will focus on the unemployment issue, which is a central concern to those who have the responsibility of managing a business.

The current joblessness in the United States is intolerable, particularly among the youth. The French scientist and philosopher René Dubos referred to the worst dangers in the world in this way:

The very worst danger, I think, is nuclear warfare. . . . I don't really know that it is the worst . . . but so many people say it is the worst . . . I am inclined to agree. I think the second worst danger is unemployment among young people. Sometimes I believe this is really the biggest problem . . . but I worry chiefly about the young. If young people feel totally cut off from our culture, which they do when they are unemployed and perhaps unemployable, then they create their own culture. I shudder to think of it.

Business *is* concerned with the pernicious impact on society of current rates of unemployment, particularly the structural unemployment of our youth. In addressing this issue, however, the bishops fail to give proper recognition to what has been accomplished in creating jobs in the United States. While they do note that our economy has created more than 20 million new jobs since 1970—the figure is actually 27 million—they neglect to point out that Europe, with a population base somewhat higher than ours, has had no net increase in jobs during the same period. European unemployment rates are high: 10.2 percent in Italy, 8.5 percent in France, 9.2 percent in Germany and 12.5 percent in Great Britain, compared with our 7 percent. Moreover, the percentage of those unemployed in Europe who are classified as long-term unemployed (12 months or more) is dramatically higher than here in the United States: Germany 32 percent, United Kingdom 40 percent, France 42 percent and the Netherlands 55 percent. The figure in the United States is 12 percent, a striking difference.

European business, labor and government leaders have been impressed by our ability to create new jobs over the past 15 years. In their travels, American businesspeople are often asked to explain how our economy deals so successfully with unemployment. Europe has not yet fully absorbed the post-war baby boom into its work force, as we have, its situation is worsening, while ours is steadily improving.

There are many reasons for our success in creating jobs. One analysis by the Business Roundtable, "Job Creation: The United States and European Experience," gives some insight to our success. It reads:

> *The ability of the U.S. economy to generate jobs and absorb an increasing supply of labor is well noted in this paper and elsewhere. Western Europe also has created new jobs. The growth of jobs in the service sector in all the major Western European countries illustrates that fact. The crux of the European problem, however, has been the failure to generate enough jobs to offset the loss of jobs and labor displacement in declining sectors of their economies—industry and agriculture— and at the same time absorb the large influx of new entrants coming into the work force.*

> *An important factor affecting job creation is the relative ease of job destruction, the ability of firms to shrink in response to changing demand. European manpower adjustment policies and other labor market rigidities, including the high cost of employment relative to other production factors, curtail employment growth in economic upswings and impede the growth of new businesses and new jobs by making it very difficult—and in some cases, almost impossible—to lay off workers in economic downturns. European policies which protect existing jobs impose heavy entry and exit costs on European businesses and discourage beneficial churning, the loss of old firms and the birth of new ones. In the United States, a significant amount of new job growth comes from the birth, and turnover, of small firms. Business entry and exit are easier and less costly in the United States, thus encouraging entrepreneurial risk and in the process creating jobs. In Europe, there is more firm stability and job security but also employment stagnation. . . .*

Although in the short run the European approach may appear to be a more humane industrial system, a longer-term view shows that these policies have institutionalized rigidities, made the European economies and labor markets more inflexible and made European firms less competitive. In the wake of these policies, economic growth slows, job creation withers and unemployment continues to grow.

A comparison of our respective performances suggests that in Europe, governments have been heavily relied on for solutions to unemployment; and although full employment is still the elusive goal of any just society, it cannot be mandated by government without threatening the very freedoms that make it possible to generate new jobs in the first place. So, there are serious concerns with this reference in the bishops' pastoral:

If we are to move toward full employment, we must first establish the right to a job for every American who wants to work. Then the burden is on all of us. . . .

After pointing out that "private initiative and entrepreneurship are essential to the task, for the private sector accounts for about 80 percent of the jobs in the United States . . ." the bishops go on to say, "Therefore, the government must act to ensure that this goal is achieved by coordinating general economic policies, by job creation programs, and by other appropriate policy measures." A review of what was attempted in postwar Europe will show that this is exactly what governments attempted to do in country after country, with poor results.

Michael S. Joyce comments on this same aspect of the bishops' pastoral:

The effect of the bishops' proposal would empower the state to take actions which would inevitably come into conflict with our fundamental human rights.

This gives rise to some disturbing questions. Would the powers granted by the bishops to our government permit the government to circumscribe plant closings? Prevent the right to lay off surplus workers? Define what are appropriate wages, work hours and benefits? Determine the extent of job creation programs? Decide which businesses would be nationalized? What effects would further government intervention have on the *creation* of productive jobs or on the creation of wealth?

It is hard to find empirical data anywhere that justify the government "ensuring" the goal of full employment. Still, this does not lessen the need for drastic and prompt action to curb the terrible blight of unemployment, especially among our minority youth. It is both morally and economically unjustifiable to have over one third of our minority youth unemployed, with many also unemployable.

The concern of René Dubos that unemployed youth would create their own culture is already a reality in the United States. The terrible scourge of drugs as well as the concomitant burgeoning costs of crime are now being woven into the fabric of an underclass in our society that all of us should deem intolerable.

This problem demands a better understanding of the underlying causes of unemployment. Therefore, we must commit ourselves to the "cooperative efforts" for which the bishops call and to the imaginative new forms of partnership they seek.

The bishops seek expansion of job-training and apprenticeship programs administered and supported jointly by business, labor unions and government. It is hoped that in the final draft the bishops will emphasize to all of us our responsibilities in this area and urge us to support aggressively a model program now in place and designed for productive cooperation between government and the private sector; specifically, the Job Training Partnership Act (JTPA), which was passed with bipartisan support by Congress in 1982 and became effective October 1, 1983. This legislation provides a new design of programs formerly operated under the Comprehensive Employment and Training Act (CETA) program and offers an important new role for the business community.

The Chamber of Commerce, the National Association of Manufacturers, the Committee for Economic Development, the National Alliance of Business and the Business Roundtable worked together for the passage of JTPA to provide an effective and flexible role for business. In essence, the JTPA provides grants to state and community agencies so they can tailor training to local needs. It is most encouraging that 70 percent of all funds in the program are spent directly on training.

Under the law, a Private Industry Council (PIC) must be established at the local level. These PICs are made up primarily of local business leaders who, along with local government officials, play a pivotal role in planning and administering the training programs. It is a true partnership, with business and political leaders working together to meet the long-term training needs of the hard to employ. With the support of business, some 8,000 corporate volunteers are now serving on more than 600 local PICs, and 1 million disadvantaged persons have enrolled in job-oriented training programs.

Although it is premature to measure the full impact of the program, over 94 percent of those served to date had been classified as economically disadvantaged. In addition, 64 percent of trained graduates have been hired by local employers. The National Alliance of Business (NAB), which traditionally has been the principal private-sector agent in matters related to training and employment of disadvantaged or dislocated workers, also indicates that the average cost per placement under JTPA amounts to only about $5,000.

In general, the program speaks well for this kind of cooperative effort and contrasts remarkably with such previous government efforts as the ill-fated CETA. As President Reagan put it, "The vital difference between this program (JTPA) and the failed ones of the past is that, this time, private employers will take the lead, not the federal government. No one knows better than private employers the skills and training needed by today's employees."

The cost of the CETA program from 1974 to 1982 amounted to some $58.4 billion, and yet during all of this time, structural unemployment grew steadily. Ray Marshall, Secretary of Labor under President Carter and one of CETA's strongest supporters, acknowledged that CETA was an extremely complex system with multiple and conflicting objectives, 50,000 subcontractors, inadequate management information systems and ridiculously short funding cycles. He also noted that the political process posed a significant barrier to success by creating timing difficulties, exaggerated expectations and a proliferation of program objectives, exacerbating problems in administration.

In contrast, JTPA to date has progressed fairly smoothly and has been twice as effective as CETA in placing program participants at half the cost. Business will soon be able to provide a realistic evaluation of the extent to which we have been able to unify and integrate various employment and training systems and coordinate public and higher education systems with employment training in every state. In addition to supporting the training aspects of JTPA, business is also committed to hiring these disadvantaged youths into real jobs and providing the support mechanisms to have them remain and grow in their work.

Companies associated with JTPA are committed to helping minority youths break the stranglehold of poverty and dependency and to assist them to move more rapidly into the mainstream of American economic life. This is precisely the kind of results the bishops are striving to achieve.

Closely related to the problems of disadvantaged youth are the disruptions taking place in our family structures. Inexplicably, the bishops fail to address to any significant extent the family factors that are seriously impairing the economic prospects of a growing number of Americans. For instance, the single-parent family, resulting largely from divorce, separation or abandonment, is increasingly being drawn into poverty and its aftermath. By contrast, in homes where both husbands and wives are present, poverty is substantially lower. Since the church traditionally places such a high value on the centrality of family, it can be expected to place greater attention on the role the breakdown of families plays in the unemployment issue, particularly among disadvantaged youth.

In the other most important area of unemployment—the displaced worker—the Business Roundtable recommends that the private sector play a strong role with government. Together, they must demonstrate a firm commitment to jobs for American workers whose employment has been interrupted by worldwide competitive forces or technological changes. In acknowledging the adverse human impact caused by the changing nature of work, the Roundtable supports the National Center on Occupational Readjustment (NaCOR), which was formed in 1983 by the business community as a private, nonprofit foundation. Its purpose is to provide a national clearinghouse and resource center available to all employees facing such economic change as plant closings and worker dislocation.

Initial funding has been provided by a demonstration grant from the Department of Labor under Title III of the Job Training Partnership Act. Paralleling many of the ideas expressed in the bishops' letter, NaCOR has prepared a guidebook to assist corporations in reaching decisions that are in the best interests of all parties. Some of the areas it examines are alternatives to the shutdown; internal company preparations, including planning, communications, notification and compensation; income assistance programs; relocation assistance; and reemployment assistance.

Another effort the Roundtable endorses is being carried forth by Secretary of Labor Brock's new Task Force on Economic Adjustment and Worker Dislocation. This group is composed of representatives from business, labor and the public sector, and is charged with studying the problem and providing the Secretary with recommendations by the end of 1986.

A substantial number of the estimated 500,000 to 1,000,000 displaced workers in the United States are out of jobs because of technological changes. The impact of these changes has not been adequately addressed by the bishops, particularly with regard to the computer and information systems revolution that is drastically altering the work habits of a large segment of the American work force. Although the pastoral speaks of a major movement away from an industrial-based, manufacturing, production-oriented economy to a knowledge-based, information–communication, science-oriented economy, there should be more discussion regarding the implications that these innovations will continue to have on our national work force. It is certain that with the acceleration in technological change and the advent of new international competition, worker displacement will be a chronic problem for the foreseeable future.

The Business Roundtable continues to address this issue and has developed special guidelines for its members to help reduce the trauma of plant closings. The booklet includes commentaries on the joint responsibilities of business, labor and government and offers suggestions on how to make the process as fair and reasonable as possible.

In truth, business, labor and government do not yet have a comprehensive understanding of the displaced worker crisis and consequently, our efforts to deal with it have clearly been inadequate. There is little disagreement that more needs to be done to understand better the problems of all kinds of unemployment, whether we label them structural, displaced worker, frictional, or seasonal. Any person who is out of work and wants a job is our collective responsibility—government, organized labor and private enterprise.

The greatest share of this responsibility should be borne by business organizations, for three reasons. The first is the fact that 80 percent of all jobs are in business, and economic growth is the "engine" of job creation. The second is that the overwhelming evidence supports the contention that our enterprise system is more effective in creating jobs than the European systems, in which governments have assumed more active roles. The third and most important reason, is that business, it can be said, has a moral obligation to seek solutions to such social problems as unemployment and the other issues identified by the bishops. It can be argued that this responsibility is implicit in the charters of all United States corporations, and there is clear evidence that those companies that organize their businesses around the broad concept of serving the public turn in superior performance for their stockholders over the long run.

How this philosophy works can best be described by recounting the experience of the following company. It begins with a quotation from a document written in the early 1940s by the late Robert Wood Johnson, son of the company's founder and the person largely responsible for the philosophies that have been key to Johnson & Johnson's success. He wrote:

Institutions, both public and private, exist because the people want them, believe in them, or at least are willing to tolerate them. The day has passed when business was a private matter—if it ever really was. In a business society, every act of business has social consequences and may arouse public interest. Every time business hires, builds, sells, or buys, it is acting for the people as well as for itself, and it must accept full responsibility for its acts. . . .

This was part of a preamble to a document that Johnson entitled simply, "Our Credo." Even though it may seem a little pretentious at first glance, its philosophical principles are pretty basic. In essence, the "Credo" articulates the company's responsibilities to all of those in society who are dependent on it.

■ First, to the consumers—doctors, nurses, patients and mothers who buy the products and services.
■ Second, to the employees, whose creative energies are responsible for those same products and services.
■ Third, to the communities—not just where the plants and offices are, but all of the various communities dealt with, including the community of man.
■ Finally, to the stockholders who invest their money in this enterprise.

The company puts the stockholders last because it believes that if it does the other jobs properly, the stockholder will be well served. The record suggests that this has been the case.

These guiding principles were disseminated among the employees, and a generation later, in 1975, some of the management became concerned about whether it was practicing what it preached. By then, the corporation had become large and complex, with well over 100 companies around the world, each with its own separate mission in the health care field. Corporate headquarters was concerned that the Credo perhaps had greater meaning there than to those who were ultimately responsible for managing the various businesses. So an experiment was tried and 24 managers from the United States and overseas were invited to a meeting to challenge the Credo. The meeting was opened with the observation that the document was displayed in most of the company's offices around the world, and if were not a commitment to it, then it was an act of pretension and ought to be ripped off the walls. The group was challenged to recommend whether it should be gotten rid of, rewritten, or committed to as it was.

The meeting was a "turn-on," a genuine happening, as managers struggled with the issues the Credo defined. When the first debate ended, the managers discovered they had a set of guiding principles far more powerful than they had imagined. Virtually everyone was energized by the idea that in their business, they were responsible to all of their constituencies—all those who were dependent on them.

This was the beginning of a series of Credo challenge meetings that took place over the next three years. They included all of key managers from the United States and overseas. In the final analysis, the philosophy remained basically unchanged, although some of the responsibilities were expanded to take cognizance of a much more complicated world. The revitalized Credo was a statement of purpose that everyone understood as well as had the chance to contribute to it. It was officially presented to the managers in June of 1979.

Commitment to the Credo was dramatically tested three years later when someone chose one of the firm's products—Tylenol—to be used as a murder weapon. The Tylenol story is well-known, but for those in management who were required to make hundreds of decisions in painfully short periods of time, it was an unrelenting nightmare. Most of the decisions involved considerable risk, and there was no historical precedent on which to rely. However, the Credo was used for guidance, and management truly believes that it played *the* most important role in the decision making and in the firm's success in reestablishing Tylenol to its preeminent position in the marketplace.

The Tylenol story is, of course, unique, but it serves to reaffirm dramatically a philosophy that is not. The most successful corporations in this country, the ones that have delivered outstanding results over a long period of time, were driven by a simple moral imperative: to serve the public in the broadest possible sense better than the competition.

Strong evidence has been developed to support this contention. Working with the Business Roundtable's Task Force on Corporate Responsibility and the Ethics Resource Center in Washington, D.C., Johnson & Johnson searched for companies that shared its beliefs about corporate responsibility for at least a generation. Found were 26 companies with a written, codified set of principles stating a philosophy that serving the public was central to their being.

The performance of these 26 companies over a 30-year period (ending in May 1985) shows their profits grew 10.7 percent a year, more than twice the growth of the gross national product during the same period.

Only 15 of these companies had comparable stock price data that could be analyzed—AT&T, Coca Cola, General Foods, Gerber Products, IBM, J. C. Penney, John Deere, Johnson & Johnson, Kodak, 3M, Pitney Bowes, Procter & Gamble, R. J. Reynolds, Sun Company and Xerox—but the results of these companies in serving their stockholders is impressive. The study was completed May 8, 1985. An investment of $30,000 in the Dow Jones averages 30 years earlier would have been worth $88,231 on that date. The same $30,000 invested—$2,000 in each of these 15 companies—would have been worth $1,033,152—almost 12 times as much!

The results are, at the very least, thought-provoking. The idea that businesses organized around the broad concept of serving the public will over the long term also provide superior results for the stockholder is a philosophy that has been embraced by the founders and builders of many of the most successful American businesses.

Although it would be naive to assume that all businesses are so "enlightened," most businesses in the United States understand the inextricable interdependence of their organizations with the rest of society. More than 2,000 years ago in Athens, Aristotle wrote, "One citizen may differ with another, but the salvation of the community is the common business of us all."

We in business have the opportunity to contribute more than most to the "common business of us all," and it is very much in our self-interest to do so. This is particularly true in addressing the needs for training the structurally unemployed and the retraining of the displaced workers.

Government can, of course, play an important role, as exemplified by the highly successful albeit very expensive Job Corps program for the hard-core unemployed and the initiation of the Job Training Partnership Act previously described. We should all, however, be very cautious in looking to government for solutions. One but needs to look at the failed welfare programs in this country. There is a growing consensus that the current system has inadvertently contributed to the breakup of families and the attendant high illegitimacy rates, thus creating an ever-growing pool of poor, uneducated and often "unemployable" youth.

Again should be urged the bishops' most thoughtful consideration of the "principle of subsidiarity" and all of us in the private sector to greater involvement in those programs that are designed for "the capacity of individuals or private groups acting independently."

Although the Job Training Partnership Act has been singled out as one that deserves broad business support, there are many other programs in the areas of education, training and job creation showing very exciting results—the "Cities & Schools" program, "Action for Excellence" and "Magnet Schools," to name just a few.

Unemployment in this country is at the crux of many of our social ills. A bishops' pastoral that exhorts all of us in business—large and small—to the moral imperative of addressing this problem vigorously could have a very tangible impact on the goal of providing "a job for every American who wants to work." On the other hand, accepting the concept currently enunciated by the bishops that "the government must act to ensure that this goal is achieved by coordinating general economic policies, by job creation programs, and by other appropriate policy measures" could mean the end of our enterprise system as we know it.

Labor Views The Pastoral Letter On The Economy

Thomas R. Donahue
Rudolph A. Oswald

The U.S. bishops' pastoral letter on "Catholic Social Teaching and the U.S. Economy" is good news to trade unionists of all religions. In their comprehensive restatement of the whole of the church's social teaching, the bishops have provided leadership that energizes the hopes and strengthens the efforts of millions who believe that America has special advantages and opportunities in fulfilling the call to create a just society, and that America's failings in achieving that society can and must be corrected.

The bishops are to be applauded for tenaciously holding their course in the face of powerful efforts to bend in one direction or another and for the integrity of purpose that shines through their work. Written large across the pastoral is the call for an experiment in economic democracy to extend and complete America's two centuries of effort to achieve political democracy. The pastoral displays the conviction that justice requires the recognition of human rights in the sphere of economics as well as in politics.

Opposition to this view, some of it hysterical, echoes the reception accorded to another pastoral letter on the U.S. economy issued two thirds of a century ago. Among the reforms proposed in the Catholic bishops' letter of 1919 were the establishment of a minimum wage; insurance against unemployment, sickness and old age; public housing for the working poor; a long-term program to increase wages; the regulation of utility rates to curb excess profits; the establishment of cooperative stores; and cooperation between workers and employers through joint enterprises and worker ownership of stock.

On many of these points, America has made much progress over the last

67 years. Back then, for advocating that progress, the bishops were denounced for their "socialistic tendencies" by a joint committee of the New York State Legislature investigating "seditious" activities, and the president of the National Association of Manufacturers had this to say:

> *It is generally assumed that the Roman Catholic church of the United States is, and always has been, unalterable in its antagonism to all forms of socialism. It is our belief that a careful reading of the [U.S. bishops'] pamphlet will lead to the conclusion we have reached, namely, that it involves what may prove to be a covert effort to disseminate partisan, pro-labor union, socialistic propaganda under the official insignia of the Roman Catholic church of America.*

While the 1986 letter's explicit reiteration of the church's consistent defense of private ownership of productive property discredits any of these knee-jerk accusations, its concept of a "social mortgage" on private property imposes clear limits on the acquisition and concentration of economic power. "The church's teaching opposes collectivist and statist economic approaches," the bishops say in summary. But it also rejects the notion that a free market automatically produces justice—and so does the AFL-CIO.

Right-wing opposition in 1986 is more subtle—the code words "central planning" do duty for "seditious" or "socialistic"—but it is no less adamant than in 1919. Before the bishops put pen to paper, they came under fire from those who appear to believe that human values exist in separate baskets and that concern for spiritual and moral matters automatically disqualifies anyone from commenting on economic and social issues. The bishops—and the AFL-CIO—say exactly the opposite, that moral leaders have an obligation to address economic issues and that to tolerate high unemployment in a society in which wages and the distribution of wealth are skewed to intolerable extremes is itself an immoral act.

Right-wing Catholic laypeople who rushed to get their objections on record before the pastoral letter was published would no doubt have welcomed a ringing endorsement of unfettered capitalism. However, they also knew the scriptural sources of Catholic doctrine and the papal encyclicals *Rerum Novarum, Quadragesimo Anno* and *Laborem Exercens* well enough to know that they were not going to get it.

These three documents present a unitary view not only of the imperative of respect for human dignity, but of the structures necessary within any nation to pursue the papal call. In the latest, *Laborem Exercens,* Pope John Paul II added the teaching that the engine of industrial democracy, trade unions, are "indispensable" to a just society.

The dimension added by the U.S. bishops is no less indispensable. That is the obligation of a social order to achieve a full employment economy. Not only the destination but the route is clearly mapped in the bishops' call for governmental support for direct job creation, expansion of job-training and apprenticeship programs, improvement in job placement services and the creation of local and state coalitions to press for all of these.

It is a blueprint for implementing Pope John Paul's call for the "indirect employer"—all of the national and international agents and agencies responsible for the whole orientation of labor policy—to get on with the processes of national and international planning.

EMPLOYMENT

The AFL-CIO concurs absolutely with the bishops' view that:

> *Full employment is the foundation of a just economy. The most urgent priority for domestic economic policy is the creation of new jobs with adequate pay and decent working conditions. We must make it possible as a nation for everyone who is seeking a job to find employment. Our emphasis on this goal is based on the conviction that human work has a special dignity and is a key to achieving justice in society.*

The urgency of that message appears lost on a majority of Americans today and certainly on political leaders who seem unable to see the 8.1 million Americans who need, want and cannot find jobs, the 1.2 million too discouraged to continue the search for work and who are therefore no longer counted, and the 5.5 million who can find only part-time jobs. As of November 1985, nearly 15 million Americans—13 percent of the work force—are wholly or partially unemployed. Even the "official" 7 percent unemployment rate at the end of 1985 is unacceptable to a humane society, but the long-range trend shows each recession starting from a higher unemployment level than the one before.

It would have been unthinkable a few short years ago to speak of "recovery" and "prosperity" while unemployment stands at 7 percent. In both 1954 and 1971, we called it recession when unemployment rose to 6.1 percent. Later in the 1970s, when the jobless rate ratcheted up, Presidents Ford and Carter launched direct job-creation programs because they, like the bishops, the AFL-CIO and the Congress that enacted the Humphrey–Hawkins Full Employment and Balanced Growth Act of 1978, accepted 3-4 percent joblessness as the upper limit for a fully employed society. That law, which requires the President to report annual numerical goals for unemployment, production, real income, productivity and prices, is annually disobeyed. Without a clear definition of full employment, we cannot have a working perspective from which to assess and address the other national needs outlined in the pastoral.

Arguments that high unemployment is a regrettable but necessary tradeoff to restrain high prices are demonstrably untrue. It is not true that high employment pushes up prices, as opponents of full-employment policies claim. Throughout the 1960s, the unemployment rate remained below 4 percent, and so did the inflation rate. Unemployment rose hand in hand with inflation during the 1970s, while inflation was fired by worldwide food shortages and huge U.S. grain sales to Russia, energy crises caused by the OPEC cartel, runaway increases in housing and health-care costs and the highest interest rates in peacetime history.

High interest rates, stemming from the nation's staggering fiscal deficit and relatively tight monetary policy, are largely responsible for high unemployment today. Home construction has declined, investment in new plant and equipment has become costlier, and the dollar has become vastly overvalued in relation to other currencies, undermining America's ability to compete with foreign producers.

Experience bears out the bishops' recommendation that "fiscal and monetary policies of the nation should be coordinated in such a way that full employment is the number one goal." However, the basic goal of fiscal policy in this country in recent years has been to cut taxes for the higher-income brackets in the mistaken belief that the benefits would trickle down to help the less fortunate in society.

Far from promoting full employment, governmental fiscal policy has undermined long-term steps to achieve full employment while specific programs to foster economic growth and employment have been scrapped. Monetary policy has been shaped by fears of inflation, not by the nation's official goal of full employment.

The bishops call for the expansion of job-training and apprenticeship programs and for direct job-creation programs targeted on the structurally unemployed, two areas that have suffered some of the biggest cuts in the federal budget between 1981 and 1985. The number of the structurally unemployed has multiplied, and those who previously were helped to get a foot on the rung of economic opportunity through public service jobs no longer have that chance because of the elimination of those programs. Clearly, governmental policies regarding training and direct job creation need to be reversed.

The pastoral letter recognizes the need to create jobs directly for the purpose of meeting society's unmet needs, and it points out the need for highways, bridges, parks, low-income housing and day care services, among others. The urgent need to improve the nation's physical infrastructure was similarly noted and spelled out in a 1983 report of the Labor–Management Group, a joint forum of the chief executive officers of the nation's largest corporations and highest elected labor leaders. The case for a major effort to match these national needs with the needs of millions of jobless workers seems rationally undeniable.

The pastoral letter's concern about plant closings and its call for effective policies to assure that workers have a voice in these decisions are not shared by the House of Representatives, which recently rejected legislation that would have required large firms to provide 60 days' advance notice of plant closings and assured workers the right to bargain with employers concerning such a decision. Recognizing the vested interest of workers who have worked for long periods for an employer, the bishops perceive the need for collective bargaining to provide a measure of protection. In labor's view, along with the training and relocation programs advocated in the letter, displaced workers should be entitled to special severance rights, pension protections, including early retirement options, and also the opportunity to purchase the plant at a fair price, if they so desire.

The new strategies recommended by the bishops to improve both the quantity and quality of jobs need more elaboration, particularly those dealing with hours of work, including job sharing, flextime, reduced workweek and limiting or abolishing compulsory overtime, all important matters to families, whether they depend on two wage earners or are headed by only one parent. Beyond these adjustments, it is surely time to reduce the standard workweek, at least to 35 hours. Reductions from the ancient sunrise-to-sunset prescription took place throughout the nineteenth and twentieth centuries up to about 1940, when the 40-hour workweek became standard. If the six-day, 72-hour workweek of a century ago were still in place, today's unemployment problem would be far worse, and the gains in productivity of nearly half a century have removed the justification of the 40-hour workweek. The AFL-CIO has long held that overtime work should be limited by raising the now obsolete overtime penalty from time-and-a-half to triple time and that overtime should be voluntary.

Although the bishops recognize the need to develop means to reduce wage differentials between men and women and to upgrade the quality of traditionally low-paying jobs, they regrettably fall short of endorsing the campaign for pay equity. Surely, jobs of comparable worth should receive the same compensation, but without a strong drive to assure pay equity, women, whose earnings average only 60 percent of men's, will continue to lag far behind men. Meanwhile, the current equal-pay-for-equal-work statute needs to be vigorously enforced.

Unaccountably, the bishops fail to emphasize the importance of adjusting the basic minimum wage to today's conditions, although in the section on poverty they note that "so long as we tolerate a situation in which people can work full-time and still be below the poverty line—a situation common among those earning the minimum wage—we will continue to have many members of the working poor." They also declare that "the provision of wages and other benefits sufficient to support a family in dignity is a basic necessity to prevent this exploitation of workers."

MINIMUM WAGE

The AFL-CIO believes that the minimum wage is an essential part of providing a floor of material well-being and that the current minimum wage is out of date. The minimum wage has deteriorated sharply in recent years. The last time Congress adjusted the minimum wage was in 1977, raising it in steps to $3.35 an hour on January 1, 1981. In the nearly six years since, the cost of living has risen some 25–27 percent, which means that to restore the same purchasing power, the minimum wage would need to be $4.25 on January 1, 1987. The minimum wage is more than $2.00 an hour below the poverty line, which is estimated to be $5.45 per hour in January 1987.

Although most workers earn more than the federal minimum, some 5-8 million are paid no more than $3.35 an hour, and some are exploited at even lower wages. Now, more than eight years since Congress last acted to adjust the minimum wage, that floor badly needs to be brought up to date. The basic idea of a minimum wage is to provide a floor to wages so human labor cannot be bought for less than a living wage and so all employers and all producers compete with one another from a base, applicable to all, which prevents exploitation. The minimum wage has fallen so far in buying power that it is in itself exploitative and no longer sufficient to support even a single person, let alone a family.

Because low-wage workers do not share in the general improvement in living standards generated by improving national productivity unless their wages rise at the same rate as other incomes, the minimum wage ought to be set in terms of average wages rather than depending on ad hoc determination by Congress. The AFL-CIO has urged that the minimum wage be set at 50 percent of the average wage paid to nonsupervisory workers. The 1949 and 1955 adjustments set the minimum at a figure equal to 52 and 54 percent of average wages, respectively. The highest relative relationship occurred with the 1967 and 1968 adjustments, at 53 and 58 percent of average wages, respectively. In 1985, the $3.35 minimum wage was only 40 percent of the average wage paid to nonsupervisory workers.

Arguments that the minimum wage is inflationary or might lead to higher unemployment are disproved by 50 years of experience showing that modest adjustments in the minimum wage brought neither widespread inflation nor massive unemployment. Recognizing that discrimination against women and minorities plays a role in the high rates of joblessness and low pay among both groups and that "discrimination against women is compounded by the lack of adequate child care services and by the unwillingness of many employers to provide flexible and part-time employment which includes fringe benefits," the bishops call for "vigorous action ... to remove barriers to full and equal employment for women and minorities." In the AFL-CIO view, the bishops pay insufficient attention to the backsliding that has been going on in the civil rights area over the past five years.

The current administration actively fails to enforce the nation's civil rights laws, gives civil rights laws and regulations the narrowest of interpretations, and presses tirelessly to reverse them. The budgets of the Equal Employment Opportunity Commission (EEOC) and other civil rights enforcement agencies have been reduced. The EEOC chair advocates a policy that would disregard statistical data showing underrepresentation as an indicator of discrimination.

Similarly, the Labor Department's Office of Federal Contract Compliance Programs has slackened enforcement of Executive Order 11246, which prohibits discrimination by federal contractors, and the Civil Rights Division of the Department of Justice opposes affirmative action and mislabels affirmative action goals and timetables as "quotas."

The AFL-CIO believes that civil rights laws must be vigorously enforced to deal with discrimination in jobs and such other areas as housing. There is a continuing serious need to put teeth into the enforcement of existing fair housing legislation.

TRADE UNIONS

The bishops, enlarging on Pope John Paul II's assertion that trade unions are "indispensable" to ensure the dignity of workers, strongly and properly criticize the work of union busters and the unfair employers whom they serve. They recognize a need for basic reform in the nation's labor laws to give workers the opportunity to exercise their rights to form and join unions.

Of the power that employers have over workers, the bishops say, "The way power is distributed in a free market economy frequently gives employers greater bargaining power than employees possess in the negotiation of wage agreements." In opposing anti-union actions, they declare, "No one may deny the right to organize for the purposes of collective bargaining without attacking human dignity itself. Therefore, we firmly oppose organized efforts, such as those regrettably now seen in this country, to use intimidation and threats to break existing unions and prevent workers" from organizing.

Reform of the nation's labor laws, which the bishops recommend "to meet these problems as well as to provide more timely and effective remedies for unfair labor practices," is urgently necessary.

Since 1957, firing for union activity and other unfair labor practices has been increasing rapidly. From 1957 to 1980, the number of unfair labor practice charges filed against employers rose from 3,655 to 31,281, while the number of elections rose from 4,729 to 7,296. In 1957, 922 illegally dismissed employees were ordered reinstated to their jobs by the National Labor Relations Board (NLRB). That number rose to 10,033 in 1980, a rise of more than tenfold. Professor Paul Weiler of Harvard University estimates that one worker is fired exercising the right to join a union for every 20 who vote in union representation elections.

As employer opposition to unions has grown, union-busting "consultants" have multiplied. Often, the hiring of these consultants signals that the employer is willing to use any method to prevent the workers from forming a union. Fear, generated through illegal firings, harassment and spying on union supporters, and intensive threats of layoffs or plant closings is a consultant's chief weapon; another is delay. Consultants orchestrate every legal objection possible in an effort to discourage workers and destroy their confidence in their union's effort to improve their situation.

An example of the widespread acceptance by business of anti-union efforts took place at the annual American Bankers Association conference in Washington, D.C., when a consulting firm openly offered attendees a "contingency plan" on "what to do if you have a union drive." For $3,000, the firm offered one day of on-site consulting, "tailoring the plan to the needs of your bank," along with comprehensive information to assist the bank's lawyers in delaying an NLRB election "to assure as much time as possible for the campaign." The intent was spelled out as to "stop any momentum gained by a union and secure the most advantageous voting unit for your bank."

The Virginia Chamber of Commerce brags that it is working "day and night" to prevent unionization in private firms, and that "At the same time, we are working day and night to prevent the organization of public employees. We have helped draft, back and pass legislation preventing collective bargaining by public employees in any area, at any level, in the Commonwealth of Virginia."

How far some firms will go in breaking the law to destroy a union is revealed in a *Charleston Gazette* news report of August 14, 1985, about a former employee of a security agency who is now seeking immunity from prosecution to tell his story. His job was to provoke violence in order to help companies get injunctions against striking unions. Besides describing actions to provoke workers on picket lines into confrontations with security guards, he tells of blowing up an electrical transformer on one occasion and setting $148,000 worth of lumber on fire on another. Both incidents were blamed on unions in order to get court injunctions.

One major conglomerate decided 20 years ago to implement its goal of a "union-free environment" by means of its merger and acquisition policies. The company began to expand in "right-to-work" states in the late 1960s and to acquire companies with anti-union policies. Finally, the company adopted the standard anti-union practices developed by union-busting consultants. As a result of the company's threats, intimidation and harassment of union supporters, unions have won only seven of 33 NLRB elections held in the company's facilities over the past 15 years. A plant in Athens, Pennsylvania, which had been with the Machinists Union for 40 years, was decertified in 1981 after an intense anti-union effort in which supervisors were instructed to grill each worker three times a week and to stress the danger of losing jobs unless the union was destroyed.

Anti-union employers break the law because it is profitable, and they will continue to do so until labor laws are reformed to penalize lawbreaking effectively and thus take the profit out of denying workers their rights. Remedies for workers illegally fired for supporting their unions must be prompt as well as effective. Current practice, requiring discharged employees to wait out lengthy court procedures to get their jobs back, creates hardship for the individual and has a chilling effect on other employees. Because the loss of a job causes family strain, humiliation, fear and intimidation as well as lost pay, then double backpay rather than merely lost wages should be required to compensate for the losses the worker suffers. Employers should also be penalized for illegally refusing to bargain. Today, all of the costs of an employer's illegal refusal to bargain rest on the employees. Violation costs lawbreaking employers nothing, even though they profit through violating the law.

The United States itself should no longer subsidize repeated, willful violations of workers' rights. For a country that preaches human rights to the rest of the world, debarment from bidding on federal contracts is a minimal action against its own human rights violators. Election procedures for workers to select a union if they so choose should be sped up or the union should be certified as bargaining agent at once if a substantial majority of the workers have signed authorization cards. These procedures would reduce the current lengthy delays that deny justice.

In stressing the importance of the right to form unions as "a specific application of the more general right to associate," the bishops touch on the AFL-CIO's conviction that democracy cannot survive the suppression of this right. Experience at home and in countries beyond our borders bears out the truth of the bishops' assertion that "violations of the freedom to associate, wherever they occur . . . are an intolerable attack on social solidarity."

THE ROLE OF UNIONS

The bishops' observation that "Perhaps the greatest challenge facing United States workers and unions today is that of developing a new vision of their role in the United States economy of the future" is timely and welcome.

Since 1982, an AFL-CIO Executive Council Committee on the Evolution of Work has been examining the changes in the work force and in the workplace. The committee issued its first report, "The Future of Work," in August 1983, then turned its attention to the implications for the trade union movement. The committee's second report, "The Changing Situation of Workers and Their Unions," issued in February 1985, has formed the basis for a self-examination by both the Federation and its affiliated unions.

The report, designed to "enable our unions to remain the authentic voice of workers and their chosen vehicle expressing their will," offered its affiliates a series of recommendations for new methods of advancing the interests of workers, ways of increasing members' participation in their unions and improving labor's communications, both internally and externally. A number of national unions have established special committees to analyze the report and discuss how its ideas might best be applied. The committee itself continues to function as a working group, assessing large numbers of new ideas and recommendations from every level of the labor movement and reviewing the implementation of earlier ones.

Also to be supported are the bishops' comments on the responsibilities of workers and trade unions:

> *Individual workers have obligations to their employers, and trade unions also have duties to society as a whole. Many U.S. unions have exercised leadership in the struggle for justice for minorities and women. Racial and sexual discrimination, however, has blotted the record of some unions. Organized labor has a responsibility to work positively toward eliminating the injustice this discrimination has caused. It should be noted, however, that wages are but one of the factors affecting the competitiveness of industry. Thus, it is unfair to expect unions to make concessions if managers and shareholders do not make at least equal sacrifices.*

Workers do care about the health of the companies in which they invest their lives. The written contract and the collective bargaining agreement are looked on not only as the cornerstone of labor–management relations, but as the basis for labor–management cooperation. The adversarial relationship that is appropriate to the negotiating process should be replaced once agreement is reached by a climate of cooperation aimed at maximizing the potential of the joint enterprise to advance the company's business and to improve the quality of workers' lives on the job and in the community. Union members care, too, about the communities in which they live. The trade union agenda includes a strong community service program as well as constructive legislative and political activities.

The labor movement does not pretend to have conquered every sign of prejudice within its ranks, but it has led the nation in rooting out systematic, institutional discrimination. These discriminatory provisions as existed in union constitutions were eliminated at the formation of the AFL-CIO in 1955, and the trade union movement became a leading participant in the civil rights coalition that secured passage of the Civil Rights Act, the Voting Rights Act, the Fair Housing Act and the Equal Pay Act. It did so because long experience has taught that equal rights are essential if workers are to achieve the solidarity that alone can make a union strong enough to win gains in the workplace. Convinced that divisiveness based on racial, ethnic, religious, or sexual distinctions has done nothing but harm to workers in their struggle for dignity in the workplace, unions have resolutely sought to eliminate these biases wherever they exist.

LABOR AROUND THE WORLD

Labor has long shared the bishops' view that to be an effective moral force, the labor movement must play a global role. American labor plays an active role in international affairs, morally and materially assisting workers in other lands to build free trade unions, especially in the developing countries of Africa, Asia and Latin America. Free and effective trade unions in those countries are essential to the defense and expansion of free and democratic societies. The U.S. labor movement also maintains relationships with other national labor organizations through the International Confederation of Free Trade Unions, the 16 international trade secretariats that group workers by their trade or industry, and the Trade Union Advisory Committee to the Organization for Economic Cooperation and Development (OECD). American unions also play a major role in the International Labor Organization (ILO).

The AFL-CIO operates international institutes that reach out to trade unions in other nations, offering on-site educational programs in collective bargaining, labor legislation and techniques of maintaining democratic unions. The institutes also offer leadership and specialized training courses at the George Meany Center for Labor Studies and provide and administer foreign aid for social projects, including the creation of credit unions and cooperatives and the construction of housing, schools and hospitals.

The AFL-CIO foreign-service institutes are the American Institute for Free Labor Development, formed in 1962 to help strengthen democratic trade unions in Latin America and the Caribbean, the Asian–American Free Labor Institute, founded in 1968 in response to the needs of democratic trade unions in Asia, and the African–American Labor Center, founded in 1964. A fourth, the Free Trade Union Institute, was created in 1977 to develop programs and projects between the AFL-CIO and European trade unions, particularly those of the newly emerging democracies of Spain and Portugal.

LABOR–MANAGEMENT RELATIONS

In developing alternative ways to improve the American economic system through labor–management partnership, the bishops point out that "Workers in firms and on farms are especially in need of stronger institutional protection, for their jobs and livelihood are particularly vulnerable to the decisions of others in today's highly competitive labor market." Labor shares their view that "The greatest challenge facing U.S. workers and unions today is that of developing a new vision of their role in the U.S. economy of the future."

All of the new approaches cited, that is, profit sharing, granting employees greater participation in determining the conditions of work, cooperative ownership and increased stock ownership, are being experimented with today in a variety of collective bargaining settings remarkable for their versatility and diversity. Each bargaining situation shapes and colors the approaches of the parties. In each, however, as the bishops rightly emphasize, "partnerships between labor and management are possible only when both groups possess real freedom and power to influence decisions," and, it could be added, "only when both sides are willing to recognize the essential validity of the other party and are willing to enter into partnership agreements." In many cases, unions are fighting for their very existence against massive attacks by employers. In recent years, such employer organizations as the National Association of Manufacturers (NAM), with its Council on a Union Free Environment, have questioned the basic legitimacy of unions. Wherever an employer pursues an active program of union avoidance or challenges a union's right to exist, cooperative approaches are simply not possible.

Happily, a number of employers have shown a willingness in recent years to enter into a broadened collective bargaining relationship that gives workers a greater voice in the day-to-day decisions that affect their work. These approaches demonstrate the positive contribution that joint decision making can bring, not only to the welfare of the workers, but also to the productivity and profitability of the firm.

At the national level, top executives of some of the largest unions and corporations meeting as the Labor–Management Group, coordinated by Harvard Economist John Dunlop, Secretary of Labor in the Ford administration, have developed a high degree of unanimity on policies to meet some of the nation's most pressing problems. Since 1982, the group has published joint recommendations on improving the nation's infrastructure, meeting the problem of illegal immigration and extending unemployment insurance for the long-term unemployed; it has also addressed such matters as energy, national tax policies and health care cost containment.

These efforts to develop national policies to deal with the nation's problems are steps toward the bishops' goal of greater cooperation and partnership: "In an advanced industrial economy like ours, all parts of society, including government, must cooperate in forming national economic policies." In all of this is the echo of John Paul II's insistence in *Laborem Exercens* on the need for all economic actors to work against unemployment in order to create a just society with human beings at its center. The bishops make it clear that their endorsement of planning "cannot be construed as an endorsement of a highly centralized form of economic planning." Rather, they say it is a call for greater coordination of the policies that affect employment and incomes, including monetary policy, domestic and defense programs, protection of the environment and worker safety and regulation of international trade. They quote Pope John Paul II's dictum that planning "cannot mean one-sided centralization by the public authorities. Instead, what is in question is a just and rational coordination within the framework of which the initiative of individuals, free groups and local work centers and complexes must be safeguarded."

AN ECONOMY WITHOUT VITALITY

Over the past few years, interest in the question of a national industrial policy had grown, along with a recognition that since the early 1970s, the American economy has shown recurring symptoms of a serious loss of vitality. The Reagan administration's devotion to "market forces" as a substitute for economic policy, though, has dampened the debate, but the consequences of this attitude are rapidly reviving interest in a national industrial policy to replace today's uncoordinated, haphazard policy that produces haphazard results.

U.S.-based multinationals have been closing plants at home and opening new ones abroad. They are encouraged by U.S. tax laws, which defer any taxation of profits from foreign operations until (or unless) those profits are brought back to the United States. This shift is further stimulated by a dollar-for-dollar credit against U.S. tax liability for income taxes paid to foreign governments.

At the same time, many other countries have implemented aggressive industrial and trade policies to improve their domestic economies at the expense of ours. In steel, auto, electronics, railcars, aircraft, semiconductors, fiber optics and a host of emerging industries, the advanced industrial countries of Europe and Japan and the newly developing industrial countries have applied a wide variety of strategic government support, from low-cost credit to protection from import competition and government assistance in technology development. The result leaves U.S. producers facing a consistently uphill battle for sales, not only abroad, but in their own national market.

Although the United States is still the greatest economic power on earth, its lead has been decreasing and its manufacturing industries have been severely damaged. The United States must begin to sort out national priorities and to channel resources into areas that will modernize private and public facilities and restore the national economy to a condition of stable growth. If we fail, the country will continue to lag in productivity growth and international trade; significant portions of its human and mechanical resources will continue to remain idle for extended periods of time, and America's standard of living will decline.

As one of the activist proponents of an industrial policy, the AFL-CIO has endorsed the creation of a tripartite industrial policy board, which would represent business, government and labor. The board would develop strategies to ensure the growth of a diversified American economy. Under the policy guidance of this board, a national development bank would invest public and private funds in necessary reindustrialization projects.

NEW DIRECTIONS

The bishops again challenge labor unions "to seek new ways of doing business. The purpose of unions is not simply to defend the existing wages and pre-rogatives of the fraction of workers who belong to them, but also to enable workers to make positive and creative contributions to the firm, the community and the larger society in an organized and cooperative way."

Hundreds of unions are cooperating in joint programs with management to meet the challenge of new technology and fierce foreign competition, to increase worker participation in job-related decision making and to humanize the workplace. Quality circles, autonomous work groups, quality of work teams, profit-sharing arrangements and other innovations testify to the search that is under way at the bargaining table and on the job to strengthen and streamline productive enterprises of all kinds.

The AFL-CIO is developing new benefit programs to bring to workers the advantage of group purchase of such programs as health, life and auto in-surance, legal assistance, credit cards, investment programs and possibly training and retraining programs. These benefits are intended not only for existing members, but also for "union associates" in order to extend these advantages more broadly throughout the community.

Over four decades of community service, the AFL-CIO has created a na-tionwide network of professionals and volunteers who work with public and private agencies to help those who need help, in programs ranging from disaster relief to alcohol and drug counseling to prisoners' aid and training for the handicapped. Union job-training programs assist minority youngsters and displaced workers in finding rewarding new careers.

TRADE

The bishops' concern for the impact of American trade policy on poor nations is entirely proper, and so is their concern for U.S. workers and their families. Trade problems stemming from the export strategies of foreign competitors, the debt burden of developing countries and the high interest rate policy of the Federal Reserve Board have had a destructive impact on American workers because of the free trade orientation of American trade policy.

Because the aggressive export policies of foreign nations are disrupting American industry, the AFL-CIO believes that the trade policies of other nations should be examined in terms of government subsidies and other practices that put American manufacturing at a disadvantage. Such practices as quotas, export subsidies, industrial targeting programs and coproduction require-ments are practically universal. The continued attempts by the United States to reduce the use of these measures by other nations have not been successful, and the U.S. market has remained open to an increasing flood of imports.

The United States is virtually alone in its belief in open markets and free competition.

In 1985, the United States merchandise trade deficit reached a record $149 billion, more than quadruple the 1980 level of $36 billion. The deficit for 1986 is expected to exceed $170 billion. For manufactured goods alone, the United States enjoyed a $12-billion surplus in 1980, which by 1985, had swung to a deficit of $113 billion and a projected deficit of more than $135 billion in 1986.

In 1960, manufactured imports were insignificant for most American industries. Imports of shoes, apparel, steel, autos, consumer electronic products and machine tools represented 6 percent or less of total U.S. consumption for each of these product areas. In 1979, the import share of the U.S. market for these products ranged from 14 percent for steel to 51 percent for consumer electronics. Since 1979, the import penetration ratios have advanced much further.

More than 1.7 million manufacturing jobs have been lost since 1979. After improving somewhat from the depths of the 1982 recession, jobs in manufacturing again began to decline in 1985, with a job loss that year of 130,000 in the first nine months. Growing problems within high-tech industries demonstrate that the newest and most advanced industries are no less vulnerable than older ones.

The most damaging influence on trade since 1980 has been the high valuation of the U.S. dollar relative to other currencies. The dollar rose 87 percent against the currencies of major U.S. trading partners from July 1980 to February 1985 and was still 54 percent above the 1980 level in November 1985. The overvaluation of the U.S. dollar is the result primarily of high U.S. interest rates, which have attracted tremendous amounts of foreign capital to this country. The rise in the value of the dollar makes imports cheaper, but makes U.S. exports vastly more expensive in foreign countries. The 54 percent rise in the value of the dollar means that an American manufacturer roughly competitive with foreign producers in 1980 is now at a 54 percent cost disadvantage. Even those who scapegoat American workers as responsible for all U.S. ills would know better than to advocate asking U.S. workers to take a 54 percent wage cut to restore them to the competitive position of 1980.

The massive borrowing of the federal government to finance the huge deficits caused by the 1981 tax cuts and the increases in defense spending have put pressure on credit markets and interest rates. At the same time, obsessed by the specter of inflation, the Federal Reserve Board has been following a tight money, high interest rate policy for most of the 1980s.

American consumers have all too frequently not benefited from the cheaper price of imports, as stores sell foreign-made shirts, shoes and other products for the same price as their U.S.-made counterparts.

The AFL-CIO believes that the current trend in trade policy means not only extreme hardship for American manufacturing workers and the communities they live in, but a loss in the real productivity of the American economy and a crippling of its ability to generate the jobs, incomes and tax revenues needed to ensure job security and an adequate standard of living for all Americans.

A fair trade policy needs to be developed in the United States that deals with the effects of an overvalued dollar, that reacts vigorously to unfair foreign trade practices, and that assures American industry adequate safeguards against a sudden or predatory undercutting of its ability to produce.

American workers and their unions have been among the strongest supporters of foreign trade and foreign aid programs designed to lift the people of developing nations out of poverty. Unfortunately, policies are now in place that countenance and even encourage the exploitation of Third World workers while undermining American jobs and living standards. As a result, America's chief constituency for effective aid to the people who need it most is being rapidly eroded.

With regard to the adjustment assistance programs in the United States that are supposed to provide supplementary unemployment benefits and training funds for workers displaced because of increased imports, the bishops say, "U.S. workers and their families who are hurt by the operation of the trading system must be helped through training and other measures to adjust to changes that advance development and decrease poverty in the Third World. . . . In our judgment, adjustment assistance programs in the United States have been poorly designed and administered, and inadequately funded."

The Reagan administration has reneged on its promise to make Trade Adjustment Assistance program funds available to those displaced from their jobs by imports and has targeted the program for extinction. The Trade Adjustment Assistance program should be retained and restored to provide adequate compensation to those unemployed because of trade and to improve training, job search and relocation aid for those displaced workers. Eligibility rules should be eased to permit workers in supplier firms and victims of foreign investments and foreign plant relocations to be covered under this program.

In condemning trade that is based on exploitive conditions in foreign countries, the bishops say, "We need to examine carefully the extent to which success in the U.S. market of certain imports is derived from exploitive labor conditions in the exporting country—conditions that may have attracted the investment in the first place" and warn that "Foreign private investment, attracted by low-wage rates, can cut jobs in the home country and aggravate the exploitation of workers in the host country."

The AFL-CIO has long urged that fair labor standards be made an integral part of U.S. trade policy in order to pressure other nations to adopt humane working standards. The AFL-CIO continues this effort within the International Confederation of Free Trade Unions, the International Labor Organization and other bodies. Fair labor standards must become a condition of the nation's overall trade with all nations; they are already required under the provisions of the Generalized System of Preferences (GSP) and the Caribbean Basin Initiative (CBI).

ECONOMIC INEQUALITY AND TAX POLICY

The bishops are rightly concerned about the economic inequality existing in the United States as a threat to human solidarity, which will lead to deep social divisions and conflict. Extreme inequality, they warn, undermines human dignity and prevents people from playing a role in social and economic life.

As the bishops point out, 28 percent of the total net wealth is held by the richest 2 percent of families in the United States, 57 percent by the top 10 percent. If homes and other real estate are excluded, 54 percent of net financial assets were held by 2 percent of all families, those whose annual income is more than $125,000. Ninety percent of all families own only 14 percent of these assets. In terms of income, the bishops note that in 1984, the bottom 20 percent of American families received only 4.7 percent of the total income in the nation and the bottom 40 percent received only 15.7 percent, the lowest share on record. In contrast, the top one fifth received 42.9 percent of the total income, the highest share since 1948.

In view of these facts, the bishops statement that "We find the disparities of income and wealth in the United States to be unacceptable" seems extremely mild. Their conclusion that "Justice requires that our society take the necessary steps to decrease these inequities" seems to us inarguable.

Economic recession, the budget cut and the tax policies of the Reagan administration have contributed to the shift of income from the poor to the wealthy. The recession and high unemployment, together with the trade problems, have put unions at a disadvantage in trying to maintain living standards. The cuts in the federal budget from 1981 to 1986 primarily hurt the poor. The tax policies of the Reagan administration have shifted the tax burden from the wealthy and corporations to low- and moderate-income wage and salary earners.

The bishops' call for a more progressive tax structure with less of a burden on the poor should be required reading on Capitol Hill. "Families below the official poverty line are, by definition, without sufficient resources to purchase the basic necessities of life. They should not be forced to bear the additional burden of paying taxes. Second, we urge that the principle of progressivity be a central guiding norm in any reforms of the tax system. Those with relatively greater financial resources should pay a higher rate of taxation, both in principle and in the actual or 'effective' tax rates paid. The inclusion of such a principle in tax policies is an important means of reducing the severe inequalities of income and wealth in the nation."

The 1981 Reagan tax cuts for the wealthy and corporations were based on the argument that the wealthy should receive larger cuts because they would save more, and those savings would be used for job-creating investment. As the AFL-CIO predicted, that argument proved false. In fact, although tremendous sums were given to the wealthy, the savings rate was no higher after the Reagan tax cuts than during the Carter administration or during the entire decade of the 1970s.

Even so, the situation has not been corrected. The revenue drain resulting from the 1981 tax cut amounted to $130 billion, or 70 percent of the expected deficit, for the fiscal year beginning in October 1985, even after taking into account the 1982 and 1984 tax legislation, which trimmed some of the abuses and recouped some of the revenue losses of the 1981 law. Corporations in 1985 are paying merely 10 percent of all federal taxes, compared to nearly 25 percent in the mid-1950s, and year after year, many highly profitable corporations pay no federal income tax at all. The 1981 reduction of the 70 percent tax bracket to 50 percent, which greatly benefits wealthy individuals, remains in place, and loopholes widened for income from capital gains and savings remain open. Still, in 1985, the President urged that the top tax rate be cut further to 35 percent.

The AFL-CIO has called for an end to the preferential double-standard that taxes workers' wages and salaries at far higher rates than "unearned income" on the savings, investments and estates of the wealthy, and for reinstatement of the corporate income tax at an equitable level. Labor further seeks the elimination of the so-called incentives that subsidize mergers, takeovers, plant shutdowns, overseas investments and other activities that conflict with the national interest, and urges that a basic structure be developed to assure that the poor are off the tax rolls and that the loopholes and escape hatches for the wealthy are closed. In its long struggle to improve the distribution of income, both through collective bargaining and legislative action, the trade union movement has been a traditional defender of the poor, disabled and retired, and has sought to ensure adequate food, housing and medical care for all.

"THE RESPONSIBILITY OF ALL, . . . THROUGH GOVERNMENT, TO ACT . . ."

Labor shares the bishops' belief that the federal government must play an active role to provide justice and fairness in American society and their rejection of any and all statist or totalitarian doctrines. Like the bishops, labor believes that government should respond to the desires of the public in a democratic framework and that it is the responsibility of all citizens to ensure that elected officials carry out a program of justice and fairness.

The bishops should be saluted for declaring "that the teachings of the church insist that government has a moral function: protecting human rights and securing basic justice for all members of the commonwealth" and that "It is government's role to guarantee the minimum conditions that make this rich social activity possible, namely, human rights and justice." In addition is their conviction that "It is the responsibility of all citizens, acting through their government, to assist and empower the poor, the disadvantaged, the handicapped and the unemployed." While steadfastly opposing totalitarian political ideologies and insisting that democracy is essential for workers to express and promote their rights, the AFL-CIO also recognizes the need for government to play an active role based on the desires of the American people to bring about full employment, improved working conditions, greater equality and to promote justice and fairness in our institutions and laws.

The American trade union movement joins wholeheartedly with the American bishops in asserting that "The economy of this nation has been built by the labor of human hands and minds. Its future will be forged by the ways persons direct all this work toward greater justice. The economy is not a machine that operates according to its own inexorable laws, and persons are not mere objects tossed about by economic forces."

Trade unions attempt to represent the interests of workers at all levels of the economic system, from the shop floor to the firm to the national and international economic policy forums. Through trade unions, workers are able to have a voice among the many forces that influence economic policy. The bishops' recognition of the role of workers and their right to participate in a democratic fashion in America's economic decision making is most welcome.

Chapter

18

The Bishops' Letter and Everyday Life
William J. Byron, S.J.

"Throughout this letter, we have stressed the special place of the disadvantaged, that is, the poor, in any ethical analysis of the U.S. economy," the U.S. bishops say in the second draft of their latest pastoral letter. "National economic policies that contribute to building a true commonwealth should reflect this by standing firmly for the rights of those who fall through the cracks of our economy: the poor, the unemployed, the homeless, the displaced. Being a citizen of this land means sharing in the responsibility to shape and implement such policies."

Therefore, being a citizen in this land involves, as the bishops see it, both a personal and a social responsibility to protect the rights of those whom the economy is not now reaching at a level of support consistent with the requirements of human dignity. Hence, the implications of this letter for the everyday life of those who would take it seriously involve, first, an assent to and assimilation of the principles on which the bishops make their argument, and then an effort, within one's personal range of influence, to "shape and implement" private practices and public policies that show a special regard for "the poor, the unemployed, the homeless, the displaced." Involved here are what the bishops call the "virtues of citizenship." These include "cooperation," "partnership," "initiative," "teamwork" and "a renewed commitment by all to the common good." The letter confronts the virtuous citizen with the challenge of economic responsibilities that relate to a specifically Christian vision. This is a vision "of the transcendent worth—the sacredness—of human beings. The dignity of the human person, realized in community with others, is the criterion against which all aspects of economic life must be measured."

If the citizen is to assent to and assimilate a set of principles, it will be helpful to assemble the set in one place. At various stages of their lengthy letter, the bishops identify principles, perspectives, priorities, themes, norms and criteria. To assemble them on one list is to assist the reader who wants

246

to cooperate with the bishops in their twofold aim in writing the letter, namely, "to help Catholics form their consciences on the moral dimensions of economic decision making and to articulate a moral perspective in the general societal and political debate that surrounds these questions":

- "Every perspective on economic life that is human, moral and Christian must be shaped by three questions: What does the economy do *for* people? What does it do *to* people? And how do people *participate* in it?"
- "The fundamental moral criterion for all economic decisions, policies and institutions is this: They must be at the service of *all people,* especially the poor."
- "The dignity of the human person, realized in community with others, is the criterion against which all aspects of economic life must be measured."
- "The norms of love, basic justice and human rights imply that personal decisions, social policies and economic institutions should be governed by several key priorities. These priorities do not specify everything that must be considered in economic decision making. They do indicate the most fundamental and urgent objectives. . . . The fulfillment of the basic needs of the poor is of the highest priority."
- "Increasing active participation in economic life by those who are presently excluded or vulnerable is a high social priority. . . . The investment of wealth, talent and human energy should be specially directed to benefit those who are poor or economically insecure. . . . These three priorities are not policies. They are norms. . . . (Later in the letter, these priorities are identified as "moral principles.")
- "Our primary criterion in judging any economy is not its adherence to a particular ideology, but the impact it has on human beings."
- "The themes of human dignity and the preferential option for the poor are at the heart of our approach. . . ."
- "The impact of national economic policies on the poor and the vulnerable is the primary criterion for judging their moral value."

In reflecting on these norms, or criteria, or whatever it pleases the reader to call them, those who are confronted by the challenges of the bishops' letter must first assess their own level of agreement with the principles. First, there is the principle of human dignity; all human rights depend on it. Next, there is the principle of solidarity; human development requires it. There is also the principle of participation; it rests on human dignity. Finally, running through the other three is the principle of preference for the poor, a biblically based, specifically Christian norm that measures the conformity of the values and choices of the Christian to the values and choices of Christ. The first implication of this letter for the everyday life of the Christian is, therefore, an exercise of reflection on the principles leading to a personal appropriation of the values they express.

No one should be surprised if this reflection prompts a call for help. Precisely how and where does the Gospel call for a preferential option for the poor? What is the link between necessary human development and life in community, the link that supports the principle of solidarity? How do human rights, particularly economic rights, flow from human dignity, and how does human dignity derive from the mere possession of human nature? What does the principle of participation really mean, and how does it relate to the rights of others as, for example, the right another might have to private ownership? Are there no limits on these rights? Or, are there identifiable limits on all rights? There are exegetical, theological and philosophical questions here. The reflective reader may indeed need help. The recognition of this need could and should lead to study projects that might best begin with chapter 2 of the letter, "The Christian Vision of Economic Life." The chapter initiates biblical, theological and philosophical reflection; its footnotes point to further readings. Both those inclined to give the bishops' principles their immediate assent and those who are respectful but not persuaded will probably agree that deeper study is desirable. Reflection will suggest a need for study—study and guided discussion of the intellectual foundations on which this letter rests. To what extent do the bishops and their people share a common vision of the Christian vision of economic life?

Reflection on the principles will prove to be a very practical first step. None of us is completely immune from the popular tendency to substitute blame for analysis. Nor is any one of us completely safe from the charge that is made occasionally, that most people confuse thinking with the re-arrangement of prejudices. It will be important not to let prejudice block the assimilation of principle or, once assimilated, impede its application in policy form.

In offering "an ethical framework that can guide economic life today," the bishops list the "duties all people have to each other and to the whole community: love of neighbor, the basic requirements of justice, and the special obligation to those who are poor and vulnerable." Corresponding to these duties, they say, are the human rights of every person, but they do not list them in parallel fashion to the obligations. They simply say, "the obligation to protect the dignity of all demands respect for these rights." But what are they? A section of the letter is titled, "Human Rights: The Minimum Conditions for Life in Community." Acknowledging that the "full range of human rights has been systematically outlined by John XXIII in his encyclical *Peace on Earth*," and noting that the encyclical "echoes" the United Nations' Universal Declaration on Human Rights, the bishops turn to human rights that "are of a specifically economic nature." It is at this point that the letter's implications for everyday life bump against reality. It should surprise no one to find that opinions will divide and arguments begin, particularly as those rights define themselves in policy proposals. The arguments, however, will be productive if they remain in the policy arena. If they deny the existence of economic rights, the arguments will block the letter's implementation. Productive debate will test the workability of policy proposals based on accepted principles. Without agreement on the principles, no productive debate is possible.

What are these economic rights? "In the first place stand the rights to life, food, clothing, shelter, rest and medical care. These are absolutely basic to the protection of human dignity. In order to ensure these basic necessities, all persons have a right to security in the event of sickness, unemployment and old age." This section of the letter goes on to call for protection of the rights to employment, to healthful working conditions, to wages and benefits that are sufficient to provide for workers and their families a standard of living in keeping with human dignity. Also called for is protection of the right to the possibility of private ownership. "These fundamental personal rights state the minimum conditions for economic institutions that respect human dignity, social solidarity and justice." In what may be the understatement of the entire letter, the bishops remark, "Securing these economic rights for all will be an arduous task." They concede that there will be "diversity of opinion" in the church and civil society on how these rights are to be protected, but they also assert, "There can be no legitimate disagreement on the basic moral objectives."

The question is one of implementation. Reflection and study are recommended here because attitudinal change will be required of most of us before we can participate in any way in the implementation process. Study is not the only route to attitudinal adjustment; experience can change our way of thinking. Reflection on experience, though, or on the content of what one studies, is necessary for the internalization, the personal appropriation of principle. Once internalized, the principles will go with us wherever we go, they will direct our attention to the nonparticipants at the margins of our economic system. The principles will help us to "see" the poor in a new light, to "notice" the unemployed as persons who have claims on us, and to regard those whose human dignity is under assault by adverse economic forces as having preferred status when questions arise concerning "the investment of wealth, talent and human energy."

Virtues are good acts internalized, principles of action and shapers of character. De Tocqueville called them "habits of the heart" and thus provided Robert Bellah and colleagues with a title for their recent study of individualism and commitment in America. Virtues of citizenship, as noted earlier in this essay and in the letter, include cooperation, partnership, initiative, teamwork and a commitment to the common good, all focused on the reduction of poverty and unemployment in the domestic economy and anywhere else in the world where human dignity is assaulted. However, yet another quality could be said to be essential for the successful implementation of this letter—creativity. Call it a virtue or any other name, but be assured that without creativity, the bishops' letter would remain merely a lengthy epistle; it would not be an occasion of social reform that benefits the poor and the unemployed. Creative implementation is imperative.

The pastoral letter encourages creativity, but it fails to demonstrate it, particularly in the portions dealing with policy. This is not a criticism, simply a commentary on the need for creativity to emerge from the imagination of those citizens who will shape and implement effective policies to help the poor, the unemployed, the homeless, the displaced.

Every citizen is a voter, consumer and potential saver. Some citizens are employers, others are employees. In the workplace, both employers and employees are workers in the basic sense of that word; all share responsibility for productivity in the workplace.

Citizens can be identified as inventors, entrepreneurs, investors, managers of resources (human, financial, material), producers of goods (ranging from works of art to loaves of bread), providers of services (that heal, instruct, transport, or entertain). Some citizens are elected or appointed to serve their fellow citizens through the art and practice of government.

No readers who happen to scan this outline of the way citizens occupy themselves in our economy will find themselves excluded, even though the specific occupation may not be mentioned. Along with "citizen," the most comprehensive category is "consumer"—it includes the unemployed and those not in the work force as well as all who are paid participants in the economy. The least comprehensive category would be "inventor," or "entrepreneur," or, if recent trends are telling us something worth noting, "saver." The point of identifying the various categories, however, is to encourage citizens to identify themselves as participants in the system, and to ask themselves: How can my participation advance the purposes of the pastoral letter?

Each one of us should save in order that investment can take place to enlarge the productive capacity of the economy. That should mean more jobs.

Each one of us will have to consume less in order to save more. That choice might occasion an examination of personal and family consumption patterns in the face of the poverty of others at home and abroad. We should take the measure of our own consumerism, surely a vice and not a virtue in our land.

Those of us who are active participants on the production side of the economy will have to face up to the issue of productivity. Whether we are unionized workers or not, sole proprietors or corporate managers, skilled professionals or part-time laborers, we have to address the issue of productivity. If wage and salary incomes rise on the average at rates not offset by equal rises in the rate of productivity, inflation will also rise and, in the process, injure those on fixed incomes and those who have to spend most of their income for the basic necessities of life. Moreover, without higher productivity in the domestic economy (economic growth at home), new job creation will lag and there will be less political inclination as well as less national product from which our nation can encourage economic growth and development abroad. In a certain sense, productivity is a function of good management, but as in so many other areas of human activity, there is simply no substitute for hard work, by everyone, if higher productivity is to be realized.

The bishops recognize that full employment is the foundation of a just economy. "The most urgent priority for domestic economic policy is the creation of new jobs with adequate pay and decent working conditions." Greater productivity on the part of present participants in the system can make this happen. There is no more effective social welfare system than a full-employment economy.

Hence, after reflection on the principles, after additional study, if necessary, to facilitate their assimilation, and after identification of one's own point or points of insertion into the economic system, the citizen concerned with the implementation of the bishops' letter must simply decide to become more productive. To the extent that individuals or groups can add creativity to their productivity, the chances of successful implementation will be correspondingly enhanced.

"All right now—be creative!" That is like ordering someone to be funny. There are, of course, command performances, but comedians and artists come to them well rehearsed. Being creative is not something that can be commanded. Nonetheless, those with creative economic potential, that is, those whose new ideas can be embodied in capital, those who see economic opportunities in unmet needs, those who can take malfunctioning economic operations and make them perform efficiently, these types of creative economic actors might well be inspired by reflecting on the problems the bishops cite, the problems of the poor, the unemployed, the homeless, the displaced. Tax incentives should be used to attract this creative potential to connect with these problems. That is perfectly appropriate in an enterprise system. Nor is it too much to expect the church to reinforce the bishops' good intent by praising this kind of activity as virtue, the virtue of citizenship. Not only is virtue involved, so is vocation in the theological meaning of the word.

The bishops encourage and support "a renewed sense of vocation in the business community"—and for good reason. All of us are called, not by chance, but by the God who holds our destiny in His hands, to be someone and to do something in our lifetime. The "someone" is, of course, each one of us; wherever we go, we are called by a God who never stops calling. Consequently, we must never stop answering. The "something" can be surgery or shoemaking, priesthood or poetry. As the bishops make plain, "Businesspeople, managers, investors and financiers follow a vital Christian vocation." Efforts to overcome injustice, they say, "are part of the Christian vocation." Priests are instructed to study the issues so they can challenge people who inhabit the secular workplace in a way that "sustains and encourages their vocations." Part of the implementation of the letter, the translation of principle to policy, will be in reawakening a sense of vocation in policymakers in both the private and public sectors. They are called, along with the rest of us, not by accident, but by the God who created them and who gives meaning to their lives, to the task of implementation.

Additional categories, not occupational but functional, through which citizens might examine their potential for participation in the implementation of the letter are voter, taxpayer and charitable contributor.

Responsible voters will carefully consider those issues that can help or hurt the poor; they will also assess the character of candidates, looking for the presence or absence of the principles the bishops have identified as important. Assimilation of the principles will put the voter on the appropriate side of the issue. Similarly, principled voters will find themselves supporting candidates with principles that match their own, just as it should be in a representative democracy.

The citizen as taxpayer has a financial interest in public policy. Not in the sense of standing to profit from this policy or that, but as one whose money is being spent and who should do all that a representative democracy permits to see that the tax dollar is spent in a way that expresses the principled convictions of the citizen. Implementing public policies that meet basic human needs is expensive. Assimilation of the principles should serve to prepare the citizen to swallow the never-pleasant dose of higher taxes when it is clear that they are fair and the programs effective. The same principles that make tax payments palatable should also fire the citizens' zeal for justice on both sides of the tax system—revenues raised and services rendered.

Citizen and conscience meet whenever the question of charitable giving comes up, and it seems to be coming up with greater frequency these days. The bishops' letter is clearly not a leave-it-to-government formula. Along with government, the letter points to citizens, owners, managers, working people and labor unions as principal agents of the necessary reforms. They also point to the church itself as faced with serious obligations in this regard. Although justice is the central theme of the letter, charity is not overlooked, nor can charity be overlooked by the citizen voter, worker, employer, or policymaker when personal participation in the effort to achieve the letter's aims is examined. "Tithing" is a word that might gain new currency as efforts are made to implement the letter. Individuals will find themselves asking, "Do I give enough?" They may decide to give more to the poor. If they decide to give to the church in order to reach the poor, through such national efforts as the Campaign for Human Development or Catholic Relief Services, or through diocesan Catholic Charities and local soup kitchens, they should also decide to track the management of their donations with the same attention they would devote as shareholders to their investments in publicly held corporations.

Bringing the letter to life in one's everyday sphere of influence means doing what one can to create new jobs. People will differ in their potential for success in job creation, but they should not preclude themselves from making a contribution in this regard. Similarly, everyone should remain alert in encouraging new job development. Bankers, for example, have daily opportunities to encourage entrepreneurs, but without depositors (and that means most of us), the bankers would not be in a position to facilitate job-creating investment. Depositors who have assimilated the principles articulated in the letter will find themselves raising the right questions about what the bankers are doing with the funds entrusted to them.

If a large enough constituency is concerned about the issues the bishops regard as important, the acoustics will improve for the discussion of new ideas: to produce jobs, improve the delivery of welfare services, increase production, improve distribution, facilitate exchange of information, discover new resources, and come up with the innovations associated with those prominent names in earlier generations in industrial America, names that still appear on products, services and, not least, the paychecks that fuel the American economy.

This quite naturally leads to the question of research. Research begins with a good question. Asking the right question requires creativity—so does answering it. Those who raise the questions must be willing to provide or participate in the search for the funds needed to support research. Opportunities abound for cooperation in this kind of activity among business, government, the foundations and the universities. The church, of course, can sponsor research, and given the issues raised in the bishops' letter, we can expect to see church support for research aimed at the reduction of unemployment and poverty. The implementation phase will give the church a fresh opportunity to encourage the researchers, motivate them in their special vocation, and remind all with ears to hear that a community of faith must always hold reason in high regard. Without the application of intellect, the problems the bishops list will remain unsolved.

One reason for the church to insert itself into this type of activity is the proliferation in America of remedies to economic problems involving gambling. States turn to lotteries to raise revenues for social programs. Casino earnings are taxed to generate funds for special societal needs. Aside from the greed that characterizes the gambling environment and the "fast-lane" behavioral problems it fosters, an economy dependent on gambling is evidence of another set of problems: the absence of creativity in finding effective and truly human economic solutions, and the decline of true charity as a response to human need. The church has reason to be concerned.

It is not enough simply to publish the pastoral letter. Implementation must now be ongoing and it should take many forms. One form of implementation that the bishops themselves could adopt would be launching a series of policy papers—technical studies of problems that received little more than a mention in the pastoral letter. As the bishops make plain, their "prudential judgments" on specific economic issues do not carry the same authority as their statements of moral principle. They should now commission policy papers written by acknowledged experts on specific economic problems. Those papers would be authoritative not because the bishops published them, but because the authors would be authorities in their fields. The appropriate role of the bishops as commissioners and publishers would be to review the work of the experts for consistency with the moral principles the bishops have articulated in their letter. If the policy proposal fits the principles, let the proposal be published so that it can be tried by government, or business, or the unions, or any appropriate economic actor. Publishing a series of policy papers would be a good way for the bishops to continue the lay colleagueship without which their letter could not have been produced and to keep alive the letter's essential ideas. Publication of the policy papers could easily span two decades. Would it also spawn arguments, or worse, charges that the bishops are captives of a particular ideology? Arguments are unavoidable in the policy arena. Policies are either workable or unworkable. Their potential in either direction is surely arguable, but the argument can only be conducted among those who agree on the basic premises; otherwise, you have not a policy debate, but a difference of principle. Moreover, charges of ideological bias can be avoided if the bishops, who are experts on the principles, remain open to policy proposals, consistent with their own clearly articulated principles, from experts in the workings of the economic machinery where those principles might be applied.

In reviewing the letter, possible topics to which policy papers might address themselves were compiled. The list is long and the titles are not in final form. Both the list and the titles serve to illustrate various routes of implementation because some of these policy papers would be used in college classrooms, while others would find their way into legislative debates, corporate strategic plans and political party platforms. Here is the list:

EMPLOYMENT AND UNEMPLOYMENT

1. "Full Employment: The Foundation of a Just Economy." (This paper would quantify the goal of full employment and specify the appropriate mix of monetary and fiscal policy.)
2. "The Impact of Joblessness on Human Lives and Dignity."
3. "Economic Distortions of the Arms Race."
4. "Creating Jobs and Curbing Inflation."
5. "How Business, Labor and Government Can Cooperate for Job-Training and Apprenticeship Programs."
6. "Plant Closings: How to Prevent Them by Bringing Labor, Management and the Local Community into the Decision-Making Process."
7. "Public Service Employment: How to Promote It; Private Employment of the Hard-to-Employ: How to Subsidize It."
8. "Job-Sharing, Flextime and Shorter Work Weeks: Defining the Circumstances Where These and Similar Devices Can Contribute to Full Employment."

POVERTY

1. "How to Promote Participation by the Poor in Economic Policy Making."
2. "How to Make Credit Unions and Consumer Cooperatives Work."
3. "Welfare Reform: Policy Recommendations."
4. "The Case for National Welfare Eligibilty Standards and Minimum Benefit Levels."
5. "Income Support through Family and Children's Allowances."

FOOD AND AGRICULTURE

1. "Are Food Prices Too Low? Would Raising Them Ease Pressures on Farmers, Save Farm Jobs, Promote Soil and Water Conservation, and Protect the Family Farm?"
2. "Are Farm Prices Too Generously Supported? Would Redirecting Support in Favor of Smaller Farms Benefit the Overall Farm Economy?"
3. "Concentration of Farm Ownership: Should It Be Controlled? Would a Progressive Land Tax Discourage Concentration?"
4. "Conservation Policy: Protecting the Land for Future Farm Production."

THE UNITED STATES AND THE WORLD ECONOMY

1. "Recommended Policies for Increasing the Participation of Poor Nations in the Global Economy."

2. "On Specifying a Percentage of Gross National Product as the Minimum Level of U.S. Development Assistance to the Third World."
3. "Design for an Equitable Trading System in a Global Economy."
4. "Recommended Adjustment-Assistance Programs for U.S. Workers Displaced by Foreign Imports."
5. "How to Express a Preferential Option for Poor Countries through Lower Interest Rates, Longer Payback Periods, and Modification of International Monetary Fund Adjustment Requirements."
6. "Public Policies to Encourage Private Investment in Developing Countries."
7. "Grain Reserves for International Food and Farm Security."
8. "Population Policy and Development Policy: Keeping Both in Balance."
9. "Defense Spending and Development Assistance: Correcting the Imbalance."

THE NEW AMERICAN EXPERIMENT

1. "Workable Models of Employee Stock Ownership."
2. "Encouraging Worker Opinion on Working Conditions: How to Improve Communication in the Workplace."
3. "New Ways of Union–Management Cooperation."
4. "The Rights of Jobholders vs. the Rights of Shareholders in Mergers and Acquisitions."
5. "Tax Reform: How Can It Express a Preferential Option for the Poor?"
6. "Policy Suggestions on Employment, Compensation, Promotion, Pensions, and Participation in Decision Making for Dioceses and Church-related Institutions."

If we had answers to these questions and clear, workable programs to address these policy issues, we would be well on our way as a nation to solving the problems that prompted the bishops to write their letter. Given the variety and interrelationship of the problems, one might envisage an infinite series of policy papers addressing an endless array of problems. Or, the extent and complexity of the challenge might simply be viewed as a mirror of the complexity of life. Everyday life cannot be lived apart from that complexity. It can, however, be lived apart from a concern for the problems identified by the bishops, all of which can be solved by persistent, day-by-day applications of creativity and commitment, two of what the bishops call "the virtues of citizenship." "Being a citizen of this land," the bishops believe, "means sharing in the responsibility to shape and implement . . . policies (that protect) the rights of those who fall through the cracks of our economy: the poor, the unemployed, the homeless, the displaced." The shaping and implementing are now on the agenda of everyday life for those who share the bishops' moral convictions.

Afterword:
A Direction For The Future

John P. Langan, S.J.

Several years ago, a student was attempting to impress on me the need for a radical change in our way of thinking about certain public policy issues, matters on which he said we need to make a 360-degree turn. I suppressed a smile and pointed out to him that a reversal of direction was actually a 180-degree turn. Since then, I have been intrigued by the possibility that in attempting abrupt and radical changes, one might actually be executing a 360-degree turn. After a period of sound and fury, excitement and promises, one might still be in the same place, facing in the same direction. Doubling the turn produces less change than a more gradual or oblique shift.

Compasses for measuring changes of direction in social and political processes that can provide us with simple quantitative measurements of where we are now heading and how much our course has changed do not exist. For that reason, it is all the more important for us to ask what difference the bishops' letter and the debate over it is likely to make. Will all this work and argument simply turn out to be a 360-degree turn? Something like this seems to be suggested by the stress that David O'Brien puts on continuities between the current pastoral and earlier statements of the U.S. bishops on economic topics. Or have we witnessed an abrupt reversal of direction in American Catholicism and its positioning of itself within the larger worlds of American society and world Catholicism? As is usual in debates of this type, in which we attempt to reaffirm and modify our norms and ideals in a way that will be both responsive to and transformative of a society that is changing in ways we do not fully or clearly grasp, we have to work out a sense of direction by looking at some of the tensions, the surprises and the limits present in what the bishops have been saying and in what various other participants in the debate, particularly those in this volume, have been saying in reply.

The first set of surprises clusters around the fact of the document itself. American Catholicism, especially in its official teaching, has not been distinguished by a spirit of intellectual adventure.[1] While it is true that over half the Catholic colleges and universities in the world are in the United States, these have served primarily to prepare the sons and daughters of immigrants to enter American middle-class life and to pursue careers in business and the professions. For a long time, American Catholics relied for intellectual stimulation and defense on such French philosophers as Jacques Maritain and Gabriel Marcel, on British converts like G. K. Chesterton and Evelyn Waugh, and on various Roman or German theologians. It was expected that those who were to lead the church administratively or intellectually would study in Rome or, if they were progressively inclined, in Louvain or Paris. A great deal of the intellectual dependence of American Catholicism on Europe continued even after Vatican II, especially in systematic or dogmatic theology, though the esteemed masters now came from northern Europe, especially Karl Rahner of Germany and Edward Schillebeeckx of the Netherlands.

The general encouragement, however, given by the council to the development of theologies that would be more responsive to diverse cultures and to contemporary experiences, along with the specific contribution made by spokesmen of American Catholicism (centrally, John Courtney Murray) to presenting and defending a strong affirmation of religious liberty, created a new situation in which all levels of the American church, from bishops to laity, felt more confidence in raising theological questions and in manifesting their dissatisfaction with traditional answers. Some of this ferment was naive and ill-informed, some of it was anti-intellectual and sentimental, or activist or both, some of its conclusions were unacceptable on intellectual, moral, or doctrinal grounds. Once this ferment was added to the spirit of free inquiry and the pragmatic frame of mind that are so prized in American cultural and intellectual life, however, the result was the overthrow of passive authoritarianism as the dominant Catholic attitude in intellectual matters. This did not imply a rebellion against traditional doctrine, but a readiness to consider the task of applying Catholic doctrine, especially the social teaching of the church, within the distinctive American context as a task for the American church in the first instance.

Encouraged both by the example of their brother bishops in Latin America, especially in their conferences at Medellin (1968) and Puebla (1979), and also by their own experience in issuing a series of pastoral letters[2] and in developing appropriate procedures and staff, the U.S. bishops were, by 1980, sufficiently confident of themselves and of their place in both U.S. society and in world Catholicism that they were ready to address two of the most pressing issues of the time, in their pastoral letters on war and peace and on the U.S. economy. They ventured to do this in a way that manifested a confidence that they had something worthwhile to say both to the U.S. Catholic community and to participants in the general debate on public policy; at the same time, the bishops showed they recognized they also had a great deal to learn about the issues and about contemporary secular ways of understanding them. A church that regards itself as intellectually dependent on Rome or Europe or that sees the American world around it as fundamentally threatening or hostile would not have been capable of addressing two such vast and controversial topics. The readiness to write the pastoral letters and the serious and generally favorable reception they encountered clearly mark a very important point in the maturation of Roman Catholicism in the United States.

The second surprising aspect of the document is the literary genre of the pastoral. The idea that public policy could be significantly affected by a church document, that members of the Joint Chiefs of Staff and directors of Fortune 500 companies would have to take seriously the reasoning and the value priorities of a statement issued by any of the Christian churches, would not have struck most observers of the American scene ten years ago as very plausible. The remarkable fact is that the bishops have produced two documents that, despite their imperfections and limitations, have succeeded in engaging the attention of large parts of the U.S. public and of significant persons in the worlds of business, the media, the academy and government. Partly, of course, this is a consequence of the size and the perceived political significance of U.S. Catholicism and the possibilities that it provides for complex and colorful conflict. As the essays in this book clearly show, however, the attention received by the pastoral on the U.S. economy (as well as by the sibling document on war and peace), is not simply a function of political muscle or media potential.

The fact is that the bishops moved into a middle ground contiguous to but not fully included within the religious, the academic and the political realms of discourse. The bishops' intention of developing and applying Catholic social teaching to U.S. economic and social realities meant that their project could not be confined to a private or separate realm of the purely religious. For this reason, the letters were criticized by both Catholics and non-Catholics as intrusions into the secular or the political. At the same time everyone, not least the bishops themselves, had to bear in mind the religious sources of their project and the continuing necessity of maintaining a religious point to the pastorals if they were to retain the support of the religious community. If this were lost, even most of their political effectiveness would evaporate. At the same time, because of the inherent demand within the Catholic theological tradition for a rational mediation and development of religious symbols and values,[3] this move from the religious to the political could not be carried on without reliance on categories and modes of understanding found in such disciplines as philosophy, economics, sociology and political science. Thus, while the letters could not ignore fundamental criticisms from experts in these disciplines, they should not be expected to achieve the standards of technical precision and intellectual rigor characteristic of the best academic argument. Indeed, one of the purposes of this volume of essays has been to indicate some of the ways in which the argument of the pastoral can be strengthened, criticized and applied by people writing from a variety of academic disciplines.

Lest this point be interpreted as either condescension or Catholic defensiveness, let me indicate four reasons why it was bound to be the case. First, the letters were the products of committees. Neither letter had a unique author who was given free rein to express his deepest understanding of the issues. Second, they had to be written to build consensus, both among the bishops and in the church at large. As a result, certain affirmations and analyses that were important potential supporters of the document had to be passed over if the basic line of argument were to be protected. Third, both documents had to meet public deadlines. There was some flexibility in the timing of the process, and the bishops were not willing to produce shoddy work to meet a self-imposed deadline, but the perfectionist pattern of indefinite deferment that marks so many doctoral dissertations and academic books was clearly inappropriate. Fourth, the scope of the project in both pastorals intentionally included the task of crossing those scholarly lines of demarcation that the experience of the academy has taught us to regard as conducive to achieving reliably excellent work. It also included the task of presenting arguments and conclusions in a way that would be accessible to the educated public. Particularly because of the lack of scholarly work by theologians with a serious interest in economics as well as the increasingly technical character of most work in contemporary economics, there was no definitive study or well-articulated scholarly consensus that could guide the bishops in shaping and presenting their views. What the two pastoral letters accomplished was not an advance along a scholarly frontier, but the creation of a common ground for Americans who are concerned about certain morally troubling aspects of our national policies, a ground on which they can freely engage in reflection and form commitments that will be religious and moral in their sources and political and economic in their effects. I believe that the character of the debate shows that this task was very largely achieved.

Two factors made this task both necessary and possible, and, in particular, urgent and surprising, at this juncture in American political history. The first of these is the tradition of Catholic social thought. This tradition has its roots in the Bible and in the writings of St. Augustine and St. Thomas Aquinas. It made creative intellectual contributions both in sixteenth-century Spain, when the foundations of modern theories of international law were laid, and in twentieth-century Europe, when Catholicism turned from its alliance with the ancien regime to an acceptance of industrial society and constitutional democracy. It has produced such great scholars such as Francisco Suàrez and Jacques Maritain, but in the past century, it found its most influential and characteristic expression in a series of papal social encyclicals beginning with *Rerum Novarum* of Leo XIII (1891), continuing through *Quadragesimo Anno* of Pius XI (1931), *Pacem in Terris* of John XXIII (1963) and *Populorum Progressio* of Paul VI (1967), to *Laborem Exercens* of John Paul II (1981). In a specially important form that reflects the church's need to deal with the increasing secularization of modern life and thought and to return to the biblical sources of Christian theology, this tradition is found in *Gaudium et Spes* (1965), the document on the church and the modern world that was issued by the Second Vatican Council and was probably the most influential statement in shaping Catholic attitudes toward political and social life in the last 20 years.[4]

This tradition, with its composite religious and philosophical foundations, its insistence on the inherently social character of human existence, its sensitivity to the need for the development and transformation of institutions, and its repeated (though often unsuccessful) efforts to adapt to changing social contexts, does not always fare well in intellectual combat with more revolutionary or more reductionist approaches to political theory, whether these come out of the contractarian tradition of the Anglophone countries or the Marxist traditions of Europe. However, it does provide an excellent base for reflections that aim at showing the relevance of religious values and concerns to the shaping of public policy and to the transformation of institutional life, especially when this is to be done in a way that stresses the continuity of Western moral values. It can be argued, of course, that this tradition has not figured prominently in the American experience, that it is an alien import from the less innovative and more security-oriented societies of Europe, and that it reflects various premodern and even antimodern influences. All of these points, it may be admitted, are true, but when they are looked at more positively, they indicate that the tradition of Catholic social teaching can provide critical distance and a point of leverage for persons who want to reflect in a fundamental way about the shape of American institutions and the direction of American policy. The Catholic tradition does include a different order of priorities among social values and a more organicist form of social imagination than have been prevalent in our legal and political traditions, yet it does not rely on a totally alien set of categories or a vastly different historical experience.

The application of Catholic social thought to the American context is, then, a challenging possibility. It is challenging because of the intellectual effort and creativity it requires, especially the necessity it imposes to creative intellectual synthesis and the demand it puts on Catholic scholars and teachers to appropriate the methods and conclusions of the social and policy sciences and to present their own views in terms that are accessible to other Americans. It is also challenging in a different sense because it does not presume or impose a harmony between the norms it proposes and existing values and policies in the United States. In contrast to the strongly voluntaristic affirmation of the compatibility between being a good American and a good Catholic, which dominated the public self-presentation of U.S. Catholicism when it was primarily a church of working-class immigrants, the church leaders and scholars who take up the challenge of applying Catholic social thought to American public policy and social institutions in the late twentieth century have to take seriously the possibility and even the likelihood of important conflicts. They do this, however, in the expectation of full consensus on such second-order values as respect for freedom of conscience, tolerance of diverse values in a pluralistic culture and a readiness to participate in and to defend democratic processes.

A certain parallel exists here to the contribution of the Jewish community to the pluralistic intellectual life of the United States. Very few would argue that the historical Jewish experience of persecution and restricted opportunity, of devotion to Torah and to learning, corresponds to the typical experience of Americans. It has to be seen as something significantly different but capable of producing a significant and valuable addition to American intellectual, political and economic life. Jewish tradition in this country undergoes transformations that make the American Jewish community recognizably different from Israel, from Soviet Jewry and from the Jewish communities in such countries as Britain and France, though also linked to them in various complex ways. The continuing presence and vitality of the Jewish tradition in both religious and secular forms, though, helps to make American Jews more creatively and actively American as participants in a democratic and pluralistic society and to increase the depth and weight of their contributions to our common society.

The presence of a significantly different tradition with its own logical implications and practical expectations within the American public debate is itself an enrichment of our common culture and public discourse. It requires a body of people who are conversant with the major documents and values of that tradition and are able to present them in terms that are intelligible even if not necessarily persuasive to the larger culture. The range and character of reactions to the pastoral letters shows that the bishops have accomplished a major breakthrough in making the tradition of Catholic social thought effectively present in American public debate and available as a continuing source of alternative criticisms and possibilities. Even for those who emphasize the incompleteness, the inadequacies and the risks of what the bishops have been doing, the letters will serve as important reference points. The tradition itself, because of its authoritative character, its historical richness, its intellectual complexity and its presentation by a distinctive international institution, provides both guidance and constraint for those Catholics and others who wish to apply it in ways that can resolve the political dilemmas of our time. Although it can be appropriated and interpreted in different ways, the Catholic tradition is not indefinitely malleable and resists exclusive manipulation by the proponents of one policy stance or the advocates of one interest group. The tradition stands as a massive reality, even though not all parts of it command equal assent, and the task of using and developing it both suggests new possibilities and requires a distinctive point of view and a breadth of vision among those who would invoke its authority.

The letter on the economy in particular impels Americans to think about fundamental aspects of their social and economic system in terms that go far beyond assessing particular policies and partisan proposals. This is, of course, a prime reason for the widespread public interest in the document, for it has been developed at a surprising time when the advocates of deregulation and supply-side economics, of privatization and of the virtues of market solutions, along with critics of the welfare state and of the surviving Great Society programs, have seemed to carry all before them in public debate and political decision. In the age of Prime Minister Thatcher and President Reagan, at a time when even many socialists have come to doubt the effectiveness of increased government intervention in the economy, in a period when the New Deal coalition seems to many to be obsolete and beyond hope of recovery, the bishops are moving in a contrary and surprising direction. To some of their critics, their policy recommendations show that they are engaged in a well-intentioned but misguided crusade to prop up declining industries and family farms that are losing economic viability as the result of technological change, increased international competition and mistaken business judgments. The bishops seem to be 20 or 50 years off in the timing of their message and to be writing a pastoral that would have been much better received in the days of Franklin Roosevelt or Lyndon Johnson.

Against this, I would argue that the bishops have articulated a moral concern about the plight of the poor and the unemployed that, while currently unfashionable, remains a permanent and disquieting matter. The bishops were ready to do this at a time when many proponents of the old remedies had fallen into ideological disarray and when many ordinary people felt their compassion drained by perplexing changes and the apparently insoluble problems that afflict so many of America's poor, especially the black poor. This readiness was the second factor that made the pastoral letter both necessary and possible. The bishops' letter has served to remind an increasingly affluent and influential Catholic community that serious problems of poverty and unemployment remain in the U.S. economy and require social action and changes in the design of our social and economic institutions. This point is now common ground for the contributors to this volume and indeed for most of the serious participants in the general debate on these issues. Insistence on it, however, remains an important service. For in the course of economic and political decisions, it is a consideration very likely to be ignored, especially when people persuade themselves that they are somehow entitled to a life of increasing affluence or when they believe that their own economic prospects are somehow threatened or diminished.

The special concern for the problems of the poor or, as the bishops put it, "a fundamental option for the poor," gives both a political direction to the bishops' argument and expresses the religious concern from which the bishops speak. This concern is a double one. It comes, first of all, from a humanitarian desire to aid the poor and "to enable them to become active participants in the life of society" (second draft, par. 90). For the bishops, this desire is not merely a personal response to their reading of scripture and their understanding of the demands of morality. It is also rooted in their task as leaders of dioceses that have to assist large numbers of poor and unemployed people, whether these be former workers at steel plants in the Northeast or new Hispanic immigrants or clients of Catholic charities. Reminding the Catholic laity and the larger society of the necessity of an option for the poor, however, also serves to meet a second responsibility of the bishops— to warn the upper and middle classes about the dangers of an increasing absorption in the consumer goods and material opportunities of our society and about the spiritual and social harm done by denying our solidarity with other human beings and assuming an adversarial attitude toward the poor.

That the bishops are right to warn us of the evils inherent in excessive reliance on material goods for our sense of worth and security and that they are right to urge us to a generous and compassionate attitude toward the poor are points that seem to me beyond criticism. They are clearly present in the teachings of Judaism, Christianity and Islam as well as in such secular moral traditions as stoicism and utilitarianism. In the pastoral letter, though, the bishops have clearly gone beyond such unexceptionable homiletic reminders. They insist that the values affirmed in the option for the poor offer a necessary, though not sufficient, guide for the formation of public policy. As they put the matter, "In summary, the norms of love, basic justice and human rights imply that personal decisions, social policies and economic institutions should be governed by several key priorities. These priorities do not specify everything that must be considered in economic decision making. They do indicate the most fundamental and urgent objectives" (second draft, par. 91).

Even if one grants, as the bishops do, that concern for the poor is not a sufficient basis for the shaping of economic policy, there is a certain risk of imbalance in assessing economic systems in terms of human rights and the special needs of the poor. This risk is in fact one of the major sources of criticism of the pastoral. For defenders of democratic capitalism, the emphasis on the poor has seemed to load the dice against any truly capitalist system. For the poor are almost by definition those who are to be regarded as the failures of the economy, those whose skills and willingness have not been put to use by the system and who are unable to obtain the resources that would enable them to live with decency and dignity.[5] To employ the notion of human rights in an economic context directs attention to those situations in which there has been failure and there is the threat or likelihood of a violation of human dignity, and is thought by many to encourage a misleading sense of entitlement. It is indeed worth remembering that the language of human rights has been developed largely in response to perceived threats or violations.[6] It is also true that capitalist economic systems do not take the protection or fulfillment of human rights as an explicit objective, but are intended, rather, to provide goods and services in an efficient way that respects the freedom of firms and individuals in the marketplace.

A concern of many conservative critics of the pastoral has been that the bishops' criteria would favor a system of social democracy or even of socialism in which there was an explicit commitment by the federal government to provide the goods and services necessary to ensure the economic rights of the poor. This is not, as I have argued elsewhere, a necessary consequence of using a human rights criterion for assessing the performance of an economic system.[7] Nor is it the intention of the bishops to alter the fundamental institutions of the American political economy. Pronouncements affirming the rights of persons to economic goods and services do not call these goods and services into being, and they do not ensure that there will be a free and just system for producing these goods. However, they do serve to remind us that there are morally urgent unmet needs.

This is in fact the use to which the notion of human rights is put in the pastoral. The bishops are not attempting to make a fundamental choice between competing economic systems. Rather, they are using the notion of human rights to point to more specific deficiencies in the performance of the U.S. economic system. This is a system that already includes many departures from the norms of pure capitalism, has various historical strengths and weaknesses, and builds on a particular culture and its values and practices. The bishops take this system so much for granted they do not even bother to offer a general justification for it. Although they offer a communal and solidaristic interpretation of the covenant with Israel and the experience of the early Christian community, particularly in the first draft, this is not used to argue, as some liberation theologians have done,[8] for socialism or communism as a way of organizing the economy. Their concern, as they put it, is to "outline an ethical framework that can guide economic life today in ways that are both faithful to the Gospel and shaped by human reason and experience" (second draft, par. 67). As a result, they fail to offer either the arguments for radical or revolutionary reconstruction of the U.S. economy that would interest Marxists and others on the far left or the fundamental justification of the system as a whole that would reassure conservatives. The reformist measures they do advocate are, if anything, more accepting of the existing patterns of U.S. capitalism than are standard presentations of Catholic social thought as a middle ground or third way between capitalism and socialism.[9]

In more practical terms, the bishops make it clear they do not want to encourage the development of a largely passive population awaiting the distribution of goods and services from an omnicompetent government. Rather, "the prime purpose of this special commitment to the poor is to enable them to become active participants in the life of society. It is to enable *all* persons to share in and contribute to the common good" (second draft, par. 90). This, it has to be admitted, is a higher and harder target to reach than setting up a comprehensive welfare system covering all the basic needs of the poor. While such a target can be defended as being worthy in itself and less expensive in the long run, it is also open to rejection on the ground that it is unattainable, given realistic limitations on our knowledge and on the efficacy of social organization and also given the necessity of respecting both human freedom and the fact of human sinfulness.

The bishops are doing three things here. They are offering an activist and participatory second stage in the social integration of the poor as a rebuttal to charges of promoting dependence on the welfare system and as evidence of their commitment to central American values of work and self-determination. They are also providing a basis for their subsequent treatment of unemployment and economic partnership. However, they are also offering an implicitly utopian resolution of the entire problem, a resolution that draws on our sense of the pathos of the human situation and our attraction to the ideal of a harmonious and integrated community in which each person flourishes. Thus, they give a softened and ironic account of the "option for the poor" that, in their view, is "not an adversarial slogan which pits one group or class against another" but "Rather, it states that the deprivation and powerlessness of the poor wounds the whole community. The extent of their suffering is a measure of how far we are from being a true community of persons."

This is a moving and important point. The difficulty with such a statement is neither its truth nor its attractiveness, but the way in which it replaces policy analysis and debate with the feelings of yearning and guilt that are appropriate when we reflect on the possibilities of an idealized society, of "a true community of persons." The policy debate, as the title of Milton Friedman's essay reminds us, is not about the desirability of such ends as full employment, social partnership and the relief of poverty, but about the means that are most capable of leading us some limited distance toward these attractive goals, given the realities of human ignorance and sinfulness, of pluralism and freedom, of human diversity and inequality, of the permanent imbalance between our desires (even our noble desires for the morally good) and our resources. The temptation to turn to ideal possibilities as a way out of the hard places in policy arguments is not always easy to distinguish from an appropriate reminder of the transcendent goal that is often lost sight of in the midst of technical complexities and political maneuvers. This distinction is not merely academic. It has to be employed in any religious approach to public policy questions, especially in the task of discerning between those evils that can be effectively resisted or eliminated without opening the way to yet greater evils, and those that are not to be tolerated or accepted without a damaging surrender of commitment to religiously significant goals. The progress of the pastoral letter on the economy reveals a somewhat unsteady oscillation between undeniably attractive goals for our economic and social life and more uncertain and controversial recommendations about policy measures with their inherent costs and negative consequences (often undesired and unintended) that are designed to bring us closer to these goals.

It would be unfair, however, to characterize the bishops as naively or uniquely utopian in their approach to shaping economic policy. That they are not uniquely utopian is, I think, manifest if one reflects on a standard defense of most economic policies that fail to achieve their intended objectives either wholly or in part. This defense usually relies on consideration of what would or should have happened under other and better conditions. In this sense, the bishops are no more utopian than are the defenders of supply-side economics or those who argue that extensive loans to developing countries were a reasonable way to invest petrodollars. The letter as a whole manifests more sensitivity to costs, to conflicting claims, to unintended consequences, to embedded interests, to structural difficulties than has been the case in previous authoritative expositions of Catholic social thought. True, the bishops have not given any comprehensive figures for the costs of what they are recommending, but they do not conceive it to be their responsibility to give a thorough assessment of the implementational difficulties that would accompany acceptance of their proposals either separately or as a whole.

This is but one aspect of the consciously planned incompleteness of their work. As has been pointed out by many of their critics, the bishops have failed to deal in any systematic way with such crucial issues as interest rates, the growth of the federal deficit and the trade deficit, the proper level of taxation, the balance between consumption and investment. A systematic treatment of these topics would be necessary if the bishops were attempting to provide comprehensive guidance for American economic policy. It can safely be said that no theologian and no church body is in a position to lay down a blueprint for a transformation of the U.S. economy that will ensure both its continued success and its meeting all the demands of social justice. It is also doubtful whether any department of economics or council of economic advisors could do so, either.

What the bishops have done is to begin the task of thinking within the Catholic tradition in a systematic way about how inadequacies and inequities within the U.S. economy are to be remedied. Thinking in a systematic way does not presuppose, as many Catholics have thought in the past, the possession of a fully elaborated intellectual construct, a system that is then to be applied to the current situation. Rather, in the present state of uncertainty and development in our economic knowledge, it involves an ability to ask systematic questions about existing and proposed policies. This involves more than a restatement of moral principles that are to be acknowledged by all. It requires a readiness to make informed choices among alternative analyses of both our current difficulties and future prospects. These choices rely on prudent judgment and cannot be derived simply from moral first principles or the principles of economics, though they should not be in contradiction to them. The controversial and creative contribution of the pastoral is to indicate ways of making those choices that are compatible with the principles of our common social morality, in particular, the norms of human rights and the principles of freedom and justice, and that are at the same time recognizable policy options within the American institutional context and in our public debate.

The bishops have made a significant and courageous decision to urge a certain policy direction on the American public and all the varied persons who play different roles in our economy. The bishops are both reminding us of moral principles and values acknowledged within the Protestant and Jewish traditions and making it clear that these principles have a cutting edge with regard to fundamental policies and daily decisions in our economic life. Their particular policy recommendations are not offered as an exercise of episcopal religious authority, but as a contribution to the public debate. They can be and are criticized, not least by many of the authors in this volume, who urge the bishops to consider alternatives to their proposals, to reexamine certain assumptions in their analyses, to look more closely at costs and negative consequences of their proposals and to recognize the inadequacy of the means they recommend to the goals they desire. This is as it should be, for the bishops are functioning both as moral teachers and citizen advocates.

The direction in which the bishops have turned should be seen neither as to the left nor to the right, but to the specific and concrete. It continues the substantive line taken earlier in papal and conciliar documents, but uses this line to pose more specific questions about the U.S. economy and to make more concrete suggestions for its future. The animated moral concern, the option for the poor, is reasonably thought to draw the bishops to the left. The decision to enter at least partially into the specifics of policy debate with the acknowledgment of limitations and tradeoffs can be seen as drawing the bishops to the right; that is, to an understanding of the characteristics and advantages of existing economic and political institutions. These labels, though, should not blind us to the possibility that the goals of leftist compassion may in the long run be more effectively achieved, as Thomas Johnson argues, by market solutions and increased production, rather than by bureaucratic allocation of resources or the possibility that solutions to the real problems of the American economy in an increasingly competitive world may require serious challenges to a variety of entrenched interests that have used political power to their own advantage. These possibilities, if they are taken seriously, disrupt efforts to portray what the bishops are saying in terms of a simple left–right polarity. In fact, the major areas of consensus between the pastoral and the letter of the Lay Commission, which was widely perceived as a reply to the pastoral from the right, show that such a simple political interpretation is not likely to be enlightening.

What the bishops have done is to move the church down into intelligent involvement with the unsolved problems of the economy and up to the high ground of economic theorizing and policy debate. Gaining access to this high ground is an important step for the Catholic community. It is a significant educational step for both Catholics and non-Catholics in making clear to them the complexity and breadth of the Catholic social agenda and in manifesting the effectiveness of the church in confronting important issues that are troubling for American society and its political and economic systems. In content, the bishops may be doing no more than a 360-degree turn, but in the audience they have reached and in their determination to share responsibility for the shape of the American economy as a whole, they have entered a new dimension, if not a new direction.

Notes

INTRODUCTION

1. Richard Easterlin, "Does Money Buy Happiness?" *The Public Interest* (Winter 1973), pp. 3–10.
2. F. A. Hayek, *New Studies in Philosophy, Politics, Economics and the History of Ideas* (Chicago: University of Chicago Press, 1978), p. 60.
3. F. A. Hayek, *The Mirage of Social Justice* (London: Routledge and Kegan Paul, 1976), pp. 15–17.
4. Karl Marx & Freidrich Engels, *The Communist Manifesto,* in Lewis S. Feuer, ed., *Marx & Engels: Basic Writings on Politics and Philosophy* (New York: Doubleday & Co., 1959), p. 9.
5. Wilhelm Ropke, *A Humane Economy: The Social Framework of the Free Market* (Chicago: Henry Regnery Co., 1960), p. 107.
6. U.S.C.C., "Catholic Social Teaching and the U.S. Economy" (second draft), *Origins* (Washington, D.C.: National Catholic Documentary Service, October 10, 1985), par. 31.
7. Pope John Paul II, *Brazil: Journey in the Light of the Eucharist* (Boston: Daughters of St. Paul, 1980), pp. 159–160.
8. National Conference of Catholic Bishops, "The Bicentennial Consultation: A Response," in *A Call to Action* (Washington, D.C.: United States Catholic Conference, 1977), p. 137.
9. Pope John Paul II, *Brazil,* p. 255.

CHAPTER 1

1. *Populorum Progressio,* par. 57.
2. Ibid, par. 58.
3. Ibid, par. 32.
4. Ibid, par 61.
5. Ibid, par. 59–61.
6. Ibid, par. 65.
7. Ibid, par. 30.
8. Ibid, par. 31.
9. *Gaudium et spes,* par. 64.

CHAPTER 2

1. There is no adequate history of American Catholic social thought and action. The best survey remains Aaron I. Abell, *American Catholicism and Social Action: A Search for Social Justice* (Garden City, N.Y.: Doubleday, 1960). Abell's edited collection, *American Catholic Thought on Social Questions* (Indianapolis, Ind.: Bobbs-Merrill, 1962), contains important texts. Charles Curran's *American Catholic Social Ethics* (Notre Dame, Ind.: University of Notre Dame Press, 1982) is a critical study of the major Catholic social commentators and movements.
2. Jay P. Dolan, *The American Catholic Experience* (Garden City, N.Y.: Doubleday, 1985), chap. 4.
3. Hugh J. Nolan has collected all the pastoral statements of the American bishops

in a four-volume set, *Pastoral Letters of the United States Catholic Bishops, 1792–1983* (Washington, D.C.: United States Catholic Conference, 1984). All quotes are taken from the texts in these volumes unless otherwise noted.

4. Jay P. Dolan, *The Immigrant Church* (Baltimore, Md.: Johns Hopkins University Press, 1970); Dolan, *Catholic Revivalism* (Notre Dame, Ind.: University of Notre Dame Press, 1975).

5. See James Roohan, "American Catholics and the Social Question, 1865–1900," unpublished Ph.D. dissertation, Yale University, 1952.

6. Henry J. Browne, *The Catholic Church and the Knights of Labor* (Washington, D.C.: Catholic University Press, 1949); Abell, *American Catholicism,* chap. 4.

7. On Ryan, see Francis L. Broderick, *The Right Reverend New Dealer: John A. Ryan* (New York: Macmillan, 1963), and O'Brien, *American Catholics and Social Reform: The New Deal Years* (New York: Oxford University Press, 1968), chap. 6.

8. This ideal of reform of the structure of the American economy enjoyed surprising support in the 1930s; see O'Brien, *American Catholics and Social Reform.*

9. On the Catholic Worker movement, see William Miller, *A Harsh and Dreadful Love* (New York: Liveright, 1974); *Dorothy Day: A Biography* (New York: Harper and Row, 1982); O'Brien, *American Catholics,* chap. 7.

10. On the reorganization of the bishops, see O'Brien, "Toward an American Catholic Church," *Cross Currents,* XXXI (Winter, 1981–1982): 457–73.

11. David Hollenbach, S.J., *Claims in Conflict* (New York: Paulist Press, 1979).

12. I have examined the church–state dimension of the bishops' teaching since Carroll in "American Catholics and American Society" in Philip J. Murnion, ed., *Catholics and Nuclear War* (New York: Seabury Press, 1983), pp. 16–29. In a forthcoming article, "Social Thought, Social Action, Social Gospel," to appear in *U.S. Catholic Historian,* I have attempted to analyze the relationship between episcopal teaching (seen best in John A. Ryan), Catholic social activism (expressed in the work of Saul Alinsky and his followers), and the newer trend toward a more prophetic approach (inspired by Dorothy Day and the Catholic Worker movement).

CHAPTER 3

1. John F. Cronin, *Social Principles and Economic Life,* rev. ed. (Milwaukee, Wis.: Bruce, 1964), pp. 30–31.

2. *Gaudium et Spes,* par. 43, in David J. O'Brien and Thomas A. Shannon, eds., *Renewing the Earth: Catholic Documents on Peace, Justice, and Liberation* (Garden City, N.Y.: Doubleday Image, 1977), p. 217.

3. Pope John XXIII, *Pacem in Terris,* especially par. 1–7, O'Brien-Shannon, pp. 124–126.

4. 1971 Synod of Bishops, *Justitia in Mundo,* in O'Brien-Shannon, , p. 391.

5. For a discussion of many aspects of this question, see Charles E. Curran and Richard A. McCormick, eds., *Readings in Moral Theology No. 2: The Distinctiveness of Christian Ethics* (New York: Paulist Press, 1980).

6. National Conference of Catholic Bishops, *Pastoral Letter on Catholic Social Teaching and the U.S. Economy: Second Draft* (Washington, D.C.: National Conference of Catholic Bishops, 1985), par. 61–62, pp. 123–124.

7. H. Richard Niebuhr, *Christ and Culture* (New York: Harper Torchbook, 1956).

8. Cronin, *Social Principles,* p. 281.

9. Rembert G. Weakland, "The Economic Pastoral: Draft Two," *America* (September 21, 1985), pp. 129–130.

10. James M. Gustafson, *Christ and the Moral life* (New York: Harper and Row, 1968), p. 240.

11. Explicit references will be to the second draft of the letter, which is all that is available at the present time. This differentiation of the four levels has been

so central to the first two drafts that one can rightly assume that the final document will follow the same approach.

12. *Second Draft,* par. 63–68, p. 20.
13. For approaches tending in this direction, see J. Brian Benestad, *The Pursuit of
    a Just Social Order: Policy Statements of the U.S. Catholic Bishops, 1966–1980*
    (Washington, D.C.: Ethics and Public Policy Center, 1982); Russell Barta, ed.,
    Challenge to the Laity (Huntington, Ind.: *Our Sunday Visitor,* 1980).
14. Pope John XXIII, *Pacem in Terris,* par. 11–27, O'Brien-Shannon, pp. 127–130.

CHAPTER 4

1. See, for example, "Catholic Social Teaching and the U.S. Economy," first draft,
   pars. 116–122, 136, 176, 243–247, 280, 310–312.
2. These three approaches to ethical issues in economic contexts are elaborated
   in Manuel Velasquez, *Business Ethics: Concepts and Cases* (Englewood Cliffs,
   N.J.: Prentice-Hall, 1982), chap. 2.
3. *Genesis,* 1:28.
4. See M. D. Chenu, *The Theology of Work* (Chicago, Ill.: Henry Regnery Co.,
   1963), pp. 9–12.
5. *Matthew,* 25:14–30.
6. *Luke,* 16:1–31; Mt. 16:26.
7. *Matthew,* 25:31–46.
8. See, for example, *The Church in the Modern World,* n. 64.
9. See in *Laborem Exercens* the opening lines of secs. 5, 6 and passim.
10. *Laborem Exercens,* sec. 6, 10.
11. Ibid., sec. 25.
12. Ibid., sec. 6.
13. *Exodus,* 22:21–24; *Deuteronomy,* 24:19–22; *Isaiah,* 1:17, 3:15; *Amos,* 2:6, 4:1,
    5:11, 8:4.
14. *Matthew,* 25:40, 45.
15. *James,* 5:1.
16. *Acts,* 2:44, 45; 4:35.
17. *Galatians,* 6:2; see *Leviticus,* 25:1–55.
18. Aquinas, *Summa Theologiae,* II-II, q. 66, a. 2.
19. *Rerum Novarum,* par. 22.
20. *Laborem Exercens,* par. 45–48.
21. *Pastoral Constitution on the Church in the Modern World,* par. 71.
22. *Laborem Exercens,* sec. 14.
23. See, for example, *Rerum Novarum,* pars. 32, 37.
24. Aquinas, *Summa Theologiae,* II–II, q. 66, a. 7.
25. *Pacem in Terris,* par. 18–22.
26. *The Church in the Modern World,* par. 69.
27. *Luke,* 8:26–33.
28. *Romans,* 6–8.
29. *James* 2:15, 16; see also *I Corinthians,* 8:9.
30. *Galatians,* 5:1, 13, 14.
31. *Laborem Exercens,* sec. 6.
32. *The Church in the Modern World,* pars. 17, 27.
33. The dominant role the large-scale corporation plays in the American economy
    is nicely described in Phillip I. Blumberg, *The Megacorporation in American
    Society: The Scope of Corporate Power* (Englewood Cliffs, N.J.: Prentice-Hall,
    Inc., 1975).
34. *Statistical Abstract of the United States, 1984,* p. 821.
35. R. Heilbroner & L. Thurow, *Economics Explained* (1982), pp. 220–221.
36. Referring to the Isaiah texts that the Easter liturgies apply to Jesus Christ, for
    example, Novak tells us, "For many years, one of my favorite texts in Scripture
    has been Isaiah 53:2–3: 'He hath no form nor comeliness; and when we shall

see him there is no beauty that we should desire him. He is despised and rejected of men; a man of sorrows, and acquainted with grief; he was despised, and we esteemed him not.' I would like to apply these words to the modern business corporation, a much despised incarnation of God's presence in this world." Michael Novak, "A Theology of the Corporation," p. 203, in Michael Novak and John W. Cooper, *The Corporation: A Theological Inquiry* (Washington, D.C.: American Enterprise Institute, 1981), pp. 203–224.

37. George Gilder, *Wealth and Poverty* (New York: Basic Books, Inc., 1981), pp. 21–27.

38. See Robert Austin Marcus, *Saeculum: History and Society in the Theology of St. Augustine* (London: Cambridge University Press, 1970).

39. "Catholic Social Teaching and the U.S. Economy," first draft, par. 95; second draft, par. 81; see also in second draft, par. 90.

40. See Adam Smith, *Inquiry into the Nature and Causes of the Wealth of Nations* [New York: Random House, 1937 (1776)]; Charles Babbage, *On the Economy of Machinery and Manufacturers* (London: Charles Knight, 1835).

41. A point that is much emphasized in Michael Novak, *The Spirit of Democratic Capitalism* (New York: Simon and Schuster, 1982), pp. 13–133.

42. Aquinas, quoted in *Rerum Novarum,* n. 37.

43. *Quadragesimo Anno,* par. 69; see also *Ibid,* par. 84.

44. The division of labor operates today in the form elaborated early this century by Frederick Taylor in his *The Principles of Scientific Management* (New York: Harper, 1911).

45. Douglas, F. Greer, *Industrial Organization and Public Policy, 2nd ed.* (New York: Macmillan, 1984), pp. 162–163.

46. The standard account of the development of the large-scale corporation in the United States is Alfred D. Chandler, Jr., *The Visible Hand: The Managerial Revolution in American Business* (Cambridge, Mass., 1977); comparable accounts of the rise of the large corporation in European economies can be found in Alfred D. Chandler, Jr. and Herman Daems, eds., *Managerial Hierarchies: Comparative Perspectives on the Rise of the Modern Industrial Enterprise* (Cambridge, Mass.: Harvard University Press, 1980); evidence on the development of large-scale enterprises in the Soviet Union and other Eastern nations can be found in Leon Smolinski, "The Scale of Soviet Industrial Establishments," *American Economic Review,* vol. 52, no. 2 (May 1962), pp. 138–148; and in Frederick L. Pryor, *Property and Industrial Organization in Communist and Capitalist Nations* (Bloomington, Ind.: Indiana University Press, 1973).

47. George Thomas Kurian, *The New Book of World Rankings* (New York: Facts On File Publications, 1984), p. 314.

48. Ibid, p. 331.

49. Ibid, p. 117.

50. Ibid, p. 96.

51. Ibid, p. 98.

52. U.S. Department of Commerce, Bureau of the Census, *Statistical Abstract of the United States, 1984,* p. 873.

53. This includes, of course, the socialist economies of Eastern Europe, which today are also dominated by the large-scale enterprise. See Frederick L. Pryor, *Property and Industrial Organization in Communist and Capitalist Nations* (Bloomington, Ind.: Indiana University Press, 1973); Leon Smolinski, "The Scale of Soviet Industrial Establishments," *American Economic Review,* vol. 52, no. 2 (May 1962), pp. 138–148, and idem., "Toward a Socialist Corporation: Soviet Industrial Reorganization of 1973," *Survey,* vol. 20, no. 1 (Winter 1974), pp. 24–35.

54. See L. W. Weiss, "Optimal Plant Size and the Extent of Suboptimal Capacity," in R. T. Masson and P. D. Qualls, eds., *Essays on Industrial Organization in Honor of Joe S. Bain,* (Cambridge, Mass.: Ballinger Publishing Co., 1976), pp. 123–141; and F. M. Scherer et al., *The Economics of Multi-Plant Operation* (Cambridge, Mass: Harvard University Press, 1975).

55. William G. Shepherd, *Market Power and Economic Welfare* (New York: Random

House, 1970), p. 198; see also the higher estimates in Keith Cowling and Dennis Mueller, "The Social Costs of Monopoly Power," *Economic Journal* (December 1978), pp. 727–748.

56. William S. Comanor and Robert H. Smiley, "Monopoly and the Distribution of Wealth," *Quarterly Journal of Economics* (May 1975), pp. 177–194.

57. *Statistical Abstract, 1984,* p. 567.

58. Jeffrey M. Netter, "Excessive Advertising: An Empirical Analysis," *Journal of Industrial Economics* (June 1982), pp. 361–373.

59. I. Lee Preston, *The Great American Blow-Up* (Madison, Wis.: University of Wisconsin Press, 1975).

60. Milton Silverman and Philip R. Lee, *Pills, Profits and Politics* (Berkeley, Calif.: University of California Press, 1974); H. J. Rotfeld and K. B. Rotzoll, "Advertising and Product Quality: Are Heavily Advertised Products Better?" *Journal of Consumer Affairs* (Summer 1976), pp. 33–47.

61. Besides weapons production, other examples are the subsidizing of the tobacco industry and of military research.

62. See F. M. Scherer, *The Weapons Acquisition Process: Economic Incentives* (Boston: Harvard University School of Business, 1963); Gordon Adams, "The Iron Triangle: Inside the Weapons Elite," *The Nation* (October 31, 1981), pp. 425, 441–444.

63. Ruth Leger Sivard, *World Military and Social Expenditures, 1983* (Washington, D.C.: World Priorities, 1983), pp. 6–7.

64. Ibid., pp. 22–26.

65. See William G. Shepherd and Clair Wilcox, *Public Policies Toward Business* (Homewood, Ill.: Richard D. Irwin, Inc., 1979), pp. 556–562. Between 1981 and 1985, all ten of the top weapons contractors were accused of various forms of waste, fraud and inefficiency, *San Jose Mercury News,* April 15, 1985, p. 1.

66. See L. Klein, *New Forms of Work Organization* (Cambridge: Cambridge University Press, 1976), p. 14; the extension of job standardization and fragmentation into white-collar work is documented in P. Kraft, *Programmers and Managers* (New York: Springer-Verlag, 1977).

67. Herbert Gintis, "The Meaning of Alienation," in Richard C. Edwards, Michael Reich, and Thomas E. Weisskopf, eds., *The Capitalist System,* 2nd ed. (Englewood Cliffs, N.J.: Prentice-Hall, 1978), p. 275; italics in original.

68. See, for example, the "human relations" literature originating with Elton Mayo's Hawthorne studies, such as E. Mayo, *The Human Problems of an Industrial Civilization* (New York: Macmillan, 1933), and the more recent literature of "industrial humanism" such as Chris Argris, *Integrating the Individual and the Organization* (New York: John Wiley & Sons, 1964), R. Likert, *The Human Organization: Its Management and Value* (New York: McGraw-Hill, 1967) and William Bennis, *Changing Organizations* (New York: McGraw-Hill, 1966).

69. See, for example, L. E. Davis, R. R. Canter, and J. Hoffman, "Current Job Design Criteria," *Journal of Industrial Engineering,* 6 (January–February, 1955):3–11, and J. C. Taylor, "Job Design Criteria Twenty Years Later," in L. E. Davis and J. C. Taylor, eds., *Design of Jobs,* 2nd ed. (Santa Monica: Goodyear, 1979), p. 61.

70. C. R. Walker and R. H. Guest, *The Man on the Assembly Line* (Cambridge, Mass.: Harvard University Press, 1952); J. R. Hackman and E. E. Lawler, "Employee Reactions to Job Characteristics," *Journal of Applied Psychology,* 55:(June, 1971), 259–286.

71. T. G. Cummings and E. S. Molloy, *Improving Productivity and the Quality of Working Life* (New York: Praeger, 1977), p. 48.

72. Later drafts acknowledged American productivity in the introductory paragraphs, but the moral aspects of productivity are never explicitly addressed nor are they directly evaluated.

73. It has been unfavorably compared with the more upbeat "lay letter" of the Lay Commission on Catholic Social Teaching and the U.S. Economy, *Toward the Future* (New York: American Catholic Committee, 1984).

74. The exception, of course, is the government enterprise, such as the General

Services Administration and the Tennessee Valley Authority. In the United States, however, such enterprises constitute a minuscule and nontraditional function of government.

75. *Laborem Exercens,* sec. 25.

76. See Phillip I. Blumberg, *The Megacorporation in American Society: The Scope of Corporate Power* (Englewood Cliffs, N.J.: Prentice-Hall, Inc., 1975), chap. 4.

77. William G. Shepherd and others have found that in manufacturing, four firm concentration ratios averaged sixty percent through the 1960s, but then declined somewhat as a result of foreign competition and enforcement of antitrust laws; see William G. Shepherd, *Market Power and Economic Welfare* (New York: Random House, 1970), pp. 106–107, and "Causes of Increased Competition in the U.S. Economy, 1939–1980," *Review of Economics and Statistics* (November 1982), p. 619. Some of the manufacturing industries that evidence especially high concentration ratios are autos, chewing gum, household refrigerators, primary aluminum, aircraft engines, explosives, sugar refining, anesthetics, antiarthritics, diabetic therapy and computers, among others. Nonmanufacturing industries that evidence high concentration ratios are local retail markets, uranium mining and insurance, among others; see Douglas F. Greer, *Industrial Organization and Public Policy* (New York: Macmillan, 1984), pp. 105–113.

78. See William G. Shepherd and Clair Wilcox, *Public Policies Toward Business* (Homewood, Ill.: Richard D. Irwin, Inc., 1979), pp. 194–254.

79. Douglas F. Greer, *Industrial Organization and Public Policy* (New York: Macmillan, 1984), pp. 51–95.

80. Shepherd and Wilcox, *Public Policies,* pp. 39–53.

81. See Charles E. Lindblom, *Politics and Markets* (Basic Books, 1977) and Samuel M. Loescher, "Corporate Giantism, Degradation of the Plane of Competition, and Countervailance", *Journal of Economic Issues,* Vol. 8 (1974):329, and "Limiting Corporate Power," *Journal of Economic Issues,* Vol. 13 (1979):557; John Kenneth Galbraith, *Economics and the Public Purpose* (Boston: Houghton Mifflin, 1973); Mark V. Nadel, *Corporations and Political Accountability* (Lexington, Mass.: D.C. Heath, 1976); Ralph Nader, Mark Green, and Joel Seligman, *Taming the Giant Corporation* (New York: Norton, 1976); Arthur S. Miller, *The Modern Corporate State: Private Governments and the American Constitution* (Westport, Conn.: Greenwood Press, 1976).

82. Edward S. Herman, *Corporate Control, Corporate Power* (New York: Cambridge University Press, 1981), pp. 177–179.

83. Ibid, pp. 174, 179–180.

84. Lester M. Salamon and John J. Siegfried, "Economic Power and Political Influence: The Impact of Industry Structure on Public Policy," *American Political Science Review,* vol. 71, (September, 1977): 1026–1043.

85. Russell Pittman, "Market Structure and Campaign Contributions," *Public Choice* 37 (Fall, 1977): 37–52.

86. Karen Orren, *Corporate Power and Social Change: The Politics of the Life Insurance Industry* (Baltimore, Md.: Johns Hopkins University Press, 1974).

87. Robert Engler, *The Brotherhood of Oil: Energy Policy and the Public Interest* (Chicago: University of Chicago Press, 1977).

88. A. Lee Fritschler, *Smoking and Politics: Policymaking and the Federal Bureaucracy* (Englewood Cliffs, N.J.: Prentice-Hall, 1969).

89. Barbara and John Ehrenreich, *The American Health Empire: Power, Profits and Politics* (New York: Random House, 1970).

90. Howard Margolis, "The Politics of Auto Emissions," *The Public Interest* No. 49, (Fall, 1977): 3–21.

91. Stephen D. Krasner, "Business-Government Relations: The Case of the International Coffee Agreement," *International Organizations* 27 (1973):495.

92. Prakash Sethi, *Advocacy Advertising and Large Corporations: Social Conflict, Big Business Image, the Mass Media and Public Policy* (1977); see also S. Prakash Sethi, "Grassroots Lobbying and the Corporation," *Business and Society Review* (November–December 1979); and U.S. Senate, 95th Congress, 2nd session,

Subcommittee on Administrative Practice and Procedure of the Committee on the Judiciary, *Sourcebook on Corporate Image and Corporate Advocacy Advertising* (1978). For an analysis of the power of sponsors over public opinion, see Eric Barnouw, *The Sponsor* (New York: Oxford University Press, 1978).

93. Robert Pitofsky, "The Political Content of Anti-Trust," University of Pennsylvania {Pa} Law Review 127 (1979):1051.

94. For a vigorous defense of this view, see Milton Friedman, "The Social Responsibility of Business Is to Make Profits."

95. See William L. Cary and Melvin Aron Eisenberg, *Cases and Materials on Corporations,* 5th ed. (Mineola, N.Y.: The Foundation Press, Inc., 1980), p. 137; and Harry G. Henn, *Handbook of the Law of Corporations* (St. Paul, Minn.: West Publishing Co., 1970), p. 95.

96. Cary and Eisenberg, *Cases and Materials.*

97. Edward S. Herman, *Corporate Control, Corporate Power* (New York: Cambridge University Press, 1981), pp. 302–323.

98. Shareholders commonly "elect" their directors by mail from a slate of candidates proposed by management. Because shareholders have little desire to interfere in the running of a business, it is rare for them to elect anyone other than the candidates proposed by managers who, presumably, know what is best for the company. Once elected, directors do not have the time, expertise, staff, or information to criticize or evaluate effectively what is going on inside a corporation. Most boards meet only about a dozen times a year, and then for only a total of perhaps 36 hours. At their meetings, they must rely on the information supplied by management, and their votes are restricted to choosing among the alternatives presented to them by management. See D. Vagts, *Basic Corporation Law,* 2nd ed. (1979), p. 211.

99. This evolution was described in the classic work of Adolf A. Berle, Jr. and Gardiner C. Means, *The Modern Corporation and Private Property* (New York: Macmillan, 1932); a superb reassessment of the Berle and Means study can be found in Edward S. Herman, *Corporate Control and Corporate Power* (New York: Cambridge University Press, 1981); see also Alfred D. Chandler, Jr., *The Visible Hand: The Managerial Revolution in American Business* (Cambridge, Mass.: Harvard University Press, 1977).

100. John A. Sussman, "Making It To the Top: A Career Profile of the Senior Executive," *Management Review,* 68 (July, 1979): 15–21.

101. Adolf Berle, in particular, has argued that the corporate manager would allocate corporate resources "on the basis of public policy rather than private cupidity." See Adolf A. Berle, Jr. and Gardiner C. Means, *The Modern Corporation and Private Property,* p. 356; Adolf A. Berle Jr., *The Twentieth Century Capitalist Revolution* (New York: Harcourt Brace, 1954); Adolf A. Berle Jr., *Power Without Property* (New York: Harcourt Brace, 1959).

102. Herman, *Corporate Control,* pp. 257–264.

103. Ibid, pp. 85–113.

104. David L. Birch, *The Job Generation Process* (Cambridge, Mass.: M.I.T. Program on Neighborhood and Region Change, 1979), appendix D.

105. See Barry Bluestone and Bennett Harrison, *The Deindustrialization of America* (New York: Basic Books, Inc., 1982), pp. 140–190.

106. Ibid, pp. 49–81.

107. Bluestone and Harrison, *Deindustrialization,* p. 235.

108. "Protecting At Will Employees Against Wrongful Discharge: The Duty to Terminate Only in Good Faith," *Harvard Law Review* 93 Vol. 93 (June 1980): 1816.

109. Lawrence E. Blades, "Employment at Will versus Individual Freedom: On Limiting the Abusive Exercise of Employer Power," *Columbia Law Review,* Vol. 67 (1967): 1405.

110. On these issues, see David Ewing, *Freedom Inside the Organization* (New York: McGraw-Hill Book Company, 1977); Mary Gibson, *Workers' Rights* (Towata, N.J.: Rowman & Allanheld, Publishers, 1983); Robert Ellis Smith, *Workrights* (New York: E. P. Dutton, Inc., 1983); Patricia H. Werhane, *Persons, Rights, & Corpo-*

rations (Englewood Cliffs, N.J.: Prentice-Hall, Inc., 1985); Alan F. Westin and Stephan Salisbury, eds., *Individual Rights in the Corporation* (New York: Pantheon Books, 1980).

111. David Ewing, "Civil Liberties in the Corporation," *New York State Bar Journal* (April 1978), pp. 188–229.

112. For example, Michael Novak, *The Spirit of Democratic Capitalism* (New York: Simon and Schuster, 1982), pp. 131–132.

CHAPTER 5

1. Joseph Schumpeter, *Capitalism, Socialism and Democracy* (New York: Harper and Row, 1940; 1975), p. 83.

2. Robert Reich, *The Next American Frontier* (New York: Penguin, 1984).

3. Mancur Olson, *The Rise and Decline of Nations* (New Haven: Yale University Press, 1982).

4. Milton Friedman, *Capitalism and Freedom* (Chicago: University of Chicago Press, 1962), pp. 175–187.

5. Walter Williams, *Youth and Minority Unemployment* (Palo Alto: Hoover Institution Press, 1977).

6. Charles Murray, *Losing Ground: American Social Policy, 1950–1980* (New York: Basic Books, 1984); Ken Auletta, *The Underclass* (New York: Random House, 1983); Walter Williams, *America: A Minority Viewpoint* (Palo Alto: Hoover Institution Press, 1977); Thomas Sowell, *Markets and Minorities* (Oxford: International Center for Economic Policy Studies, 1981); *Ethnic America* (New York: Basic Books, 1981), *The Economics and Politics of Race* (New York: Morrow, 1983), and *Civil Rights: Rhetoric or Reality?* (New York: Morrow, 1984).

CHAPTER 6

1. Walter Block, "The Jews and Capitalism," *Vital Speeches,* February 15, 1985, p. 284.

2. The matter of trends in Jewish voting is enormously complicated. In 1980, largely because of their relative dissatisfaction with President Jimmy Carter and their attraction to the independent John Anderson, Jews appeared to have deserted the Democratic party in larger numbers than ever before. However, this trend appears to have been reversed in the 1984 election, with 66% of Jewish voters casting their ballot for Mondale versus only 32% for Reagan. In the same election, white Catholics voted 41% for Mondale versus 58% for Reagan (*The New York Times,* Sunday, November 25, 1984, section 4, p. 23). A number of explanations for this continuing Democratic affiliation have been offered, including Charles Silberman's emphasis on Jews' endemic sense of social insecurity and their corresponding "cultural liberalism" and preference for political parties that support tolerance and diversity. [For a discussion of this matter, see his *A Certain People* (New York: Summit Books, 1985), pp. 345–359.] Nevertheless, apart from the immediate fluctuations of election campaigns and the attraction offered by specific candidates, many commentators agree that deep social and economic forces are working against traditional Jewish liberalism and Jews' affiliation with less-fortunate groups in the New Deal coalition.

3. Milton Friedman, "Capitalism and the Jews," in *Religion, Economics and Social Thought* quoted in Block (n. 1), p. 284.

4. *Catholic Social Teaching and the U.S. Economy* (second draft), Publication No. 968, Washington, D.C.: National Conference of Catholic Bishops, 1985, pp. 1, 10f.

5. Ibid., pp. 1, 22f.

6. Ibid., p. 12.

7. Ibid., pp. 8, 18.

8. Ibid., pp. 66–68.

9. Roger Brooks, *Support for the Poor in the Mishnaic Law of Agriculture: Tractate Peah* (Chico, California: Scholars Press, 1983), p. 18.

10. For a fuller discussion of the theme of common ownership of the created goods of the world as this teaching emerged in the early church, see William J. Walsh and John P. Langan, "Patristic Social Consciousness—The Church and the Poor," in John C. Haughey, ed., *The Faith that Does Justice* (New York: Paulist Press, 1977), pp. 113–151.

11. Ephraim Frisch, *An Historical Survey of Jewish Philanthropy* (New York: Macmillan, 1924), p. 9.

12. Discussions of classical Jewish approaches to the issue of social welfare include Israel Abrahams, *Jewish Life in the Middle Ages* (London: Edward Goldston, 1932); Salo W. Baron, *The Jewish Community* (Philadelphia: Jewish Publication Society of America, 1942), vol. 2, chap. 16; Ephraim Frisch, *Survey of Jewish Philanthropy*; Kaufman Kohler, "The Historical Development of Jewish Charity," *Hebrew Union College and Other Addresses* (Cincinnati, 1916), pp. 229–252; Solomon Schechter, "Notes of Lectures on Jewish Philanthropy," *Studies in Judaism*, 3rd series (Philadelphia: Jewish Publication Society of America, 1934), pp. 238–276; Isadore Twersky, "Some Aspects of the Jewish Attitude Toward the Welfare State," *Tradition* 5:2 (Spring 1963), pp. 137–158. Also, the articles in the *Encyclopedia Judaica* on "Charity," "The Poor" and "Gemilut Hasadim."

13. "Some Aspects of the Jewish Attitude toward the Welfare State," *Tradition* 5:1 (Spring 1963), p. 146.

14. TB Pe'ah, 8:7. All references to the Babylonian Talmud are to the Soncino edition, I. Epstein, ed. (London: Soncino Press, 1935–520).

15. *The Code of Maimonides,* Book Seven, *The Book of Agriculture,* Isaac Klein, trans. (New Haven: Yale University Press, 1979), Treatise II, "Laws Concerning Gifts to the Poor," chap. 9, par. 3, p. 85.

16. Frisch, *Survey of Jewish Philanthropy,* p. 39.

17. To give a tenth of one's wealth to charity was regarded as a moderate contribution, a twentieth or less was judged to be "mean." The rabbis also stipulated that during their lifetime, persons might not contribute more than one fifth of their wealth to charity lest their families suffer impoverishment, but bequests at death might exceed this amount (TB Kethubot 50a, 67b).

18. TB Pe'ah, 8:8.

19. This was done to spare them undue psychological suffering. A precedent for this practice was found in a famous Talmudic story about Hillel the Elder who provided for an impoverished but formerly well-to-do man the best of food and drink and a horse and footman for his journeys. One day, according to the story, the sage was unable to locate a footman and performed this service himself (TB Kethubot, 67b).

20. The rule was laid down that relief was to be withheld from those who went begging door to door, although a compromise was arrived at, allowing some giving to such mendicants (TB Baba Bathra, 9a).

21. Talmud Yerushalmi, Pe'ah viii, sec. 9, f. 21b, line 13. This selection from the Jerusalem Talmud is translated in Montefiore and Lowe, *A Rabbinic Anthology,* p. 418. Cf. *The Code of Maimonides,* vol. 6; *The Book of Seasons,* Hyman Klein, ed. (New Haven: Yale University Press, 1961), chaps. 2, 16 (p. 462). At the same time, the rabbis repeatedly warned against deception in matters of eligibility for public relief. The constant teaching was that "if a man accepts charity and is not in need of it, his end [will be that] he will not pass out of the world before he comes to such a condition" (TB Kethubot, 68a).

22. Solomon Schechter observes that this same understanding forms the basis for the recitation of a benediction and saying grace before and after meals. According to the Talmud, "One who enjoys of the good things of this world without saying grace, is as though he robbed the Holy One. . . ." "Notes of Lectures on Jewish Philanthropy," p. 243.

23. TB Kethubot, 67b. Compare this anecdote with Ambrose's admonition to the

avaricious to make restitution by giving alms: "You are not making a gift of your possessions to the poor person. You are handing over to him what is his." *Naboth* 55, quoted in Walsh and Langan (n. 10), "Patristic Social Consciousness," p. 128.

24. Frisch, *Survey of Jewish Philanthropy,* p. 79.

25. Frisch, *Survey of Jewish Philanthropy,* p. 79, paraphrasing *The Code of Maimonides,* Book Seven, Treatise II, 1:1–6 and 7:10.

26. TB Gittin, 7a. Cf. *The Code of Maimonides,* Book Seven, Treatise II, 9:18 (p. 49f.).

27. TB Ḳethubot, 49b; *The Code of Maimonides,* Book Seven, Treatise II, 7:10 (p. 79).

28. TB Sukkah, 49b.

29. Hence, the teaching that "Loving-kindness is much greater than charity" (TB Sukkah, 49b). For a discussion of comparisons between *Zedakah* and *Gemilut Hasadim,* see Frisch, *Survey of Jewish Philanthropy,* p. 92f.

30. Twersky, "Aspects of the Jewish Attitude," p. 149.

31. *Exodus Rabbah,* S. M. Lehrman, trans. (London: Soncino Press, 1939), Mishpatim, xxxi, 14 (p. 395).

32. Although such Jewish ascetic groups as the Essenes existed, they always constituted fringe movements within orthodox Judaism. For a fuller treatment of asceticism and the Jewish tradition, see Schechter (n. 12), "Lectures on Jewish Philanthropy," pp. 267f. This relative absence of an ascetic tradition is an important contrast to Christian thought. As a result, Judaism's heritage of social concern tends to be rooted in compassion for the poor and insistence on their rights, rather than in the kind of discomfort over attachment to material goods in Christian teaching. For a discussion of this motif, see Walsh and Langan (n. 10), "Patristic Social Consciousness," pp. 119–126.

33. TB Kethubot, 67b.

34. TB Hagigah, 5a.

35. TJ Pe'ah, 8:9, 21b.

36. This concept is borrowed from Richard Titmuss, *The Gift Relationship* (New York: Pantheon Books, 1971), chapter 13.

37. According to R. Eliezer, the "secret giver" is greater than Moses (TB Baba Bathra, 9b). The practice of secret giving is indicated in the Mishnah, in which it is said that the Temple had a chamber of "secret gifts" where donations to the poor could be deposited and collected anonymously (TB Shekalim, 5:6).

38. TB Shabbath, 104a.

39. *The Code of Maimonides,* Book Seven, Treatise II, 10:7 (p. 91). Sifre, ed. Friedmann, p. 98a, nn. 11–12. Cf. TB Baba Mezià, 31b. The Talmud records the remark of R. Abba said, in the name of R. Simeon ben Lakesh, that "He who advances a loan is greater than he who gives charity, and he who puts in capital for partnership (with the person in distress) is more meritorious than all others" (TB Shabbath, 63a).

40. "If a man has no means and does not wish to be maintained [out of poor funds] he should be granted [the sum he requires] as a loan. . . ." "If he has no means and does not wish to be maintained [out of the poor funds] he is told, 'Bring a pledge and you will receive [a loan]' in order to raise thereby his [drooping] spirit" (TB Kethubot, 67b).

41. TB Kiddushin, 29b.

42. TB Pesahim, 113a.

43. *Catholic Social Teaching and the U.S. Economy* (second draft), p. 66.

44. Max Weber, *Ancient Judaism* (New York: The Free Press, 1952), chap. 13.

45. Abrahams (n. 12), *Jewish Life in the Middle Ages,* pp. 359ff.

46. Frisch, *Survey of Jewish Philanthropy,* p. 117.

47. Baron, *The Jewish Community,* pp. 339–343.

48. TB Baba Mezi'a, 71a.

49. Joseph Karo, Shulhan Àruk, Yoreh Deàh, 251:3.

50. Frisch, *Survey of Jewish Philanthropy,* p. 117.

51. Talmud Yerushalmi, Demai, IV, sec. 6, f. 24a, line 67. Montefiore and Lowe, trans., *A Rabbinic Anthology*, p. 424, and TB Gittin, 61a.

52. "In every generation, let each man look on himself as if *he* had come forth out of Egypt." *The Passover Haggadah*, Nahum N. Glatzer, ed. (New York: Schocken Books, 1969), p. 49.

CHAPTER 7

1. See Rose D. Friedman, *Poverty: Definition and Perspective* (Washington, D.C.: American Enterprise Institute, 1965).

2. In the second draft, the words "food prices" and "pricing policies" occur in a sentence in the section added on "Food and Agriculture" (par. 217). The sentence itself is bad economics, reversing cause and effect. The bishops regard relatively "low food prices" as a result of "pricing policies" that "put pressure on farmers to increase output and lower costs," whereas the low prices result primarily from technological developments that have lowered costs and led to sharply expanded output. Government "pricing policies" have been directed at keeping prices up rather than driving them down!

   The words "fair prices" occur in the discussion of trade with other countries (p. 261) without any analysis whatsoever of what the term means. To an economist, it has no objective meaning; its meaning is entirely in the eye of the beholder.

   To the best of my knowledge, these are the only occurrences of the word "price" or "pricing" in the document.

3. See Milton Friedman and Rose D. Friedman, *Free to Choose* (New York and London: Harcourt Brace Jovanovich, 1980; paperback ed., New York: Avon Books, 1981), chap. 1.

4. *The Economist*, October 19, 1985, p. 117; fuller data in Statistical Office of the European Communities, *Unemployment: Monthly Bulletin* (Luxembourg).

5. See Milton Friedman, "Nobel Lecture: Inflation and Unemployment," *Journal of Political Economy*, 85 (June 1977): 451–472.

6. See Finis Welch, *Minimum Wages: Issues and Evidence* (Washington, D.C.: American Enterprise Institute, 1978); Thomas Sowell, *Markets and Minorities* (New York: Basic Books, 1981).

7. See Martin Anderson, *The Federal Bulldozer: A Critical Analysis of Urban Renewal, 1949–1962* (Cambridge Mass.: Massachusetts Institute of Technology Press, 1964).

8. W. H. Hutt, *The Economics of the Colour Bar* (London: Andre Deutsch for The Institute of Economic Affairs, 1964).

9. Charles Murray, *Losing Ground* (New York: Basic Books, 1984).

10. Critics have pointed out that the changing demographic structure of the population as a result of the baby boom at the one end and the lengthening of life at the other has played a significant role in those developments. That may partly explain, but does not alter, the discrepancy between the claims made for the "war on poverty" and the results. The fact remains that market forces were more effective than governmental measures, and that governmental measures had effects very different from those intended by their well-meaning sponsors.

11. See Peter T. Bauer, *Equality, the Third World, and Economic Delusion,* and *Dissent on Development* (Cambridge, Mass.: Harvard University Press, 1981 and 1976); Melvyn B. Krauss, *Development Without Aid: Growth, Poverty and Government* (New York: McGraw-Hill for The Manhattan Institute, 1983); see also Milton Friedman, "Foreign Economic Aid: Means and Objectives," *Yale Review* 47 (Summer 1958): pp. 500–516, and "Myths That Keep People Hungry," *Harper's Magazine*, April 1967, pp. 16–24.

12. See Milton Friedman, *Capitalism and Freedom* (Chicago: University of Chicago Press, 1962; reissued, 1982), chap. 1; Friedman and Friedman, *Free to Choose*,

pp. 298–309; Martin Anderson, "An Economic Bill of Rights," in *To Promote Prosperity: U.S. Domestic Policy in the Mid-1980s,* John H. Moore, ed. (Stanford, Calif.: Hoover Institution Press, 1984), pp. 1–22.

CHAPTER 8

1. National Conference of Catholic Bishops, *Pastoral Letter on Catholic Social Teaching and the U.S. Economy,* October 7, 1985.
2. Michael Harrington, *The Vast Majority* (New York: Simon and Schuster, 1977).
3. William C. Birdsall, "The Value of the Official Poverty Statistics," Sixth Annual Research Conference of the Association for Public Policy and Management, New Orleans, 1984.
4. Mary Corcoran et al., "Myth and Reality: The Causes and Persistence of Poverty," *Journal of Policy Analysis and Management,* 1985, 4:516–536.
5. Corcoran, et al., "Myth and Reality," p. 26.

CHAPTER 9

1. Lay Commission on Catholic Social Teaching and the U.S. Economy, Toward the Future: Catholic Social Thought and the U.S. Economy: A Lay Letter (New York, 1984).
2. U.S. President, Economic Report (Washington, D.C.: U.S. Government Printing Office, 1972 and 1985).
3. Milton Friedman, "The Role of Monetary Policy," *American Economic Review,* 58 (March 1968):1–17.
4. Paul McCracken et al. *Towards Full Employment and Price Stability* (Paris, OECD, 1977).
5. U.S. President, Economic Report.
6. Martin Feldstein, "The Economics of the New Unemployment," *Public Interest,* No. 33 (Fall 1973), pp. 3–42.
7. Martin Feldstein, "Temporary Layoffs in the Theory of Unemployment," *Journal of Political Economy,* 84 (October 1976):427–457.
8. Martin Feldstein, "The Effect of Unemployment Insurance on Temporary Layoff Unemployment," *American Economic Review,* 68 (December 1978):834–846.
9. Robert H. Topel, "On Layoffs and Unemployment Insurance," *American Economic Review,* 73 (September 1983):541–559.
10. Kenneth W. Clarkson, and Roger E. Meiners [1979], "Institutional Changes, Reported Unemployment, and Induced Institutional Changes," Karl Brunner and Allan H. Meltzer, eds., *Three Aspects of Policy and Policymaking: Knowledge, Data and Institutions,* vol. 10, pp. 205–235, in the Carnegie-Rochester Conference Series on Public Policy: a supplementary series to the *Journal of Monetary Economics* (Amsterdam: North-Holland Publishing Co., 1979).
11. U.S. President, Economic Report.
12. John Rawls, *A Theory of Justice* (Cambridge, Mass.: Harvard University Press, 1971).
13. Carl F. Christ and Alan A. Walters, "The Mythology of Tax Cuts," *Policy Review* (Spring 1981), pp. 73–86.
14. Both Houses of Congress have passed mildly progressive tax bills that would: (1) close or narrow many loopholes, (2) raise exemptions so as to free many low income persons from the income tax completely, and (3) lower the highest personal tax rate, to 38 percent under the House bill and to 32 percent under the Senate bill. The Senate bill has four tax brackets, with tax rates (from the lowest to the highest incomes) to 12 percent, 27 percent, 32 percent, and again 27 percent. The total tax would be exactly 27 percent of total income for persons in the highest income bracket, and would always be less than 27 percent for those in the lower brackets.

CHAPTER 10

1. Kent A. Price, ed., *The Dilemmas of Choice* (Washington, D.C.: Resources for the Future, 1985).
2. Pierre R. Crosson and S. Brubaker, *Resource and Environmental Effects of U.S. Agriculture* (Washington, D.C.: Resources for the Future, 1982).
3. Kenneth R. Farrell, F. Sanderson, and T. T. Vo, "Meeting Future Needs for United States Food, Fiber, and Forest Products," in *Reference Document: Needs Assessment for the Food and Agricultural Sciences* (Washington, D.C.: Joint Council on Food Agricultural Sciences, 1984).
4. Kenneth R. Farrell and S. M. Capalbo, "Natural Resource and Environmental Dimensions of Agricultural Development," paper presented at International Association of Agricultural Economists, Malaga, Spain, August 26–September 2, 1985 (proceedings forthcoming).
5. Gordon C. Rausser, and Kenneth R. Farrell, eds., *Alternative Agricultural and Food Policies and the 1985 Farm Bill* (Berkeley, Calif.: Giannini Foundation of Agricultural Economics, University of California, 1984).

CHAPTER 11

1. This chapter is based on presentations, papers and conversations during meetings of the Latin American Econometric Society in recent years. The author makes no claim for originality. This paper should be seen as an exposition and popular amplification of the ideas of Carlos Diaz-Alejandro, Rudiger Dornbusch, Edmar Bacha, Mario Simonsen, Lance Taylor and John Taylor. The words "old style" and "new style" have been used by Diaz-Alejandro and Dornbusch in slightly different ways to describe macro policy in South America. This paper uses "old style" and "new style" according to the definitions of Dornbusch.
2. See Jan Tinbergen, *On the Theory of Economic Policy* (Amsterdam: North-Holland Publishing Co., 1952); James Meade, *The Balance of Payments* (New York: Oxford University Press, 1951); and Robert A. Mundell, "The Appropriate Use of Monetary and Fiscal Policy for Internal and External Stability," *International Monetary Fund Staff Papers*, vol. 9 (1962).
3. This exchange rate policy works only if the export and import goods in question are sufficiently sensitive to price, so that a price change would lower demand for imports and raise demand for exports. This condition of "sufficient price sensitivity" is called the Marshall-Lerner condition.
4. Rudiger Dornbusch made these points in his analysis of old style programs. He called fiscal reform and the policy of "setting prices right" through currency devaluation "euphemisms" for a reduced standard of living. See Dornbusch, "Stabilization Policies in Developing Countries: What Have We Learned?" *World Development* Vol. 10 (September, 1982) pp. 701–708; see also W. N. Corden, "The Geometric Representation of Policies to Attain Internal and External Balance," *Review of Economic Studies*, vol. 28 (1960).
5. Dornbusch emphasized that the new style program of preannounced target exchange rates is a direct means to anchor expectations and thus provide a "direct, strongly visible" means for disinflation. See Dornbusch, "Stabilization Policies."
6. See Mario Henrique Simonsen's paper in Dornbusch and Simonsen, *Inflation Debt, and Indexation* (Cambridge, Mass.: Massachusetts Institute of Technology Press, 1983).
7. This is the judgment of Carlos Diaz-Alejandro in his thorough evaluation of Southern Cone policies in his roundtable presentation at the Bogota Meeting of the Latin American Econometric Society in July 1984.
8. Observations about Argentina come from Guillermo Calvo and Carlos Rodriguez and about Brazil from Jose Julio Senna and Francisco Lopes, in private conversation.

9. Both Dornbusch and Calvo emphasized these points about the Argentinian stabilization program. See Guillermo Calvo "Trying to Stabilize" in Aspilla, Dornbusch, and Obstfeld, *Financial Integration and World Capital Markets* (Chicago: University of Chicago Press, 1984).

10. Edmar Bacha described the Delfim Netto policy as a "one-sided" or an "unbalanced" growth policy in private conversation.

11. Carlos Diaz-Alejandro raised some of these points about the income distribution effects of new style programs.

12. According to Dornbusch ("Stabilization Policies"), maintaining a normal rate of interest during the disinflation process would involve high nominal money growth. See Dornbusch.

13. Bacha called attention to the profit-motivated markup process, while Dornbusch stressed inflationary inertia and the need for wage controls, excess profit taxes and the fixing of public-sector prices. Bacha made this point in a seminar, while Dornbusch's points appear in Dornbusch, "Stabilization Policies."

14. These are some of the findings of Cleometrics, an application to economic history of econometric methods. See Christina Romer, "Spurious Volatility in Historical Unemployment Data," *Journal of Political Economy* (February 1986), pp. 1–36.

AFTERWORD

1. John Tracy Ellis, "American Catholics and the Intellectual Life" *Thought* 30 (1955), 351–388.

2. A useful collection of relevant papal, conciliar and episcopal statements prior to the current pastoral on the economy can be found in *Justice in the Marketplace: Collected Statements of the Vatican and the United States Catholic Bishops on Economic Policy, 1891–1984,* David Byers, ed. (Washington, D.C.: United States Catholic Conference, 1985).

3. Charles Curran, *American Catholic Social Ethics* (Notre Dame, Ind.: Notre Dame University Press, 1982) pp. 17–20.

4. See John P. Langan, "Political Tasks, Political Hopes," in *Questions of Special Urgency,* Judith Dwyer, ed. (Washington, D.C.: Georgetown University Press, 1986, pp. 99–121) for an overview of some of the impact of *Gaudium et Spes.*

5. For a concise and helpful treatment of the role these notions play in establishing a moral minimum, see Drew Christiansen, S.J., "Basic Needs: Criterion for the Legitimacy of Development" in *Human Rights in the Americas: The Struggle for Consensus,* Alfred Hennelly, S.J. and John P. Langan, S.J. ed. (Washington, D.C.: Georgetown University Press, 1982), pp. 260–262.

6. On the function of rights in providing protection against standard threats, see Henry Shue, *Basic Rights* (Princeton, N.J.: Princeton University Press, 1980), pp. 13–18.

7. John P. Langan, S. J., "Defining Human Rights: A Revision of the Liberal Tradition" in Hennelly and Langan, *Human Rights,* pp. 69–101.

8. For a straightforward argument that Christian faith requires a political choice for socialism over capitalism, see Juan Luis Segundo, "Capitalism Versus Socialism: Crux Theologica," in *Frontiers of Theology in Latin America,* Rosino Gibellini, ed., John Drury, tran. (Maryknoll, NY: Orbis, 1979), pp. 240–259.

9. For contrasting general interpretations of Catholic social teaching, see David Hollenbach, S.J., *Claims in Conflict: Retrieving and Renewing the Catholic Human Rights Tradition* (New York: Paulist Press, 1979), and Michael Novak, *Freedom with Justice: Catholic Social Thought and Liberal Institutions* (San Francisco: Harper & Row, 1984).

Index

Economic Justice for All: Catholic Social Teaching and the U.S. Economy

ECONOMIC JUSTICE FOR ALL

Brothers and Sisters in Christ:

1. We are believers called to follow Our Lord Jesus Christ and proclaim his Gospel in the midst of a complex and powerful economy. This reality poses both opportunities and responsibilities for Catholics in the United States. Our faith calls us to measure this economy, not only by what it produces, but also by how it touches human life and whether it protects or undermines the dignity of the human person. Economic decisions have human consequences and moral content; they help or hurt people, strengthen or weaken family life, advance or diminish the quality of justice in our land.

2. This is why we have written *Economic Justice for All: A Pastoral Letter on Catholic Social Teaching and the U.S. Economy.* This letter is a personal invitation to Catholics to use the resources of our faith, the strength of our economy, and the opportunities of our democracy to shape a society that better protects the dignity and basic rights of our sisters and brothers, both in this land and around the world.

3. The pastoral letter has been a work of careful inquiry, wide consultation, and prayerful discernment. The letter has been greatly enriched by this process of listening and refinement. We offer this introductory pastoral message to Catholics in the United States seeking to live their faith in the marketplace—in homes, offices, factories, and schools; on farms and ranches; in boardrooms and union halls; in service agencies and legislative chambers. We seek to explain why we wrote the pastoral letter, to introduce its major themes, and to share our hopes for the dialogue and action it might generate.

WHY WE WRITE

4. We write to share our teaching, to raise questions, to challenge one another to live our faith in the world. We write as heirs of the biblical prophets who summon us "to do the right, and to love goodness, and to walk humbly with your God" (Mi 6:8). We write as followers of Jesus who told us in the Sermon on the Mount: "Blessed are the poor in spirit. . . . Blessed are the meek. . . . Blessed are they who hunger and thirst for righteousness. . . . You are the salt of the earth. . . . You are the light of the world" (Mt 5:1-6,13-14). These words challenge us not only as believers but also as consumers, citizens, workers, and owners. In the parable of the Last Judgment, Jesus said, "For I was hungry and you gave me food, I was thirsty and you gave me drink. . . . As often as you did it for one of my least brothers, you did it for me" (Mt 25:35-40). The challenge for us is to discover in our own place and time what it means to be "poor in spirit" and "the salt of the earth" and what it means to serve "the least among us" and to "hunger and thirst for righteousness."

5. Followers of Christ must avoid a tragic separation between faith and everyday life. They can neither shirk their earthly duties nor, as the Second Vatican Council declared, "immerse [them]selves in earthly activities as if these latter were utterly foreign to religion, and religion were nothing more than the fulfillment of acts of worship and the observance of a few moral obligations" (*Pastoral Constitution on the Church in the Modern World,* no. 43).

6. Economic life raises important social and moral questions for each of us and for society as a whole. Like family life, economic life is one of the chief areas where we live out our faith, love our neighbor, confront temptation, fulfill God's creative design, and achieve our holiness. Our economic activity in factory, field, office, or shop feeds our families—or feeds our anxieties. It exercises our talents—or wastes them. It raises our hopes—or crushes them. It brings us into cooperation with others—or sets us at odds. The Second Vatican Council instructs us "to preach the message of Christ in such a way that the light of the Gospel will shine on all activities of the faithful" (*Pastoral Constitution,* no. 43). In this case, we are trying to look at economic life through the eyes of faith, applying traditional church teaching to the U.S. economy.

7. In our letter, we write as pastors, not public officials. We speak as moral teachers, not economic technicians. We seek not to make some political or ideological point but to lift up the human and ethical dimensions of economic life, aspects too often neglected in public discussion. We bring to this task a dual heritage of Catholic social teaching and traditional American values.

8. As *Catholics,* we are heirs of a long tradition of thought and action on the moral dimensions of economic activity. The life and words of Jesus and the teaching of his Church call us to serve those in need and to work actively for social and economic justice. As a community of believers, we know that our faith is tested by the quality of justice among us, that we can best measure our life together by how the poor and the vulnerable are treated. This is not a new concern for us. It is as old as the Hebrew prophets, as compelling as the Sermon on the Mount, and as current as the powerful voice of Pope John Paul II defending the dignity of the human person.

9. As *Americans,* we are grateful for the gift of freedom and committed to the dream of "liberty and justice for all." This nation, blessed with extraordinary resources, has provided an unprecedented standard of living for millions of people. We are proud of the strength, productivity, and creativity of our economy, but we also remember those who have been left behind in our progress. We believe that we honor our history best by working for the day when all our sisters and brothers share adequately in the American dream.

10. As bishops, in proclaiming the Gospel for these times we also manage institutions, balance budgets, meet payrolls. In this we see the human face of our economy. We feel the hurts and hopes of our people. We feel the pain of our sisters and brothers who are poor, unemployed, homeless, living on the edge. The poor and vulnerable are on our doorsteps, in our parishes, in our service agencies, and in our shelters. We see too much hunger and injustice, too much suffering and despair, both in our own country and around the world.

11. As pastors, we also see the decency, generosity, and vulnerability of our people. We see the struggles of ordinary families to make ends meet and to provide a better future for their children. We know the desire of managers, professionals, and business people to shape what they do by what they believe. It is the faith, good will, and generosity of our people that gives us hope as we write this letter.

PRINCIPAL THEMES OF THE PASTORAL LETTER

12. The pastoral letter is not a blueprint for the American economy. It does not embrace any particular theory of how the economy works, nor does it attempt to resolve the disputes between different schools of economic thought. Instead, our letter turns to Scripture and to the social teachings of the Church. There, we discover what our economic life must serve, what standards it must meet. Let us examine some of these basic moral principles.

13. *Every economic decision and institution must be judged in light of whether it protects or undermines the dignity of the human person.* The pastoral letter begins with the human person. We believe the person is sacred—the clearest reflection of God among us. Human dignity comes from God, not from nationality, race, sex, economic status, or any human accomplishment. We judge any economic system by what it does *for* and *to* people and by how it permits all to *participate* in it. The economy should serve people, not the other way around.

14. Human dignity can be realized and protected only in community. In our teaching, the human person is not only sacred but also social. How we organize our society—in economics and politics, in law and policy—directly affects human dignity and the capacity of individuals to grow in community. The obligation to "love our neighbor" has an individual dimension, but it also requires a broader social commitment to the common good. We have many partial ways to measure and debate the health of our economy: Gross National Product, per capita income, stock market prices, and so forth. The Christian vision of economic life looks beyond them all and asks, Does economic life enhance or threaten our life together as a community?

15. All people have a right to participate in the economic life of society. Basic justice demands that people be assured a minimum level of participation in the economy. It is wrong for a person or group to be excluded unfairly or to be unable to participate or contribute to the economy. For example, people who are both able and willing, but cannot get a job are deprived of the participation that is so vital to human development. For, it is through employment that most individuals and families meet their material needs, exercise their talents, and have an opportunity to contribute to the larger community. Such participation has a special significance in our tradition because we believe that it is a means by which we join in carrying forward God's creative activity.

16. All members of society have a special obligation to the poor and vulnerable. From the Scriptures and church teaching, we learn that the justice of a society is tested by the treatment of the poor. The justice that was the sign of God's covenant with Israel was measured by how the poor and unprotected—the widow, the orphan, and the stranger—were treated. The kingdom that Jesus proclaimed in his word and ministry excludes no one. Throughout Israel's history and in early Christianity, the poor are agents of God's transforming power. "The Spirit of the Lord is upon me, therefore he has anointed me. He has sent me to bring glad tidings to the poor"(Lk 4:18). This was Jesus' first public utterance. Jesus takes the side of those most in need. In the Last Judgment, so dramatically described in St. Matthew's Gospel, we are told that we will be judged according to how we respond to the hungry, the thirsty, the naked, the stranger. As followers of Christ, we are challenged to make a fundamental "option for the poor"—to speak for the voiceless, to defend the defenseless, to assess life styles, policies, and social institutions in terms of their impact on the poor. This "option for the poor" does not mean pitting one group against another, but rather, strengthening the whole community by assisting those who are most vulnerable. As Christians, we are called to respond to the needs of *all* our brothers and sisters, but those with the greatest needs require the greatest response.

17. Human rights are the minimum conditions for life in community. In Catholic teaching, human rights include not only civil and political rights but also economic rights. As Pope John XXIII declared, "all people have a right to life, food, clothing, shelter, rest, medical care, education, and employment." This means that when people are without a chance to earn a living, and must go hungry and homeless, they are being denied basic rights. Society must ensure that these rights are protected. In this way, we will ensure that the minimum conditions of economic justice are met for all our sisters and brothers.

18. Society as a whole, acting through public and private institutions, has the moral responsibility to enhance human dignity and protect human rights. In addition to the clear responsibility of private institutions, government has an essential responsibility in this area. This does not mean that government has the primary or exclusive role, but it does have a positive moral responsibility in safeguarding human rights and ensuring that the minimum conditions of human dignity are met for all. In a democracy, government is a means by which we can act together to protect what is important to us and to promote our common values.

19. These six moral principles are not the only ones presented in the pastoral letter, but they give an overview of the moral vision that we are trying to share. This vision of economic life cannot exist in a vacuum; it must be translated into concrete measures. Our pastoral letter spells out some specific applications of Catholic moral principles. We call for a new national commitment to full employment. We say it is a social and moral scandal that one of every seven Americans is poor, and we call for concerted efforts to eradicate poverty. The fulfillment of the basic needs of the poor is of the highest priority. We urge that all economic policies be evaluated in light of their impact on the life and stability of the family. We support measures to halt the loss of family farms and to resist the growing concentration in the ownership of agricultural resources. We specify ways in which the United States can do far more to relieve the plight of poor nations and assist in their development. We also reaffirm church teaching on the rights of workers, collective bargaining, private property, subsidiarity, and equal opportunity.

20. We believe that the recommendations in our letter are reasonable and balanced. In analyzing the economy, we reject ideological extremes and start from the fact that ours is a "mixed" economy, the product of a long history of reform and adjustment. We know that some of our specific recommendations are controversial. As bishops, we do not claim to make these prudential judgments with the same kind of authority that marks our declarations of principle. But, we feel obliged to teach by example how Christians can undertake concrete analysis and make specific judgments on economic issues. The Church's teachings cannot be left at the level of appealing generalities.

21. In the pastoral letter, we suggest that the time has come for a "New American Experiment"—to implement economic rights, to broaden the sharing of economic power, and to make economic decisions more accountable to the common good. This experiment can create new structures of economic partnership and participation within firms at the regional level, for the whole nation, and across borders.

22. Of course, there are many aspects of the economy the letter does not touch, and there are basic questions it leaves to further exploration. There are also many specific points on which men and women of good will may disagree. We look for a fruitful exchange among differing viewpoints. We pray only that all will take to heart the urgency of our concerns; that together we will test our views by the Gospel and the Church's teaching; and that we will listen to other voices in a spirit of mutual respect and open dialogue.

A CALL TO CONVERSION AND ACTION

23. We should not be surprised if we find Catholic social teaching to be demanding. The Gospel is demanding. We are always in need of conversion, of a change of heart. We are richly blessed, and as St. Paul assures us, we are destined for glory. Yet, it is also true that we are sinners; that we are not always wise or loving or just; that, for all our amazing possibilities, we are incompletely born, wary of life, and hemmed in by fears and empty routines. We are unable to entrust ourselves fully to the living God, and so we seek substitute forms of security in material things, in power, in indifference, in popularity, in pleasure. The Scriptures warn us that these things can become forms of idolatry. We know that, at times, in order to remain truly a community of Jesus' disciples, we will have to say "no" to certain aspects in our culture, to certain trends and ways of acting that are opposed to a life of faith, love, and justice. Changes in our hearts lead naturally to a desire to change how we act. With what care, human kindness, and justice do I conduct myself at work? How will my economic decisions to buy, sell, invest, divest, hire, or fire serve human dignity and the common good? In what career can I best exercise my talents so as to fill the world with the Spirit of Christ? How do my economic choices contribute to the strength of my family and community, to the values of my children, to a sensitivity to those in need? In this consumer society, how can I develop a healthy detachment from things and avoid the temptation to assess who I am by what I have? How do I strike a balance between labor and leisure that enlarges my capacity for friendships, for family life, for community? What government policies should I support to attain the well-being of all, especially the poor and vulnerable?

24. The answers to such questions are not always clear—or easy to live out. But, conversion is a lifelong process. And, it is not undertaken alone. It occurs with the support of the whole believing community, through baptism, common prayer, and our daily efforts, large and small, on behalf of justice. As a Church, we must be people after God's own heart, bonded by the Spirit, sustaining one another in love, setting our hearts on God's kingdom, committing ourselves to solidarity with those who suffer, working for peace and justice, acting as a sign of Christ's love and justice in the world. The Church cannot redeem the world from the deadening effects of sin and injustice unless it is working to remove sin and injustice in its own life and institutions. All of us must help the Church to practice in its own life what it preaches to others about economic justice and cooperation.

25. The challenge of this pastoral letter is not merely to think differently, but also to act differently. A renewal of economic life depends on the conscious choices and commitments of individual believers who practice their faith in the world. The road to holiness for most of us lies in our secular vocations. We need a spirituality that calls forth and supports lay initiative and witness not just in our churches but also in business, in the labor movement, in the professions, in education, and in public life. Our faith is not just a weekend obligation, a mystery to be celebrated around the altar on Sunday. It is a pervasive reality to be practiced every day in homes, offices, factories, schools, and businesses across our land. We cannot separate what we believe from how we act in the marketplace and the broader community, for this is where we make our primary contribution to the pursuit of economic justice.

26. We ask each of you to read the pastoral letter, to study it, to pray about it, and match it with your own experience.

We ask you to join with us in service to those in need. Let us reach out personally to the hungry and the homeless, to the poor and the powerless, and to the troubled and the vulnerable. In serving them, we serve Christ. Our service efforts cannot substitute for just and compassionate public policies, but they can help us practice what we preach about human life and human dignity.

27. The pursuit of economic justice takes believers into the public arena, testing the policies of government by the principles of our teaching. We ask you to become more informed and active citizens, using your voices and votes to speak for the voiceless, to defend the poor and the vulnerable and to advance the common good. We are called to shape a constituency of conscience, measuring every policy by how it touches the least, the lost, and the left-out among us. This letter calls us to conversion and common action, to new forms of stewardship, service, and citizenship.

28. The completion of a letter such as this is but the beginning of a long process of education, discussion, and action. By faith and baptism, we are fashioned into new creatures, filled with the Holy Spirit and with a love that compels us to seek out a new profound relationship with God, with the human family, and with all created things. Jesus has entered our history as God's anointed son who announces the coming of God's kingdom, a kingdom of justice and peace and freedom. And, what Jesus proclaims, he embodies in his actions. His ministry reveals that the reign of God is something more powerful than evil, injustice, and the hardness of hearts. Through his crucifixion and resurrection, he reveals that God's love is ultimately victorious over all suffering, all horror, all meaninglessness, and even over the mystery of death. Thus, we proclaim words of hope and assurance to all who suffer and are in need.

29. We believe that the Christian view of life, including economic life, can transform the lives of individuals, families, schools, and our whole culture. We believe that with your prayers, reflection, service, and action, our economy can be shaped so that human dignity prospers and the human person is served. This is the unfinished work of our nation. This is the challenge of our faith.

Chapter I

THE CHURCH AND THE FUTURE OF THE U.S. ECONOMY

1. Every perspective on economic life that is human, moral, and Christian must be shaped by three questions: What does the economy do *for* people? What does it do *to* people? And how do people *participate* in it? The economy is a human reality: men and women working together to develop and care for the whole of God's creation. All this work must serve the material and spiritual well-being of people. It influences what people hope for themselves and their loved ones. It affects the way they act together in society. It influences their very faith in God.[1]

2. The Second Vatican Council declared that "the joys and hopes, the griefs and anxieties of the people of this age, especially those who are poor or in any way afflicted, these too are the joys and hopes, the griefs and anxieties of the followers of Christ."[2] There are many signs of hope in U.S. economic life today:

- Many fathers and mothers skillfully balance the arduous responsibilities of work and family life. There are parents who pursue a purposeful and modest way of life and by their example encourage their children to follow a similar path. A large number of women and men, drawing on their religious tradition, recognize the challenging vocation of family life and child rearing in a culture that emphasizes material display and self-gratification.
- Conscientious business people seek new and more equitable ways to organize resources and the workplace. They face hard choices over expanding or retrenching, shifting investments, hiring or firing.
- Young people choosing their life's work ask whether success and security are compatible with service to others.
- Workers whose labor may be toilsome or repetitive try daily to ennoble their work with a spirit of solidarity and friendship.
- New immigrants brave dislocations while hoping for the opportunities realized by the millions who came before them.

3. These signs of hope are not the whole story. There have been failures—some of them massive and ugly:

- Poor and homeless people sleep in community shelters and in our church basements; the hungry line up in soup lines.
- Unemployment gnaws at the self-respect of both middle-aged persons who have lost jobs and the young who cannot find them.
- Hardworking men and women wonder if the system of enterprise that helped them yesterday might destroy their jobs and their communities tomorrow.
- Families confront major new challenges: dwindling social supports for family stability; economic pressures that force both parents of young children to work outside

the home; a driven pace of life among the successful that can sap love and commitment; lack of hope among those who have less or nothing at all. Very different kinds of families bear different burdens of our economic system.

- Farmers face the loss of their land and way of life; young people find it difficult to choose farming as a vocation; farming communities are threatened; migrant farmworkers break their backs in serf-like conditions for disgracefully low wages.

4. And beyond our own shores, the reality *of 800 million people living in absolute poverty and 450 million malnourished or facing starvation casts an ominous shadow over all these hopes and problems at home.*

5. Anyone who sees all this will understand our concern as pastors and bishops. People shape the economy and in turn are shaped by it. Economic arrangements can be sources of fulfillment, of hope, of community—or of frustration, isolation, and even despair. They teach virtues—or vices—and day by day help mold our characters. They affect the quality of people's lives; at the extreme even determining whether people live or die. Serious economic choices go beyond purely technical issues to fundamental questions of value and human purpose.[3] We believe that in facing these questions the Christian religious and moral tradition can make an important contribution.

A. THE U.S. ECONOMY TODAY: MEMORY AND HOPE

6. The United States is among the most economically powerful nations on earth. In its short history the U.S. economy has grown to provide an unprecedented standard of living for most of its people. The nation has created productive work for millions of immigrants and enabled them to broaden their freedoms, improve their families' quality of life, and contribute to the building of a great nation. Those who came to this country from other lands often understood their new lives in the light of biblical faith. They thought of themselves as entering a promised land of political freedom and economic opportunity. The United States *is* a land of vast natural resources and fertile soil. It *has* encouraged citizens to undertake bold ventures. Through hard work, self-sacrifice, and cooperation, families have flourished; towns, cities, and a powerful nation have been created.

7. But we should recall this history with sober humility. The American experiment in social, political, and economic life has involved serious conflict and suffering. Our nation was born in the face of injustice to native Americans, and its independence was paid for with the blood of revolution. Slavery stained the commercial life of the land through its

first two hundred and fifty years and was ended only by a violent civil war. The establishment of women's suffrage, the protection of industrial workers, the elimination of child labor, the response to the Great Depression of the 1930s, and the civil rights movement of the 1960s all involved a sustained struggle to transform the political and economic institutions of the nation.

8. The U.S. value system emphasizes economic freedom. It also recognizes that the market is limited by fundamental human rights. Some things are never to be bought or sold.[4] This conviction has prompted positive steps to modify the operation of the market when it harms vulnerable members of society. Labor unions help workers resist exploitation. Through their government, the people of the United States have provided support for education, access to food, unemployment compensation, security in old age, and protection of the environment. The market system contributes to the success of the U. S. economy, but so do many efforts to forge economic institutions and public policies that enable *all* to share in the riches of the nation. The country's economy has been built through a creative struggle; entrepreneurs, business people, workers, unions, consumers, and government have all played essential roles.

9. The task of the United States today is as demanding as that faced by our forebears. Abraham Lincoln's words at Gettysburg are a reminder that complacency today would be a betrayal of our nation's history: "It is for us, the living, rather to be dedicated here to the unfinished work . . . they have thus far nobly advanced."[5] There is unfinished business in the American experiment in freedom and justice for all.

B. URGENT PROBLEMS OF TODAY

10. The preeminent role of the United States in an increasingly interdependent global economy is a central sign of our times.[6] The United States is still the world's economic giant. Decisions made here have immediate effects in other countries; decisions made abroad have immediate consequences for steelworkers in Pittsburgh, oil company employees in Houston, and farmers in Iowa. U.S. economic growth is vitally dependent on resources from other countries and on their purchases of our goods and services. Many jobs in U.S. industry and agriculture depend on our ability to export manufactured goods and food.

11. In some industries the mobility of capital and technology makes wages the main variable in the cost of production. Overseas competitors with the same technology but with wage rates as low as one-tenth of ours put enormous pressure on U.S. firms to cut wages, relocate abroad, or close. U.S. workers and their communities should not be expected to bear these burdens alone.

12. All people on this globe share a common ecological environment that is under increasing pressure. Depletion of soil, water, and other natural resources endangers the future. Pollution of air and water threatens the delicate balance of the biosphere on which future generations will depend.[7] The resources of the earth have been created by God for the benefit of all, and we who are alive today hold them in trust. This is a challenge to develop a new ecological ethic that will help shape a future that is both just and sustainable.

13. In short, nations separated by geography, culture, and ideology are linked in a complex commercial, financial, technological, and environmental network. These links have two direct consequences. First, they create hope for a new form of community among all peoples, one built on dignity, solidarity, and justice. Second, this rising global awareness calls for greater attention to the stark inequities across countries in the standards of living and control of resources. We must not look at the welfare of U.S. citizens as the only good to be sought. Nor may we overlook the disparities of power in the relationships between this nation and the developing countries. The United States is the major supplier of food to other countries, a major source of arms sales to developing nations, and a powerful influence in multilateral institutions such as the International Monetary Fund, the World Bank, and the United Nations. What Americans see as a growing interdependence is regarded by many in the less developed countries as a pattern of domination and dependence.

14. Within this larger international setting, there are also a number of challenges to the domestic economy that call for creativity and courage. The promise of the "American dream"—freedom for all persons to develop their God-given talents to the full—remains unfulfilled for millions in the United States today.

15. Several areas of U.S. economic life demand special attention. Unemployment is the most basic. Despite the large number of new jobs the U.S. economy has generated in the past decade, approximately 8 million people seeking work in this country are unable to find it, and many more are so discouraged they have stopped looking.[8] Over the past two decades the nation has come to tolerate an increasing level of unemployment. The 6 to 7 percent rate deemed acceptable today would have been intolerable twenty years ago. Among the unemployed are a disproportionate number of blacks, Hispanics, young people, or women who are the sole support of their families.[9] Some cities and states have many more unemployed persons than others as a result of economic forces that have little to do with people's desire to work. Unemployment is a tragedy no matter whom it strikes, but the tragedy is compounded by the unequal and unfair way it is distributed in our society.

16. Harsh poverty plagues our country despite its great wealth. More than 33 million Americans are poor; by any reasonable standard another 20 to 30 million are needy. Poverty is increasing in the United States, not decreasing.[10] For a people who believe in "progress," this should be cause for alarm. These burdens fall most heavily on blacks, Hispanics, and

Native Americans. Even more disturbing is the large increase in the number of women and children living in poverty. Today children are the largest single group among the poor. This tragic fact seriously threatens the nation's future. That so many people are poor in a nation as rich as ours is a social and moral scandal that we cannot ignore.

17. Many working people and middle-class Americans live dangerously close to poverty. A rising number of families must rely on the wages of two or even three members just to get by. From 1968 to 1978 nearly a quarter of the U. S. population was in poverty part of the time and received welfare benefits in at least one year.[11] The loss of a job, illness, or the breakup of a marriage may be all it takes to push people into poverty.

18. The lack of a mutually supportive relation between family life and economic life is one of the most serious problems facing the United States today.[12] The economic and cultural strength of the nation is directly linked to the stability and health of its families.[13] When families thrive, spouses contribute to the common good through their work at home, in the community, and in their jobs; and children develop a sense of their own worth and of their responsibility to serve others. When families are weak or break down entirely, the dignity of parents and children is threatened. High cultural and economic costs are inflicted on society at large.

19. The precarious economic situation of so many people and so many families calls for examination of U.S. economic arrangements. Christian conviction and the American promise of liberty and justice for all give the poor and the vulnerable a special claim on the nation's concern. They also challenge all members of the Church to help build a more just society.

20. The investment of human creativity and material resources in the production of weapons of war makes these economic problems even more difficult to solve. Defense Department expenditures in the United States are almost $300 billion per year. The rivalry and mutual fear between superpowers divert into projects that threaten death, minds and money that could better human life. Developing countries engage in arms races they can ill afford, often with the encouragement of the superpowers. Some of the poorest countries of the world use scarce resources to buy planes, guns, and other weapons when they lack the food, education, and health care their people need. Defense policies must be evaluated and assessed in light of their real contribution to freedom, justice, and peace for the citizens of our own and other nations. We have developed a perspective on these multiple moral concerns in our 1983 pastoral letter, *The Challenge of Peace: God's Promise and Our Response.*[14] When weapons or strategies make questionable contributions to security, peace, and justice and will also be very expensive, spending priorities should be redirected to more pressing social needs.[15]

21. Many other social and economic challenges require careful analysis: the movement of many industries from the Snowbelt to the Sunbelt, the federal deficit and interest rates, corporate mergers and takeovers, the effects of new technologies such as robotics and information systems in U.S. industry, immigration policy, growing international traffic in

drugs, and the trade imbalance. All of these issues do not provide a complete portrait of the economy. Rather they are symptoms of more fundamental currents shaping U.S. economic life today: the struggle to find meaning and value in human work, efforts to support individual freedom in the context of renewed social cooperation, the urgent need to create equitable forms of global interdependence in a world now marked by extreme inequality. These deeper currents are cultural and moral in content. They show that the long-range challenges facing the nation call for sustained reflection on the values that guide economic choices and are embodied in economic institutions. Such explicit reflection on the ethical content of economic choices and policies must become an integral part of the way Christians relate religious belief to the realities of everyday life. In this way, the "split between the faith which many profess and their daily lives,"[16] which Vatican II counted among the more serious errors of the modern age, will begin to be bridged.

C. THE NEED FOR MORAL VISION

22. Sustaining a common culture and a common commitment to moral values is not easy in our world. Modern economic life is based on a division of labor into specialized jobs and professions. Since the industrial revolution, people have had to define themselves and their work ever more narrowly to find a niche in the economy. The benefits of this are evident in the satisfaction many people derive from contributing their specialized skills to society. But the costs are social fragmentation, a decline in seeing how one's work serves the whole community, and an increased emphasis on personal goals and private interests.[17] This is vividly clear in discussions of economic justice. Here it is often difficult to find a common ground among people with different backgrounds and concerns. One of our chief hopes in writing this letter is to encourage and contribute to the development of this common ground.[18]

23. Strengthening common moral vision is essential if the economy is to serve all people more fairly. Many middle-class Americans feel themselves in the grip of economic demands and cultural pressures that go far beyond the individual family's capacity to cope. Without constructive guidance in making decisions with serious moral implications, men and women who hold positions of responsibility in corporations or government find their duties exacting a heavy price. We want these reflections to help them contribute to a more just economy.

24. The quality of the national discussion about our economic future will affect the poor most of all, in this country and throughout the world. The life and dignity of millions of men, women, and children hang in the balance. Decisions must be judged in light of what they do *for* the poor, what they do *to* the poor, and what they enable the poor to do *for themselves.* The fundamental moral criterion for all economic decisions, policies, and institutions is this: They must be at the service of *all people, especially the poor.*

25. This letter is based on a long tradition of Catholic social thought, rooted in the Bible and developed over the past century by the popes and the Second Vatican Council in re-

sponse to modern economic conditions. This tradition insists that human dignity, realized in community with others and with the whole of God's creation, is the norm against which every social institution must be measured.[19]

26. This teaching has a rich history. It is also dynamic and growing.[20] Pope Paul VI insisted that all Christian communities have the responsibility "to analyze with objectivity the situation which is proper to their own country, to shed on it the light of the Gospel's unalterable words and to draw principles of reflection, norms of judgment, and directives for action from the social teaching of the Church."[21] Therefore, we build on the past work of our own bishops' conference, including the 1919 Program of Social Reconstruction and other pastoral letters.[22] In addition many people from the Catholic, Protestant, and Jewish communities, in academic, business or political life, and from many different economic backgrounds have also provided guidance. We want to make the legacy of Christian social thought a living, growing resource that can inspire hope and help shape the future.

27. We write, then, first of all to provide guidance for members of our own Church as they seek to form their consciences about economic matters. No one may claim the name Christian and be comfortable in the face of the hunger, homelessness, insecurity, and injustice found in this country and the world. At the same time, we want to add our voice to the public debate about the directions in which the U.S. economy should be moving. We seek the cooperation and support of those who do not share our faith or tradition. The common bond of humanity that links all persons is the source of our belief that the country can attain a renewed public moral vision. The questions are basic and the answers are often elusive; they challenge us to serious and sustained attention to economic justice.

Chapter II

THE CHRISTIAN VISION OF ECONOMIC LIFE

28. The basis for all that the Church believes about the moral dimensions of economic life is its vision of the transcendent worth—the sacredness—of human beings. *The dignity of the human person, realized in community with others, is the criterion against which all aspects of economic life must be measured.*[1] All human beings, therefore, are ends to be served by the institutions that make up the economy, not means to be exploited for more narrowly defined goals. Human personhood must be respected with a reverence that is religious. When we deal with each other, we should do so with the sense of awe that arises in the presence of something holy and sacred. For that is what human beings are: we are created in the image of God (Gn 1:27). Similarly, all economic institutions must support the bonds of community and solidarity that are essential to the dignity of persons. Wherever our economic arrangements fail to conform to the demands of human dignity lived in community, they must be questioned and transformed. These convictions have a biblical basis. They are also supported by a long tradition of theological and philosophical reflection and through the reasoned analysis of human experience by contemporary men and women.

29. In presenting the Christian moral vision, we turn first to the Scriptures for guidance. Though our comments are necessarily selective, we hope that pastors and other church members will become personally engaged with the biblical texts. The Scriptures contain many passages that speak directly of economic life. We must also attend to the Bible's deeper vision of God, of the purpose of creation, and of the dignity of human life in society. Along with other churches and ecclesial communities who are "strengthened by the grace of Baptism and the hearing of God's Word," we strive to become faithful hearers and doers of the word.[2] We also claim the Hebrew Scriptures as common heritage with our Jewish brothers and sisters, and we join with them in the quest for an economic life worthy of the divine revelation we share.

A. BIBLICAL PERSPECTIVES

30. The fundamental conviction of our faith is that human life is fulfilled in the knowledge and love of the living God in communion with others. The Sacred Scriptures offer guidance so that men and women may enter into full communion with God and with each other, and witness to God's saving acts. We discover there a God who is creator of heaven and earth, and of the human family. Though our first parents reject the God who created them, God does not abandon them, but from Abraham and Sarah forms a people of promise. When this people is enslaved in an alien land, God delivers them and makes a covenant with them in which they are summoned to be faithful to the *torah* or sacred teaching. The focal points of Israel's faith—creation,

covenant, and community—provide a foundation for reflection on issues of economic and social justice.

1. CREATED IN GOD'S IMAGE

31. After the exile, when Israel combined its traditions into a written *torah*, it prefaced its history as a people with the story of the creation of all peoples and of the whole world by the same God who created them as a nation (Gn 1-11). God is the creator of heaven and earth (Gn 14:19-22; Is 40:28; 45:18); creation proclaims God's glory (Ps 89:6-12) and is "very good" (Gn 1:31). Fruitful harvests, bountiful flocks, a loving family are God's blessings on those who heed God's word. Such is the joyful refrain that echoes throughout the Bible. One legacy of this theology of creation is the conviction that no dimension of human life lies beyond God's care and concern. God is present to creation, and creative engagement with God's handiwork is itself reverence for God.

32. At the summit of creation stands the creation of man and woman, made in God's image (Gn 1:26-27). *As such every human being possesses an inalienable dignity that stamps human existence prior to any division into races or nations and prior to human labor and human achievement (Gn 4-11).* Men and women are also to share in the creative activity of God. They are to be fruitful, to care for the earth (Gn 2:15), and to have "dominion" over it (Gn 1:28), which means they are "to govern the world in holiness and justice and to render judgment in integrity of heart" (Wis 9:3). Creation is a gift; women and men are to be faithful stewards in caring for the earth. They can justly consider that by their labor they are unfolding the Creator's work.[3]

33. The narratives of Genesis 1-11 also portray the origin of the strife and suffering that mar the world. Though created to enjoy intimacy with God and the fruits of the earth, Adam and Eve disrupted God's design by trying to live independently of God through a denial of their status as creatures. They turned away from God and gave to God's creation the obedience due to God alone. For this reason the prime sin in so much of the biblical tradition is idolatry: service of the creature rather than of the creator (Rom 1:25), and the attempt to overturn creation by making God in human likeness. The Bible castigates not only the worship of idols, but also manifestations of idolatry, such as the quest for unrestrained power and the desire for great wealth (Is 40:12-20; 44:1-20; Wis 13:1-14:31; Col 3:5, "the greed that is idolatry"). The sin of our first parents had other consequences as well. Alienation from God pits brother against brother (Gn 4:8-16), in a cycle of war and vengeance (Gn 4:22-23). Sin and evil abound, and the primeval history culminates with another assault on the heavens, this time ending in a babble of tongues scattered over the face of the earth (Gn 11:1-9). Sin simultaneously

alienates human beings from God and shatters the solidarity of the human community. Yet this reign of sin is not the final word. The primeval history is followed by the call of Abraham, a man of faith, who was to be the bearer of the promise to many nations (Gn 12:1-4). Throughout the Bible we find this struggle between sin and repentance. God's judgment on evil is followed by God's seeking out a sinful people.

34. The biblical vision of creation has provided one of the most enduring legacies of Church teaching. To stand before God as the creator is to respect God's creation, both the world of nature and of human history. *From the patristic period to the present, the Church has affirmed that misuse of the world's resources or appropriation of them by a minority of the world's population betrays the gift of creation since "whatever belongs to God belongs to all."*[4]

2. A PEOPLE OF THE COVENANT

35. When the people of Israel, our forerunners in faith, gathered in thanksgiving to renew their covenant (Jos 24:1-15), they recalled the gracious deeds of God (Dt 6:20-25; 26: 5-11). When they lived as aliens in a strange land and experienced oppression and slavery, they cried out. The Lord, the God of their ancestors, heard their cries, knew their afflictions, and came to deliver them (Ex 3:7-8). By leading them out of Egypt, God created a people that was to be the Lord's very own (Jer 24:7; Hos 2:25). They were to imitate God by treating the alien and the slave in their midst as God had treated them (Ex 22:20-22; Jer 34:8-14).

36. In the midst of this saving history stands the covenant at Sinai (Ex 19-24). It begins with an account of what God has done for the people (Ex 19:1-6; cf. Jos 24:1-13) and includes from God's side a promise of steadfast love (*hesed*) and faithfulness ('*emeth*, Ex 34:5-7). The people are summoned to ratify this covenant by faithfully worshiping God alone and by directing their lives according to God's will, which was made explicit in Israel's great legal codes such as the Decalogue (Ex 20:1-17) and the Book of the Covenant (Ex 20:22-23:33). Far from being an arbitrary restriction on the life of the people, these codes made life in community possible.[5] The specific laws of the covenant protect human life and property, demand respect for parents and the spouses and children of one's neighbor, and manifest a special concern for the vulnerable members of the community: widows, orphans, the poor, and strangers in the land. Laws such as that for the Sabbath year when the land was left fallow (Ex 23:11; Lv 25:1-7) and for the year of release of debts (Dt 15:1-11) summoned people to respect the land as God's gift and reminded Israel that as a people freed by God from bondage they were to be concerned for the poor and oppressed in their midst. Every fiftieth year a jubilee was to be proclaimed as a year of "liberty throughout the land" and property was to be restored to its original owners (Lv 25:8-17, cf. Is 61:1-2; Lk 4:18-19).[6] The codes of Israel reflect the norms of the covenant: reciprocal responsibility, mercy, and truthfulness. They embody a life in freedom from oppression: worship of the One God, rejection of idolatry, mutual respect among people, care and protection for every member of the social body. Being free and being a co-responsible community are God's intentions for us.

37. When the people turn away from the living God to serve idols and no longer heed the commands of the covenant, God sends prophets to recall his saving deeds and to summon them to return to the one who betrothed them "in right and in justice, in love and in mercy" (Hos 2:21). The substance of prophetic faith is proclaimed by Micah: "to do justice and to love kindness, and to walk humbly with your God" (Mi 6:8, RSV). Biblical faith in general, and prophetic faith especially, insist that fidelity to the covenant joins obedience to God with reverence and concern for the neighbor. The biblical terms which best summarize this double dimension of Israel's faith are *sedaqah*, justice (also translated as righteousness), and *mishpat* (right judgment or justice embodied in a concrete act or deed). The biblical understanding of justice gives a fundamental perspective to our reflections on social and economic justice.[7]

38. God is described as a "God of justice" (Is 30:18) who loves justice (Is 61:8, cf. Pss 11:7; 33:5; 37:28; 99:4) and delights in it (Jer 9:23). God demands justice from the whole people (Dt 16:20) and executes justice for the needy (Ps 140:13). Central to the biblical presentation of justice is that the justice of a community is measured by its treatment of the powerless in society, most often described as the widow, the orphan, the poor, and the stranger (non-Israelite) in the land. The Law, the Prophets, and the Wisdom literature of the Old Testament all show deep concern for the proper treatment of such people.[8] What these groups of people have in common is their vulnerability and lack of power. They are often alone and have no protector or advocate. Therefore, it is God who hears their cries (Pss 109:21; 113:7), and the king who is God's anointed is commanded to have special concern for them.

39. Justice has many nuances.[9] Fundamentally, it suggests a sense of what is right or of what should happen. For example, paths are just when they bring you to your destination (Gn 24:48; Ps 23:3), and laws are just when they create harmony within the community, as Isaiah says: "Justice will bring about peace; right will produce calm and security" (Is 32:17). God is "just" by acting as God should, coming to the people's aid and summoning them to conversion when they stray. People are summoned to be "just," that is, to be in a proper relation to God, by observing God's laws which form them into a faithful community. Biblical justice is more comprehensive than subsequent philosophical definitions. It is not concerned with a strict definition of rights and duties, but with the rightness of the human condition before God and within society. Nor is justice opposed to love; rather, it is both a manifestation of love

and a condition for love to grow.[10] Because God loves Israel, he rescues them from oppression and summons them to be a people that "does justice" and loves kindness. The quest for justice arises from loving gratitude for the saving acts of God and manifests itself in wholehearted love of God and neighbor.

40. These perspectives provide the foundation for a biblical vision of economic justice. Every human person is created as an image of God, and the denial of dignity to a person is a blot on this image. Creation is a gift to all men and women, not to be appropriated for the benefit of a few; its beauty is an object of joy and reverence. The same God who came to the aid of an oppressed people and formed them into a covenant community continues to hear the cries of the oppressed and to create communities which are responsive to God's word. God's love and life are present when people can live in a community of faith and hope. These cardinal points of the faith of Israel also furnish the religious context for understanding the saving action of God in the life and teaching of Jesus.

3. THE REIGN OF GOD AND JUSTICE

41. Jesus enters human history as God's anointed son who announces the nearness of the reign of God (Mk 1:9-14). This proclamation summons us to acknowledge God as creator and covenant partner and challenges us to seek ways in which God's revelation of the dignity and destiny of all creation might become incarnate in history. It is not simply the promise of the future victory of God over sin and evil, but that this victory has already begun—in the life and teaching of Jesus.

42. What Jesus proclaims by word, he enacts in his ministry. He resists temptations of power and prestige, follows his Father's will, and teaches us to pray that it be accomplished on earth. He warns against attempts to "lay up treasures on earth" (Mt 6:19) and exhorts his followers not to be anxious about material goods but rather to seek first God's reign and God's justice (Mt 6:25-33). His mighty works symbolize that the reign of God is more powerful than evil, sickness, and the hardness of the human heart. He offers God's loving mercy to sinners (Mk 2:17), takes up the cause of those who suffered religious and social discrimination (Lk 7:36-50; 15:1-2), and attacks the use of religion to avoid the demands of charity and justice (Mk 7:9-13; Mt 23:23).

43. When asked what was the greatest commandment, Jesus quoted the age-old Jewish affirmation of faith that God alone is One and to be loved with the whole heart, mind, and soul (Dt 6:4-5) and immediately adds: "You shall love your neighbor as yourself" (Lv 19:18, Mk 12:28-34). This dual command of love that is at the basis of all Christian morality is illustrated in the Gospel of Luke by the parable of a Samaritan who interrupts his journey to come to the aid of a dying man (Lk 10:29-37). Unlike the other wayfarers who look on the man and pass by, the Samaritan "was moved with compassion at the sight"; he stops, tends the wounded man, and takes him to a place of safety. In this parable compassion is the bridge between mere seeing and action; love is made real through effective action.[11]

44. Near the end of his life, Jesus offers a vivid picture of the last judgment (Mt 25: 31-

46). All the nations of the world will be assembled and will be divided into those blessed who are welcomed into God's kingdom or those cursed who are sent to eternal punishment. The blessed are those who fed the hungry, gave drink to the thirsty, welcomed the stranger, clothed the naked, and visited the sick and imprisoned; the cursed are those who neglected these works of mercy and love. Neither the blessed nor the cursed are astounded that they are judged by the Son of Man, nor that judgment is rendered according to works of charity. The shock comes when they find that in neglecting the poor, the outcast, and the oppressed, they were rejecting Jesus himself. Jesus who came as "Emmanuel" (God with us, Mt 1:23) and who promises to be with his people until the end of the age (Mt 28:20) is hidden in those most in need; to reject them is to reject God made manifest in history.

4. CALLED TO BE DISCIPLES IN COMMUNITY

45. Jesus summoned his first followers to a change of heart and to take on the yoke of God's reign (Mk 1:14-15; Mt 11:29). They are to be the nucleus of that community which will continue the work of proclaiming and building God's kingdom through the centuries. As Jesus called the first disciples in the midst of their everyday occupations of fishing and tax collecting; so he again calls people in every age in the home, in the workplace, and in the marketplace.

46. The Church is, as Pope John Paul II reminded us, "a community of disciples" in which "we must see first and foremost Christ saying to each member of the community: follow me."[12] To be a Christian is to join with others in responding to this personal call and in learning the meaning of Christ's life. It is to be sustained by that loving intimacy with the Father that Jesus experienced in his work, in his prayer, and in his suffering.

47. Discipleship involves imitating the pattern of Jesus' life by openness to God's will in the service of others (Mk 10:42-45). Disciples are also called to follow him on the way of the cross, and to heed his call that those who lose their lives for the sake of the Gospel will save them (Mk 8:34-35). Jesus' death is an example of that greater love which lays down one's life for others (cf. Jn 15:12-18). It is a model for those who suffer persecution for the sake of justice (Mt 5:10). The death of Jesus was not the end of his power and presence, for he was raised up by the power of God. Nor did it mark the end of the disciples' union with him. After Jesus had appeared to them and when they received the gift of the Spirit (Acts 2:1-12), they became apostles of the good news to the ends of the earth. In the face of poverty and persecution they transformed human lives and formed communities which became signs of the power and presence of God. Sharing in this same resurrection faith, contemporary followers of Christ can face the struggles and challenges that await those who bring the gospel vision to bear on our complex economic and social world.

5. POVERTY, RICHES, AND THE CHALLENGE OF DISCIPLESHIP

48. The pattern of Christian life as presented in the Gospel of Luke has special relevance

today. In her *Magnificat*, Mary rejoices in a God who scatters the proud, brings down the mighty, and raises up the poor and lowly (Lk 1:51-53). The first public utterance of Jesus is "The Spirit of the Lord is upon me, because he has anointed me to preach the good news to the poor" (Lk 4:18 cf. Is 61:1-2). Jesus adds to the blessing on the poor a warning, "Woe to you who are rich, for you have received your consolation" (Lk 6:24). He warns his followers against greed and reliance on abundant possessions and underscores this by the parable of the man whose life is snatched away at the very moment he tries to secure his wealth (Lk 12:13-21). In Luke alone, Jesus tells the parable of the rich man who does not see the poor and suffering Lazarus at his gate (Lk 16:19-31). When the rich man finally "sees" Lazarus, it is from the place of torment and the opportunity for conversion has passed. Pope John Paul II has often recalled this parable to warn the prosperous not to be blind to the great poverty that exists beside great wealth.[13]

49. Jesus, especially in Luke, lives as a poor man, like the prophets takes the side of the poor, and warns of the dangers of wealth.[14] The terms used for poor, while primarily describing lack of material goods, also suggest dependence and powerlessness. The poor are also an exiled and oppressed people whom God will rescue (Is 51:21-23) as well as a faithful remnant who take refuge in God (Zep 3:12-13). Throughout the Bible, material poverty is a misfortune and a cause of sadness. A constant biblical refrain is that the poor must be cared for and protected and that when they are exploited, God hears their cries (Prv 22:22-23). Conversely, even though the goods of the earth are to be enjoyed and people are to thank God for material blessings, wealth is a constant danger. The rich are wise in their own eyes (Prv 28:11), and are prone to apostasy and idolatry (Am 5:4-13; Is 2:6-8), as well as to violence and oppression (Jas 2:6-7).[15] Since they are neither blinded by wealth nor make it into an idol, the poor can be open to God's presence; throughout Israel's history and in early Christianity the poor are agents of God's transforming power.

50. The poor are often related to the lowly (Mt 5:3,5) to whom God reveals what was hidden from the wise (Mt 11:25-30). When Jesus calls the poor "blessed," he is not praising their condition of poverty, but their openness to God. When he states that the reign of God is theirs, he voices God's special concern for them, and promises that they are to be the beneficiaries of God's mercy and justice. When he summons disciples to leave all and follow him, he is calling them to share his own radical trust in the Father and his freedom from care and anxiety (cf. Mt 6:25-34). The practice of evangelical poverty in the Church has always been a living witness to the power of that trust and to the joy that comes with that freedom.

51. Early Christianity saw the poor as an object of God's special love, but it neither canonized material poverty nor accepted deprivation as an inevitable fact of life. Though few early Christians possessed wealth or power (1 Cor 1:26-28; Jas 2:5), their communities had well-off members (Acts 16:14; 18:8). Jesus' concern for the poor was continued in different forms in the early Church.

The early community at Jerusalem distributed its possessions so that "there was no needy person among them," and held "all things in common"—a phrase that suggests not only shared material possessions, but more fundamentally, friendship and mutual concern among all its members (Acts 4:32-34; 2:44). While recognizing the dangers of wealth, the early Church proposed the proper use of possessions to alleviate need and suffering, rather than universal dispossession. Beginning in the first century and throughout history, Christian communities have developed varied structures to support and sustain the weak and powerless in societies that were often brutally unconcerned about human suffering.

52. Such perspectives provide a basis today for what is called the "preferential option for the poor."[16] Though in the Gospels and in the New Testament as a whole the offer of salvation is extended to all peoples, Jesus takes the side of those most in need, physically and spiritually. The example of Jesus poses a number of challenges to the contemporary Church. It imposes a prophetic mandate to speak for those who have no one to speak for them, to be a defender of the defenseless, who in biblical terms are the poor. It also demands a compassionate vision that enables the Church to see things from the side of the poor and powerless and to assess lifestyle, policies, and social institutions in terms of their impact on the poor. It summons the Church also to be an instrument in assisting people to experience the liberating power of God in their own lives so that they may respond to the Gospel in freedom and in dignity. Finally, and most radically, it calls for an emptying of self, both individually and corporately, that allows the Church to experience the power of God in the midst of poverty and powerlessness.

6. A COMMUNITY OF HOPE

53. The biblical vision of creation, covenant, and community, as well as the summons to discipleship, unfolds under the tension between promise and fulfillment. The whole Bible is spanned by the narratives of the first creation (Gn 1-3) and the vision of a restored creation at the end of history (Rv 21:1-4). Just as creation tells us that God's desire was one of wholeness and unity between God and the human family and within this family itself, the images of a new creation give hope that enmity and hatred will cease and justice and peace will reign (Is 11:4-6; 25:1-8). Human life unfolds "between the times," the time of the first creation and that of a restored creation (Rom 8:18-25). Although the ultimate realization of God's plan lies in the future, Christians in union with all people of good will are summoned to shape history in the image of God's creative design, and in response to the reign of God proclaimed and embodied by Jesus.

54. A Christian is a member of a new community, "God's own people" (1 Pt 2:9-10), who, like the people of Exodus, owes its existence to the gracious gift of God and is summoned to respond to God's will made manifest in the life and teaching of Jesus. A Christian walks in the newness of life (Rom 6:4), and is "a new creation; the old has passed away, the new has come" (2 Cor 5:17). This new creation in Christ proclaims that God's creative love is constantly at work, offers sinners forgiveness, and reconciles a

broken world. Our action on behalf of justice in our world proceeds from the conviction that, despite the power of injustice and violence, life has been fundamentally changed by the entry of the Word made flesh into human history.

55. Christian communities that commit themselves to solidarity with those suffering and to confrontation with those attitudes and ways of acting which institutionalize injustice, will themselves experience the power and presence of Christ. They will embody in their lives the values of the new creation while they labor under the old. The quest for economic and social justice will always combine hope and realism, and must be renewed by every generation. It involves diagnosing those situations that continue to alienate the world from God's creative love as well as presenting hopeful alternatives that arise from living in a renewed creation. This quest arises from faith and is sustained by hope as it seeks to speak to a broken world of God's justice and loving kindness.

7. A LIVING TRADITION

56. Our reflection on U.S. economic life today must be rooted in this biblical vision of the kingdom and discipleship, but it must also be shaped by the rich and complex tradition of Catholic life and thought. Throughout its history, the Christian community has listened to the words of Scripture and sought to enact them in the midst of daily life in very different historical and cultural contexts.

57. In the first centuries, when Christians were a minority in a hostile society, they cared for one another through generous almsgiving. In the patristic era, the church fathers repeatedly stressed that the goods of the earth were created by God for the benefit of every person without exception, and that all have special duties toward those in need. The monasteries of the Middle Ages were centers of prayer, learning, and education. They contributed greatly to the cultural and economic life of the towns and cities that sprang up around them. In the twelfth century the new mendicant orders dedicated themselves to following Christ in poverty and to the proclamation of the good news to the poor.

58. These same religious communities also nurtured some of the greatest theologians of the Church's tradition, thinkers who synthesized the call of Christ with the philosophical learning of Greek, Roman, Jewish, and Arab worlds. Thomas Aquinas and the other scholastics devoted rigorous intellectual energy to clarifying the meaning of both personal virtue and justice in society. In more recent centuries Christians began to build a large network of hospitals, orphanages, and schools, to serve the poor and society at large. And beginning with Leo XIII's *Rerum Novarum*, down to the writings and speeches of John Paul II, the popes have more systematically addressed the rapid change of modern society in a series of social encyclicals. These teachings of modern popes and of the Second Vatican Council are especially significant for efforts to respond to the problems facing society today.[17]

59. We also have much to learn from the strong emphasis in Protestant traditions on the vocation of lay people in the world and from ecumenical efforts to develop an economic ethic that addresses newly emergent problems.

And in a special way our fellow Catholics in developing countries have much to teach us about the Christian response to an ever more interdependent world.

60. Christians today are called by God to carry on this tradition through active love of neighbor, a love that responds to the special challenges of this moment in human history. The world is wounded by sin and injustice, in need of conversion and of the transformation that comes when persons enter more deeply into the mystery of the death and Resurrection of Christ. The concerns of this pastoral letter are not at all peripheral to the central mystery at the heart of the Church.[18] They are integral to the proclamation of the Gospel and part of the vocation of every Christian today.[19]

B. ETHICAL NORMS FOR ECONOMIC LIFE

61. These biblical and theological themes shape the overall Christian perspective on economic ethics. This perspective is also subscribed to by many who do not share Christian religious convictions. Human understanding and religious belief are complementary, not contradictory. For human beings are created in God's image, and their dignity is manifest in the ability to reason and understand, in their freedom to shape their own lives and the life of their communities, and in the capacity for love and friendship. In proposing ethical norms, therefore, we appeal both to Christians and to all in our pluralist society to show that respect and reverence owed to the dignity of every person. Intelligent reflection on the social and economic realities of today is also indispensable in the effort to respond to economic circumstances never envisioned in biblical times. Therefore, we now want to propose an ethical framework that can guide economic life today in ways that are both faithful to the Gospel and shaped by human experience and reason.

62. First we outline the *duties* all people have to each other and to the whole community: love of neighbor, the basic requirements of justice, and the special obligation to those who are poor or vulnerable. Corresponding to these duties are the *human rights* of every person; the obligation to protect the dignity of all demands respect for these rights. Finally these duties and rights entail several *priorities* that should guide the economic choices of individuals, communities, and the nation as a whole.

1. THE RESPONSIBILITIES OF SOCIAL LIVING

63. Human life is life in community. Catholic social teaching proposes several complementary perspectives that show how moral responsibilities and duties in the economic sphere are rooted in this call to community.

a. LOVE AND SOLIDARITY

64. *The commandments to love God with all one's heart and to love one's neighbor as oneself are the heart and soul of Christian morality.* Jesus offers himself as the model of this all-inclusive love: ". . . Love one another as I have loved you" (Jn 15:12). These commands point out the path toward true human fulfillment and happiness. They are not arbitrary restrictions on human freedom. Only active love of God and neighbor makes the fullness of community happen. Christians

look forward in hope to a true communion among all persons with each other and with God. The Spirit of Christ labors in history to build up the bonds of solidarity among all persons until that day on which their union is brought to perfection in the Kingdom of God.[20] Indeed Christian theological reflection on the very reality of God as a trinitarian unity of persons—Father, Son, and Holy Spirit—shows that being a person means being united to other persons in mutual love.[21]

65. What the Bible and Christian tradition teach, human wisdom confirms. Centuries before Christ, the Greeks and Romans spoke of the human person as a "social animal" made for friendship, community, and public life. These insights show that human beings achieve self-realization not in isolation, but in interaction with others.[22]

66. The virtues of citizenship are an expression of Christian love more crucial in today's interdependent world than ever before. These virtues grow out of a lively sense of one's dependence on the commonweal and obligations to it. This civic commitment must also guide the economic institutions of society. In the absence of a vital sense of citizenship among the businesses, corporations, labor unions, and other groups that shape economic life, society as a whole is endangered. Solidarity is another name for this social friendship and civic commitment that make human moral and economic life possible.

67. The Christian tradition recognizes, of course, that the fullness of love and community will be achieved only when God's work in Christ comes to completion in the kingdom of God. This kingdom has been inaugurated among us, but God's redeeming and transforming work is not yet complete. Within history, knowledge of how to achieve the goal of social unity is limited. Human sin continues to wound the lives of both individuals and larger social bodies and places obstacles in the path toward greater social solidarity. If efforts to protect human dignity are to be effective, they must take these limits on knowledge and love into account. Nevertheless, sober realism should not be confused with resigned or cynical pessimism. It is a challenge to develop a courageous hope that can sustain efforts that will sometimes be arduous and protracted.

b. JUSTICE AND PARTICIPATION

68. Biblical justice is the goal we strive for. This rich biblical understanding portrays a just society as one marked by the fullness of love, compassion, holiness, and peace. On their path through history, however, sinful human beings need more specific guidance on how to move toward the realization of this great vision of God's Kingdom. This guidance is contained in the norms of basic or minimal justice. These norms state the *minimum* levels of mutual care and respect that all persons owe to each other in an imperfect world.[23] Catholic social teaching, like much philosophical reflection, distinguishes three dimensions of basic justice: commutative justice, distributive justice, and social justice.[24]

69. *Commutative justice calls for fundamental fairness in all agreements and exchanges between individuals or private social groups.* It demands respect for the equal human dignity

of all persons in economic transactions, contracts, or promises. For example, workers owe their employers diligent work in exchange for their wages. Employers are obligated to treat their employees as persons, paying them fair wages in exchange for work done and establishing conditions and patterns of work that are truly human.[25]

70. *Distributive justice requires that the allocation of income, wealth, and power in society be evaluated in light of its effects on persons whose basic material needs are unmet.* The Second Vatican Council stated: "The right to have a share of earthly goods sufficient for oneself and one's family belongs to everyone. The fathers and doctors of the Church held this view, teaching that we are obliged to come to the relief of the poor and to do so not merely out of our superfluous goods."[26] Minimum material resources are an absolute necessity for human life. If persons are to be recognized as members of the human community, then the community has an obligation to help fulfill these basic needs unless an absolute scarcity of resources makes this strictly impossible. No such scarcity exists in the United States today.

71. Justice also has implications for the way the larger social, economic, and political institutions of society are organized. *Social justice implies that persons have an obligation to be active and productive participants in the life of society and that society has a duty to enable them to participate in this way.* This form of justice can also be called "contributive," for it stresses the duty of all who are able to help create the goods, services, and other nonmaterial or spiritual values necessary for the welfare of the whole community. In the words of Pius XI, "It is of the very essence of social justice to demand from each individual all that is necessary for the common good."[27] Productivity is essential if the community is to have the resources to serve the well-being of all. Productivity, however, cannot be measured solely by its output in goods and services. Patterns of production must also be measured in light of their impact on the fulfillment of basic needs, employment levels, patterns of discrimination, environmental quality, and sense of community.

72. The meaning of social justice also includes a duty to organize economic and social institutions so that people can contribute to society in ways that respect their freedom and the dignity of their labor. Work should enable the working person to become "more a human being," more capable of acting intelligently, freely, and in ways that lead to self-realization.[28]

73. Economic conditions that leave large numbers of able people unemployed, underemployed, or employed in dehumanizing conditions fail to meet the converging demands of these three forms of basic justice. Work with adequate pay for all who seek it is the primary means for achieving basic justice in our society. Discrimination in job opportunities or income levels on the basis of race, sex, or other arbitrary standards can never be justified.[29] It is a scandal that such discrimination continues in the United States today. Where the effects of past discrimination persist, society has the obligation to take positive steps to overcome the legacy of injustice. Judiciously administered affirmative action pro-

grams in education and employment can be important expressions of the drive for solidarity and participation that is at the heart of true justice. Social harm calls for social relief.

74. Basic justice also calls for the establishment of a floor of material well-being on which all can stand. This is a duty of the whole of society and it creates particular obligations for those with greater resources. This duty calls into question extreme inequalities of income and consumption when so many lack basic necessities. Catholic social teaching does not maintain that a flat, arithmetical equality of income and wealth is a demand of justice, but it does challenge economic arrangements that leave large numbers of people impoverished. Further, it sees extreme inequality as a threat to the solidarity of the human community, for great disparities lead to deep social divisions and conflict.[30]

75. This means that all of us must examine our way of living in light of the needs of the poor. Christian faith and the norms of justice impose distinct limits on what we consume and how we view material goods. The great wealth of the United States can easily blind us to the poverty that exists in this nation and the destitution of hundreds of millions of people in other parts of the world. Americans are challenged today as never before to develop the inner freedom to resist the temptation constantly to seek more. Only in this way will the nation avoid what Paul VI called "the most evident form of moral underdevelopment," namely greed.[31]

76. These duties call not only for individual charitable giving but also for a more systematic approach by businesses, labor unions, and the many other groups that shape economic life—as well as government. The concentration of privilege that exists today results far more from institutional relationships that distribute power and wealth inequitably than from differences in talent or lack of desire to work. These institutional patterns must be examined and revised if we are to meet the demands of basic justice. For example, a system of taxation based on assessment according to ability to pay[32] is a prime necessity for the fulfillment of these social obligations.

c. OVERCOMING MARGINALIZATION AND POWERLESSNESS

77. These fundamental duties can be summarized this way: *Basic justice demands the establishment of minimum levels of participation in the life of the human community for all persons.* The ultimate injustice is for a person or group to be treated actively or abandoned passively as if they were nonmembers of the human race. To treat people this way is effectively to say that they simply do not count as human beings. This can take many forms, all of which can be described as varieties of marginalization, or exclusion from social life.[33] This exclusion can occur in the political sphere: restriction of free speech, concentration of power in the hands of a few, or outright repression by the state. It can also take economic forms that are equally harmful. Within the United States, individuals, families, and local communities fall victim to a downward cycle of poverty generated by economic forces they are powerless to influence. The poor, the disabled, and the unemployed too often are simply left behind. This pattern is even more severe beyond our borders in the least-developed countries. Whole nations are

prevented from fully participating in the international economic order because they lack the power to change their disadvantaged position. Many people within the less developed countries are excluded from sharing in the meager resources available in their homelands by unjust elites and unjust governments. These patterns of exclusion are created by free human beings. In this sense they can be called forms of social sin.[34] Acquiescence in them or failure to correct them when it is possible to do so is a sinful dereliction of Christian duty.

78. Recent Catholic social thought regards the task of overcoming these patterns of exclusion and powerlessness as a most basic demand of justice. Stated positively, justice demands that social institutions be ordered in a way that guarantees all persons the ability to participate actively in the economic, political, and cultural life of society.[35] The level of participation may legitimately be greater for some persons than for others, but there is a basic level of access that must be made available for all. Such participation is an essential expression of the social nature of human beings and of their communitarian vocation.

2. HUMAN RIGHTS: THE MINIMUM CONDITIONS FOR LIFE IN COMMUNITY

79. Catholic social teaching spells out the basic demands of justice in greater detail in the human rights of every person. These fundamental rights are prerequisites for a dignified life in community. The Bible vigorously affirms the sacredness of every person as a creature formed in the image and likeness of God. The biblical emphasis on covenant and community also shows that human dignity can only be realized and protected in solidarity with others. In Catholic social thought, therefore, respect for human rights and a strong sense of both personal and community responsibility are linked, not opposed. Vatican II described the common good as "the sum of those conditions of social life which allow social groups and their individual members relatively thorough and ready access to their own fulfillment."[36] These conditions include the rights to fulfillment of material needs, a guarantee of fundamental freedoms, and the protection of relationships that are essential to participation in the life of society.[37] These rights are bestowed on human beings by God and grounded in the nature and dignity of human persons. They are not created by society. Indeed society has a duty to secure and protect them.

80. The full range of human rights has been systematically outlined by John XXIII in his encyclical *Peace on Earth*. His discussion echoes the United Nations Universal Declaration of Human Rights and implies that internationally accepted human rights standards are strongly supported by Catholic teaching. These rights include the civil and political rights to freedom of speech, worship, and assembly. A number of human rights also concern human welfare and are of a specifically economic nature. First among these are the rights to life, food, clothing, shelter, rest, medical care, and basic education. These are indispensable to the protection of human dignity. In order to ensure these necessities, all persons have a right to earn a living, which for most people in our economy is through remunerative employment. All persons also have a right to security in the event of sickness, unemployment, and old age. Participa-

tion in the life of the community calls for the protection of this same right to employment, as well as the right to healthful working conditions, to wages, and other benefits sufficient to provide individuals and their families with a standard of living in keeping with human dignity, and to the possibility of property ownership.[39] These fundamental personal rights—civil and political as well as social and economic—state the minimum conditions for social institutions that respect human dignity, social solidarity, and justice. They are all essential to human dignity and to the integral development of both individuals and society, and are thus moral issues.[40] Any denial of these rights harms persons and wounds the human community. Their serious and sustained denial violates individuals and destroys solidarity among persons.

81. Social and economic rights call for a mode of implementation different from that required to secure civil and political rights. Freedom of worship and of speech imply immunity from interference on the part of both other persons and the government. The rights to education, employment, and social security, for example, are empowerments that call for positive action by individuals and society at large.

82. However, both kinds of rights call for positive action to create social and political institutions that enable all persons to become active members of society. Civil and political rights allow persons to participate freely in the public life of the community, for example, through free speech, assembly, and the vote. In democratic countries these rights have been secured through a long and vigorous history of creating the institutions of constitutional government. In seeking to secure the full range of social and economic rights today, a similar effort to shape new economic arrangements will be necessary.

83. The first step in such an effort is the development of a new cultural consensus that the basic economic conditions of human welfare are essential to human dignity and are due persons by right. Second, the securing of these rights will make demands on *all* members of society, on all private sector institutions, and on government. A concerted effort on all levels in our society is needed to meet these basic demands of justice and solidarity. Indeed political democracy and a commitment to secure economic rights are mutually reinforcing.

84. Securing economic rights for all will be an arduous task. There are a number of precedents in U.S. history, however, which show that the work has already begun.[41] The country needs a serious dialogue about the appropriate levels of private and public sector involvement that are needed to move forward. There is certainly room for diversity of opinion in the Church and in U.S. society on *how* to protect the human dignity and economic rights of all our brothers and sisters.[42] In our view, however, there can be no legitimate disagreement on the basic moral objectives.

3. MORAL PRIORITIES FOR THE NATION

85. *The common good demands justice for all, the protection of the human rights of all.*[43] Making cultural and economic institutions more supportive of the freedom, power, and security of individuals and families must be a central, long-range objective for the na-

tion. Every person has a duty to contribute to building up the commonweal. All have a responsibility to develop their talents through education. Adults must contribute to society through their individual vocations and talents. Parents are called to guide their children to the maturity of Christian adulthood and responsible citizenship. Everyone has special duties toward the poor and the marginalized. Living up to these responsibilities, however, is often made difficult by the social and economic patterns of society. Schools and educational policies both public and private often serve the privileged exceedingly well, while the children of the poor are effectively abandoned as second-class citizens. Great stresses are created in family life by the way work is organized and scheduled, and by the social and cultural values communicated on TV. Many in the lower middle class are barely getting by and fear becoming victims of economic forces over which they have no control.

86. *The obligation to provide justice for all means that the poor have the single most urgent economic claim on the conscience of the nation.* Poverty can take many forms, spiritual as well as material. All people face struggles of the spirit as they ask deep questions about their purpose in life. Many have serious problems in marriage and family life at some time in their lives, and all of us face the certain reality of sickness and death. The Gospel of Christ proclaims that God's love is stronger than all these forms of diminishment. Material deprivation, however, seriously compounds such sufferings of the spirit and heart. To see a loved one sick is bad enough, but to have no possibility of obtaining health care is worse. To face family problems, such as the death of a spouse or a divorce, can be devastating, but to have these lead to the loss of one's home and end with living on the streets is something no one should have to endure in a country as rich as ours. In developing countries these human problems are even more greatly intensified by extreme material deprivation. This form of human suffering can be reduced if our own country, so rich in resources, chooses to increase its assistance.

87. As individuals and as a nation, therefore, we are called to make a fundamental "option for the poor."[44] The obligation to evaluate social and economic activity from the viewpoint of the poor and the powerless arises from the radical command to love one's neighbor as one's self. Those who are marginalized and whose rights are denied have privileged claims if society is to provide justice for *all*. This obligation is deeply rooted in Christian belief. As Paul VI stated:

In teaching us charity, the Gospel instructs us in the preferential respect due the poor and the special situation they have in society: the more fortunate should renounce some of their rights so as to place their goods more generously at the service of others.[45]

John Paul II has described this special obligation to the poor as "a call to have a special openness with the small and the weak, those that suffer and weep, those that are humiliated and left on the margin of society, so as to help them win their dignity as human persons and children of God."[46]

88. The prime purpose of this special commitment to the poor is to enable them to become active participants in the life of society.

It is to enable *all* persons to share in and contribute to the common good.[47] The "option for the poor," therefore, is not an adversarial slogan that pits one group or class against another. Rather it states that the deprivation and powerlessness of the poor wounds the whole community. The extent of their suffering is a measure of how far we are from being a true community of persons. These wounds will be healed only by greater solidarity with the poor and among the poor themselves.

89. In summary, the norms of love, basic justice, and human rights imply that personal decisions, social policies, and economic institutions should be governed by several key priorities. These priorities do not specify everything that must be considered in economic decision making. They do indicate the most fundamental and urgent objectives.

90.a.*The fulfillment of the basic needs of the poor is of the highest priority.* Personal decisions, policies of private and public bodies, and power relationships must all be evaluated by their effects on those who lack the minimum necessities of nutrition, housing, education, and health care. In particular, this principle recognizes that meeting fundamental human needs must come before the fulfillment of desires for luxury consumer goods, for profits not conducive to the common good, and for unnecessary military hardware.

91.b.*Increasing active participation in economic life by those who are presently excluded or vulnerable is a high social priority.* The human dignity of all is realized when people gain the power to work together to improve their lives, strengthen their families, and contribute to society. Basic justice calls for more than providing help to the poor and other vulnerable members of society. It recognizes the priority of policies and programs that support family life and enhance economic participation through employment and widespread ownership of property. It challenges privileged economic power in favor of the well-being of all. It points to the need to improve the present situation of those unjustly discriminated against in the past. And it has very important implications for both the domestic and the international distribution of power.

92.c.*The investment of wealth, talent, and human energy should be specially directed to benefit those who are poor or economically insecure.* Achieving a more just economy in the United States and the world depends in part on increasing economic resources and productivity. In addition, the ways these resources are invested and managed must be scrutinized in light of their effects on nonmonetary values. Investment and management decisions have crucial moral dimensions: they create jobs or eliminate them; they can push vulnerable families over the edge into poverty or give them new hope for the future; they help or hinder the building of a more equitable society. Indeed they can have either positive or negative influence on the fairness of the global economy. Therefore, this priority presents a strong moral challenge to policies that put large amounts of talent and capital into the production of luxury consumer goods and military technology while failing to invest sufficiently in education, health, the basic infrastructure of our society, and economic sectors that produce urgently needed jobs, goods, and services.

93.d.*Economic and social policies as well as the organization of the work world should be continually evaluated in light of their impact on the strength and stability of family life.* The long-range future of this nation is intimately linked with the well-being of families, for the family is the most basic form of human community.[48] Efficiency and competition in the marketplace must be moderated by greater concern for the way work schedules and compensation support or threaten the bonds between spouses and between parents and children. Health, education, and social service programs should be scrutinized in light of how well they ensure both individual dignity and family integrity.

94. These priorities are not policies. They are norms that should guide the economic choices of all and shape economic institutions. They can help the United States move forward to fulfill the duties of justice and protect economic rights. They were strongly affirmed as implications of Catholic social teaching by Pope John Paul II during his visit to Canada in 1984: "The needs of the poor take priority over the desires of the rich; the rights of workers over the maximization of profits; the preservation of the environment over uncontrolled industrial expansion; production to meet social needs over production for military purposes."[49] There will undoubtedly be disputes about the concrete applications of these priorities in our complex world. We do not seek to foreclose discussion about them. However, we believe that an effort to move in the direction they indicate is urgently needed.

95. The economic challenge of today has many parallels with the political challenge that confronted the founders of our nation. In order to create a new form of political democracy they were compelled to develop ways of thinking and political institutions that had never existed before. Their efforts were arduous and their goals imperfectly realized, but they launched an experiment in the protection of civil and political rights that has prospered through the efforts of those who came after them. *We believe the time has come for a similar experiment in securing economic rights: the creation of an order that guarantees the minimum conditions of human dignity in the economic sphere for every person.* By drawing on the resources of the Catholic moral-religious tradition, we hope to make a contribution through this letter to such a new "American Experiment": a new venture to secure economic justice for all.

C. WORKING FOR GREATER JUSTICE: PERSONS AND INSTITUTIONS

96. The economy of this nation has been built by the labor of human hands and minds. Its future will be forged by the ways persons direct all this work toward greater justice. The economy is not a machine that operates according to its own inexorable laws, and persons are not mere objects tossed about by economic forces. Pope John Paul II has stated that "human work is a key, probably the essential key, to the whole social question."[50] The Pope's understanding of work includes virtually all forms of productive human activity: agriculture, entrepreneurship, industry, the care of children, the sustaining of family life, politics, medical care, and scientific research. Leisure, prayer, celebration, and the

arts are also central to the realization of human dignity and to the development of a rich cultural life. It is in their daily work, however, that persons become the subjects and creators of the economic life of the nation.[51] Thus, it is primarily through their daily labor that people make their most important contributions to economic justice.

97. All work has a threefold moral significance. First, it is a principal way that people exercise the distinctive human capacity for self-expression and self-realization. Second, it is the ordinary way for human beings to fulfill their material needs. Finally, work enables people to contribute to the well-being of the larger community. Work is not only for one's self. It is for one's family, for the nation, and indeed for the benefit of the entire human family.[52]

98. These three moral concerns should be visible in the work of all, no matter what their role in the economy: blue collar workers, managers, homemakers, politicians, and others. They should also govern the activities of the many different, overlapping communities and institutions that make up society: families, neighborhoods, small businesses, giant corporations, trade unions, the various levels of government, international organizations, and a host of other human associations including communities of faith.

99. Catholic social teaching calls for respect for the full richness of social life. The need for vital contributions from different human associations—ranging in size from the family to government—has been classically expressed in Catholic social teaching in the "principle of subsidiarity":

> Just as it is gravely wrong to take from individuals what they can accomplish by their own initiative and industry and give it to the community, so also it is an injustice and at the same time a grave evil and disturbance of right order to assign to a greater and higher association what lesser and subordinate organizations can do. For every social activity ought of its very nature to furnish help (*subsidium*) to the members of the body social, and never destroy and absorb them.[53]

100.This principle guarantees institutional pluralism. It provides space for freedom, initiative, and creativity on the part of many social agents. At the same time, it insists that *all* these agents should work in ways that help build up the social body. Therefore, in all their activities these groups should be working in ways that express their distinctive capacities for action, that help meet human needs, and that make true contributions to the common good of the human community. The task of creating a more just U.S. economy is the vocation of all and depends on strengthening the virtues of public service and responsible citizenship in personal life and on all levels of institutional life.[54]

101.Without attempting to describe the tasks of all the different groups that make up society, we want to point to the specific rights and duties of some of the persons and institutions whose work for justice will be particularly important to the future of the United States economy. These rights and duties are among the concrete implications of the principle of subsidiarity. Further implications will be discussed in Chapter IV of this letter.

1. WORKING PEOPLE AND LABOR UNIONS

102.Though John Paul II's understanding of

work is a very inclusive one, it fully applies to those customarily called "workers" or "labor" in the United States. Labor has great dignity, so great that all who are able to work are obligated to do so. The duty to work derives both from God's command and from a responsibility to one's own humanity and to the common good.[55] The virtue of industriousness is also an expression of a person's dignity and solidarity with others. All working people are called to contribute to the common good by seeking excellence in production and service.

103.Because work is this important, people have a right to employment. In return for their labor, workers have a right to wages and other benefits sufficient to sustain life in dignity. As Pope Leo XIII stated, every working person has "the right of securing things to sustain life."[56] The way power is distributed in a free market economy frequently gives employers greater bargaining power than employees in the negotiation of labor contracts. Such unequal power may press workers into a choice between an inadequate wage and no wage at all. But justice, not charity, demands certain minimum guarantees. The provision of wages and other benefits sufficient to support a family in dignity is a basic necessity to prevent this exploitation of workers. The dignity of workers also requires adequate health care, security for old age or disability, unemployment compensation, healthful working conditions, weekly rest, periodic holidays for recreation and leisure, and reasonable security against arbitrary dismissal.[57] These provisions are all essential if workers are to be treated as persons rather than simply as a "factor of production."

104.The Church fully supports the right of workers to form unions or other associations to secure their rights to fair wages and working conditions. This is a specific application of the more general right to associate. In the words of Pope John Paul II, "The experience of history teaches that organizations of this type are an indispensable element of social life, especially in modern industrialized societies."[58] Unions may also legitimately resort to strikes where this is the only available means to the justice owed to workers.[59] No one may deny the right to organize without attacking human dignity itself. Therefore, we firmly oppose organized efforts, such as those regrettably now seen in this country, to break existing unions and prevent workers from organizing. Migrant agricultural workers today are particularly in need of the protection, including the right to organize and bargain collectively. U.S. labor law reform is needed to meet these problems as well as to provide more timely and effective remedies for unfair labor practices.

105.Denial of the right to organize has been pursued ruthlessly in many countries beyond our borders. We vehemently oppose violations of the freedom to associate, wherever they occur, for they are an intolerable attack on social solidarity.

106.Along with the rights of workers and unions go a number of important responsibilities. Individual workers have obligations to their employers, and trade unions also have duties to society as a whole. Union management in particular carries a strong responsibility for the good name of the entire union movement. Workers must use their collective

power to contribute to the well-being of the whole community and should avoid pressing demands whose fulfillment would damage the common good and the rights of more vulnerable members of society.[60] It should be noted, however, that wages paid to workers are but one of the factors affecting the competitiveness of industries. Thus, it is unfair to expect unions to make concessions if managers and shareholders do not make at least equal sacrifices.

107.Many U.S. unions have exercised leadership in the struggle for justice for minorities and women. Racial and sexual discrimination, however, have blotted the record of some unions. Organized labor has a responsibility to work positively toward eliminating the injustice this discrimination has caused.

108.Perhaps the greatest challenge facing United States workers and unions today is that of developing a new vision of their role in the United States economy of the future. The labor movement in the United States stands at a crucial moment. The dynamism of the unions that led to their rapid growth in the middle decades of this century has been replaced by a decrease in the percentage of U.S. workers who are organized. American workers are under heavy pressures today that threaten their jobs. The restrictions on the right to organize in many countries abroad make labor costs lower there, threaten American workers and their jobs, and lead to the exploitation of workers in these countries. In these difficult circumstances, guaranteeing the rights of U.S. workers calls for imaginative vision and creative new steps, not reactive or simply defensive strategies. For example, organized labor can play a very important role in helping to provide the education and training needed to help keep workers employable. Unions can also help both their own members and workers in developing countries by increasing their international efforts. A vital labor movement will be one that looks to the future with a deepened sense of global interdependence.

109.There are many signs that these challenges are being discussed by creative labor leaders today. Deeper and broader discussions of this sort are needed. This does not mean that only organized labor faces these new problems. All other sectors and institutions in the U.S. economy need similar vision and imagination. Indeed new forms of cooperation among labor, management, government, and other social groups are essential, and will be discussed in Chapter IV of this letter.

2. OWNERS AND MANAGERS

110.The economy's success in fulfilling the demands of justice will depend on how its vast resources and wealth are managed. Property owners, managers, and investors of financial capital must all contribute to creating a more just society. Securing economic justice depends heavily on the leadership of men and women in business and on wise investment by private enterprises. Pope John Paul II has pointed out, "The degree of well-being which society today enjoys would be unthinkable without the dynamic figure of the business person, whose function consists of organizing human labor and the means of production so as to give rise to the goods and services necessary for the prosperity and progress of the community."[61] The freedom of entrepreneurship, business, and finance should be protected, but the accountability of this freedom to the common good and the norms of justice must be assured.

111. Persons in management face many hard choices each day, choices on which the well-being of many others depends. Commitment to the public good and not simply the private good of their firms is at the heart of what it means to call their work a vocation and not simply a career or a job. We believe that the norms and priorities discussed in this letter can be of help as they pursue their important tasks. The duties of individuals in the business world, however, do not exhaust the ethical dimensions of business and finance. The size of a firm or bank is in many cases an indicator of relative power. Large corporations and large financial institutions have considerable power to help shape economic institutions within the United States and throughout the world. With this power goes responsibility and the need for those who manage it to be held to moral and institutional accountability.

112. Business and finance have the duty to be faithful trustees of the resources at their disposal. No one can ever own capital resources absolutely or control their use without regard for others and society as a whole.[62] This applies first of all to land and natural resources. Short-term profits reaped at the cost of depletion of natural resources or the pollution of the environment violate this trust.

113. Resources created by human industry are also held in trust. Owners and managers have not created this capital on their own. They have benefited from the work of many others and from the local communities that support their endeavors.[63] They are accountable to these workers and communities when making decisions. For example, reinvestment in technological innovation is often crucial for the long-term viability of a firm. The use of financial resources solely in pursuit of short-term profits can stunt the production of needed goods and services; a broader vision of managerial responsibility is needed.

114. The Catholic tradition has long defended the right to private ownership of productive property.[64] This right is an important element in a just economic policy. It enlarges our capacity for creativity and initiative.[65] Small and medium-sized farms, businesses, and entrepreneurial enterprises are among the most creative and efficient sectors of our economy. They should be highly valued by the people of the United States, as are land ownership and home ownership. Widespread distribution of property can help avoid excessive concentration of economic and political power. For these reasons ownership should be made possible for a broad sector of our population.[66]

115. The common good may sometimes demand that the right to own be limited by public involvement in the planning or ownership of certain sectors of the economy. Support of private ownership does not mean that anyone has the right to unlimited accumulation of wealth. "Private property does not constitute for anyone an absolute or unconditioned right. No one is justified in keeping for his exclusive use what he does not need, when others lack necessities."[67] Pope John Paul II has referred to limits placed on ownership in the duty to serve the common good as a "social mortgage" on private property.[68] For example, these limits are the basis of society's exercise of eminent domain over privately owned land needed for roads or other essen-

tial public goods. The Church's teaching opposes collectivist and statist economic approaches. But it also rejects the notion that a free market automatically produces justice. Therefore, as Pope John Paul II has argued, "One cannot exclude the socialization, in suitable conditions, of certain means of production."[69] The determination of when such conditions exist must be made on a case by case basis in light of the demands of the common good.

116. United States business and financial enterprises can also help determine the justice or injustice of the world economy. They are not all-powerful, but their real power is unquestionable. Transnational corporations and financial institutions can make positive contributions to development and global solidarity. Pope John Paul II has pointed out, however, that the desire to maximize profits and reduce the cost of natural resources and labor has often tempted these transnational enterprises to behavior that increases inequality and decreases the stability of the international order.[70] By collaborating with those national governments that serve their citizens justly and with intergovernmental agencies, these corporations can contribute to overcoming the desperate plight of many persons throughout the world.

117. Business people, managers, investors, and financiers follow a vital Christian vocation when they act responsibly and seek the common good. We encourage and support a renewed sense of vocation in the business community. We also recognize that the way business people serve society is governed and limited by the incentives which flow from tax policies, the availability of credit, and other public policies.

118. Businesses have a right to an institutional framework that does not penalize enterprises that act responsibly. Governments must provide regulations and a system of taxation which encourage firms to preserve the environment, employ disadvantaged workers, and create jobs in depressed areas. Managers and stockholders should not be torn between their responsibilities to their organizations and their responsibilities toward society as a whole.

3. CITIZENS AND GOVERNMENT

119. In addition to rights and duties related to specific roles in the economy, everyone has obligations based simply on membership in the social community. By fulfilling these duties, we create a true commonwealth. Volunteering time, talent, and money to work for greater justice is a fundamental expression of Christian love and social solidarity. All who have more than they need must come to the aid of the poor. People with professional or technical skills needed to enhance the lives of others have a duty to share them. And the poor have similar obligations: to work together as individuals and families to build up their communities by acts of social solidarity and justice. These voluntary efforts to overcome injustice are part of the Christian vocation.

120. Every citizen also has the responsibility to work to secure justice and human rights through an organized social response. In the words of Pius XI, "Charity will never be true charity unless it takes justice into account. . . . Let no one attempt with small gifts of charity to exempt himself from the great duties imposed by justice."[71] The guar-

anteeing of basic justice for all is not an optional expression of largesse but an inescapable duty for the whole of society.

121. The traditional distinction between society and the state in Catholic social teaching provides the basic framework for such organized public efforts. The Church opposes all statist and totalitarian approaches to socioeconomic questions. Social life is richer than governmental power can encompass. All groups that compose society have responsibilities to respond to the demands of justice. We have just outlined some of the duties of labor unions and business and financial enterprises. These must be supplemented by initiatives by local community groups, professional associations, educational institutions, churches, and synagogues. All the groups that give life to this society have important roles to play in the pursuit of economic justice.

122. For this reason, it is all the more significant that the teachings of the Church insist that *government has a moral function: protecting human rights and securing basic justice for all members of the commonwealth.*[72] Society as a whole and in all its diversity is responsible for building up the common good. But it is government's role to guarantee the minimum conditions that make this rich social activity possible, namely, human rights and justice.[73] This obligation also falls on individual citizens as they choose their representatives and participate in shaping public opinion.

123. More specifically, it is the responsibility of all citizens, acting through their government, to assist and empower the poor, the disadvantaged, the handicapped, and the unemployed. Government should assume a positive role in generating employment and establishing fair labor practices, in guaranteeing the provision and maintenance of the economy's infrastructure, such as roads, bridges, harbors, public means of communication, and transport. It should regulate trade and commerce in the interest of fairness.[74] Government may levy the taxes necessary to meet these responsibilities, and citizens have a moral obligation to pay those taxes. The way society responds to the needs of the poor through its public policies is the litmus test of its justice or injustice. The political debate about these policies is the indispensable forum for dealing with the conflicts and trade-offs that will always be present in the pursuit of a more just economy.

124. The primary norm for determining the scope and limits of governmental intervention is the "principle of subsidiarity" cited above. This principle states that, in order to protect basic justice, government should undertake only those initiatives which exceed the capacity of individuals or private groups acting independently. Government should not replace or destroy smaller communities and individual initiative. Rather it should help them to contribute more effectively to social well-being and supplement their activity when the demands of justice exceed their capacities. This does not mean, however, that the government that governs least governs best. Rather it defines good government intervention as that which truly "helps" other social groups contribute to the common good by directing, urging, restraining, and regulating economic activity as "the occasion requires and necessity demands."[75] This calls for cooperation and consensus-building among the diverse

agents in our economic life, including government. The precise form of government involvement in this process cannot be determined in the abstract. It will depend on an assessment of specific needs and the most effective ways to address them.

D. CHRISTIAN HOPE AND THE COURAGE TO ACT

125.The Christian vision is based on the conviction that God has destined the human race and all creation for "a kingdom of truth and life, of holiness and grace, of justice, love, and peace."[76] This conviction gives Christians strong hope as they face the economic strug- gles of the world today. This hope is not a naive optimism that imagines that simple formulas for creating a fully just society are ready at hand. The Church's experience through history and in nations throughout the world today has made it wary of all ideologies that claim to have the final answer to humanity's problems.[77] Christian hope has a much stronger foundation than such ideologies, for it rests on the knowledge that God is at work in the world, "preparing a new dwelling place and a new earth where justice will abide."[78]

126.This hope stimulates and strengthens Christian efforts to create a more just eco- nomic order in spite of difficulties and setbacks.[79] Christian hope is strong and resilient, for it is rooted in a faith that knows that the fullness of life comes to those who follow Christ in the way of the Cross. In pursuit of concrete solutions, all members of the Christian community are called to an ever finer discernment of the hurts and opportunities in the world around them, in order to respond to the most pressing needs and thus build up a more just society.[80] This is a communal task calling for dialogue, experimentation, and imagination. It also calls for deep faith and courageous love.

Chapter III

SELECTED ECONOMIC POLICY ISSUES

*127.*We have outlined this moral vision as a guide to all who seek to be faithful to the Gospel in their daily economic decisions and as a challenge to transform the economic arrangements that shape our lives and our world. These arrangements embody and communicate social values and therefore have moral significance both in themselves and in their effects. Christians, like all people, must be concerned about how the concrete outcomes of their economic activity serve human dignity; they must assess the extent to which the structures and practices of the economy support or undermine their moral vision.

*128.*Such an assessment of economic practices, structures, and outcomes leads to a variety of conclusions. Some people argue that an unfettered free-market economy, where owners, workers, and consumers pursue their enlightened self-interest, provides the greatest possible liberty, material welfare, and equity. The policy implication of this view is to intervene in the economy as little as possible because it is such a delicate mechanism that any attempt to improve it is likely to have the opposite effect. Others argue that the capitalist system is inherently inequitable and therefore contradictory to the demands of Christian morality, for it is based on acquisitiveness, competition, and self-centered individualism. They assert that capitalism is fatally flawed and must be replaced by a radically different system that abolishes private property, the profit motive, and the free market.

*129.*Catholic social teaching has traditionally rejected these ideological extremes because they are likely to produce results contrary to human dignity and economic justice.[1] Starting with the assumption that the economy has been created by human beings and can be changed by them, the Church works for improvement in a variety of economic and political contexts; but it is not the Church's role to create or promote a specific new economic system. Rather, the Church must encourage all reforms that hold out hope of transforming our economic arrangements into a fuller systemic realization of the Christian moral vision. The Church must also stand ready to challenge practices and institutions that impede or carry us farther away from realizing this vision.

*130.*In short, the Church is not bound to any particular economic, political, or social system; it has lived with many forms of economic and social organization and will continue to do so, evaluating each according to moral and ethical principles: What is the impact of the system on people? Does it support or threaten human dignity?

*131.*In this document we offer reflections on the particular reality that is the U.S. economy. In doing so we are aware of the need to address not only individual issues within the economy but also the larger question of the economic system itself. Our approach in analyzing the U.S. economy is pragmatic and evolutionary in nature. We live in a "mixed"

economic system which is the product of a long history of reform and adjustment. It is in the spirit of this American pragmatic tradition of reform that we seek to continue the search for a more just economy. Our nation has many assets to employ in this quest—vast economic, technological, and human resources and a system of representative government through which we can all help shape economic decisions.

*132.*Although we have chosen in this chapter to focus primarily on some aspects of the economy where we think reforms are realistically possible, we also emphasize that Catholic social teaching bears directly on larger questions concerning the economic system itself and the values it expresses—questions that cannot be ignored in the Catholic vision of economic justice.[2] For example, does our economic system place more emphasis on maximizing profits than on meeting human needs and fostering human dignity? Does our economy distribute its benefits equitably or does it concentrate power and resources in the hands of a few? Does it promote excessive materialism and individualism? Does is adequately protect the environment and the nation's natural resources? Does it direct too many scarce resources to military purposes? These and other basic questions about the economy need to be scrutinized in light of the ethical norms we have outlined. We urge continuing exploration of these systemic questions in a more comprehensive way than this document permits.

*133.*We have selected the following subjects to address here: 1) employment, 2) poverty, 3) food and agriculture, and 4) the U.S. role in the global economy. These topics were chosen because of their relevance to both the economic "signs of the times" and the ethical norms of our tradition. Each exemplifies U.S. policies that are basic to the establishment of economic justice in the nation and the world, and each illustrates key moral principles and norms for action from Catholic social teaching. Our treatment of these issues does not constitute a comprehensive analysis of the U.S. economy. We emphasize that these are illustrative topics intended to exemplify the interaction of moral values and economic issues in our day, not to encompass all such values and issues. This document is not a technical blueprint for economic reform. Rather, it is an attempt to foster a serious moral analysis leading to a more just economy.

*134.*In focusing on some of the central economic issues and choices in American life in the light of moral principles, we are aware that the movement from principle to policy is complex and difficult and that although moral values are essential in determining public policies, they do not dictate specific solutions. They must interact with empirical data, with historical, social, and political realities, and with competing demands on limited resources. The soundness of our prudential judgments

depends not only on the moral force of our principles, but also on the accuracy of our information and the validity of our assumptions.

*135.*Our judgments and recommendations on specific economic issues, therefore, do not carry the same moral authority as our statements of universal moral principles and formal church teaching; the former are related to circumstances which can change or which can be interpreted differently by people of good will. We expect and welcome debate on our specific policy recommendations. Nevertheless, we want our statements on these matters to be given serious consideration by Catholics as they determine whether their own moral judgments are consistent with the Gospel and with Catholic social teaching. We believe that differences on complex economic questions should be expressed in a spirit of mutual respect and open dialogue.[3]

A. EMPLOYMENT

*136.*Full employment is the foundation of a just economy. The most urgent priority for domestic economic policy is the creation of new jobs with adequate pay and decent working conditions. We must make it possible as a nation for every one who is seeking a job to find employment within a reasonable amount of time. Our emphasis on this goal is based on the conviction that human work has a special dignity and is a key to achieving justice in society.[4]

*137.*Employment is a basic right, a right which protects the freedom of all to participate in the economic life of society. It is a right which flows from the principles of justice which we have outlined above. Corresponding to this right is the duty on the part of society to ensure that the right is protected. The importance of this right is evident in the fact that for most people employment is crucial to self-realization and essential to the fulfillment of material needs. Since so few in our economy own productive property, employment also forms the first line of defense against poverty. Jobs benefit society as well as workers, for they enable more people to contribute to the common good and to the productivity required for a healthy economy.

1. THE SCOPE AND EFFECTS OF UNEMPLOYMENT

*138.*Joblessness is becoming a more widespread and deep-seated problem in our nation. There are about 8 million people in the United States looking for a job who cannot find one. They represent about 7 percent of the labor force.[5] The official rate of unemployment does not include those who have given up looking for work or those who are working part-time, but want to work full-time. When these categories are added, it becomes clear that about one-eighth of the workforce is directly affected by unemployment.[6] The severity of the unemployment problem is compounded by the fact that almost three-fourths of those who are unemployed receive no unemployment insurance benefits.[7]

*139.*In recent years there has been a steady trend toward higher and higher levels of unemployment, even in good times. Between 1950 and 1980 the annual unemployment rate exceeded current levels only during the recession years of 1975 and 1976. Periods of economic recovery during these three decades brought unemployment rates down to 3 and 4 percent. Since 1979, however, the rate has generally been above 7 percent.

*140.*Who are the unemployed? Blacks, Hispanics, Native Americans, young adults, female heads of households, and those who are inadequately educated are represented disproportionately among the ranks of the unemployed. The unemployment rate among minorities is almost twice as high as the rate among whites. For female heads of households the unemployment rate is over 10 percent. Among black teenagers, unemployment reaches the scandalous rate of more than one in three.[8]

*141.*The severe human costs of high unemployment levels become vividly clear when we examine the impact of joblessness on human lives and human dignity. It is a deep conviction of American culture that work is central to the freedom and well-being of people. The unemployed often come to feel they are worthless and without a productive role in society. Each day they are unemployed our society tells them: We don't need your talent. We don't need your initiative. We don't need *you.* Unemployment takes a terrible toll on the health and stability of both individuals and families. It gives rise to family quarrels, greater consumption of alcohol, child abuse, spouse abuse, divorce, and higher rates of infant mortality.[9] People who are unemployed often feel that society blames them for being unemployed. Very few people survive long periods of unemployment without some psychological damage even if they have sufficient funds to meet their needs.[10] At the extreme, the strains of job loss may drive individuals to suicide.[11]

*142.*In addition to the terrible waste of individual talent and creativity, unemployment also harms society at large. Jobless people pay little or no taxes, thus lowering the revenues for cities, states, and the federal government. At the same time, rising unemployment requires greater expenditures for unemployment compensation, food stamps, welfare, and other assistance. It is estimated that in 1986, for every one percentage point increase in the rate of unemployment, there will be roughly a $40 billion increase in the federal deficit.[12] The costs to society are also evident in the rise in crime associated with joblessness. The Federal Bureau of Prisons reports that increases in unemployment have been followed by increases in the prison population. Other studies have shown links between the rate of joblessness and the frequency of homicides, robberies, larcenies, narcotics arrests, and youth crimes.[13]

*143.*Our own experiences with the individuals, families, and communities that suffer the burdens of unemployment compel us to the conviction that as a nation we simply cannot afford to have millions of able-bodied men and women unemployed. We cannot afford the economic costs, the social dislocation, and the enormous human tragedies caused by un-

employment. In the end, however, what we can least afford is the assault on human dignity that occurs when millions are left without adequate employment. Therefore, we cannot but conclude that current levels of unemployment are intolerable, and they impose on us a moral obligation to work for policies that will reduce joblessness.

2. UNEMPLOYMENT IN A CHANGING ECONOMY

*144.*The structure of the U.S. economy is undergoing a transformation that affects both the quantity and the quality of jobs in our nation. The size and makeup of the workforce, for example, have changed markedly in recent years. For a number of reasons, there are now more people in the labor market than ever before in our history. Population growth has pushed up the supply of potential workers. In addition, large numbers of women have entered the labor force not only in order to put their talents and education to greater use, but also out of economic necessity. Many families need two salaries if they are to live in a decently human fashion. Female-headed households often depend heavily on the mother's income to stay off the welfare rolls. Immigrants seeking a better existence in the United States have also added to the size of the labor force. These demographic changes, however, cannot fully explain the higher levels of unemployment.

*145.*Technological changes are also having dramatic impacts on the employment picture in the United States. Advancing technology brings many benefits, but it can also bring social and economic costs, including the downgrading and displacement of workers. High technology and advanced automation are changing the very face of our nation's industries and occupations. In the 1970s, about 90 percent of all new jobs were in service occupations. By 1990, service industries are expected to employ 72 percent of the labor force. Much of the job growth in the 1980s is expected to be in traditionally low-paying, high-turnover jobs such as sales, clerical, janitorial, and food service.[14] Too often these jobs do not have career ladders leading to higher skilled, higher paying jobs. Thus, the changing industrial and occupational mix in the U.S. economy could result in a shift toward lower paying and lower skilled jobs.

*146.*Increased competition in world markets is another factor influencing the rate of joblessness in our nation. Many other exporting nations have acquired and developed up-to-the-minute technology, enabling them to increase productivity dramatically. Combined with very low wages in many nations, this has allowed them to gain a larger share of the U.S. market to cut into U.S. export markets. At the same time many corporations have closed plants in the United States and moved their capital, technology, and jobs to foreign affiliates.

*147.*Discrimination in employment is one of the causes for high rates of joblessness and low pay among racial minorities and women. Beyond the normal problems of locating a job, blacks, Hispanics, Native Americans, immigrants, and other minorities bear this added burden of discrimination. Discrimination against women is compounded by the lack of adequate child care services and by the unwillingness of many employers to provide

flexible employment or extend fringe benefits to part-time employees.

*148.*High levels of defense spending also have an effect on the number of jobs in our economy. In our pastoral letter, *The Challenge of Peace,* we noted the serious economic distortions caused by the arms race and the disastrous effects that it has on society's ability to care for the poor and the needy. Employment is one area in which this interconnection is very evident. The hundreds of billions of dollars spent by our nation each year on the arms race cause a massive drain on the U.S. economy as well as a very serious "brain drain." Such spending on the arms race means a net loss in the number of jobs created in the economy, because defense industries are less labor-intensive than other major sectors of the economy.[15] Moreover, nearly half of the American scientific and engineering force works in defense-related programs and over 60 percent of the entire federal research and development budget goes to the military.[16] We must ask whether our nation will ever be able to modernize our economy and achieve full employment if we continue to devote so much of our financial and human resources to defense-related activities.

*149.*These are some of the factors that have driven up the rate of unemployment in recent years. Although our economy has created more than 20 million new jobs since 1970,[17] there continues to be a chronic and growing job shortage. In the face of this challenge, our nation's economic institutions have failed to adapt adequately and rapidly enough. For example, failure to invest sufficiently in certain industries and regions, inadequate education and training for new workers, and insufficient mechanisms to assist workers displaced by new technology have added to the unemployment problem.

*150.*Generating an adequate number of jobs in our economy is a complex task in view of the changing and diverse nature of the problem. It involves numerous trade-offs and substantial costs. Nevertheless, it is not an impossible task. Achieving the goal of full employment may require major adjustments and creative strategies that go beyond the limits of existing policies and institutions, but it is a task we must undertake.

3. GUIDELINES FOR ACTION

*151.*We recommend that the nation make a major new commitment to achieve full employment. At present there is nominal endorsement of the full employment ideal, but no firm commitment to bringing it about. If every effort were now being made to create the jobs required, one might argue that the situation today is the best we can do. But such is not the case. The country is doing far less than it might to generate employment.

*152.*Over the last decade, economists, policy makers, and the general public have shown greater willingness to tolerate unemployment levels of 6 to 7 percent or even more.[18] Although we recognize the complexities and trade-offs involved in reducing unemployment, we believe that 6 to 7 percent unemployment is neither inevitable nor acceptable. While a zero unemployment rate is clearly impossible in an economy where people are constantly entering the job market and others are changing jobs, appropriate policies and concerted private and public action can improve the situation considerably, if we have the will to do so. No economy can be considered truly healthy when so many millions of people are denied jobs by forces outside their control. The acceptance of present unemployment rates would have been unthinkable twenty years ago. It should be regarded as intolerable today.

153.We must first establish a consensus that everyone has a right to employment. Then the burden of securing full employment falls on all of us—policy makers, business, labor, and the general public—to create and implement the mechanisms to protect that right. We must work for the formation of a new national consensus and mobilize the necessary political will at all levels to make the goal of full employment a reality.

154.Expanding employment in our nation will require significant steps in both the private and public sectors, as well as joint action between them. Private initiative and entrepreneurship are essential to this task, for the private sector accounts for about 80 percent of the jobs in the United States, and most new jobs are being created there.[19] Thus, a viable strategy for employment generation must assume that a large part of the solution will be with private firms and small businesses. At the same time, it must be recognized that government has a prominent and indispensable role to play in addressing the problem of unemployment. The market alone will not automatically produce full employment. Therefore, the government must act to ensure that this goal is achieved by coordinating general economic policies, by job creation programs, and by other appropriate policy measures.

155.Effective action against unemployment will require a careful mix of general economic policies and targeted employment programs. Taken together, these policies and programs should have full employment as their number one goal.

a. GENERAL ECONOMIC POLICIES

156.The general or macroeconomic policies of the federal government are essential tools for encouraging the steady economic growth that produces more and better jobs in the economy. *We recommend that the fiscal and monetary policies of the nation—such as federal spending, tax, and interest rate policies—should be coordinated so as to achieve the goal of full employment.*

157.General economic policies that attempt to expand employment must also deal with the problem of inflation.[20] The risk of inflationary pressures resulting from such expansionary policies is very real. Our response to this risk, however, must not be to abandon the goal of full employment, but to develop effective policies that keep inflation under control.

158.While economic growth is an important and necessary condition for the reduction of unemployment, it is not sufficient in and of itself. In order to work for full employment and restrain inflation, it is also necessary to adopt more specific programs and policies targeted toward particular aspects of the unemployment problem.[21]

b. TARGETED EMPLOYMENT PROGRAMS

159.(1) *We recommend expansion of job-training and apprenticeship programs in the private sector administered and supported jointly by business, labor unions, and govern-*

ment. Any comprehensive employment strategy must include systematic means of developing the technical and professional skills needed for a dynamic and productive economy. Investment in a skilled work force is a prerequisite both for sustaining economic growth and achieving greater justice in the United States. The obligation to contribute to this investment falls on both the private and public sectors. Today business, labor, and government need to coordinate their efforts and pool their resources to promote a substantial increase in the number of apprenticeship programs and to expand on-the-job training programs. We recommend a national commitment to eradicate illiteracy and to provide people with the skills necessary to adapt to the changing demands of employment.

160.With the rapid pace of technological change, continuing education and training are even more important today than in the past. Businesses have a stake in providing it, for skilled workers are essential to increased productivity. Labor unions should support it, for their members are increasingly vulnerable to displacement and job loss unless they continue to develop their skills and their flexibility on the job. Local communities have a stake as well, for their economic well-being will suffer serious harm if local industries fail to develop and are forced to shut down.

161.The best medicine for the disease of plant-closings is prevention. Prevention depends not only on sustained capital investment to enhance productivity through advanced technology but also on the training and retraining of workers within the private sector. In circumstances where plants are forced to shut down, management, labor unions, and local communities must see to it that workers are not simply cast aside. Retraining programs will be even more urgently needed in these circumstances.

162.(2) *We recommend increased support for direct job creation programs targeted on the long-term unemployed and those with special needs.* Such programs can take the form of direct public service employment and also of public subsidies for employment in the private sector. Both approaches would provide jobs for those with low skills less expensively and with less inflation than would general stimulation of the economy.[22] The cost of providing jobs must also be balanced against the savings realized by the government through decreased welfare and unemployment insurance expenditures and increased revenues from the taxes paid by the newly employed.

163.Government funds, if used effectively, can also stimulate private sector jobs for the long-term unemployed and for groups particularly hard to employ. Experiments need to be conducted on the precise ways such subsidies would most successfully attract business participation and ensure the generation of permanent jobs.

164.These job generation efforts should aim specifically at bringing marginalized persons into the labor force. They should produce a net increase in the number of jobs rather than displacing the burden of unemployment from one group of persons to another. They should also be aimed at long-term jobs and should include the necessary supportive services to assist the unemployed in finding and keeping jobs.

165.Jobs that are created should produce

goods and services needed and valued by society. It is both good common sense and sound economics to create jobs directly for the purpose of meeting society's unmet needs. Across the nation, in every state and locality, there is ample evidence of social needs that are going unmet. Many of our parks and recreation facilities are in need of maintenance and repair. Many of the nation's bridges and highways are in disrepair. We have a desperate need for more low-income housing. Our educational systems, day-care services, senior citizen services, and other community programs need to be expanded. These and many other elements of our national life are areas of unmet need. At the same time, there are more than 8 million Americans looking for productive and useful work. Surely we have the capacity to match these needs by giving Americans who are anxious to work a chance for productive employment in jobs that are waiting to be done. The overriding moral value of enabling jobless persons to achieve a new sense of dignity and personal worth through employment also strongly recommends these programs.

166.These job creation efforts will require increased collaboration and fresh alliances between the private and public sectors at all levels. There are already a number of examples of how such efforts can be successful.[23] We believe that the potential of these kinds of partnerships has only begun to be tapped.

c. EXAMINING NEW STRATEGIES

167.In addition to the actions suggested above, we believe there is also a need for careful examination and experimentation with alternative approaches that might improve both the quantity and quality of jobs. More extensive use of job sharing, flex time, and a reduced work week are among the topics that should continue to be on the agenda of public discussion. Consideration should also be given to the possibility of limiting or abolishing compulsory overtime work. Similarly, methods might be examined to discourage the overuse of part-time workers, who do not receive fringe benefits.[24] New strategies also need to be explored in the area of education and training for the hard-to-employ, displaced workers, the handicapped, and others with special needs. Particular attention is needed to achieve pay equity between men and women, as well as upgrading the pay scale and working conditions of traditionally low-paying jobs. The nation should renew its efforts to develop effective affirmative action policies that assist those who have been excluded by racial or sexual discrimination in the past. New strategies for improving job placement services at the national and local levels are also needed. Improving occupational safety is another important concern that deserves increased attention.

168.Much greater attention also needs to be devoted to the long-term task of converting some of the nation's military production to more peaceful and socially productive purposes. The nation needs to seek more effective ways to retool industries, to retrain workers, and to provide the necessary adjustment assistance for communities affected by this kind of economic conversion.

169.These are among the avenues that need to be explored in the search for just employment policies. A belief in the inherent dignity of human work and in the right to employment should motivate people in all sectors of society to carry on that search in new and creative ways.

B. POVERTY

*170.*More than 33 million Americans—about one in every seven people in our nation—are poor by the government's official definition. The norms of human dignity and the preferential option for the poor compel us to confront this issue with a sense of urgency. Dealing with poverty is not a luxury to which our nation can attend when it finds the time and resources. Rather, it is a moral imperative of the highest priority.

*171.*Of particular concern is the fact that poverty has increased dramatically during the last decade. Since 1973 the poverty rate has increased by nearly a third. Although the recent recovery has brought a slight decline in the rate, it remains at a level that is higher than at almost any other time during the last two decades.[25]

*172.*As pastors we have seen firsthand the faces of poverty in our midst. Homeless people roam city streets in tattered clothing and sleep in doorways or on subway grates at night. Many of these are former mental patients released from state hospitals. Thousands stand in line at soup kitchens because they have no other way of feeding themselves. Millions of children are so poorly nourished that their physical and mental development are seriously harmed.[26] We have also seen the growing economic hardship and insecurity experienced by moderate-income Americans when they lose their jobs and their income due to forces beyond their control. These are alarming signs and trends. They pose for our nation an urgent moral and human challenge: to fashion a society where no one goes without the basic material necessities required for human dignity and growth.

*173.*Poverty can be described and defined in many different ways. It can include spiritual as well as material poverty. Likewise, its meaning changes depending on the historical, social, and economic setting. Poverty in our time is different from the more severe deprivation experienced in earlier centuries in the U.S. or in Third World nations today. Our discussion of poverty in this chapter is set within the context of present-day American society. By poverty, we are referring here to the lack of sufficient material resources required for a decent life. We use the government's official definition of poverty, although we recognize its limits.[27]

1. CHARACTERISTICS OF POVERTY

*174.*Poverty is not an isolated problem existing solely among a small number of anonymous people in our central cities. Nor is it limited to a dependent underclass or to specific groups in the United States. It is a condition experienced at some time by many people in different walks of life and in different circumstances. Many poor people are working but at wages insufficient to lift them out of poverty.[28] Others are unable to work and therefore dependent on outside sources of support. Still others are on the edge of poverty; although not officially defined as poor, they are economically insecure and at risk of falling into poverty.

*175.*While many of the poor manage to escape from beneath the official poverty line,

others remain poor for extended periods of time. Long-term poverty is concentrated among racial minorities and families headed by women. It is also more likely to be found in rural areas and in the South.[29] Of the long-term poor, most are either working at wages too low to bring them above the poverty line or are retired, disabled, or parents of pre-school children. Generally they are not in a position to work more hours than they do now.[30]

a. CHILDREN IN POVERTY

*176.*Poverty strikes some groups more severely than others. Perhaps most distressing is the growing number of children who are poor. Today one in every four American children under the age of six, and one in every two black children under six, are poor. The number of children in poverty rose by four million over the decade between 1973 and 1983, with the result that there are now more poor children in the United States than at any time since 1965.[31] The problem is particularly severe among female-headed families, where more than half of all children are poor. Two-thirds of black children and nearly three-quarters of Hispanic children in such families are poor.

*177.*Very many poor families with children receive no government assistance, have no health insurance, and cannot pay medical bills. Less than half are immunized against preventable diseases such as diphtheria and polio.[32] Poor children are disadvantaged even before birth; their mothers' lack of access to high quality prenatal care leaves them at much greater risk of premature birth, low-birth weight, physical and mental impairment, and death before their first birthday.

b. WOMEN AND POVERTY

*178.*The past twenty years have witnessed a dramatic increase in the number of women in poverty.[33] This includes women raising children alone as well as women with inadequate income following divorce, widowhood, or retirement. More than one-third of all female-headed families are poor. Among minority families headed by women the poverty rate is over 50 percent.[34]

*179.*Wage discrimination against women is a major factor behind these high rates of poverty. Many women are employed but remain poor because their wages are too low. Women who work outside their homes full-time and year-round earn only 61 percent of what men earn. Thus, being employed full-time is not by itself a remedy for poverty among women. Hundreds of thousands of women hold full-time jobs but are still poor. Sixty percent of all women work in only ten occupations, and most new jobs for women are in areas with low pay and limited chances of advancement. Many women suffer discrimination in wages, salaries, job classifications, promotions, and other areas.[35] As a result, they find themselves in jobs that have low status, little security, weak unionization, and few fringe benefits. Such discrimination is immoral and efforts must be made to overcome the effects of sexism in our society.

*180.*Women's responsibilities for childrearing are another important factor to be considered. Despite the many changes in marriage and family life in recent decades, women continue to have primary responsibility in this area.

When marriages break up, mothers typically take custody of the children and bear the major financial responsibility for supporting them. Women often anticipate that they will leave the labor force to have and raise children, and often make job and career choices accordingly. In other cases they are not hired or promoted to higher paying jobs because of their childrearing responsibilities. In addition, most divorced or separated mothers do not get child support payments. In 1983, less than half of women raising children alone had been awarded child support, and of those, only half received the full amount to which they were entitled. Even fewer women (14 percent) are awarded alimony, and many older women are left in poverty after a lifetime of homemaking and childrearing.[36] Such women have great difficulty finding jobs and securing health insurance.

c. RACIAL MINORITIES AND POVERTY

*181.*Most poor people in our nation are white, but the rates of poverty in our nation are highest among those who have borne the brunt of racial prejudice and discrimination. For example, blacks are about three times more likely to be poor than whites. While one out of every nine white Americans is poor, one of every three blacks and Native Americans and more than one of every four Hispanics are poor.[37] While some members of minority communities have successfully moved up the economic ladder, the overall picture indicates that black family income is only 55 percent of white family income, reflecting an income gap that is wider now than at any time in the last fifteen years.[38]

*182.*Despite the gains which have been made toward racial equality, prejudice and discrimination in our own time as well as the effects of past discrimination continue to exclude many members of racial minorities from the mainstream of American life. Discriminatory practices in labor markets, in educational systems, and in electoral politics create major obstacles for blacks, Hispanics, Native Americans, and other racial minorities in their struggle to improve their economic status.[39] Such discrimination is evidence of the continuing presence of racism in our midst. In our pastoral letter, *Brothers and Sisters to Us*, we have described this racism as a sin—"a sin that divides the human family, blots out the image of God among specific members of that family, and violates the fundamental human dignity of those called to be children of the same Father."[40]

2. ECONOMIC INEQUALITY

*183.*Important to our discussion of poverty in America is an understanding of the degree of economic inequality in our nation. Our economy is marked by a very uneven distribution of wealth and income. For example, it is estimated that 28 percent of the total net wealth is held by the richest 2 percent of families in the United States. The top ten percent holds 57 percent of the net wealth.[41] If homes and other real estate are excluded, the concentration of ownership of "financial wealth" is even more glaring. In 1983, 54 percent of the total net financial assets were held by 2 percent of all families, those whose annual income is over $125,000. Eighty-six percent of these assets were held by the top 10 percent of all families.[42]

184.Although disparities in the distribution of income are less extreme, they are still striking. In 1984 the bottom 20 percent of American families received only 4.7 percent of the total income in the nation and the bottom 40 percent received only 15.7 percent, the lowest share on record in U.S. history. In contrast, the top one-fifth received 42.9 percent of the total income, the highest share since 1948.[43] These figures are only partial and very imperfect measures of the inequality in our society.[44] However, they do suggest that the degree of inequality is quite large. In comparison with other industrialized nations, the United States is among the more unequal in terms of income distribution.[45] Moreover, the gap between rich and poor in our nation has increased during the last decade.[46] These inequities are of particular concern because they reflect the uneven distribution of power in our society. They suggest that the level of participation in the political and social spheres is also very uneven.

185.Catholic social teaching does not require absolute equality in the distribution of income and wealth. Some degree of inequality not only is acceptable, but also may be considered desirable for economic and social reasons, such as the need for incentives and the provision of greater rewards for greater risks. However, unequal distribution should be evaluated in terms of several moral principles we have enunciated: the priority of meeting the basic needs of the poor and the importance of increasing the level of participation by all members of society in the economic life of the nation. These norms establish a strong presumption against extreme inequality of income and wealth as long as there are poor, hungry, and homeless people in our midst. They also suggest that extreme inequalities are detrimental to the development of social solidarity and community. In view of these norms we find the disparities of income and wealth in the United States to be unacceptable. Justice requires that all members of our society work for economic, political, and social reforms that will decrease these inequities.

3. GUIDELINES FOR ACTION

186.Our recommendations for dealing with poverty in the United States build upon several moral principles that were explored in chapter two of this letter. The themes of human dignity and the preferential option for the poor are at the heart of our approach; they compel us to confront the issue of poverty with a real sense of urgency.

187.The principle of social solidarity suggests that alleviating poverty will require fundamental changes in social and economic structures that perpetuate glaring inequalities and cut off millions of citizens from full participation in the economic and social life of the nation. The process of change should be one that draws together all citizens, whatever their economic status, into one community.

188.The principle of participation leads us to the conviction that the most appropriate and fundamental solutions to poverty will be those that enable people to take control of their own lives. For poverty is not merely the lack of adequate financial resources. It entails a more profound kind of deprivation, a denial of full participation in the economic, social, and political life of society and an inability to influ-

ence decisions that affect one's life. It means being powerless in a way that assaults not only one's pocketbook but also one's fundamental human dignity. Therefore, we should seek solutions that enable the poor to help themselves through such means as employment. Paternalistic programs which do too much *for* and too little *with* the poor are to be avoided.

189.The responsibility for alleviating the plight of the poor falls upon all members of society. As individuals, all citizens have a duty to assist the poor through acts of charity and personal commitment. But private charity and voluntary action are not sufficient. We also carry out our moral responsibility to assist and empower the poor by working collectively through government to establish just and effective public policies.

190.Although the task of alleviating poverty is complex and demanding, we should be encouraged by examples of our nation's past successes in this area. Our history shows that we can reduce poverty. During the 1960s and early 1970s, the official poverty rate was cut in half, due not only to a healthy economy, but also to public policy decisions that improved the nation's income transfer programs. It is estimated, for example, that in the late 1970s federal benefit programs were lifting out of poverty about 70 percent of those who would have otherwise been poor.[47]

191.During the last twenty-five years, the Social Security Program has dramatically reduced poverty among the elderly.[48] In addition, in 1983 it lifted out of poverty almost 1.5 million children of retired, deceased, and disabled workers.[49] Medicare has enhanced the life expectancy and health status of elderly and disabled people, and Medicaid has reduced infant mortality and greatly improved access to health care for the poor.[50]

192.These and other successful social welfare programs are evidence of our nation's commitment to social justice and a decent life for everyone. They also indicate that we have the capacity to design programs that are effective and provide necessary assistance to the needy in a way that respects their dignity. Yet it is evident that not all social welfare programs have been successful. Some have been ill-designed, ineffective, and wasteful. No one has been more aware of this than the poor themselves, who have suffered the consequences. Where programs have failed, we should discard them, learn from our mistakes, and fashion a better alternative. Where programs have succeeded, we should acknowledge that fact and build on those successes. In every instance, we must summon a new creativity and commitment to eradicate poverty in our midst and to guarantee all Americans their right to share in the blessings of our land.

193.Before discussing directions for reform in public policy, we must speak frankly about misunderstandings and stereotypes of the poor. For example, a common misconception is that most of the poor are racial minorities. In fact, about two-thirds of the poor are white.[51] It is also frequently suggested that people stay on welfare for many years, do not work, could work if they wanted to, and have children who will be on welfare. In fact, reliable data show that these are not accurate descriptions of most people who are poor and on welfare. Over a decade people move on and off welfare, and less than 1 percent ob-

tain these benefits for all ten years.[52] Nor is it true that the rolls of Aid to Families with Dependent Children (AFDC) are filled with able-bodied adults who could but will not work. The majority of AFDC recipients are young children and their mothers who must remain at home.[53] These mothers are also accused of having more children so that they can raise their allowances. The truth is that 70 percent of AFDC families have only one or two children and that there is little financial advantage in having another. In a given year, almost half of all families who receive AFDC include an adult who has worked full or part-time.[54] Research has consistently demonstrated that people who are poor have the same strong desire to work that characterizes the rest of the population.[55]

194.We ask everyone to refrain from actions, words, or attitudes that stigmatize the poor, that exaggerate the benefits received by the poor, and that inflate the amount of fraud in welfare payments.[56] These are symptoms of a punitive attitude towards the poor. The belief persists in this country that the poor are poor by choice or through laziness, that anyone can escape poverty by hard work, and that welfare programs make it easier for people to avoid work. Thus, public attitudes toward programs for the poor tend to differ sharply from attitudes about other benefits and programs. Some of the most generous subsidies for individuals and corporations are taken for granted and are not even called benefits but entitlements.[57] In contrast, programs for the poor are called handouts and receive a great deal of critical attention, even though they account for less than 10 percent of the federal budget.[58]

195.We now wish to propose several elements which we believe are necessary for a national strategy to deal with poverty. We offer this not as a comprehensive list but as an invitation for others to join the discussion and take up the task of fighting poverty.

196.a. *The first line of attack against poverty must be to build and sustain a healthy economy that provides employment opportunities at just wages for all adults who are able to work.* Poverty is intimately linked to the issue of employment. Millions are poor because they have lost their jobs or because their wages are too low. The persistent high levels of unemployment during the last decade are a major reason why poverty has increased in recent years.[59] Expanded employment especially in the private sector would promote human dignity, increase social solidarity, and promote self-reliance of the poor. It should also reduce the need for welfare programs and generate the income necessary to support those who remain in need and cannot work: elderly, disabled, and chronically ill people, and single parents of young children. It should also be recognized that the persistence of poverty harms the larger society because the depressed purchasing power of the poor contributes to the periodic cycles of stagnation in the economy.

197.In recent years the minimum wage has not been adjusted to keep pace with inflation. Its real value has declined by 24 percent since 1981. We believe Congress should raise the minimum wage in order to restore some of the purchasing power it has lost due to inflation.

198.While job creation and just wages are

major elements of a national strategy against poverty, they are clearly not enough. Other more specific policies are necessary to remedy the institutional causes of poverty and to provide for those who cannot work.

199.b. Vigorous action should be undertaken to remove barriers to full and equal employment for women and minorities. Too many women and minorities are locked into jobs with low pay, poor working conditions, and little opportunity for career advancement. So long as we tolerate a situation in which people can work full-time and still be below the poverty line—a situation common among those earning the minimum wage—too many will continue to be counted among the "working poor." Concerted efforts must be made through job training, affirmative action, and other means to assist those now prevented from obtaining more lucrative jobs. Action should also be taken to upgrade poorer paying jobs and to correct wage differentials that discriminate unjustly against women.

200.c. Self-help efforts among the poor should be fostered by programs and policies in both the private and public sectors. We believe that an effective way to attack poverty is through programs that are small in scale, locally based, and oriented toward empowering the poor to become self-sufficient. Corporations, private organizations, and the public sector can provide seed money, training and technical assistance, and organizational support for self-help projects in a wide variety of areas such as low-income housing, credit unions, worker cooperatives, legal assistance, and neighborhood and community organizations. Efforts that enable the poor to participate in the ownership and control of economic resources are especially important.

*201.*Poor people must be empowered to take charge of their own futures and become responsible for their own economic advancement. Personal motivation and initiative, combined with social reform, are necessary elements to assist individuals in escaping poverty. By taking advantage of opportunities for education, employment, and training, and by working together for change, the poor can help themselves to be full participants in our economic, social, and political life.

202.d. The tax system should be continually evaluated in terms of its impact on the poor. This evaluation should be guided by three principles. First, the tax system should raise adequate revenues to pay for the public needs of society, especially to meet the basic needs of the poor. Secondly, the tax system should be structured according to the principle of progressivity, so that those with relatively greater financial resources pay a higher rate of taxation. The inclusion of such a principle in tax policies is an important means of reducing the severe inequalities of income and wealth in the nation. Action should be taken to reduce or offset the fact that most sales taxes and payroll taxes place a disproportionate burden on those with lower incomes. Thirdly, families below the official poverty line should not be required to pay income taxes. Such families are, by definition, without sufficient resources to purchase the basic necessities of life. They should not be forced to bear the additional burden of paying income taxes.[60]

203.e. All of society should make a much stronger commitment to education for the poor. Any long-term solution to poverty in this country must pay serious attention to education, public and private, in school and out of school. Lack of adequate education, especially in the inner city setting, prevents many poor people from escaping poverty. In addition, illiteracy, a problem that affects tens of millions of Americans, condemns many to joblessness or chronically low wages. Moreover, it excludes them in many ways from sharing in the political and spiritual life of the community.[61] Since poverty is fundamentally a problem of powerlessness and marginalization, the importance of education as a means of overcoming it cannot be overemphasized.

*204.*Working to improve education in our society is an investment in the future, an investment that should include both the public and private school systems. Our Catholic schools have the well-merited reputation of providing excellent education, especially for the poor. Catholic inner-city schools provide an otherwise unavailable educational alternative for many poor families. They provide one effective vehicle for disadvantaged students to lift themselves out of poverty. We commend the work of all those who make great sacrifices to maintain these inner-city schools. We pledge ourselves to continue the effort to make Catholic schools models of education for the poor.

*205.*We also wish to affirm our strong support for the public school system in the United States. There can be no substitute for quality education in public schools, for that is where the large majority of all students, including Catholic students, are educated. In Catholic social teaching, basic education is a fundamental human right.[62] In our society a strong public school system is essential if we are to protect that right and allow everyone to develop to their maximum ability. Therefore, we strongly endorse the recent calls for improvements in and support for public education, including improving the quality of teaching and enhancing the rewards for the teaching profession.[63] At all levels of education we need to improve the ability of our institutions to provide the personal and technical skills that are necessary for participation not only in today's labor market but also in contemporary society.

206.f. Policies and programs at all levels should support the strength and stability of families, especially those adversely affected by the economy. As a nation, we need to examine all aspects of economic life and assess their effects on families. Employment practices, health insurance policies, income security programs, tax policy, and service programs can either support or undermine the abilities of families to fulfill their roles in nurturing children and caring for infirm and dependent family members.

*207.*We affirm the principle enunciated by John Paul II that society's institutions and policies should be structured so that mothers of young children are not forced by economic necessity to leave their children for jobs outside the home.[64] The nation's social welfare and tax policies should support parents' decisions to care for their own children and should recognize the work of parents in the home because of its value for the family and for society.

*208.*For those children whose parents do work outside the home, there is a serious shortage of affordable, quality day care. Employers, governments, and private agencies need to improve both the availability and the quality of child care services. Likewise, families could be assisted by the establishment of parental leave policies that would assure job security for new parents.

*209.*The high rate of divorce and the alarming extent of teenage pregnancies in our nation are distressing signs of the breakdown of traditional family values. These destructive trends are present in all sectors of society: rich and poor; white, black, and brown; urban and rural. However, for the poor they tend to be more visible and to have more damaging economic consequences. These destructive trends must be countered by a revived sense of personal responsibility and commitment to family values.

210.g. A thorough reform of the nation's welfare and income-support programs should be undertaken. For millions of poor Americans the only economic safety net is the public welfare system. The programs that make up this system should serve the needs of the poor in a manner that respects their dignity and provides adequate support. In our judgment the present welfare system does not adequately meet these criteria.[65] We believe that several improvements can and should be made within the framework of existing welfare programs. However, in the long run, more far-reaching reforms that go beyond the present system will be necessary. Among the immediate improvements that could be made are the following:

211.(1) Public assistance programs should be designed to assist recipients, wherever possible, to become self-sufficient through gainful employment. Individuals must be no worse off economically when they get jobs than when they rely only on public assistance. Under current rules, people who give up welfare benefits to work in low-paying jobs soon lose their Medicaid benefits. To help recipients become self-sufficient and reduce dependency on welfare, public assistance programs should work in tandem with job creation programs that include provisions for training, counseling, placement, and child care. Jobs for recipients of public assistance should be fairly compensated so that workers receive the full benefits and status associated with gainful employment.

212.(2) Welfare programs should provide recipients with adequate levels of support. This support should cover basic needs in food, clothing, shelter, health care, and other essentials. At present only 4 percent of poor families with children receive enough cash welfare benefits to lift them out of poverty.[66] The combined benefits of AFDC and food stamps typically come to less than three-fourths of the official poverty level.[67] Those receiving public assistance should not face the prospect of hunger at the end of the month, homelessness, sending children to school in ragged clothing, or inadequate medical care.

213.(3) National eligibility standards and a national minimum benefit level for public assistance programs should be established. Currently welfare eligibility and benefits vary greatly among states. In 1985 a family of three with no earnings had a maximum AFDC benefit of $96 a month in Mississippi and $558 a month in Vermont.[68] To remedy these great disparities, which are far larger than the regional differences in the cost of living, and to assure a floor of benefits for all needy people, our nation should establish and fund national minimum benefit levels and eligibility standards in cash assistance programs.[69] The benefits should also be indexed to reflect changes in the cost of living. These changes reflect standards that our nation has already put in place for aged and disabled people and veterans. Is it not possible to do the same for the children and their mothers who receive public assistance?

214.(4) *Welfare programs should be available to two-parent as well as single-parent families.* Most states now limit participation in AFDC to families headed by single parents, usually women.[70] The coverage of this program should be extended to two-parent families so that fathers who are unemployed or poorly paid do not have to leave home in order for their children to receive help. Such a change would be a significant step toward strengthening two-parent families who are poor.

4. CONCLUSION

215.The search for a more human and effective way to deal with poverty should not be limited to short-term reform measures. The agenda for public debate should also include serious discussion of more fundamental alternatives to the existing welfare system. We urge that proposals for a family allowance or a children's allowance be carefully examined as a possible vehicle for ensuring a floor of income support for all children and their families.[71] Special attention is needed to develop new efforts that are targeted on long-term poverty, which has proven to be least responsive to traditional social welfare programs. The "negative income tax" is another major policy proposal that deserves continued discussion.[72] These and other proposals should be part of a creative and ongoing effort to fashion a system of income support for the poor that protects their basic dignity and provides the necessary assistance in a just and effective manner.

C. FOOD AND AGRICULTURE

216.The fundamental test of an economy is its ability to meet the essential human needs of this generation and future generations in an equitable fashion. Food, water, and energy are essential to life; their abundance in the United States has tended to make us complacent. But these goods—the foundation of God's gift of life—are too crucial to be taken for granted. God reminded the people of Israel that "the land is mine; for you are strangers and guests with me" (Lv 25:23, RSV). Our Christian faith calls us to contemplate God's creative and sustaining action and to measure our own collaboration with the Creator in using the earth's resources to meet human needs. While Catholic social teaching on the care of the environment and the management of natural resources is still in the process of development, a Christian moral perspective clearly gives weight and urgency to their use in meeting human needs.

217.No aspect of this concern is more pressing than the nation's food system. We are concerned that this food system may be in jeopardy as increasing numbers of farm bankruptcies and foreclosures result in increased concentration of land ownership.[73] We are likewise concerned about the increasing damage to natural resources resulting from many modern agricultural practices: the overconsumption of water, the depletion of topsoil, and the pollution of land and water. Finally, we are concerned about the stark reality of world hunger in spite of food surpluses. Our food production system is clearly in need of evaluation and reform.

1. U.S. AGRICULTURE—PAST AND PRESENT

218.The current crisis has to be assessed in the context of the vast diversity of U.S. crops and climates. For example, subsistence farming in Appalachia, where so much of the land is absentee-owned and where coal mining and timber production are the major economic interests, has little in common with family farm grain production in the central Midwest or ranching in the Great Plains. Likewise, large-scale irrigated fruit, vegetable, and cotton production in the central valley of California is very different from dairy farming in Wisconsin or tobacco and peanut production in the Southeast.

219.Two aspects of the complex history of U.S. land and food policy are particularly relevant. First, the United States entered this century with the ownership of productive land widely distributed. The Preemption Acts of the early 19th century and the Homestead Act of 1862 were an important part of that history. Wide distribution of ownership was reflected in the number and decentralization of farms in the United States, a trend that reached its peak in the 1930s. The U.S. farm system included nearly 7 million owner-operators in 1935.[74] By 1983 the number of U.S. farms had declined to 2.4 million, and only about 3 percent of the population were engaged in producing food.[75] Second, U.S. food policy has had a parallel goal of keeping the consumer cost of food low. As a result, Americans today spend less of their disposable income on food than people in any other industrialized country.[76]

220.These outcomes require scrutiny. First of all, the loss of farms and the exodus of farmers from the land have led to the loss of a valued way of life, the decline of many rural communities, and the increased concentration of land ownership. Secondly, while low food prices benefit those who are left with additional income to spend on other goods, these pricing policies put pressure on farmers to increase output and hold down costs. This has led them to replace human labor with cheaper energy, expand farm size to employ new technologies favoring larger scale operations, neglect soil and water conservation, underpay farmworkers, and oppose farmworker unionization.[77]

221.Today nearly half of U.S. food production comes from the 4 percent of farms with over $200,000 in gross sales.[78] Many of these largest farms are no longer operated by families, but by managers hired by owners.[79] Nearly three-quarters of all farms, accounting for only 13 percent of total farm sales, are comparatively small. They are often run by part-time farmers who derive most of their income from off-farm employment. The remaining 39 percent of sales comes from the 24 percent of farms grossing between $40,000 and $200,000. It is this group of farmers, located throughout the country and caught up in the long-term trend toward fewer and larger farms, who are at the center of the present farm crisis.

222.During the 1970s new markets for farm exports created additional opportunities for profit and accelerated the industrialization of agriculture, a process already stimulated by new petroleum-based, large-scale technologies that allowed farmers to cultivate many more acres. Federal tax policies and farm programs fostered this tendency by encouraging too much capital investment in agriculture and overemphasizing large-scale technologies.[80] The results were greater production, increases in the value of farmland, and heavy borrowing to finance expansion. In the 1980s, with export markets shrinking and commodity prices and land values declining, many farmers cannot repay their loans.

223.Their situation has been aggravated by certain "external" factors: persistent high interest rates that make it difficult to repay or refinance loans, the heavy debt burden of food-deficient countries, the high value of the dollar, dramatically higher U.S. budget and trade deficits, and generally reduced international trade following the worldwide recession of the early 1980s. The United States is unlikely to recapture its former share of the world food and fiber trade, and it is not necessarily an appropriate goal to attempt to do so. Exports are not the solution to U.S. farm problems. Past emphasis on producing for overseas markets has contributed to the strain on our natural resource base and has also undermined the efforts of many less developed countries in attaining self-reliance in feeding their own people. In attempting to correct these abuses, however, we must not reduce our capability to help meet emergency food needs.

224.Some farmers face financial insolvency because of their own eagerness to take advantage of what appeared to be favorable investment opportunities. This was partly in response to the encouragement of public policy incentives and the advice of economists and financiers. Nevertheless, farmers should share some responsibility for their current plight.

225.Four other aspects of the current situation concern us: first, land ownership is becoming further concentrated as units now facing bankruptcy are added to existing farms and non-farm corporations. Diversity of ownership and widespread participation are declining in this sector of the economy as they have in others. Since differing scales of operation and the investment of family farm labor have been important for American farm productivity, this increasing concentration of ownership in almost all sectors of agriculture points to an important change in that system.[81] Of particular concern is the growing phenomenon of "vertical integration" whereby companies gain control of two or three of the links in the food chain: as suppliers of farm inputs, landowners, and food processors. This increased concentration could also adversely affect food prices.

226.Second, diversity and richness in American society are lost as farm people leave the land and rural communities decay. It is not just a question of coping with additional unemployment and a need for retraining and relocation. It is also a matter of maintaining opportunities for employment and human development in a variety of economic sectors and cultural contexts.

227.Third, although the United States has set a world standard for food production, it has not done so without cost to our natural resource base.[82] On nearly one-quarter of our most productive cropland, topsoil erosion currently exceeds the rate at which it can be replaced by natural processes. Similarly, underground water supplies are being depleted in areas where food production depends on irrigation. Furthermore, chemical fertilizers, pesticides, and herbicides, considered now almost essential to today's agriculture, pollute the air, water, and soil, and pose countless health hazards. Finally, where the expansion of residential, industrial, and recreational areas makes it rewarding to do so, vast acreages of prime farmland, three million acres per year by some estimates, are converted to nonfarm use. The continuation of these practices, reflecting short-term investment interests or immediate income needs of farmers and other landowners, constitutes a danger to future food production because these practices are not sustainable.

228.Farm owners and farmworkers are the immediate stewards of the natural resources required to produce the food that is necessary to sustain life. These resources must be understood as gifts of a generous God. When they are seen in that light and when the human race is perceived as a single moral community, we gain a sense of the substantial responsibility we bear as a nation for the world food system. Meeting human needs today and in the future demands an increased sense of stewardship and conservation from owners, managers, and regulators of all resources, especially those required for the production of food.

229.Fourth, the situation of racial minorities in the U.S. food system is a matter of special pastoral concern. They are largely excluded from significant participation in the farm economy. Despite the agrarian heritage of so many Hispanics, for example, they operate only a minute fraction of America's farms.[83] Black-owned farms, at one time a significant resource for black participation in the economy, have been disappearing at a dramatic rate in recent years,[84] a trend that the U.S. Commission on Civil Rights has warned "can only serve to further diminish the stake of blacks in the social order and reinforce their skepticism regarding the concept of equality under the law."[85]

230.It is largely as hired farm laborers rather than farm owners that minorities participate in the farm economy. Along with many white farmworkers, they are, by and large, the poorest paid and least benefited of any laboring group in the country. Moreover, they are not as well protected by law and public policy as other groups of workers; and their efforts to organize and bargain collectively have been systematically and vehemently resisted, usually by farmers themselves. Migratory field workers are particularly susceptible to exploitation. This is reflected not only in their characteristically low wages but also in the low standards of housing, health care, and education made available to these workers and their families.[86]

2. GUIDELINES FOR ACTION

231.We are convinced that current trends in the food sector are not in the best interests of the United States or of the global community. The decline in the number of moderate-sized farms, increased concentration of land ownership, and the mounting evidence of poor resource conservation raise serious questions of morality and public policy. As pastors, we cannot remain silent while thousands of farm families caught in the present crisis lose their homes, their land, and their way of life. We approach this situation, however, aware that it reflects longer-term conditions that carry consequences for the food system as a whole and for the resources essential for food production.

232.While much of the change needed must come from the cooperative efforts of farmers themselves, we strongly believe that there is an important role for public policy in the protection of dispersed ownership through family farms, as well as in the preservation of natural resources. We suggest three guidelines for both public policy and private efforts aimed at shaping the future of American agriculture.

233.*First, moderate-sized farms operated by families on a full-time basis should be preserved and their economic viability protected.* Similarly, small farms and part-time farming, particularly in areas close to cities, should be encouraged. As we have noted elsewhere in this pastoral letter,[87] there is genuine social and economic value in maintaining a wide distribution in the ownership of productive property. The democratization of decision making and control of the land resulting from wide distribution of farm ownership are protections against concentration of power and a consequent possible loss of responsiveness to public need in this crucial sector of the economy.[88] Moreover, when those who work in an enterprise also share in its ownership, their active commitment to the purpose of the endeavor and their participation in it are enhanced. Ownership provides incentives for diligence and is a source of an increased sense that the work being done is one's own. This is particularly significant in a sector as vital to human well-being as agriculture.

234.Furthermore, diversity in farm ownership tends to prevent excessive consumer dependence on business decisions that seek maximum return on invested capital, thereby making the food system overly susceptible to fluctuations in the capital markets. This is particularly relevant in the case of nonfarm corporations that enter agriculture in search of high profits. If the return drops substantially, or if it appears that better profits can be obtained by investing elsewhere, the corporation may cut back or even close down operations without regard to the impact on the community or on the food system in general. In similar circumstances full-time farmers, with a heavy personal investment in their farms and strong ties to the community, are likely to persevere in the hope of better times. Family farms also make significant economic and social contributions to the life of rural communities.[89] They support farm suppliers and other local merchants, and their farms support the tax base needed to pay for roads, schools, and other vital services.

235.This rural interdependence has value beyond the rural community itself. Both Catholic social teaching and the traditions of our country have emphasized the importance of maintaining the rich plurality of social institutions that enhances personal freedom and increases the opportunity for participation in community life. Movement toward a smaller number of very large farms employing wage workers would be a movement away from this institutional pluralism. By contributing to the vitality of rural communities, full-time residential farmers enrich the social and political life of the nation as a whole. Cities, too, benefit soundly and economically from a vibrant rural economy based on family farms. Because of out-migration of farm and rural people, too much of this enriching diversity has been lost already.

236.*Second, the opportunity to engage in farming should be protected as a valuable form of work.* At a time when unemployment in the country is already too high, any unnecessary increase in the number of unemployed people, however small, should be avoided. Farm unemployment leads to further rural unemployment as rural businesses lose their customers and close down. The loss of people from the land also entails the loss of expertise in farm and land management and creates a need for retraining and relocating another group of displaced workers.

237.Losing any job is painful, but losing one's farm and having to leave the land can be tragic. It often means the sacrifice of a family heritage and a way of life. Once farmers sell their land and their equipment, their move is practically irreversible. The costs of returning are so great that few who leave ever come back. Even the small current influx of people into agriculture attracted by lower land values will not balance this loss. Society should help those who would and could continue effectively in farming.

238.*Third, effective stewardship of our natural resources should be a central consideration in any measures regarding U.S. agriculture.* Such stewardship is a contribution to the common good that is difficult to assess in purely economic terms, because it involves the care of resources entrusted to us by our Creator for the benefit of all. Responsibility for the stewardship of these resources rests on society as a whole. Since farmers make their living from the use of this endowment, however, they bear a particular obligation to be caring stewards of soil and water. They fulfill this obligation by participating in soil and water conservation programs, using farm practices that enhance the quality of the resources, and maintaining prime farmland in food production rather than letting it be converted to nonfarm uses.

3. POLICIES AND ACTIONS

239.The human suffering involved in the present situation and the long-term structural changes occurring in this sector call for responsible action by the whole society. A half-century of federal farm-price supports, subsidized credit, production-oriented research and extension services, and special tax policies for farmers have made the federal government a central factor in almost every aspect of American agriculture.[90] No redirection of current trends can occur without giving close attention to these programs.

240.A prime consideration in all agricultural trade and food assistance policies should be the contribution our nation can make to global food security. This means continuing and increasing food aid without depressing Third World markets or using food as a weapon in international politics. It also means not subsidizing exports in ways that lead to trade wars and instability in international food markets.

241.We offer the following suggestions for governmental action with regard to the farm and food sector of the economy.

242.a. The current crisis calls for special measures to assist otherwise viable family farms that are threatened with bankruptcy or foreclosure. Operators of such farms should have access to emergency credit, reduced rates of interest, and programs of debt restructuring. Rural lending institutions facing problems because of nonpayment or slow payment of large farm loans should also have access to temporary assistance. Farmers, their families, and their communities will gain immediately from these and other short-term measures aimed at keeping these people on the land.

243.b. Established federal farm programs, whose benefits now go disproportionately to the largest farmers,[91] should be reassessed for their long-term effects on the structure of agriculture. Income-support programs that help farmers according to the amount of food they produce or the number of acres they farm should be subject to limits that ensure a fair income to all farm families and should restrict participation to producers who genuinely need such income assistance. There should also be a strict ceiling on price-support payments which assist farmers in times of falling prices, so that benefits go to farms of moderate or small size. To succeed in redirecting the benefits of these programs while holding down costs to the public, consideration should be given to a broader application of mandatory production control programs.[92]

244.c. We favor reform of tax policies which now encourage the growth of large farms, attract investments in agriculture by nonfarmers seeking tax shelters, and inequitably benefit large and well-financed farming operations.[93] Offsetting nonfarm income with farm "losses" has encouraged high-income investors to acquire farm assets with no intention of depending on them for a living as family farmers must. The ability to depreciate capital equipment faster than its actual decline in value has benefited wealthy investors and farmers. Lower tax rates on capital gains have stimulated farm expansion and larger investments in energy-intensive equipment and technologies as substitutes for labor. Changes in estate tax laws have consistently favored the largest estates. All of these results have demonstrated that reassessment of these and similar tax provisions is needed.[94] We continue, moreover, to support a progressive land tax on farm acreage to discourage the accumulation of excessively large holdings.[95]

245.d. Although it is often assumed that farms must grow in size in order to make the most efficient and productive use of sophisticated and costly technologies, numerous studies have shown that medium-sized commercial farms achieve most of the technical cost efficiencies available in agriculture today. We, therefore, recommend that the research and extension resources of the federal government and the nation's land grant colleges and universities be redirected toward improving the productivity of small and medium-sized farms.[96]

246.e. Since soil and water conservation, like other efforts to protect the environment, are contributions to the good of the whole society, it is appropriate for the public to bear a share of the cost of these practices and to set standards for environmental protection. Gov-

ernment should, therefore, encourage farmers to adopt more conserving practices and distribute the costs of this conservation more broadly.

247.f. Justice demands that worker guarantees and protections such as minimum wages and benefits and unemployment compensation be extended to hired farmworkers on the same basis as all other workers. There is also an urgent need for additional farmworker housing, health care, and educational assistance.

4. SOLIDARITY IN THE FARM COMMUNITY

248.While there is much that government can and should do to change the direction of farm and food policy in this country, that change in direction also depends upon the cooperation and good will of farmers. The incentives in our farm system to take risks, to expand farm size, and to speculate in farmland values are great. Hence, farmers and ranchers must weigh these incentives against the values of family, rural community, care of the soil, and a food system responsive to long-term as well as short-term food needs of the nation and the world. The ever present temptation to individualism and greed must be countered by a determined movement toward solidarity in the farm community. Farmers should approach farming in a cooperative way, working with other farmers in the purchase of supplies and equipment and in the marketing of produce. It is not necessary for every farmer to be in competition against every other farmer. Such cooperation can be extended to the role farmers play through their various general and community organizations in shaping and implementing governmental farm and food policies.[97] Likewise, it is possible to seek out and adopt technologies that reduce costs and enhance productivity without demanding increases in farm size. New technologies are not forced on farmers; they are chosen by farmers themselves.

249.Farmers also must end their opposition to farmworker unionization efforts. Farmworkers have a legitimate right to belong to unions of their choice and to bargain collectively for just wages and working conditions. In pursuing that right they are protecting the value of labor in agriculture, a protection that also applies to farmers who devote their own labor to their farm operations.

5. CONCLUSION

250.The U.S. food system is an integral part of the larger economy of the nation and the world. As such this integral role necessitates the cooperation of rural and urban interests in resolving the challenges and problems facing agriculture. The very nature of agricultural enterprise and the family farm traditions of this country have kept it a highly competitive sector with a widely dispersed ownership of the most fundamental input to production, the land. That competitive, diverse structure, proven to be a dependable source of nutritious and affordable food for this country and millions of people in other parts of the world, is now threatened. The food necessary for life, the land and water resources needed to produce that food, and the way of life of the people who make the land productive are at risk. Catholic social and ethical traditions attribute moral significance to each of these. Our response to the present situation should reflect a sensitivity to that moral significance,

a determination that the United States will play its appropriate role in meeting global food needs, and a commitment to bequeath to future generations an enhanced natural environment and the same ready access to the necessities of life that most of us enjoy today. To farmers and farm workers who are suffering because of the farm crisis, we promise our solidarity, prayers, counseling and the other spiritual resources of our Catholic faith.

D. THE U.S. ECONOMY AND THE DEVELOPING NATIONS: COMPLEXITY, CHALLENGE, AND CHOICES

1. THE COMPLEXITY OF ECONOMIC RELATIONS IN AN INTERDEPENDENT WORLD

251.The global economy is made up of national economies of industrialized countries of the North and the developing countries of the South, together with the network of economic relations that link them. It constitutes the framework in which the solidarity we seek on a national level finds its international expression. Traditional Catholic teaching on this global interdependence emphasizes the dignity of the human person, the unity of the human family, the universally beneficial purpose of the goods of the earth, the need to pursue the international common good, as well as the good of each nation, and the imperative of distributive justice. The United States plays a leading role in the international economic system, and we are concerned that U.S. relations with all nations—Canada, Europe, Japan, and our other trading partners, as well as the socialist countries—reflect this teaching and be marked by fairness and mutual respect.

252.Nevertheless, without in the least discounting the importance of these linkages, our emphasis on the preferential option for the poor moves us to focus our attention mainly on U.S. relations with the Third World. Unless conscious steps are taken toward protecting human dignity and fostering human solidarity in these relationships, we can look forward to increased conflict and inequity, threatening the fragile economies of these relatively poor nations far more than our own relatively strong one. Moreover, equity requires, even as the fact of interdependence becomes more apparent, that the *quality* of interdependence be improved, in order to eliminate "the scandal of the shocking inequality between the rich and the poor"[98] in a world divided even more sharply between them.

253.Developing countries, moreover, often perceive themselves more as *dependent* on the industrialized countries, especially the United States, because the international system itself, as well as the way the United States acts in it, subordinates them. The prices at which they must sell their commodity exports and purchase their food and manufactured imports, the rates of interest they must pay and the terms they must meet to borrow money, the standards of economic behavior of foreign investors, the amounts and conditions of external aid, etc., are essentially determined by the industrialized world. Moreover, their traditional cultures are increasingly susceptible to the aggressive cultural penetration of Northern (especially U.S.) advertising and media programing. The developing countries are junior partners at best.

254.The basic tenets of church teaching take on a new moral urgency as we deepen our understanding of how disadvantaged large numbers of people and nations are in this interdependent world. Half the world's people, nearly two and a half billion, live in countries where the annual per capita income is $400 or less.[99] At least 800 million people in those countries live in absolute poverty, "beneath any rational definition of human decency."[100] Nearly half a billion are chronically hungry, despite abundant harvests worldwide.[101] Fifteen out of every 100 children born in those countries die before the age of five, and millions of the survivors are physically or mentally stunted. No aggregate of individual examples could portray adequately the appalling inequities within those desperately poor countries and between them and our own. And their misery is not the inevitable result of the march of history or of the intrinsic nature of particular cultures, but of human decisions and human institutions.

255.On the international economic scene three main sets of actors warrant particular attention: individual nations, which retain great influence; multilateral institutions, which channel money, power, ideas, and influence; transnational corporations and banks, which have grown dramatically in number, size, scope, and strength since World War II.[102] In less identifiable ways trade unions, popular movements, private relief and development agencies, and regional groupings of nations also affect the global economy. The interplay among all of them sets the context for policy choices that determine whether genuine interdependence is promoted or the dependence of the disadvantaged is deepened.

256.In this arena, where fact and ethical challenges intersect, the moral task is to devise rules for the major actors that will move them toward a just international order. One of the most vexing problems is that of reconciling the transnational corporations' profit orientation with the common good that they, along with governments and their multilateral agencies, are supposed to serve.

257.The notion of interdependence erases the fading line between domestic and foreign policy. Many foreign policy decisions (for example, on trade, investment, and immigration) have direct and substantial impact on domestic constituencies in the United States. Similarly, many decisions thought of as domestic (for example, on farm policy, interest rates, the federal budget, or the deficit) have important consequences for other countries. This increasingly recognized link of domestic and foreign issues poses new empirical and moral questions for national policy.

2. THE CHALLENGE OF CATHOLIC SOCIAL TEACHING

258.Catholic teaching on the international economic order recognizes this complexity, but does not provide specific solutions. Rather, we seek to ensure that moral considerations are taken into account. All of the elements of the moral perspective we have outlined above have important implications for international relationships. (1) The demands of *Christian love* and *human solidarity* challenge all economic actors to choose community over chaos. They require a definition of political community that goes beyond national sovereignty to policies that recognize

the moral bonds among all people. (2) *Basic justice* implies that all peoples are entitled to participate in the increasingly interdependent global economy in a way that ensures their freedom and dignity. When whole communities are effectively left out or excluded from equitable participation in the international order, basic justice is violated. We want a world that works fairly for all. (3) *Respect for human rights*, both political and economic, implies that international decisions, institutions, and policies must be shaped by values that are more than economic. The creation of a global order in which these rights are secure for all must be a prime objective for all relevant actors on the international stage. (4) *The special place of the poor* in this moral perspective means that meeting the basic needs of the millions of deprived and hungry people in the world must be the number one objective of international policy.

259.These perspectives constitute a call for fundamental reform in the international economic order. Whether the problem is preventing war and building peace, or addressing the needs of the poor, Catholic teaching emphasizes not only the individual conscience, but also the political, legal, and economic structures through which policy is determined and issues are adjudicated.[103] We do not seek here to evaluate the various proposals for international economic reform or deal here with economic relations between the United States and other industrialized countries. We urge, as a basic and overriding consideration, that both empirical and moral evidence, especially the precarious situation of the developing countries, calls for the renewal of the dialogue between the industrialized countries of the North and the developing countries of the South, with the aim of reorganizing international economic relations to establish greater equity and help meet the basic human needs of the poor majority.[104]

260.Here, as elsewhere, the preferential option for the poor is the central priority for policy choice. It offers a unique perspective on foreign policy in whose light U.S. relationships, especially with developing countries, can be reassessed. Standard foreign policy analysis deals with calculations of power and definitions of national interest; but the poor are, by definition, not powerful. If we are to give appropriate weight to their concerns, their needs, and their interests, we have to go beyond economic gain or national security as a starting point for the policy dialogue. We want to stand with the poor everywhere, and we believe that relations between the U.S. and developing nations should be determined in the first place by a concern for basic human needs and respect for cultural traditions.

3. THE ROLE OF THE UNITED STATES IN THE GLOBAL ECONOMY: CONSTRUCTIVE CHOICES

261.As we noted in *The Challenge of Peace,* recent popes have strongly supported the United Nations as a crucial step forward in the development and organization of the human community; we share their regret that no political entity now exists with the responsibility and power to promote the global common good, and we urge the United States to support UN efforts to move in that direction. Building a just world economic order in the absence of such an authority demands that na-

tional governments promote public policies that increase the ability of poor nations and marginalized people to participate in the global economy. Because no other nation's economic power yet matches ours, we believe that this responsibility pertains especially to the United States; but it must be carried out in cooperation with other industrialized countries as in the case of halting the rise of the dollar. This is yet another evidence of the fact of interdependence. Joint action toward these goals not only promotes justice and reduces misery in the Third World, but also is in the interest of the United States and other industrialized nations.

262.Yet in recent years U.S. policy toward development in the Third World has become increasingly one of selective assistance based on an East-West assessment of North-South problems, at the expense of basic human needs and economic development. Such a view makes national security the central policy principle.[105] Developing countries have become largely testing grounds in the East-West struggle; they seem to have meaning or value mainly in terms of this larger geopolitical calculus. The result is that issues of human need and economic development take second place to the political-strategic argument. This tendency must be resisted.

263.Moreover, U.S. performance in North-South negotiations often casts us in the role of resisting developing-country proposals without advancing realistic ones of our own.[106] North-South dialogue is bound to be complex, protracted, and filled with symbolic and often unrealistic demands; but the situation has now reached the point where the rest of the world expects the United States to assume a reluctant, adversarial posture in such discussions. The U.S. approach to the developing countries needs urgently to be changed; a country as large, rich, and powerful as ours has a moral obligation to lead in helping to reduce poverty in the Third World.

264.We believe that U.S. policy toward the developing world should reflect our traditional regard for human rights and our concern for social progress. In economic policy, as we noted in our pastoral letter on nuclear war, the major international economic relationships of aid, trade, finance, and investment are interdependent among themselves and illustrate the range of interdependence issues facing U.S. policy. All three of the major economic actors are active in all these relationships. Each relationship offers us the possibility of substantial, positive movement toward increasing social justice in the developing world; in each, regrettably, we fall short. It is urgent that immediate steps be taken to correct these deficiencies.

265.a. *Development Assistance:* The official development assistance that the industrialized and the oil-producing countries provide the Third World in the form of grants; low-interest, long-term loans; commodities; and technical assistance is a significant contribution to their development. Although the annual share of U.S. gross national product (GNP) devoted to foreign aid is now less than one-tenth of that of the Marshall Plan, which helped rebuild devastated but advanced European economies, we remain the largest donor country. We still play a critical role in these resource transfers, but we no longer set an example for other donors. We lag proportionately behind most other industrial nations in providing resources and seem to care less than before about development in the Third World. Our bilateral aid has become increasingly militarized and security-related and our contributions to multilateral agencies have been reduced in recent years.[107] Not all of these changes are justifiable. The projects of the International Development Agency, for example, seem worthy of support.

266.This is a grave distortion of the priority that development assistance should command. We are dismayed that the United States, once the pioneer in foreign aid, is almost last among the seventeen industrialized nations in the Organization for Economic Cooperation and Development (OECD) in percentage of GNP devoted to aid. Reduction of the U.S. contribution to multilateral development institutions is particularly regrettable, because these institutions are often better able than the bilateral agencies to focus on the poor and reduce dependency in developing countries.[108] This is also an area in which, in the past, our leadership and example have had great influence. A more affirmative U.S. role in these institutions, which we took the lead in creating, could improve their performance, send an encouraging signal of U.S. intentions, and help reopen the dialogue on the growing poverty and dependency of the Third World.

267.b. *Trade:* Trade continues to be a central component of international economic relations. It contributed in a major way to the rapid economic growth of many developing countries in the 1960s and 1970s and will probably continue to do so, though at a slower rate. The preferential option for the poor does not, by itself, yield a trade policy; but it does provide a frame of reference. In particular, an equitable trading system that will help the poor should allocate its benefits fairly and ensure that exports from developing countries receive fair prices reached by agreement among all trading partners. Developing nations have a right to receive a fair price for their raw materials that allows for a reasonable degree of profit.

268.Trade policy illustrates the conflicting pressures that interdependence can generate: claims of injustice from developing countries denied market access are countered by claims of injustice in the domestic economies of industrialized countries when jobs are threatened and incomes fall. Agricultural trade and a few industrial sectors present particularly acute examples of this.

269.We believe the ethical norms we have applied to domestic economic questions are equally valid here.[109] As in other economic matters, the basic questions are: Who benefits from the particular policy measure? How can any benefit or adverse impact be equitably shared? We need to examine, for example, the extent to which the success in the U.S. market of certain imports is derived from exploitative labor conditions in the exporting country, conditions that in some cases have attracted the investment in the first place. The United States should do all it can to ensure that the trading system treats the poorest segments of developing countries' societies fairly and does not lead to human rights violations. In particular the United States should seek effective special measures under the General Agreement on Tariffs and Trade (GATT)[110] to benefit the poorest countries.

270.At the same time, U.S. workers and their families hurt by the operation of the trading system must be helped through training and other measures to adjust to changes that advance development and decrease poverty in the Third World. This is a very serious, immediate, and intensifying problem. In our judgment, adjustment assistance programs in the United States have been poorly designed and administered, and inadequately funded. A society and an economy such as ours can better adjust to trade dislocations than can poverty-ridden developing countries.

271.c. *Finance:* Aid and trade policies alone, however enlightened, do not constitute a sufficient approach to the developing countries; they must also be looked at in conjunction with international finance and investment. The debtor-creditor relationship well exemplifies both the interdependence of the international economic order and its asymmetrical character, i.e., the *dependence* of the developing countries. The aggregate external debt of the developing countries now approaches $1 trillion,[111] more than one-third of their combined GNP; this total doubled between 1979 and 1984 and continues to rise. On average, the first 20 percent of export earnings goes to service that debt without significantly reducing the principal; in some countries debt service is nearly 100 percent of such earnings, leaving scant resources available for the countries' development programs.

272.The roots of this very complex debt crisis are both historic and systemic. *Historically,* the three major economic actors share the responsibility for the present difficulty because of decisions made and actions taken during the 1970s and 1980s. In 1972 the Soviet Union purchased the entire U.S. grain surplus, and grain prices trebled. Between 1973 and 1979, the Organization of Petroleum Exporting Countries raised the price of oil eightfold and thereafter deposited most of the profits in commercial banks in the North. In order to profit from the interest-rate spread on these deposits, the banks pushed larger and larger loans on eager Third World borrowers needing funds to purchase more and more expensive oil. A second doubling of oil prices in 1979 forced many of these countries to refinance their loans and borrow more money at escalating interest rates. A global recession beginning in 1979 caused the prices of Third World export commodities to fall and thus reduced the ability to meet the increasingly burdensome debt payments out of export earnings.

273.The global *system* of finance, development, and trade established by the Bretton Woods Conference in 1944—the World Bank, the International Monetary Fund (IMF), and the GATT—was created by the North to prevent a recurrence of the economic problems that were perceived to have led to World War II. Forty years later that system seems incapable, without basic changes, of helping the debtor countries—which had no part in its creation—manage their increasingly untenable debt situation effectively and equitably. The World Bank, largest of these institutions, has been engaged primarily in lending for specific projects rather than for general economic health. The IMF was intended to be a short-term lender that would help out with temporary balance of payments, or cash-flow problems; but in the current situation it has come

to the fore as a monitor of commercial financial transactions and an evaluator of debtors' creditworthiness—and therefore the key institution for resolving these problems. The GATT, which is not an institution, had been largely supplanted, as trade monitor for the developing countries, by UNCTAD[112] in which the latter have more confidence.

274.This crisis, however, goes beyond the system; it affects people. It afflicts and oppresses large numbers of people who are already severely disadvantaged. That is the scandal: it is the poorest people who suffer most from the austerity measures required when a country seeks the IMF "seal of approval" which establishes its creditworthiness for a commercial loan (or perhaps an external aid program). It is these same people who suffer most when commodity prices fall, when food cannot be imported or they cannot buy it, and when natural disasters occur. Our commitment to the preferential option for the poor does not permit us to remain silent in these circumstances. Ways must be found to meet the immediate emergency—moratorium on payments, conversion of some dollar-denominated debt into local-currency debt, creditors' accepting a share of the burden by partially writing-down selected loans, capitalizing interest, or perhaps outright cancellation.

275.The poorest countries, especially those in sub-Saharan Africa which are least developed, most afflicted by hunger and malnutrition, and most vulnerable to commodity price declines, are in extremely perilous circumstances.[113] Although their aggregate debt of more than $100 billion (much of it owed to multilateral institutions), is about one-quarter that of Latin America, their collateral (oil, minerals, manufactures, grain, etc.) is much less adequate, their ability to service external debt much weaker, and the possibility of their rescheduling it very small. For low-income countries like these, the most useful immediate remedies are longer payment periods, lower interest rates, and modification of IMF adjustment requirements that exacerbate the already straitened circumstances of the poor.[114] Especially helpful for some African countries would be cancellation of debts owed to governments, a step already taken by some creditor nations.

276.Better off debtor countries also need to be able to adjust their debts without penalizing the poor. Although the final policy decisions about the allocation of adjustment costs belong to the debtor government, internal equity considerations should be taken into account in determining the conditions of debt rescheduling and additional lending; for example, wage reductions should not be mandated, basic public services to the poor should not be cut, and measures should be required to reduce the flight of capital. Since this debt problem, like most others, is systemic, a case-by-case approach is not sufficient: lending policies and exchange-rate considerations are not only economic questions, but are thoroughly and intensely political.

277.Beyond all this, the growing external debt that has become the overarching economic problem of the Third World also requires systemic change to provide immediate relief and to prevent recurrence. The Bretton Woods institutions do not adequately represent Third World debtors, and their policies are not dealing effectively with problems affecting those nations. These institutions need to be substantially reformed and their policies reviewed at the same time that the immediate problem of Third World debt is being dealt with. The United States should promote, support, and participate fully in such reforms and reviews. Such a role is not only morally right, but is in the economic interest of the United States; more than a third of this debt is owed to U.S. banks. The viability of the international banking system (and of those U.S. banks) depends in part on the ability of debtor countries to manage those debts. Stubborn insistence on full repayment could force them to default—which would lead to economic losses in the United States. In this connection, we should not overlook the impact of U.S. budget and trade deficits on interest rates. These high interest rates exacerbate the already difficult debt situation. They also attract capital away from investment in economic development in Third World countries.

278.d. *Foreign Private Investment:* Although direct private investment in the developing countries by U.S.-based transnational corporations has declined in recent years, it still amounts to about $60 billion and accounts for sizeable annual transfers. Such investment in developing countries should be increased, consistent with the host country's development goals and with benefits equitably distributed. Particular efforts should be made to encourage investments by medium-sized and small companies, as well as to joint ventures, which may be more appropriate to the developing country's situation. For the foreseeable future, however, private investment will probably not meet the infrastructural needs of the poorest countries—roads, transportation, communications, education, health, etc.— since these do not generally show profits and therefore do not attract private capital. Yet without this infrastructure, no real economic growth can take place.
279.Direct foreign investment, risky though it may be for both the investing corporation and the developing country, can provide needed capital, technology, and managerial expertise. Care must be taken lest such investment create or perpetuate dependency, harming especially those at the bottom of the economic ladder. Investments that sustain or worsen inequities in a developing country, that help to maintain oppressive elites in power, or that increase food dependency by encouraging cash cropping for export at the expense of local needs, should be discouraged. Foreign investors, attracted by low wage rates in less developed countries, should consider both the potential loss of jobs in the home country and the potential exploitation of workers in the host country.[115] Both the products and the technologies of the investing firms should be appropriate to the developing country, neither catering just to a small number of high-income consumers, nor establishing capital-intensive processes that displace labor, especially in the agricultural sector.[116]
280.Such inequitable results, however, are not necessary consequences of transnational corporate activity. Corporations can contribute to development by attracting and training high-caliber managers and other personnel, by helping organize effective marketing systems, by generating additional capital, by introducing or reinforcing financial accountability, and by sharing the knowledge gained from their

own research and development activities. Although the ability of the corporations to plan, operate, and communicate across national borders without concern for domestic considerations makes it harder for governments to direct their activities toward the common good, the effort should be made; the Christian ethic is incompatible with a primary or exclusive focus on maximization of profit. We strongly urge U.S. and international support of efforts to develop a code of conduct for foreign corporations that recognizes their quasi-public character and encourages both development and the equitable distribution of their benefits. Transnational corporations should be required to adopt such a code, and to conform their behavior to its provisions.

281.e. *The World Food Problem—A Special Urgency:* These four resource transfer channels—aid, trade, finance, and investment—intersect and overlap in all economic areas, but in none more clearly than in the international food system. The largest single segment of development assistance support goes to the agricultural sector and to food aid for short-term emergencies and vulnerable groups; food constitutes one of the most critical trade sectors; developing countries have borrowed extensively in the international capital markets to finance food imports; and a substantial portion of direct private investment flows into the agricultural sector.
282.The development of U.S. agriculture has moved the United States into a dominant position in the international food system. The best way to meet the responsibilities this dominance entails is to design and implement a U.S. food and agriculture policy that contributes to increased food security—that is, access by everyone to an adequate diet. A world with nearly half a billion hungry people is not one in which food security has been achieved. The problem of hunger has a special significance for those who read the Scriptures and profess the Christian faith. From the Lord's command to feed the hungry, to the Eucharist we celebrate as the Bread of Life, the fabric of our faith demands that we be creatively engaged in sharing the food that sustains life. There is no more basic human need. The gospel imperative takes on new urgency in a world of abundant harvests where hundreds of millions of people face starvation. Relief and prevention of their hunger cannot be left to the arithmetic of the marketplace.[117]
283.The chronic hunger of those who live literally from day to day is only one symptom of the underlying problem of poverty; relieving and preventing hunger is part of a larger, coordinated strategy to attack poverty itself. People must be enabled either to grow or to buy the food they need, without depending on an indefinite dole; there is no substitute for long-term agricultural and food-system development in the nations now caught in the grip of hunger and starvation. Most authorities agree that the key to this development is the small farmers, most of whom are prevented from participating in the food system by the lack of a market incentive resulting from the poverty of the bulk of the populations and by the lack of access to productive agricultural inputs, especially land, resulting mainly from their own poverty. In these poor, food-deficit countries, no less than in our own, the small family farm deserves support and protection.
284.But recognizing the long-term problem

does not dissolve the short-term obligation of the world's major food-exporting nation to provide food aid sufficient to meet the nutritional needs of poor people, and to provide it not simply to dispose of surpluses but in a way that does not discourage local food production. There can be no successful solution to the problem of hunger in the world without U.S. participation in a cooperative effort that simultaneously increases food aid and launches a long-term program to help develop food self-reliance in food-deficit developing countries.
285.Hunger is often seen as being linked with the problem of population growth, as effect to cause. While this relationship is sometimes presented in oversimplified fashion, we cannot fail to recognize that the earth's resources are finite and that population tends to grow rapidly. Whether the world can provide a truly human life for twice as many people or more as now live in it (many of whose lives are sadly deficient today) is a matter of urgent concern that cannot be ignored.[118]
286.Although we do not believe that people are poor and hungry primarily because they have large families, the Church fully supports the need for all to exercise responsible parenthood. Family size is heavily dependent on levels of economic development, education, respect for women, availability of health care, and the cultural traditions of communities. Therefore, in dealing with population growth we strongly favor efforts to address these social and economic concerns.
287.Population policies must be designed as part of an overall strategy of integral human development. They must respect the freedom of parents and avoid coercion. As Pope Paul VI has said concerning population policies:

> "It is true that too frequently an accelerated demographic increase adds its own difficulties to the problems of development: the size of the population increases more rapidly than available resources, and things are found to have reached apparently an impasse. From that moment the temptation is great to check the demographic increase by means of radical measures. It is certain that public authorities can intervene, within the limit of their competence, by favoring the availability of appropriate information and by adopting suitable measures, provided that these be in conformity with the moral law and that they respect the rightful freedom of married couples. Where the inalienable right to marriage and procreation is lacking, human dignity has ceased to exist."[119]

4. U.S. RESPONSIBILITY FOR REFORM IN THE INTERNATIONAL ECONOMIC SYSTEM

288.The United States cannot be the sole savior of the developing world, nor are Third World countries entirely innocent with respect to their own failures or totally helpless to achieve their own destinies. Many of these countries will need to initiate positive steps to promote and sustain development and economic growth—streamline bureaucracies, account for funds, plan reasonable programs, and take further steps toward empowering their people. Progress toward development will surely require them to take some tough remedial measures as well: prevent the flight of capital, reduce borrowing, modify price discrimination against rural areas, eliminate corruption in the use of funds and other resources, and curtail spending on inefficient public enterprises. The pervasive U.S. presence in many parts of our interdependent world, however, also creates a responsibility for us to increase the use of U.S. economic power—not just aid—in the service of human dignity and human rights, both political and economic.

289.In particular, as we noted in our earlier letter, *The Challenge of Peace*, the contrast between expenditures on armaments and on development reflects a shift in priorities from meeting human needs to promoting "national security" and represents a massive distortion of resource allocations. In 1982, for example, the military expenditures of the industrialized countries were seventeen times larger than their foreign assistance; in 1985 the United States alone budgeted more than twenty times as much for defense as for foreign assistance, and nearly two-thirds of the latter took the form of military assistance (including subsidized arms sales) or went to countries because of their perceived strategic value to the United States.[120] *Rather than promoting U.S. arms sales, especially to countries that cannot afford them, we should be campaigning for an international agreement to reduce this lethal trade.*

290.In short, the international economic order, like many aspects of our own economy, is in crisis; the gap between rich and poor countries and between rich and poor people within countries is widening. The United States represents the most powerful single factor in the international economic equation. But even as we speak of crisis, we see an opportunity for the United States to launch a worldwide campaign for justice and economic rights to match the still incomplete, but encouraging, political democracy we have achieved in the United States with so much pain and sacrifice.

291.To restructure the international order along lines of greater equity and participation and apply the preferential option for the poor to international economic activity will require sacrifices of at least the scope of those we have made over the years in building our own nation. We need to call again upon the qualities of leadership and vision that have marked our history when crucial choices were demanded. As Pope John Paul II said during his 1979 visit to the United States, "America, which in the past decades has demonstrated goodness and generosity in providing food for the hungry of the world, will, I am sure, be able to match this generosity with an equally convincing contribution to the establishing of a world order that will create the necessary economic and trade conditions for a more just relationship between all the nations of the world."[121]

292.We share his conviction that most of the policy issues generally called economic are, at root, moral and therefore require the application of moral principles derived from the Scriptures and from the evolving social teaching of the Church and other traditions.[122] We also recognize that we are dealing here with sensitive international issues that cross national boundaries. Nevertheless, in order to pursue justice and peace on a global scale, *we call for a U.S. international economic policy designed to empower people everywhere and enable them to continue to develop a sense of their own worth, improve the quality of their lives, and ensure that the benefits of economic growth are shared equitably.*

E. CONCLUSION

293.None of the issues we have addressed in this chapter can be dealt with in isolation. They are interconnected, and their resolution requires difficult trade-offs among competing interests and values. The changing international economy, for example, greatly influences efforts to achieve full employment in the United States and to maintain a healthy farm sector. Similarly, as we have noted, policies and programs to reduce unemployment and poverty must not ignore a potential inflationary impact. These complexities and trade-offs are real and must be confronted, but they are not an excuse for inaction. They should not paralyze us in our search for a more just economy.

294.Many of the reforms we have suggested in this chapter would be expensive. At a time when the United States has large annual deficits some might consider these costs too high. But this discussion must be set in the context of how our resources are allocated and the immense human and social costs of failure to act on these pressing problems. We believe that the question of providing adequate revenues to meet the needs of our nation must be faced squarely and realistically. Reforms in the tax code which close loopholes and generate new revenues, for example, are among the steps that need to be examined in order to develop a federal budget that is both fiscally sound and socially responsible. The cost of meeting our social needs must also be weighed against the $300 billion a year allocated for military purposes. Although some of these expenditures are necessary for the defense of the nation, some elements of the military budget are both wasteful and dangerous for world peace.[123] Careful reductions should be made in these areas in order to free up funds for social and economic reforms. In the end, the question is not whether the United States can provide the necessary funds to meet our social needs, but whether we have the political will to do so.

Chapter IV

A NEW AMERICAN EXPERIMENT: PARTNERSHIP FOR THE PUBLIC GOOD

295.For over two hundred years the United States has been engaged in a bold experiment in democracy. The founders of the nation set out to establish justice, promote the general welfare, and secure the blessings of liberty for themselves and their posterity. Those who live in this land today are the beneficiaries of this great venture. Our review of some of the most pressing problems in economic life today shows, however, that this undertaking is not yet complete. Justice for all remains an aspiration; a fair share in the general welfare is denied to many. In addition to the particular policy recommendations made above, a long-term and more fundamental response is needed. This will call for an imaginative vision of the future that can help shape economic arrangements in creative new ways. We now want to propose some elements of such a vision and several innovations in economic structures that can contribute to making this vision a reality.

296.Completing the unfinished business of the American experiment will call for new forms of cooperation and partnership among those whose daily work is the source of the prosperity and justice of the nation. The United States prides itself on both its competitive sense of initiative and its spirit of teamwork. Today a greater spirit of partnership and teamwork is needed; competition alone will not do the job. It has too many negative consequences for family life, the economically vulnerable, and the environment. Only a renewed commitment by all to the common good can deal creatively with the realities of international interdependence and economic dislocations in the domestic economy. The virtues of good citizenship require a lively sense of participation in the commonwealth and of having obligations as well as rights within it.[1] The nation's economic health depends on strengthening these virtues among all its people, and on the development of institutional arrangements supportive of these virtues.[2]

297.The nation's founders took daring steps to create structures of participation, mutual accountability, and widely distributed power to ensure the political rights and freedoms of all. We believe that similar steps are needed today to expand economic participation, broaden the sharing of economic power, and make economic decisions more accountable to the common good. As noted above, the principle of subsidiarity states that the pursuit of economic justice must occur on all levels of society. It makes demands on communities as small as the family, as large as the global society and on all levels in between. There are a number of ways to enhance the cooperative participation of these many groups in the task of creating this future. Since there is no single innovation that will solve all problems, we recommend careful experimentation with several possibilities that hold considerable hope for increasing partnership and strengthening mutual responsibility for economic justice.

A. COOPERATION WITHIN FIRMS AND INDUSTRIES

298.A new experiment in bringing democratic ideals to economic life calls for serious exploration of ways to develop new patterns of partnership among those working in individual firms and industries.[3] Every business, from the smallest to the largest, including farms and ranches, depends on many different persons and groups for its success: workers, managers, owners or shareholders, suppliers, customers, creditors, the local community, and the wider society. Each makes a contribution to the enterprise, and each has a stake in its growth or decline. Present structures of accountability, however, do not acknowledge all these contributions or protect these stakes. A major challenge in today's economy is the development of new institutional mechanisms for accountability that also preserve the flexibility needed to respond quickly to a rapidly changing business environment.[4]

299.New forms of partnership between workers and managers are one means for developing greater participation and accountability within firms.[5] Recent experience has shown that both labor and management suffer when the adversarial relationship between them becomes extreme. As Pope Leo XIII stated, "Each needs the other completely: capital cannot do without labor, nor labor without capital."[6] The organization of firms should reflect and enhance this mutual partnership. In particular, the development of work patterns for men and women that are more supportive of family life will benefit both employees and the enterprises they work for.

300.Workers in firms and on farms are especially in need of stronger institutional protection, for their jobs and livelihood are particularly vulnerable to the decisions of others in today's highly competitive labor market. Several arrangements are gaining increasing support in the United States: profit sharing by the workers in a firm; enabling employees to become company stockholders; granting employees greater participation in determining the conditions of work; cooperative ownership of the firm by all who work within it; and programs for enabling a much larger number of Americans, regardless of their employment status, to become shareholders in successful corporations. Initiatives of this sort can enhance productivity, increase the profitability of firms, provide greater job security and work satisfaction for employees, and reduce adversarial relations.[7] In our 1919 Program of Social Reconstruction, we observed "the full possibilities of increased production will not be realized so long as the majority of workers remain mere wage earners. The majority must somehow become owners, at least in part, of the instruments of production."[8]

We believe this judgment remains generally valid today.

301.None of these approaches provides a panacea, and all have certain drawbacks. Nevertheless we believe that continued research and experimentation with these approaches will be of benefit. Catholic social teaching has endorsed on many occasions innovative methods for increasing worker participation within firms.[9] The appropriateness of these methods will depend on the circumstances of the company or industry in question and on their effectiveness in actually increasing a genuinely cooperative approach to shaping decisions. The most highly publicized examples of such efforts have been in large firms facing serious financial crises. If increased participation and collaboration can help a firm avoid collapse, why should it not give added strength to healthy businesses? Cooperative ownership is particularly worthy of consideration in new entrepreneurial enterprises.[10]

302.Partnerships between labor and management are possible only when both groups possess real freedom and power to influence decisions. This means that unions ought to continue to play an important role in moving toward greater economic participation within firms and industries. Workers rightly reject calls for less adversarial relations when they are a smokescreen for demands that labor make all the concessions. For partnership to be genuine it must be a two-way street, with creative initiative and a willingness to cooperate on all sides.

303.When companies are considering plant closures or the movement of capital, it is patently unjust to deny workers any role in shaping the outcome of these difficult choices.[11] In the heavy manufacturing sector today, technological change and international competition can be the occasion of painful decisions leading to the loss of jobs or wage reductions. While such decisions may sometimes be necessary, a collaborative and mutually accountable model of industrial organization would mean that workers not be expected to carry all the burdens of an economy in transition. Management and investors must also accept their share of sacrifices, especially when management is thinking of closing a plant or transferring capital to a seemingly more lucrative or competitive activity. The capital at the disposal of management is in part the product of the labor of those who have toiled in the company over the years, including currently employed workers.[12] As a minimum, workers have a right to be informed in advance when such decisions are under consideration, a right to negotiate with management about possible alternatives, and a right to fair compensation and assistance with retraining and relocation expenses should these be necessary. Since even these minimal rights are jeopardized without collective negotiation, industrial cooperation requires a strong role for labor unions in our changing economy.

304.Labor unions themselves are challenged by the present economic environment to seek new ways of doing business. The purpose of unions is not simply to defend the existing wages and prerogatives of the fraction of workers who belong to them, but also to enable workers to make positive and creative contributions to the firm, the community, and the larger society in an organized and cooperative way.[13] Such contributions call for experiments with new directions in the U.S. labor movement.

305.The parts played by managers and shareholders in U.S. corporations also need careful examination. In U.S. law, the primary responsibility of managers is to exercise prudent business judgment in the interest of a profitable return to investors. But morally this legal responsibility may be exercised only within the bounds of justice to employees, customers, suppliers, and the local community. Corporate mergers and hostile takeovers may bring greater benefits to shareholders, but they often lead to decreased concern for the well-being of local communities and make towns and cities more vulnerable to decisions made from afar.

306.Most shareholders today exercise relatively little power in corporate governance.[14] Although shareholders can and should vote on the selection of corporate directors and on investment questions and other policy matters, it appears that return on investment is the governing criterion in the relation between them and management. We do not believe this is an adequate rationale for shareholder decisions. The question of how to relate the rights and responsibilities of shareholders to those of the other people and communities affected by corporate decisions is complex and insufficiently understood. We, therefore, urge serious, long-term research and experimentation in this area. More effective ways of dealing with these questions are essential to enable firms to serve the common good.

B. LOCAL AND REGIONAL COOPERATION

307.The context within which U.S. firms do business has direct influence on their ability to contribute to the common good. Companies and indeed whole industries are not sole masters of their own fate. Increased cooperative efforts are needed to make local, regional, national, and international conditions more supportive of the pursuit of economic justice.

308.In the principle of subsidiarity, Catholic social teaching has long stressed the importance of small- and intermediate-sized communities or institutions in exercising moral responsibility. These mediating structures link the individual to society as a whole in a way that gives people greater freedom and power to act.[15] Such groups include families, neighborhoods, church congregations, community organizations, civic and business associations, public interest and advocacy groups, community development corporations, and many other bodies. All these groups can play a crucial role in generating creative partnerships for the pursuit of the public good on the local and regional level.

309.The value of partnership is illustrated by considering how new jobs are created. The development of new businesses to serve the local community is key to revitalizing areas hit hard by unemployment.[16] The cities and

regions in greatest need of these new jobs face serious obstacles in attracting enterprises that can provide them. Lack of financial resources, limited entrepreneurial skill, blighted and unsafe environments, and a deteriorating infrastructure create a vicious cycle that makes new investment in these areas more risky and therefore less likely.

310.Breaking out of this cycle will require a cooperative approach that draws on all the resources of the community.[17] Community development corporations can keep efforts focused on assisting those most in need. Existing business, labor, financial, and academic institutions can provide expertise in partnership with innovative entrepreneurs. New cooperative structures of local ownership will give the community or region an added stake in businesses and even more importantly give these businesses a greater stake in the community.[18] Government on the local, state, and national levels must play a significant role, especially through tax structures that encourage investment in hard hit areas and through funding aimed at conservation and basic infrastructure needs. Initiatives like these can contribute to a multilevel response to the needs of the community.

311.The Church itself can work as an effective partner on the local and regional level. First-hand knowledge of community needs and commitment to the protection of the dignity of all should put Church leaders in the forefront of efforts to encourage a community-wide cooperative strategy. Because churches include members from many different parts of the community, they can often serve as mediator between groups who might otherwise regard each other with suspicion. We urge local church groups to work creatively and in partnership with other private and public groups in responding to local and regional problems.

C. PARTNERSHIP IN THE DEVELOPMENT OF NATIONAL POLICIES

312.The causes of our national economic problems and their possible solutions are the subject of vigorous debate today. The discussion often turns on the role the national government has played in creating these problems and could play in remedying them. We want to point to several considerations that could help build new forms of effective citizenship and cooperation in shaping the economic life of our country.

313.First, while economic freedom and personal initiative are deservedly esteemed in our society, we have increasingly come to recognize the inescapably social and political nature of the economy. The market is always embedded in a specific social and political context. The tax system affects consumption, saving, and investment. National monetary policy, domestic and defense programs, protection of the environment and worker safety, and regulation of international trade all shape the economy as a whole. These policies influence domestic investment, unemployment rates, foreign exchange, and the health of the entire world economy.

314.The principle of subsidiarity calls for government intervention when small or intermediate groups in society are unable or unwilling to take the steps needed to promote basic justice. Pope John XXIII observed that the growth of more complex relations of inter-

dependence among citizens has led to an increased role for government in modern societies.[19] This role is to work *in partnership with* the many other groups in society, helping them fulfill their tasks and responsibilities more effectively, not replacing or destroying them. The challenge of today is to move beyond abstract disputes about whether more or less government intervention is needed, to consideration of creative ways of enabling government and private groups to work together effectively.

315.It is in this light that we understand Pope John Paul II's recommendation that "society make provision for overall planning" in the economic domain.[20] Planning must occur on various levels, with the government ensuring that basic justice is protected and also protecting the rights and freedoms of all other agents. In the Pope's words:

> In the final analysis this overall concern weighs on the shoulders of the state, but it cannot mean one-sided centralization by the public authorities. Instead what is in question is a just and rational coordination within the framework of which the initiative of individuals, free groups, and local work centers and complexes must be safeguarded.[21]

316.We are well aware that the mere mention of economic planning is likely to produce a strong negative reaction in U.S. society. It conjures up images of centralized planning boards, command economies, inefficient bureaucracies, and mountains of government paperwork. It is also clear that the meaning of "planning" is open to a wide variety of interpretations and takes very different forms in various nations.[22] The Pope's words should not be construed as an endorsement of a highly centralized form of economic planning, much less a totalitarian one. His call for a "just and rational coordination" of the endeavors of the many economic actors is a call to seek creative new partnership and forms of participation in shaping national policies.

317.There are already many forms of economic planning going on within the U.S. economy today. Individuals and families plan for their economic future. Management and labor unions regularly develop both long- and short-term plans. Towns, cities, and regions frequently have planning agencies concerned with their social and economic future. When state legislatures and the U.S. Congress vote on budgets or on almost any other bill that comes before them, they are engaged in a form of public planning. Catholic social teaching does not propose a single model for political and economic life by which these levels are to be institutionally related to each other. It does insist that reasonable coordination among the different parts of the body politic is an essential condition for achieving justice. This is a moral precondition of good citizenship that applies to both individual and institutional actors. In its absence no political structure can guarantee justice in society or the economy. Effective decisions in these matters will demand greater cooperation among all citizens. To encourage our fellow citizens to consider more carefully the appropriate balance of private and local initiative with national economic policy, we make several recommendations.

318.First, in an advanced industrial economy like ours, all parts of society, including government, must cooperate in forming national economic policies. Taxation, monetary policy, high levels of government spending, and many other forms of governmental regulation are here to stay. A modern economy without governmental interventions of the sort we have alluded to is inconceivable. These interventions, however, should help, not replace, the contributions of other economic actors and institutions and should direct them to the common good. The development of effective new forms of partnership between private and public agencies will be difficult in a situation as immensely complex as that of the United States in which various aspects of national policy seem to contradict one another.[23] On the theoretical level, achieving greater coordination will make demands on those with the technical competence to analyze the relationship among different parts of the economy. More practically, it will require the various subgroups within our society to sharpen their concern for the common good and moderate their efforts to protect their own short-term interests.

319.*Second, the impact of national economic policies on the poor and the vulnerable is the primary criterion for judging their moral value.* Throughout this letter we have stressed the special place of the poor and the vulnerable in any ethical analysis of the U. S. economy. National economic policies that contribute to building a true commonwealth should reflect this by standing firmly for the rights of those who fall through the cracks of our economy: the poor, the unemployed, the homeless, the displaced. Being a citizen of this land means sharing in the responsibility for shaping and implementing such policies.

320.*Third, the serious distortion of national economic priorities produced by massive national spending on defense must be remedied.* Clear-sighted consideration of the role of government shows that government and the economy are already closely intertwined through military research and defense contracts. Defense-related industries make up a major part of the U.S. economy and have intimate links with both the military and civilian government; they often depart from the competitive model of free-market capitalism. Moreover, the dedication of so much of the national budget to military purposes has been disas-

trous for the poor and vulnerable members of our own and other nations. The nation's spending priorities need to be revised in the interests of both justice and peace.[24]

321.We recognize that these proposals do not provide a detailed agenda. We are also aware that there is a tension between setting the goals for coherent policies and actually arriving at them by democratic means. But if we can increase the level of commitment to the common good and the virtues of citizenship in our nation, the ability to achieve these goals will greatly increase. It is these fundamental moral concerns that lead us as bishops to join the debate on national priorities.

D. COOPERATION AT THE INTERNATIONAL LEVEL

322.If our country is to guide its international economic relationships by policies that serve human dignity and justice, we must expand our understanding of the moral responsibility of citizens to serve the common good of the entire planet. Cooperation is not limited to the local, regional, or national level. Economic policy can no longer be governed by national goals alone. The fact that the "social question has become worldwide"[25] challenges us to broaden our horizons and enhance our collaboration and sense of solidarity on the global level. The cause of democracy is closely tied to the cause of economic justice. The unfinished business of the American experiment includes the formation of new international partnerships, especially with the developing countries, based on mutual respect, cooperation, and a dedication to fundamental justice.

323.The principle of subsidiarity calls for government to intervene in the economy when basic justice requires greater social coordination and regulation of economic actors and institutions. In global economic relations, however, no international institution provides this sort of coordination and regulation. The U.N. system, including the World Bank, the International Monetary Fund, and the General Agreement on Tariffs and Trade, does not possess the requisite authority. Pope John XXIII called this institutional weakness a "structural defect" in the organization of the human community. The structures of world

order, including economic ones, "no longer correspond to the objective requirements of the universal common good."[26]

324.Locked together in a world of limited material resources and a growing array of common problems, we help or hurt one another by the economic policies we choose. All the economic agents in our society, therefore, must consciously and deliberately attend to the good of the whole human family. We must all work to increase the effectiveness of international agencies in addressing global problems that cannot be handled through the actions of individual countries. In particular we repeat our plea made in *The Challenge of Peace* urging "that the United States adopt a stronger supportive leadership role with respect to the United Nations."[27] In the years following World War II, the United States took the lead in establishing multilateral bodies to deal with postwar economic problems. Unfortunately, in recent years this country has taken steps that have weakened rather than strengthened multilateral approaches. This is a shortsighted policy and should be reversed if the long-term interests of an interdependent globe are to be served.[28] In devising more effective arrangements for pursuing international economic justice, the overriding problem is how to get from where we are to where we ought to be. Progress toward that goal demands positive and often difficult action by corporations, banks, labor unions, governments, and other major actors on the international stage. But whatever the difficulty, the need to give priority to alleviating poverty in developing countries is undeniable; and the cost of continued inaction can be counted in human lives lost or stunted, talents wasted, opportunities foregone, misery and suffering prolonged, and injustice condoned.

325.Self-restraint and self-criticism by all parties are necessary first steps toward strengthening the international structures to protect the common good. Otherwise, growing interdependence will lead to conflict and increased economic threats to human dignity. This is an important long-term challenge to the economic future of this country and its place in the emerging world economic community.

Chapter V

A COMMITMENT TO THE FUTURE

326.Because Jesus' command to love our neighbor is universal, we hold that the life of each person on this globe is sacred. This commits us to bringing about a just economic order where all, without exception, will be treated with dignity and to working in collaboration with those who share this vision. The world is complex and this may often tempt us to seek simple and self-centered solutions; but as a community of disciples we are called to a new hope and to a new vision that we must live without fear and without oversimplification. Not only must we learn more about our moral responsibility for the larger economic issues that touch the daily life of each and every person on this planet, but we also want to help shape the Church as a model of social and economic justice. Thus, this chapter deals with the Christian vocation in the world today, the special challenges to the Church at this moment of history, ways in which the themes of this letter should be followed up, and a call to the kind of commitment that will be needed to reshape the future.

A. THE CHRISTIAN VOCATION IN THE WORLD TODAY

327.This letter has addressed many matters commonly regarded as secular, for example, employment rates, income levels, and international economic relationships. Yet, the affairs of the world, including economic ones, cannot be separated from the spiritual hunger of the human heart. We have presented the biblical vision of humanity and the Church's moral and religious tradition as a framework for asking the deeper questions about the meaning of economic life and for actively responding to them. But words alone are not enough. The Christian perspective on the meaning of economic life must transform the lives of individuals, families, in fact, our whole culture. The Gospel confers on each Christian the vocation to love God and neighbor in ways that bear fruit in the life of society. That vocation consists above all in a change of heart: a conversion expressed in praise of God and in concrete deeds of justice and service.

1. CONVERSION

328.The transformation of social structures begins with and is always accompanied by a conversion of the heart.[1] As disciples of Christ each of us is called to a deep personal conversion and to "action on behalf of justice and participation in the transformation of the world."[2] By faith and baptism we are fashioned into a "new creature"; we are filled with the Holy Spirit and a new love that compels us to seek out a new profound relationship with God, with the human family, and with all created things.[3] Renouncing self-centered desires, bearing one's daily cross, and imitating Christ's compassion, all involve a personal struggle to control greed and selfishness, a personal commitment to rever-

ence one's own human dignity and the dignity of others by avoiding self-indulgence and those attachments that make us insensitive to the conditions of others and that erode social solidarity. Christ warned us against attachments to material things, against total self-reliance, against the idolatry of accumulating material goods and seeking safety in them. We must take these teachings seriously and in their light examine how each of us lives and acts towards others. But personal conversion is not gained once and for all. It is a process that goes on through our entire life. Conversion, moreover, takes place in the context of a larger faith community: through baptism into the Church, through common prayer, and through our activity with others on behalf of justice.

2. WORSHIP AND PRAYER

329.Challenging U.S. economic life with the Christian vision calls for a deeper awareness of the integral connection between worship and the world of work. Worship and common prayer are the wellsprings that give life to any reflection on economic problems and that continually call the participants to greater fidelity to discipleship. To worship and pray to the God of the universe is to acknowledge that the healing love of God extends to all persons and to every part of existence, including work, leisure, money, economic and political power and their use, and to all those practical policies that either lead to justice or impede it. Therefore, when Christians come together in prayer, they make a commitment to carry God's love into all these areas of life.

330.The unity of work and worship finds expression in a unique way in the Eucharist. As people of a new covenant, the faithful hear God's challenging word proclaimed to them—a message of hope to the poor and oppressed—and they call upon the Holy Spirit to unite all into one body of Christ. For the Eucharist to be a living promise of the fullness of God's Kingdom, the faithful must commit themselves to living as redeemed people with the same care and love for all people that Jesus showed. The body of Christ which worshipers receive in Communion is also a reminder of the reconciling power of his death on the Cross. It empowers them to work to heal the brokenness of society and human relationships and to grow in a spirit of self-giving for others.

331.The liturgy teaches us to have grateful hearts: to thank God for the gift of life, the gift of this earth, and the gift of all people. It turns our hearts from self-seeking to a spirituality that sees the signs of true discipleship in our sharing of goods and working for justice. By uniting us in prayer with all the people of God, with the rich and the poor, with those near and dear, and with those in distant lands, liturgy challenges our way of living and refines our values. Together in the community of worship, we are encouraged to use the goods of this earth for the benefit of all. In

worship and in deeds for justice, the Church becomes a "sacrament," a visible sign of that unity in justice and peace that God wills for the whole of humanity.[4]

3. CALL TO HOLINESS IN THE WORLD

332.Holiness is not limited to the sanctuary or to moments of private prayer; it is a call to direct our whole heart and life toward God and according to God's plan for this world. For the laity holiness is achieved in the midst of the world, in family, in community, in friendships, in work, in leisure, in citizenship. Through their competency and by their activity, lay men and women have the vocation to bring the light of the Gospel to economic affairs, "so that the world may be filled with the Spirit of Christ and may more effectively attain its destiny in justice, in love, and in peace."[5]

333.But as disciples of Christ we must constantly ask ourselves how deeply the biblical and ethical vision of justice and love permeates our thinking. How thoroughly does it influence our way of life? We may hide behind the complexity of the issues or dismiss the significance of our personal contribution; in fact, each one has a role to play, because every day each one makes economic decisions. Some, by reason of their work or their position in society, have a vocation to be involved in a more decisive way in those decisions that affect the economic well-being of others. They must be encouraged and sustained by all in their search for greater justice.

334.At times we will be called upon to say no to the cultural manifestations that emphasize values and aims that are selfish, wasteful, and opposed to the Scriptures. Together we must reflect on our personal and family decisions and curb unnecessary wants in order to meet the needs of others. There are many questions we must keep asking ourselves: Are we becoming ever more wasteful in a "throw-away" society? Are we able to distinguish between our true needs and those thrust on us by advertising and a society that values consumption more than saving? All of us could well ask ourselves whether as a Christian prophetic witness we are not called to adopt a simpler lifestyle, in the face of the excessive accumulation of material goods that characterizes an affluent society.

335.Husbands and wives, in particular, should weigh their needs carefully and establish a proper priority of values as they discuss the questions of both parents working outside the home and the responsibilities of raising children with proper care and attention. At times we will be called as individuals, as families, as parishes, as Church, to identify more closely with the poor in their struggle for participation and to close the gap of understanding between them and the affluent. By sharing the perspectives of those who are suffering, we can come to understand economic and social problems in a deeper way, thus leading us to seek more durable solutions.

336.In the workplace the laity are often called to make tough decisions with little information about the consequences that such decisions have on the economic lives of others. Such times call for collaborative dialogue together with prayerful reflection on Scripture and ethical norms. The same can be said of the need to elaborate policies that will reflect sound ethical principles and that can become a part of our political and social system. Since this is a part of the lay vocation and its call to holiness, the laity must seek to instill a moral and ethical dimension into the public debate on these issues and help enunciate the ethical questions that must be faced. To weigh political options according to criteria that go beyond efficiency and expediency requires prayer, reflection, and dialogue on all the ethical norms involved. Holiness for the laity will involve all the sacrifices needed to lead such a life of prayer and reflection within a worshiping and supporting faith community. In this way the laity will bridge the gap that so easily arises between the moral principles that guide the personal life of the Christian and the considerations that govern decisions in society in the political forum and in the marketplace.

4. LEISURE

337.Some of the difficulty in bringing Christian faith to economic life in the United States today results from the obstacles to establishing a balance of labor and leisure in daily life. Tedious and boring work leads some to look for fulfillment only during time off the job. Others have become "workaholics," people who work compulsively and without reflection on the deeper meaning of life and their actions. The quality and pace of work should be more human in scale enabling people to experience the dignity and value of their work and giving them time for other duties and obligations. This balance is vitally important for sustaining the social, political, educational, and cultural structures of society. The family, in particular, requires such balance. Without leisure there is too little time for nurturing marriages, for developing parent-child relationships, and for fulfilling commitments to other important groups: the extended family, the community of friends, the parish, the neighborhood, schools, and political organizations. Why is it one hears so little today about shortening the work week, especially if both parents are working? Such a change would give them more time for each other, for their children, and for their other social and political responsibilities.
338.Leisure is connected to the whole of one's value system and influenced by the general culture one lives in. It can be trivialized into boredom and laziness, or end in nothing but a desire for greater consumption and waste. For disciples of Christ, the use of leisure may demand being countercultural. The Christian tradition sees in leisure, time to build family and societal relationships and an opportunity for communal prayer and worship, for relaxed contemplation and enjoyment of God's creation, and for the cultivation of the arts which help fill the human longing for wholeness. Most of all, we must be convinced that economic decisions affect our use of leisure and that such decisions are also to be based on moral and ethical considerations. In this area of leisure we must be on our

guard against being swept along by a lack of cultural values and by the changing fads of an affluent society. In the creation narrative God worked six days to create the world and rested on the seventh (Gn 2:1-4). We must take that image seriously and learn how to harmonize action and rest, work and leisure, so that both contribute to building up the person as well as the family and community.

B. CHALLENGES TO THE CHURCH

339.The Church is all the people of God, gathered in smaller faith communities, guided and served by a pope and a hierarchy of bishops, ministered to by priests, deacons, religious, and laity, through visible institutions and agencies. Church is, thus, primarily a communion of people bonded by the Spirit with Christ as their Head, sustaining one another in love, and acting as a sign or sacrament in the world. By its nature it is people called to a transcendent end; but, it is also a visible social institution functioning in this world. According to their calling, members participate in the mission and work of the Church and share, to varying degrees, the responsibility for its institutions and agencies.[6]

At this moment in history, it is particularly important to emphasize the responsibilities of the whole Church for education and family life.

1. EDUCATION

340.We have already emphasized the commitment to quality education that is necessary if the poor are to take their rightful place in the economic structures of our society. We have called the Church to remember its own obligation in this regard and we have endorsed support for improvements in public education.
341.The educational mission of the Church is not only to the poor but to all its members. We reiterate our 1972 statement: "Through education, the Church seeks to prepare its members to proclaim the Good News and to translate this proclamation into action. Since the Christian vocation is a call to transform oneself and society with God's help, the educational efforts of the Church must encompass the twin purposes of personal sanctification and social reform in the light of Christian values."[7] Through her educational mission the Church seeks: to integrate knowledge about this world with revelation about God; to understand God's relationship to the human race and its ultimate destiny in the Kingdom of God; to build up human communities of justice and peace; and to teach the value of all creation. By inculcating these values the educational system of the Church contributes to society and to social justice. Economic questions are, thus, seen as a part of a larger vision of the human person and the human family, the value of this created earth, and the duties and responsibilities that all have toward each other and toward this universe.

342.For these reasons the Church must incorporate into all levels of her educational system the teaching of social justice and the biblical and ethical principles that support it. We call on our universities, in particular, to make Catholic social teaching and the social encyclicals of the popes a part of their curriculum, especially for those whose vocation will call them to an active role in U.S. economic and political decision making. Faith

and technological progress are not opposed one to another, but this progress must not be channeled and directed by greed, self-indulgence, or novelty for its own sake, but by values that respect human dignity and foster social solidarity.
343.The Church has always held that the first task and responsibility for education lies in the hands of parents: they have the right to choose freely the schools or other means necessary to educate their children in the faith.[8] The Church also has consistently held that public authorities must ensure that public subsidies for the education of children are allocated so that parents can freely choose to exercise this right without incurring unjust burdens. This parental right should not be taken from them. We call again for equitable sharing in public benefits for those parents who choose private and religious schools for their children. Such help should be available especially for low-income parents. Though many of these parents sacrifice a great deal for their children's education, others are effectively deprived of the possibility of exercising this right.

2. SUPPORTING THE FAMILY

344.Economic life has a profound effect on all social structures and particularly on the family. A breakdown of family life often brings with it hardship and poverty. Divorce, failure to provide support to mothers and children, abandonment of children, pregnancies out of wedlock, all contribute to the amount of poverty among us. Though these breakdowns of marriage and the family are more visible among the poor, they do not affect only that one segment of our society. In fact, one could argue that many of these breakdowns come from the false values found among the more affluent—values which ultimately pervade the whole of society.
345.More studies are needed to probe the possible connections between affluence and family and marital breakdowns. The constant seeking for self-gratification and the exaggerated individualism of our age, spurred on by false values often seen in advertising and on television, contribute to the lack of firm commitment in marriage and to destructive notions of responsibility and personal growth.[9]
346.With good reason, the Church has traditionally held that the family is the basic building block of any society. In fighting against economic arrangements that weaken the family, the Church contributes to the well-being of society. The same must be said of the Church's teaching on responsible human sexuality and its relationship to marriage and family. Economic arrangements must support the family and promote its solidity.

3. THE CHURCH AS ECONOMIC ACTOR
347.Although all members of the Church are economic actors every day in their individual lives, they also play an economic role united together as Church. On the parish and diocesan level, through its agencies and institutions, the Church employs many people; it has investments; it has extensive properties for worship and mission. *All the moral principles that govern the just operation of any economic endeavor apply to the Church and its agencies and institutions; indeed the Church should be exemplary.* The Synod of Bishops in 1971 worded this challenge most aptly:

"While the Church is bound to give witness to justice, she recognizes that anyone who ventures to speak to people about justice must first be just in their eyes. Hence, we must undertake an examination of the modes of acting and of the possessions and lifestyle found within the Church herself."[10]

348.Catholics in the United States can be justly proud of their accomplishments in building and maintaining churches and chapels, and an extensive system of schools, hospitals, and charitable institutions. Through sacrifices and personal labor our immigrant ancestors built these institutions. For many decades religious orders of women and men taught in our schools and worked in our hospitals with very little remuneration. Right now, we see the same spirit of generosity among the religious and lay people even as we seek to pay more adequate salaries.

349.We would be insincere were we to deny a need for renewal in the economic life of the Church itself and for renewed zeal on the part of the Church in examining its role in the larger context of reinforcing in U.S. society and culture those values that support economic justice.[11]

350.We select here five areas for special reflection: (1) wages and salaries, (2) rights of employees, (3) investments and property, (4) works of charity, and (5) working for economic justice.

351.We bishops commit ourselves to the principle that those who serve the Church—laity, clergy, and religious—should receive a sufficient livelihood and the social benefits provided by responsible employers in our nation. These obligations, however, cannot be met without the increased contributions of all the members of the Church. We call on all to recognize their responsibility to contribute monetarily to the support of those who carry out the public mission of the Church. Sacrificial giving or tithing by all the People of God would provide the funds necessary to pay these adequate salaries for religious and lay people; the lack of funds is the usual underlying cause for the lack of adequate salaries. The obligation to sustain the Church's institutions—education and health care, social service agencies, religious education programs, care of the elderly, youth ministry, and the like—falls on all the members of the community because of their baptism; the obligation is not just on the users or on those who staff them. Increased resources are also needed for the support of elderly members of religious communities. These dedicated women and men have not always asked for or received the stipends and pensions that would have assured their future. It would be a breach of our obligations to them to let them or their communities face retirement without adequate funds.

352.Many volunteers provide services to the Church and its mission which cannot be measured in dollars and cents. These services are important to the life and vitality of the Church in the United States and carry on a practice that has marked the history of the Church in this country since its founding. In this tradition, we ask young people to make themselves available for a year or more of voluntary service before beginning their training for more specific vocations in life; we also recommend expanding voluntary service roles for retired persons; we encourage those who have accepted this challenge.

353.All church institutions must also fully recognize the rights of employees to organize and bargain collectively with the institution through whatever association or organization they freely choose.[12] In the light of new creative models of collaboration between labor and management described earlier in this letter, we challenge our church institutions to adopt new fruitful modes of cooperation. Although the Church has its own nature and mission that must be respected and fostered, we are pleased that many who are not of our faith, but who share similar hopes and aspirations for the human family, work for us and with us in achieving this vision. In seeking greater justice in wages, we recognize the need to be alert particularly to the continuing discrimination against women throughout Church and society, especially reflected in both the inequities of salaries between women and men and in the concentration of women in jobs at the lower end of the wage scale.

354.Individual Christians who are shareholders and those responsible within church institutions that own stocks in U.S. corporations must see to it that the invested funds are used responsibly. Although it is a moral and legal fiduciary responsibility of the trustees to ensure an adequate return on investment for the support of the work of the Church, their stewardship embraces broader moral concerns. As part-owners, they must cooperate in shaping the policies of those companies through dialogue with management, through votes at corporate meetings, through the introduction of resolutions, and through participation in investment decisions. We praise the efforts of dioceses and other religious and ecumenical bodies that work together toward these goals. We also praise efforts to develop alternative investment policies, especially those which support enterprises that promote economic development in depressed communities and which help the Church respond to local and regional needs.[13] When the decision to divest seems unavoidable, it should be done after prudent examination and with a clear explanation of the motives.

355.The use of church property demands special attention today. Changing demographic patterns have left many parishes and institutions with empty or partially used buildings. The decline in the number of religious who are teaching in the schools and the reduction in the number of clergy often result in large residences with few occupants. In this regard, the Church must be sensitive to the image the possession of such large facilities often projects, namely, that it is wealthy and extravagant in the use of its resources. This image can be overcome only by clear public accountability of its financial holdings, of its properties and their use, and of the services it renders to its members and to society at large. We support and encourage the creative use of these facilities by many parishes and dioceses to serve the needs of the poor.

356.The Church has a special call to be a servant of the poor, the sick, and the marginalized, thereby becoming a true sign of the Church's mission—a mission shared by every member of the Christian community. The Church now serves many such people through one of the largest private human services delivery systems in the country. The networks of agencies, institutions, and programs provide services to millions of persons of all faiths. Still we must be reminded that in our day our Christian concerns must increase and extend beyond our borders, because everyone in need is our neighbor. We must also be reminded that charity requires more than alleviating misery. It demands genuine love for the person in need. It should probe the meaning of suffering and provoke a response that seeks to remedy causes. True charity leads to advocacy.

357.Yet charity alone is not a corrective to all economic social ills. All citizens, working through various organizations of society and through government, bear the responsibility of caring for those who are in need. The Church, too, through all its members individually and through its agencies, must work to alleviate injustices that prevent some from participating fully in economic life. Our experience with the Campaign for Human Development confirms our judgment about the validity of self-help and empowerment of the poor. The campaign, which has received the positive support of American Catholics since it was launched in 1970, provides a model that we think sets a high standard for similar efforts. We bishops know of the many faithful in all walks of life who use their skills and their compassion to seek innovative ways to carry out the goals we are proposing in this letter. As they do this, they *are* the Church acting for economic justice. At the same time, we hope they will join together with us and their priests to influence our society so that even more steps can be taken to alleviate injustices. Grassroots efforts by the poor themselves, helped by community support, are indispensable. The entire Christian community can learn much from the way our deprived brothers and sisters assist each other in their struggles.

358.In addition to being an economic actor, the Church is a significant cultural actor concerned about the deeper cultural roots of our economic problems. As we have proposed a new experiment in collaboration and participation in decision making by all those affected at all levels of U. S. society, so we also commit the Church to become a model of collaboration and participation.

C. THE ROAD AHEAD

359.The completion of a letter such as this one is but the beginning of a long process of education, discussion and action; its contents must be brought to all members of the Church and of society.

360.In this respect we mentioned the twofold aim of this pastoral letter: to help Catholics form their consciences on the moral dimensions of economic decision making and to articulate a moral perspective in the general societal and political debate that surrounds these questions. These two purposes help us to reflect on the different ways the institutions and ministers of the Church can assist the laity in their vocation in the world. Renewed emphasis on Catholic social teaching in our schools, colleges, and universities; special seminars with corporate officials, union leaders, legislators, bankers, and the like; the organization of small groups composed of people from different ways of life to meditate together on the Gospel and ethical norms; speakers' bureaus; family programs; clearinghouses of available material; pulpit aids for priests; diocesan television and radio programs; research projects in our universities—all of these are appropriate means for continued discussion and action. Some of these are done best on the parish level, others by the state Catholic conferences, and others by the National Conference of Catholic Bishops. These same bodies can assist the laity in the many difficult decisions that deal with political options that affect economic decisions. Where many options are available, it must be the concern of all in such debates that we as Catholics do not become polarized. All must be challenged to show how the decisions they make and the policies they suggest flow from the ethical moral vision outlined here. As new problems arise, we hope through our continual reflection that we will be able to help refine Catholic social teaching and contribute to its further development.

*361.*We call upon our priests, in particular, to continue their study of these issues, so that they can proclaim the gospel message in a way that not only challenges the faithful but also sustains and encourages their vocation in and to the world. Priestly formation in our seminaries will also have to prepare candidates for this role.

*362.*We wish to emphasize the need to undertake research into many of the areas this document could not deal with in depth and to continue exploration of those we have dealt with. We encourage our Catholic universities, foundations, and other institutions to assist in these necessary projects. The following areas for further research are merely suggestive, not exhaustive: the impact of arms production and large military spending on the domestic economy and on culture; arms production and sales as they relate to Third World poverty; tax reforms to express the preferential option for the poor; the rights of women and minorities in the work force; the development of communications technology and its global influences; robotics, automation, and reduction

of defense industries as they will affect employment; the economy and the stability of the family; legitimate profit versus greed; securing economic rights; environmental and ecological questions; future roles of labor and unions; international financial institutions and Third World debt; our national deficit; world food problems; "full employment" and its implementation; plant closings and dealing with the human costs of an evolving economy; cooperatives and new modes of sharing; welfare reform and national eligibility standards; income support systems; concentration of land ownership; assistance to Third World nations; migration and its effects; population policies and development; the effects of increased inequality of incomes in society.

D. COMMITMENT TO A KINGDOM OF LOVE AND JUSTICE

*363.*Confronted by this economic complexity and seeking clarity for the future, we can rightly ask ourselves one single question: How does our economic system affect the lives of people—*all* people? Part of the American dream has been to make this world a better place for people to live in; at this moment of history that dream must include everyone on this globe. Since we profess to be members of a "catholic" or universal Church, we all must raise our sights to a concern for the well-being of everyone in the world. Third World debt becomes our problem. Famine and starvation in sub-Saharan Africa become our concern. Rising military expenditures everywhere in the world become part of our fears for the future of this planet. We cannot be content if we see ecological neglect or the squandering of natural resources. In this letter we bishops have spoken often of economic interdependence; now is the moment when all of us must confront the reality of such economic bonding and its consequences and see it as a moment of grace—a

kairos—that can unite all of us in a common community of the human family. We commit ourselves to this global vision.

*364.*We cannot be frightened by the magnitude and complexity of these problems. We must not be discouraged. In the midst of this struggle, it is inevitable that we become aware of greed, laziness, and envy. No utopia is possible on this earth; but as believers in the redemptive love of God and as those who have experienced God's forgiving mercy, we know that God's providence is not and will not be lacking to us today.

*365.*The fulfillment of human needs, we know, is not the final purpose of the creation of the human person. We have been created to share in the divine life through a destiny that goes far beyond our human capabilities and before which we must in all humility stand in awe. Like Mary in proclaiming her *Magnificat*, we marvel at the wonders God has done for us, how God has raised up the poor and the lowly and promised great things for them in the Kingdom. God now asks of us sacrifices and reflection on our reverence for human dignity—in ourselves and in others—and on our service and discipleship, so that the divine goal for the human family and this earth can be fulfilled. Communion with God, sharing God's life, involves a mutual bonding with all on this globe. Jesus taught us to love God and one another and that the concept of neighbor is without limit. We know that we are called to be members of a new covenant of love. We have to move from our devotion to independence, through an understanding of interdependence, to a commitment to human solidarity. That challenge must find its realization in the kind of community we build among us. Love implies concern for all—especially the poor—and a continued search for those social and economic structures that permit everyone to share in a community that is a part of a redeemed creation (Rom 8:21-23).

END NOTES

CHAPTER I

[1] Vatican Council II, *The Pastoral Constitution on the Church in the Modern World*, 33. [Note: This pastoral letter frequently refers to documents of the Second Vatican Council, papal encyclicals, and other official teachings of the Roman Catholic Church. Most of these texts have been published by the United States Catholic Conference Office of Publishing and Promotion Services; many are available in collections, though no single collection is comprehensive. See Selected Bibliography.]

[2] *Pastoral Constitution*, 1.

[3] See ibid., 10, 42, 43; Congregation for the Doctrine of the Faith, *Instruction on Christian Freedom and Liberation*, (Washington, D.C.: USCC Office of Publishing and Promotion Services, 1986), 34-36.

[4] See Pope John Paul II, *On Human Work* (1981), 14; and Pope Paul VI, *Octogesima Adveniens* (1971), 35. See also Arthur Okun, *Equality and Efficiency: The Big Tradeoff* (Washington, D.C.: The Brookings Institution, 1975), ch. 1; Michael Walzer, *Spheres of Justice: A Defense of Pluralism and Equality* (New York: Basic Books, 1983), ch. 4; Jon P. Gunnemann, "Capitalism and Commutative Justice," paper presented at the 1985 meeting of the Society of Christian Ethics.

[5] Abraham Lincoln, Address at Dedication of National Cemetery at Gettysburg, November 19, 1863.

[6] Pope John XXIII, *Peace on Earth* (1963), 130-131.

[7] Synod of Bishops, *Justice in the World* (1971), 8; Pope John Paul II, *Redeemer of Man* (1979), 15.

[8] U.S. Department of Labor, Bureau of Labor Statistics, *The Employment Situation: August 1985* (September 1985), Table A-1.

[9] Ibid.

[10] U.S. Bureau of the Census, Current Population Reports, Series P-60, 145, *Money Income and Poverty Status of Families and Persons in the United States: 1983* (Washington, D.C.: U.S. Government Printing Office, 1984), 20.

[11] Greg H. Duncan, *Years of Poverty, Years of Plenty: The Changing Economic Fortunes of American Workers and Their Families* (Ann Arbor, Mich.: Institute for Social Research, University of Michigan, 1984).

[12] See Pope John Paul II, *Familiaris Consortio* (1981), 46.

[13] *Pastoral Constitution*, 47.

[14] National Conference of Catholic Bishops, *The Challenge of Peace: God's Promise and Our Response* (Washington, D.C.: USCC Office of Publishing and Promotion Services, 1983).

[15] Cardinal Joseph L. Bernardin and Cardinal John J. O'Connor, Testimony before the House Foreign Relations Committee, June 26, 1984, *Origins* 14:10 (August 10, 1984): 157.

[16] *Pastoral Constitution*, 43.

[17] See, for example, Peter Berger, Brigitte Berger, and Hansfried Kellner, *The Homeless Mind: Modernization and Consciousness* (New York: Vintage, 1974).

[18] For a recent study of the importance and difficulty of achieving such a common language and vision see Robert N. Bellah, Richard Madsen, William M. Sullivan, Ann Swidler, and Stephen M. Tipton, *Habits of the Heart: Individualism and Commitment in American Life* (Berkeley, Calif.: University of California Press, 1985). See also Martin E. Marty, *The Public Church* (New York: Crossroads, 1981).

[19] Pope John XXIII, *Mater et Magistra* (1961), 219; *Pastoral Constitution*, 40.

[20] Congregation for the Doctrine of the Faith, *Instruction on Certain Aspects of the Theology of Liberation* (Washington, D.C.: USCC Office of Publishing and Promotion Services, 1984); Pope Paul VI, *Octogesima Adveniens* (1971), 42.

[21] *Octogesima Adveniens*, 4.

[22] Administrative Committee of the National Catholic War Council, *Program of Social Reconstruction*, February 12, 1919. Other notable statements on the economy are our predecessors are *The Present Crisis*, April 25, 1933; *Statement on Church and Social Order*, February 4, 1940; *The Economy: Human Dimensions*, November 20, 1975. These and numerous other statements of the U.S. Catholic episcopate can be found in Hugh J. Nolan, ed., *Pastoral Letters of the United States Catholic Bishops*, 4 vols. (Washington, D.C.: USCC Office of Publishing and Promotion Services, 1984).

CHAPTER II

[1] *Mater et Magistra*, 219-220. See *Pastoral Constitution*, 63.

[2] Vatican Council II, *Decree on Ecumenism*, 22-23.

[3] C. Westermann, *Creation* (Philadelphia: Fortress Press, 1974); and B. Vawter, *On Genesis: A New Reading* (Garden City, N.Y.: Doubleday, 1977). See also *Pastoral Constitution*, 34.

[4] St. Cyprian, *On Works and Almsgiving*, 25, trans. R. J. Deferrari, *St. Cyprian: Treatises*, 36 (New York: Fathers of the Church, 1958), 251. Original text in Migne, *Patrologia Latina*, vol. 4, 620. On the Patristic teaching, see C. Avila, *Ownership: Early Christian Teaching* (Maryknoll, N.Y.: Orbis Books, 1983). Collection of original texts and translations.

[5] T. Ogletree, *The Use of the Bible in Christian Ethics* (Philadelphia: Fortress Press, 1983), 47-85.

[6] Though scholars debate whether the Jubilee was a historical institution or an ideal, its images were continually evoked to stress God's sovereignty over the land and God's concern for the poor and the oppressed (e.g., Is 61:1-2; Lk 4:16-19). See R. North, *Sociology of the Biblical Jubilee* (Rome: Biblical Institute, 1954); S. Ringe, *Jesus, Liberation and the Biblical Jubilee: Images for Ethics and Christology* (Philadelphia: Fortress Press, 1985).

[7] On justice, see J. R. Donahue, "Biblical Perspectives on Justice," in Haughey, ed., *The Faith That Does Justice* (New York: Paulist Press,

1977), 68-112; and S. C. Mott, *Biblical Ethics and Social Change* (New York: Oxford University Press, 1982).

[8] See Ex 22:20-26; Dt 15:1-11; Jb 22:12-17; Pss 69:34; 72:2, 4, 12-24; 82:3-4; Prv 14:21, 31; Is 3:14-15; 10:2; Jer 22:16; Zec 7:9-10.

[9] J. Pedersen, *Israel: Its Life and Culture*, vol. I-II (London: Oxford University Press, 1926), 337-340.

[10] J. Alfaro, *Theology of Justice in the World* (Rome: Pontifical Commission on Justice and Peace, 1973), 40-41; E. McDonagh, *The Making of Disciples* (Wilmington, Del.: Michael Glazier, 1982), 119.

[11] Pope John Paul II has drawn on this parable to exhort us to have a "compassionate heart" to those in need in his Apostolic Letter "On the Christian Meaning of Human Suffering" (*Salvifici Doloris*) (Washington, D.C.: USCC Office of Publishing and Promotion Services, 1984), 34-39.

[12] *Redeemer of Man*, 21.

[13] Address to Workers at Sao Paulo, 8, *Origins* 10:9 (July 31, 1980): 139; and Address at Yankee Stadium, *Origins* 9:19 (October 25, 1979): 311-312.

[14] J. Dupont and A. George, eds., *La pauvrete evangelique* (Paris: Cerf, 1971); M. Hengel, *Property and Riches in the Early Church* (Philadelphia: Fortress Press, 1974); L. Johnson, *Sharing Possessions: Mandate and Symbol of Faith* (Philadelphia: Fortress Press, 1981); D. L. Mealand, *Poverty and Expectation in the Gospels* (London: SPCK, 1980); W. Pilgrim, *Good News to the Poor: Wealth and Poverty in Luke-Acts* (Minneapolis: Augsburg, 1981); and W. Stegemann, *The Gospel and the Poor* (Philadelphia: Fortress Press, 1984).

[15] See Am 4:1-3; Jb 20:19; Sir 13:4-7; Jas 2:6; 5:1-6; Rv 18:11-19.

[16] See paras. 86-90.

[17] See Selected Bibliography.

[18] Extraordinary Synod of Bishops (1985) *The Final Report*, II, A (Washington, D.C.: USCC Office of Publishing and Promotion Services, 1986).

[19] Pope Paul VI, *On Evangelization in the Modern World*, 31.

[20] Ibid., 24.

[21] *Pastoral Constitution*, 32.

[22] Ibid., 25.

[23] See para. 39.

[24] Josef Pieper, *The Four Cardinal Virtues* (Notre Dame, Ind.: University of Notre Dame Press, 1966), 43-116; David Hollenbach, "Modern Catholic Teachings concerning Justice," in John C. Haughey ed., *The Faith That Does Justice* (New York: Paulist Press, 1977), 207-231.

[25] Jon P. Gunnemann, "Capitalism and Commutative Justice," presented at the 1985 meeting of the Society of Christian Ethics, forthcoming in *The Annual of the Society of Christian Ethics*.

[26] *Pastoral Constitution*, 69.

[27] Pope Pius XI, *Divini Redemptoris*, 51. See John A. Ryan, *Distributive Justice*, third edition (New York: Macmillan, 1942), 188. The term "social justice" has been used in several different but related ways in the Catholic ethical tradition. See William Ferree, "The Act of Social Justice," *Philosophical Studies*, vol. 72 (Washington, D.C.: The Catholic University of America Press, 1943).

[28] *On Human Work*, 6, 9.

[29] *Pastoral Constitution*, 29.

[30] Ibid. See below, paras. 180-182.

[31] Pope Paul VI, *On the Development of Peoples* (1967), 19.

[32] *Mater et Magistra*, 132.

[33] *Justice in the World*, 10, 16; and *Octogesima Adveniens*, 15.

[34] *Pastoral Constitution*, 25; *Justice in the World*, 51; Pope John Paul II, *The Gift of the Redemption* Apostolic Exhortation on Reconciliation and Penance (Washington, D.C: USCC Office of Publishing and Promotion Services, 1984), 16; Congregation for the Doctrine of the Faith, *Instruction on Christian Freedom and Liberation*, 42, 74.

[35] In the words of the 1971 Synod of Bishops: "Participation constitutes a right which is to be applied in the economic and in the social and political field," *Justice in the World*, 18.

[36] *Pastoral Constitution*, 26.

[37] Pope John Paul II, Address at the General Assembly of the United Nations (October 2, 1979), 13, 14.

[38] See Pope Pius XII, 1941 Pentecost Address, in V. Yzermans, *The Major Addresses of Pope Pius XII*, vol. I (St. Paul: North Central, 1961), 32-33.

[39] *Peace on Earth*, 8-27. See *On Human Work*, 18-19. *Peace on Earth* and other modern papal statements refer explicitly to the "right to work" as one of the fundamental economic rights. Because of the ambiguous meaning of the phrase in the United States, and also because the ordinary way people earn their living in our society is through paid employment, the NCCB has affirmed previously that the protection of human dignity demands that the right to useful employment be secured for all who are able and willing to work. See NCCB, *The Economy: Human Dimensions* (November 20, 1975), 5, in NCCB, *Justice in the Marketplace*, 470. See also Congregation for the Doctrine of the Faith, *Instruction on Christian Freedom and Liberation*, 85.

[40] *The Development of Peoples*, 14.

[41] Martha H. Good, "Freedom from Want: The Failure of United States Courts to Protect Subsistence Rights," *Human Rights Quarterly* 6 (1984): 335-365.

[42] *Pastoral Constitution*, 43.

[43] *Mater et Magistra*, 65.

[44] On the recent use of this term see: Congregation for the Doctrine of the Faith, *Instruction on Christian Freedom and Liberation*, 46-50, 66-68; *Evangelization in Latin America's Present and Future*, Final Document of the Third General Conference of the Latin American Episcopate (Puebla, Mexico, January 27-February 13, 1979), esp. part VI, ch. 1, "A Preferential Option for the Poor," in J. Eagleson and P. Scharper, eds., *Puebla and Beyond* (Maryknoll: Orbis Books, 1979), 264-267; Donal Dorr, *Option for the Poor: A Hundred Years of Vatican*

Social Teaching (Dublin: Gill and Macmillan/Maryknoll, N.Y.: Orbis Books, 1983).

45 *Octogesima Adveniens,* 23.

46 Address to Bishops of Brazil, 6, 9, *Origins* 10:9 (July 31, 1980): 135.

47 Pope John Paul II, Address to Workers at Sao Paulo, 4, *Origins,* 10:9 (July 31, 1980): 138; Congregation for the Doctrine of the Faith, *Instruction on Christian Freedom and Liberation,* 66-68.

48 *Pastoral Constitution,* 47.

49 Address on Christian Unity in a Technological Age (Toronto, September 14, 1984) in *Origins* 14:16 (October 4, 1984): 248.

50 *On Human Work,* 3.

51 Ibid., 5, 6.

52 Ibid., 6, 10.

53 *Quadragesimo Anno,* 79. The meaning of this principle is not always accurately understood. For studies of its interpretation in Catholic teaching see: Calvez and Perrin in John F. Cronin, *Catholic Social Principles,* (Milwaukee: Bruce, 1950), 328-342; Johannes Messner, "Freedom as a Principle of Social Order: An Essay in the Substance of Subsidiary Function," *Modern Schoolman* 28 (1951): 97-110; Richard E. Mulcahy, "Subsidiarity," *New Catholic Encyclopedia* vol. 13 (New York: McGraw-Hill, 1966), 762; Franz H. Mueller, "The Principle of Subsidiarity in Christian Tradition," *American Catholic Sociological Review)* 4 (October 1943): 144-157; Oswald von Nell-Breuning, "Zur Sozialreform, Erwagungen zum Subsidiaritatsprinzip," *Stimmen der Zeit* 157, Bd. 81 (1955-1956): 1-11; id., "Subsidiarity," *Sacramentum Mundi,* vol. 6 (New York: Herder and Herder, 1970), 6, 114-116; Arthur Fridolin Utz, *Formen und Grenzen des Subsidiaritatsprinzips* (Heidelberg: F. H. Kerle Verlag, 1956); id., "The Principle of Subsidiarity and Contemporary Natural Law," *Natural Law Forum* 3 (1958): 170-183; id., *Grundsatze der Sozialpolitik: Solidaritat und Subsidiaritat in der Alterversicherung* (Stuttgart: Sewald Verlag, 1969).

54 *Pastoral Constitution,* 31.

55 *On Human Work,* 16.

56 *Rerum Novarum,* 62; see also 9.

57 *On Human Work,* 19.

58 Ibid., 20.

59 Ibid.

60 Ibid.

61 Pope John Paul II, Address to Business Men and Economic Managers (Milan, May 22, 1983) in *L'Osservatore Romano,* weekly edition in English (June 20, 1983): 9:1.

62 Thomas Aquinas, *Summa Theologiae,* IIa, IIae, q. 66.

63 As Pope John Paul II has stated: "This gigantic and powerful instrument—the whole collection of the means of production that in a sense are considered synonymous with 'capital'—is the result of work and bears the signs of human labor" *On Human Work,* 12.

64 *Rerum Novarum,* 10, 15, 36.

65 *Mater et Magistra,* 109.

66 *Rerum Novarum,* 65, 66; *Mater et Magistra,* 115.

67 *On the Development of Peoples,* 23.

68 Pope John Paul II, Opening Address at the Puebla Conference (Puebla, Mexico, January 28, 1979) in John Eagleson and Philip Scharper, eds., *Puebla and Beyond,* 67.

69 *On Human Work,* 14.

70 Ibid., 17.

71 *Divini Redemptoris,* 49.

72 *Peace on Earth,* 60-62.

73 Vatican Council II, *Declaration on Religious Freedom (Dignitatis Humanae),* 6. See John Courtney Murray, *The Problem of Religious Freedom,* Woodstock Papers, no. 7 (Westminster, Md.: Newman Press, 1965).

74 *Peace on Earth,* 63-64. *Quadragesimo Anno,* 80. In *Rerum Novarum* Pope Leo XIII set down the basic norm that determines when government intervention is called for: "If, therefore, any injury has been done to or threatens either the common good or the interests of individual groups, which injury cannot in any other way be repaired or prevented, it is necessary for public authority to intervene" *Rerum Novarum,* 52. Pope John XXIII synthesized the Church's understanding of the function of governmental intervention this way: "The State, whose purpose is the realization of the common good in the temporal order, can by no means disregard the economic activity of its citizens. Indeed it should be present to promote in suitable manner the production of a sufficient supply of material goods, . . . contribute actively to the betterment of the living conditions of workers, . . . see to it that labor agreements are entered into according to the norms of justice and equity, and that in the environment of work the dignity of the human being is not violated either in body or spirit" *Mater et Magistra,* 20-21.

75 *Quadragesimo Anno,* 79.

76 Preface for the Feast of Christ the King, *The Sacramentary of the Roman Missal.*

77 *Octogesima Adveniens,* 26-35.

78 *Pastoral Constitution,* 39.

79 Ibid.

80 *Octogesima Adveniens,* 42.

CHAPTER III

1 *Octogesima Adveniens,* 26-41; and *On Human Work,* 7, 13.

2 *Program of Social Reconstruction,* 33-40.

3 See *The Challenge of Peace: God's Promise and Our Response,* 9-10.

4 *On Human Work,* 3.

5 U.S. Department of Labor, Bureau of Labor Statistics, *The Employment Situation: April 1986* (May 1986).

6 Full Employment Action Council, *Employment in America: Illusory Recovery in a Decade of Decline* (Washington, D.C., February 1985),

19. Calculations based on data from the U.S. Department of Labor's Bureau of Labor Statistics.

7 U.S. Department of Labor, Bureau of Labor Statistics, *The Employment Situation: August 1985;* and U. S. Department of Labor, Employment and Training Administration, *Unemployment Insurance Claims,* Reference week of June 22, 1985.

8 *The Employment Situation: August 1985.*

9 Brenner, "Fetal, Infant and Maternal Mortality during Periods of Economic Instability," *International Journal of Health Services* (Summer 1973); P. H. Ellison, "Neurology of Hard Times," *Clinical Pediatrics* (March 1977); S. V. Kasl and S. Cobb, "Some Mental Health Consequences of Plant Closings and Job Loss," in L. Ferman and J. P. Gordus, eds., *Mental Health and the Economy* (Kalamazoo, Mich.: W. E. Upjohn Institute for Employment Research, 1979), 255-300; L. E. Kopolow and F. M. Ochberg, "Spinoff from a Downward Swing," *Mental Health* 59 (Summer 1975); D. Shaw, "Unemployment Hurts More than the Pocketbook," *Today's Health* (March 1978).

10 Richard M. Cohn, *The Consequences of Unemployment on Evaluation of Self,* Doctoral dissertation, Department of Psychology (University of Michigan, 1977); John A. Garraty, *Unemployment in History: Economic Thought and Public Policy* (New York: Harper and Row, 1978); Harry Maurer, *Not Working: An Oral History of the Unemployed* (New York: Holt, Rinehart, and Winston, 1979).

11 M. Harvey Brenner, *Estimating the Social Cost of National Economic Policy* (U.S. Congress, Joint Economic Committee, 1976); see Brenner, *Mental Illness and the Economy* (Cambridge, Mass.: Harvard University Press, 1973).

12 Congressional Budget Office, *Economic and Budget Outlook: FY 1986—FY 1990* (Washington, D.C., February 1985), 75.

13 *Correlation of Unemployment and Federal Prison Population* (Washington, D.C.: U.S. Bureau of Prisons, March 1975); M. Yeager, "Unemployment and Imprisonment," *Journal of Criminal Law and Criminology* 70:4 (1979); Testimony of M. H. Brenner in *Unemployment and Crime* (U.S. Congress, House Hearings, 1977,) 25.

14 Committee on the Evolution of Work, AFL-CIO, *The Future of Work* (Washington, D.C.: AFL-CIO, 1983), 11.

15 Congressional Budget Office, *Defense Spending and the Economy* (Washington, D.C.: Government Printing Office, 1983). See also Michael Edelstein, *The Economic Impact of Military Spending* (New York: Council on Economic Priorities, 1977); and Robert De Grasse, Jr., *Military Expansion, Economic Decline* (New York: Council on Economic Priorities, 1983). See also U.S. Department of Labor, Bureau of Labor Statistics Report, "Structure of the U.S. Economy in 1980 and 1985" (Washington, D.C.: Government Printing Office, 1975); and Marion Anderson, *The Empty Pork Barrel* (Lansing, Mich.: Employment Research Associates, 1982).

16 U.S. Office of Management and Budget, *Historical Tables,* Budget of the United States Government Fiscal Year 1986 (Washington, D.C.: U.S. Government Printing Office, 1985). Table 10.2, 10.2(3). See also, National Science Foundation Report, "Characteristics of Experienced Scientists and Engineers" (1978), Detailed Statistical Tables (Washington, D.C.: U.S. Government Printing Office, 1978).

17 "Statistical Supplement to International Comparison of Unemployment," Bureau of Labor Statistics, (May 1984): 7. Unpublished.

18 Isabel V. Sawhill and Charles F. Stone state the prevailing view among economists this way: "High employment is usually defined as the rate of unemployment consistent with no additional inflation, a rate currently believed by many, but not all, economists to be in the neighborhood of 6 percent." "The Economy: The Key to Success," in John L. Palmer and Isabel V. Sawhill, eds., *The Reagan Record: An Assessment of America's Changing Domestic Priorities* (Cambridge, Mass.: Bollinger, 1984), 72. See also Stanley Fischer and Rudiger Dornbusch, *Economics* (New York: McGraw-Hill, 1983), 731-743.

19 W. L. Birch, "Who Creates Jobs?," *The Public Interest* 65 (Fall 1981): 3-14.

20 Martin Neil Baily and Arthur M. Okun, eds., *The Battle Against Unemployment and Inflation,* third edition (New York: Norton, 1982); and Martin Neil Baily, "Labor Market Performance, Competition and Inflation," in Baily, ed., *Workers, Jobs and Inflation* (Washington, D.C.: The Brookings Institution, 1982). See also, Lawrence Klein, "Reducing Unemployment Without Inflation"; and James Tobin, "Unemployment, Poverty, and Economic Policy," testimony before the Subcommittee on Economic Stabilization, U.S. House of Representatives Committee on Banking, Finance and Urban Affairs (March 19, 1985), serial no. 99-5 (Washington, D.C.: U.S. Government Printing Office, 1985), 15-18, 31-33.

21 Tobin, "Unemployment, Poverty, and Economic Policy"; and Klein, "Reducing Unemployment Without Inflation."

22 Robert H. Haveman, "Toward Efficiency and Equity through Direct Job Creation," *Social Policy* 11:1 (May/June 1980): 48.

23 William H. McCarthy, *Reducing Urban Unemployment: What Works at the Local Level* (Washington, D.C.: National League of Cities, October 1985); William Schweke, "States that Take the Lead on a New Industrial Policy," in Betty G. Lall, ed., *Economic Dislocation and Job Loss* (New York: Cornell University, New York State School of Industrial and Labor Relations, 1985), 97-106; David Robinson, *Training and Jobs Programs in Action: Case Studies in Private Sector Initiatives for the Hard to Employ* (New York: Committee for Economic Development, 1978). See also ch. IV of this pastoral letter.

24 Rudy Oswald, "The Economy and Workers' Jobs, The Living Wage and a Voice," in John W. Houch and Oliver F. Williams, eds., *Catholic Social Teaching and the U.S. Economy: Working Papers for a Bishops' Pastoral* (Washington, D.C.: University Press of America, 1984), 77-89. On the subject of shortening the work week, Oswald points out that in the first 40 years of this century, the average work week fell from 60 hours to 40 hours. However, the standard work week has been unchanged now for almost 50 years.

25 U.S. Bureau of the Census, Current Population Reports, Series P-60, no. 149, *Money Income and Poverty Status of Families in the United States: 1984* (Washington, D.C.: U.S. Government Printing Office, 1985).

26 Massachusetts Department of Public Health, *Massachusetts Nutrition Survey* (Boston, Mass.: 1983).

27 There is considerable debate about the most suitable definition of poverty. Some argue that the government's official definition understates the number of the poor, and that a more adequate definition would indicate that as many as 50 million Americans are poor. For example, they note that the poverty line has declined sharply as a percent of median family income—from 48% in 1959 to 35% in 1983. Others argue that the official indicators should be reduced by the amount of in-kind benefits received by the poor, such as food stamps. By some calculations that would reduce the number counted as poor to about 12 million. We conclude that for present purposes the official government definition provides a suitable middle ground. That definition is based on a calculation that multiplies the cost of USDA's lowest cost food plan times three. The definition is adjusted for inflation each year.

Among other reasons for using the official definition is that it allows one to compare poverty figures over time. For additional readings on this topic see: L. Rainwater, *What Money Buys: Inequality and the Social Meanings of Income* (New York: Basic Books, 1975); id., *Persistent and Transitory Poverty: A New Look* (Cambridge, Mass.: Joint Center for Urban Studies, 1980); M. Orshansky, "How Poverty is Measured," *Monthly Labor Review* 92 (1969): 37-41; M. Anderson, *Welfare* (Stanford, Calif.: Hoover Institution Press, 1978); and Michael Harrington, *The New American Poverty* (New York: Holt, Rinehart, and Winston, 1984), 81-82.

28 Of those in poverty, 3 million work year-round and are still poor. Of the 22.2 million poor who are 15 years or over, more than 9 million work sometime during the year. Since 1979, the largest increases of poverty in absolute terms have been among those who work and are still poor. U.S. Bureau of the Census, *Money, Income and Poverty*.

29 U.S. Bureau of the Census, Current Population Reports, series P-60, no. 149, 19. Blacks make up about 12% of the entire population but 62% of the long-term poor. Only 19% of the overall population live in families headed by women, but they make up 61% of the long-term poor. Twenty-eight percent of the nation's total population reside in nonmetropolitan areas, but 34% of the nation's poor live in these areas.

30 G. J. Duncan et al., *Years of Poverty, Years of Plenty: The Changing Economic Fortunes of American Workers and Their Families* (Ann Arbor, Mich.: Institute for Social Research, The University of Michigan, 1984). This book is based on the Panel Study of Income Dynamics, a survey of 5,000 American families conducted annually by the Survey Research Center of the University of Michigan. See G. J. Duncan and J. N. Morgan, *Five Thousand American Families—Patterns of Economic Progress* vol. III (Ann Arbor: University of Michigan, 1975).

31 Congressional Research Service and Congressional Budget Office, *Children in Poverty* (Washington, D.C., May 22, 1985), 57. This recent study also indicates that children are now the largest age group in poverty. We are the first industrialized nation in the world in which children are the poorest age group. See Daniel Patrick Moynihan, *Family and Nation* (New York: Harcourt, Brace, Jovanovich, 1986), 112.

32 Children's Defense Fund, *American Children in Poverty* (Washington, D.C., 1984).

33 This trend has been commonly referred to as the "feminization of poverty." This term was coined by Dr. Diana Pierce in the *1980 Report to the President* of the National Advisory Council on Economic Opportunity to describe the dramatic increase in the proportion of the poor living in female-headed households.

34 U.S. Bureau of the Census, Technical Paper 55, *Estimates of Poverty Including the Value of Non-Cash Benefits: 1984* (Washington, D.C., August 1985), 5, 23.

35 Barbara Raskin and Heidi Hartmann, *Women's Work, Men's Work, Sex Segregation on the Job,* National Academy of Sciences (Washington, D.C.: National Academy Press, 1986), pp. 10–126.

36 U.S. Bureau of the Census, series P-23, no. 124, *Special Study Child Support and Alimony: 1981 Current Population Report* (Washington, D.C., 1981).

37 U.S. House of Representatives Subcommittee on Oversight and Public Assistance and Unemployment Compensation, Committee on Ways and Means, *Background Material on Poverty* (Washington, D.C., October, 1983). See also Committee on Ways and Means, U.S. House of Representatives, *Children in Poverty,* 3.

38 The National Urban League, *The Status of Black America 1984* (New York, January 1984).

39 Ibid.

40 NCCB, *Brothers and Sisters to Us* Pastoral Letter on Racism in Our Day (Washington, D.C.: USCC Office of Publishing and Promotion Services, 1979).

41 Federal Reserve Board, "Survey of Consumer Finances, 1983: A Second Report," reprint from the *Federal Reserve Bulletin* (Washington, D.C., December 1984), 857-868. This survey defines net worth as the difference between gross assets and gross liabilities. The survey's estimates include all financial assets, equity in homes and other real property, as well as all financial liabilities such as consumer credit and other debts.

42 Ibid., 863-864.

43 U.S. Bureau of the Census, series P-60, no. 149, 11.

44 Income distribution figures give only a static picture of income shares. They do not reflect the significant movement of families into and out of different income categories over an extended period of time. See *Years of Poverty, Years of Plenty,* 13. It should also be noted that these figures reflect pre-tax incomes. However, since the national tax structure is proportional for a large segment of the population, it does not have a significant impact on the distribution of income. See Joseph Pechman, *Who Paid Taxes, 1966-85?* (Washington, D.C.: The Brookings Institution, 1985), 51.

45 Lars Osberg, *Economic Inequality in the United States* (New York: M. E. Sharpe, Inc., 1984), 24-28.

46 U.S. Bureau of the Census, series P-60, no. 149, 11.

47 "Poverty in the United States: Where Do We Stand Now?" *Focus* (University of Wisconsin: Institute for Research on Poverty, Winter 1984). See also Danzinger and Gottschalk, "The Poverty of Losing Ground," *Challenge* 28:2 (May/June 1985). As these studies indicate, the slowing of the economy after 1969 tended to push more people into poverty, a trend that was offset to a great extent by the broadening of federal benefit programs. Likewise, the cutbacks in federal programs for the poor in recent years have contributed to the increase in poverty. For other analyses of the causes and cures of poverty see Charles Murray, *Losing Ground: American Social Policy 1950-1980* (New York: Basic Books, Inc., 1984); Ben J. Wattenberg, *The Good News Is the Bad News Is Wrong* (New York: Simon and Shuster, 1984); and Michael Harrington, *The New American Poverty* (New York: Holt, Rinehart, and Winston, 1984).

48 *Family and Nation,* 111-113.

49 Committee on Ways and Means, *Children In Poverty*. Calculation based on Tables 6-1 and 6-2, 180-181; and estimates of social insurance transfers on 221-222.

50 Paul Starr, *The Social Transformation of American Medicine* (New York: Basic Books, Inc., 1982), 373.

51 U.S. Bureau of the Census, series P-60, no. 149, 11.

52 *Years of Poverty, Years of Plenty,* 13.

53 Center on Social Welfare Policy and Law, *Beyond the Myths: The Families Helped by the AFDC Program* (New York, 1985).

54 Ibid. This booklet cites Census Bureau data showing that in 1980 about 45% of those families who received AFDC also had earned income during that year, and that the average number of weeks worked during the year was 32.1.

55 Leonard Goodwin, *Causes and Cures of Welfare* (Lexington, Mass.: Lexington Books, 1983), ch. 1. See also Leonard Goodwin, "Can Workfare Work?" *Public Welfare* 39 (Fall 1981): 19-25.

56 *Beyond the Myths*. With respect to error and fraud rates in AFDC, this booklet notes that erroneous payments in the AFDC program account for less than 10% of the benefits paid. No more than 8.1% of the families on AFDC received overpayments as a result of client error. In less than 4.5% of all AFDC cases nationally are questions of fraud raised. Moreover, in over 40% of these cases, a review of the facts indicated that there was insufficient evidence to support an allegation of fraud.

57 P. G. Peterson, "No More Free Lunch for the Middle Class," *New York Times Magazine* (January 17, 1982).

58 Interfaith Action for Economic Justice, *End Results: The Impact of Federal Policies Since 1980 on Low-Income Americans* (Washington, D.C.), 2.

59 "The Poverty of Losing Ground," 32-38.

60 The tax reform legislation of 1986 did a great deal to achieve this goal. It removed from the federal income tax rolls virtually all families below the official poverty line.

61 Jonathan Kozol, *Illiterate America* (New York: Anchor Press/Doubleday, 1985).

62 *Peace on Earth,* 13.

63 These reports and studies include: E. Boyer, *High School: A Report on Secondary Education in America* (Princeton: Carnegie Foundation for the Advancement of Teaching, 1983); P. Cusick, *The American High School and the Egalitarian Ideal* (New York: Longman, 1983); J. I. Goodlad, *A Place Called School: Prospects for the Future* (New York: McGraw-Hill, 1983); The National Commission on Excellence in Education, *A Nation at Risk: The Imperative for Educational Reform* (Washington, D.C.: U.S. Department of Education, 1983); D. Ravitch, *The Troubled Crusade: American Education, 1945-1980* (New York: Basic Books, 1983); T. R. Sizer, *Horace's Compromise: The Dilemma of the American High School* (Boston: Houghton Mifflin, 1984); Task Force on Education for Economic Growth, *Action for Excellence: A Comprehensive Plan to Improve our Nation's Schools* (Denver: Education Commission of the States, 1983); and The Twentieth Century Fund Task Force on Federal Elementary and Secondary Education Policy, *Making the Grade* (New York: Twentieth Century Fund, 1983). For a discussion of the issues raised in these reports see *Harvard Educational Review* 54:1 (February 1984): 1-31.

64 The Vatican, *Charter of the Rights of the Family* (Washington, D.C.: USCC Office of Publishing and Promotion Services, 1983). See also *On Human Work,* 19; *Familiaris Consortio,* 23, 81; and "Christian Solidarity Leads to Action," Address to Austrian Workers (Vienna, September 1983) in *Origins* 13:16 (September 29, 1983): 275.

65 H. R. Rodgers, Jr., *The Cost of Human Neglect: America's Welfare* (Armonk, N.Y.: W. E. Sharpe, Inc., 1982); C. T. Waxman, *The Stigma of Poverty,* second edition (New York: Pergamon Press, 1983), especially ch. 5; and S. A. Levitan and C. M. Johnson, *Beyond the Safety Net: Reviving the Promise of Opportunity in America* (Cambridge, Mass.: Ballinger, 1984).

66 *Children in Poverty.*

67 U.S. House of Representatives Committee on Ways and Means, *Background Materials and Data on Programs Within the Jurisdiction of the Committee on Ways and Means* (Washington, D.C., February 22, 1985), 345-346.

68 Ibid., 347-348.

69 In 1982, similar recommendations were made by eight former Secretaries of Health, Education, and Welfare (now Health and Human Services). In a report called "Welfare Policy in the United States," they suggested a number of ways in which national minimal standards might be set and strongly urged the establishment of a floor for all states and territories.

70 Committee on Ways and Means, *Background Materials and Data on Programs.*

71 France adopted a "family" or "children's" allowance in 1932, followed by Italy in 1936, The Netherlands in 1939, the United Kingdom in 1945, and Sweden in 1947. Arnold Heidenheimer, Hugh Heclo, and Carolyn Teich Adams, *Comparative Public Policy: The Politics of Social Choice in Europe and America* (New York: St. Martin's Press, 1975), 189, 199. See Also Robert Kuttner, *The Economic Illusion* (Boston: Houghton Mifflin Co., 1984), 243-246; and Joseph Piccione, *Help for Families on the Front Lines: The Theory and Practice of Family Allowances* (Washington, D.C.: The Free Congress Research and Education Foundation, 1983).

72 Milton Friedman, *Capitalism and Freedom* (University of Chicago Press, 1962), 190-195.

73 *The Current Financial Condition of Farmers and Farm Lenders*, Ag. Info. Bulletin no. 490 (Washington, D.C.: U.S. Department of Agriculture Economic Research Service, March 1985), viii-x.

74 Data on farms and farm population are drawn from *Agricultural Statistics,* annual reports of the U.S. Department of Agriculture, Wash-

ington, D.C.

[75] Irma T. Elo and Calvin L. Beale, *Rural Development, Poverty, and Natural Resources* (Washington, D.C.: National Center for Food and Agricultural Policy, Resources for the Future, 1985).

[76] *National Food Review*, USDA, no. 29 (Winter/Spring 1985). In 1984 Americans were spending 15.1% of their disposable income on food. This is an average figure. Many low-income people spent a good deal more and others much less.

[77] Luther Tweeten, *Causes and Consequences of Structural Change in the Farming Industry* (Washington, D.C.: National Planning Association, 1984), 7.

[78] *Economic Indicators of the Farm Sector: Income and Balance Sheet Statistics, 1983*, ECIFS 3-3 (Washington, D.C.: U.S. Department of Agriculture Economic Research Service, September 1984).

[79] Marion Clawson, *Ownership Patterns of Natural Resources in America: Implications for Distribution of Wealth and Income* (Washington, D.C.: Resources for the Future, Summer 1983).

[80] *Causes and Consequences*, 7; and *A Time to Choose: Summary Report on the Structure of Agriculture* (Washington, D.C.: U.S. Department of Agriculture, January 1981).

[81] The nature of this transformation and its implications have been addressed previously by the USCC Committee on Social Development and World Peace in a February 1979 statement *The Family Farm* and again in May 1980 by the bishops of the Midwest in a joint pastoral letter *Strangers and Guests: Toward Community in the Heartland*.

[82] *Soil Conservation in America: What Do We Have To Lose?* (Washington, D.C.: American Farmland Trust, 1984); E. Philip LeVeen, "Domestic Food Security and Increasing Competition for Water," in Lawrence Busch and William B. Lacy, eds., *Food Security in the United States* (Boulder, Colo.: Westview Press, 1984), 52. See also *America's Soil and Water: Condition and Trends* (Washington, D.C.: U.S. Department of Agriculture Soil Conservation Service, 1981).

[83] *1982 Census of Agriculture*.

[84] U.S. Commission on Civil Rights, *The Decline of Black Farming in America* (Washington, D.C.: U.S. Commission on Civil Rights, February 1982), esp. 65-69 regarding their property.

[85] Ibid., 8.

[86] U.S. Department of Labor, *Hearings Concerning Proposed Full Sanitation Standards*, document no. H-308 (Washington, D.C., 1984).

[87] Ch. II, para. 112.

[88] *A Time to Choose*, 148.

[89] Luther Tweeten, "The Economics of Small Farms," *Science* vol. 219 (March 4, 1983): 1041.

[90] U.S. Department of Agriculture, *History of Agricultural Price-Support and Adjustment Programs, 1933-1984*, Ag. Info. Bulletin no. 485 (Washington, D.C.: U.S. Department of Agriculture Economic Research Service, December 1984).

[91] *The Distribution of Benefits from the 1982 Federal Crop Programs* (Washington, D.C.: U.S. Senate Committee on the Budget, November 1984).

[92] "The Great Debate on Mandatory Production Controls" in *Farm Policy Perspectives: Setting the Stage for 1985 Agricultural Legislation* (Washington, D.C.: U.S. Senate Committee on Agriculture, Nutrition, and Forestry, April 1984).

[93] *A Time to Choose*, 91.

[94] Richard Dunford, *The Effects of Federal Income Tax Policy on U.S. Agriculture* (Washington, D.C.: Subcommittee on Agriculture and Transportation of the Joint Economic Committee of the Congress of the United States, December 21, 1984).

[95] This proposal was put forward thirteen years ago in *Where Shall the People Live?* A Special Message of the United States Catholic Bishops (Washington, D.C.: USCC Office of Publishing and Promotion Services, 1972).

[96] Thomas E. Miller, et al., *Economies of Size in U.S. Field Crop Farming* (Washington, D.C.: U.S. Department of Agriculture Economic Research Service, July 1981).

[97] See ch. IV.

[98] *Instruction on Certain Aspects of the Theology of Liberation*, I:6. See also *Peace on Earth*, 130-131; and *On Human Work*, 11.

[99] Overseas Development Council, *U.S. Policy and the Third World: Agenda 1985-1986*.

[100] Robert S. McNamara, *Address to the Board of Governors of the World Bank* (Washington, D.C.: World Bank, September 30, 1980).

[101] U.N./Food and Agricultural Organization, *Dimensions of Need*, E 9 (Rome, 1982). The U.N. World Food Council uses this figure consistently, most recently at its 11th annual meeting in Paris.

[102] Joseph Greenwald and Kenneth Flamm, *The Global Factory* (Washington, D.C.: The Brookings Institution, 1985); see also Ronald Muller and Richard Barnet, *Global Reach* (New York: Simon and Schuster, 1974); Raymond Vernon, *The Economic and Political Consequences of Multinational Enterprise* (Cambridge, Mass.: Harvard University Press, 1972); the United Nations Center on Transnational Corporations maintains current data on these institutions.

[103] *Peace on Earth*, 56-63.

[104] *On the Development of Peoples*, 44, 58-63; quoted also by Pope John Paul II, *Origins* 14:16 (October 4, 1984): 247.

[105] President's Commission on Security and Economic Assistance (Carlucci Commission), *A Report to the Secretary of State* (Washington, D.C., November 1983).

[106] For example: After a dozen years of negotiations, during which nearly all of the issues were resolved to U.S. satisfaction, the United States refused to sign the Law of the Seas treaty; only the United States failed to support the U.N. infant formula resolution; the United States has not ratified the two UN Covenants on Human Rights, etc.

[107] U.S. Agency for International Development, *Congressional Presentation, Fiscal Year 1986, Main Volume* (Washington, D.C., 1985).

[108] The clients of the International Development Association, the "soft loan window" of the World Bank, are the poorest countries. The United States insisted upon—and obtained—a 25% reduction in IDA's current (seventh) replenishment. Taking inflation into account, this meant a 40% drop in real terms at exactly the moment when developing-country debt levels are punishingly high and the prices of their export commodities are almost at rock bottom.

[109] See ch. II.

[110] The GATT, third of the Bretton Woods "institutions" (with the World Bank and the IMF) is in fact a treaty, monitored and supported by a secretariat located in Geneva, Switzerland. Periodic "rounds" of negotiations among its several score members, North and South, modify and extend its provisions and regulations.

[111] Debt figures have been compiled from data published by the World Bank, the IMF, and the Bank for International Settlements.

[112] The United Nations Conference on Trade and Development (UNCTAD) originated in Geneva in 1964 at a meeting convened by the U.N. to discuss trade, development, and related problems of low-income countries. It established a quadrennial meeting and created permanent machinery in the U.N. to deal with these problems. A Trade and Development Board (TDB), with standing committees, meets every two years; and there is a small secretariat to staff it. UNCTAD is viewed as representing the developing countries' continuing effort to have a larger voice in international decisions affecting trade and development and to secure more favorable terms of trade.

[113] *U.S. Policy and the Third World*, Table B-5.

[114] When the IMF helps a country adjust to balance-of-payments problems (e.g., by assisting in the rescheduling of its external debt), it negotiates certain conditions with the debtor country in order to improve its immediate financial position. In general, these require the borrowing country to earn and save more. The adjustments, usually referred to as "conditionality," tend to fall most heavily on the poor through reduction of government spending on consumer subsidies and public services, and often of wages.

[115] North American Coalition for Human Rights in Korea, *Testimony before the U. S. Trade Representative*, June 24, 1985.

[116] E. F. Schumacher, *Small Is Beautiful: Economics As If People Mattered* (New York: Harper and Row, 1973).

[117] *On the Development of Peoples*, 44, 58-63.

[118] Ibid., 37; *Pastoral Constitution*, 87.

[119] *On the Development of Peoples*, 37.

[120] Ruth Leger Sivard, *World Military and Social Expenditures 1983* (Washington D.C.: World Priorities, 1983), 23.

[121] Pontifical Commission Justitia et Pax, *The Social Teaching of John Paul II*, 6 (October 6, 1979).

[122] *On the Development of Peoples*, 44, 58-63.

[123] See "Testimony on U. S. Arms Control Policy," *Origins* 14:10 (August 9, 1984): 154ff.

CHAPTER IV

[1] *Octogesima Adveniens*, 24.

[2] For different analyses along these lines with quite different starting points see Martin Carnoy, Derek Shearer, and Russell Rumberger, *A New Social Contract* (New York: Harper and Row, 1983); Amatai Etzioni, *An Immodest Agenda: Reconstructing America before the Twenty-First Century* (New York: McGraw-Hill, 1983); Charles E. Lindblom, *Politics and Markets* (New York: Basic Books, 1977), esp. 346-348; George C. Lodge, *The New American Ideology* (New York: Alfred A. Knopf, 1975); Douglas Sturm, "Corporations, Constitutions, and Covenants," *Journal of the American Academy of Religion*, 41 (1973): 331-55; Lester Thurow, *The Zero-Sum Society* (New York: Basic Books, 1980), esp. ch. 1; Roberto Mangabeira Unger, *Knowledge and Politics* (New York: Free Press, 1975); George F. Will, *Statecraft as Soulcraft: What Government Does* (New York: Simon and Schuster, 1982), esp. ch. 6.

[3] *Pastoral Constitution*, 68. See *Mater et Magistra*, 75-77.

[4] Charles W. Powers provided a helpful discussion of these matters in a paper presented at a conference on the first draft of this pastoral letter sponsored by the Harvard University Divinity School and the Institute for Policy Studies, Cambridge, Massachusetts, March 29-31, 1985.

[5] See John Paul II, "The Role of Business in a Changing Workplace," 3, *Origins* 15 (February 6, 1986): 567.

[6] *Rerum Novarum*, 28. For an analysis of the relevant papal teachings on institutions of collaboration and partnership, see John Cronin, *Catholic Social Principles: The Social Teaching of the Catholic Church Applied to American Economic Life* (Milwaukee: Bruce, 1950), ch. VII; Oswald von Nell-Breuning, *Reorganization of Social Economy: The Social Encyclical Developed and Explained*, trans. Bernard W. Dempsey (Milwaukee: Bruce, 1936), chs. X-XII; Jean-Yves Calvez and Jacques Perrin, *The Church and Social Justice*, trans. J. R. Kirwan (Chicago: Regnery, 1961), ch. XIX.

[7] Michael Conte, Arnold S. Tannenbaum, and Donna McCulloch, *Employee Ownership*, Research Report Series, Institute for Social Research (Ann Arbor, Mich.: University of Michigan, 1981); Robert A. Dahl, *A Preface to Economic Democracy* (Berkeley: University of California Press, 1985); Harvard Business School, "The Mondragon Cooperative Movement," case study prepared by David P. Ellerman (Cambridge, Mass.: Harvard Business School, n.d.); Robert Jackall and Henry M. Levin, eds., *Worker Cooperatives in America* (Berkeley: University of California Press, 1984); Derek Jones and Jan Svejnar, eds., *Participatory and Self-Managed Firms: Evaluating Economic Performance* (Lexington, Mass.: D. C. Heath, 1982); Irving H. Siegel and Edgar Weinberg, *Labor-Management Cooperation: The American Experience* (Kalamazoo, Mich.: W. E. Upjohn Institute for Employment Research, 1982); Stuart M. Speiser, "Broadened Capital Ownership—The Solution to Major Domestic and International Problems," *Journal of Post Keynesian Economics* VIII (1985): 426-434; Jaroslav Vanek, ed., *Self-Management: Economic Liberation of Man* (London: Penguin, 1975); Martin L. Weitzman, *The Share Economy* (Cambridge, Mass.: Harvard University Press, 1984).

[8] *Program of Social Reconstruction* in *Justice in the Marketplace*, 381.

[9] *Mater et Magistra*, 32, 77, 85-103; *On Human Work*, 14.

[10] For examples of worker-owned and operated enterprises supported by the Campaign for Human Development's revolving loan fund see CHD's *Annual Report* (Washington, D.C.: USCC).

[11] *Quadragesimo Anno* states the basic norm on which this conclusion

is based: "It is wholly false to ascribe to property alone or to labor alone whatever has been obtained through the combined effort of both, and it is wholly unjust for either, denying the efficacy of the other, to arrogate to itself whatever has been produced" (53).

[12] *On Human Work*, 12.

[13] Ibid., 20. This point was well made by John Cronin twenty-five years ago: "Even if most injustice and exploitation were removed, unions would still have a legitimate place. They are the normal voice of labor, necessary to organize social life for the common good. There is positive need for such organization today, quite independently of any social evils which may prevail. Order and harmony do not happen; they are the fruit of conscious and organized effort. While we may hope that the abuses which occasioned the rise of unions may disappear, it does not thereby follow that unions will have lost their function. On the contrary, they will be freed from unpleasant, even though temporarily necessary, tasks and able to devote all their time and efforts to a better organization of social life" *Catholic Social Principles*, 418. See also AFL-CIO Committee on the Evolution of Work, *The Future of Work* (Washington, D.C.: AFL-CIO, 1983).

[14] For a classic discussion of the relative power of managers and shareholders see A. A. Berle and Gardiner C. Means, *The Modern Corporation and Private Property* (New York, Macmillan, 1932).

[15] Peter L. Berger and Richard John Neuhaus, *To Empower People: The Role of Mediating Structures in Public Policy* (Washington, D.C.: American Enterprise Institute, 1977).

[16] United States Small Business Administration, *1978 Annual Report* (Washington, D.C.: Government Printing Office, 1979).

[17] For recent discussion from a variety of perspectives see: Robert Friedman and William Schweke, eds., *Expanding the Opportunity to Produce: Revitalizing the American Economy through New Enterprise Development: A Policy Reader* (Washington, D.C.: Corporation for New Enterprise Development, 1981); Jack A. Meyer, ed., *Meeting Human Needs: Toward a New Public Philosophy* (Washington, D.C.: American Enterprise Institute, 1982); Committee for Economic Development, *Jobs for the Hard-to-Employ: New Directions for a Public-Private Partnership* (New York: Committee for Economic Development, 1978); Gar Alperovitz and Jeff Faux, *Rebuilding America: A Blueprint for the New Economy* (New York: Pantheon Books, 1984).

[18] Christopher Mackin, *Strategies for Local Ownership and Control: A Policy Analysis* (Somerville, Mass.: Industrial Cooperative Association, 1983).

[19] *Mater et Magistra*, 59, 62.

[20] *On Human Work*, 18.

[21] Ibid.

[22] For examples and analysis of different meanings of economic planning see Naomi Caiden and Aaron Wildavsky, *Planning and Budgeting in Poor Countries* (New York: Wiley, 1974); Robert Dahl and Charles E. Lindblom, *Politics, Economics and Welfare: Planning and Politico-Economic Systems Resolved into Basic Social Processes* (Chicago: University of Chicago Press, 1976); Stephen S. Cohen, *Modern Capitalist Planning: The French Model* (Berkeley: University of California Press, 1977); Albert Waterston, *Development Planning: Lessons of Experience* (Baltimore: Johns Hopkins Press, 1965); *Rebuilding America*, chs. 14, 15.

[23] For example, many students of recent policy point out that monetary policy on the one hand and fiscal policies governing taxation and government expenditures on the other have been at odds with each other, with larger public deficits and high interest rates as the outcome. See Alice M. Rivlin, ed., *Economic Choices 1984* (Washington, D.C.: The Brookings Institution, 1984), esp. ch. 2.

[24] *The Challenge of Peace*, 270-271.

[25] *On the Development of Peoples*, 3.

[26] *Peace on Earth*, 134-135.

[27] *The Challenge of Peace*, 268.

[28] See Robert O. Keohane and Joseph S. Nye, Jr., "Two Cheers for Multilateralism," *Foreign Policy* 60 (Fall 1985): 148-167.

CHAPTER V

[1] *Reconciliation and Penance*, 13.

[2] *Justice in the World*, 6.

[3] Medellin Documents: *Justice* (1968), 4.

[4] *Dogmatic Constitution on the Church*, 1; *Pastoral Constitution*, 42, 45; *Constitution on the Liturgy*, 26; *Decree on the Church's Missionary Activity*, 5; *Liturgy and Social Justice*, ed. by Mark Searle, (Collegeville, Minn.: Liturgical Press, 1980); National Conference of Catholic Bishops, *The Church at Prayer* (Washington, D.C.: USCC Office of Publishing and Promotion Services, 1983).

[5] *Dogmatic Constitution on the Church*, 36.

[6] *Justice in the World*, 41.

[7] National Conference of Catholic Bishops, *To Teach as Jesus Did*, A Pastoral Message on Education (Washington, D.C.: USCC Office of Publishing and Promotion Services, 1972), 7.

[8] Cf. Vatican Council II, *Declaration on Christian Education*, 3, 6. See also, *Charter of the Rights of the Family*, 5b; *Instruction on Christian Freedom and Liberation*, 94.

[9] Pope John Paul II, *On the Family* (Washington, D.C.: USCC Office of Publishing and Promotion Services, 1981), 6. See also Robert N. Bellah, Richard Madsen, William M. Sullivan, Ann Swidler, Steven M. Tipton, *Habits of the Heart: Individualism and Commitment in American Life* (Berkeley: University of California Press, 1985); *The Family Today and Tomorrow: The Church Addresses Her Future* (Boston, Mass.: The Pope John Center, 1985).

[10] *Justice in the World*, 40.

[11] *Dogmatic Constitution on the Church*, 8.

[12] National Conference of Catholic Bishops, *Health and Health Care* (Washington, D.C.: USCC Office of Publishing and Promotion Services, 1981), 50.

[13] See ch. IV of this pastoral letter.

SELECTED BIBLIOGRAPHY

PAPAL AND VATICAN DOCUMENTS

Pope Leo XIII. *Rerum Novarum (On the Condition of Workers)*, May 15, 1891.

Pope Pius XI. *Quadragesimo Anno (On Reconstructing the Social Order)*, May 15, 1931.

————. *Divini Redemptoris (On Atheistic Communism)*, March 19, 1937.

Pope John XXIII. *Mater et Magistra (On Christianity and Social Progress)*, May 15, 1961.

————. *Pacem in Terris (On Establishing Universal Peace in Truth, Justice, Charity and Liberty*, April 11, 1963.

Second Vatican Council. *Lumen Gentium (Dogmatic Constitution on the Church)*, November 21, 1964.

————. *Dei Verbum (Dogmatic Constitution on Divine Revelation)*, November 18, 1965.

————. *Dignitatis Humanae (Declaration on Religious Freedom)*, December 7, 1965.

————. *Gaudium et Spes (Pastoral Constitution on the Church in the Modern World)*, December 7, 1965.

Pope Paul VI, *Populorum Progressio (On Promoting the Development of Peoples)*, March 26, 1967.

————. *Octogesima Adveniens (On the Occasion of the Eightieth Anniversary of the Encyclical Rerum Novarum)*, May 14, 1971.

————. *Evangelii Nuntiandi (On Evangelization in the Modern World)*, December 8, 1975.

Synod of Bishops, *Justice in the World (Justitia in Mundo)*. 1971.

Pope John Paul II, *Redemptor Hominis (Redeemer of Man)*, March 4, 1979.

————. *Dives in Misericordia (Rich in Mercy)*, November 30, 1980.

————. *Laborem Exercens (On Human Work)*, September 14, 1981.

————. *Salvifici Doloris (On the Christian Meaning of Human Suffering)*, February 11, 1984.

COLLECTIONS AND COMMENTARIES

Abbott, Walter M., SJ, ed. *The Documents of Vatican II*, Very Rev. Msgr. Joseph Gallagher, trans. New York: America Press, 1966.

Baum, Gregory. *The Priority of Labor: A Commentary on "Laborem Exercens."* New York: Paulist Press, 1982.

Benestad, J. Brian, Ph.D., and Francis J. Butler, S.T.D., eds., *Quest for Justice: A Compendium of the Statements of the United States Catholic Bishops on the Political and Social Order, 1966-1980.* Washington, D.C.: USCC Office of Publishing and Promotion Services, 1981.

Byers, David M., ed. *Justice in the Marketplace: Collected Statements of the Vatican and the U.S. Catholic Bishops on Economic Policy, 1891-1984*, with commentary by John T. Pawlikowski, OSM, Ph.D. Washington, D.C.: USCC Office of Publishing and Promotion Services, 1985.

Calvez, Jean-Yves. *The Social Thought of John XXIII: "Mater et Magistra,"* George McKenzie, trans. Chicago: Regnery, 1964.

Calvez, Jean-Yves and Jacques Perrin. *The Church and Social Justice,* J. R. Kirwan, trans. Chicago: Regnery, 1961.

Camp, Richard L. *The Papal Ideology of Social Reform.* Leiden: Brill, 1969.

Cronin, John F. *Catholic Social Principles.* Milwaukee: Bruce, 1950.

Dorr, Donald. *Option for the Poor: A Hundred Years of Vatican Social Teaching.* Dublin: Gillord McMillan/Maryknoll, N.Y.: Orbis Books, 1983.

Flannery, Austin, OP, ed. *Vatican Council II: The Conciliar and Post Conciliar Documents.* Vatican Collection, Vol. 1. Northport, N.Y.: Costello Publishing Company, 1975.

————. *Vatican Council II: More Post Conciliar Documents.* Vatican Collection, Vol. 2. Northport, N.Y.: Costello Publishing Company, 1982.

Gibbons, William J., ed. *Seven Great Encyclicals.* New York: Paulist Press, 1963.

Gremillion, Joseph, ed. *The Gospel of Peace and Justice: Catholic Social Teaching Since Pope John XXIII.* Maryknoll, N.Y.: Orbis Books, 1976.

Gudorf, Christine, E. *Catholic Social Teaching on Liberation Themes.* Lanham, Md.: University Press of America, 1980.

Heckel, Roger. *The Social Teaching of John Paul II: The Use of the Expression "Social Doctrine" of the Church.* Vatican City: Pontifical Commission Justitia et Pax, 1980.

Holland, Joe and Peter Henriot. *Social Analysis: Linking Faith and Justice.* Washington, D.C.: Center for Concern, 1980.

Hollenbach, David. *Claims in Conflict.* New York: Paulist Press, 1979.

Moody, Joseph N. *Church and Society: Catholic Social and Political Thought and Movements, 1789-1950.* New York: Arts, 1953.

Nell-Breuning, Oswald von. *Reorganization of Social Economy,* B. W. Dempsey, trans. Milwaukee: Bruce, 1936.

Novak, Michael. *Freedom with Justice: Catholic Social Thought and Liberal Institutions.* San Francisco: Harper and Row, 1984.

O'Brien, David J. and Thomas A. Shannon, eds. *Renewing the Earth: Catholic Documents on Peace, Justice, and Liberation.* Garden City, N.Y.: Doubleday, 1977.

Ryan, John A. *A Living Wage.* New York: Macmillan, 1906.

————. *Distributive Justice,* Third Edition. New York: Macmillan, 1942.

Schotte, Jan P. *Reflections on "Laborem Exercens."* (Vatican City: Pontifical Commission Justitia et Pax, 1982.

Vidler, Alec R. *A Century of Social Catholicism.* London: SPCK, 1964.

Walsh, Michael and Brian Davies, eds. *Proclaiming Justice and Peace: Documents from John XXIII-John Paul II.* Mystic, Conn.: Twenty-Third Publications, 1984.